AMERICAN ISSUES

Second Edition

AMERICAN ISSUES

A Primary Source Reader
in United States History

Volume II: Since 1865

Edited by

Irwin Unger
New York University

and

Robert R. Tomes
St. John's University

Prentice Hall, Upper Saddle River, New Jersey 07458

Library of Congress Cataloging-in-Publication Data

American issues : a primary source reader in United States history /
    edited by Irwin Unger and Robert R. Tomes.
        p.   cm.
    Contents: v. 1. To 1877 —v. 2. Since 1865.
    ISBN 0–13–775545–7 (v. 1). —ISBN 0–13–775552–X (v. 2)
    1. United States—History—Sources.   I. Unger, Irwin.   II. Tomes,
Robert R.
E173.A745   1999
973—dc21   98–42413
                                                                CIP

Editor in Chief: *Charlyce Jones-Owen*
Executive Editor: *Todd Armstrong*
Editorial Assistant: *Holly Jo Brown*
Senior Managing Editor: *Jan Stephan*
Production Liaison: *Fran Russello*
Project Manager: *Marianne Hutchinson (Pine Tree Composition)*
AVP/Director of Manufacturing and Production: *Barbara Kittle*
Prepress and Manufacturing Buyer: *Lynn Pearlman*
Art Director: *Jayne Conte*

This book was set in 10/12 Times Roman by Pine Tree Composition
and was printed and bound by Courier Companies, Inc.
The cover was printed by Phoenix Color Corp.

© 1999, 1994 by Prentice-Hall, Inc.
Upper Saddle River, New Jersey 07458

Printed in the United States of America

10 9 8 7 6 5

ISBN 0-13-775552-X

Prentice-Hall International (UK) Limited, *London*
Prentice-Hall of Australia Pty. Limited, *Sydney*
Prentice-Hall Canada Inc., *Toronto*
Prentice-Hall Hispanoamericana, S.A., *Mexico*
Prentice-Hall of India Private Limited, *New Delhi*
Prentice-Hall of Japan, Inc., *Tokyo*
Prentice-Hall Asia Pte. Ltd., *Singapore*
Editora Prentice-Hall do Brasil, Ltda., *Rio de Janeiro*

Brief Contents

VOLUME I

Chapter 1   The Settlement Enterprise   1

Chapter 2   America: Paradise or Hell?   24

Chapter 3   Native Americans   41

Chapter 4   Colonial Religious Toleration   66

Chapter 5   Patriot versus Loyalist   85

Chapter 6   The Constitution   112

Chapter 7   Federalist versus Republican   127

Chapter 8   Pioneers and Native Americans   155

Chapter 9   Capital versus Labor   165

Chapter 10   Jacksonian Democracy   179

Chapter 11   The Ferment of Reform   197

Chapter 12   Defining the American Character   218

Chapter 13   The Mexican War   239

Chapter 14   Slavery and the "Old South"   254

Chapter 15   The Clash of Sections   274

Chapter 16   The Civil War   299

Chapter 17   Reconstruction   329

VOLUME II

Chapter 1   Reconstruction   1

Chapter 2   An Urban and Industrial Nation   33

Chapter 3   The Last West and Populism   62
Chapter 4   Outward Thrust   88
Chapter 5   The Progressive Impulse   100
Chapter 6   Race and Ethnicity   124
Chapter 7   World War I   148
Chapter 8   The Twenties Culture War   173
Chapter 9   The New Deal   192
Chapter 10   World War II   207
Chapter 11   The Fifties   230
Chapter 12   The Cold War   248
Chapter 13   The Civil Rights Revolution   271
Chapter 14   The Great Society   287
Chapter 15   The New Feminism   306
Chapter 16   The Vietnam War   324
Chapter 17   Watergate   342
Chapter 18   The Reagan Revolution   356
Chapter 19   The New Environmentalism   379
Chapter 20   Defining America at the Century's End   401

Contents

Preface   xi

Chapter 1   **Reconstruction**   **1**

    1.1:   Harsh versus Lenient Victors (1865)   2

    1.2:   The White South Responds (1865, 1866, 1868, 1874)   10

    1.3:   The Black Response (1865, 1868, 1866)   21

Chapter 2   **An Urban and Industrial Nation**   **33**

    2.1:   The Industrial Status Quo Defended (1883)   34

    2.2:   The Industrial Worker (1885, 1878)   38

    2.3:   Labor Rejects Capitalism (1912)   45

    2.4:   The Cities Acclaimed (1905)   50

    2.5:   The Cities Deplored (1890)   54

    2.6:   City Government (1905)   56

Chapter 3   **The Last West and Populism**   **62**

    3.1:   The Mining Frontier (1864)   63

    3.2:   The Buffalo Destroyed (1876–1877)   66

    3.3:   The Cattle Kingdom (1888)   69

    3.4:   Native Americans (1877, 1881)   75

3.5:   The Populist Party Platform (1892)   80

3.6:   William Allen White and the Kansas Populists
       (1896)   84

Chapter 4   Outward Thrust   88

4.1:   Racial Destiny (1885)   88

4.2:   Manhood and Imperialism (1899)   92

4.3:   Trade and Markets (1900)   94

4.4:   The Anti-Imperialists (1899)   97

Chapter 5   The Progressive Impulse   100

5.1:   The Danger of Concentrated Wealth (1912, 1913)   100

5.2:   Conservation and Efficiency (1908, 1912)   112

5.3:   Social Justice Progressivism (1892, 1906, 1908)   118

Chapter 6   Race and Ethnicity   124

6.1:   The Great Migration: The Dark Side (1905, 1919)   125

6.2:   Black Americans Respond (1905, 1923)   132

6.3:   The New Immigration and American Toleration (1912,
       1916)   137

6.4:   Asian-American Immigration (1882, 1908)   145

Chapter 7   World War I   148

7.1:   The Submarine Dimension (1915)   149

7.2:   Voices for Intervention (1915)   154

7.3:   Opponents of Intervention (1917)   161

7.4:   Idealism and Disillusionment (1918, 1920)   166

Chapter 8   The Twenties Culture War   173

8.1:   Sacco-Vanzetti (1927)   174

8.2: The Ku Klux Klan (1924, 1921)   182

8.3: Wets versus Drys (1915, 1924)   186

Chapter 9   The New Deal   192

9.1: Roosevelt Explains His Policies (1934)   193

9.2: The New Deal and the "Common Man" (1934, 1936)   196

9.3: Attack from the Right (1932, 1936)   200

9.4: Thunder from the Left (1934)   203

Chapter 10   World War II   207

10.1: Isolationism (1935, 1939)   209

10.2: Interventionists (1935)   213

10.3: America First versus Aid to Britain (1940, 1941)   216

10.4: Undeclared War (1941)   222

10.5: A New American Internationalism (1941)   226

Chapter 11   The Fifties   230

11.1: Suburbia (1954, 1957)   231

11.2: The Red Scare (1950)   237

Chapter 12   The Cold War   248

12.1: "Mr. X" and the Soviet Menace (1947, 1952)   249

12.2: The Truman Doctrine and the Marshall Plan (1947, 1949)   259

Chapter 13   The Civil Rights Revolution   271

13.1: School Desegregation (1954, 1965)   272

13.2: Christian Love versus Racial Anger (1964, 1967)   278

Chapter 14   The Great Society   287

14.1: Defenders (1964)   288
14.2: The Attack from the Right (1964)   291
14.3: The Attack from the Left (1962)   295

Chapter 15   The New Feminism   306

15.1: The National Organization for Women's Bill of Rights (1967)   307
15.2: Radical Feminism (1969, 1968)   309
15.3: The Counterattack (1977)   314
15.4: *Roe* v. *Wade* (1973)   318

Chapter 16   The Vietnam War   324

16.1: The Hawk Position (1954, 1965)   327
16.2: The North Vietnamese Analyze American Intervention (1965)   333
16.3: The Antiwar Movement Strikes Back (1965, 1966)   336

Chapter 17   Watergate   342

17.1: The Tapes (1972)   344
17.2: Nixon Defends Himself (1973)   348
17.3: The Vote for Impeachment (1974)   352

Chapter 18   The Reagan Revolution   356
18.1: The New Right (1981, 1980, 1978)   357
18.2: The Liberals Hit Back (1982, 1981)   369

Chapter 19   The New Environmentalism   379
19.1: The Ecology Ethic (1949, 1975, 1973)   380
19.2: The Critics (1971, 1970)   391

Chapter 20   Defining America at the Century's End   401

Preface

Americans worry about the state of education in the United States today. Recently we have been told how little students know about science, geography, mathematics, and history; we fear that our country will be unprepared to compete against the other advanced industrial societies in years to come. We are also concerned that the new generation will lack the shared civic knowledge essential for a functioning democratic system.

There is indeed reason to be dismayed by how small a stock of historical information young Americans possess. But it is important also to realize that education is not just transmission of data. It is also the fostering of critical thinking. The most encyclopedic knowledge does students little good if they cannot use it to reach valid and useful conclusions. It is this belief that has inspired *American Issues*. This two-volume work will stimulate critical thinking and active learning about American history—leading students to reject received ideas when appropriate, relate the past to their own experience, and reach conclusions on the basis of evidence. At times, no doubt, students will have to do additional reading beyond this textbook; that, of course, is all to the good.

American Issues is not a compendium of scholars' views. It is constructed out of *primary documents,* the raw material of history. In its pages participants and contemporary observers express their opinions, make their observations, and reach their conclusions about events and issues of their own day that affected the nation and American society. The selections do not point in one direction on any given issue. On the contrary, they were chosen to raise questions and force the student to confront disparity, complexity, and apparent contradiction. *American Issues* avoids giving students the "simple bottom line." Rather, it compels them to grapple with the same ambiguous raw materials that historians process to reach their conclusions. To further the engagement process, each selection asks specific questions of the student. The approach resembles that of the 1950 Japanese movie *Rashomon,* in which an event was depicted from the perspectives of several participants and viewers were expected to reach their own conclusions. That approach, we believe, is an incomparable way to enlighten students about the rich complexity and fullness of historical reality.

We would like to acknowledge the following reviewers of this text: Stephen H. Coe, Eastern Kentucky University; Samuel Crompton, Holyoke Community College; Anthony O. Edmonds, Ball State University; John A. Hall, Albion College; Edward L. Schapsmeier, Illinois State University; Rebecca S. Shoemaker, Indiana State University; and Donald G. Sofchalk, Mankato State University.

The selections in Volume I and Volume II range widely in subject matter across the American past. Besides the key political questions, they deal with the social, cultural, economic, and gender problems our predecessors faced. *American Issues* is guided by the sense that America has always been a heterogeneous society whose inhabitants led their lives in many ways. Yet it does not abandon the view that all of our forebears were also part of the same American experience and shared many concerns of their era.

What can we expect from conscientious use of *American Issues*? No single text can turn a passive human sponge into an active seeker and thinker. But *American Issues* can, we believe, engage college students' natural curiosity and tendency to differ and encourage the habit of critical appraisal. Instructors and students alike will find *American Issues* a stimulating and challenging introduction to informed and discriminating thinking about the American past.

Irwin Unger
Robert R. Tomes

AMERICAN ISSUES

☆ **1** ☆

Reconstruction

In April 1865 the nation faced colossal problems of readjustment and repair. The South was a devastated region, its railroads, its banking system, and many of its towns and cities reduced to ruins. The human cost in the former Confederacy had been enormous. Thousands of young southern men had died or been maimed. Most difficult of all, in some ways, 4 million former slaves had been wrenched from their accustomed place within the South's social and labor systems and left without clear roles and firm moorings.

The new circumstances also raised urgent constitutional problems for the nation as a whole. Having fought to leave the Union, the South was now out of constitutional alignment with the rest of the states. Should the North accept the logic of its own position—that secession was illegal—and simply allow the former Confederate states to return to full constitutional status without conditions? That response would go easy on the ex-rebels and at the same time allow the southern states a free hand in dealing with the newly freed men and women. Could white southerners be trusted to be fair to the former slaves? Should erstwhile Confederates be allowed to resume their place in the Union without punishment for committing atrocities against Union prisoners, for violating federal oaths of office, for creating the mountain of dead and wounded the American people had suffered?

For over a decade following Confederate defeat, the nation's politics would be roiled by the debate over how to manage the Reconstruction process. Americans would be deeply divided. Congress would battle the president, southerners would battle northerners, whites would battle blacks, Democrats would battle Republicans. On each issue there would often be a bewildering array of positions not easily categorized as pro or con.

The documents below express a range of views on important Reconstruction problems. They do not exhaust the full spectrum of either opinions or issues on this complex event in our history; they are only a sample of how Americans thought. As you read the selections that follow, try to determine the gist of each argument and try to understand why particular individuals felt the way they did.

1.1:   Harsh versus Lenient Victors (1865)

Besides being influenced by differing ideologies or philosophies, northern leaders were swayed in their approaches to Reconstruction by differences of temperament and personality. Abraham Lincoln, a pragmatist and a compassionate man, was inclined to make the return of the southern states to full constitutional equality a relatively easy process. In several states that had been occupied by Union forces before the final Confederate surrender, he was able to put his lenient policies in effect.

The first selection below is an excerpt from Lincoln's last recorded address, remarks he made from the White House balcony to a group of citizens who had come to "serenade" him just four days before his death by an assassin's bullet. Lincoln discusses the issue of the constitutional status of the seceded states, a legalistic issue that had important implications for policy. If it was held that the southern states had never actually left the Union, then they remained sovereign entities like the other states, and Washington had only limited powers over them. But if it was decided that they had left the Union and reverted to territorial status, as some believed, then Congress could constitutionally impose a wide range of conditions on them.

What does Lincoln say about this issue? What is his overall tone? Was his estimate of the best thing for the nation to do valid in light of all that followed? How would you characterize Lincoln's views of the rights of the former slaves?

The second selection is a May 1865 proclamation by President Andrew Johnson establishing a provisional government for South Carolina. In the next two months Johnson issued six other proclamations establishing governments for other former Confederate states.

Johnson was himself a southerner (from Tennessee), but a strong unionist who had refused to disavow his government when his state seceded. Like Lincoln, he believed the southern states should be readmitted to the Union with as few preconditions as possible. What preconditions are imposed by the president's proclamation? Are they severe?

What obvious conditions that might have been imposed are omitted? Is there any mention of a role for Congress in the Reconstruction process? Should Johnson have assumed sole leadership in this all-important matter?

The third selection is from a speech by Representative Thaddeus Stevens of Pennsylvania. Stevens was a "Radical Republican." During the war he had, as other Radicals, pushed for the early emancipation of the slaves and aggressive policies against the Confederacy and its leaders. After the war he and his fellow Radicals would demand that the South be compelled to repudiate its prewar planter leadership and guarantee equal social and political rights for the freedmen.[1] Southerners and conservative northerners, mostly Democrats, would call Stevens and his colleagues mean-spirited "vindictives," who lacked Christian compassion toward their former enemies and were moved primarily by partisan political ends.

After Lincoln's assassination, Stevens rallied the congressional opposition to President Johnson's lenient Reconstruction policy. He and his supporters would seize from the president the management of the Reconstruction process. Ultimately they would break completely with Johnson, and in 1868 the Radical-controlled Congress would impeach the president—although not convict him—for defying the will and the laws of Congress.

From the excerpt below, would you say that Stevens deserves to be considered vindictive? Do his sympathies for the freed slaves seem sincere? Does his reference to "perpetual ascendency to the party of the Union" seem like a blatant grab for power by Republicans? Putting yourself in Stevens's shoes, how can such a partisan position be justified?

Reconstruction Must Be Gradual and Careful

ABRAHAM LINCOLN

I have been shown a letter . . . in which the writer expresses regret that my mind has not seemed to be definitely fixed upon the question whether the seceded States, so called, are in the Union or out of it. I would perhaps add astonishment to his regret were he to learn that since I have found professed Union men endeavoring to answer that question, I have purposely forborne any public expression upon it. As ap-

[1] Though the term might seem sexist today it was used to refer to *all* the freed slaves after 1865, and it is still so used—ED.

Arthur B. Lapsley, *Writings of Abraham Lincoln*, (New York: G. P. Putnam's Sons, 1906), vol. 7, pp. 362–68.

pears to me, that question has not been nor yet is a practically material one, and that any discussion of it, while it thus remains practically immaterial, could have no effect other than the mischievous one of dividing our friends. As yet, whatever it may become, that question is bad as the basis of a controversy, and good for nothing at all—a merely pernicious abstraction. We all agree that the seceded States, so called, are out of their proper practical relation with the Union, and that the sole object of the Government, civil and military, in regard to these States, is to again get them into their proper practical relation. I believe that is not only possible, but in fact [it is] easier to do this without deciding or even considering whether these States have ever been out of the Union, than with it. Finding themselves safely at home, it would be utterly immaterial whether they have been abroad. Let us all join in doing the act necessary to restore the proper practical relations between these States and the Union, and each forever after innocently indulge his own opinion whether, in doing the acts, he brought the States from without the Union, or only gave them proper assistance, they never having been out of it. The amount of constituency, so to speak, on which the Louisiana government rests, would be more satisfactory to all if it contained fifty thousand, or thirty thousand, or even twenty thousand, instead of twelve thousand, as it does. It is also unsatisfactory to some that the elective franchise is not given to the colored man. I would myself prefer that it were now conferred on the very intelligent, and on those who serve our cause as soldiers. Still, the question is not whether the Louisiana government, as it stands, is quite all that is desirable. The question is, Will it be wiser to take it as it is and help to improve it, or to reject and disperse [sic]? Can Louisiana be brought into proper practical relation with the Union sooner by sustaining or by discarding her new State government? Some twelve thousand voters in the heretofore Slave State of Louisiana have sworn allegiance to the Union, assumed to be the rightful political power of the State, held elections, organized a State government, adopted a Free State constitution, giving the benefit of public schools equally to black and white, and empowering the Legislature to confer the elective franchise upon the colored man. This Legislature has already voted to ratify the Constitutional Amendment recently passed by Congress, abolishing slavery throughout the nation. These twelve thousand persons are thus fully committed to the Union, and to perpetuate freedom in the State—committed to the very things, and nearly all things, the nation wants—and they ask the nation's recognition and its assistance to make good this committal. Now, if we reject and spurn them, we do our utmost to disorganize and disperse them. We, in fact, say to the white man: You are worthless or worse; we will neither help you nor be helped by you. To the blacks we say: This cup of liberty which these, your old masters, held to your lips, we will dash from you, and leave you to the chances of gathering the spilled and scattered contents in some vague and undefined when, where, and how. If this course, discouraging and paralyzing both white and black, has any tendency to bring Louisiana into proper practical relations with the Union, I have so far been unable to perceive it. If, on the contrary, we recognize and sustain the new government of Louisiana, the converse of all this is made true. We encourage the hearts and nerve the arms of twelve thousand to adhere to their work, and argue for it, and proselyte for it, and fight for it, and feed it, and grow it, and ripen it to a complete success. <u>The colored man, too, in seeing all united for him, is inspired with vigilance, and energy, and daring to the same end</u>. Grant that he desires the elective franchise, will he not attain it sooner by saving the already advanced steps towards it, than by running backward over them? Concede that the new government of Louisiana is only to what it should be as the egg is to the fowl, we shall sooner have the fowl by hatching the egg than by smashing it. Again, if we reject Louisiana, we also reject one vote in favor of the proposed amendment to the National Constitution. To meet this proposition, it has been argued that no more than three fourths of those States which have not attempted secession are necessary to validly ratify the amendment. I do not commit myself against this, further than to say that such a ratification would be questionable, and sure to be persistently questioned, while a ratification by three fourths of all the States would be unquestioned and unquestionable. <u>I repeat the question, Can Louisiana be brought into proper practical relation with the Union sooner by sustaining or by discarding her new State government?</u> What has been said of Louisiana will apply to other States. And yet so great peculiarities pertain to each State, and such important and sudden changes occur in the same State, and withal so new and unprecedented is the whole case, that no exclusive and inflexible plan can safely be prescribed as to details and collaterals. Such exclusive and inflexible plan would surely become a new entanglement. Important principles may and must be inflexible. In the present situation as the phrase goes, it may be my duty to make some new announcement to the people of the South. I am considering, and shall not fail to act, when satisfied that action will be proper.

Amnesty Proclamation

ANDREW JOHNSON

By the President of the United States of America. A Proclamation.

Whereas the fourth section of the fourth article of the Constitution of the United States declares that the United States shall guarantee to every State in the Union a republican form of government and shall protect each of them against invasion and domestic violence; and

Whereas the President of the United States is by the Constitution made Commander in Chief of the Army and Navy, as well as chief civil executive officer of the United States, and is bound by solemn oath faithfully to execute the office of President of the United States and to take care that the laws be faithfully executed; and

Whereas the rebellion which has been waged by a portion of the people of the United States against the properly constituted authorities of the Government thereof in the most violent and revolting form, but whose organized and armed forces have

James D. Richardson, ed., *A Compilation the Messages and Papers of the Presidents* (New York: Bureau of National Literature, 1897), vol. 8, pp. 3508–10.

now been almost entirely overcome, has in its revolutionary progress deprived the people of the State of South Carolina of all civil government; and

Whereas it becomes necessary and proper to carry out and enforce the obligations of the United States to the people of South Carolina in securing them in the enjoyment of a republican form of government:

Now, therefore, in obedience to the high and solemn duties imposed upon me by the Constitution of the United States and for the purpose of enabling the loyal people of said State to organize a State government whereby justice may be established, domestic tranquillity insured, and loyal citizens protected in all their rights of life, liberty, and property, I, Andrew Johnson, President of the United States and Commander in Chief of the Army and Navy of the United States, do hereby appoint Benjamin F. Perry, of South Carolina, provisional governor of the State of South Carolina, whose duty it shall be, at the earliest practicable period, to prescribe such rules and regulations as may be necessary and proper for convening a convention composed of delegates to be chosen by that portion of the people of said State who are loyal to the United States, and no others, for the purpose of altering or amending the constitution thereof, and with authority to exercise within the limits of said State all the powers necessary and proper to enable such loyal people of the State of South Carolina to restore said State to its constitutional relations to the Federal Government and to present such a republican form of State government as will entitle the State to the guaranty of the United States therefor and its people to protection by the United States against invasion, insurrection, and domestic violence: *Provided,* That in any election that may be hereafter held for choosing delegates to any State convention as aforesaid no person shall be qualified as an elector or shall be eligible as a member of such convention unless he shall have previously taken and subscribed the oath of amnesty as set forth in the President's proclamation of May 29, A.D. 1865, and is a voter qualified as prescribed by the constitution and laws of the State of South Carolina in force immediately before the 17th day of November, A.D. 1860, the date of the so-called ordinance of secession; and the said convention, when convened, or the legislature that may be thereafter assembled, will prescribe the qualification of electors and the eligibility of persons to hold office under the constitution and laws of the State—a power the people of the several States composing the Federal Union have rightfully exercised from the origin of the Government to the present time.

And I do hereby direct—

First. That the military commander of the department and all officers and persons in the military and naval service aid and assist the said provisional governor in carrying into effect this proclamation; and they are enjoined to abstain from in any way hindering, impeding, or discouraging the loyal people from the organization of a State government as herein authorized.

Second. That the Secretary of State proceed to put in force all laws of the United States the administration whereof belongs to the State Department applicable to the geographical limits aforesaid.

Third. That the Secretary of the Treasury proceed to nominate for appointment assessors of taxes and collectors of customs and internal revenue and such other officers of the Treasury Department as are authorized by law and put in execution the revenue laws of the United States within the geographical limits aforesaid. In making appointments the preference shall be given to qualified loyal persons residing within the districts where their respective duties are to be performed; but if suitable residents of the districts shall not be found, then persons residing in other States or districts shall be appointed.

Fourth. That the Postmaster-General proceed to establish post-offices and post routes and put into execution the postal laws of the United States within the said State, giving to loyal residents the preference of appointment; but if suitable residents are not found, then to appoint agents, etc., from other States.

Fifth. That the district judge for the judicial district in which South Carolina is included proceed to hold courts within said State in accordance with the provisions of the act of Congress. The Attorney-General will instruct the proper officers to libel and bring to judgment, confiscation, and sale property subject to confiscation and enforce the administration of justice within said State in all matters within the cognizance and jurisdiction of the Federal courts.

Sixth. That the Secretary of the Navy take possession of all public property belonging to the Navy Department within said geographical limits and put in operation all acts of Congress in relation to naval affairs having application to the said State.

Seventh. That the Secretary of the Interior put in force the laws relating to the Interior Department applicable to the geographical limits aforesaid.

We Must Have a Radical Reconstruction

THADDEUS STEVENS

It is obvious . . . that the first duty of Congress is to pass a law declaring the condition of these outside or defunct States, and providing proper civil governments for them. Since the conquest they have been governed by martial law. Military rule is necessarily despotic, and ought not to exist longer than is absolutely necessary. As there are no symptoms that the people of these provinces will be prepared to participate in constitutional government for some years, I know of no arrangement so proper for them as territorial governments. There they can learn the principles of freedom and eat the fruit of foul rebellion. Under such governments, while electing members to the Territorial Legislatures, they will necessarily mingle with those to whom Congress shall extend the right of suffrage. In Territories Congress fixes the qualifications of electors; and I know of no better place nor better occasion for the conquered rebels and the conqueror to practice justice to all men, and accustom themselves to make and to obey equal laws.

As these fallen rebels cannot at their option reënter the heaven which they have disturbed, the garden of Eden which they have deserted, and flaming swords are set

Congressional Globe, 39th Cong., 1st sess., December 18, 1865, pp. 72–75.

at the gates to secure their exclusion, it becomes important to the welfare of the nation to inquire when the doors shall be reopened for their admission.

According to my judgment they ought never to be recognized as capable of acting in the Union, or of being counted as valid States, until the Constitution shall have been so amended as to make it what its framers intended; and so as to secure perpetual ascendency to the party of the Union; and so as to render our republican Government firm and stable forever. The first of those amendments is to change the basis of representation among the States from Federal numbers to actual voters. Now all the colored freemen in the slave States, and three fifths of the slaves, are represented, though none of them have votes. The States have nineteen representatives of colored slaves. If the slaves are now free then they can add, for the other two fifths, thirteen more, making the slave representation thirty-two. I suppose the free blacks in those States will give at least five more, making the representation of non-voting people of color about thirty-seven. The whole number of representatives now from the slave States is seventy. Add the other two fifths and it will be eighty-three.

If the amendment prevails, and those States withhold the right of suffrage from persons of color, it will deduct about thirty-seven, leaving them but forty-six. With the basis unchanged, the eighty-three southern members, with the Democrats that will in the best times be elected from the North, will always give them a majority in Congress and in the Electoral College. They will at the very first election take possession of the White House and the halls of Congress. I need not depict the ruin that would follow. Assumption of the rebel debt or repudiation of the Federal debt would be sure to follow. The oppression of the freedmen; the reamendment of their State constitutions, and the reëstablishment of slavery would be the inevitable result. That they would scorn and disregard their present constitutions, forced upon them in the midst of martial law, would be both natural and just. No one who has any regard for freedom of elections can look upon those governments, forced upon them in duress, with any favor. If they should grant the right of suffrage to persons of color, I think there would always be Union white men enough in the South, aided by the blacks, to divide the representation, and thus continue the Republican ascendency. If they should refuse to thus alter their election laws it would reduce the representatives of the late slave States to about forty-five and render them powerless for evil.

It is plain that this amendment must be consummated before the defunct States are admitted to be capable of State action, or it never can be. . . .

But this is not all that we ought to do before these inveterate rebels are invited to participate in our legislation. We have turned, or are about to turn, loose four million slaves without a hut to shelter them or a cent in their pockets. The infernal laws of slavery have prevented them from acquiring an education, understanding the commonest laws of contract, or of managing the ordinary business of life. This Congress is bound to provide for them until they can take care of themselves. If we do not furnish them with homesteads, and hedge them around with protective laws; if we leave them to the legislation of their late masters, we had better have left them in bondage. Their condition would be worse than that of our prisoners at Andersonville. If we fail in this great duty now, when we have the power, we shall deserve and receive the execration of history and of all future ages. . . .

This Congress owes it to its own character to set the seal of reprobation upon a doctrine which is becoming too fashionable, and unless rebuked will be the recognized principle of our Government. Governor Perry[1] and other provisional governors and orators proclaim that "this is the white man's Government." The whole copperhead party, pandering to the lowest prejudices of the ignorant, repeat the cuckoo cry, "This is the white man's Government." Demagogues of all parties, even some high in authority, gravely shout, "This is the white man's Government." What is implied by this? That one race of men are to have the exclusive right forever to rule this nation, and to exercise all acts of sovereignty, while all other races and nations and colors are to be their subjects, and have no voice in making the laws and choosing the rulers by whom they are to be governed. Wherein does this differ from slavery except in degree? Does not this contradict all the distinctive principles of the Declaration of Independence? When the great and good men promulgated that instrument, and pledged their lives and sacred honors to defend it, it was supposed to form an epoch in civil government. Before that time it was held that the right to rule was vested in families, dynasties, or races, not because of superior intelligence or virtue, but because of a divine right to enjoy exclusive privileges.

Our fathers repudiated the whole doctrine of the legal superiority of families or races, and proclaimed the equality of men before the law. Upon that they created a revolution and built the Republic. They were prevented by slavery from perfecting the superstructure whose foundation they had thus broadly laid. For the sake of the Union they consented to wait, but never relinquished the idea of its final completion. The time to which they looked forward with anxiety has come. It is our duty to complete their work. If this Republic is not now made to stand on their great principles, it has no honest foundation, and the Father of all men will still shake it to its center. If we have not yet been sufficiently scourged for our national sin to teach us to do justice to all God's creatures, without distinction of race or color, we must expect the still more heavy vengeance of an offended Father, still increasing his inflictions as he increased the severity of the plagues of Egypt until the tyrant consented to do justice. And when that tyrant repented of his reluctant consent, and attempted to re-enslave the people, as our southern tyrants are attempting to do now, he filled the Red sea with broken chariots and drowned horses, and strewed the shores with dead carcasses.

Mr. Chairman, I trust the Republican party will not be alarmed at what I am saying. I do not profess to speak their sentiments, nor must they be held responsible for them. I speak for myself, and take the responsibility, and will settle with my intelligent constituents.

This is not a "white man's Government," in the exclusive sense in which it is used. To say so is political blasphemy, for it violates the fundamental principles of our gospel of liberty. This is man's Government; the Government of all men alike;

---

[1]Benjamin F. Perry of South Carolina, a Unionist rewarded by Johnson with an appointment as provisional governor of the state—ED.

not that all men will have equal power and sway within it. Accidental circumstances, natural and acquired endowment and ability, will vary their fortunes. But equal rights to all the privileges of the Government is innate in every immortal being, no matter what the shape or color of the tabernacle which it inhabits.

If equal privileges were granted to all, I should not expect any but white men to be elected to office for long ages to come. The prejudice engendered by slavery would not soon permit merit to be preferred to color. But it would still be beneficial to the weaker races. In a country where political divisions will always exist, their power, joined with just white men, would greatly modify, if it did not entirely prevent, the injustice of majorities. Without the right of suffrage in the late slave States, (I do not speak of the free States.) I believe the slaves had far better been left in bondage. I see it stated that very distinguished advocates of the right of suffrage lately declared in this city that they do not expect to obtain it by congressional legislation, but only by administrative action, because, as one gallant gentleman said, the States had not been out of the Union. Then they will never get it. The President is far sounder than they. He sees that administrative action has nothing to do with it. If it ever is to come, it must be constitutional amendments or congressional action in the Territories, and in enabling acts.

How shameful that men of influence should mislead and miseducate the public mind! They proclaim, "This is the white man's Government," and the whole coil of copperheads echo the same sentiment, and upstart, jealous Republicans join the cry. Is it any wonder ignorant foreigners and illiterate natives should learn this doctrine, and be led to despise and maltreat a whole race of their fellow-men?

Sir, this doctrine of a white man's Government is as atrocious as the infamous sentiment that damned the late Chief Justice [Roger Taney] to everlasting fame; and, I fear, to everlasting fire.

1.2: The White South Responds
(1865, 1866, 1868, 1874)

White southerners were themselves divided over Reconstruction. In the immediate aftermath of Confederate surrender, many were too stunned to resist the North's dictation. But that mood did not last very long. In a matter of months many southern leaders, including former Confederate officials, had regained their composure and were preparing to salvage what they could from the shambles of defeat. Under the state governments reestablished under President Johnson's auspices, they resisted major changes in relations between the races and refused to express contrition at their section's secessionist past. When Thaddeus Stevens and his Radical allies in Congress imposed more stringent conditions, they fought back even harder.

The first selection below is an example of the Black Codes passed by the conservative southern state governments established under Johnson's 1865 proclamations. These state laws were designed to regularize legal relations between blacks and the dominant white society now that slavery was gone. They accepted the end of slavery, but in most cases they cast blacks as inferior beings, not full citizens, and even placed them in jeopardy of quasi-reenslavement.

Among the harshest of the state Black Codes was that of Mississippi, a state, like South Carolina, with a black majority in its population. What elements of this code implied recognition of the end of the slave system? What provisions suggest that white Mississippians were not willing to accord the freed men and women full equality? Can you see from this document why black leaders and Radical Republicans considered Johnson's Reconstruction policy too lenient?

A substantial minority of native-born white southerners for a time came to terms with the Radical state administrations imposed by Congress when it seized control of Reconstruction policy. Called "scalawags," these Republican voters were particularly numerous in the former nonslaveholding parts of the South and among businessmen of Whig antecedents. To scalawags, the enemy was often the former planter elite that had pulled the South into a disastrous war, not the Republican politicians in Washington. Joining with blacks, newly enfranchised under the Fourteenth and Fifteenth Amendments to the Constitution, and with "carpetbaggers"—northern whites who came South to make their fortunes after 1865—they won control for a time over the state governments established under the Reconstruction Acts.

The second document is by a scalawag. James W. Hunnicutt was a South Carolina Baptist minister who had originally supported secession and then changed his mind. The selection is his testimony before the congressional Joint Committee on Reconstruction in early 1866. Why does Hunnicutt emphasize the treatment of white unionists in the South? Do you feel that the questioner, Radical Republican Senator Jacob Howard of Michigan, is leading the witness?

The third item in this section represents the position of the "redeemers," the ardent white conservatives who fought to wrest political supremacy from the Radical Republicans who controlled the state Reconstruction governments.

An editorial from the Atlanta News *of September 10, 1874, it charges the Republicans and blacks with barbarism. Were the charges valid? Do you know if the Radical regimes in the South were more corrupt, wasteful, and incompetent than state governments elsewhere dur-*

ing this era? Were the charges based more on race prejudice than on reality? How do you explain the vitriol of the conservative southern attack on the Radical regimes?

Mississippi Black Code

MISSISSIPPI LEGISLATURE

1. Civil Rights of Freedmen in Mississippi

Sec. 1. *Be it enacted,* . . . That all freedmen, free negroes, and mulattoes may sue and be sued, implead and be impleaded, in all the courts of law and equity of this State, and may acquire personal property, and choses [sic] in action, by descent or purchase, and may dispose of the same in the same manner and to the same extent that white persons may: *Provided,* That the provisions of this section shall not be so construed as to allow any freedman, free negro, or mulatto to rent or lease any lands or tenements except in incorporated cities or towns, in which places the corporate authorities shall control the same. . . .

Sec. 3. . . . All freedmen, free negroes, or mulattoes who do now and have here-before lived and cohabited together as husband and wife shall be taken and held in law as legally married, and the issue shall be taken and held as legitimate for all purposes; that it shall not be lawful for any freedman, free negro, or mulatto to intermarry with any white person; nor for any white person to intermarry with any freedman, free negro, or mulatto; and any person who shall so intermarry, shall be deemed guilty of felony, and on conviction thereof shall be confined in the State penitentiary for life; and those shall be deemed freedmen, free negroes, and mulattoes who are of pure negro blood, and those descended from a negro to the third generation, inclusive, though one ancestor in each generation may have been a white person.

Sec. 4. . . . In addition to cases in which freedmen, free negroes, and mulattoes are now by law competent witnesses, freedmen, free negroes, or mulattoes shall be competent in civil cases, when a party or parties to the suit, either plaintiff or plaintiffs, defendant or defendants, and a white person or white persons, is or are the opposing party or parties, plaintiff or plaintiffs, defendant or defendants. They shall also be competent witnesses in all criminal prosecutions where the crime charged is alleged to have been committed by a white person upon or against the person or property of a freedman, free negro, or mulatto: *Provided,* that in all cases said witnesses shall be examined in open court, on the stand; except, however, they may be examined before the grand jury, and shall in all cases be subject to the rules and tests of the common law as to competency and credibility. . . .

Laws of the State of Mississippi Passed at the Regular Session of the Mississippi Legislature, Held in the City of Jackson, October–December, 1865 (Jackson: J. J. Shannon and Company, 1866), pp. 82–93.

Sec. 6. . . . All contracts for labor made with freedmen, free negroes, and mulattoes for a longer period than one month shall be in writing, and in duplicate, attested and read to said freedman, free negro, or mulatto by a beat, city or county officer, or two disinterested white persons of the county in which the labor is to be performed, of which each party shall have one; and said contracts shall be taken and held as entire contracts, and if the laborer shall quit the service of the employer before the expiration of his term of service, without good cause, he shall forfeit his wages for that year up to the time of quitting.

Sec. 7. . . . Every civil officer shall, and every person may, arrest and carry back to his or her legal employer any freedman, free negro, or mulatto who shall have quit the service of his or her employer before the expiration of his or her term of service without good cause; and said officer and person shall be entitled to receive for arresting and carrying back every deserting employe aforesaid the sum of five dollars, and ten cents per mile from the place of arrest to the place of delivery; and the same shall be paid by the employer, and held as a set-off for so much against the wages of said deserting employe: *Provided,* that said arrested party, after being so returned, may appeal to the justice of the peace or member of the board of police of the county, who, on notice to the alleged employer, shall try summarily whether said appellant is legally employed by the alleged employer, and has good cause to quit said employer; either party shall have the right of appeal to the county court, pending which the alleged deserter shall be remanded to the alleged employer or otherwise disposed of, as shall be right and just; and the decision of the county court shall be final. . . .

Sec. 9. . . . If any person shall persuade or attempt to persuade, entice, or cause any freedman, free negro, or mulatto to desert from the legal employment of any person before the expiration of his or her term of service, or shall knowingly employ any such deserting freedman, free negro, or mulatto, or shall knowingly give or sell to any such deserting freedman, free negro, or mulatto, any food, raiment, or other thing, he or she shall be guilty of a misdemeanor, and, upon conviction, shall be fined not less than twenty-five dollars and not more than two hundred dollars and the costs; and if said fine and costs shall not be immediately paid, the court shall sentence said convict to not exceeding two months' imprisonment in the county jail, and he or she shall moreover be liable to the party injured in damages: *Provided,* if any person shall, or shall attempt to, persuade, entice, or cause any freedman, free negro, or mulatto to desert from any legal employment of any person, with the view to employ said freedman, free negro, or mulatto without the limits of this State, such person, on conviction, shall be fined not less than fifty dollars, and not more than five hundred dollars and costs; and if said fine and costs shall not be immediately paid, the court shall sentence said convict to not exceeding six months imprisonment in the county jail. . . .

2. Mississippi Apprentice Law

Sec. 1. . . . It shall be the duty of all sheriffs, justices of the peace, and other civil officers of the several counties in this State, to report to the probate courts of their respective counties semi-annually, at the January and July terms of said courts, all freedmen, free negroes, and mulattoes, under the age of eighteen, in their respective counties, beats or districts, who are orphans, or whose parent or parents have not the means or who refuse to provide for and support said minors; and thereupon it shall be the duty of said probate court to order the clerk of said court to apprentice said minors to some competent and suitable person, on such terms as the court may direct, having a particular care to the interest of said minor: *Provided,* that the former owner of said minors shall have the preference when, in the opinion of the court, he or she shall be a suitable person for that purpose.

Sec. 2. . . . The said court shall be fully satisfied that the person or persons to whom said minor shall be apprenticed shall be a suitable person to have the charge and care of said minor, and fully to protect the interest of said minor. The said court shall require the said master or mistress to execute bond and security, payable to the State of Mississippi, conditioned that he or she shall furnish said minor with sufficient food and clothing; to treat said minor humanely; furnish medical attention in case of sickness; teach, or cause to be taught, him or her to read and write, if under fifteen years old, and will conform to any law that may be hereafter passed for the regulation of the duties and relation of master and apprentice. . . .

Sec. 3. . . . In the management and control of said apprentice, said master or mistress shall have the power to inflict such moderate corporal chastisement as a father or guardian is allowed to inflict on his or her child or ward at common law: *Provided,* that in no case shall cruel or inhuman punishment be inflicted.

Sec. 4. . . . If any apprentice shall leave the employment of his or her master or mistress, without his or her consent, said master or mistress may pursue and recapture said apprentice, and bring him or her before any justice of the peace of the county, whose duty it shall be to remand said apprentice to the service of his or her master or mistress; and in the event of a refusal on the part of said apprentice so to return, then said justice shall commit said apprentice to the jail of said county, on failure to give bond, to the next term of the county court; and it shall be the duty of said court at the first term thereafter to investigate said case, and if the court shall be of opinion that said apprentice left the employment of his or her master or mistress without good cause, to order him or her to be punished, as provided for the punishment of hired freedmen, as may be from time to time provided for by law for desertion, until he or she shall agree to return to the service of his or her master or mistress: . . . if the court shall believe that said apprentice had good cause to quit his said master or mistress, the court shall discharge said apprentice from said indenture, and also enter a judgment against the master or mistress for not more than one hundred dollars, for the use and benefit of said apprentice. . . .

3. Mississippi Vagrant Law

Sec. 1. *Be it enacted,* etc., . . . That all rogues and vagabonds, idle and dissipated persons, beggars, jugglers, or persons practicing unlawful games or plays, runaways, common drunkards, common night-walkers, pilferers, lewd, wanton, or lascivious persons, in speech or behavior, common railers and brawlers, persons who neglect their calling or employment, misspend what they earn, or do not provide for the support of themselves or their families, or dependents, and all other idle and disorderly persons, including all who neglect all lawful business, habitually misspend their time by frequenting houses of ill-fame, gaming-houses, or tippling shops, shall be deemed and considered vagrants, under the provisions of this act, and upon conviction thereof shall be fined not exceeding one hundred dollars, with all accruing costs, and be imprisoned at the discretion of the court, not exceeding ten days.

Sec. 2. . . . All freedmen, free negroes and mulattoes in this State, over the age of eighteen years, found on the second Monday in January, 1866, or thereafter, with no lawful employment or business, or found unlawfully assembling themselves together, either in the day or night time, and all white persons so assembling themselves with freedmen, free negroes or mulattoes, or usually associating with freedmen, free negroes or mulattoes, on terms of equality, or living in adultery or fornication with a freed woman, free negro or mulatto, shall be deemed vagrants, and on conviction thereof shall be fined in a sum not exceeding, in the case of a freedman, free negro or mulatto, fifty dollars, and a white man two hundred dollars, and imprisoned at the discretion of the court, the free negro not exceeding ten days, and the white man not exceeding six months. . . .

Sec. 7. . . . If any freedman, free negro, or mulatto shall fail or refuse to pay any tax levied according to the provisions of the sixth section of this act, it shall be *prima facie* evidence of vagrancy, and it shall be the duty of the sheriff to arrest such freedman, free negro, or mulatto or such person refusing or neglecting to pay such tax, and proceed at once to hire for the shortest time such delinquent tax-payer to any one who will pay the said tax, with accruing costs, giving preference to the employer, if there be one. . . .

4. Penal Laws of Mississippi

Sec. 1. *Be it enacted,* . . . That no freedman, free negro or mulatto, not in the military service of the United States government, and not licensed so to do by the board of police of his or her county, shall keep or carry fire-arms of any kind, or any ammunition, dirk or bowie knife, and on conviction thereof in the county court shall be punished by fine, not exceeding ten dollars, and pay the costs of such proceedings, and all such arms or ammunition shall be forfeited to the informer; and it shall be the duty of every civil and military officer to arrest any freedman, free negro, or mulatto found with any such arms or ammunition, and cause him or her to be committed to trial in default of bail.

[Sec.] 2. . . . Any freedman, free negro, or mulatto committing riots, routs, affrays, trespasses, malicious mischief, cruel treatment to animals, seditious speeches, insulting gestures, language, or acts, or assaults on any person, disturbance of the peace, exercising the function of a minister of the Gospel without a license from some regularly organized church, vending spirituous or intoxicating liquors, or committing any other misdemeanor, the punishment of which is not specifically provided for by law, shall, upon conviction thereof in the county court, be fined not less than ten dollars, and not more than one hundred dollars, and may be imprisoned at the discretion of the court, not exceeding thirty days.

Sec. 3. . . . If any white person shall sell, lend, or give to any freedman, free negro, or mulatto any fire-arms, dirk or bowie knife, or ammunition, or any spirituous or intoxicating liquors, such person or persons so offending, upon conviction thereof in the county court of his or her county, shall be fined not exceeding fifty dollars, and may be imprisoned, at the discretion of the court, not exceeding thirty days. . . .

Sec. 5. . . . If any freedman, free negro, or mulatto, convicted of any of the misdemeanors provided against in this act, shall fail or refuse for the space of five days, after conviction, to pay the fine and costs imposed, such person shall be hired out by the sheriff or other officer, at public outcry, to any white person who will pay said fine and all costs, and take said convict for the shortest time.

Johnson's Policies Criticized

JAMES W. HUNNICUTT

Mr. [Jacob] Howard: What is the effect of President Johnson's policy of reconstruction there? [South Carolina]—*A.:* . . . They are all in favor of President Johnson's policy of reconstruction. As soon as they get their ends served by him they would not touch him, but he is their man now. They say that in 1868 the South will be a unit, and that with the help of the copperhead party of the North they will elect a President. They do not care to have slavery back, but they will try and make the federal government pay them for their slaves. A man from Virginia told me today that they would be paid for their Negroes. This gentleman lost forty Negroes. This is their idea; they do not want slavery back, but they want to be paid for their slaves. They say that unless you accept their debt they will repudiate yours. They say they are not interested in this government.

Q.: They would be glad to have Uncle Sam assume the payment of the Confederate debt?—*A.:* Yes, sir, and to pay them for their Negroes and to indemnify them for their loss of property in the war. It is an impression of most of them, men, women, and children, that they are going to be paid for every rail burned, for every stick of timber destroyed, and for every Negro lost. One man told me in my house that as soon as they could get the reins of government in their hands they would undo everything that this administration has done, with an awful adjective prefixed to the word "administration." He said, "We have as much right to undo what the administration has done as they have to destroy the government of the Constitution"— as they claim the administration has done.

Q.: They propose to get back into the Union for the purpose of restoring the Constitution?—*A.:* Yes, sir; and the testimony of the Negroes will not be worth a snap of your finger, and all this is done for policy. A Negro can come and give his testimony, and it passes for what it is worth with the courts. They can do what they please with it; there are the judges, the lawyers, and the jury against the Negro, and

Report of the Joint Committee on Reconstruction, (Washington, D.C.: Government Printing Office, 1866) pt. 2, pp. 150–51.

perhaps every one of them is sniggering and laughing while the Negro is giving his testimony.

Q.: Has not the liberal policy of President Johnson in granting pardons and amnesties rather tended to soothe and allay their feelings towards the government of the United States?—*A.:* No, sir, not towards the government of the United States nor towards the Union men.

Q.: What effect has it had in that respect?—*A.:* It has made them more impudent. They were once humble and felt that they had done wrong, but this policy has emboldened them, and they are more impudent today, more intolerant, and more proscriptive than they were in 1864. They say that we are the traitors and went over to the damned Yankees. Our present mayor [of Fredericksburg] Slaughter, had sixty men of Grant's army, who were wounded in the wilderness and sent to Fredericksburg, forwarded to General [Robert E.] Lee as prisoners-of-war. When Fredericksburg fell into our hands Slaughter made his escape. The federals arrested sixty citizens of Fredericksburg to be held as hostages for these sixty soldiers whom Slaughter had sent to the enemy, and among them was my wife's brother, who was living in Fredericksburg, and yet that same Slaughter was reelected mayor of Fredericksburg last summer after the collapse of the rebellion. Old Tom Barton, the commonwealth's attorney, said in 1861 (and I suppose his feelings are the same still) that all these Union shriekers ought to be hung as high as Haman, and this old man was reelected commonwealth attorney by the people of the county. Every member of the rebel common council was reelected. One of the men who were elected members of the common council from that district stated that none of the Union men who went over to the Yankees during the war should be allowed to return to Fredericksburg; he was also appointed director of a bank there. These are the men we have got over us, and what kind of justice can we expect in the courts?

Q.: You will probably get pretty summary justice?—*A.:* I think so; these are facts.

Q.: Where is Slaughter now?—*A.:* He is now mayor of Fredericksburg and will be reelected next month; we need not run a Union man there; we are disfranchised.

Q.: Is not Slaughter a good Union man?—*A.:* Oh! He has been notoriously Union all the time, as the papers say—notoriously Union! I saw that stated in a Fredericksburg paper; it stated that they had been persecuting Mayor Slaughter, who had been notoriously Union all the time.

Q.: You have not a great deal of confidence in the truthfulness of secession?—*A.:* No, sir; I have not.

Q.: Where their political standing is concerned?—*A.:* I used to have some confidence, not in secession, but in the people; but it seems to me that their whole nature and character has been changed, and that when treason enters a man's heart, every virtue he has departs.

Q.: Could Jefferson Davis be convicted of treason in that part of Virginia?—*A.:* As I went home last Sunday week in the boat, I was in company with a delegation from the Virginia legislature which waited upon President Johnson, and I heard one of them say that there could not be a jury obtained south of the Potomac who would convict Jeff Davis, and that the man who would write down there that Jeff Davis should be punished would be in danger. Jeff Davis cannot be punished down there, and they would elect Lee tomorrow, if there were no difficulty in the way, governor of Virginia. There is no question about that in my mind.

Q.:   Do you think of anything that you wish to relate?—*A.:* No, sir; I simply wish to state that I make these remarks conscientiously. I was born and raised in the South; my interests of every kind, social, financial, religious and political, are in the South; my church is in the South, and I am going soon to Richmond to edit a paper. Nothing but the good of the country, my own safety, and the safety of my children, and of Union men and of freedmen, could have induced me to come before you and make this statement. I am a friend of the South. I have written for the South, and I shall write in behalf of the South, but the South is one thing, and traitors and treason in the South are different things.

White People Must Regain Control of Their States

EDITOR, *ATLANTA NEWS*

Let there be White Leagues formed in every town, village and hamlet of the South, and let us organize for the great struggle which seems inevitable. If the October elections which are to be held at the North are favorable to the radicals, the time will have arrived for us to prepare for the very worst. The radicalism of the republican party must be met by the radicalism of white men. We have no war to make against the United States Government, but against the republican party our hate must be unquenchable, our war interminable and merciless. Fast fleeting away is the day of wordy protests and idle appeals to the magnanimity of the republican party. By brute force they are endeavoring to force us into acquiescence to their hideous programme. We have submitted long enough to indignities, and it is time to meet brute-force with brute-force. Every Southern State should swarm with White Leagues, and we should stand ready to act the moment [President Ulysses S.] Grant signs the civil-rights bill.[1] It will not do to wait till radicalism has fettered us to the car of social equality before we make an effort to resist it. The signing of the bill will be a declaration of war against the southern whites. It is our duty to ourselves, it is our duty to our children, it is our duty to the white race whose prowess subdued the wilderness of this continent, whose civilization filled it with cities and towns and villages, whose mind gave it power and grandeur, and whose labor imparted to it prosperity, and whose love made peace and happiness dwell within its homes, to take the gage of battle the moment it is thrown down. If the white democrats of the

Walter L. Fleming, ed., *Documentary History of Reconstruction: Political, Military, and Industrial, 1865 to the Present Time* (Cleveland: The Arthur H. Clark Company, 1907), vol. 2, pp. 387–88.

[1]A bill proposed by Charles Sumner in 1870–71 that sought to guarantee blacks non-segregated, equal access to all public accommodations—ED.

North are men, they will not stand idly by and see us borne down by northern radicals and half-barbarous negroes. But no matter what they may do, it is time for us to organize. We have been temporizing long enough. Let northern radicals understand that military supervision of southern elections and the civil-rights bill mean war, that war means bloodshed, and that we are terribly in earnest, and even they, fanatical as they are, may retrace their steps before it is too late.

Organization and Principles of the Ku Klux Klan (1868)

Organization and Principles of the Ku Klux Klan

Appellation

This Organization shall be styled and denominated, the Order of the * * *

Creed

We, the Order of the * * * , reverentially acknowledge the majesty and supremacy of the Divine Being, and recognize the goodness and providence of the same. And we recognize our relation to the United States Government, the supremacy of the Constitution, the Constitutional Laws thereof, and the Union of States thereunder.

Character and Objects of the Order

This is an institution of Chivalry, Humanity, Mercy, and Patriotism; embodying in its genius and its principles all that is chivalric in conduct, noble in sentiment, generous in manhood, and patriotic in purpose; its peculiar objects being

First: To protect the weak, the innocent, and the defenseless, from the indignities, wrongs, and outrages of the lawless, the violent, and the brutal; to relieve the injured and oppressed; to succor the suffering and unfortunate, and especially the widows and orphans of Confederate soldiers.

Second: To protect and defend the Constitution of the United States, and all laws passed in conformity thereto, and to protect the States and the people thereof from all invasion from any source whatever.

Third: To aid and assist in the execution of all constitutional laws, and to protect the people from unlawful seizure, and from trial except by their peers in conformity to the laws of the land.

Titles

Sec. 1. The officers of this Order shall consist of a Grand Wizard of the Empire, and his ten Genii; a Grand Dragon of the Realm, and his eight Hydras: a Grand Titan of the Dominion, and his six Furies; a Grand Giant of the Province, and his four Goblins; a Grand Cyclops of the Den, and his two Night Hawks; a Grand Magi, a Grand Monk, a Grand Scribe, a Grand Exchequer, a Grand Turk, and a Grand Sentinel.

U.S. 42nd Congress, 2nd Session, Senate Report, No. 41 on the Ku Klux Klan, Washington, DC, 1871.

Sec. 2. The body politic of this Order shall be known and designated as "Ghouls."

Territory and its Divisions

Sec. 1. The territory embraced within the jurisdiction of this Order shall be coterminous with the States of Maryland, Virginia. North Carolina, South Carolina, Georgia, Florida, Alabama, Mississippi, Louisiana, Texas, Arkansas, Missouri, Kentucky, and Tennessee; all combined constituting the Empire.

Sec. 2. The Empire shall be divided into four departments, the first to be styled the Realm, and coterminous with the boundaries of the several States; the second to be styled the Dominion and to be coterminous with such counties as the Grand Dragons of the several Realms may assign to the charge of the Grand Titan. The third to be styled the Province, and to be coterminous with the several counties: *provided* the Grand Titan may, when he deems it necessary, assign two Grand Giants to one Province, prescribing, at the same time, the jurisdiction of each. The fourth department to be styled the Den, and shall embrace such part of a Province as the Grand Giant shall assign to the charge of a Grand Cyclops. . . .

Interrogations to be Asked

1st. Have you ever been rejected, upon application for membership in the * * * , or have you ever been expelled from the same?

2d. Are you now, or have you ever been, a member of the Radical Republican party, or either of the organizations known as the "Loyal League" and the "Grand Army of the Republic?"

3d. Are you opposed to the principles and policy of the Radical party, and to the Loyal League. and the Grand Army of the Republic, so far as you are informed of the character and purposes of those organizations?

4th. Did you belong to the Federal army during the late war, and fight against the South during the existence of the same?

5th. Are you opposed to negro equality, both social and political?

6th. Are you in favor of a white man's government in this country?

7th. Are you in favor of Constitutional liberty, and a Government of equitable laws instead of a Government of violence and oppression ?

8th. Are you in favor of maintaining the Constitutional rights of the South?

9th. Are you in favor of the re-enfranchisement and emancipation of the white men of the South, and the restitution of the Southern people to all their rights, alike proprietary, civil, and political?

10th. Do you believe in the inalienable right of self-preservation of the people against the exercise of arbitrary and unlicensed power? . . .

. . . 9. The most profound and rigid secrecy concerning any and everything that relates to the Order, shall at all times be maintained.

10. Any member who shall reveal or betray the secrets of this Order, shall suffer the extreme penalty of the law.

1.3: The Black Response (1865, 1868, 1866)

Emancipation and Union victory liberated almost 4 million black Americans from bondage. What role would they now play in the life of their region? Would they be citizens and voters? How would they earn a living? What claim did they have on their communities for education and other services? These and other questions confronted northern policy makers and voters after Confederate defeat.

To educated blacks, many of them former "free people of color," the most important right that the government could confer was that of suffrage, the right to vote. In the first selection below, Frederick Douglass, the prominent black abolitionist, argues for the necessity of giving the vote to the newly freed slaves. What are Douglass's arguments? This address was greeted with applause by his audience, but he was speaking to a Boston abolitionist convention. How do you think white southerners felt about suffrage for blacks? Do you know how most white northerners felt about giving black men the vote at this time—Douglass's Boston audience notwithstanding? Note Douglass's reference to woman suffrage. Why does he believe black males should be given the vote before white women?

The second selection is an excerpt from a debate at the 1868 South Carolina constitutional convention, which was called after Congress refused to accept the state's "Johnson government" and established stricter rules for southern readmission to the Union.

One of the many topics the convention delegates debated was land ownership. If conservative southern whites sought to reestablish a system of near slavery, blacks and some of their Radical defenders wanted what seemed to many contemporaries to be the other extreme: to create a black farm-owner class by redistributing white-owned land. The participants in the selection below are Richard H. Cain, a black minister originally from New York; Francis L. Cardozo, a South Carolinian of mixed race, also a minister; and N. G. Parker and C. P. Leslie, white carpetbaggers. Their debate focuses on a resolution asking the federal Congress to appropriate $1 million to be used to buy small homesteads for South Carolina freed men and women. What are the arguments pro and con? What is the reference to "confiscation"? Congress never made the appropriation.

Can you guess why from the evidence in this debate? What would have been the advantage to the nation at large if ideas such as Cardozo's and Cain's had been enacted?

The third selection adds education to the "wish list" of Southern blacks during Reconstruction. Why were they so eager for education? Did they have access to education in slave days? Was their faith in education as salvation part of the American tradition? Was it misguided or exaggerated?

What the Black Man Wants

FREDERICK DOUGLASS

Mr. President,—I came here [to the annual meeting of the Massachusetts Anti-Slavery Society at Boston], as I come always to the meetings in New England, as a listener, and not as a speaker; and one of the reasons why I have not been more frequently to the meetings of this society, has been because of the disposition on the part of some of my friends to call me out upon the platform, even when they knew that there was some difference of opinion and of feeling between those who rightfully belong to this platform and myself; and for fear of being misconstrued, as desiring to interrupt or disturb the proceedings of these meetings, I have usually kept away, and have thus been deprived of that educating influence, which I am always free to confess is of the highest order, descending from this platform. I have felt, since I have lived out West, that in going there I parted from a great deal that was valuable; and I feel, every time I come to these meetings, that I have lost a great deal by making my home west of Boston, west of Massachusetts; for, if anywhere in the country there is to be found the highest sense of justice, or the truest demands for my race, I look for it in the East, I look for it here. The ablest discussions of the whole question of our rights occur here, and to be deprived of the privilege of listening to those discussions is a great deprivation.

I do not know, from what has been said, that there is any difference of opinion as to the duty of abolitionists, at the present moment. How can we get up any difference at this point, or at any point, where we are so united, so agreed? I went especially, however, with that word of Mr. [Wendell] Phillips, which is the criticism of Gen. Banks and Gen. Banks's policy. I hold that that policy is our chief danger at the present moment; that it practically enslaves the negro, and makes the [Emancipation] Proclamation of 1863 a mockery and delusion. What is freedom? It is the right to choose one's own employment. Certainly it means that, if it means any thing; and when any individual or combination of individuals, undertakes to decide for any man when he shall work, where he shall work, at what he shall work, and for what he shall work, he or they practically reduce him to slavery. (Applause.) He is a slave. That I understand Gen. Banks to do—to determine for the so-called freedman, when, and where, and at what, and for how much he shall work, when he shall be punished, and by whom punished. It is absolute slavery. It defeats the

William D. Kelley, Wendell Phillips, and Frederick Douglass, *The Equality of Men before the Law Claimed and Defended* (Boston: n.p., 1865), pp. 36–39.

beneficent intentions of the Government, if it has beneficent intentions, in regard to the freedom of our people.

I have had but one idea for the last three years, to present to the American people, and the phraseology in which I clothe it is the old abolition phraseology. I am for the "immediate, unconditional, and universal" enfranchisement of the black man, in every State in the Union. (Loud applause.) Without this, his liberty is a mockery; without this, you might as well almost retain the old name of slavery for his condition; for, in fact, if he is not the slave of the individual master, he is the slave of society, and holds his liberty as a privilege, not as a right. He is at the mercy of the mob, and has no means of protecting himself.

It may be objected, however, that this pressing of the negro's right to suffrage is premature. Let us have slavery abolished, it may be said, let us have labor organized, and then, in the natural course of events, the right of suffrage will be extended to the negro. I do not agree with this. The constitution of the human mind is such, that if it once disregards the conviction forced upon it by a revelation of truth, it requires the exercise of a higher power to produce the same conviction afterwards. The American people are now in tears. The Shenandoah has run blood—the best blood of the North. All around Richmond, the blood of New England and of the North has been shed—of your sons, your brothers and your fathers. We all feel, in the existence of this Rebellion, that judgments terrible, wide-spread, far-reaching, overwhelming, are abroad in the land; and we feel, in view of these judgments, just now, a disposition to learn righteousness. This is the hour. Our streets are in mourning, tears are falling at every fireside, and under the chastisement of this Rebellion we have almost come up to the point of conceding this great, this all-important right of suffrage. I fear that if we fail to do it now, if abolitionists fail to press it now, we may not see, for centuries to come, the same disposition that exists at this moment. (Applause.) Hence, I say, now is the time to press this right.

It may be asked, "Why do you want it? Some men have got along very well without it. Women have not this right." Shall we justify one wrong by another? That is a sufficient answer. Shall we at this moment justify the deprivation of the negro of the right to vote, because some one else is deprived of that privilege? I hold that women, as well as men, have the right to vote (applause), and my heart and my voice go with the movement to extend suffrage to woman; but that question rests upon another basis than that on which our right rests. We may be asked, I say, why we want it. I will tell you why we want it. We want it because it is our *right,* first of all. (Applause.) No class of men can, without insulting their own nature, be content with any deprivation of their rights. We want it, again, as a means for educating our race. Men are so constituted that they derive their conviction of their own possibilities largely from the estimate formed of them by others. If nothing is expected of a people, that people will find it difficult to contradict that expectation. By depriving us of suffrage, you affirm our incapacity to form an intelligent judgment respecting public men and public measures; you declare before the world that we are unfit to exercise the elective franchise, and by this means lead us to undervalue ourselves, to put a low estimate upon ourselves, and to feel that we have no possibilities like other men. Again, I want the elective franchise, for one, as a colored man, because ours is a peculiar government, based upon a peculiar idea, and that idea is universal suffrage. If I were in a monarchical government, or an autocratic or aristocratic government, where the few bore rule and the many were subject, there would be no special stigma resting upon me, because I did not exercise the elective franchise. It would do me no great violence. Mingling with the mass, I should partake of the strength of the mass; I should be supported by the mass, and I should have the same incentives to endeavor with the mass of my fellow-men; it would be no particular burden, no particular deprivation; but here, where universal suffrage is the rule, where that is the fundamental idea of the Government, to rule us out is to make us an exception, to brand us with the stigma of inferiority, and to invite to our heads the missiles of those about us; therefore, I want the franchise for the black man.

There are, however, other reasons, not derived from any consideration merely of our rights, but arising out of the condition of the South, and of the country—considerations which have already been referred to by Mr. Phillips—considerations which must arrest the attention of statesmen. I believe that when the tall heads of this Rebellion shall have been swept down, as they will be swept down, when the [Jefferson] Davises and [Robert] Toombses and [Alexander] Stephenses, and others who are leading in this Rebellion shall have been blotted out, there will be this rank undergrowth of treason, to which reference has been made, growing up there, and interfering with, and thwarting the quiet operation of the Federal Government in those States. You will see those traitors handing down, from sire to son, the same malignant spirit which they have manifested, and which they are now exhibiting, with malicious hearts, broad blades, and bloody hands in the field, against our sons and brothers. That spirit will still remain; and whoever sees the Federal Government extended over those Southern States will see that Government in a strange land, and not only in a strange land, but in an enemy's land. A post-master of the United States in the South will find himself surrounded by a hostile spirit; a collector in a Southern port will find himself surrounded by a hostile spirit; a United States marshal or United States judge will be surrounded there by a hostile element. That enmity will not die out in a year, will not die out in an age. The Federal Government will be looked upon in those States precisely as the Governments of Austria and France are looked upon in Italy at the present moment. They will endeavor to circumvent, they will endeavor to destroy, the peaceful operation of this Government. Now, where will you find the strength to counterbalance this spirit, if you do not find it in the negroes of the South? They are your friends, and have always been your friends. They were your friends even when the Government did not regard them as such. They comprehended the genius of this war before you did. It is a significant fact, it is a marvellous fact, it seems almost to imply a direct interposition of Providence, that this war, which began in the interest of slavery on both sides, bids fair to end in the interest of liberty on both sides. (Applause.) It was begun, I say, in the interest of slavery on both sides. The South was fighting to take slavery out of the Union, and the North fighting to keep it in the Union; the South fighting to get it beyond the limits of the United-States Constitution, and the North fighting to retain it within those limits; the South fighting for new guarantees, and the North fighting for the old guarantees;—both despising the negro, both insulting the negro.

Yet, the negro, apparently endowed with wisdom from on high, saw more clearly the end from the beginning than we did. When [William] Seward said the status of no man in the country would be changed by the war, the negro did not believe him. (Applause.) When our generals sent their underlings in shoulder-straps to hunt the flying negro back from our lines into the jaws of slavery, from which he had escaped, the negroes thought that a mistake had been made, and that the intentions of the Government had not been rightly understood by our officers in shoulder-straps, and they continued to come into our lines, threading their way through bogs and fens, over briers and thorns, fording streams, swimming rivers, bringing us tidings as to the safe path to march, and pointing out the dangers that threatened us. They are our only friends in the South, and we should be true to them in this their trial hour, and see to it that they have the elective franchise.

I know that we are inferior to you in some things—virtually inferior. We walk about among you like dwarfs among giants. Our heads are scarcely seen above the great sea of humanity. The Germans are superior to us; the Irish are superior to us; the Yankees are superior to us (laughter); they can do what we cannot, that is, what we have not hitherto been allowed to do. But while I make this admission, I utterly deny that we are originally, or naturally, or practically, or in any way, or in any important sense, inferior to anybody on this globe. (Loud applause.) This charge of inferiority is an old dodge. It has been made available for oppression on many occasions. It is only about six centuries since the blue-eyed and fair-haired Anglo-Saxons were considered inferior by the haughty Normans, who once trampled upon them. If you read the history of the Norman Conquest, you will find that this proud Anglo-Saxon was once looked upon as of coarser clay than his Norman master, and might be found in the highways and byways of old England laboring with a brass collar on his neck, and the name of his master marked upon it. *You* were down then! (Laughter and applause.) You are up now. I am glad you are up, and I want you to be glad to help us up also. (Applause.)

The story of our inferiority is an old dodge, as I have said; for wherever men oppress their fellows, wherever they enslave them, they will endeavor to find the needed apology for such enslavement and oppression in the character of the people oppressed and enslaved. When we wanted, a few years ago, a slice of Mexico, it was hinted that the Mexicans were an inferior race, that the old Castilian blood had become so weak that it would scarcely run down hill, and that Mexico needed the long, strong and beneficent arm of the Anglo-Saxon care extended over it. We said that it was necessary to its salvation, and a part of the "manifest destiny" of this Republic, to extend our arm over that dilapidated government. So, too, when Russia wanted to take possession of a part of the Ottoman Empire, the Turks were "an inferior race." So, too, when England wants to set the heel of her power more firmly in the quivering heart of old Ireland, the Celts are an "inferior race." So, too, the negro, when he is to be robbed of any right which is justly his, is an "inferior man." It is said that we are ignorant; I admit it. But if we know enough to be hung, we know enough to vote. If the negro knows enough to pay taxes to support the government, he knows enough to vote; taxation and representation should go together. If he knows enough to shoulder a musket and fight for the flag, fight for the government, he knows enough to vote. If he knows as much when he is sober as an Irishman knows when drunk, he knows enough to vote, on good American principles. (Laughter and applause.)

But I was saying that you needed a counterpoise in the persons of the slaves to the enmity that would exist at the South after the Rebellion is put down. I hold that the American people are bound, not only in self-defence, to extend this right to the freedmen of the South, but they are bound by their love of country, and by all their regard for the future safety of those Southern States, to do this—to do it as a measure essential to the preservation of peace there. But I will not dwell upon this. I put it to the American sense of honor. The honor of a nation is an important thing. It is said in the Scriptures, "What doth it profit a man if he gain the whole world and lose his own soul?" It may be said, also, What doth it profit a nation if it gain the whole world, but lose its honor? I hold that the American government has taken upon itself a solemn obligation of honor, to see that this war—let it be long or let it be short, let it cost much or let it cost little—that this war shall not cease until every freedman at the South has the right to vote. (Applause.) It has bound itself to it. What have you asked the black men of the South, the black men of the whole country, to do? Why, you have asked them to incur the deadly enmity of their masters, in order to befriend you and to befriend this Government. You have asked us to call down, not only upon ourselves, but upon our children's children, the deadly hate of the entire Southern people. You have called upon us to turn our backs upon our masters, to abandon their cause and espouse yours; to turn against the South and in favor of the North; to shoot down the Confederacy and uphold the flag—the American flag. You have called upon us to expose ourselves to all the subtle machinations of their malignity for all time. And now, what do you propose to do when you come to make peace? To reward your enemies, and trample in the dust your friends? Do you intend to sacrifice the very men who have come to the rescue of your banner in the South, and incurred the lasting displeasure of their masters thereby? Do you intend to sacrifice them and reward your enemies? Do you mean to give your enemies the right to vote, and take it away from your friends? Is that wise policy? Is that honorable? Could American honor withstand such a blow? I do not believe you will do it. I think you will see to it that we have the right to vote. There is something too mean in looking upon the negro, when you are in trouble, as a citizen, and when you are free from trouble, as an alien. When this nation was in trouble, in its early struggles, it looked upon the negro as a citizen. In 1776 he was a citizen. At the time of the formation of the Constitution the negro had the right to vote in eleven States out of the old thirteen. In your trouble you have made us citizens. In 1812 Gen. [Andrew] Jackson addressed us as citizens—"fellow-citizens." He wanted us to fight. We were citizens then! And now, when you come to frame a conscription bill, the negro is a citizen again. He has been a citizen just three times in the history of this government, and it has always been in time of trouble. In time of trouble we are citizens. Shall we be citizens in war, and aliens in peace? Would that be just?

I ask my friends who are apologizing for not insisting upon this right, where can the black man look, in this country, for the assertion of this right, if he may not look to the Massachusetts Anti-Slavery Society? Where under the whole heavens can he look for sympathy, in asserting this right, if he may not look to this platform? Have you lifted us up to a certain height to see that we are men, and then are any disposed to leave us there, without seeing that we are put in possession of all our rights? We look naturally to this platform for the assertion of all our rights, and for this one especially. I understand the anti-slavery societies of this country to be based on two principles,—first, the freedom of the blacks of this country; and, second, the elevation of them. Let me not be misunderstood here. I am not asking for sympathy at the hands of abolitionists, sympathy at the hands of any. I think the American people are disposed often to be generous rather than just. I look over this country at the present time, and I see Educational Societies, Sanitary Commissions, Freedmen's Associations, and the like,—all very good: but in regard to the colored people there is always more that is benevolent, I perceive, than just, manifested towards us. What I ask for the negro is not benevolence, not pity, not sympathy, but simply *justice.* (Applause.) The American people have always been anxious to know what they shall do with us. Gen. Banks was distressed with solicitude as to what he should do with the negro. Everybody has asked the question, and they learned to ask it early of the abolitionists, "What shall we do with the negro?" I have had but one answer from the beginning. Do nothing with us! Your doing with us has already played the mischief with us. Do nothing with us! If the apples will not remain on the tree of their own strength, if they are worm-eaten at the core, if they are early ripe and disposed to fall, let them fall! I am not for tying or fastening them on the tree in any way, except by nature's plan, and if they will not stay there, let them fall. And if the negro cannot stand on his own legs, let him fall also. All I ask is, give him a chance to stand on his own legs! Let him alone! If you see him on his way to school, let him alone,—don't disturb him! If you see him going to the dinner-table at a hotel, let him go! If you see him going to the ballot-box, let him alone,—don't disturb him! (Applause.) If you see him going into a work-shop, just let him alone,—your interference is doing him a positive injury. Gen. Banks's "preparation" is of a piece with this attempt to prop up the negro. Let him fall if he cannot stand alone! If the negro cannot live by the line of eternal justice, so beautifully pictured to you in the illustration used by Mr. Phillips, the fault will not be yours, it will be his who made the negro, and established that line for his government. (Applause.) Let him live or die by that. If you will only untie his hands, and give him a chance, I think he will live. He will work as readily for himself as the white man. A great many delusions have been swept away by this war. One was, that the negro would not work; he has proved his ability to work. Another was, that the negro would not fight; that he possessed only the most sheepish attributes of humanity; was a perfect lamb, or an "Uncle Tom"; disposed to take off his coat whenever required, fold his hands, and be whipped by anybody who wanted to whip him. But the war has proved that there is a great deal of human nature in the negro, and that "he will fight," as Mr. Quincy, our President, said, in earlier days than these, "when there is a reasonable probability of his whipping anybody." (Laughter and applause.)

The Ex-Slaves Should Have Land

Mr. [Richard H.] Cain: I offer this resolution with good intentions. I believe that there is need for immediate relief to the poor people of the State. I know from my experience among the people, there is a pressing need of some measures to meet the wants of the utterly destitute. The gentleman [C. P. Leslie] says that it will only take money out of the Treasury. Well, that is the intention. I do not expect to get it anywhere else. I expect to get the money, if at all, through the Treasury of the United States, or some other department. It certainly must come out of the Government. I believe such an appropriation would remove a great many of the difficulties now in the State and do a vast amount of good to poor people. It may be that we will not get it, but that will not debar us from asking. It is our privilege and right. Other Conventions have asked from Congress appropriations. Georgia and other States have sent in their petitions. One has asked for $30,000,000 to be appropriated to the Southern States. I do not see any inconsistency in the proposition presented by myself.

Mr. C. P. Leslie: Suppose I should button up my coat and march up to your house and ask you for money or provisions, when you had none to give, what would you think of me.

Mr. Cain: You would do perfectly right to run the chance of getting something to eat. This is a measure of relief to those thousands of freed people who now have no lands of their own. I believe the possession of lands and homesteads is one of the best means by which a people is made industrious, honest and advantageous to the State. I believe it is a fact well known, that over three hundred thousand men, women and children are homeless, landless. The abolition of slavery has thrown these people upon their own resources. How are they to live. I know the philosopher of the New York Tribune says, "root hog or die"; but in the meantime we ought to have some place to root. My proposition is simply to give the hog some place to root. I believe if the proposition is sent to Congress, it will certainly receive the attention of our friends. I believe the whole country is desirous to see that this State shall return to the Union in peace and quiet, and that every inhabitant of the State shall be made industrious and profitable to the State. I am opposed to this Bureau system.[1] I want a system adopted that will do away with the Bureau, but I cannot see how it can be done unless the people have homes. As long as people are working on shares and contracts, and at the end of every year are in debt, so long will they and the country suffer. But give them a chance to buy lands, and they become steady, industrious men. That is the reason I desire to bring this money here and to assist them to buy lands. . . .

I do not desire to have a foot of land in this State confiscated. I want every man to stand upon his own character. I want these lands purchased by the government, and

Proceedings of the Constitutional Convention of South Carolina, 1868 (New York: Arno Press, 1968), pp. 378–424.
[1]Cain probably means the work of the Freedmen's Bureau in negotiating labor contracts for the ex-slaves, contracts that were difficult to enforce—ED.

the people afforded an opportunity to buy from the government. I believe every man ought to carve out for himself a character and position in this life. I believe every man ought to be made to work by some means or other, and if he does not, he must go down. . . . I want to have the satisfaction of showing that the freedmen are as capable and willing to work as any men on the face of the earth. This measure will save the State untold expenses. I believe there are hundreds of persons in the jail and penitentiary cracking rock to-day who have all the instincts of honesty, and who, had they an opportunity of making a living, would never have been found in such a place. I think if Congress will accede to our request, we shall be benefited beyond measure, and save the State from taking charge of paupers, made such by not having the means to earn a living for themselves. . . .

Mr. C. P. Leslie: . . . I assert that time will prove that the petition offered, and the addresses made here to-day, were most inopportune. These addresses have been listened to by a large concourse of spectators, and have held out to them that within a very short time they are to get land. We all know that the colored people want land. Night and day they think and dream of it. It is their all in all. As these men retire from the hall and go home, the first thing they do is to announce to the people "joy on earth, and good will to all mankind." We are all going to have a home. . . . And when I know as they know, that without land a race of people, four millions in number, travelling up and down the earth without a home are suffering, I cannot but denounce those who would, for political purposes, add to their misery by raising expectations that could never be realized. . . .

Let us have a little more light upon the subject. Parson French, who, it is well known, has the welfare of the colored people at heart, did go to Washington and portrayed to leading Senators and members of Congress the terrible predicament of the colored people in the State. He said that cotton had sold so low that all the people were poverty stricken. The white people, he told them, were not able to plant, and there being no necessity to employ laborers, the colored people were turned out of house and home, and he begged them to loan the people, or the State, a million of dollars. Their answer was, "Mr. French, for God's sake, send up no petitions for money, for we cannot give one dollar." . . .

Mr. F[rancis] L. Cardozo: . . . The poor freedmen were induced, by many Congressmen even, to expect confiscation. They held out the hope of confiscation. [Union] General [William Tecumseh] Sherman did confiscate, gave the lands to the freedmen; and if it were not for President Johnson, they would have them now. The hopes of the freedmen have not been realized, and I do not think that asking for a loan of one million, to be paid by a mortgage upon the land, will be half as bad as has been supposed. I have been told by the Assistant Commissioner that he has been doing on a private scale what this petition proposes to do. I say every opportunity for helping the colored man should be seized upon. I think the adoption of this measure will do honor to the Convention. We should certainly vote for some measure of relief for the colored men, as we have to the white men, who mortgaged their property to perpetuate slavery, and whom they have liberated from their bonds.

Mr. N. G. Parker: I am glad that the gentleman who has just taken his seat has distinctly laid down the proposition that any member who votes against this petition votes against the colored man. I am a friend to the colored man, and he knows it. I have a record extending back for twenty years that shows it. . . .

I tell you, Mr. President, that the destitution that prevails this winter in those snow clad [Northern and Western] States is greater than it has ever been before. Thousands, yes millions, are out of employment, and what is the cause of it. I cannot stop now to elaborate the causes, but I will only briefly allude to them. War and its results are directly the cause of it. One of the results of the war, and the principal one, was the overthrow of slavery and tyranny in the Southern States; this was the good result of it; but the expense it caused the nation to do this, and the debt it incurred, and the overthrow of the labor system and consequent disturbance of trade and commerce, was the immediate evils. The burdensome taxation which followed is another principle cause of distress which now prevails in the Northern and Western States. The fact is patent that all the manufacturing States need aid; and let me tell you if the Congress of the United States grants additional aid to any of the unreconstructed States, for anything further than to perfect the reconstruction already half consummated, and the support of the Military and the Freedmen's Bureau, that in my opinion such a howl will go up as never was heard before, and I for one, would despair of success.

Our friends are trembling at Washington to-day, and all over the country, lest New Hampshire should cast a Democratic vote at her approaching election. I am of the opinion that if Congress should pass the appropriation called for just at this particular time, that every State from Maine to California would roll up such a Democrat vote in the coming election that was never heard of, or dreamt of, by the most ardent Democrat in this country. The result of the elections for the last year should not be unheeded.

Where would be our reconstruction if Andrew Johnson and the Democratic party had the handling of us? . . .

The Treasury of the United States has already as many drafts upon it as it can well bear. They have no money to purchase lands in South Carolina to sell on a credit—it is asking too much. Look at the almost overwhelming debt of the nation, and would you colored men, or white men, seek to increase it? For what was it contracted? and what keeps the expenses of Government to-day so large? It was contracted to make you free, and it is continually increased to preserve, protect and defend your freedom.

There never was a more liberal and humane government, nor never one that made such herculian [*sic*] efforts to retrieve the past as she has made and is making. We cannot ask her to do more than she is doing. There is such a thing as disgusting our friends. Do not let us weary them. If she will continue to afford us the protection she has afforded us in the past three years, if she will continue to the end in sustaining the reconstruction she commenced, if she will sustain the Freedmen's Bureau as long as it is a necessity, and give us the military necessary to protect and defend us, in God's name let us be satisfied. . . .

Mr. R. H. Cain: This measure, if carried out, therefore, will meet a want which the Bureau never can meet. A man may have rations to-day and not tomorrow, but when he gets land and a homestead, and is once fixed on that land, he never will want to go to the Commissary again. It is said that I depicted little farms by the roadside, chickens roosting on the fence, and all those poetical beauties. . . . I prefer this to seeing strong men working for the paltry sum of five or ten dollars a month, and some for even three dollars a month. How can a man live at that rate. I hate the contract system as I hate the being of whom my friend from Orangeburg (Mr. [Benjamin F.] Randolph) spoke last week (the devil). It has ruined the people. After fifty men have gone on a plantation, worked the whole year at raising twenty thousand bushels of rice, and then go to get their one-third, by the time they get through the division, after being charged by the landlord twenty-five or thirty cents a pound for bacon, two or three dollars for a pair of brogans that costs sixty cents, for living that costs a mere song, two dollars a bushel for corn that can be bought for one dollar; after I say, these people have worked the whole season, and at the end make up their accounts, they find themselves in debt. . . . I want to see a change in this country. Instead of the colored people being always penniless, I want to see them coming in with their mule teams and ox teams. I want to see them come with their corn and potatoes and exchange for silks and satins. I want to see school houses and churches in every parish and township. I want to see children coming forth to enjoy life as it ought to be enjoyed. This people know nothing of what is good and best for mankind until they get homesteads and enjoy them.

With these remarks, I close. I hope the Convention will vote for the proposition. Let us send up our petition. The right to petition is a jealous right. It was a right guaranteed to the Barons of England. The American people have always been jealous of that right, and regarded it as sacred and inviolate. That right we propose to maintain. It is said here that some high officers are opposed to it. I do not care who is opposed to it. It is none of their business. I do not care whether General [Robert K.] Scott, General [Ulysses S.] Grant or General anybody else is opposed to it, we will petition in spite of them. I appeal to the delegates to pass this resolution. It will do no harm if it does no good, and I am equally confident that some gentleman will catch what paddy gave the drum when they go back to their constituents.

The Ex-Slaves Crave Education

The Desire of the Blacks for Education

Senate Ex. Doc. no. 27, 39 Cong., 1 Sess. Report of J. W. Alvord, Superintendent of Schools for the Freedmen's Bureau

January 1, 1866

A general desire for education is everywhere manifested. In some instances, as in Halifax county [Virginia], very good schools were found taught and paid for by the colored people themselves. Said a gentleman to me, "I constantly see in the streets and on the door-steps opposite my dwelling groups of little negroes studying their spelling-books." . . .

Walter L. Fleming, ed., *Documentary History of Reconstruction: Political, Military, and Industrial, 1865 to the Present Time* (Cleveland: The Arthur H. Clark Company, 1907), vol. 2, pp. 182–83.

Not only are individuals seen at study, and under the most untoward circumstances, but in very many places I have found what I will call "native schools," often rude and very imperfect, but there they are, a group, perhaps, of all ages, trying to learn. Some young man, some woman, or old preacher, in cellar, or shed, or corner of a negro meeting-house, with the alphabet in hand, or a torn spelling-book, is their teacher. All are full of enthusiasm with the new knowledge the book is imparting to them.

Freedmen's Bureau Schools in North Carolina

Senate Ex. Doc. no. 6, 39 Cong., 2 Sess., p. 104. Report of Gen[eral] John C. Robinson of the Freedmen's Bureau

1866

It is no unfrequent occurrence to witness in the same rooms, and pursuing the same studies, the child and parent—youth and gray hairs—all eagerly grasping for that by which, obtained, they are intellectually regenerated. . . .

As an evidence of the great interest manifested for acquiring knowledge, an instance, probably never before equalled in the history of education, is to be found in one of the schools of this State, where side by side sat representatives of four generations in a direct line, viz.: a child six years old, her mother, grandmother, and great-grandmother, the latter over 75 years of age. All commenced their alphabet together, and each one can read the Bible fluently.

Night schools have met with gratifying success, and are eagerly sought for by those whose labors are of such a character as to prevent their attendance during the day. . . .

Sunday schools have been established at many points where teachers reside. . . . It is evident much good has been accomplished by their establishment, and no estimate can be made of the beneficial results of their full development.

☆ **2** ☆

An Urban and Industrial Nation

During the thirty-five years following the Civil War, the United States became the world's richest and most productive industrial nation. The drive to industrial supremacy was not effortless or untroubled, however. It was accompanied by greed, corruption, and exploitation; it also threatened older patterns of living, degraded the physical environment, and weakened traditional political values.

Yet most Americans of the day probably thought of the sweeping economic and social changes of this era as progress. We today, although we are the beneficiaries of our predecessors' sacrifices, are perhaps more skeptical. Do our greater doubts derive from our ability to see further and clearer than our forebears? Or have we, without knowing what it was really like, romanticized preindustrial rural life?

There was a vast churning of American population after 1865. As some Americans moved west, others moved to the cities. Urban growth during the half-century following the Civil War was spectacular. In 1870 a little over a quarter of all Americans lived in cities; in 1920 over half. In sheer numbers this meant an increase from 10 million to over 54 million city dwellers.

These people came from several sources. City folk begat city folk; many urbanites were the children of urbanites. Most, however, were newcomers, people born in rural communities who moved to the cities. They came from many parts of the world. One giant contingent consisted of native-born citizens from America's own farms and villages. Most of the remainder came from Europe's farms and villages and, after about 1890, predominantly from the rural areas of southern and eastern Europe.

The mass migration to the cities was part of the great shift in the Atlantic world's economy from agriculture to commerce and industry. Most of the newcomers were drawn by the economic advantages of the cities over their rural homes. Since the movement continued over many decades, we must assume that the urban edge in jobs and living standards persisted year after year.

Yet this is not to say that the newcomers found their new urban environment ideal. The cities of America were less than perfect places to live. To use a modern phrase, they had a "deficient infrastructure," especially early in this period. Housing, sanitation, health, and transportation facilities could not meet the surging demand. The cities' institutions also were imperfect. City governments were feeble and corrupt. They lacked the power to do what was needed, and what they did do was often accomplished at high cost. The cities were also deficient in civility. Anonymity, diversity, and poverty generated crime, disorder, and social breakdown. Urban law authorities were often unable to ensure safety for life and property. Churches and philanthropic organizations tried to help but were often pushed beyond their capacities.

Yet at worst Americans had mixed feelings about their cities, for despite their drawbacks, they also had advantages. What follows is an assortment of contemporary views, pro and con, of cities and city life in the period 1870–1920.

In the selections below Americans who lived through the late nineteenth-century surge of growth describe their experiences or evaluate the processes that swept them along. In considering what these people said, remember that no one individual could see more than a tiny part of what was a truly massive event. Where some workers may have experienced hardship, for example, others may have found the good life. (In this connection, see if you can determine from the work of economic historians whether income per person in America was growing or declining in this period. You may also want to know what was happening to "real" annual wages, that is, the total buying power of wage earners' yearly wages.)

2.1: **The Industrial Status Quo Defended (1883)**

Among the educated middle class, there was little doubt that the changes underway during the late nineteenth century were an enormous boon to humankind. A member of this group defends both the achievement and the way it was accomplished.

William Graham Sumner was an Episcopal minister who taught economics and sociology at Yale University. Sumner was a deeply committed "social Darwinist." His views derived from the theories of English naturalist Charles Darwin, who believed that the competition for survival among living things was the mechanism for increasing biological complexity and ensuring biological advance. In late nineteenth-century America, Darwin's influential ideas were increasingly applied to validate views that in human society, as in nature, competition and struggle were the proper vehicles for progress. Any attempt to soften their effects, said the social Darwinists, was misguided and would in the end do more harm than good.

What are the basic precepts of Sumner's views? How might they have been used to support the economic status quo in late nineteenth-century America? Is there any validity to Sumner's ideas? Have opinions like his been used in recent years to support unfettered economic competition? If so, by whom?

We Must Not Help the Weak at the Expense of the Strong

WILLIAM GRAHAM SUMNER

Certain ills belong to the hardships of human life. They are natural. They are part of the struggle with Nature for existence. We cannot blame our fellow-men for our share of these. My neighbor and I are struggling to free ourselves from these ills. The fact that my neighbor has succeeded in this struggle better than I constitutes no grievance for me. Certain other ills are due to the malice of men, and to the imperfections or errors of civil institutions. These ills are an object of agitation, and a subject of discussion. The former class of ills is to be met only by manly effort and energy; the latter may be corrected by associated effort. The former class of ills is constantly grouped and generalized, and made the object of social schemes. We shall see, as we go on, what that means. The second class of ills falls on certain social classes, and reform will take the form of interference by other classes in favor of that one. The last fact is, no doubt, the reason why people have been led . . . to believe that the same method was applicable to the other class of ills. The distinction here made between the ills which belong to the struggle for existence and those which are due to the faults of human institutions is of prime importance. . . .

The question whether voluntary charity is mischievous or not is one thing; the question whether legislation which forces one man to aid another is right and wise, as well as economically beneficial, is quite another question. Great confusion and consequent error is [*sic*] produced by allowing these two questions to become entangled in the discussion. Especially we shall need to notice the attempts to apply legislative methods of reform to the ills which belong to the order of Nature.

There is no possible definition of "a poor man." A pauper is a person who cannot earn his living; whose producing powers have fallen positively below his necessary consumption; who cannot, therefore, pay his way. A human society needs the active co-operation and productive energy of every person in it. A man who is present as a

William Graham Sumner, *What Social Classes Owe to Each Other* (New York: Harper and Brothers, 1883), pp. 17–27, 138–145.

consumer, yet does not contribute either by land, labor, or capital, to the work of society, is a burden. On no sound political theory ought such a person share in the political power of the State. He drops out of the ranks of workers and producers. Society must support him. It accepts the burden, but he must be cancelled from the ranks likewise. About him no more need be said. But he is not the "poor man." The "poor man" is an elastic term, under which any number of social fallacies may be hidden.

Neither is there any possible definition of "the weak." Some are weak in one way, some in another; and those who are weak in one sense are strong in another. In general, however, it may be said that those whom humanitarians and philanthropists call the weak are the ones through whom the productive and conservative forces of society are wasted. They constantly neutralize and destroy the finest efforts of the wise and industrious, and are a dead-weight on the society in all its struggles to realize any better things. Whether the people who mean no harm, but are weak in the essential powers necessary to the performance of one's duties in life, or those who are malicious and vicious, do the more mischief, is a question not easy to answer. . . .

The humanitarians, philanthropists, and reformers, looking at the facts of life as they present themselves, find enough which is sad and unpromising in the condition of many members of society. They see wealth and poverty side by side. They note great inequality of social position and social chances. They eagerly set about the attempt to account for what they see, and to devise schemes for remedying what they do not like. In their eagerness to recommend the less fortunate classes to pity and consideration they forget all about the rights of other classes; they gloss over all the faults of the classes in question, and they exaggerate their misfortunes and their virtues. They invent new theories of property, distorting rights and perpetrating injustice, as any one is sure to do who sets about the re-adjustment of social relations with the interests of one group distinctly before his mind, and the interests of all other groups thrown into the background. When I have read certain of these discussions I have thought that it must be quite disreputable to be respectable, quite dishonest to own property, quite unjust to go one's own way and earn one's own living, and that the only really admirable person was the good-for-nothing. The man who by his own effort raises himself above poverty appears, in these discussions, to be of no account. The man who has done nothing to raise himself above poverty finds that the social doctors flock about him, bringing the capital which they have collected from the other class, and promising him the aid of the State to give him what the other had to work for. In all these schemes and projects the organized intervention of society through the State is either planned or hoped for, and the State is thus made to become the protector and guardian of certain classes. . . .

Social improvement is not to be won by direct effort. It is secondary, and results from physical or economic improvements. That is the reason why schemes of direct social amelioration always have an arbitrary, sentimental, and artificial character, while true social advance must be a product and a growth. The efforts which are being put forth for every kind of progress in the arts and sciences are, therefore, contributing to true social progress. Let any one learn what hardship was involved, even for a wealthy person, a century ago, in crossing the Atlantic, and then let him compare that hardship even with a steerage passage at the present time, considering time and money cost. This improvement in transportation by which "the poor and weak" can be carried from the crowded centres of population to the new land is worth more to them than all the schemes of all the social reformers. An improvement in surgical instruments or in anæsthetics really does more for those who are not well off than all the declamations of the orators and pious wishes of the reformers. Civil service reform would be a greater gain to the laborers than innumerable factory acts and eight-hour laws. Free trade would be a greater blessing to "the poor man" than all the devices of all the friends of humanity if they could be realized. If the economists could satisfactorily solve the problem of the regulation of paper currency, they would do more for the wages class than could be accomplished by all the artificial doctrines about wages which they seem to feel bound to encourage. If we could get firm and good laws passed for the management of savings-banks, and then refrain from the amendments by which those laws are gradually broken down, we should do more for the non-capitalist class than by volumes of laws against "corporations" and the "excessive power of capital." . . .

We each owe it to the other to guarantee rights. Rights do not pertain to *results,* but only to *chances.* They pertain to the *conditions* of the struggle for existence, not to any of the results of it; to the *pursuit* of happiness, not to the possession of happiness. It cannot be said that each one has a right to have some property, because if one man had such a right some other man or men would be under a corresponding obligation to provide him with some property. Each has a right to acquire and possess property if he can. It is plain what fallacies are developed when we overlook this distinction. Those fallacies run through *all* socialistic schemes and theories. If we take rights to pertain to results, and then say that rights must be equal, we come to say that men have a right to be equally happy, and so on in all the details. Rights should be equal, because they pertain to chances, and all ought to have equal chances so far as chances are provided or limited by the action of society. This, however, will not produce equal results, but it is right just because it will produce unequal results—that is, results which shall be proportioned to the merits of individuals. We each owe it to the other to guarantee mutually the chance to earn, to possess, to learn, to marry, etc., etc., against any interference which would prevent the exercise of those rights by a person who wishes to prosecute and enjoy them in peace for the pursuit of happiness. If we generalize this, it means that All-of-us ought to guarantee rights to each of us. But our modern free, constitutional States are constructed entirely on the notion of rights, and we regard them as performing their functions more and more perfectly according as they guarantee rights in consonance with the constantly corrected and expanded notions of rights from one generation to another. Therefore, when we say that we owe it to each other to guarantee rights we only say that we ought to prosecute and improve our political science.

If we have in mind the value of chances to earn, learn, possess, etc., for a man of independent energy, we can go one step farther in our deductions about help. The only help which is generally expedient, even within the limits of the private and personal relations of two persons to each other, is that which consists in helping a man to help himself. This always consists in opening the chances. A man of assured position can, by an effort which is of no appreciable importance to him, give aid which is of incalculable value to a man who is all ready to make his own career if he can only get a chance. The truest and deepest pathos in this world is not that of suffering but that of brave struggling. The truest sympathy is not compassion, but a fellow-feeling with courage and fortitude in the midst of noble effort.

Now, the aid which helps a man to help himself is not in the least akin to the aid which is given in charity. If alms are given, or if we "make work" for a man, or "give him employment," or "protect" him, we simply take a product from one and give it to another. If we help a man to help himself, by opening the chances around him, we put him in a position to add to the wealth of the community by putting new powers in operation to produce. It would seem that the difference between getting something already in existence from the one who has it, and producing a new thing by applying new labor to natural materials, would be so plain as never to be forgotten; but the fallacy of confusing the two is one of the commonest in all social discussions. . . .

Instead of endeavoring to redistribute the acquisitions which have been made between the existing classes, our aim should be to *increase, multiply, and extend the chances.* Such is the work of civilization. Every old error or abuse which is removed opens new chances of development to all the new energy of society. Every improvement in education, science, art, or government expands the chances of man on earth. Such expansion is no guarantee of equality. On the contrary, if there be liberty, some will profit by the chances eagerly and some will neglect them altogether. Therefore, the greater the chances the more unequal will be the fortune of these two sets of men. So it ought to be, in all justice and right reason. The yearning after equality is the offspring of envy and covetousness, and there is no possible plan for satisfying that yearning which can do aught else than rob A to give to B; consequently all such plans nourish some of the meanest vices of human nature, waste capital, and overthrow civilization. But if we can expand the chances we can count on a general and steady growth of civilization and advancement of society by and through its best members. In the prosecution of these chances we all owe to each other good-will, mutual respect, and mutual guarantees of liberty and security. Beyond this nothing can be affirmed as a duty of one group to another in a free state.

2.2: **The Industrial Worker (1885, 1878)**

Although real wages had been rising for American wage earners in the half-century following the Civil War, they remained low compared to the incomes of the professional and business classes. That gap in itself would undoubtedly have produced social resentment, but there were other aspects of wage earners' lives that also created discontent. The work day was long and mind-deadening, on-the-job health conditions were poor, industrial accidents were frequent, unemployment was common. Laboring people at times responded to these conditions by strikes and riots. Some also turned to trade unionism to solve their difficulties. A small but significant minority even questioned the validity of private property rights and the basic assumptions of capitalism.

The first selection below is the testimony of a New York tailor, Conrad Carl, to a U.S. Senate committee investigating the conditions of labor and the relations of capital and labor in 1885. Carl's work experience bridged the important change from hand to machine labor in the garment industry. He obviously was not happy about the change. Why not? Does his description allow, however, for the possibility that the changes were good for consumers or the economy as a whole, although not necessarily for Carl's fellow garment workers? Were the circumstances of the garment workers typical of labor in this period?

The second selection is from the constitution of the Knights of Labor, a trade union organization of national scope that flourished for a time in the 1880s. The Knights were not a modern trade union. Their goals went beyond the higher wages, shorter hours, and improved working conditions demanded by such "pure and simple" trade unions as the American Federation of Labor. Still, the selection expresses eloquently the yearnings of wage earners exposed to the hazards and challenges of post–Civil War industrial life. What vision of society is implicit in the document below? Does it seem to foreshadow later reform movements? How do you explain the Knights' reluctance to employ strikes?

How Changes in the Garment Industry Have Harmed Labor

CONRAD CARL

CONRAD CARL sworn and examined.
By Mr. PUGH:

Question: How long have you resided in this city?—*Answer:*   Nearly thirty years.

Q.:   What has been your profession or occupation?—*A.:*   I have been a tailor since boyhood.

Q.:   Are you an employé or an employer?—*A.:*   An employé.

Q.:   Have you been an employé during the whole time you have been in the business?—*A.:*   The whole time.

Senate Committee on the Relations between Capital and Labor (Washington, DC: Government Printing Office, 1885), vol. 2, pp. 413–21.

Q.:   Please give us any information that you may have as to the relation existing between the employers and the employés in the tailoring business in this city, as to wages, as to treatment of the one by the other class, as to the feeling that exists between the employers and the employed generally, and all that you know in regard to the subject that we are authorized to inquire into?

A.:   During the time I have been here the tailoring business is altered in three different ways. Before we had sewing-machines we worked piece-work with our wives, and very often our children. We had no trouble then with our neighbors, nor with the landlord, because it was a very still business, very quiet; but in 1854 or 1855, and later, the sewing-machine was invented and introduced, and it stitched very nicely, nicer than the tailor could do; and the bosses said: "We want you to use the sewing-machine; you have to buy one." Many of the tailors had a few dollars in the bank, and they took the money and bought machines. Many others had no money, but must help themselves; so they brought their stitching, the coat or vest, to the other tailors who had sewing-machines, and paid them a few cents for the stitching. Later, when the money was given out for the work, we found out that we could earn no more than we could without the machine; but the money for the machine was gone now, and we found that the machine was only for the profit of the bosses; that they got their work quicker, and it was done nicer.

Q.:   How about the average wages?—*A.:*   The average wages before the [Civil] war (that marks an epoch, you know) was [*sic*] from $8 to $10 a week for a man working with his wife.

Q.:   Is the work graded in any way? Do certain employés do certain kinds of work? Is the work classified in the shop?—*A.:*   At that time it was divided among vest-makers, pants-makers, and coat-makers.

Q.:   You have cutters, I suppose?—*A.:*   The cutter was in the shop, in the boss's shop. We worked at home in our rooms. We had to buy fuel to heat the irons for pressing, and light in the winter; and we worked very deep in the night. The hours of working at that time were about fifteen to twenty hours a day.

Q.:   You worked by the day then, and not by the piece?—*A.:*   Piece-work, only piece-work, in our own rooms.

Q.:   Was working that length of time voluntary, or was it required by the employer?—*A.:*   He had no place to put us in. He would not pay out the money to hire a large room or hall to put his tailors in to make the coats or vests, and the tailor himself had to give his room for the business and had to buy coal and furnish the light to do the work for the boss.

Q.:   And then the tailors bought sewing-machines to do the work?—*A.:*   Yes.

Q.:   You say they worked from fifteen to eighteen hours a day before the war; how is it now?—*A.:*   Now they have to work quicker, because they can not work so long. The machine makes too much noise in the place, and the neighbors want to sleep, and we have to stop sewing earlier; so we have to work faster. We work now in excitement—in a hurry. It is hunting; it is not work at all; it is a hunt.

Q.:   You turn out two or three times as much work per day now as you did in prior times before the war?—*A.:*   Yes, sir; two or three times as much; and we have to do it, because the wages are two-thirds lower than they were five or ten years back. . . .

Q.:   How much wages were paid a day after the war?—*A.:*   From 1864 to 1873, . . . they ran from $20 to $25 a week for a tailor and his wife. A tailor is nothing without a wife, and very often a child. If the child is old enough, about twelve or fourteen years, it is employed in the tailor's business; but the children often go out into the factories to earn something.

Q.:   How much did you make after the war, from 1864 to 1873?—*A.:*   I made boys' fine fancy jackets and could get from $2 to $3.50 or $4 apiece for them.

Q.:   Was that for the jacket, or for the making of it?—*A.:*   For the making of it.

Q.:   How much are you paid for making a vest of the same sort now?—*A.:*   The highest is $1.

Q.:   For what sort of a vest?—*A.:*   Not vests—jackets.

Q.:   How much were you paid for pants from 1864 to 1873?—*A.:*   From five shillings to a dollar or nine shillings apiece.[1]

Q.:   Now how much is paid?—*A.:*   It is from 15 to 28 cents.

Q.:   On what sort of material do you work?—*A.:*   All wool.

Q.:   What was paid for making a coat, from 1864 to 1873?—*A.:*   From 12 shillings to three or four dollars.

Q.:   How much is paid now?—*A.:*   From 40 cents to a dollar.

Q.:   You state, then, that there has been a reduction of two-thirds in the pay for some kinds of work?—*A.:*   Yes, sir.

By Mr. GEORGE:

Q.:   Is that owing to the change from hand work to machine work, or is it a reduction from the prices paid for machine work before the war?—*A.:*   From machine work to machine work. Hand work was before the war.

Q.:   Are the machines on which the work is done now the same as those that were used formerly?—*A.:*   They have better machines now—quicker.

Q.:   Did you do that fast work of which you have told us from 1864 to 1873?—*A.:*   No, sir; the fast work began about five or six years ago, when the wages lowered.

Q.:   You, of course, make more pieces in a given time than you did by hand; what is the difference between the amount of work that you can turn out with a machine

---

[1]A "shilling," as money of account, was about 10 cents—ED.

and the amount you could turn out by hand?—*A.:*   I have to make now four jackets a day, with my wife and daughter's assistance.

Q.:   You do that with the machine?—*A.:*   All machine work.

Q.:   Working by hand, how many could you turn out?—*A.:*   Oh, with the hand I could make only one.

Q.:   Have you any idea of the number of tailors, men and women, who are engaged in that work in this city?—*A.:*   You mean in the clothing business—in the custom trade? That is another part of the business.

Q.:   I understand that. How many do you think there are?—*A.:*   I don't know; eighteen or twenty thousand.

Q.:   What proportion of them are women and what proportion men, according to your best judgment?—*A.:*   I guess there are many more women than men.

Q.:   The pay of the women is the same as the pay of the men for the same quantity of work, I suppose?—*A.:*   Yes; in cases where a manufacturer—that is, a middleman—gets work from the shop and brings it into his store and employs hands to make it, women get paid by the piece also. If the manufacturer gets 25 cents for a piece, he pays for the machine work on that piece so many cents to the machine-worker, he pays so many cents to the presser, so many cents to the finisher, and so many to the button-sewer—so much to each one—and what remains is to pay his rent and to pay for the machinery.

Q.:   What is your knowledge as to the amount that workers of that class are able to save from their wages?—*A.:*   I don't know any one that does save except those manufacturers.

Q.:   As a class, then, the workers save nothing?—*A.:*   No.

Q.:   What sort of house-room do they have? What is the character, in general, of the food and clothing which they are able to purchase with what they can make by their labor?—*A.:*   They live in tenement houses four or five stories high, and have two or three rooms.

Q.:   What is the character of their clothing?—*A.:*   They buy the clothing that they make—the cheapest of it.

Q.:   What about the character of food that they are able to provide for themselves?—*A.:*   Food? They have no time to eat dinner. They have a sandwich in the middle of the day, and in the evening when they go away from work it is the same, and they drink lager or anything they can get.

Q.:   They are kept busy all the time and have but little opportunity for rest?—*A.:* Yes.

Q.:   What is the state of feeling between the employers and their employés in that business? How do you workingmen feel towards the people who employ you and pay you?—*A.:*   Well, I must say the workingmen are discouraged. If I speak with them they go back and don't like to speak much about the business and the pay. They fear that if they say how it is they will get sent out of the shop. They hate the bosses and the foremen more than the bosses, and that feeling is deep.

Q.: Why do they feel so towards the foremen?—*A.:* They know that they do a wrong onto them; they know that.

Q.: Do not the foremen act under the instruction of the bosses?—*A.:* Well, it seems so.

Q.: Could not the boss correct the wrong that the foreman does, if it is a wrong?— *A.:* Well, when we complain that the foreman is so and so, the boss says, "Oh, I have nothing to do with it; I don't know; go to the foreman; it is the foreman's business." Then when we go to the foreman he says, "Oh, I can't pay more; these are my rules; if you don't like it, go to the boss."

Q.: And when you do go to the boss he sends you back to the foreman?—*A.:* Yes; he says, "I have nothing to do with this; that is my foreman's business; go to him." Therefore the workmen hate them both.

Q.: But can you explain why they hate the foremen, as you say they do, more than the bosses, when the bosses keep the foremen there and could discharge them and get better ones in the places if they desired?—*A.:* Gentlemen, if I say all this here—if it is made public I come out of work.

By Mr. PUGH:

Q.: Then you are testifying here under the apprehension of punishment for what you have stated?—*A.:* Well, I have no fear for any one, you know, and if you think it is better that I say it, I do so.

Q.: What is your feeling of restraint in testifying? What injury would you be subjected to for telling the truth? Would the workingmen in your business testify under a fear of being punished by their employers for telling the truth?—*A.:* Yes. It is nothing but fear.

By the CHAIRMAN:

Q.: What are the hours of work in winters?—*A.:* They make a light in the morning and they have a light burning until 9 or 10 o'clock in the evening. . . .

Q.: Are not the tailors the hardest-worked and poorest-paid class of laborers in the city?—*A.:* The hardest worked, the longest hours, and the poorest paid.

Q.: What proportion of them belong to labor unions? Do all or most of them belong to the unions?—*A.:* No. They are all dispersed—they are all discouraged; they have no union at all.

Q.:   To what do you attribute that? What is the reason of it?—*A.:*   Well, they have not had success in getting higher wages. As often as they came together or went on a strike, they lost, always.

Q.:   And their wages, you say, have been gradually reduced?—*A.:*   Yes, and some of them that have houses, they are hungrier than the others; they corrupt the foremen, give them money, and get more work for themselves, and take it home and employ poor men and women.

Q.:   You say there is no separate union of the tailors?—*A.:*   No. It was, but it is not now.

Q.:   There are, you say, between eighteen and twenty thousand working tailors in this city?—*A.:*   Yes. I was very glad when the act of the legislature came that cigar-making in tenement houses is forbidden.

Q.:   What is your idea of the value of strikes as a means of remedying your troubles?—*A.:*   It is not always of great value, but it is a necessity. It springs from necessity, and the sooner the workingman will go on strike when he cannot remain on the work—so poor as the workingmen are, they cannot carry that on—the burden is too great.

Preamble to the Constitution of the Knights of Labor[1]

The recent alarming development and aggression of aggregated wealth, which, unless checked, will invariably lead to the pauperization and hopeless degradation of the toiling masses, render it imperative, if we desire to enjoy the blessings of life, that a check should be placed upon its power and upon unjust accumulation, and a system adopted which will secure to the laborer the fruits of his toil; and as this much-desired object can only be accomplished by the thorough unification of labor, and the united efforts of those who obey the divine injunction that "In the sweat of thy brow shalt thou eat bread," we have formed the————with a view of securing the organization and direction, by co-operative effort, of the power of the industrial classes; and we submit to the world the objects sought to be accomplished by our organization, calling upon all who believe in securing "the greatest good to the greatest number" to aid and assist us:

    I.   To bring within the folds of organization every department of productive industry, making knowledge a stand-point for action, and industrial and moral worth, not wealth, the true standard of individual and national greatness.
    II.   To secure to the toilers a proper share of the wealth that they create; more of the leisure that rightfully belongs to them; more societary advantages; more of the benefits, privileges, and emoluments of the world; in a word, all those rights and privileges necessary to make them capable of enjoying, appreciating, defending, and perpetuating the blessing of good government.

Terence V. Powderly, *Thirty Years of Labor* (Columbus: Excelsior Publishing House, 1889), pp. 243–45.
[1]Footnotes deleted.

III.   To arrive at the true condition of the producing masses in their educational, moral, and financial condition, by demanding from the various governments the establishment of bureaus of Labor and Statistics.

IV.   The establishment of co-operative institutions, productive and distributive.

V.   The reserving of the public lands—-the heritage of the people—for the actual settler; not another acre for railroads or speculators.

VI.   The abrogation of all laws that do not bear equally upon capital and labor, the removal of unjust technicalities, delays, and discriminations in the administration of justice, and the adopting of measures providing for the health and safety of those engaged in mining, manufacturing, or building pursuits.

VII.   The enactment of laws to compel chartered corporations to pay their employes weekly, in full, for labor performed during the preceding week, in the lawful money of the country.

VIII.   The enactment of laws giving mechanics and laborers first lien on their work for their full wages.

IX.   The abolishment of the contract system on national, State, and municipal work.

X.   The substitution of arbitration for strikes, whenever and wherever employers and employes are willing to meet on equitable grounds.

XI.   The prohibition of the employment of children in workshops, mines and factories before attaining their fourteenth year.

XII.   To abolish the system of letting out by contract the labor of convicts in our prisons and reformatory institutions.

XIII.   To secure for both sexes equal pay for equal work.

XIV.   The reduction of the hours of labor to eight per day, so that the laborers may have more time for social enjoyment and intellectual improvement, and be enabled to reap the advantages conferred by the labor-saving machinery which their brains have created.

XV.   To prevail upon governments to establish a purely national circulating medium, based upon the faith and resources of the nation, and issued directly to the people, without the intervention of any system of banking corporations, which money shall be legal tender in payment of all debts, public or private.

2.3:   Labor Rejects Capitalism (1912)

Disenchantment with the existing industrial regime led some wage earners to disavow capitalism itself. During the last years of the old century and the opening years of the new, socialist parties were usually the medium through which such root discontent expressed itself. The largest and most durable of these organizations was the Socialist Party of America (SPA), formed in 1901 from an amalgamation of several older socialist groups. For much of its early life the SPA was headed by the eloquent and magnetic Eugene V. Debs, a native-born trade union leader who had led the railroad workers' Pullman Strike in 1894, been jailed, and later become a Socialist.

The following is the text of the SPA's platform of 1912, when, with Debs as its presidential candidate, it won almost 900,000 votes. The document embraces a theory of history. What is this theory? Do the So-

cialists anywhere in this platform endorse the use of force and violence? In what ways did the SPA's specific demands overlap those of liberal political groups that accepted capitalism? What evidence is there in the platform that the Socialists were radicals, interested in fundamental social change? Clearly the Socialists spoke in the name of the wage-earner class. Did they also receive wide wage-earner support? Which groups in contemporary America supported socialist ideas?

Socialist Party Platform of 1912

The Socialist party declares that the capitalist system has outgrown its historical function, and has become utterly incapable of meeting the problems now confronting society. We denounce this outgrown system as incompetent and corrupt and the source of unspeakable misery and suffering to the whole working class.

Under this system the industrial equipment of the nation has passed into the absolute control of a plutocracy which exacts an annual tribute of hundreds of millions of dollars from the producers. Unafraid of any organized resistance, it stretches out its greedy hands over the still undeveloped resources of the nation—the land, the mines, the forests and the water powers of every State of the Union.

In spite of the multiplication of labor-saving machines and improved methods in industry which cheapen the cost of production, the share of the producers grows ever less, and the prices of all the necessities of life steadily increase. The boasted prosperity of this nation is for the owning class alone. To the rest it means only greater hardship and misery. The high cost of living is felt in every home. Millions of wage-workers have seen the purchasing power of their wages decrease until life has become a desperate battle for mere existence.

Multitudes of unemployed walk the streets of our cities or trudge from State to State awaiting the will of the masters to move the wheels of industry.

The farmers in every state are plundered by the increasing prices exacted for tools and machinery and by extortionate rents, freight rates and storage charges.

Capitalist concentration is mercilessly crushing the class of small business men and driving its members into the ranks of propertyless wage-workers. The overwhelming majority of the people of America are being forced under a yoke of bondage by this soulless industrial despotism.

It is this capitalist system that is responsible for the increasing burden of armaments, the poverty, slums, child labor, most of the insanity, crime and prostitution, and much of the disease that afflicts mankind.

Under this system the working class is exposed to poisonous conditions, to frightful and needless perils to life and limb, is walled around with court decisions, injunctions and unjust laws, and is preyed upon incessantly for the benefit of the controlling oligarchy of wealth. Under it also, the children of the working class are doomed to ignorance, drudging toil and darkened lives.

Kirk Harold Porter, ed., *National Party Platforms* (New York: The Macmillan Company, 1924), pp. 361–68.

In the face of these evils, so manifest that all thoughtful observers are appalled at them, the legislative representatives of the Republican and Democratic parties remain the faithful servants of the oppressors. Measures designed to secure to the wage-earners of this Nation as humane and just treatment as is already enjoyed by the wage-earners of all other civilized nations have been smothered in committee without debate, the laws ostensibly designed to bring relief to the farmers and general consumers are juggled and transformed into instruments for the exaction of further tribute. The growing unrest under oppression has driven these two old parties to the enactment of a variety of regulative measures, none of which has limited in any appreciable degree the power of the plutocracy, and some of which have been perverted into means of increasing that power. Anti-trust laws, railroad restrictions and regulations, with the prosecutions, indictments and investigations based upon such legislation, have proved to be utterly futile and ridiculous.

Nor has this plutocracy been seriously restrained or even threatened by any Republican or Democratic executive. It has continued to grow in power and insolence alike under the administration of [Presidents] Cleveland, McKinley, Roosevelt and Taft.

We declare, therefore, that the longer sufferance of these conditions is impossible, and we purpose to end them all. We declare them to be the product of the present system in which industry is carried on for private greed, instead of for the welfare of society. We declare, furthermore, that for these evils there will be and can be no remedy and no substantial relief except through Socialism under which industry will be carried on for the common good and every worker receive the full social value of the wealth he creates.

Society is divided into warring groups and classes, based upon material interests. Fundamentally, this struggle is a conflict between the two main classes, one of which, the capitalist class, owns the means of production, and the other, the working class, must use these means of production, on terms dictated by the owners.

The capitalist class, though few in numbers, absolutely controls the government, legislative, executive and judicial. This class owns the machinery of gathering and disseminating news through its organized press. It subsidizes seats of learning—the colleges and schools—and even religious and moral agencies. It has also the added prestige which established customs give to any order of society, right or wrong.

The working class, which includes all those who are forced to work for a living whether by hand or brain, in shop, mine or on the soil, vastly outnumbers the capitalist class. Lacking effective organization and class solidarity, this class is unable to enforce its will. Given such a class solidarity and effective organization, the workers will have the power to make all laws and control all industry in their own interest. All political parties are the expression of economic class interests. All other parties than the Socialist party represent one or another group of the ruling capitalist class. Their political conflicts reflect merely superficial rivalries between competing capitalist groups. However they result, these conflicts have no issue of real value to the workers. Whether the Democrats or Republicans win politically, it is the capitalist class that is victorious economically.

The Socialist party is the political expression of the economic interests of the workers. Its defeats have been their defeats and its victories their victories. It is a party founded on the science and laws of social development. It proposes that, since all social necessities to-day are socially produced, the means of their production and distribution shall be socially owned and democratically controlled.

In the face of the economic and political aggressions of the capitalist class the only reliance left the workers is that of their economic organizations and their political power. By the intelligent and class conscious use of these, they may resist successfully the capitalist class, break the fetters of wage slavery, and fit themselves for the future society, which is to displace the capitalist system. The Socialist party appreciates the full significance of class organization and urges the wage-earners, the working farmers and all other useful workers to organize for economic and political action, and we pledge ourselves to support the toilers of the fields as well as those in the shops, factories and mines of the nation in their struggles for economic justice.

In the defeat or victory of the working class party in this new struggle for freedom lies the defeat or triumph of the common people of all economic groups, as well as the failure or triumph of popular government. Thus the Socialist party is the party of the present day revolution which makes the transition from economic individualism to socialism, from wage slavery to free co-operation, from capitalist oligarchy to industrial democracy.

Working Program

As measures calculated to strengthen the working class in its fight for the realization of its ultimate aim, the co-operative commonwealth, and to increase its power against capitalist oppression, we advocate and pledge ourselves and our elected officers to the following program:

Collective Ownership

1. The collective ownership and democratic management of railroads, wire and wireless telegraphs and telephones, express service, steamboat lines, and all other social means of transportation and communication and of all large scale industries.
2. The immediate acquirement by the municipalities, the states or the federal government of all grain elevators, stock yards, storage warehouses, and other distributing agencies, in order to reduce the present extortionate cost of living.
3. The extension of the public domain to include mines, quarries, oil wells, forests and water power.
4. The further conservation and development of natural resources for the use and benefit of all the people: . . .
5. The collective ownership of land wherever practicable, and in cases where such ownership is impracticable, the appropriation by taxation of the annual rental value of all the land held for speculation and exploitation.
6. The collective ownership and democratic management of the banking and currency system.

Unemployment

The immediate government relief of the unemployed by the extension of all useful public works. All persons employed on such works to be engaged directly by the government under a work day of not more than eight hours and at not less than the prevailing union wages. The government also to establish employment bureaus; to lend money to states and municipalities without interest for the purpose of carrying on public works, and to take such other measures within its power as will lessen the widespread misery of the workers caused by the misrule of the capitalist class.

Industrial Demands

The conservation of human resources, particularly of the lives and well-being of the workers and their families:

1. By shortening the work day in keeping with the increased productiveness of machinery.
2. By securing for every worker a rest period of not less than a day and a half in each week.
3. By securing a more effective inspection of workshops, factories and mines.
4. By the forbidding the employment of children under sixteen years of age.
5. By the co-operative organization of the industries in the federal penitentiaries for the benefit of the convicts and their dependents.
6. By forbidding the interstate transportation of the products of child labor, of convict labor and of all uninspected factories and mines.
7. By abolishing the profit system in government work and substituting either the direct hire of labor or the awarding of contracts to co-operative groups of workers.
8. By establishing minimum wage scales.
9. By abolishing official charity and substituting a non-contributary system of old age pensions, a general system of insurance by the State of all its members against unemployment and invalidism and a system of compulsory insurance by employers of their workers, without cost to the latter, against industrial diseases, accidents and death.

Political Demands

1. The absolute freedom of press, speech and assemblage.
2. The adoption of a graduated income tax and the extension of inheritance taxes, graduated in proportion to the value of the estate and to nearness of kin—the proceeds of these taxes to be employed in the socialization of industry.
3. The abolition of the monopoly ownership of patents and the substitution of collective ownership, with direct rewards to inventors by premiums or royalties.
4. Unrestricted and equal suffrage for men and women.
5. The adoption of the initiative, referendum and recall and of proportional representation, nationally as well as locally.
6. The abolition of the Senate and of the veto power of the President.
7. The election of the President and Vice-President by direct vote of the people.
8. The abolition of the power usurped by the Supreme Court of the United States to pass upon the constitutionality of the legislation enacted by Congress. National laws to be repealed only by act of Congress or by a referendum vote of the whole people.
9. Abolition of the present restrictions upon the amendment of the constitution, so that instrument may be made amendable by a majority of the voters in a majority of the States.
10. The granting of the right of suffrage in the District of Columbia with representation in Congress and a democratic form of municipal government for purely local affairs.
11. The extension of democratic government to all United States territory.
12. The enactment of further measures for the conservation of health. The creation of an independent bureau of health, with such restrictions as will secure full liberty to all schools of practice.

13. The enactment of further measures for general education and particularly for vocational education in useful pursuits. The Bureau of Education to be made a department.
14. The separation of the present Bureau of Labor from the Department of Commerce and Labor and its elevation to the rank of a department.
15. Abolition of all federal district courts and the United States circuit court of appeals. State courts to have jurisdiction in all cases arising between citizens of several states and foreign corporations. The election of all judges for short terms.
16. The immediate curbing of the power of the courts to issue injunctions.
17. The free administration of the law.
18. The calling of a convention for the revision of the constitution of the U.S.

Such measures of relief as we may be able to force from capitalism are but a preparation of the workers to seize the whole powers of government, in order that they may thereby lay hold of the whole system of socialized industry and thus come to their rightful inheritance.

2.4: The Cities Acclaimed (1905)

Cities have always been problematical to country folk. Americans, moreover, even more than most other Western peoples, have long prized the Arcadian ideal of a happy, virtuous, prosperous society set in the unspoiled countryside.

Frederic C. Howe was a widely published journalist-reformer who flourished during the Progressive Era early in this century. The Progressives were preponderantly urban dwellers, and they did much of their work as reformers within the urban setting. It was thus natural for them to regard the cities as showcases for the virtues and values of the new, reformed society. In the following selection, what does Howe foresee for the city in the near future? Has much of what he anticipated come to pass? Have the changes he describes produced the results he expected?

The Hope of Democracy

FREDERIC C. HOWE

The city is not only the problem of our civilization, it is the hope of the future. In the city democracy is awakening, it is beginning to assert itself. Here life is free and eager and countless agencies coöperate to create a warmer sympathy, a broader sense of responsibility, and a more intelligent political sense. Already the city has attained a higher degree of political responsiveness than has the commonwealth

Frederic C. Howe, *The City: The Hope of Democracy* (New York: Charles Scribner's Sons, 1905), pp. 280–287, 292–293, 298–299.

which gave it being and which jealously resents its growing independence. In many instances it is better governed than is the state or the nation at large. It is freer from the more subtle forms of corruption. For the open bribe, the loan, or even the game of poker in which the ignorant councilman is permitted to win a handsome stake are not the only means employed. Self-interest, a class-conscious feeling, the fancied advantage of party may be as powerful a motive for evil as the more vulgar methods with which we are familiar. The sinister influences bent on maintaining the *status quo,* on the prevention of necessary legislation, the control of the party, the caucus, or the convention; methods which are in vogue in national and state affairs, may be even more dangerous to democracy than the acts which violate the criminal code and which are becoming intolerable to public opinion. Moreover, in national affairs, the public is less alert, much less able to act collectively or to concentrate attention upon a given issue. The same is true in state affairs, where the divergent interests of the country and the city render united action well-nigh impossible.

The city is also being aroused to social and economic issues as well as to political ones. It is constantly taking on new activities and assuming new burdens. Everything tends to encourage this, while many things render it imperative. By necessity we are forced to meet the burdens of a complex life. We cannot live in close association without common activities, without abandoning some of our liberties to regulation. Not only do health, comfort, and happiness demand this, self-protection necessitates it.

Some of the activities which the city has assumed, or will assume, have been suggested. Through them many of the losses which the city has created will be made good. By these means the city will become fuller of opportunity than the scattered rural life which it has displaced. A conscious housing policy will be adopted. The tenement will become habitable, comfortable, and safe. Cheap and rapid transit will lure the population from the crowded slum into smaller suburban centres. For the city of the future will cover a wide area.

The same motives that have opened up breathing spots in the form of parks, as well as public baths and gymnasiums, in the crowded quarters will, in time, lead to the establishment of city clubhouses, winter recreation centres, where such advantages as are now found in the social settlement will be offered. About these centres the life of the community will focus for study, play, recreation, and political activity. Here concerts, lectures, and human intercourse will be offered. A sense of the city as a home, as a common authority, a thing to be loved and cared for, will be developed. In the city club the saloon will find a rival. From such centres charity work will be carried on. Here neglected children will be cared for, here the boys and girls will find an opportunity of escape from the street, and the mother and father a common meeting ground which is now denied them. For city life not only destroys the home of the poor, it promotes divorce. The tenement drives its dwellers to the streets and to the saloon. Private philanthropy has done much to relieve this condition through the settlement, but the service it renders is as much a public one as are the parks, the hospitals, or the schools. For the settlement is the equivalent of the outdoor park. Even from a pecuniary point of view it is a good investment to the city. The settlement promotes order, it lessens crime, it reduces petty misdemeanors, and organizes the life and energy of the slum and turns it into good channels. The uniform testimony of police officials is to the effect that a settlement or a playground is as good as a half-dozen policemen.

When the city becomes its own factory inspector, the problem of school attendance will be simplified. Then the city will be able to coördinate its administration and enforce its own ordinances. With reduced cost of transportation, through the public ownership of the means of transit, with free books and possibly free luncheons to school children, compulsory education will become a possibility. For the problem of education is largely economic or industrial. Our cities are now in the illogical position of enforcing school attendance upon those who cannot afford even the insignificant cost of the same.

These reforms will be possible through home rule, through the city-republic. With the city free in these regards it will be able to raise the educational age, adopt manual-training and trades' schools, fit its instruction to local needs, and ultimately elevate the standard of life of all classes. With the city free, the administration of our correctional institutions may be fitted to the crime. Probation courts and city farm schools may then be established and provision made for those of tender years who, in many cities, are still imprisoned with criminals, branded with the mark of crime, a brand which they can never outlive, a memory which they can never forget, an influence that can never be eradicated. Then the city will be able to discriminate between the offences of ignorance and poverty and those of instinct. Today they are all classed together. The poor who have unwittingly violated some local ordinance, such as blocking a sidewalk, driving a garbage cart without a license, failing to remove rubbish, or the like, when arrested, if unable to find bail, are cast into jail to await trial or to serve their time. An examination of the police-court blotter of the average city leads one to wonder if the offences of society against its own do not equal those of the individual against his fellows. Justice, as administered in these courts, probably hurts quite as much as it helps, and society, by its thoughtlessness, creates as much crime as it prevents. The solicitude of the common law for the occasional innocent has not been extended to the thousands of real innocents, to the children, the unfortunate, the ignorant, whom indifference punishes and, in punishing, destroys. Thousands of men and women are sent to the jails, workhouses, and penitentiary every year who should have been sent to the hospital, to an inebriate asylum, to the country, or, much better, given work. Their offence is of a negative sort. It is not wilful. It is industrial or economic; they could not catch on.

By natural processes inability to maintain life in store, factory, or sweat-shop produces the outcast woman, just as sickness, irregular employment, hard times yield their unvarying harvest of vagrants, with the sequence of the lodging house, the street, and ultimately a life of petty crime. Such a career is not often taken from choice, but by misfortune. And society often arrests, sentences, and punishes, when it should help and endeavor to reclaim by work, kindness, and assistance.

We have had our public schools for so long that we accept them as a commonplace. But we do not appreciate that the high schools are raising millions of citizens to an educated estate which was known to but a limited number a few years ago. The effect of this infusion of culture into our life is beginning to make itself felt. And in the years to come, when education has, in fact, become compulsory, and the school age has been raised to a higher standard, the effect will be tremendous. Along with the schools go the public libraries. Branches and distributing agencies are extending their influence into every part of the city. Through them opportunity is offered for a continuation of study, even after the door of the school has closed.

Provision for public concerts in summer as well as in winter has already found a place in many municipal budgets. With the development of the city club there will come public orchestras, art exhibitions, and the like that will brighten the life of the community. Something like this is already being done through the libraries which are being constructed with assembly halls and meeting rooms for this purpose. Here and there the idea is taking form of utilizing the public-school buildings as local clubs. The basement, gymnasiums, and assembly rooms are being opened in the evening and during the summer months. In time there will be a modification in their architecture, equipment, and facilities, so that they will be available for a multitude of purposes instead of the limited one of education. In New York City the school buildings are already being erected with roof-gardens, where music, recreation, and a common centre for the life of the locality are offered.

These are some of the things the new city will do. It will also care for the sick, as it now does in many cities, through district physicians or visiting nurses attached to the school departments. It will find work and maintain employment agencies. It will supervise factories, mills, and work-shops. The latter function is now inadequately performed by the state at large, and the inefficiency of its performance is largely attributable to the fact that the state is attempting to supervise a matter of local concern. The regulation of the conditions of employment is as much a city function as is the preservation of the health and well-being of the community. It is also a necessary part of school administration. . . .

It is along these lines that the advance of society is to be made. It is to come about through the city. For here life is more active, while the government is close to the people. It is already manifest on every hand. Through the divorce of the city from state control this progress will be stimulated. The city will become a centre of pride and patriotism. Here art and culture will flourish. The citizen will be attached to his community just as were the burghers of the mediaeval towns. Through direct legislation the city will be democratized. Public opinion will be free to act. Then the official will be holden to a real responsibility, while national politics will no longer dominate local affairs, for the test of the candidate for office will be his citizenship in the community which he serves. . . .

. . . The city will cease to be a necessary abyss of poverty. It is our institutions and our laws, not a divine ordinance or the inherent viciousness of humankind, that are at fault. Our evils are economic, not personal. Relief is possible through a change in our laws, in an increase in the positive agencies of the government, and the taxing for the common weal of those values which are now responsible for much of the common woe. It is not personal goodness that is demanded so much as public intelligence. For the worst of the evils under which America suffers are traceable to laws creating privileges. The evils can be largely corrected through their abolition. This is most easily obtainable in the city, for it is in the city that democracy is organizing and the power of privilege most rampant.

2.5: The Cities Deplored (1890)

Post–Civil War American cities were rife with problems.

The Danish-born journalist Jacob Riis focuses on the housing problems of America's growing urban centers. The cities by and large were able to meet the housing needs of the middle class. Builders constructed numerous brick, stone, and wooden homes on shady streets for the cities' professional and business families. They also began to put up large apartment buildings with spacious "flats" for those prosperous urbanites who liked to live close to the center of town.

The housing needs of wage earners were less successfully met, however. Most working-class people were unable to pay more than modest rents, and many blue-collar families and individuals were forced to live with others for financial reasons. Some had to live in cellars and the cast-off, minimally reworked former homes of the middle class who left for better neighborhoods. There was a supply of new apartments for the working class, but these were usually shoddily constructed tenements, thrown up by speculative builders, that often lacked heat and full interior plumbing. They quickly deteriorated into slums.

The selection below is from Riis's account of the tenements of lower Manhattan in New York City during the late 1880s. What do you deduce from his description of the causes of poverty and ill health in the slums? Did the slums cause the social and physical problems of the poor? Or did poverty cause their dreadful housing conditions? Why were the cities unable to solve the housing problem? Were all cities as deficient in housing as New York?

The Bend[1]

JACOB RIIS

Where Mulberry Street crooks like an elbow within hail of the old depravity of the Five Points, is "the Bend," foul core of New York's slums. . . . Never was change more urgently needed. Around "the Bend" cluster the bulk of the tenements that are

Jacob Riis, *How the Other Half Lives: Studies among the Tenements of New York* (New York: Charles Scribner's Sons, 1903), pp. 55, 61, 65.

[1]Footnotes deleted.

stamped as altogether bad, even by the optimists of the Health Department. Incessant raids cannot keep down the crowds that make them their home. In the scores of back alleys, of stable lanes and hidden byways, of which the rent collector alone can keep track, they share such shelter as the ramshackle structures afford with every kind of abomination rifled from the dumps and ash-barrels of the city. . . .

In the street, where the city wields the broom, there is at least an effort at cleaning up. There has to be, or it would be swamped in filth overrunning from the courts and alleys where the ragpickers live. It requires more than ordinary courage to explore these on a hot day. The undertaker has to do it then, the police always. Right here, in this tenement on the east side of the street, they found little Antonia Candia, victim of fiendish cruelty, "covered," says the account found in the records of the Society for the Prevention of Cruelty to Children, "with sores, and her hair matted with dried blood." Abuse is the normal condition of "the Bend," murder its everyday crop, with the tenants not always the criminals. In this block between Bayard, Park, Mulberry, and Baxter Streets, "the Bend" proper, the late Tenement House Commission counted 155 deaths of children in a specimen year (1882). Their percentage of the total mortality in the block was 68.28, while for the whole city the proportion was only 46.20. The infant mortality in any city or place as compared with the whole number of deaths is justly considered a good barometer of its general sanitary condition. Here, in this tenement, No. 59½ next to Bandit's Roost, fourteen persons died that year, and eleven of them were children; in No. 61 eleven, and eight of them not yet five years old. According to the records in the Bureau of Vital Statistics only thirty-nine people lived in No. 59½ in the year 1888, nine of them little children. There were five baby funerals in that house the same year. Out of the alley itself, No. 59, nine dead were carried in 1888, five in baby coffins. . . . The general death-rate for the whole city that year was 26.27.

These figures speak for themselves, when it is shown that in the model tenement across the way at Nos. 48 and 50, where the same class of people live in greater swarms (161, according to the record), but under good management, and in decent quarters, the hearse called that year only twice, once for a baby. The agent of the Christian people who built that tenement will tell you that Italians are good tenants, while the owner of the alley will oppose every order to put his property in repair with the claim that they are the worst of a bad lot. Both are right, from their different stand-points. It is the stand-point that makes the difference—and the tenant.

What if I were to tell you that this alley, and more tenement property in "the Bend," all of it notorious for years as the vilest and worst to be found anywhere, stood associated on the taxbooks all through the long struggle to make its owners responsible, which has at last resulted in a qualified victory for the law, with the name of an honored family, one of the "oldest and best," rich in possessions and in influence, and high in the councils of the city's government? It would be but the plain truth. Nor would it be the only instance by very many that stand recorded on the Health Department's books of a kind that has come near to making the name of landlord as odious in New York as it has become in Ireland.

Well do I recollect the visit of a health inspector to one of these tenements on a July day when the thermometer outside was climbing high in the nineties; but inside, in that awful room, with half a dozen persons washing, cooking, and sorting rags, lay the dying baby alongside the stove, where the doctor's thermometer ran up to 115°! Perishing for the want of a breath of fresh air in this city of untold charities! Did not the manager of the Fresh Air Fund write to the pastor of an Italian Church only last year that "no one asked for Italian children," and hence he could not send any to the country?

.   .   .   .

... In the stifling July nights, when the big barracks are like fiery furnaces, their very walls giving out absorbed heat, men and women lie in restless, sweltering rows, panting for air and sleep. Then every truck in the street, every crowded fire-escape, becomes a bedroom, infinitely preferable to any the house affords. A cooling shower on such a night is hailed as a heaven-sent blessing in a hundred thousand homes.

Life in the tenements in July and August spells death to an army of little ones whom the doctor's skill is powerless to save. When the white badge of mourning flutters from every second door, sleepless mothers walk the streets in the gray of the early dawn, trying to stir a cooling breeze to fan the brow of the sick baby. There is no sadder sight than this patient devotion striving against fearfully hopeless odds. Fifty "summer doctors," especially trained to this work, are then sent into the tenements by the Board of Health, with free advice and medicine for the poor. Devoted women follow in their track with care and nursing for the sick. Fresh-air excursions run daily out of New York on land and water; but despite all efforts the grave-diggers in Calvary work over-time, and little coffins are stacked mountain-high on the deck of the Charity Commissioners' boat when it makes its semi-weekly trips to the city cemetery.

Under the most favorable circumstances, an epidemic, which the well-to-do can afford to make light of as a thing to be got over or avoided by reasonable care, is excessively fatal among the children of the poor, by reason of the practical impossibility of isolating the patient in a tenement. The measles, ordinarily a harmless disease, furnishes a familiar example. Tread it ever so lightly on the avenues, in the tenements it kills right and left. ... The records showed that respiratory diseases, the common heritage of the grippe and the measles, had caused death in most cases, discovering the trouble to be, next to the inability to check the contagion in those crowds, in the poverty of the parents and the wretched home conditions that made proper care of the sick impossible. ...

That ignorance plays its part, as well as poverty and bad hygienic surroundings, in the sacrifice of life is of course inevitable. They go usually hand in hand.

2.6:   City Government (1905)

Historians have been of two minds about city government in the late nineteenth and early twentieth centuries. On the one hand, it was corrupt and inefficient, providing poor services at high cost. On the other hand, in the absence of formal welfare agencies, these corrupt govern-ments, ruled by political machines, were more generous, more com-passionate, and more effective than the reform administrations that periodically, and temporarily, replaced them.

The selection below is an account of how a precinct captain ("ward heeler"), early in this century, helped build and retain voter loyalty for Tammany Hall, the venal machine of the Democratic Party in New York City. Some of it comes from the diary of George Washington Plunkitt, a Tammany leader, but most is comment by the journalist William L. Riordan, who interviewed Plunkitt extensively.

How would you characterize the way Plunkitt goes about his job? Judging from this description, could the Tammany machine, with a lit-tle stretching, be characterized as a social welfare organization? Were there other agencies at this time that performed these same functions? Does Plunkitt's account suggest anything significant about the rela-tions of immigrants to the city machines? Did city dwellers pay an ex-cessively high price for the machine's help?

Strenuous Life of the Tammany District Leader[1]

WILLIAM L. RIORDAN

The life of the Tammany district leader is strenuous. To his work is due the wonder-ful recuperative power of the organization.

One year it goes down to defeat and the prediction is made that it will never again raise its head. The district leader undaunted by defeat, collects his scattered forces, organizes them as only Tammany knows how to organize, and in a little while the organization is as strong as ever.

No other politician in New York or elsewhere is exactly like the Tammany dis-trict leader or works as he does. As a rule, he has no business or occupation other than politics. He plays politics every day and night in the year, and his headquarters bears the inscription, "Never closed."

Everybody in the district knows him. Everybody knows where to find him, and nearly everybody goes to him for assistance of one sort or another, especially the poor of the tenements.

He is always obliging. He will go to the police courts to put in a good word for the "drunks and disorderlies" or pay their fines, if a good word is not effective. He will attend christenings, weddings, and funerals. He will feed the hungry and help bury the dead.

William L. Riordan, *Plunkitt of Tammany Hall: Plain Talks and Practical Politics* (New York: McClure Phillips and Company, 1905), pp. 167–183, *passim*.

[1]This chapter is based on extracts from [George Washington] Plunkitt's Diary and on my daily observa-tion of the work of the district leader.—*W.L.R.*

A philanthropist? Not at all. He is playing politics all the time.

Brought up in Tammany Hall, he has learned how to reach the heart of the great mass of voters. He does not bother about reaching their heads. It is his belief that arguments and campaign literature have never gained votes.

He seeks direct contact with the people, does them good turns when he can, and relies on their not forgetting him on election day. His heart is always in his work, too, for his subsistence depends on its results.

If he holds his district and Tammany is in power, he is amply rewarded by a good office and the opportunities that go with it. What these opportunities are has been shown by the quick rise to wealth of so many Tammany district leaders. With the examples before him of Richard Croker, once leader of the Twentieth District; John F. Carroll, formerly leader of the Twenty-ninth; Timothy ("Dry Dollar") Sullivan, late leader of the Sixth, and many others, he can always look forward to riches and ease while he is going through the drudgery of his daily routine.

This is a record of a day's work by Plunkitt:

2 A.M.: Aroused from sleep by the ringing of his door bell; went to the door and found a bartender, who asked him to go to the police station and bail out a saloon-keeper who had been arrested for violating the excise law. Furnished bail and returned to bed at three o'clock.

6 A.M.: Awakened by fire engines passing his house. Hastened to the scene of the fire, according to the custom of the Tammany district leaders, to give assistance to the fire sufferers, if needed. Met several of his election district captains who are always under orders to look out for fires, which are considered great vote-getters. Found several tenants who had been burned out, took them to a hotel, supplied them with clothes, fed them, and arranged temporary quarters for them until they could rent and furnish new apartments.

8:30 A.M.: Went to the police court to look after his constituents. Found six "drunks." Secured the discharge of four by a timely word with the judge, and paid the fines of two.

9 A.M.: Appeared in the Municipal District Court. Directed one of his district captains to act as counsel for a widow against whom dispossess proceedings had been instituted and obtained an extension of time. Paid the rent of a poor family about to be dispossessed and gave them a dollar for food.

11 A.M.: At home again. Found four men waiting for him. One had been discharged by the Metropolitan Railway Company for neglect of duty, and wanted the district leader to fix things. Another wanted a job on the road. The third sought a place on the Subway and the fourth, a plumber, was looking for work with the Consolidated Gas Company. The district leader spent nearly three hours fixing things for the four men, and succeeded in each case.

3 P.M.: Attended the funeral of an Italian as far as the ferry. Hurried back to make his appearance at the funeral of a Hebrew constituent. Went conspicuously to the front booth in the Catholic church and the synagogue, and later attended the Hebrew confirmation ceremonies in the synagogue.

7 P.M.: Went to district headquarters and presided over a meeting of election district captains. Each captain submitted a list of all the voters in his district, reported on their attitude toward Tammany, suggested who might be won over and how they could be won, told who were in need, and who were in trouble of any kind and the best way to reach them. District leader took notes and gave orders.

8 P.M.: Went to a church fair. Took chances on everything, bought ice-cream for the young girls and the children. Kissed the little ones, flattered their mothers and took their fathers out for something down at the corner.

9 P.M.: At the club-house again. Spent $10 on tickets for a church excursion and promised a subscription for a new church-bell. Bought tickets for a base-ball game to be played by two nines from his district. Listened to the complaints of a dozen push-cart peddlers who said they were persecuted by the police and assured them he would go to Police Headquarters in the morning and see about it.

10:30 P.M.: Attended a Hebrew wedding reception and dance. Had previously sent a handsome wedding present to the bride.

12 P.M.: In bed.

That is the actual record of one day in the life of Plunkitt. He does some of the same things every day, but his life is not so monotonous as to be wearisome.

Sometimes the work of a district leader is exciting, especially if he happens to have a rival who intends to make a contest for the leadership at the primaries. In that case, he is even more alert, tries to reach the fires before his rival, sends our runners to look for "drunks and disorderlies" at the police stations, and keeps a very close watch on the obituary columns of the newspapers.

A few years ago there was a bitter contest for the Tammany leadership of the Ninth District between John C. Sheehan and Frank J. Goodwin. Both has had long experience in Tammany politics and both understood every move of the game.

Every morning their agents went to their respective headquarters before seven o'clock and read through the death notices in all the morning papers. If they found that anybody in the district had died, they rushed to the homes of their principals with information and then there was a race to the house of the deceased to offer condolences, and, if the family were poor, something more substantial.

On the day of the funeral there was another contest. Each faction tried to surpass the other in the number and appearance of the carriages it sent to the funeral, and more than once they almost came to blows at the church or in the cemetery.

On one occasion the Goodwinites played a trick on their adversaries which has since been imitated in other districts. A well-known liquor dealer who had a considerable following died, and both Sheehan and Goodwin were eager to become his political heir by making a big showing at the funeral.

Goodwin managed to catch the enemy napping. He went to all the livery stables in the district, hired all the carriages for the day, and gave orders to two hundred of his men to be on hand as mourners.

Sheehan had never had any trouble about getting all the carriages that he wanted, so he let the matter go until the night before the funeral. Then he found that he could not hire a carriage in the district.

He called his district committee together in a hurry and explained the situation to them. He could get all the vehicles he needed in the adjoining district, he said, but if he did that, Goodwin would rouse the voters of the Ninth by declaring that he (Sheehan), had patronized foreign industries.

Finally, it was decided that there was nothing to do but go over to Sixth and Broadway for carriages. Sheehan made a fine turnout at the funeral, but the deceased was hardly in his grave before Goodwin raised the cry of "Protection to home industries," and denounced his rival for patronizing livery-stable keepers outside of his district. The cry had its effect in the primary campaign. At all events, Goodwin was elected leader.

A recent contest for the leadership of the Second District illustrated further the strenuous work of the Tammany district leaders. The contestants were Patrick Divver, who had managed the district for years, and Thomas F. Foley.

Both were particularly anxious to secure the large Italian vote. They not only attended all the Italian christenings and funerals, but also kept a close lookout for the marriages in order to be on hand with wedding presents.

At first, each had his own reporter in the Italian quarter to keep track of the marriages. Later, Foley conceived a better plan. He hired a man to stay all day at the City Hall marriage bureau, where most Italian couples go through the civil ceremony, and telephone to him at his saloon when anything was doing at the bureau.

Foley had a number of presents ready for use and, whenever he received a telephone message from his man, he hastened to the City Hall with a ring or a watch or a piece of silver and handed it to the bride with his congratulations. As a consequence, when Divver got the news and went to the home of the couple with the present, he always found that Foley had been ahead of him. Toward the end of that campaign, Divver also stationed a man at the marriage bureau and then there were daily foot races and fights between the two leaders.

Sometimes the rivals come into conflict at the death-bed. One night a poor Italian peddler died in Roosevelt Street. The news reached Divver and Foley about the same time, and as they knew the family of the man was destitute, each went to an undertaker and brought him to the Roosevelt tenement.

The rivals and the undertakers met at the house and an altercation ensued. After much discussion the Divver undertaker was selected. Foley had more carriages at the funeral, however, and he further impressed the Italian voters by paying the widow's rent for a month, and sending her half a ton of coal and a barrel of flour.

The rivals were put on their mettle toward the end of the campaign by the wedding of a daughter of one of the original Cohens of the Baxter Street region. The Hebrew vote in the district is nearly as large as the Italian vote, and Divver and Foley set out to capture the Cohens and their friends.

They stayed up nights thinking what they would give the bride. Neither knew how much the other was prepared to spend on a wedding present, or what form it would take; so spies were employed by both sides to keep watch on the .jewelry stores, and the jewelers of the district were bribed by each side to impart the desired information.

At last Foley heard that Divver had purchased a set of silver knives, forks, and spoons. He at once bought a duplicate set and added a silver tea service. When the presents were displayed at the home of the bride Divver was not in a pleasant mood and he charged his jeweler with treachery. It may be added that Foley won at the primaries.

One of the fixed duties of a Tammany district leader is to give two outings every summer, one for the men of his district and the other for the women and children, and a beefsteak dinner and a ball every winter. The scene of the outings is, usually, one of the groves along the [Long Island] Sound.

The ambition of the district leader on these occasions is to demonstrate that his men have broken all records in the matter of eating and drinking. He gives out the exact number of pounds of beef, poultry, butter, etc., that they have consumed and professes to know how many potatoes and ears of corn have been served.

According to his figures, the average eating record of each man at the outing is about ten pounds of beef, two or three chickens, a pound of butter, a half peck of potatoes, and two dozen ears of corn. The drinking records, as given out, are still more phenomenal. For some reason, not yet explained, the district leader thinks that his popularity will be greatly increased if he can show that his followers can eat and drink more than the followers of any district leader.

The same idea governs the beefsteak dinners in the winter. It matters not what sort of steak is served or how it is cooked; the district leader considers only the question of quantity, and when he excels all others in this particular, he feels, somehow, that he is a bigger man, and deserves more patronage than his associates in the Tammany Executive Committee.

As to the balls, they are the events of the winter in the extreme East Side and West Side society. Mamie and Maggie and Jennie prepare for them months in advance, and their young men save up for the occasion just as they save for the summer trips to Coney Island.

The district leader is in his glory at the opening of the ball. He leads the cotillion with the prettiest woman present—his wife, if he has one, permitting—and spends almost the whole night shaking hands with his constituents. The ball costs him a pretty penny, but he has found that the investment pays.

By these means the Tammany district leader reaches out into the homes of his district, keeps watch not only on the men, but also on the women and children; knows their needs, their likes and dislikes, their troubles and their hopes, and places himself in a position to use his knowledge for the benefit of his organization and himself. Is it any wonder that scandals do not permanently disable Tammany and that it speedily recovers from what seems to be crushing defeat?

☆ **3** ☆

The Last West and Populism

During the half-century following the Civil War, the huge expanse of territory between the Missouri River and the Pacific slope was absorbed into the national economy. This was a region of wide deserts and rugged mountains, fertile plains and valleys, dense timber stands, and rich mineral deposits. In 1865 it was thinly peopled by scores of Native American tribes living primarily as nomadic hunters and foragers who relied on the teeming herds of bison (buffalo) for the food and materiel of their lives.

White Americans, regarded the "last West," as previous "Wests," as a land of opportunity to be conquered and exploited by the plow, the cow, the spade, and the ax. The Native Americans seemed an impediment to be swept aside or forced to yield to "civilization."

The first set of documents that follow reflect the views of Americans, whites and Indians, of the settlement and exploitation of the trans-Missouri region after 1865. They represent disparate responses to a vast land of diverse terrain, climate, and resources. When you read these selections, as before, see if you can detect the preconceptions and values that informed the views expressed.

Agriculture also made an important contribution to the economic surge of the post–Civil War years. From the nation's farms, plantations, and ranches poured an ever-widening flood of wheat, corn, cotton, fruit, vegetables, beef, pork, and dairy products. Many Americans—and people around the world—benefited from this torrent of food and fiber. Yet the farmers were not happy. As production rose, farm prices fell, farm debt soared, and land values stagnated. Many farmers and farm leaders denounced the economic and political arrangements they believed had contributed to their plight.

During the 1870s farm discontent expressed itself through the Granger Movement that blamed agriculture's troubles on "monopolies," especially those in transportation and farm machinery manufacture, and advocated marketing by farmers themselves rather than through various middlemen. The Grangers organized independent farmers' parties in the midwest and helped enact state laws regulating railroads and other business groups that distributed farm products.

By the late 1880s, with farm prices still declining, the Grangers gave way to the Alliances, farmers' organizations, mainly in the South and the Plains, which sought to check deflation and provide relief to farm debtors through manipulation of the money supply. In early 1892 a number of insurgent groups, including the Alliances, the Knights of Labor, and various independent reformers, joined to form the People's Party, usually called the Populists.

The new party embraced the Alliance programs but with special emphasis on "free silver"—that is, the U.S. Treasury's coinage into dollars of all silver bullion brought to it, with sixteen ounces of silver to equal one ounce of gold. Free silver, said the reformers, would pump up the money supply and so increase prices, make credit cheaper, and relieve debtors of their crippling burdens.

In 1892 the People's Party challenged the two major parties at the polls, running candidates for state offices and for Congress and president. The Populist national ticket of James B. Weaver and James G. Field garnered over a million popular votes, about 9 per cent of the total, and won the electoral vote of several western states.

The year 1892 was the high-water mark of the People's Party; thereafter its support declined, but not its influence. The Populists gave voice to a widespread mood of the day that economic inequality and the dominance of wealth had progressed too far and should be reversed. Following the Panic of 1893, Populist ideas invaded the Democratic Party, especially in the West and South, where it expressed in part festering sectional resentment against the power centers of the East.

In some of the selections below you will encounter the views of Populists and Populist-influenced Democrats as well as their opponents. Consider, as previously, the spirit as well as the logic behind the arguments advanced.

3.1: The Mining Frontier (1864)

Among the trans-Missouri West's most coveted resources were its minerals, especially its precious metals, silver and gold. These were a powerful magnet that drew thousands from the East and from foreign lands. The lure of gold, particularly, set off a succession of pell-mell "rushes" that overnight created flourishing and vibrant communities in the mining regions. Most of these boom towns were mushroom growths that withered in a matter of months. A few, however, became the seeds of permanent cities like Denver, Helena, Tucson, and Boise.

The following account captures many of the qualities of the typical Rocky Mountain mining community. Its author is Granville Stuart, who, along with his brother, James, struck gold in 1863 at Alder Gulch in Montana, near the headwaters of the Missouri River. The brothers' efforts to keep their strike secret failed, and in a matter of months the rush of miners to the Gulch had created the community of Virginia City with 4,000 inhabitants. In the next few years the miners extracted $30 million of gold dust and nuggets from the region.

How do you explain the special characteristics of Virginia City? How did such a community govern itself? There is at most only an oblique mention of women in Stuart's account. Do you suppose there were any in Virginia City? What roles might they have served in such a community?

Gold Rush Days

GRANVILLE STUART

The winter of 1863–64 was a mild one, building and mining operations were carried on with but little interruption all winter and before spring every branch of business was represented. Gold was coming out in large quantities. The district extended from the foot of Old Baldy to twelve miles down the creek. The bed of the creek and the bars on both sides were uniformly rich; the bed rock being literally paved with gold. The Alder gulch diggings were the richest gold placer diggings ever discovered in the world.

Freight teams from Salt Lake arrived until late in the fall, bringing in supplies; and while we were not provided with luxuries there was no suffering from food shortage. . . .

There was a great number of saloons and each dispenser of liquid refreshments had the formula for making "tanglefoot:"—a quantity of boiled mountain sage, two plugs tobacco steeped in water, box cayenne pepper, one gallon water; so if any one got low in whiskey he promptly manufactured more. Saloons, gambling houses, public dance halls (hurdy gurdies) ran wide open and here, as in California, gold dust flowed in a yellow stream from the buckskin bags of the miners into the coffers of the saloons, dance halls, and gambling dens. Gold dust was the sole medium of exchange and it was reckoned at $18.00 an ounce. Every business house had gold scales for weighing the dust. If a man was under the influence of liquor, the bar keepers were not averse to helping themselves liberally to the man's dust, when paying himself for drinks and he more often took $1.00 for a drink than the going

Granville Stuart, *Forty Years on the Frontier as Seen in the Journals and Reminiscences of Granville Stuart,* Paul C. Phillips, ed. (Cleveland: The Arthur H. Clark Company, 1925), vol. 1, pp. 264–72.

price of twenty-five cents. A dance at one of the hurdy gurdies cost one dollar and as each dance wound up with an invitation to visit the bar where drinks for self and partner were expected, the cost of a waltz, schottische, or quadrille was usually $1.50. Dances kept up all night long but were usually orderly. If a man was found to be getting too much under the influence of liquor, some obliging friend would expel him from the hall. Every sort of gambling game was indulged in and it was no uncommon thing to see one thousand dollars staked on the turn of a monte card. The miner who indulged in gambling usually worked six days, then cleaned up his dust; and placing it in a buckskin sack hied himself to the nearest gambling house where he remained until he had transferred the contents of the sack to the professional gambler. If he played in luck he could usually stay in the game twenty-four hours. He would then return to his "diggins" without money and often with little grub; a sadder but no wiser man, for he would repeat the same thing over and over as long as his claim lasted and would then start out, blankets on his back, in search of new "diggins". . . .

About the middle of January, 1864, a regular stampede craze struck Virginia City. The weather had been quite cold and work in the mines was temporarily suspended. A large number of idle men were about town and it required no more than one man with an imaginative mind to start half the population off on a wild goose chase. Somebody would say that somebody said, that somebody had found a good thing and without further inquiry a hundred or more men would start out for the reported diggings.

One report of a discovery on Gallatin river started a large party out in that direction. Every horse that could be found fit to ride was made ready. We had some horses on a ranch near town and brought them in and in less than an hour we had sold them all for about twice what they would have sold for at any other time. Four hundred men left town in mid-winter, with the ground covered with snow, for some place on the Gallatin river; no one seemed to know exactly where they were going, but most of them brought up at Gallatin City. Many, who could not get horses, started on foot. The first night out brought them to a realization of the futility of such a trip and they turned back.

Late in the evening on January 22, a rumor started that a big discovery had been made on Wisconsin creek, a distance of thirty miles from Virginia City. The report said that as much as one hundred dollars to the pan had been found; and away the people flew all anxious to be first on the ground, where they could "just shovel up gold." Virginia City was almost deserted: men did not stop for horses, blankets, or provisions, the sole aim was to get there first and begin to shovel it out at the rate of one hundred to the pan. Fortunately the distance was not great and the weather was mild. Robert Dempsey had a ranch nearby and the stampeders got a supply of beef from him to last them back to town. It is needless to say that they found no diggings and all returned to Virginia in a few days.

The next great excitement was caused by a rumor of new rich discoveries on Boulder creek, a branch of the Jefferson. We sold every horse that we would spare at about three times its real value. Reece Anderson was among those taken with the fever and he joined the expedition. He had a good saddle and pack horses and plenty of food and blankets. There were so many in this stampede who started with little or nothing that those who had good outfits were obliged to share food with those who had none to keep them from starving and in the long run those with good outfits did not fare much better than those who started with none. Our friend, Reece Anderson, returned in about two weeks without having found any big thing in the way of gold mines, but he had accumulated quite a valuable stock of experience and got his nose, ears, and fingers badly frost-bitten.

The next big excitement started right in town. Somebody reported a "find" at the edge of town and in the morning claims were being staked off the main streets and on the rear of all of our lots. One enthusiastic man began to sink a hole in the street, just above the store and it began to look like we would be dug up and washed out without ceremony. Of course there was no gold found and mining operations in the streets and back yards was soon suspended.

A grand stampede to the Prickley Pear valley in which more than six hundred people took part was the last of the season. Away they went, crossing the hills into Boulder valley. They found the snow very deep, but fortunately not cold. Some good mines had been discovered on one bar about six hundred feet long, but all good ground had been taken when the stampeders arrived. The little army of disappointed men turned around and returned home once more.

3.2: The Buffalo Destroyed (1876–1877)

Much of the trans-Missouri region was too rugged or too dry for conventional agriculture, but in many places it produced an annual crop of short grass that provided forage for grazing animals. Before the arrival of white people the eastern half of the region, the high Plains, supported enormous herds of buffalo, and these in turn provided the Native American tribes with food (their flesh), clothing (their hides), rope (their sinews), and fuel (their droppings). By the late 1870s most of the buffalo were gone, leaving the land for domestic cattle and depriving the Indians of a basic necessity.

The destruction of the buffalo is not a pretty page in our history. In the following selection a professional buffalo hunter describes his occupation during the late 1870s. What were the hunter's motives? What part might the transcontinental railroads have played in the destruction of the buffalo herds? Some scholars believe that the slaughter of the buffalo was part of a deliberate policy designed to "tame" the nomadic Plains Indians. Was it?

The Destruction of the Plains Buffalo

W. SKELTON GLENN

There was several methods to kill [buffalos] and each [hunter] adopted his own course and plan. They would get together and while one gained a point from another, he, in turn, would gain a point from him. One method was to run beside them, shooting them as they ran. Another was to shoot from the rear, what was termed tail shooting: [always shooting] the hindmost buffalo and when a day's hunt was done, they would be strung on the ground for a mile or more, from ten to fifteen yards apart.

We first noticed that the buffaloes always went around a ravine or gulch, unless going for water straight down a bluff; and as the buffalo always followed these trails a man on foot by a mere cut-off of a hundred yards could cut him off. That is why they was so far apart in tail-hunting, as it was called.

.   .   .   .

Another method of hunting was to leave your horse out of sight after you had determined the direction and course of the wind, and then get as near as possible. If the herd was lying at rest, he would pick out some buffalo that was standing up on watch and shoot his ball in the side of him so that it would not go through, but would lodge in the flesh; as on many times it had been proven by men [who were] well hid and the wind taking the sound of the gun and the whizz of the bullet off, [that] if a ball passed through a buffalo the herd would stampede and run for miles. A buffalo shot in this manner would merely hump up his back as if he had the colic and commence to mill round and round in a slow walk. The other buffalo sniffing the blood and following would not be watching the hunter, and he would continue to shoot the outside cow buffalo; if there were old cows they would take them as there would be some two or three offsprings following her. If she would hump up, he would know that he had the range, and in this way hold the herd as long as they acted in this way as well as the well trained cowpuncher would hold his herd, only the hunter would use his gun. This was termed mesmerising the buffalo so that we could hold them on what we termed a stand, which afterwards proved to be the most successful way of killing the buffalo.

It was not always the best shot but the best hunter that succeeded, that is, the man who piled his buffalo in a pile so as to be more convenient for the skinner to get at and not have to run all over the country.

.   .   .   .

The hunter was hired by the piece: if robe hides were worth $3.00, [he was] given twenty-five cents for every one that he killed and was brought in by the skinners— was tallied up at camp. It was the camp rustler's business to keep tally of the num-

Rex W. Strickland, ed., "The Recollections of W. S. Glenn, Buffalo Hunter," *Panhandle Plains Historical Review,* vol. 22 (1949), pp. 20–26.

ber of hides killed each day. If the hides were worth $2.50, he [the hunter] got 20 cents; $2.00, he got 15 cents; $1.50, he got 10 cents; and $1.00, he got 5 cents.

.   .   .   .

I have seen their bodies so thick after being skinned, that they would look like logs where a hurricane had passed through a forrest [sic]. If they were lying on a hillside, the rays of the sun would make it look like a hundred glass windows. These buffalo would lie in this way until warm weather, drying up, and I have seen them piled fifty or sixty in a pile where the hunter had made a stand. As the skinner commenced on the edge, he would have to roll it out of the way to have room to skin the next, and when finished they would be rolled up as thick as saw logs around a mill. In this way a man could ride over a field and pick out the camps that were making the most money out of the hunt.

These hides, like all other commodities would rise and fall in price and we had to be governed by the prices [in the] East. This man, J. R. Loganstein, that run the hunt, has known them to be shipped to New York, then to Liverpool and back again in order to raise the price or corner the market. . . .

We will now describe a camp outfit. They would range from six to a dozen men, there being one hunter who killed the buffalo and took out the tongues, also the tallow. As the tallow was of an oily nature, it was equal to butter; [it was used] for lubricating our guns and we loaded our own shells, each shell had to be lubricated and [it] was used also for greasing wagons and also for lights in camp. Often chunks as large as an ear of corn were thrown on the fire to make heat. This [i.e., the removal of the tallow] had to be done while the meat was fresh, the hunter throwing it into a tree to wind dry; if the skinner forgot it, it would often stay there all winter and still be good to eat in the spring and better to eat after hanging there in the wind a few days.

We will return to the wagon man. [There were] generally two men to the wagon and their business was to follow up the hunter, if they were not in sight after the hunter had made a killing, he would proceed in their direction until he had met them, and when they would see him, he would signal with his hat where the killing was. If they got to the buffalo when they were fresh, their duty was to take out all the humps, tongues and tallow from the best buffalo. The hunter would then hunt more if they did not have hides enough to make a load or finish their day's work.

A remarkable good hunter would kill seventy-five to a hundred in a day, an average hunter about fifty, and a common one twenty-five, some hardly enough to run a camp. It was just like in any other business. A good skinner would skin from sixty to seventy-five, an average man from thirty to forty, and a common one from fifteen to twenty-five. These skinners were also paid by the hide[,] about five cents less than the hunter was getting for killing, being furnished with a grind stone, knives and steel and a team and wagon. The men were furnished with some kind of a gun, not as valuable as Sharp's rifle, to kill cripples with, also kips and calves that were standing around. In several incidents [instances?] it has been known to happen while the skinner was busy, they would slip up and knock him over. Toward the latter part of the hunt, when all the big ones were killed, I have seen as many as five hundred up to a thousand in a bunch, nothing but calves and have ridden right up to them, if the wind was right.

3.3: The Cattle Kingdom (1888)

Domestic cattle were introduced into the southern Plains well before 1860. At the end of the Civil War, Texas found itself with a tremendous excess of animals, and in 1866 Texas cattlemen began to drive their herds northward in the spring to the east-west railroads that were beginning to inch across the Plains.

These drives were hard and hazardous. Cowboys and trail bosses often had to fend off unfriendly Indians and irate farmers while dealing with the uncertainties of weather and skittish cattle, prone to stampedes. Arriving at railhead—a succession of "cow towns" along the Missouri Pacific, Kansas Pacific, and Santa Fe railroads—the drivers sold their animals to merchants specializing in cattle marketing. The cowhands were then paid, and, typically, after a wild spree in the dance halls, saloons, and bawdy houses, returned home to prepare for the following spring drive.

In the 1870s, after the railroads had pushed beyond the Missouri, the cattle industry spread to the northern Plains. There—in Montana, Wyoming, Idaho, and the Dakotas—enterprising cattlemen established ranches stocked with hardy longhorns imported from Texas. The ranchers had few expenses. The cattle grazed on public land and did not require shelter, even in winter. In the spring they were rounded up, and the newborn calves were branded with each rancher's characteristic mark. They were then sold to buyers and shipped east to the feedlots of the Corn Belt or the slaughterhouses of Chicago and St. Louis.

For a time the Plains cattle industry drew entrepreneurs and capital from the East and even from Europe. Beef prices were high; costs were low; profits inevitably were good. Moreover, the life of a rancher was exciting and glamorous.

One easterner attracted to the ranching life was Theodore Roosevelt. A New Yorker from an elite Knickerbocker family, Roosevelt went to Dakota Territory in 1884 and established the Elkhorn ranch on the Little Missouri River. In the selection below he describes the way the cattle business was conducted in the mid-1880s, with special emphasis on the roundup, the centerpiece of the ranchers' year.

Do you have any sense while reading Roosevelt's account that he is engaged in special pleading? Does his description seem to be romanticized? Would an account written by one of the ranch hands who earned forty dollars a month be as positive as that of the rancher him-self? Do you think Roosevelt was ever a real rancher, or was he only an "eastern dude" "who played at the business?"

A Round-up on the Plains

THEODORE ROOSEVELT

Cattle-ranching can only be carried on in its present form while the population is scanty; and so in stock-raising regions, pure and simple, there are usually few towns, and these are almost always at the shipping points for cattle. . . .

A true "cow town" is worth seeing,—such a one as Miles City, for instance, especially at the time of the annual meeting of the great Montana Stock-raisers' Association. Then the whole place is full to overflowing, the importance of the meeting and the fun of the attendant frolics, especially the horse-races, drawing from the surrounding ranch country many hundreds of men of every degree, from the rich stock-owner worth his millions to the ordinary cowboy who works for forty dollars a month. It would be impossible to imagine a more typically American assemblage, for although there are always a certain number of foreigners, usually English, Irish, or German, yet they have become completely Americanized; and on the whole it would be difficult to gather a finer body of men, in spite of their numerous short-comings. The ranch-owners differ more from each other than do the cowboys; and the former certainly compare very favorably with similar classes of capitalists in the East. Anything more foolish than the demagogic outcry against "cattle kings" it would be difficult to imagine. Indeed, there are very few businesses so absolutely legitimate as stock-raising and so beneficial to the nation at large; and a successful stock-grower must not only be shrewd, thrifty, patient, and enterprising, but he must also possess qualities of personal bravery, hardihood, and self-reliance to a degree not demanded in the least by any mercantile occupation in a community long settled. Stockmen are in the West the pioneers of civilization, and their daring and adventurousness make the after settlement [*sic*] of the region possible. The whole country owes them a great debt.

The stock-growers of Montana, of the western part of Dakota, and even of portions of extreme northern Wyoming,—that is, of all the grazing lands lying in the basin of the Upper Missouri,—have united, and formed themselves into the great Montana Stock-growers' Association. Among the countless benefits they have derived from this course, not the least has been the way in which the various round-ups work in with and supplement one another. At the spring meeting of the association, the entire territory mentioned above, including perhaps a hundred thousand square miles, is mapped out into round-up districts, which generally are changed but slightly from year to year, and the times and places for the round-ups to begin refixed so that those of adjacent districts may be run with a view to the best interests of all. . . .

Theodore Roosevelt, "Ranch Life in the Far West," *Century Magazine*, vol. 35 (February–April 1888), pp. 500, 850–55.

The captain or foreman of the round-up, upon whom very much of its efficiency and success depends, is chosen beforehand. He is, of course, an expert cowman, thoroughly acquainted with the country; and he must also be able to command and to keep control of the wild rough-riders he has under him—a feat needing both tact and firmness.

At the appointed day all meet at the place from which the round-up is to start. Each ranch, of course, has most work to be done in its own round-up district, but it is also necessary to have representatives in all those surrounding it. A large outfit may employ a dozen cowboys, or over, in the home district, and yet have nearly as many more representing its interest in the various ones adjoining. Smaller outfits generally club together to run a wagon and send outside representatives, or else go along with their stronger neighbors, they paying part of the expenses. A large outfit, with a herd of twenty thousand cattle or more, can, if necessary, run a round-up entirely by itself, and is able to act independently of outside help; it is therefore at a great advantage compared with those that can take no step effectively without their neighbors' consent and assistance.

If the starting-point is some distance off, it may be necessary to leave home three or four days in advance. Before this we have got everything in readiness; have overhauled the wagons, shod any horse whose forefeet are tender,—as a rule, all our ponies go barefooted,—and left things in order at the ranch. Our outfit may be taken as a sample of every one else's. We have a stout four-horse wagon to carry the bedding and the food; in its rear a mess-chest is rigged to hold the knives, forks, cans, etc. All our four team-horses are strong, willing animals, though of no great size, being originally just "broncos," or unbroken native horses, like the others. The teamster is also cook: a man who is a really first-rate hand at both driving and cooking—and our present teamster is both—can always command his price. Besides our own men, some cowboys from neighboring ranches and two or three representatives from other round-up districts are always along, and we generally have at least a dozen "riders," as they are termed,—that is, cowboys, or "cow-punchers," who do the actual cattle-work,—with the wagon. Each of these has a string of eight or ten ponies; and to take charge of the saddle-band, thus consisting of a hundred odd head, there are two herders, always known as "horse-wranglers"—one for the day and one for the night.

At the meeting-place there is usually a delay of a day or two to let every one come in; and the plain on which the encampment is made becomes a scene of great bustle and turmoil. The heavy four-horse wagons jolt in from different quarters, the horse-wranglers rushing madly to and fro in the endeavor to keep the different saddle-bands from mingling, while the "riders," or cowboys, with each wagon jog along in a body. The representatives from outside districts ride in singly or by twos and threes, every man driving before him his own horses, one of them loaded with his bedding. Each wagon wheels out of the way into some camping-place not too near the others, the bedding is tossed out on the ground, and then every one is left to do what he wishes, while the different wagon bosses, or foremen, seek out the captain of the round-up to learn what his plans are.

There is a good deal of rough but effective discipline and method in the way in which a round-up is carried on. The captain of the whole has as lieutenants the various wagon foremen and in making demands for men to do some special service he will usually merely designate some foreman to take charge of the work and let him parcel it out among his men to suit himself. The captain of the round-up or the foreman of a wagon may himself be a ranchman; if such is not the case, and the ranchman nevertheless comes along, he works and fares precisely as do the other cowboys.

There is no eight-hour law in cowboy land: during round-up time we often count ourselves lucky if we get off with much less than sixteen hours; but the work is done in the saddle, and the men are spurred on all the time by the desire to outdo one another in feats of daring and skillful horsemanship. There is very little quarreling or fighting; and though the fun often takes the form of rather rough horse-play, yet the practice of carrying dangerous weapons makes cowboys show far more rough courtesy to each other and far less rudeness to strangers than is the case among, for instance, Eastern miners, or even lumbermen. When a quarrel may very probably result fatally, a man thinks twice before going into it.

The method of work is simple. The mess-wagons and loose horses, after breaking camp in the morning, move on in a straight line for some miles, going into camp again before midday; and the day herd, consisting of all the cattle that have been found far off their range, and which are to be brought back there, and of any others that it is necessary to gather, follows on afterwards. Meanwhile the cowboys scatter out and drive in all the cattle from the country round about, going perhaps ten or fifteen miles back from the line of march, and meeting at the place where camp has already been pitched. The wagons always keep some little distance from one another, and the saddle-bands do the same, so that the horses may not get mixed.

The speed and thoroughness with which a country can be worked depends, of course, very largely upon the number of riders. Ours is probably about an average round-up as regards size. The last spring I was out, there were half a dozen wagons along; the saddle-bands numbered about a hundred each; and the morning we started, sixty men in the saddle splashed across the shallow ford of the river that divided the plain where we had camped from the valley of the long winding creek up which we were first to work.

In the morning the cook is preparing breakfast long before the first glimmer of dawn. As soon as it is ready, probably about 3 o'clock, he utters a long-drawn shout, and all the sleepers feel it is time to be up on the instant, for they know there can be no such thing as delay on the round-up, under penalty of being set afoot. . . . The meal is not an elaborate one; nevertheless a man will have a hurry if he wishes to eat it before hearing the foreman sing out, "Come, boys, catch your horses"; when he must drop everything and run out to the wagon with his lariat. When all are saddled, many of the horses bucking and dancing about, the riders from the different wagons all assemble at the one where the captain is sitting, already mounted. He waits a very short time—for laggards receive but scant mercy—before announcing the proposed camping-place and parceling out the work among those present. If, as is usually the case, the line of march is along a river or creek, he appoints some man to take a dozen others and drive down (or up) it ahead of the day herd, so that the latter will not have to travel through other cattle; the day herd itself being driven and guarded by a dozen men detached for that purpose. The rest of the riders are divided into two bands, placed under men who know the country, and start out, one on each side, to bring in every head for fifteen miles back. The captain then himself rides down to the new camping-place, so as to be there as soon as any cattle are brought in.

Meanwhile the two bands, a score of riders in each, separate and make their way in opposite directions. The leader of each tries to get such a "scatter" on his men that they will cover completely all the land gone over. This morning work is called circle riding, and is peculiarly hard in the Bad Lands on account of the remarkably broken, rugged nature of the country. The men come in on lines that tend to a common center—as if the sticks of a fan were curved. As the band goes out, the leader from time to time detaches one or two men to ride down through certain sections of the country, making the shorter, or what are called inside, circles, while he keeps on; and finally, retaining as companions the two or three whose horses are toughest, makes the longest or outside circle himself, going clear back to the divide, or whatever the point may be that marks the limit of the round-up work, and then turning and working straight to the meeting-place. Each man, of course, brings in every head of cattle he can see.

When the men on the outside circle have reached the bound set them,—whether it is a low divide, a group of jagged hills, the edge of the rolling, limitless prairie, or the long, waste reaches of alkali and sage brush,—they turn their horses' heads and begin to work down the branches of the creeks, one or two riding down the bottom, while the others keep off to the right and the left, a little ahead and fairly high up on the side hills, so as to command as much of a view as possible. . . . All the cattle are carried on ahead down the creek; and it is curious to watch the different behavior of the different breeds. A cowboy riding off to one side of the creek, and seeing a number of long-horned Texans grazing in the branches of a set of coulees, has merely to ride across the upper ends of these, uttering the drawn-out "ei-koh-h-h," so familiar to the cattle-men, and the long-horns will stop grazing, stare fixedly at him, and then, wheeling, strike off down the coulees at a trot, tails in air, to be carried along by the center riders when they reach the main creek into which the coulees lead. . . . Every little bunch of stock is thus collected, and all are driven along together. At the place where some large fork joins the main creek another band may be met, driven by some of the men who have left earlier in the day to take one of the shorter circles; and thus, before coming down to the bottom where the wagons are camped and where the actual "round-up" itself is to take place, this one herd may include a couple of thousand head; or, on the other hand, the longest ride may not result in the finding of a dozen animals. As soon as the riders are in, they disperse to their respective wagons to get dinner and change horses, leaving the cattle to be held by one or two of their number. If only a small number of cattle have been gathered, they will all be run into one herd; if there are many of them, however, the different herds will be held separate.

As soon as, or even before, the last circle riders have come in and have snatched a few hasty mouthfuls to serve as their mid-day meal, we begin to work the herd—or herds, if the one herd would be of too unwieldy size. The animals are held in a compact bunch, most of the riders forming a ring outside, while a couple from each ranch successively look the herds through and cut out those marked with their own brand. It is difficult, in such a mass of moving beasts,—for they do not stay still, but keep weaving in and out among each other,—to find all of one's own animals: a man must have natural gifts, as well as great experience, before he becomes a good brand-reader and is able to "clean up a herd"—that is, be sure he has left nothing of his own in it.

All this time the men holding the herd have their hands full, for some animal is continually trying to break out, when the nearest man flies at it at once and after a smart chase brings it back to its fellows. As soon as all the cows, calves, and whatever else is being gathered have been cut out, the rest are driven clear off the ground and turned loose, being headed in the direction contrary to that in which we travel the following day. Then the riders surround the next herd, the men holding cuts move them up near it, and the work is begun anew.

As soon as all the brands of cattle are worked, and the animals that are to be driven along have been put in the day herd, attention is turned to the cows and calves, which are already gathered in different bands, consisting each of all the cows of a certain brand and all the calves that are following them. If there is a corral, each band is in turn driven into it; if there is none, a ring of riders does duty in its place. A fire is built, the irons heated, and a dozen men dismount to, as it is called, "wrestle" the calves. The best two ropers go in on their horses to catch the latter; one man keeps tally, a couple put on the brands, and the others seize, throw, and hold the little unfortunates.

Every morning certain riders are detached to drive and to guard the day herd, which is most monotonous work, the men being on from 4 in the morning till 8 in the evening, the only rest coming at dinner-time, when they change horses.

From 8 in the evening till 4 in the morning the day herd becomes a night herd. Each wagon in succession undertakes to guard it for a night, dividing the time into watches of two hours apiece, a couple of riders taking each watch. This is generally chilly and tedious; but at times it is accompanied by intense excitement and danger, when the cattle become stampeded, whether by storm or otherwise. The first and the last watches are those chosen by preference; the others are disagreeable, the men having to turn out cold and sleepy, in the pitchy darkness, the two hours of chilly wakefulness completely breaking the night's rest.

But though there is much work and hardship, rough fare, monotony, and exposure connected with the round-up, yet there are few men who do not look forward to it and back to it with pleasure. The only fault to be found is that the hours of work are so long that one does not usually have enough time to sleep. The food, if rough, is good: beef, bread, pork, beans, coffee or tea, always canned tomatoes, and often rice, canned corn, or sauce made from dried apples. The men are good-humored, bold, and thoroughly interested in their business, continually vying with one another in the effort to see which can do the work best. It is superbly health-giving, and is full of excitement and adventure, calling for the exhibition of pluck, self-reliance, hardihood, and dashing horsemanship; and of all forms of physical labor the easiest and pleasantest is to sit in the saddle.

3.4: Native Americans (1877, 1881)

*The most resistant barrier to white exploitation of the "last West"
were the Native American peoples who, until the 1850s, occupied the
Great Plains as "One Big Reservation." These were formidable
mounted warriors capable of firing a shower of deadly arrows at a
target while riding their ponies at full gallop. Yet in the end, they could
not stand up to the superior organization and numbers of the whites
who coveted their lands.*

*Beginning in the 1850s the federal government, responding to the
demands of western farmers, miners, and railroad promoters, began to
force the Plains tribes into smaller and smaller reservations. Using
bribery, deception, and threats, the federal government strong-armed
the Indians into treaties that reduced their lands to ever-more limited
tracts, often arid and rugged terrain that no one else wanted. The Indians resisted, and between 1866 and 1890 the Plains tribes and the
U.S. Army fought a series of wars in which the Indians often gave as
good as they got. In 1866 the Sioux killed 82 soldiers under the command of Captain W. J. Fetterman; in 1876, commanded by Chiefs Sitting Bull and Crazy Horse, they were again victorious, killing all 265
men under the command of the foolhardy army general George
Custer, at the Little Big Horn River.*

*The first selection below is Sitting Bull's account of the battle on the
Little Big Horn as given to a New York newspaper reporter. Why, according to Sitting Bull, were the Indians able to destroy Custer's
force? What does the chief's description reveal of Indian values? Do
you know if Custer and his men were badly outnumbered? Why, do
you think, past generations romanticized Custer? Is he still considered
a tragic hero?*

*The second selection is a portion of President Chester A. Arthur's
1881 State of the Union Address in which Arthur, an easterner, says
that the government must cease to treat the Indians as collective members of separate, autonomous nations, and deal with them instead as
individuals to be absorbed into mainstream American life. In what way
can Arthur's approach be considered generous and enlightened for the
day? Is there any significance in the fact that Arthur was an easterner? (The "severalty" proposal for land ownership by individual
families, as contrasted with the former communal ownership by tribes,
was finally enacted by Congress in 1887 as the Dawes Act.)*

*Do you know if the Indians benefited or lost under the new policy?
What is the significance of Arthur's suggestion concerning education for
the Indians? What sort of education, do you suppose, he had in mind?*

Sitting Bull Tells How He Defeated Custer

SITTING BULL

"When the fight commenced here," I asked, pointing to the spot where Custer advanced beyond the Little Big Horn, "what happened?"

"Hell!"

"You mean, I suppose, a fierce battle?"

"I mean a thousand devils."

"The village was by this time thoroughly aroused?"

"The squaws were like flying birds; the bullets were like humming bees."

"You say that when the first attack was made, up here on the right of the map, the old men and the squaws and children ran down the valley toward the left. What did they do when this second attack came from up here toward the left?"

"They ran back again to the right, here and here," answered Sitting Bull, placing his swarthy finger on the place where the words "Abandoned Lodges" are.

"And where did the warriors run?"

"They ran to the fight—the big fight."

"So that, in the afternoon, after the fight, on the right hand side of the map was over, and after the big fight toward the left hand side began, you say that the squaws and children all returned to the right hand side, and that the warriors, the fighting men of all the Indian camps, ran to the place where the big fight was going on?"

"Yes."

"Why was that? Were not some of the warriors left in front of these intrenchments on the bluffs, near the right side of the map? Did not you think it necessary—did not your war chiefs think it necessary—to keep some of your young men there to fight the troops who had retreated to those intrenchments?"

"No."

"Why?"

"You have forgotten."

"How?"

"You forget that only a few soldiers were left by the Long Hair[1] on those bluffs. He took the main body of his soldiers with him to make the big fight down here on the left."

"So there were no soldiers to make a fight left in the intrenchments on the right hand bluffs?"

"I have spoken. It is enough. The squaws could deal with them. There were none but squaws and pappooses in front of them that afternoon."

"Well then," I inquired of Sitting Bull, "Did the cavalry, who came down and made the big fight, fight?"

Again Sitting Bull smiled.

New York Herald, November 16, 1877.
[1]Custer, who wore his hair down his back—ED.

"They fought. Many young men are missing from our lodges. But is there an American squaw who has her husband left? Were there any Americans left to tell the story of that day? No."

"How did they come on to the attack?"

"I have heard that there are trees which tremble."

"Do you mean the trees with trembling leaves?"

"Yes."

"They call them in some parts of the western country Quaking Asps; in the eastern part of the country they call them Silver Aspens."

"Hah! A great white chief, whom I met once, spoke these words 'Silver Aspens,' trees that shake; these were the Long Hair's soldiers."

"You do not mean that they trembled before your people because they were afraid?"

"They were brave men. They were tired. They were too tired."

"How did they act? How did they behave themselves?"

At this Sitting Bull again arose. I also arose from my seat, as did the other persons in the room, except the stenographer.

"Your people," said Sitting Bull, extending his right hand, "were killed. I tell no lies about deadmen. These men who came with the Long Hair were as good men as ever fought. When they rode up their horses were tired and they were tired. When they got off from their horses they could not stand firmly on their feet. They swayed to and fro—so my young men have told me—like the limbs of cypresses in a great wind. Some of them staggered under the weight of their guns. But they began to fight at once; but by this time, as I have said, our camps were aroused, and there were plenty of warriors to meet them. They fired with needle guns. We replied with magazine guns—repeating rifles. It was so (and here Sitting Bull illustrated by patting his palms together with the rapidity of a fusilade). Our young men rained lead across the river and drove the white braves back."

"And then?"

"And then, they rushed across themselves."

"And then?"

"And then they found that they had a good deal to do."

"Was there at that time some doubt about the issue of the battle, whether you would whip the Long Hair or not?"

"Where was so much doubt about it that I started down there (here again pointing to the map) to tell the squaws to pack up the lodges and get ready to move away."

"You were on that expedition, then, after the big fight had fairly begun?"

"Yes."

"You did not personally witness the rest of the big fight? You were not engaged in it?"

"No. I have heard of it from the warriors."

"When the great crowds of your young men crossed the river in front of the Long Hair what did they do? Did they attempt to assault him directly in his front?"

"At first they did, but afterward they found it better to try and get around him. They formed themselves on all sides of him except just at his back."

"How long did it take them to put themselves around his flanks?"

"As long as it takes the sun to travel from here to here" (indicating some marks upon his arm with which apparently he is used to gauge the progress of the shadow of his lodge across his arm, and probably meaning half an hour. An Indian has no more definite way than this to express the lapse of time).

"The trouble was with the soldiers," he continued; "they were so exhausted and their horses bothered them so much that they could not take good aim. Some of their horses broke away from them and left them to stand and drop and die. When the Long Hair, the General, found that he was so outnumbered and threatened on his flanks, he took the best course he could have taken. The bugle blew. It was an order to fall back. All the men fell back fighting and dropping. They could not fire fast enough, though. But from our side it was so," said Sitting Bull, and here he clapped his hands rapidly twice a second to express with what quickness and continuance the balls flew from the Henry and Winchester rifles wielded by the Indians. "They could not stand up under such a fire," he added.

"Were any military tactics shown? Did the Long Haired Chief make any disposition of his soldiers, or did it seem as though they retreated all together, helter skelter, fighting for their lives?"

"They kept in pretty good order. Some great chief must have commanded them all the while. They would fall back across a *coulee* and make a fresh stand beyond on higher ground. The map is pretty nearly right. It shows where the white men stopped and fought before they were all killed. I think that is right—down there to the left, just above the Little Big Horn. There was one part driven out there, away from the rest, and there a great many men were killed. The places marked on the map are pretty nearly the places where all were killed."

"Did the whole command keep on fighting until the last?"

"Every man, so far as my people could see. There were no cowards on either side."

The Indians Must Be Assimilated

CHESTER A. ARTHUR

Prominent among the matters which challenge the attention of Congress at its present session is the management of our Indian affairs. While this question has been a cause of trouble and embarrassment from the infancy of the Government, it is but recently that any effort has been made for its solution at once serious, determined, consistent, and promising success.

James D. Richardson, ed., *A Compilation of the Messages and Papers of the Presidents* (New York: Bureau of National Literature, 1897), vol. 10, pp. 4641–43.

It has been easier to resort to convenient makeshifts for tiding over temporary difficulties than to grapple with the great permanent problem, and accordingly the easier course has almost invariably been pursued.

It was natural, at a time when the national territory seemed almost illimitable and contained many millions of acres far outside the bounds of civilized settlements, that a policy should have been initiated which more than aught else has been the fruitful source of our Indian complications.

I refer, of course, to the policy of dealing with the various Indian tribes as separate nationalities, of relegating them by treaty stipulations to the occupancy of immense reservations in the West, and of encouraging them to live a savage life, undisturbed by any earnest and well-directed efforts to bring them under the influences of civilization.

The unsatisfactory results which have sprung from this policy are becoming apparent to all.

As the white settlements have crowded the borders of the reservations, the Indians, sometimes contentedly and sometimes against their will, have been transferred to other hunting grounds, from which they have again been dislodged whenever their new-found homes have been desired by the adventurous settlers.

These removals and the frontier collisions by which they have often been preceded have led to frequent and disastrous conflicts between the races.

It is profitless to discuss here which of them has been chiefly responsible for the disturbances whose recital occupies so large a space upon the pages of our history.

We have to deal with the appalling fact that though thousands of lives have been sacrificed and hundreds of millions of dollars expended in the attempt to solve the Indian problem, it has until within the past few years seemed scarcely nearer a solution than it was half a century ago. But the Government has of late been cautiously but steadily feeling its way to the adoption of a policy which has already produced gratifying results, and which, in my judgment, is likely, if Congress and the Executive accord in its support, to relieve us ere long from the difficulties which have hitherto beset us.

For the success of the efforts now making to introduce among the Indians the customs and pursuits of civilized life and gradually to absorb them into the mass of our citizens, sharing their rights and holden to their responsibilities, there is imperative need for legislative action.

My suggestions in that regard will be chiefly such as have been already called to the attention of Congress and have received to some extent its consideration.

First. I recommend the passage of an act making the laws of the various States and Territories applicable to the Indian reservations within their borders and extending the laws of the State of Arkansas to the portion of the Indian Territory not occupied by the Five Civilized Tribes.

The Indian should receive the protection of the law. He should be allowed to maintain in court his rights of person and property. He has repeatedly begged for this privilege. Its exercise would be very valuable to him in his progress toward civilization.

Second. Of even greater importance is a measure which has been frequently recommended by my predecessors in office, and in furtherance of which several bills have been from time to time introduced in both Houses of Congress. The enactment of a general law permitting the allotment in severalty, to such Indians, at least, as desire it, of a reasonable quantity of land secured to them by patent, and for their own protection made inalienable for twenty or twenty-five years, is demanded for their present welfare and their permanent advancement.

In return for such considerate action on the part of the Government, there is reason to believe that the Indians in large numbers would be persuaded to sever their tribal relations and to engage at once in agricultural pursuits. Many of them realize the fact that their hunting days are over and that it is now for their best interests to conform their manner of life to the new order of things. By no greater inducement than the assurance of permanent title to the soil can they be led to engage in the occupation of tilling it.

The well-attested reports of their increasing interest in husbandry justify the hope and belief that the enactment of such a statute as I recommend would be at once attended with gratifying results. A resort to the allotment system would have a direct and powerful influence in dissolving the tribal bond, which is so prominent a feature of savage life, and which tends so strongly to perpetuate it.

Third. I advise a liberal appropriation for the support of Indian schools, because of my confident belief that such a course is consistent with the wisest economy.

3.5: The Populist Party Platform (1892)

Meeting at Omaha in July 1892, the People's Party adopted a platform that went beyond the demands of the dirt farmers' leaders to express the concerns of social critics and reformers who foresaw imminent social catastrophe for America if something were not done soon. The preamble of this platform was written by Ignatius Donnelly, novelist, journalist, intellectual, and former Republican congressman from Minnesota.

How do you explain the platform's apocalyptic tone? In what ways does it seek to create a farmer-labor alliance? It has been said that Populism foreshadowed twentieth-century liberalism. Is there anything in the platform that reminds you of later Progressive and New Deal policies and programs?

The Preamble of the Platform of the People's Party

Assembled upon the 116th anniversary of the Declaration of Independence, the People's Party of America, in their first national convention, invoking upon their

Edward McPherson, *A Handbook of Politics for 1892* (Washington DC: James J. Chapman, 1892), pp. 269–271.

action the blessing of Almighty God, puts forth, in the name and on behalf of the people of this country, the following preamble and declaration of principles:—The conditions which surround us best justify our cooperation: we meet in the midst of a nation brought to the verge of moral, political, and material ruin. Corruption dominates the ballot-box, the legislatures, the Congress, and even touches the ermine of the bench. The people are demoralized; most of the states have been compelled to isolate the voters at the polling-places to prevent universal intimidation or bribery. The newspapers are largely subsidized or muzzled; public opinion silenced; business prostrated; our homes covered with mortgages; labor impoverished; and the land concentrating in the hands of the capitalists. The urban workmen are denied the right of organization for self-protection; imported pauperized labor beats down their wages; a hireling standing army, unrecognized by our laws, is established to shoot them down, and they are rapidly degenerating into European conditions. The fruits of the toil of millions are boldly stolen to build up colossal fortunes for a few, unprecedented in the history of mankind; and the possessors of these, in turn, despise the Republic and endanger liberty. From the same prolific womb of governmental injustice we breed two great classes—tramps and millionaires.

The national power to create money is appropriated to enrich bondholders; a vast public debt, payable in legal tender currency, has been funded into gold bearing bonds, thereby adding millions to the burdens of the people. Silver, which has been accepted as coin since the dawn of history, has been demonetized to add to the purchasing power of gold by decreasing the value of all forms of property as well as human labor; and the supply of currency is purposely abridged to fatten usurers, bankrupt enterprise, and enslave industry. A vast conspiracy against mankind has been organized on two continents, and it is rapidly taking possession of the world. If not met and overthrown at once, it forebodes [*sic*] terrible convulsions, the destruction of civilization, or the establishment of an absolute despotism.

We have witnessed for more than a quarter of a century the struggles of the two great political parties for power and plunder, while grievous wrongs have been inflicted upon the suffering people. We charge that the controlling influences dominating both these parties have permitted the existing dreadful conditions to develop without serious effort to prevent or restrain them. Neither do they now promise us any substantial reform. They have agreed together to ignore in the coming campaign every issue but one. They propose to drown the outcries of a plundered people with the uproar of a sham battle over the tariff, so that capitalists, corporations, national banks, rings, trusts, watered stock, the demonetization of silver, and the oppressions of the usurers may all be lost sight of. They propose to sacrifice our homes, lives and children on the altar of mammon; to destroy the multitude in order to secure corruption funds from the millionaires.

Assembled on the anniversary of the birthday of the nation, and filled with the spirit of the grand general and chieftain who established our independence, we seek to restore the government of the Republic to the hands of "the plain people," with whose class it originated. We assert our proposes to be identical with the purposes of the National Constitution, "to form a more perfect union and establish justice, insure domestic tranquility, provide for the common defence, promote the general welfare, and secure the blessings of liberty for ourselves and our posterity." We declare that this republic can only endure as a free government while built upon the love of the whole people for each other and for the nation; that it cannot be pinned together by bayonets; that the civil war is over, and that every passion and resentment which grew out of it must die with it; and that we must be in fact, as we are in name, one united brotherhood of freemen.

Our country finds itself confronted by conditions for which there is no precedent in the history of the world; our annual agricultural productions amount to billions of dollars in value, which must in a few weeks or months, be exchanged for billions of dollars of commodities consumed in their production; the existing currency supply is wholly inadequate to make this exchange; the results are falling prices, the formation of combines and rings, the impoverishment of the producing class. We pledge ourselves, if given power, we will labor to correct these evils by wise and reasonable legislation, in accordance with the terms of our platform. We believe that the powers of government—in other words, of the people—should be expanded (as in the case of the postal service) as rapidly and as far as the good sense of an intelligent people and the teachings of experience shall justify, to the end that oppression, injustice, and poverty shall eventually cease in the land.

While our sympathies as a party of reform are naturally upon the side of every proposition which will tend to make men intelligent, virtuous, and temperate, we nevertheless regard these questions—important as they are—as secondary to the great issues now pressing for solution, and upon which not only our individual prosperity but the very existence of free institutions depends; and we ask all men to first help us to determine whether we are to have a republic to administer before we differ as to the conditions upon which it is to be administered; believing that the forces of reform this day organized will never cease to move forward until every wrong is remedied, and equal rights and equal privileges securely established for all the men and women of this country.

We declare, therefore,—

First—That the union of the labor forces of the United States this day consummated shall be permanent and perpetual; may its spirit enter all hearts for the salvation of the republic and the uplifting of mankind!

Second—Wealth belongs to him who creates it, and every dollar taken from industry without an equivalent is robbery. "If any will not work, neither shall he eat." The interests of rural and civic labor are the same; their enemies are identical.

Third—We believe that the time has come when the railroad corporations will either own the people or the people must own the railroads; and, should the government enter upon the work of owning and managing all railroads, we should favor an amendment to the Constitution by which all persons engaged in the government service shall be placed under a civil service regulation of the most rigid character, so as to prevent the increase of the power of the national administration by the use of such additional government employees.

First, *Money*—We demand a national currency, safe, sound, and flexible, issued by the general government only, a full legal tender for all debts, public and private, and that, without the use of banking corporations, a just, equitable, and efficient means of distribution direct to the people, at a tax not to exceed two per cent per annum, to be provided as set forth in the sub-treasury plan of the Farmers' Alliance, or a better system; also, by payments in discharge of its obligation for public improvements.

a. We demand free and unlimited coinage of silver and gold at the present legal ratio of sixteen to one.
b. We demand that the amount of circulating medium be speedily increased to not less than fifty dollars per capita.
c. We demand a graduated income tax.
d. We believe that the money of the country should be kept as much as possible in the hands of the people, and hence we demand that all state and national revenues shall be limited to the necessary expenses of the government economically and honestly administered.
e. We demand that postal savings banks be established by the government for the safe deposit of the earnings of the people and to facilitate exchange.

Second, *Transportation*—Transportation being a means of exchange and a public necessity, the government should own and operate the railroads in the interest of the people.

Third, *Land,*—The land, including all the natural sources of wealth, is the heritage of the people, and should not be monopolized for speculative purposes, and alien ownership of land should be prohibited. All land now held by railroads and other corporations in excess of their actual needs, and all lands now owned by aliens, should be reclaimed by the government and held for actual settlers only.

Resolutions

Whereas, Other questions have been presented for our considerations, we hereby submit the following, not as part of the platform of the People's party, but as resolutions of the sentiment of this convention.

1. *Resolved,* That we demand a free ballot and a fair count in all elections, and pledge ourselves to secure it to every legal voter without federal intervention, through the adoption by the States of the unperverted Australian or secret ballot system.

2. *Resolved,* That the revenue derived from a graduated income tax should be applied to the reduction of the burden of taxation now resting upon the domestic industries of this country.

3. *Resolved,* That we pledge our support to fair and liberal pensions to ex-Union soldiers and sailors.

4. *Resolved,* That we condemn the fallacy of protecting American labor under the present system, which opens our ports to the pauper and criminal classes of the world, and crowds out our wage-earners; and we denounce the present ineffective laws against contract labor, and demand the further restriction of undesirable immigration.

5. *Resolved,* That we cordially sympathize with the efforts of organized workingmen to shorten the hours of labor, and demand a rigid enforcement of the existing eighthour law on government work, and ask that a penalty clause be added to said law.

6. *Resolved,* That we regard the maintenance of a large standing army of mercenaries, known as the Pinkerton system, as a menace to our liberties, and we demand its abolition; and we condemn the recent invasion of the Territory of Wyoming by the hired assassins of the plutocracy, assisted by federal officials.

7. *Resolved,* That we commend to the favorable consideration of the people and the reform press the legislative system known as the initiative and referendum.

8. *Resolved,* That we favor a constitutional provision limiting the office of President and Vice-President to one term, and providing for the election of senators of the United States by a direct vote of the people.

9. *Resolved,* That we oppose any subsidy or national aid to any private corporation for any purpose.

10. *Resolved,* That this convention sympathizes with the Knights of Labor and their righteous contest with the tyrannical combine of clothing manufacturers of Rochester, and declares it to be the duty of all who hate tyranny and oppression to refuse to purchase the goods made by said manufacturers, or to patronize any merchants who sell such goods.

3.6: William Allen White and the Kansas Populists (1896)

In 1896, when he wrote the article below, William Allen White was the twenty-eight-year-old editor of the Emporia Gazette, *a newspaper in a small city in Kansas. The son of a doctor, White would later become a champion of social and political reform, but at this point he despised the home-grown reformers who called themselves Populists. The following essay was published during the heat of the presidential contest between William Jennings Bryan and William McKinley and immediately attracted national attention as a biting critique of midwestern Populism by a midwesterner. Republican newspapers by the score promptly reprinted the essay, and the McKinley campaign people distributed it as an anti-Bryan broadside.*

What are White's chief complaints about the Kansas Populists? Were his charges valid? What social factors in White's background might explain why this son of Kansas was so hostile to the farmers' party of his state?

What's the Matter with Kansas?

WILLIAM ALLEN WHITE

Today the Kansas Department of Agriculture sent out a statement which indicates that Kansas has gained less than two thousand people in the past year. There are about two hundred and twenty-five thousand families in this state, and there were

William Allen White, *The Autobiography of William Allen White* (New York: The Macmillan Company, 1946), pp. 280–283. Reprinted with permission of Barbara White Walker.

ten thousand babies born in Kansas, and yet so many people have left the state that the natural increase is cut down to less than two thousand net.

This has been going on for eight years.

If there had been a high brick wall around the state eight years ago, and not a soul had been admitted or permitted to leave, Kansas would be a half million souls better off than she is today. And yet the nation has increased in population. In five years ten million people have been added to the national population, yet instead of gaining a share of this—say, half a million—Kansas has apparently been a plague spot and, in the very garden of the world, has lost population by ten thousands every year.

Not only has she lost population, but she has lost money. Every moneyed man in the state who could get out without loss has gone. Every month in every community sees someone who has a little money pack up and leave the state. This has been going on for eight years. Money has been drained out all the time. In towns where ten years ago there were three or four or half a dozen money-lending concerns, stimulating industry by furnishing capital, there is now none, or one or two that are looking after the interest and principal already outstanding.

No one brings any money into Kansas any more. What community knows over one or two men who have moved in with more than $5,000 in the past three years? And what community cannot count half a score of men in that time who have left, taking all the money they could scrape together?

Yet the nation has grown rich; other states have increased in population and wealth—other neighboring states. Missouri has gained over two million, while Kansas has been losing half a million. Nebraska has gained in wealth and population while Kansas has gone downhill. Colorado has gained every way, while Kansas has lost every way since 1888.

What's the matter with Kansas?

There is no substantial city in the state. Every big town save one has lost in population. Yet Kansas City, Omaha, Lincoln, St. Louis, Denver, Colorado Springs, Sedalia, the cities of the Dakotas, St. Paul and Minneapolis and Des Moines—all cities and towns in the West—have steadily grown.

Take up the government blue book [which lists federal officeholders] and you will see that Kansas is virtually off the map. Two or three little scrubby consular places in yellow-fever-stricken communities that do not aggregate ten thousand dollars a year is all the recognition that Kansas has. Nebraska draws about one hundred thousand dollars; little old North Dakota draws about fifty thousand dollars; Oklahoma doubles Kansas; Missouri leaves her a thousand miles behind; Colorado is almost seven times greater than Kansas—the whole west is ahead of Kansas.

Take it by any standard you please, Kansas is not in it.

Go east and you hear them laugh at Kansas; go west and they sneer at her; go south and they "cuss" her; go north and they have forgotten her. Go into any crowd of intelligent people gathered anywhere on the globe, and you will find the Kansas man on the defensive. The newspaper columns and magazines once devoted to praise of her, to boastful facts and startling figures concerning her resources, are now filled with cartoons, jibes and Pefferian speeches. Kansas just naturally isn't in it. She has traded places with Arkansas and Timbuctoo.

What's the matter with Kansas?

We all know; yet here we are at it again. We have an old mossback Jacksonian who snorts and howls because there is a bathtub in the State House; we are running that old jay for Governor. We have another shabby, wild-eyed, rattle-brained fanatic who has said openly in a dozen speeches that "the rights of the user are paramount to the rights of the owner"; we are running him for Chief Justice, so that capital will come tumbling over itself to get into the state. We have raked the old ash heap of failure in the state and found an old human hoop skirt who has failed as a business-man, who has failed as an editor, who has failed as a preacher, and we are going to run him for Congressman-at-Large. He will help the looks of the Kansas delegation at Washington. Then we have discovered a kid without a law practice and have de-cided to run him for Attorney General. Then, for fear some hint that the state had become respectable might percolate through the civilized portions of the nation, we have decided to send three or four harpies out lecturing, telling the people that Kansas is raising hell and letting the corn go to weed.

Oh, this is a state to be proud of! We are a people who can hold up our heads! What we need is not more money, but less capital, fewer white shirts and brains, fewer men with business judgment, and more of those fellows who boast that they are "just ordinary clodhoppers, but they know more in a minute about finance than John Sherman"; we need more men who are "posted," who can bellow about the crime of '73, who hate prosperity, and who think, because a man believes in na-tional honor, he is a tool of Wall Street. We have had a few of them—some hundred fifty thousand—but we need more.

We need several thousand gibbering idiots to scream about the "Great Red Dragon" of Lombard Street [a term for the British Wall Street]. We don't need pop-ulation, we don't need wealth, we don't need well-dressed men on the streets, we don't need cities on the fertile prairies; you bet we don't! What we are after is the money power. Because we have become poorer and ornerier and meaner than a spavined, distempered mule, we, the people of Kansas, propose to kick; we don't care to build up, we wish to tear down.

"There are two ideas of government," said our noble [William Jennings] Bryan at Chicago. "There are those who believe that if you legislate to make the well-to-do prosperous, this prosperity will leak through on those below. The Democratic idea has been that if you legislate to make the masses prosperous their prosperity will find its way up and through every class and rest upon them."

That's the stuff! Give the prosperous man the dickens! Legislate the thriftless man into ease, whack the stuffing out of the creditors and tell the debtors who bor-rowed the money five years ago when money "per capita" was greater than it is now, that the contraction of currency gives him a right to repudiate.

Whoop it up for the ragged trousers; put the lazy, greasy fizzle, who can't pay his debts on the altar, and bow down and worship him. Let the state ideal be high. What we need is not the respect of our fellow men, but the chance to get something for nothing.

Oh, yes, Kansas is a great state. Here are people fleeing from it by the score every day, capital going out of the state by the hundreds of dollars; and every industry but farming paralyzed, and that crippled, because its products have to go across the ocean before they can find a laboring man at work who can afford to buy them. Let's don't stop this year. Let's drive all the decent, self-respecting men out of the state. Let's keep the old clodhoppers who know it all. Let's encourage the man who is "posted." He can talk, and what we need is not mill hands to eat our meat, nor factory hands to eat our wheat, nor cities to oppress the farmer by consuming his butter and eggs and chickens and produce. What Kansas needs is men who can talk, who have large leisure to argue the currency question while their wives wait at home for a nickel's worth of bluing.

What's the matter with Kansas?

Nothing under the shining sun. She is losing her wealth, population and standing. She has got her statesmen, and the money power is afraid of her. Kansas is all right. She has started in to raise hell as Mrs. [Mary Ellen] Lease advised, and she seems to have an over-production. But that doesn't matter. Kansas never did believe in diversified crops. Kansas is all right. There is absolutely nothing wrong with Kansas. "Every prospect pleases and only man is vile."

☆ **4** ☆

Outward Thrust

For a time during the closing years of the nineteenth century, the United States joined the big power race for overseas markets and colonies. Although the country had acquired Alaska and several small islands soon after the Civil War, until the 1890s most of its expansionist energies had been expended on settling and exploiting the broad expanse within its own national boundaries. Numerous, rich, and aggressive, Americans had not been averse to bullying weaker neighbors and forcibly dispossessing the Native Americans. Still, they had avoided acquiring territory detached from the North American continent. Nor had they been particularly interested in overseas investment or, with the notable exception of the South's cotton, in overseas markets. All told, as the nation entered the post-Reconstruction era, the inward-looking United States was a relatively minor player on world economic and political stages.

These attitudes soon changed. The documents that follow address the issues of why this occurred. They suggest why the self-satisfied and prosperous republic abandoned its inward focus and, at least for a time, dreamed of an empire. In the selections below you will encounter a range of opinion on America's outward thrust of the 1890s that culminated in the Spanish-American War and the acquisition of the Philippines, Puerto Rico, Hawaii, and other lands beyond the nation's continental borders.

4.1: Racial Destiny (1885)

Darwinian survival-of-the-fittest ideas not only sanctioned laissez-faire (free market) economics but also encouraged American expansionism. Nations and races, like individuals, differed in natural talent and abilities, many Darwinists believed. Some nations and races were superior, and, like superior individuals, deserved to rule the rest. Writing in 1885, the Congregational minister Josiah Strong depicted in Darwinian terms the triumph of the American branch of the Anglo-Saxon race over all its competitors and its ultimate dominion over much of the world. Historians note that in his book Our Country, *which is excerpted below, Strong put into words what many educated Americans implicitly believed in this period.*

Is it surprising that a Protestant minister should announce views such as those Strong expressed? Are they Christian beliefs? Would it be fair to liken the notion of Anglo-Saxon superiority that Strong asserts to the views of Aryan supremacy that German Nazis disseminated during the 1930s and 1940s? What do you suppose foreigners thought of Strong's vision of an American-dominated world? It is interesting that Strong was a part of the reformist Social Gospel trend in organized Protestantism, which sought to improve social conditions for the poor and for labor. Do his statements seem compatible with this position? How could he maintain the two perspectives simultaneously?

Why the Anglo-Saxons Will Triumph

JOSIAH STRONG

It is not necessary to argue to those for whom I write that the two great needs of mankind, that all men may be lifted up into the light of the highest Christian civilization, are, first, a pure, spiritual Christianity, and, second, civil liberty. Without controversy, these are the forces which, in the past, have contributed most to the elevation of the human race, and they must continue to be, in the future, the most efficient ministers to its progress. It follows, then, that the Anglo-Saxon, as the great representatives of these two ideas, the depositary of these two greatest blessings, sustains peculiar relations to the world's future, is divinely commissioned to be, in a peculiar sense, his brother's keeper. Add to this the fact of his rapidly increasing strength in modern times, and we have well nigh a demonstration of his destiny. . . .

There can be no reasonable doubt that North America is to be the great home of the Anglo-Saxon, the principal seat of his power, the center of his life and influence. Not only does it constitute seven-elevenths of his possessions, but his empire is unsevered, while the remaining four-elevenths are fragmentary and scattered over the earth. . . .

But we are to have not only the larger portion of the Anglo-Saxon race for generations to come, we may reasonably expect to develop the highest type of Anglo-Saxon civilization. If human progress follows a law of development, if

Josiah Strong, *Our Country* (New York: Baker and Taylor, for the Home Missionary Society, 1885), pp. 161, 165, 168, 170–171, 172–175.

"Time's noblest offspring is the last,"

our civilization should be the noblest; for we are

"The heirs of all the ages in the foremost files of time,"

and not only do we occupy the latitude of power, but *our land is the last to be occupied in that latitude.* There is no other virgin soil in the North Temperate Zone. If the consummation of human progress is not to be looked for here, if there is yet to flower a higher civilization, where is the soil that is to produce it? . . .

Mr. Darwin is not only disposed to see, in the superior vigor of our people, an illustration of his favorite theory of natural selection, but even intimates that the world's history thus far has been simply preparatory for our future, and tributary to it. He says: "There is apparently much truth in the belief that the wonderful progress of the United States, as well as the character of the people, are the results of natural selection; for the more energetic, restless and courageous men from all parts of Europe have emigrated during the last ten or twelve generations to that great country, and have there succeeded best. Looking at the distant future, I do not think that the Rev. Mr. Zincke takes an exaggerated view when he says: 'All other series of events—as that which resulted in the culture of mind in Greece, and that which resulted in the Empire of Rome—only appear to have purpose and value when viewed in connection with, or rather as subsidiary to, the great stream of Anglo-Saxon emigration to the West.'"

There is abundant reason to believe that the Anglo-Saxon race is to be, is, indeed, already becoming, more effective here than in the mother country. . . .

It may be easily shown, and is of no small significance, that the two great ideas of which the Anglo-Saxon is the exponent are having a fuller development in the United States than in Great Britain. There the union of Church and State tends strongly to paralyze some of the members of the body of Christ. Here there is no such influence to destroy spiritual life and power. Here, also, has been evolved the form of government consistent with the largest possible civil liberty. Furthermore, it is significant that the marked characteristics of this race are being here emphasized most. Among the most striking features of the Anglo-Saxon is his money-making power—a power of increasing importance in the widening commerce of the world's future. . . . [A]lthough England is by far the richest nation of Europe we have already outstripped her in the race after wealth, and we have only begun the development of our vast resources.

Again, another marked characteristic of the Anglo-Saxon is what may be called an instinct of genius for colonizing. His unequaled energy, his indomitable perseverance, and his personal independence, made him a pioneer. He excels all others in pushing his way into new countries. It was those in whom this tendency was strongest that came to America, and this inherited tendency has been further developed by the westward sweep of successive generations across the continent. So noticeable has this characteristic become that English visitors remark it. Charles Dickens once said that the typical American would hesitate to enter heaven unless assured that he could go further west.

Again, nothing more manifestly distinguishes the Anglo-Saxon than his intense and persistent energy; and he is developing in the United States an energy which, in eager activity and effectiveness, is peculiarly American. This is due partly to the fact that Americans are much better fed than Europeans, and partly to the undeveloped resources of a new country, but more largely to our climate, which acts as a constant stimulus. Ten years after the landing of the Pilgrims, the Rev. Francis Higginson, a good observer, wrote: "A sup of New England air is better than a whole flagon of English ale." Thus early had the stimulating effect of our climate been noted. Moreover, our social institutions are stimulating. In Europe the various ranks of society are, like the strata of the earth, fixed and fossilized. There can be no great change without a terrible upheaval, a social earthquake. Here society is like the waters of the sea, mobile; as General [James] Garfield said, and so signally illustrated in his own experience, that which is at the bottom today may one day flash on the crest of the highest wave. Every one is free to become whatever he can make of himself; free to transform himself from a rail-splitter or a tanner or a canal-boy, into the nation's President. Our aristocracy, unlike that of Europe, is open to all comers. Wealth, position, influence, are prizes offered for energy; and every farmer's boy, every apprentice and clerk, every friendless and penniless immigrant, is free to enter the lists. Thus many causes co-operate to produce here the most forceful and tremendous energy in the world.

What is the significance of such facts? These tendencies infold the future; they are the mighty alphabet with which God writes his prophecies. May we not, by a careful laying together of the letters, spell out something of his meaning? It seems to me that God, with infinite wisdom and skill, is training the Anglo-Saxon race for an hour sure to come in the world's future. Heretofore there has always been in the history of the world a comparatively unoccupied land westward, into which the crowded countries of the East have poured their surplus populations. But the widening waves of migration, which millenniums ago rolled east and west from the valley of the Euphrates, meet today on our Pacific coast. There are no more new worlds. The unoccupied arable lands of the earth are limited, and will soon be taken. The time is coming when the pressure of population on the means of subsistence will be felt here as it is now felt in Europe and Asia. Then will the world enter upon a new stage of its history—*the final competition of races, for which the Anglo-Saxon is being schooled.* Long before the thousand millions are here, the mighty *centrifugal* tendency, inherent in this stock and strengthened in the United States, will assert itself. Then this race of unequaled energy, with all the majesty of numbers and the might of wealth behind it—the representative, let us hope, of the largest liberty, the purest Christianity, the highest civilization—having developed peculiarly aggressive traits calculated to impress its institutions upon mankind, will spread itself over the earth. If I read not amiss, this powerful race will move down upon Mexico, down upon Central and South America, out upon the islands of the sea, over upon Africa and beyond. And can any one doubt that the result of this competition of races will be the "survival of the fittest"?

4.2:   Manhood and Imperialism (1899)

One of the most vigorous proponents of American expansion was the young politician Theodore Roosevelt. During the early 1880s he had tried his hand at ranching in the Dakotas. In 1897 he became assistant secretary of the navy under President William McKinley and in that capacity in 1898 dispatched the American Pacific fleet to the Philippines to prepare for war with Spain. During the Spanish-American War Roosevelt quit his navy post to organize a cavalry regiment, known as the Rough Riders, for service in Cuba. TR returned from Cuba a war hero and in 1899 ran successfully for governor of New York. Eventually, of course, he became president of the United States.

In the selection below, written before he was elected to high office, Roosevelt expresses views that would influence how many Americans regarded the rest of the world. How would you characterize these attitudes? Can you see any connection between these opinions and Roosevelt's interest in ranching? Can you guess what a modern feminist might say about the source of Roosevelt's views? Why does TR believe that unpatriotic attitudes were especially widespread among the educated? Can Roosevelt's opinions be found among Americans today?

Manhood and Foreign Policy

THEODORE ROOSEVELT

It is a matter of serious concern to every college man, and, indeed, to every man who believes in the good effects of a liberal education, to see the false views which seem to obtain among so many of the leaders of educated thought, not only upon the Monroe Doctrine, but upon every question which involves the existence of a feeling of robust Americanism. Every educated man who puts himself out of touch with the current of American thought, and who on conspicuous occasions assumes an attitude hostile to the interest of America, is doing what he can to weaken the influence of educated men in American life. The crude, ill-conditioned jealousy of education, which is so often and so lamentably shown by large bodies of our people, is immensely stimulated by the action of those prominent educated men in whom education seems to have destroyed the strong, virile virtues and especially the spirit of Americanism.

.   .   .   .

There are many upright and honorable men who take the wrong side, that is, the anti-American side, of the Monroe Doctrine because they are too short-sighted or

Theodore Roosevelt, *American Ideals* (New York: G. P. Putnam's Sons, 1897), pp. 240–245.

too unimaginative to realize the hurt to the nation that would be caused by the adoption of their views. There are other men who take the wrong view simply because they have not thought much of the matter, or are in unfortunate surroundings, by which they have been influenced to their own moral hurt. There are yet other men in whom the mainspring of the opposition to that branch of American policy known as the Monroe Doctrine is sheer timidity. This is sometimes the ordinary timidity of wealth. Sometimes, however, it is peculiarly developed among educated men whose education has tended to make them over-cultivated and over-sensitive to foreign opinion. They are generally men who undervalue the great fighting qualities, without which no nation can ever rise to the first rank.

The timidity of wealth is proverbial, and it was well illustrated by the attitude taken by too many people of means at the time of the Venezuela trouble.[1] Many of them, including bankers, merchants, and railway magnates, criticized the action of the President and the Senate, on the ground that it had caused business disturbance. Such a position is essentially ignoble. When a question of national honor or of national right or wrong, is at stake, no question of financial interest should be considered for a moment. Those wealthy men who wish the abandonment of the Monroe Doctrine because its assertion may damage their business, bring discredit to themselves, and, so far as they are able, discredit to the nation of which they are a part.

It is an evil thing for any man of education to forget that education should intensify patriotism, and that patriotism must not only be shown by striving to do good to the country from within, but by readiness to uphold its interests and honor, at any cost, when menaced from without. Educated men owe to the community the serious performance of this duty. We need not concern ourselves with the *emigré* educated man, the American who deliberately takes up his permanent abode abroad, whether in London or Paris; he is usually a man of weak character, unfitted to do good work either abroad or at home, who does what he can for his country by relieving it of his presence. But the case is otherwise with the American who stays at home and tries to teach the youth of his country to disbelieve in the country's rights, as against other countries, and to regard it as the sign of an enlightened spirit to decry the assertion of those rights by force of arms. This man may be inefficient for good; but he is capable at times of doing harm, because he tends to make other people inefficient likewise. . . . Similarly the anæmic man of refinement and cultivation, whose intellect has been educated at the expense of his character, and who shrinks from all these struggles through which alone the world moves on to greatness, is inclined to consider any expression of the Monroe Doctrine as truculent and ill advised.

.   .   .   .

. . . No triumph of peace is quite so great as the supreme triumphs of war. The courage of the soldier, the courage of the statesman who has to meet storms which

---

[1] A confrontation between the U.S. and Britain in 1895 over the Venezuela-British Guiana boundary—ED.

can be quelled only by soldierly qualities—this stands higher than any quality called out merely in time of peace. . . .

.   .   .   .

. . . It is through strife, or the readiness for strife, that a nation must win greatness. We ask for a great navy, partly because we think that the possession of such a navy is the surest guaranty of peace, and partly because we feel that no national life is worth having if the nation is not willing, when the need shall arise, to stake everything on the supreme arbitrament of war, and to pour out its blood, its treasure, and its tears like water, rather than submit to the loss of honor and renown.

4.3: Trade and Markets (1900)

If most Americans in 1898 felt Spain's brutality against the Cuban people and its apparent sabotage of the American battleship Maine[1] *in Havana harbor were ample justifications for war, the American business community, just pulling out of the mid-1890s depression, felt otherwise. War, many business leaders feared, would create further economic uncertainty. Yet America's quick victory over Spain changed the minds of many industrialists and bankers. Perhaps, they now felt, an emerging American empire would create new trade opportunities, especially in east Asia, and save the nation from market saturation at home. Particularly intriguing were the possibilities of the formerly Spanish-ruled Philippines, just a few hundred miles off the East Asian coast, which had fallen into American hands soon after the declaration of war.*

Albert Beveridge, a young Republican Senator from Indiana, was not a businessman, but he believed that the Philippines were a potentially valuable economic asset for America. In the following selection, Beveridge argues for retaining the islands rather than surrendering them or permitting them to become an independent country. What were the supposed economic advantages of retaining the Philippines? Has history shown Beveridge to be correct regarding the important commercial role of the Philippines? What other arguments for keeping the islands in American hands does he marshal? The senator seems uneasy about fitting colonies into the American constitutional system. Why would new colonies challenge American constitutional precedents?

---

[1] An American naval commission investigated the *Maine* disaster and concluded that the explosion came from outside the vessel's hull. Although the commission could not fix blame for the tragedy, most Americans assumed that a deliberately set Spanish mine was responsible.

Why We Must Keep the Philippines

ALBERT BEVERIDGE

Mr. President, I address the Senate at this time because Senators and Members of the House on both sides have asked that I give to Congress and the country my observations in the Philippines and the far East, and the conclusions which those observations compel. . . .

Mr. President, the times call for candor. The Philippines are ours forever, "territory belonging to the United States," as the Constitution calls them. And just beyond the Philippines are China's illimitable markets. We will not retreat from either. We will not repudiate our duty in the archipelago. We will not abandon our opportunity in the Orient. We will not renounce our part in the mission of our race, trustee, under God, of the civilization of the world. And we will move forward to our work, not howling out regrets like slaves whipped to their burdens, but with gratitude for a task worthy of our strength, and thanksgiving to Almighty God that He has marked us as His chosen people, henceforth to lead in the regeneration of the world.

This island empire is the last land left in all the oceans. If it should prove a mistake to abandon it, the blunder once made would be irretrievable. If it proves a mistake to hold it, the error can be corrected when we will. Every other progressive nation stands ready to relieve us.

But to hold it will be no mistake. Our largest trade henceforth must be with Asia. The Pacific is our ocean. More and more Europe will manufacture the most it needs, secure from its colonies the most it consumes. Where shall we turn for consumers of our surplus"? Geography answers the question. China is our natural customer. She is nearer to us than to England, Germany, or Russia, the commercial powers of the present and the future. They have moved nearer to China by securing permanent bases on her borders. The Philippines give us a base at the door of all the East.

Lines of navigation from our ports to the Orient and Australia; from the Isthmian Canal to Asia; from all Oriental ports to Australia, converge at and separate from the Philippines. They are a self-supporting, dividend-paying fleet, permanently anchored at a spot selected by the strategy of Providence, commanding the Pacific. And the Pacific is the ocean of the commerce of the future. Most future wars will be conflicts for commerce. The power that rules the Pacific, therefore, is the power that rules the world. And, with the Philippines, that power is and will forever be the American Republic. . . .

Nothing is so natural as trade with one's neighbors. The Philippines make us the nearest neighbors of all the East. Nothing is more natural than to trade with those you know. This is the philosophy of all advertising. The Philippines bring us permanently face to face with the most sought-for customers of the world. National prestige, national propinquity, these and commercial activity are the elements of com-

Congressional Globe, 56th Cong., 1st sess., 1900, 33, pt. O: 704–712.

mercial success. The Philippines give the first; the character of the American people supply the last. It is a providential conjunction of all the elements of trade, of duty, and of power. If we are willing to go to war rather than let England have a few feet of frozen Alaska, which affords no market and commands none, what should we not do rather than let England, Germany, Russia, or Japan have all the Philippines? And no man on the spot can fail to see that this would be their fate if we retired. . . .

Here, then, Senators, is the situation. Two years ago there was no land in all the world which we could occupy for any purpose. Our commerce was daily turning toward the Orient, and geography and trade developments made necessary our commercial empire over the Pacific. And in that ocean we had no commercial, naval, or military base. To-day we have one of the three great ocean possessions of the globe, located at the most commanding commercial, naval, and military points in the eastern seas, within hail of India, shoulder to shoulder with China, richer in its own resources than any equal body of land on the entire globe, and peopled by a race which civilization demands shall be improved. Shall we abandon it? That man little knows the common people of the Republic, little understands the instincts of our race, who thinks we will not hold it fast and hold it forever, administering just government by simplest methods. We may trick up devices to shift our burden and lessen our opportunity; they will avail us nothing but delay. We may tangle conditions by applying academic arrangements of self-government to a crude situation; their failure will drive us to our duty in the end. . . .

But, Senators, it would be better to abandon this combined garden and Gibraltar of the Pacific, and count our blood and treasure already spent a profitable loss, than to apply any academic arrangement of self-government to these children. They are not capable of self-government. How could they be? They are not of a self-governing race. They are Orientals, Malays, instructed by Spaniards in the latter's worst estate.

They know nothing of practical government except as they have witnessed the weak, corrupt, cruel, and capricious rule of Spain. What magic will anyone employ to dissolve in their minds and characters those impressions of governors and governed which three centuries of misrule has created? What alchemy will change the oriental quality of their blood and set the self-governing currents of the American pouring through their Malay veins? How shall they, in the twinkling of an eye, be exalted to the heights of self-governing peoples which required a thousand years for us to reach, Anglo-Saxon though we are? . . .

Blind indeed is he who sees not the hand of God in events so vast, so harmonious, so benign. Reactionary indeed is the mind that perceives not that this vital people is the strongest of the saving forces of the world; that our place, therefore, is at the head of the constructing and redeeming nations of the earth; and that to stand aside while events march on is a surrender of our interests, a betrayal of our duty as blind as it is base. Craven indeed is the heart that fears to perform a work so golden and so noble; that dares not win a glory so immortal. . . .

Mr. President and Senators, adopt the resolution offered, that peace may quickly come and that we may begin our saving, regenerating, and uplifting work. . . . Re-

ject it, and the world, history, and the American people will know where to forever
fix the awful responsibility for the consequences that will surely follow such failure
to do our manifest duty. How dare we delay when our soldiers' blood is flowing?
[Applause in the galleries].

4.4: The Anti-Imperialists (1899)

*Most Americans undoubtedly supported the decision to go to war with
Spain in 1898. But what transpired in the Philippines after the American occupation did not seem very different from Spanish rule in Cuba.
The Filipinos quickly came to resent the American presence and rose
up against the new oppressor. For two years Americans and Filipinos
fought a nasty and brutal guerrilla war to determine the islands' fate.
In the end American troops put down the Filipino fighters and imposed
U.S. rule on the archipelago. But the Philippine Insurrection made a
mockery of benevolent American claims.*

*Many Americans strongly opposed their nation's role in the Philip-
pines, and in November 1898 a group of reformers, journalists, acade-
mics, clergy, business leaders, and maverick politicians formed the
Anti-Imperialist League to resist the colonialist drift. The League initially campaigned to defeat the annexation of the Philippines. Once the
annexation treaty was ratified, however, it turned its efforts against
the cruel war to subdue the Filipinos. The following selection is the
platform adopted by the Anti-Imperialist League in 1899.*

*What is the League leaders' intellectual strategy in appealing to the
American people? Is their statement effective propaganda? Do you
know whether views such as theirs influenced the way Americans responded to the Filipinos? What future course did Filipino American
relations take? What are those relations like now?*

We Must Perfect Imperialism

ANTI-IMPERIALIST LEAGUE

We hold that the policy known as imperialism is hostile to liberty and tends toward
militarism, an evil from which it has been our glory to be free. We regret that it has
become necessary in the land of Washington and Lincoln to reaffirm that all men,

---

The text of the platform is included in Carl Schurz, "The Policy of Imperialism." In Frederic Bancroft,
ed. *Speeches, Correspondence, and Political Papers of Carl Schurz* (New York: G. P. Putnam's Sons,
1913), pp. 77–79.

of whatever race or color, are entitled to life, liberty, and the pursuit of happiness. We maintain that governments derive their just powers from the consent of the governed. We insist that the subjugation of any people is "criminal aggression" and open disloyalty to the distinctive principles of our government.

We earnestly condemn the policy of the present National Administration in the Philippines. It seeks to extinguish the spirit of 1776 in those islands. We deplore the sacrifice of our soldiers and sailors, whose bravery deserves admiration even in an unjust war. We denounce the slaughter of the Filipinos as a needless horror. We protest against the extension of American sovereignty by Spanish methods.

We demand the immediate cessation of the war against liberty, begun by Spain and continued by us. We urge that Congress be promptly convened to announce to the Filipinos our purpose to concede to them the independence for which they have so long fought and which of right is theirs.

The United States have always protested against the doctrine of international law which permits the subjugation of the weak by the strong. A self-governing state cannot accept sovereignty over an unwilling people. The United States cannot act upon the ancient heresy that might makes right.

Imperialists assume that with the destruction of self-government in the Philippines by American hands, all opposition here will cease. This is a grievous error. Much as we abhor the war of "criminal aggression" in the Philippines, greatly as we regret the blood of the Filipinos is on American hands, we more deeply resent the betrayal of American institutions at home. The real firing line is not in the suburbs of Manila. The foe is of our own household. The attempt of 1861 was to divide the country. That of 1899 is to destroy its fundamental principles and noblest ideals.

Whether the ruthless slaughter of the Filipinos shall end next month or next year is but an incident in a contest that must go on until the Declaration of Independence and the Constitution of the United States are rescued from the hands of their betrayers. Those who dispute about standards of value while the Republic is undermined will be listened to as little as those who would wrangle about the small economies of the household while the house is on fire. The training of a great people for a century, the aspiration for liberty of a vast immigration are forces that will hurl aside those who in the delirium of conquest seek to destroy the character of our institutions.

We deny that the obligation of all citizens to support their Government in times of grave National peril applies to the present situation. If an Administration may with impunity ignore the issues upon which it was chosen, deliberately create a condition of war anywhere on the face of the globe, debauch the civil service for spoils to promote the adventure, organize a truth-suppressing censorship and demand of all citizens a suspension of judgment and their unanimous support while it chooses to continue the fighting, representative government itself is imperiled.

We propose to contribute to the defeat of any person or party that stands for the forcible subjugation of any people. We shall oppose for reelection all who in the White House or in Congress betray American liberty in pursuit of un-American gains. We still hope that both of our great political parties will support and defend the Declaration of Independence in the closing campaign of the century.

We hold, with Abraham Lincoln, that "no man is good enough to govern another man without that man's consent. When the white man governs himself, that is self-government, but when he governs himself and also governs another man, that is more than self-government—that is despotism." "Our reliance is in the love of liberty which God has planted in us. Our defense is in the spirit which prizes liberty as the heritage of all men in all lands. Those who deny freedom to others deserve it not for themselves, and under a just God cannot long retain it."

We cordially invite the cooperation of all men and women who remain loyal to the Declaration of Independence and the Constitution of the United States.

☆ **5** ☆

The Progressive Impulse

During the first two decades of the twentieth century, as the country shifted from rural to urban, its political structure also altered. More prosperous than ever, many Americans nevertheless felt uneasy over the rapid economic and social changes taking place. Their discomfort with the unfamiliar spawned a many-sided reform movement we call Progressivism.

Progressivism has long been a puzzle to scholars. Its shape seems fuzzy and changing, including within its boundaries a wide range of views, programs, and personnel. Its origins too seem unclear. Who favored reform during the early twentieth century? Were they the same people who had supported Populist political insurgency during the 1890s? And why did the movement appear when it did?

The selections below represent different and often competing aspects of Progressive thought. As you read these, you might consider whether there is a single thread connecting all of them, or whether Progressivism is just a convenient name for a grab bag of reformist demands that fortuitously surfaced together in the decade preceding World War I.

5.1: The Danger of Concentrated Wealth (1912, 1913)

The wave of business combinations formed between 1898 and 1903 was a response to the single national market that emerged following completion of the transportation and communications network. Deprived of local monopoly power and forced into cutthroat competition with aggressive distant firms, business leaders sought to consolidate their operations. In the six-year period straddling the turn of the cen-

tury, there were 234 industrial mergers representing some $6 billion in capital.

The merger movement dismayed the public. How could small producers survive in an era of huge trusts? How severely would consumers be hurt by price fixing when competition waned? How could representative government fend off giant business firms when they sought favors?

The four selections below reflect various views of business consolidation. The first two, by Theodore Roosevelt and Woodrow Wilson, represent different Progressive responses. The third, by the J. P. Morgan firm, is the reply of the leading American investment bankers to the conclusions of the Pujo Committee, a subcommittee of the House of Representatives that, in its report of 1913, had declared that financial power was dangerously concentrated in the hands of a small number of northeastern banks. The last selection is by another Progressive, Walter Weyl, who emphasizes the dangers to consumers from the monopoly power of big business.

As you read the Roosevelt and Wilson pieces, consider the differences in approach of the two political leaders, who were both within the Progressive orbit. Do they have identical attitudes toward concentrated business power? How are their prescriptions for cure related to their long-term party allegiances? Has the passage of eighty years since the speeches were delivered demonstrated which of the formulas for dealing with concentrated economic power is more effective in protecting the public interest? As for the remarks of J. P. Morgan, should we reject his position out of hand? He was, after all, the chief target of the Pujo investigators.

The selection by Progressive journalist Walter Weyl is especially interesting. We know that a consumer movement first appeared during the Progressive Era. Two important measures—the Pure Food and Drug Act and the Meat Inspection Act (both passed in 1906)— attest to the Progressives' concern for consumer welfare. But Weyl makes a larger point than the mere need for consumer protection measures, for he sees consumer concerns as the common thread that bound diverse Progressives and distinguished them from their Populist predecessors. How might consumer concerns have united various reform groups during these years? What other aspects of the Progressive program besides the 1906 measures had consumer relevance? According to Weyl, what other element in the American economy, in addition to big business, threatened consumer interests? Is his analysis valid?

Republican Anti-Trust

THEODORE ROOSEVELT

An important volume entitled "Concentration and Control" has just been issued by President Charles R. Van Hise of the University of Wisconsin. The University of Wisconsin has been more influential than any other agency in making Wisconsin what it has become, a laboratory for wise social and industrial experiment in the betterment of conditions. President Van Hise is one of those thoroughgoing but sane and intelligent radicals from whom much of leadership is to be expected in such a matter. The sub-title of his book shows that his endeavor is to turn the attention of his countrymen toward practically solving the trust problem of the United States.

In his preface he states that his aim is to suggest a way to gain the economic advantages of the concentration of industry and at the same time to guard the interests of the public and to assist in the rule of enlightenment, reason, fair play, mutual consideration, and toleration. In sum, he shows that unrestrained competition as an economic principle has become too destructive to be permitted to exist, and that the small men must be allowed to co-operate under penalty of succumbing before their big competitors; and yet such co-operation, vitally necessary to the small man, is criminal under the present law. He says:

> With the alternative before the business men of co-operation or failure, we may be sure that they will co-operate. Since the law is violated by practically every group of men engaged in trade from one end of the country to the other, they do not feel that in combining they are doing a moral wrong. The selection of the individual or corporation for prosecution depends upon the arbitrary choice of the Attorney General, perhaps somewhat influenced by the odium which attaches to some of the violators of the law. They all take their chance, hoping that the blow will fall elsewhere. With general violation and sporadic enforcement of an impracticable law, we cannot hope that our people will gain respect for it.
>
> In conclusion, there is presented as the solution of the difficulties of the present industrial situation, concentration, co-operation, and control. Through concentration we may have the economic advantages coming from magnitude of operations. Through co-operation we may limit the wastes of the competitive system. Through control by commission we may secure freedom for fair competition, elimination of unfair practices, conservation of our natural resources, fair wages, good social conditions, and reasonable prices.
>
> Concentration and co-operation in industry in order to secure efficiency are a world-wide movement. The United States cannot resist it. If we isolate ourselves and insist upon the subdivision of industry below the highest economic efficiency, and do not allow co-operation, we shall be defeated in the world's markets. We cannot adopt an economic system less efficient than our great competitors, Germany, England, France, and Austria. Either we must modify our present obsolete laws regarding concentration and co-operation so as to conform with the world movement, or else fall behind in the race for the world's markets. Concentration and co-operation are con-

ditions imperatively essential for industrial advance; but if we allow concentration and co-operation there must be control in order to protect the people, and adequate control is only possible through the administrative commission. Hence concentration, co-operation, and control are the keywords for a scientific solution of the mighty industrial problem which now confronts this Nation. . . .

We Progressives stand for the rights of the people. When these rights can best be secured by insistence upon States' rights, then we are for States' rights; when they can best be secured by insistence upon National rights, then we are for National rights. Inter-State commerce can be effectively controlled only by the Nation. The States cannot control it under the Constitution, and to amend the Constitution by giving them control of it would amount to a dissolution of the Government. The worst of the big trusts have always endeavored to keep alive the feeling in favor of having the States themselves, and not the Nation, attempt to do this work, because they know that in the long run such effort would be ineffective. There is no surer way to prevent all successful effort to deal with the trusts than to insist that they be dealt with by the States rather than by the Nation, or to create a conflict between the States and the Nation on the subject. The well-meaning ignorant man who advances such a proposition does as much damage as if he were hired by the trusts themselves, for he is playing the game of every big crooked corporation in the country. The only effective way in which to regulate the trusts is through the exercise of the collective power of our people as a whole through the Governmental agencies established by the Constitution for this very purpose.

Grave injustice is done by the Congress when it fails to give the National Government complete power in this matter; and still graver injustice by the Federal courts when they endeavor in any way to pare down the right of the people collectively to act in this matter as they deem wise; such conduct does itself tend to cause the creation of a twilight zone in which neither the Nation nor the States have power. Fortunately, the Federal courts have more and more of recent years tended to adopt the true doctrine, which is that all these matters are to be settled by the people themselves, and that the conscience of the people, and not the preferences of any servants of the people, is to be the standard in deciding what action shall be taken by the people. As Lincoln phrased it: "The [question] of National power and State rights as a principle is no other than the principle of generality and locality. Whatever concerns the whole should be confided to the whole—to the General Government; while whatever concerns only the State should be left exclusively to the State."

It is utterly hopeless to attempt to control the trusts merely by the antitrust law, or by any law the same in principle, no matter what the modifications may be in detail. In the first place, these great corporations cannot possibly be controlled merely by a succession of lawsuits. The administrative branch of the Government must exercise such control. The preposterous failure of the Commerce Court has shown that only damage comes from the effort to substitute judicial for administrative control of great corporations. In the next place, a loosely drawn law which promises to do everything would reduce business to complete ruin if it were not also so drawn as to accomplish almost nothing. . . .

Contrast what has actually been accomplished under the inter-State commerce law with what has actually been accomplished under the anti-trust law. The first has, on the whole, worked in a highly efficient manner and achieved real and great results; and it promises to achieve even greater results, (although I firmly believe that if the power of the Commissioners grows greater it will be necessary to make them and their superior, the President, even more completely responsible to the people for their acts). The second has occasionally done good, has usually accomplished nothing, but generally left the worst conditions wholly unchanged, and has been responsible for a considerable amount of downright and positive evil.

What is needed is the application to all industrial concerns and all cooperating interests engaged in inter-State commerce in which there is either monopoly or control of the market of the principles on which we have gone in regulating transportation concerns engaged in such commerce. The anti-trust law should be kept on the statute books and strengthened so as to make it genuinely and thoroughly effective against every big concern tending to monopoly or guilty of anti-social practices.

At the same time, a National industrial commission should be created which should have complete power to regulate and control all the great industrial concerns engaged in inter-State business—which practically means all of them in this country. This commission should exercise over these industrial concerns like powers to those exercised over the railways by the Inter-State Commerce Commission, and over the National banks by the Controller of the Currency, and additional powers if found necessary. The establishment of such a commission would enable us to punish the individual rather than merely the corporation, just as we now do with banks, where the aim of the Government is not to close the bank but to bring to justice personally any bank official who has gone wrong.

This commission should deal with all the abuses of the trusts—all the abuses such as those developed by the Government suit against the Standard Oil and Tobacco Trusts—as the Inter-State Commerce Commission now deals with rebates. It should have complete power to make the capitalization absolutely honest and put a stop to all stock watering. Such supervision over the issuance of corporate securities would put a stop to exploitation of the people by dishonest capitalists desiring to declare dividends on watered securities, and would open this kind of industrial property to ownership by the people at large. It should have free access to the books of each corporation and power to find out exactly how it treats its employees, its rivals, and the general public. It should have power to compel the unsparing publicity of all the acts of any corporation which goes wrong.

The regulation should be primarily under the administrative branch of the Government and not by lawsuit. It should prohibit and effectually punish monopoly achieved through wrong, and also actual wrongs done by industrial corporations which are not monopolies, such as the artificial raising of prices, the artificial restriction on productivity, the elimination of competition by unfair or predatory practices, and the like; leaving industrial organizations free within the limits of fair and honest dealing to promote through the inherent efficiency of organization the power of the United States as a competitive Nation among Nations, and the greater abundance at home that will come to our people from that power wisely exercised.

Democratic Anti-Trust

WOODROW WILSON

I take my stand absolutely, where every Progressive ought to take his stand, on the proposition that private monopoly is indefensible and intolerable. And there I will fight my battle. And I know how to fight it. Everybody who has even read the newspapers knows the means by which these men built up their power and created these monopolies. Any decently equipped lawyer can suggest to you statutes by which the whole business can be stopped. What these gentlemen do not want is this: they do not want to be compelled to meet all comers on equal terms. I am perfectly willing that they should beat any competitor by fair means; but I know the foul means they have adopted, and I know that they can be stopped by law. If they think that coming into the market upon the basis of mere efficiency, upon the mere basis of knowing how to manufacture goods better than anybody else and to sell them cheaper than anybody else, they can carry the immense amount of water that they have put into their enterprises in order to buy up rivals, then they are perfectly welcome to try it. But there must be no squeezing out of the beginner, no crippling his credit; no discrimination against retailers who buy from a rival; no threats against concerns who sell supplies to a rival; no holding back of raw material from him; no secret arrangements against him. All the fair competition you choose, but no unfair competition of any kind. And then when unfair competition is eliminated, let us see these gentlemen carry their tanks of water on their backs. All that I ask and all I shall fight for is that they shall come into the field against merit and brains everywhere. If they can beat other American brains, then they have got the best brains.

But if you want to know how far brains go, as things now are, suppose you try to match your better wares against these gentlemen, and see them undersell you before your market is any bigger than the locality and make it absolutely impossible for you to get a fast foothold. If you want to know how brains count, originate some invention which will improve the kind of machinery they are using, and then see if you can borrow enough money to manufacture it. You may be offered something for your patent by the corporation,—which will perhaps lock it up in a safe and go on using the old machinery; but you will not be allowed to manufacture. I know men who have tried it, and they could not get the money, because the great money lenders of this country are in the arrangement with the great manufacturers of this country, and they do not propose to see their control of the market interfered with by outsiders. And who are outsiders? Why, all the rest of the people of the United States are outsiders.

They are rapidly making us outsiders with respect even of the things that come from the bosom of the earth, and which belong to us in a peculiar sense. Certain monopolies in this country have gained almost complete control of the raw material, chiefly in the mines, out of which the great body of manufactures are carried on, and they now discriminate, when they will, in the sale of that raw material between those who are rivals of the monopoly and those who submit to the monopoly. We

Woodrow Wilson, *The New Freedom* (New York: Doubleday, Page and Company, 1913), pp. 167–175, 176–177, 179–181.

must soon come to the point where we shall say to the men who own these essentials of industry that they have got to part with these essentials by sale to all citizens of the United States with the same readiness and upon the same terms. Or else we shall tie up the resources of this country under private control in such fashion as will make our independent development absolutely impossible.

There is another injustice that monopoly engages in. The trust that deals in the cruder products which are to be transformed into the more elaborate manufactures often will not sell these crude products except upon the terms of monopoly—that is to say, the people that deal with them must buy exclusively from them. And so again you have the lines of development tied up and the connections of development knotted and fastened so that you cannot wrench them apart.

Again, the manufacturing monopolies are so interlaced in their personal relationships with the great shipping interests of this country, and with the great railroads, that they can often largely determine the rates of shipment. . . .

And when you reflect that the twenty-four men who control the United States Steel Corporation, for example, are either presidents or vice-presidents or directors in 55 per cent of the railways of the United States, reckoning by the valuation of those railroads and the amount of their stock and bonds, you know just how close the whole thing is knitted together in our industrial system, and how great the temptation is. These twenty-four gentlemen administer that corporation as if it belonged to them. The amazing thing to me is that the people of the United States have not seen that the administration of a great business like that is not a private affair; it is a public affair. . . .

The big trusts, the big combinations, are the most wasteful, the most uneconomical, and, after they pass a certain size, the most inefficient, way of conducting the industries of this country.

A notable example is the way in which Mr. Carnegie was bought out of the steel business. Mr. Carnegie could build better mills and make better steel rails and make them cheaper than anybody else connected with what afterward became the United States Steel Corporation. They didn't dare leave him outside. He had so much more brains in finding out the best processes; he had so much more shrewdness in surrounding himself with the most successful assistants; he knew so well when a young man who came into his employ was fit for promotion and was ripe to put at the head of some branch of his business and was sure to make good, that he could undersell every mother's son of them in the market for steel rails. And they bought him out at a price that amounted to three or four times,—I believe actually five times,—the estimated value of his properties and of his business, because they couldn't beat him in competition. And then in what they charged afterward for their product,—the product of his mills included,—they made us pay the interest on the four or five times the difference.

That is the difference between a big business and a trust. A trust is an arrangement to get rid of competition, and a big business is a business that has survived competition by conquering in the field of intelligence and economy. A trust does not bring efficiency to the aid of business; it *buys efficiency out of business*. I am for big business, and I am against the trusts. Any man who can survive by his brains, any man who can put the others out of the business by making the thing cheaper to the consumer at the same time that he is increasing its intrinsic value and quality, I take off my hat to, and I say: "You are the man who can build up the United States, and I wish there were more of you." . . .

We have restricted credit, we have restricted opportunity, we have controlled development, and we have come to be one of the worst ruled, one of the most completely controlled and dominated, governments in the civilized world—no longer a government by free opinion, no longer a government by conviction and the vote of the majority, but a government by the opinion and the duress of small groups of dominant men.

If the government is to tell big business men how to run their business, then don't you see that big business men have to get closer to the government even than they are now? Don't you see that they must capture the government, in order not to be restrained too much by it? Must capture the government? They have already captured it. Are you going to invite those inside to stay inside? They don't have to get there. They are there. Are you going to own your own premises, or are you not? That is your choice. Are you going to say: "You didn't get into the house the right way, but you are in there, God bless you; we will stand out here in the cold and you can hand us out something once in a while"?

At the least, under the plan I am opposing, there will be an avowed partnership between the government and the trusts. I take it that the firm will be ostensibly controlled by the senior member. For I take it that the government of the United States is at least the senior member, though the younger member has all along been running the business. But when all the momentum, when all the energy, when a great deal of the genius, as so often happens in partnerships the world over, is with the junior partner, I don't think that the superintendence of the senior partner is going to amount to very much. And I don't believe that benevolence can be read into the hearts of the trusts by the superintendence and suggestions of the federal government; because the government has never within my recollection had its suggestions accepted by the trusts. On the contrary, the suggestions of the trusts have been accepted by the government.

There is no hope to be seen for the people of the United States until the partnership is dissolved. And the business of the party now entrusted with power is going to be to dissolve it.

The "Monopolists" Respond

J. P. MORGAN AND COMPANY

To Honorable A. P. Pujo, Chairman,
Committee on Banking and Currency
House of Representatives,
Washington, D.C.

Dear Sir:

You have invited us to supplement the recent inquiry of your committee by presenting "such considerations as may occur to you (us) bearing upon the question of concentration and control of money and credit." . . .

Letter from Messrs. J. P. Morgan and Company (New York: privately printed, February 25, 1913), pp. 1–13 *passim.*

We would suggest, . . . with the utmost respect, that a large part of the valuable time of your Committee, in our belief, has been consumed in an endeavor to piece out a certain theory as to money and credit, which theory it will be impossible ever to demonstrate; for its establishment is, and always will be, prevented by economic laws which have operated ever since the beginnings of barter and trade.

We suggest to you that such ills—and they are neither few nor trifling—as are existent in this country's financial affairs are the outcome of a clumsy and outworn banking system rather than of the schemes of men; and that to eradicate such ills at their source, there is needed not legislation upon some one or more isolated symptoms, but rather a careful diagnosis of our whole banking system; a study of the successful system of other countries which for decades have been free from periodic panics which have distressed this country; and finally cooperation among all committees in Congress which consider this subject to the one end of wise and comprehensive—as contrasted with piecemeal—legislation . . . such "concentration" as has taken place in New York and other financial centres has been due, not to the purposes and activities of men, but primarily to the operation of our antiquated banking system which automatically compels interior banks to concentrate in New York City hundreds of millions of reserve funds; and next, to economic laws which in every country create some one city as the great financial centre, and which draw to it, in enormous volume, investment funds for the development of industrial enterprises throughout the country. . . .

We lay especial stress upon this point of economic rule, for the reason that not only the Resolution (H. Res. 504) under which your Committee acts, but many questions to witnesses, indicated a belief that for their own selfish ends certain men, or a group of them, have succeeded in transcending the laws of supply and demand (which operate all over the world) and in establishing new economic laws. . . .

If any one man, or group of men had the ability and resources—which they do not—to withhold credits in any one market like New York, the situation would ordinarily be promptly relieved by the automatic inflow of credits from some altogether foreign source. . . .

For the maintenance of such an impossible economic theory there have been spread before your Committee elaborate tables of so-called interlocking directorates from which exceedingly mistaken inferences have been publicly drawn. In these tables it is shown that 180 bankers and bank directors serve upon the boards of corporations having resources aggregating twenty-five billion dollars, and it is implied that this vast aggregate of the country's wealth is at the disposal of these 180 men. But such an implication rests solely upon the untenable theory that these men, living in different parts of the country, in many cases personally unacquainted with each other, and in most cases associated only in occasional transactions, vote always for the same policies and control with united purpose the directorates of the 132 corporations on which they serve. The testimony failed to establish any concerted policy or harmony of action binding these 180 men together, and as a matter of fact no such policy exists. The absurdity of the assumption of such control becomes more apparent when one considers that on the average these directors represent only one quarter of the memberships of their boards. It is preposterous to suppose that every "interlocking" director has full control in every organization with which he is connected, and that the majority of directors who are not "interlocking" are mere figureheads, subject to the will of a small minority of their boards. . . .

Such growth in the size of banks in New York and Chicago has frequently been erroneously designated before your Committee as "concentration," whereas we have hitherto pointed out the growth of banking resources in New York City has been less rapid than that of the rest of the country. But increase of capital and merger of two or more banks into one institution (with the same resources as the aggregate of the banks merging into it) has [sic] been frequent, especially since January 1, 1908.

These mergers, however, are a development due simply to the demand for larger banking facilities to care for the growth of the country's business. As our cities double and treble in size and importance, as railroads extend and industrial plants expand, not only is it natural, but it is necessary that our banking institutions should grow in order to care for the increased demands put upon them. Perhaps it is not known as well as it should be that in New York City the largest banks are far inferior in size to banks in the commercial capitals of other and much smaller countries. . . . [The letter then points out that it takes either large banks to finance large enterprises or cooperation between several smaller ones.]

For a private banker to sit upon . . . a directorate is in most instances a duty, not a privilege. Inquiry will readily develop the fact that the members of the leading banking houses in this country—and it was the leading houses only against which animadversions were directed—are besought continually to act as directors in various corporations, whose securities they handle, and that in general they enter only those boards which the opinion of the investing public requires them to enter, as an evidence of good faith that they are willing to have their names publicly associated with the management.

Yet, before your Committee, this natural and eminently desirable relationship was made to appear almost sinister and no testimony whatever was adduced to show the actual working of such relationships. . . . [The letter concludes with an explanation as to why banks felt it necessary to sell securities, appoint fiscal agents, and maintain such close scrutiny over corporations, and a comment that unlimited liability and the force of public opinion prevented most banks from malpractice.]

Respectfully submitted,
(Signed) J. P. MORGAN & CO.
New York City
February 25, 1913.

The Consumer Factor

WALTER WEYL

The plutocracy is more and more opposed by an ever larger number of social groups and individuals, not only for what it does and for what it is, but for the deeper economic tendencies which it represents. Different men are arrayed against the plutocracy for different reasons. While, however, such common hostility is a sufficient

Walter Weyl, *The New Democracy* (New York: Macmillan, 1912), pp. 249–254.

stimulus to an aggressive campaign, it is not a basis broad enough for a constructive program. Unless the opponents of the plutocracy have some common positive aim, their antagonism will dissipate itself in abortive assaults and waste heat, without permanent influence upon social conditions.

There exists, however, such a common aim. This aim, which holds together the opponents of an intrenched plutocracy, is the attainment of a common share in the conquered continent, in the material and moral accumulations of a century. When the trust raises prices, obtains valuable franchises or public lands, escapes taxation, secures bounties, lowers wages, evades factory laws, or makes other profitable maneuvers, it is diverting a part of the social surplus from the general community to itself. The public pays the higher prices, loses the franchises or lands, pays higher taxes, suffers in wages (and pays for the ill effects of low wages), and generally makes up dollar for dollar for all such gains. In all these things the people have a perceivable interest. The great mass is injured in its capacity of wage earner, salary earner, taxpayer, and consumer.

Of these capacities that of the consumer is the most universal, since even those who do not earn wages or pay direct taxes consume commodities. In America today the unifying economic force, about which a majority, hostile to the plutocracy, is forming, is the common interest of the citizen as a consumer of wealth, and incidentally as an owner of (undivided) national possessions. The producer (who is only the consumer in another rôle) is highly differentiated. He is banker, lawyer, soldier, tailor, farmer, shoeblack, messenger boy. He is capitalist, workman, money lender, money borrower, urban worker, rural worker. The consumer, on the other hand, is undifferentiated. All men, women, and children who buy shoes (except only the shoe manufacturer) are interested in cheap good shoes. The consumers of most articles are overwhelmingly superior in numbers to the producers.

Despite this overwhelming superiority in numbers, the consumer, finding it difficult to organize, has often been worsted in industrial battles. In our century-long tariff contests, a million inaudible consumers have often counted less than has a petty industry in a remote district. The consumer thought of himself as a producer, and he united only with men of his own productive group. For a time there was a certain reason for such an alignment. It was a period of falling prices, of severe competition, in which the whole organization of industry favored the consumer. In fact, the unorganized and ruthless consumer was blamed—and rightly blamed (as he is still rightly blamed to-day)—for many of the evils of industry. The curse of the sweatshop and of the starving seamstress, sewing by candle-light, was fairly brought to the doors of the bargain-hunting housewife. The consumer, though acting singly, felt himself secure.

Even when prices began to rise, consumers remained quiescent. There was greater difficulty in resisting price advances, because the loss to each individual from each increase was so infinitesimal. The reverse of the overwhelming numbers of the consumers was the small individual interest of each in each transaction. Wages affected a man far more sensibly than did prices. If a motorman's wages were reduced one cent an hour he might lose thirty dollars a year; a rise of ten cents in the price of shoes, on the other hand, meant a loss of, at most, two dollars a year.

A man could not spend his lifetime fighting ten-cent increases. The cure for high prices was high wages.

As prices continue to rise, however, as a result (among other causes) of our gradually entering into a monopoly period, a new insistence is laid upon the rights of the consumer, and political unity is based upon him. Where formerly production seemed to be the sole governing economic fact of a man's life, to-day many producers have no direct interest in their product. It is a very attenuated interest which the Polish slag-worker has in the duty on steel billets, but the Polish slag-worker and the Boston salesgirl and the Oshkosh lawyer have a similar interest (and a common cause of discontent) as consumers of the national wealth. The universality of the rise of prices has begun to affect the consumer as though he were attacked by a million gnats. The chief offense of the trust becomes its capacity to injure the consumer. Therefore the consumer, disinterred from his grave, reappears in the political arena as the "common man," the "plain people," the "strap-hanger," "the man on the street," "the taxpayer," the "ultimate consumer." Men who voted as producers are now voting as consumers.

We are now beginning to appeal to the "ultimate consumer," the man who actually eats, wears, or uses the article. A generation ago we legislated for the penultimate shopkeeper, or the ante-penultimate manufacturer. Our contest for railroad rate regulation was formerly waged in the interest of the producer or shipper, and not primarily in the interest of the consumer. The rates in question were freight, not passenger, rates, and the great problem was not so much low freight rates (which more immediately benefited the consumer) as equal freight rates, in which the competing manufacturer was primarily interested.

It is difficult for the consumer to act industrially in concert. The "rent strikes" on the East Side of New York have always been unsuccessful. The meat strikes have been equally without result. The work of the Consumers' Leagues has been chiefly a humanitarian labor for the benefit of producers, and we have never successfully developed in America great coöperative associations of workingmen consumers, like those of England, Belgium, France, and Germany. The appeal to the consumer has therefore been made on the political field. . . .

Of all the hard blows which the course of American political and economic development has dealt the traditional system of political ideas and institutions, perhaps the hardest is this demand for discrimination on behalf of union labor. It means that the more intelligent and progressive American workingmen are coming to believe that the American political and economic organization does not sufficiently secure the material improvement of the wage-earner. This conviction may be to a large extent erroneous. Certain it is that the wages of unorganized farm laborers have been increasing as rapidly during the past thirty years as have the wages of the organized mechanics. But whether erroneous or not, it is widespread and deep-rooted; and whatever danger it possesses is derived from the fact that it affords to a substantially revolutionary purpose a large and increasing popular following. The other instances of organization for special purposes which have been remarked have superficially, at least, been making for conservatism. The millionaire and the professional politician want above all things to be let alone, and to be allowed to enjoy the benefit of their conquests. But the labor organizations cannot exercise the power necessary in their opinion to their interests without certain radical changes in the political and economic order; and inasmuch as their power is likely to increase rather than diminish, the American people are confronted with the prospect of persistent, unscrupulous, and increasing agitation on behalf of an economic and political reorganization in favor of one class of citizens.

The large corporations and the unions occupy in certain respects a similar relation to the American political system. Their advocates both believe in associated action for themselves and in competition for their adversaries. They both demand governmental protection and recognition, but resent the notion of efficient governmental regulation. They have both reached their existing power, partly because of the weakness of the state governments, to which they are legally subject, and they both are opposed to any interference by the Federal government—except exclusively on their own behalf. Yet they both have become so very powerful that they are frequently too strong for the state governments, and in different ways they both traffic for their own benefit with the politicians, who so often control those governments. Here, of course, the parallelism ends and the divergence begins. The corporations have apparently the best of the situation, because existing institutions are more favorable to the interests of the corporations than to the interests of the unionists; but on the other hand, the unions have the immense advantage of a great and increasing numerical strength. They are beginning to use the suffrage to promote a class interest, though how far they will travel on this perilous path remains doubtful. In any event, it is obvious that the development in this country of two such powerful and unscrupulous and well-organized special interests has created a condition which the founders of the Republic never anticipated, and which demands as a counterpoise a more effective body of national opinion, and a more powerful organization of the national interest.

5.2: Conservation and Efficiency (1908, 1912)

A recent school of historians has emphasized the importance of "efficiency" in the Progressive agenda. Progressives were not so much defenders of the weak against the strong, they say, as missionaries for applying expert knowledge to administration—even if the weak suffered.

This aspect of Progressivism can, in fact, be detected in several realms—business regulation, scientific management, and municipal government, for example. But it appeared most clearly in the conservation movement, where the mainstream, led by Roosevelt and his friend and ally Gifford Pinchot, emphasized the use of the nation's natural endowment in a prudent and effective manner to maximize its commercial returns and extend its life.

These "utilitarian" conservationists competed with a wing of the natural resources movement moved by a different rationale and set of goals. "Preservationists" cherished unspoiled nature for its aesthetic and "spiritual" values and wished to keep it inviolate for future generations, even if this meant forgoing economic advantage. The most prominent preservationist was John Muir, a Scottish-born naturalist whose experiences in California in the late 1860s stimulated his love of nature. The differences between the preservationists and utilitarians did not prevent Muir and Roosevelt from being friends.

The two selections below bracket the utilitarian-preservationist controversy. The first is a statement composed by a conference of governors in 1908. The second, by Muir, is an attack on the plans of San Francisco officials to dam the Tuolumne River in the Sierras in order to supply water to the fast-growing Bay City. (The city won.)

What are the differences in tone and emphasis between the two statements? In what ways does the first document express the utilitarian conservationist viewpoint? How does the battle over the Tuolumne dam reveal the strain between the two positions on the nation's natural endowment? In what ways do the documents reveal a tension between the "efficiency" and the moral dimensions of Progressivism? Which of the two positions comes closest to the philosophy of the ecology movement of today?

Conservation Statement

GOVERNORS OF THE STATES

Declaration

We the Governors of the States and Territories of the United States of America, in Conference assembled, do hereby declare the conviction that the great prosperity of our country rests upon the abundant resources of the land chosen by our forefathers for their homes and where they laid the foundation of this great Nation.

We look upon these resources as a heritage to be made use of in establishing and promoting the comfort, prosperity, and happiness of the American People, but not to be wasted, deteriorated, or needlessly destroyed.

Proceedings of a Conference of Governors in The White House May 13–15, 1908 (Washington: Government Printing Office, 1909), pp. 192–193.

We agree that our country's future is involved in this; that the great natural resources supply the material basis on which our civilization must continue to depend, and on which the perpetuity of the Nation itself rests.

We agree, in the light of facts brought to our knowledge and from information received from sources which we can not doubt, that this material basis is threatened with exhaustion. Even as each succeeding generation from the birth of the Nation has performed its part in promoting the progress and development of the Republic, so do we in this generation recognize it as a high duty to perform our part; and this duty in large degree lies in the adoption of measures for the conservation of the natural wealth of the country.

We declare our firm conviction that this conservation of our natural resources is a subject of transcendent importance, which should engage unremittingly the attention of the Nation, the States, and the People in earnest cooperation. These natural resources include the land on which we live and which yields our food; the living waters which fertilize the soil, supply power, and form great avenues of commerce; the forests which yield the materials for our homes, prevent erosion of the soil, and conserve the navigation and other uses of our streams; and the minerals which form the basis of our industrial life, and supply us with heat, light, and power.

We agree that the land should be so used that erosion and soil-wash shall cease; that there should be reclamation of arid and semi-arid regions by means of irrigation, and of swamp and overflowed regions by means of drainage; that the waters should be so conserved and used as to promote navigation, to enable the arid regions to be reclaimed by irrigation, and to develop power in the interests of the People; that the forests which regulate our rivers, support our industries, and promote the fertility and productiveness of the soil should be preserved and perpetuated; that the minerals found so abundantly beneath the surface should be so used as to prolong their utility; that the beauty, healthfulness, and habitability of our country should be preserved and increased; that the sources of national wealth exist for the benefit of the People, and that monopoly thereof should not be tolerated.

We commend the wise forethought of the President in sounding the note of warning as to the waste and exhaustion of the natural resources of the country, and signify our high appreciation of his action in calling this Conference to consider the same and to seek remedies therefore through cooperation of the Nation and the States.

We agree that this cooperation should find expression in suitable action by the Congress within the limits of and coextensive with the national jurisdiction of the subject, and, complementary thereto, by the legislatures of the several States within the limits of and coextensive with their jurisdiction.

We declare the conviction that in the use of the natural resources our independent States are interdependent and bound together by ties of mutual benefits, responsibilities and duties.

We agree in the wisdom of future conferences between the President, Members of Congress, and the Governors of States on the conservation of our natural resources with a view of continued cooperation and action on the lines suggested; and to this end we advise that from time to time, as in his judgment may seem wise, the President call the Governors of the States and Members of Congress and others into conference.

We agree that further action is advisable to ascertain the present condition of our natural resources and to promote the conservation of the same; and to that end we recommend the appointment by each State of a Commission on the Conservation of Natural Resources, to cooperate with each other and with any similar commission of the Federal Government.

We urge the continuation and extension of forest policies adapted to secure the husbanding and renewal of our diminishing timber supply, the prevention of soil erosion, the protection of headwaters, and the maintenance of the purity and navigability of our streams. We recognize that the private ownership of forest lands entails responsibilities in the interests of all the People, and we favor the enactment of laws looking to the protection and replacement of privately owned forests.

We recognize in our waters a most valuable asset of the People of the United States, and we recommend the enactment of laws looking to the conservation of water resources for irrigation, water supply, power, and navigation, to the end that navigable and source streams may be brought under complete control and fully utilized for every purpose. We especially urge on the Federal Congress the immediate adoption of a wise, active, and thorough waterway policy, providing for the prompt improvement of our streams and the conservation of their watersheds required for the uses of commerce and the protection of the interests of our People.

We recommend the enactment of laws looking to the prevention of waste in the mining and extraction of coal, oil, gas, and other minerals with a view to their wise conservation for the use of the People, and to the protection of human life in the mines.

Let us conserve the foundations of our prosperity.

Respectfully submitted,
[Signatures]

Hetch Hetchy

JOHN MUIR

Yosemite[1] is so wonderful that we are apt to regard it as an exceptional creation, the only valley of its kind in the world; but Nature is not so poor as to have only one of anything. Several other yosemites have been discovered in the Sierra that occupy the same relative positions on the Range and were formed by the same forces in the same kind of granite. One of these, the Hetch Hetchy Valley, is in the Yosemite Na-

John Muir, *The Yosemite* (New York: The Century Company, 1912), pp. 249–262.
[1]The Yosemite is the beautiful Sierra Valley in California set aside as a national park in 1890 through the efforts of Muir and others—ED.

tional Park about twenty miles from Yosemite and is easily accessible to all sorts of travelers by road and trail. . . .

I have always called it the "Tuolomne Yosemite," for it is a wonderfully exact counterpart of the Merced Yosemite not only in its sublime rocks and waterfalls but in the gardens, groves and meadows of its flowery park-like floor. . . .

Imagine yourself in Hetch Hetchy on a sunny day in June, standing waist-deep in grass and flowers . . . while the great pines sway dreamily with scarcely perceptible motion. Looking northward across the Valley you see a plain, gray granite cliff arising abruptly out of the gardens and groves to a height of 1800 feet, and in front of it Tueeulala's silvery scarf burning with irised sun-fire. In the first white outburst at the head there is an abundance of visible energy, but it is speedily hushed and concealed in divine repose, and its tranquil progress to the base of the cliff is like that of a downy feather in a still room. Now observe the fineness and marvelous distinctiveness of the various sun-illumined fabrics into which the water is woven; they sift and float from form to form down the face of that grand gray rock in so leisurely and unconfused a manner that you can examine their texture, and patterns of and tones of color as you would a piece of embroidery held in the hand. Toward the top of the fall you see groups of booming, comet-like masses, their solid white heads separate, their tails like combed silk interlacing among delicate gray and purple shadows, ever forming and dissolving, worn out by friction in their rush through the air. . . . Near the bottom the width of the fall has increased from about twenty-five feet to a hundred feet. Here it is composed of even finer tissues, and is still without a trace of disorder—air, water and sunlight woven into stuff that spirits might wear. . . .

It appears, therefore, that Hetch Hetchy Valley, far from being a plain, common, rock-bound meadow, as many who have not seen it seem to suppose, is a grand landscape garden, one of Nature's rarest and most precious mountain temples. As in Yosemite, the sublime rocks of its walls seem to glow with life, whether leaning back in repose or standing erect in thoughtful attitudes, giving welcome to storms and calms alike, their brows in the sky, their feet set in the groves and gay flowery meadows, while birds, bees and butterflies help the river and waterfalls to stir all the air into music—things frail and fleeting and types of permanence meeting here and blending, just as they do at Yosemite, to draw her lovers into close and confiding communion with her.

Sad to say, this most precious and sublime feature of the Yosemite National Park, one of the greatest of all our natural resources for the uplifting joy and peace and health of the people, is in danger of being dammed and made into a reservoir to help supply San Francisco with water and light, thus flooding it from wall to wall and burying its gardens and groves one or two hundred feet deep. This grossly destructive commercial scheme has long been planned and urged (though water as pure and abundant can be got from sources outside of the people's park, in a dozen different places), because of the comparative cheapness of the dam and of the territory which it is sought to divert from the great uses to which it was dedicated in the Act of 1890 establishing the Yosemite National Park.

The making of gardens and parks goes on with civilization all over the world, and they increase both in size and number as their value is recognized. Everybody needs beauty as well as bread, places to play in and pray in, where Nature may heal and cheer and give strength to body and soul alike. This natural beauty-hunger is made manifest in the little window-sill gardens of the poor, though perhaps only a geranium slip in a broken cup, as well as in the carefully tended rose and lily gardens of the rich, the thousands of spacious city parks and botanical gardens, and in our magnificent National parks—the Yellowstone, Yosemite, Sequoia, etc.—Nature's sublime wonderlands, the admiration and joy of the world. Nevertheless, like anything else worth while, from the very beginning, however well guarded, they have always been subject to attack by despoiling gain-seekers and mischief-makers of every degree from Satan to Senators, eagerly trying to make everything immediately and selfishly commercial, with schemes disguised in smug-smiling philanthropy, industriously, shampiously crying, "Conservation, conservation, panutilization," that man and beast may be fed and the dear Nation made great. Thus long ago a few enterprising merchants utilized the Jerusalem temple as a place of business instead of a place of prayer, changing money, buying and selling cattle and sheep and doves; and earlier still, the first forest reservation, including only one tree, was likewise despoiled. Ever since the establishment of the Yosemite National Park, strife has been going on around its borders and I suppose this will go on as part of the universal battle between right and wrong, however much its boundaries may be shorn, or its wild beauty destroyed.

The first application to the Government by the San Francisco Supervisors for the commercial use of Lake Eleanor and the Hetch Hetchy Valley was made in 1903, and on December 22nd of that year it was denied by the Secretary of the Interior, Mr. Hitchcock, who truthfully said:

> Presumably the Yosemite National Park was created such by law because of the natural objects of varying degrees of scenic importance located within its boundaries, inclusive alike of its beautiful small lakes, like Eleanor, and its majestic wonders, like Hetch Hetchy and Yosemite Valley. It is the aggregation of such natural scenic features that makes the Yosemite Park a wonderland which the Congress of the United States sought by law to reserve for all coming time as nearly as practicable in the condition fashioned by the hand of the Creator— a worthy object of National pride and a source of healthful pleasure and rest for the thousands of people who may annually sojourn there during the heated months.

In 1907 when Mr. Garfield became Secretary of the Interior the application was renewed and granted; but under his successor, Mr. Fisher, the matter has been referred to a Commission, which as this volume goes to press still has it under consideration. . . .

That any one would try to destroy such a place seems incredible; but sad experience shows that there are people good enough and bad enough for anything. The proponents of the dam scheme bring forward a lot of bad arguments to prove that the only righteous thing to do with the people's parks is to destroy them bit by bit as they are able. Their arguments are curiously like those of the devil, devised for the destruction of the first garden—so much of the very best Eden fruit going to waste; so much of the best Tuolumne water and Tuolumne scenery going to waste. Few of their statements are even partly true, and all are misleading.

Thus, Hetch Hetchy, they say, is a "low-lying meadow." On the contrary, it is a high-lying natural landscape garden, as the photographic illustrations show.

"It is a common minor feature, like thousands of others." On the contrary it is a very uncommon feature; after Yosemite, the rarest and in many ways the most important in the National Park.

"Damming and submerging it 175 feet deep would enhance its beauty by forming a crystal-clear lake." Landscape gardens, places of recreation and worship, are never made beautiful by destroying and burying them. The beautiful sham lake, forsooth, would be only an eyesore, a dismal blot on the landscape, like many others to be seen in the Sierra. For, instead of keeping it at the same level all the year, allowing Nature centuries of time to make new shores, it would, of course, be full only a month or two in the spring, when the snow is melting fast; then it would be gradually drained, exposing the slimy sides of the basin and shallower parts of the bottom, with the gathered drift and waste, death and decay of the upper basins, caught here instead of being swept on to decent natural burial along the banks of the river or in the sea. Thus the Hetch Hetchy dam-lake would be only a rough imitation of a natural lake for a few of the spring months, an open sepulcher for the others.

"Hetch Hetchy water is the purest of all to be found in the Sierra, unpolluted, and forever unpollutable." On the contrary, excepting that of the Merced below Yosemite, it is less pure than that of most of the other Sierra streams, because of the sewerage of camp grounds draining into it, especially of the Big Tuolumne Meadows camp ground, occupied by hundreds of tourists and mountaineers, with their animals, for months every summer, soon to be followed by thousands from all the world.

These temple destroyers, devotees of ravaging commercialism, seem to have a perfect contempt for Nature, and, instead of lifting their eyes to the God of the mountains, lift them to the Almighty Dollar.

Dam Hetch Hetchy! As well dam for water-tanks the people's cathedrals and churches, for no holier temple has ever been consecrated by the heart of man.

5.3:   Social Justice Progressivism (1892, 1906, 1908)

Although efficient administration may have been the core issue for some Progressives, others were moved by broader social sympathies. These social justice reformers were particularly numerous among the settlement house workers—middle-class men and women who estab-

lished community centers in the urban slums where the poor, many of them foreign born, could learn skills, absorb American ways, and find refuge from the harsh city environment. The settlements were actually precursors of Progressivism. Many were established in the 1890s, but their impact on the larger society awaited the stirring of the urban middle class in the new century.

The social justice Progressives did not confine their labors to the settlement houses. Many were active in city-wide good-government movements and efforts on the state and national levels to shelter women and child workers from exploitation, reduce the hazards of dangerous occupations, improve protection for consumers, and make government machinery more responsive to voter majorities than to special interests.

The first selection below, by Jane Addams, describes the activities of Hull House, the settlement she founded in the Chicago slums in 1889. It has been said that the white middle-class settlement workers patronized the people they sought to help and failed to respect their values and traditions. Does this attitude come through in Addams's description? Or does she seem alert to this danger and seek to avoid it? Did most slum dwellers in early twentieth-century America themselves want to assimilate middle-class "American" values?

Children made up a significant portion of the human fuel consumed to power the nation's mighty industrial engine. In The Bitter Cry of the Children, *John Spargo charged that child labor was an abusive practice that occurred in all regions of the country and in multiple sectors of the economy. The U.S. Bureau of Labor later confirmed his findings as basically accurate. The selection on children in textile factories conveys an abysmal vision of the human price of economic success. What disturbs you most about this account? Was it necessary to end child labor through legal and legislative action, or might the system have come to its own natural end? Child labor is now illegal in the United States, but what is its current global status?*

Finally, not only political reformers called for change. A rising interest in what became known as the "Social Gospel" swept through many of the established churches. Stated briefly, these religious reformers hoped to apply the principles of Christianity to the world around them. They sought to organize and institutionalize charitable and humanitarian efforts. The "Social Creed of the Churches" reflects this concern. Would you label this document idealistic or practical? In addition to economic woes, what other problems did industrialization unleash that these clergymen attempted to address?

Hull House, Chicago: An Effort toward Social Democracy[1]

JANE ADDAMS

Hull House, Chicago's first Social Settlement, was established in September, 1889. It . . . was opened by two women, supported by many friends, in the belief that the mere foothold of a house, easily accessible, ample in space, hospitable and tolerant in spirit, situated in the midst of the large foreign colonies which so easily isolate themselves in American cities, would be in itself a serviceable thing for Chicago. . . . It was opened on the theory that the dependence of classes on each other is reciprocal; and that as "the social relation is essentially a reciprocal relation, it gave a form of expression that has peculiar value." . . .

Hull House is an ample old residence, well built and somewhat ornately decorated after the manner of its time, 1856. . . . It once stood in the suburbs, but the city has steadily grown up around it and its site now has corners on three or four distinct foreign colonies. Between Halsted Street and the river live about ten thousand Italians. . . . To the south on Twelfth Street are many Germans, and side streets are given over almost entirely to Polish and Russian Jews. Further south, these Jewish colonies merge into a huge Bohemian colony, so vast that Chicago ranks as the third Bohemian city in the world. To the northwest are many Canadian-French, . . . and to the north are many Irish and first-generation Americans. . . .

The streets are inexpressibly dirty, the number of schools inadequate, factory legislation unenforced, the street-lighting bad, and paving miserable, . . . and the stables defy all laws of sanitation. . . . The Hebrews and Italians do the finishing for the great clothing-manufacturers. . . . As the design of the sweating system is the elimination of rent from the manufacture of clothing, the "outside work" is begun after the clothing leaves the cutter. For this work no basement is too dark, no stable loft too foul, no rear shanty too provisional, no tenement room too small, as these conditions imply low rental. Hence these shops abound in the worst of the foreign districts, where the sweater easily finds his cheap basement and his home finishers. . . .

This site for a Settlement was selected . . . because of its diversity and the variety of activity for which it presented an opportunity. It has been the aim of the residents to respond to all sides of the neighborhood life. . . . One thing seemed clear in regard to entertaining these foreigners: to preserve and keep for them whatever of value their past life contained and to bring them into contact with a better type of Americans. For two years, every Saturday evening, our Italian neighbors were our guests; entire families came . . . and the house became known as a place where Italians were welcome and where national holidays were observed. They came to us with their petty law-suits, sad relics of the *vendetta,* with their incorrigible boys, with their hospital cases, with their aspirations for American clothes, and with their needs for an interpreter. . . .

Jane Addams, "Hull House, Chicago: An Effort toward Social Democracy," *Forum,* vol. 14 (October 1892), pp. 226–241.
[1]Footnotes deleted.

But our social evenings are by no means confined to foreigners. Our most successful clubs are entirely composed of English speaking and American-born young people. . . . The boys who are known as the Young Citizens' Club are supposed to inform themselves on municipal affairs. . . . The gymnasium is a somewhat pretentious name for a building next door which was formerly a saloon, but which we rented last fall, repaired, and fitted up with simple apparatus. . . . The more definite humanitarian effect of Hull House has taken shape in a day nursery. . . . During two months of this summer the reports sent in from Hull House to the Municipal Order League and through it to the Health Department were one thousand and thirty-seven, . . . and a marked improvement has taken place in the scavenger service and in the regulation of the small stables of the ward. . . .

Last May twenty girls from a knitting factory who struck because they were docked for loss of time when they were working by the piece, came directly from the factory to Hull House. . . . They had heard that we "stood by working people." We were able to have the strike arbitrated . . . and we had the satisfaction of putting on record one more case of arbitration in the slowly growing list. . . . It is difficult to classify the Working Peoples' Social Science Club, which meets weekly at Hull House. It is social, educational, and civic in character, the latter because it strongly connects the house with the labor problems in their political and social aspects. . . .

I am always sorry to have Hull House regarded as philanthropy, although it doubtless has strong philanthropic tendencies. . . . Working people live in the same streets with those in need of charity, but they themselves require and want none of it. As one of their number has said, they require only that their aspirations be recognized and stimulated and the means of attaining them put at their disposal. Hull House makes a constant effort to secure these means, but to call that effort philanthropy is to use the word unfairly and to underestimate the duties of good citizenship.

The Bitter Cry of the Children (1906)

JOHN SPARGO

There are more than 80,000 children employed in the textile industries of the United States, according to the very incomplete census returns, most of them being little girls. In these industries conditions are undoubtedly worse in the Southern states than elsewhere, though I have witnessed many pitiable cases of child slavery in Northern mills which equalled almost anything I have ever seen in the South. During the Philadelphia textile workers' strike in 1903, I saw at least a score of children ranging from eight to ten years of age who had been working in the mills prior to the strike. One little girl of nine I saw in the Kensington Labor Lyceum. She had been working for almost a year before the strike began, she said,

John Spargo, *The Bitter Cry of the Children* (New York: Macmillan, 1906), pp. 152–153.

and careful inquiry proved her story to be true. When "Mother" Mary Jones started with her little "army" of child toilers to march to Oyster Bay, in order that the President of the United States might see for himself some of the little ones who had actually been employed in the mills of Philadelphia, I happened to be engaged in assisting the strikers. For two days I accompanied the little "army" on its march, and thus had an excellent opportunity of studying the children. Amongst them were several from eight to eleven years of age, and I remember one little girl who was not quite eleven telling me with pride that she had "worked two years and never missed a day."

One evening, not long ago, I stood outside of a large flax mill in Paterson, N. J., while it disgorged its crowd of men, women, and children employees. All the afternoon, as I lingered in the tenement district near the mills, the comparative silence of the streets oppressed me. There were many babies and very small children, but the older children, whose boisterous play one expects in such streets, were wanting. "If thow'lt bide till th' mills shut for th' day, thow'lt see plenty on 'em—big kids as plenty as small taties," said one old woman to whom I spoke about it. She was right. At six o'clock the whistles shrieked, and the streets were suddenly filled with people, many of them mere children. Of all the crowd of tired, pallid, and languid-looking children I could only get speech with one, a little girl who claimed thirteen years, though she was smaller than many a child of ten. Indeed, as I think of her now, I doubt whether she would have come up to the standard of normal physical development either in weight or stature for a child of ten. One learns, however, not to judge the ages of working children by their physical appearance, for they are usually behind other children in height, weight, and girth of chest,—often as much as two or three years. If my little Paterson friend was thirteen, perhaps the nature of her employment will explain her puny, stunted body. She works in the "steaming room" of the flax mill. All day long, in a room filled with clouds of steam, she has to stand barefooted in pools of water twisting coils of wet hemp. When I saw her she was dripping wet, though she said that she had worn a rubber apron all day. In the coldest evenings of winter little Marie, and hundreds of other little girls, must go out from the superheated steaming rooms into the bitter cold in just that condition. No wonder that such children are stunted and underdeveloped!

In textile mill towns like Biddeford, Me., Manchester, N. H., Fall River and Lawrence, Mass., I have seen many such children, who, if they were twelve or fourteen according to their certificates and the companies' registers, were not more than ten or twelve in reality. I have watched them hurrying into and away from the mills, "those receptacles, in too many instances, for living human skeletons, almost disrobed of intellect," as Robert Owen's burning phrase describes them. I do not doubt that, upon the whole, conditions in the textile industries are better in the North than in the South, but they are nevertheless too bad to permit of self-righteous boasting and complacency. And in several other departments of industry conditions are no whit better in the North than in the South. The child-labor problem is not sectional, but national. . . .

The Social Creed of the Churches Statement Adopted by the General Conference of the Methodist Episcopal Church, May 1908.

The Methodist Episcopal Church stands:

For equal rights and complete justice for all men in all stations of life.

For the principle of conciliation and arbitration in industrial dissensions.

For the protection of the worker from dangerous machinery, occupational disease, injuries and mortality.

For the abolition of child labor.

For such regulation of the conditions of labor for women as shall safeguard the physical and moral health of the community.

For the suppression of the "sweating system."

For the gradual and reasonable reduction of the hours of labor to the lowest practical point, with work for all; and for that degree of leisure for all which is the condition of the highest human life.

For a release from employment one day in seven.

For a living wage in every industry.

For the highest wage that each industry can afford, and for the most equitable division of the products in industry that can ultimately be devised.

For the recognition of the Golden Rule, and the mind of Christ as the supreme law of society and the sure remedy for all social ills.

General Conference of the Methodist Episcopal Church. The Social Creed of the Churches adopted May 1908. Quoted from *A Year Book of the Church and Social Service in the United States,* ed. by H. F. Ward, 1916, p. 197–198.

☆ **6** ☆

Race and Ethnicity

The two decades on either side of 1900 witnessed a vast turnover of nationalities and races in America. As noted, sometime in the 1890s the source of immigrants to America shifted decisively from western and northern Europe to eastern and southern Europe. Particularly after 1900, far fewer proportionately of the newcomers came from Britain, Germany, Ireland, and Scandinavia and far more from Poland, Russia, Austria-Hungary, Greece, and Italy. Meanwhile, in the years just preceding World War I, there began a migration to northern cities of African American people, until then tied overwhelmingly, as during slavery days, to the rural South.

There were important differences between these two human streams. The people from the southern countryside who came to New York, Chicago, Philadelphia, and Cleveland were English-speaking, Protestant, American citizens. The transatlantic arrivals were, of course, foreigners, who spoke alien tongues, and were predominantly Catholic, Greek Orthodox, or Jewish. The migrants from the rural South were black; the newcomers from Europe were white. Race would make a difference.

But there were also significant overlaps between the two groups. Both were rural peoples, new to city life and city ways. Both were predominantly unskilled workers who found their economic niches in the mines, factories, and construction sites doing the hard, dirty, menial labor the industrial society of the day required. Both met prejudice and bigotry from old-stock white Americans already on the scene, although African Americans undoubtedly suffered more than immigrants.

The selections that follow depict how the post-1890 newcomers to northern cities were perceived and received. The new arrivals were not uniformly scorned. There remained among old-stock white Americans a residue of good will toward immigrants and black people based on the nation's democratic, egalitarian traditions. Many business leaders welcomed the newcomers, especially the white immigrants, as a source of cheap labor. Still, the balance was clearly tipped against a generous toleration, as the documents below suggest.

6.1: The Great Migration: The Dark Side (1905, 1919)

Southern black people began to move north in substantial numbers in the earliest years of this century. The trickle became a torrent after 1915, when World War I blocked the normal flow of European immigrants and created major labor shortages in northern industry.

Jobs, however, were not the only magnet drawing rural African Americans northward. The North also promised to be freer and less repressive than Dixie, where segregation by race, known as "Jim Crow," remained entrenched, and violence against blacks had accelerated.

Ray Stannard Baker's article in McClure's *describes a lynching in Springfield, Ohio. Are you surprised by this account? Was white racial supremacy and mob violence confined to the South?*

One of the black newcomers' favorite destinations was booming Chicago, where the stockyards and the city's many industrial plants provided employment. By 1920 the Windy City had almost 110,000 African American residents, almost four times the number in 1900.

The first selection below describes the Chicago "Black Belt" shortly after the turn of the century. Even in this early period some of the major problems that would continue to plague black urban dwellers in the North had surfaced. What are some of these? What does the reference to "strike-breakers" suggest? What are some of the hopeful aspects of life in the "Black Belt" as described here? What are some of the sources of racial tension?

The second selection depicts the savage Chicago race riot of 1919, fourteen years after the scene described in the previous document. This was one of a dozen shameful racial disorders that erupted in the first two decades of the twentieth century. Can you deduce from the account the causes of the barbaric behavior described? Group antagonisms have been very widespread in America, but they were seldom so brutal and destructive as those between whites and blacks in the cities, especially in the early part of this century. What explains this ferocity? Did race riots continue long past this period? Have recent racial disorders been similar to the Chicago riot of 1919?

What Is a Lynching? A Study of Mob Justice, South and North

RAY STANNARD BAKER

I cite these facts to show the underlying conditions in Springfield;[1] a soil richly prepared for an outbreak of mob law—with corrupt politics, vile saloons, the law paralysed by non-enforcement against vice, a large venal Negro vote, lax courts of justice.

Gathering of the Lynching Mob

Well, on Monday afternoon the mob began to gather. At first it was an absurd, ineffectual crowd, made up largely of lawless boys of sixteen to twenty—a pronounced feature of every mob—with a wide fringe of more respectable citizens, their hands in their pockets and no convictions in their souls, looking on curiously, helplessly. They gathered hooting around the jail, cowardly, at first, as all mobs are, but growing bolder as darkness came on and no move was made to check them. The murder of Collis was not a horrible, soul-rending crime like that at Statesboro, Georgia; these men in the mob were not personal friends of the murdered man; it was a mob from the back rooms of the swarming saloons of Springfield; and it included also the sort of idle boys "who hang around cigar stores," as one observer told me. The newspaper reports are fond of describing lynching mobs as "made up of the foremost citizens of the town." In no cases that I know of, either South or North, . . . has a mob been made up of what may be called the best citizens; but the best citizens have often stood afar off "decrying the mob"—as a Springfield man told me piously—and letting it go on. A mob is the method by which good citizens turn over the law and the government to the criminal or irresponsible classes.

And no official in direct authority in Springfield that evening, apparently, had so much as an ounce of grit within him. The sheriff came out and made a weak speech in which he said he "didn't want to hurt anybody." They threw stones at him and broke his windows. The chief of police sent eighteen men to the jail but did not go near himself. All of these policemen undoubtedly sympathised with the mob in its efforts to get at the slayer of their brother officer; at least, they did nothing effective to prevent the lynching. An appeal was made to the Mayor to order out the engine companies that water might be turned on the mob. He said he didn't like to; *the hose might be cut!* The local militia company was called to its barracks, but the officer in charge hesitated, vacillated, doubted his authority, and objected finally because he had no ammunition *except* Krag-Jorgenson cartridges, which, if fired into a mob, would kill too many people! The soldiers did not stir that night from the safe and comfortable precincts of their armory.

Ray Stannard Baker, "What Is a Lynching? A Study of Mob Justice, North and South," *McClure's*, February, 1905.
[1]Springfield, Ohio.

A sort of dry rot, a moral paralysis, seems to strike the administrators of law in a town like Springfield. What can be expected of officers who are not accustomed to enforce the law, or of a people not accustomed to obey it—or who make reservations and exceptions when they do enforce it or obey it?

Threats to Lynch the Judges

When the sheriff made his speech to the mob, urging them to let the law take its course they jeered him. The law! When, in the past, had the law taken its proper course in Clark County? Someone shouted, referring to Dixon:

"He'll only get fined for shooting in the city limits."

"He'll get ten days in jail and suspended sentence."

Then there were voices:

"Let's go hang Mower and Miller"—the two judges.

This threat, indeed, was frequently repeated both on the night of the lynching and on the day following.

So the mob came finally, and cracked the door of the jail with a railroad rail. This jail is said to be the strongest in Ohio, and having seen it, I can well believe that the report is true. But steel bars have never yet kept out a mob; it takes something a good deal stronger: human courage backed up by the consciousness of being right.

They murdered the Negro in cold blood in the jail doorway; then they dragged him to the principal business street and hung him to a telegraph-pole, afterward riddling his lifeless body with revolver shots.

Lesson of a Hanging Negro

That was the end of that! Mob justice administered! And there the Negro hung until daylight the next morning—an unspeakably grisly, dangling horror, advertising the shame of the town. His head was shockingly crooked to one side, his ragged clothing, cut for souvenirs, exposed in places his bare body: he dripped blood. And, with the crowds of men both here and at the morgue where the body was publicly exhibited, came young boys in knickerbockers, and little girls and women by scores, horrified but curious. They came even with baby carriages! Men made jokes: "A dead nigger is a good nigger." And the purblind, dollars-and-cents man, most despicable of all, was congratulating the public:

"It'll save the county a lot of money!"

Significant lessons, these, for the young!

But the mob wasn't through with its work. Easy people imagine that, having hanged a Negro, the mob goes quietly about its business; but that is never the way of the mob. Once released, the spirit of anarchy spreads and spreads, not subsiding until it has accomplished its full measure of evil.

Mob Burning of Negro Saloons

All the following day a rumbling, angry crowd filled the streets of Springfield, threatening to burn out the notorious Levee, threatening Judges Mower and Miller, threatening the "niggers." The local troops—to say nothing of the police force—

which might easily have broken up the mob, remained sedulously in their armories, vacillating, doubtful of authority, knowing that there were threats to burn and destroy, and making not one move toward the protection of the public. One of the captains was even permitted to go to a neighboring city to a dance! At the very same time the panic-stricken officials were summoning troops from other towns. So night came on, the mob gathered around the notorious dives, someone touched a match, and the places of crime suddenly disgorged their foul inhabitants. Black and white, they came pouring out and vanished into the darkness where they belonged and whence they have not yet returned. Eight buildings went up in smoke, the fire department deliberating—intentionally, it is said—until the flames could not be controlled. The troops, almost driven out by the county prosecutor, McGrew, appeared after the mob had completed its work.

Good work, badly done, a living demonstration of the inevitability of law—if not orderly, decent law, then of mob-law.

For days following the troops filled Springfield, costing the state large sums of money, costing the county large sums of money. They chiefly guarded the public fountain; the mob had gone home—until next time.

Efforts to Punish the Mob

What happened after that? A perfunctory court-martial that did absolutely nothing. A grand jury of really good citizens that sat for weeks, off and on; and like the mountain that was in travail and brought forth a mouse, they indicted two boys and two men out of all that mob, not for murder but for "breaking into jail." And, curiously enough, it developed—how do such things develop?—that every man on the grand jury was a Republican, chosen by Republican county officers, and in their report they severely censored police force (Democratic), and the mayor (Democratic), and had not one word of disapproval for the sheriff (Republican). Curiously enough, also, the public did not become enthusiastic over the report of that grand jury. . . .

But the worst feature of all in this Springfield lynching was the apathy of the public. No one really seemed to care. A "nigger" had been hanged: what of it? But the law itself had been lynched. What of that? I had just come from the South, where I had found the people of several lynching towns in a state of deep excitement—moral excitement if you like, thinking about this problem, quarrelling about it, expelling men from the church, impeaching sheriffs, dishonourably discharging whole militia companies. Here in Springfield, I found cold apathy, except for a few fine citizens, one of whom City Solicitor Stewart L. Tatum, promptly offered his services to the sheriff and assisted in a vain effort to remove the Negro in a closed carriage and afterward at the risk of personal assault earnestly attempted to defeat the purposes of the mob. Another of these citizens, the Rev. Father Cogan, pleaded with the mob on the second night of the rioting at risk to himself; another withdrew from the militia company because it had not done its duty. And afterward the city officials were stirred by the faintest of faint spasms of righteousness; some of the Negro saloons were closed up, but within a month, the most notorious of all the dive-keepers, Hurley, the Negro political boss, was permitted to open an establishment—through the medium of a brother-in-law!

If there ever was an example of good citizenship lying flat on its back with political corruption squatting on its neck, Springfield furnished an example of that condition.

Social Bonds in the "Black Belt" of Chicago: Negro Organizations and the New Spirit Pervading Them[1]

FANNIE BARRIER WILLIAMS

The last federal census [1900] showed the Negro population of Chicago to be about 35,000. The present population is estimated to be over 50,000, an increase of about forty per cent in five years. The colored people who are thus crowding into Chicago come mostly from the states of Kentucky, Tennessee, Alabama, Mississippi, Louisiana, Arkansas, and Missouri. . . . [The] many industrial strikes . . . in the last ten years have brought thousands of colored people to Chicago, either for immediate work as strikebreakers, or with the prospect of employment for both skilled and unskilled workers . . . ; thousands of Negro men and women are now employed in the stockyards and other large industrial plants where ten years ago this would not have been thought of.

This increase of Negro population has brought with it problems that directly affect the social and economic life of the newcomers. Prevented from mingling easily and generally with the rest of the city's population, according to their needs and deservings, but with no preparation made for segregation . . . they have been subject to more social ills than any other nationality among us. . . . The real problem of the social life of the colored people in Chicago, as in all northern cities, lies in the fact of their segregation. While they do not occupy all the worst streets and live in all the unsanitary houses in Chicago, what is known as the "Black Belt" is altogether forbidding and demoralizing. . . .

The organizations created and maintained by them in Chicago are numerous and touch almost every phase of our social life. . . . First in importance is the Negro church. There are 25 regularly organized colored churches. This number includes 9 Methodist, 8 Baptist, 1 Catholic, 1 Episcopal, 1 Christian and 1 Presbyterian. In addition to these there are numerous missions in various parts of the "Black Belt." . . . Most of these churches are burdened with oppressive indebtedness, and because of this their usefulness as agents of moral up-lift is seriously handicapped. . . . Thousands of Negroes know and care for no other entertainment than that furnished by the church. . . .

Next to the Negro church, in importance, as affecting the social life of the people are the secret orders, embracing such organizations as the Masons, Odd Fellows, Knights of Pythias, True Reformers, the United Brotherhood, . . . the Ancient Order

---

Fannie Barrier Williams, "Social Bonds in the 'Black Belt' of Chicago: Negro Organizations and the New Spirit Pervading Them," *Charities,* October 7, 1905, pp. 40–44.
[1]Footnotes deleted.

of Foresters, and the Elks. Nearly all of these secret orders have auxiliary associations composed of women. . . .

In the matter of employment, the colored people of Chicago have lost in the last ten years nearly every occupation of which they once had almost a monopoly. There is now scarcely a Negro barber left in the business district. Nearly all the janitor work in the large buildings has been taken away from them by the Swedes. White men and women as waiters have supplanted colored men in nearly all the first-class hotels and restaurants. Practically all the shoe polishing is now done by Greeks. Negro coachmen and expressmen and teamsters are seldom seen in the business districts. It scarcely need be stated that colored young men and women are almost never employed as clerks and bookkeepers in business establishments. . . .

The increase of the Negro population in Chicago . . . has not tended to liberalize public sentiment; in fact hostile sentiment has been considerably intensified by the importation from time to time of colored men as strikebreakers. Then again a marked increase of crime among the Negro population has been noted in recent years. All these things have tended to put us in a bad light, resulting in an appreciable loss of friends and well-wishers.

Chicago Commission on Race Relations: Causes of the Race Riot

Sunday afternoon, July 27, 1919, hundreds of white and Negro bathers crowded the lake-front beaches at Twenty-sixth and Twenty-ninth streets. This is the eastern boundary of the thickest Negro residence area. At Twenty-sixth Street Negroes were in great majority; at Twenty-ninth Street there were more whites. An imaginary line in the water separating the two beaches had been generally observed by the two races. Under the prevailing relations, aided by wild rumors and reports, this line served virtually as a challenge to either side to cross it. Four Negroes who attempted to enter the water from the "white" side were driven away by the whites. They returned with more Negroes, and there followed a series of attacks with stones, first one side gaining the advantage, then the other.

Eugene Williams, a Negro boy of seventeen, entered the water from the side used by Negroes and drifted across the line supported by a railroad tie. He was observed by the crowd on the beach and promptly became a target for stones. He suddenly released the tie, went down and was drowned. Guilt was immediately placed on Stauber, a young white man, by Negro witnesses who declared that he threw the fatal stone.[1]

White and Negro men dived for the boy without result. Negroes demanded that the policeman present arrest Stauber. He refused; and at this crucial moment ar-

Chicago Commission on Race Relations: The Negro in Chicago (Chicago: University of Chicago Press, 1927), pp. 596–598. © University of Chicago Press.
[1]A jury later determined that Williams had drowned because he was kept from coming ashore by the white stone-throwers—ED.

rested a Negro on a white man's complaint. Negroes then attacked the officer. These two facts, the drowning and the refusal of the policeman to arrest Stauber, together marked the beginning of the riot.

Two hours after the drowning, a Negro, James Crawford, fired into a group of officers summoned by the policeman at the beach and was killed by a Negro policeman. Reports and rumors circulated rapidly, and new crowds began to gather. Five white men were injured in clashes near the beach. As darkness came Negroes in white districts to the west suffered severely. Between 9:00 P.M. and 3:00 A.M. twenty-seven Negroes were beaten, seven stabbed, and four shot. Monday morning was quiet, and Negroes went to work as usual.

Returning from work in the afternoon many Negroes were attacked by white ruffians. Street-car routes, especially at transfer points, were the centers of lawlessness. Trolleys were pulled from the wires, and Negro passengers were dragged into the street, beaten, stabbed, and shot. The police were powerless to cope with these numerous assaults. During Monday, four Negro men and one white assailant were killed, and thirty Negroes were severely beaten in street-car clashes. Four white men were killed, six stabbed, five shot, and nine severely beaten. It was rumored that the white occupants of the Angelus Building at Thirty-fifth Street and Wabash Avenue had shot a Negro. Negroes gathered about the building. The white tenants sought police protection, and one hundred policemen, mounted and on foot, responded. In a clash with the mob the police killed four Negroes and injured many.

Raids into the Negro residence area then began. Automobiles sped through the streets, the occupants shooting at random. Negroes retaliated by "sniping" from ambush. At midnight surface and elevated car service was discontinued because of a strike for wage increases, and thousands of employees were cut off from work.

On Tuesday, July 29, Negro men en route on foot to their jobs through hostile territory were killed. White soldiers and sailors in uniform, aided by civilians, raided the "Loop" business section, killing two Negroes and beating and robbing several others. Negroes living among white neighbors in Englewood, far to the south, were driven from their homes, their household goods were stolen, and their houses were burned or wrecked. On the West Side an Italian mob, excited by a false rumor that an Italian girl had been shot by a Negro, killed Joseph Lovings, a Negro.

Wednesday night at 10:30 Mayor [William] Thompson yielded to pressure and asked the help of the three regiments of militia which had been stationed in nearby armories during the most severe rioting, awaiting the call. They immediately took up positions throughout the South Side. A rainfall Wednesday night and Thursday kept many people in their homes, and by Friday the rioting had abated. On Saturday incendiary fires burned forty-nine houses in the immigrant neighborhood west of the Stock Yards. Nine hundred and forty-eight people, mostly Lithuanians, were made homeless, and the property loss was about $250,000. Responsibility for the fires was never fixed.

The total casualties of this reign of terror were thirty-eight deaths—fifteen white, twenty-three Negro—and 537 people injured. Forty-one per cent of the reported clashes occurred in the white neighborhood near the Stock Yards between the south branch of the Chicago River and Fifty-fifth Street, Wentworth Avenue and the city limits, and 34 per cent in the "Black Belt" between Twenty-second and Thirty-ninth streets, Wentworth Avenue and Lake Michigan. Others were scattered.

Responsibility for many attacks was definitely placed by many witnesses upon the [white] "athletic clubs," including "Ragen's Colts," the "Hamburgers," "Aylwards," "Our Flag," the "Standard," the "Sparklers," and several others. The mobs were made up for the most part of boys between fifteen and twenty-two. Older persons participated, but the youth of the rioters was conspicuous in every clash. Little children witnessed the brutalities and frequently pointed out the injured when the police arrived.

6.2:   Black Americans Respond (1905, 1923)

People of good will, black and white, were appalled by what one Progressive called "the race war in the North." In 1909, soon after a shocking race riot in Springfield, Illinois, a group of reformers established the National Association for the Advancement of Colored People (NAACP) to work for better black-white relations and for improved economic conditions for black workers.

The NAACP represented a union of two elements: white Progressives and a new African American leadership, northern-born and northern-educated. Many of the latter were members of the Niagara Movement, a black defense group established in 1905 that rejected the acquiescence in segregation and second-class citizenship associated with Booker T. Washington, head of Tuskegee Institute in Alabama.[1]
The leading figure in the Niagara Movement was W.E.B. Du Bois, a brilliant black scholar who had earned a doctorate in history at Harvard and gone on to a successful academic career. Du Bois became the head of publicity and research for the NAACP and remained with it as a leading militant voice for over twenty years.

The first selection below is a statement composed by Du Bois for the Niagara Movement. What changes in the treatment of black Americans does it demand? How does Du Bois seek to awaken the support

[1]Washington was author of the so-called Atlanta Compromise that pledged black Americans to abandon claims to suffrage rights and social equality in exchange for economic opportunity. Its pronouncement at the 1895 Cotton States Exposition in Atlanta won wide applause from the white community and made Washington a "leader" of his race in the eyes of whites.

of the white majority? Why would contemporaries have considered a statement like this a bold departure from the past? Why does it end with a pledge that blacks themselves will seek to fulfill certain obligations?

The second selection is by Marcus Garvey, a black West Indian who came to the United States in 1916 with his plan for a Universal Negro Improvement Association. Garvey was a nationalist who sought to awaken black racial pride, establish ties between blacks of the Americas and Africa, and encourage the independence of black Africa, then almost totally under European colonial dominion. He too opposed Booker T. Washington's timid approach to race improvement, but his alternative was different from Du Bois's.

In the United States Garvey proved an effective voice of black pride, and thousands of urban blacks joined the Universal Negro Improvement Association and contributed to several of Garvey's black run commercial and political ventures. Eventually opposition from established black leaders, including Du Bois, and from the federal government led to Garvey's conviction for mail fraud. He died in obscurity in London in 1940.

How would you characterize the essential differences between the Du Bois and the Garvey responses to racial oppression? Whose recent views do Garvey's foreshadow? Were Garvey's plans practical ones? Why did they appeal to black city dwellers in the 1920s?

What Black Americans Want

W.E.B. DU BOIS

We believe that [Negro-American] citizens should protest emphatically and continually against the curtailment of their political rights. We believe in manhood suffrage: we believe that no man is so good, intelligent or wealthy as to be entrusted wholly with the welfare of his neighbor.

We believe also in protest against the curtailment of our civil rights. All American citizens have the right to equal treatment in places of public entertainment according to their behavior and deserts.

We especially complain against the denial of equal opportunities to us in economic life; in the rural districts of the south this amounts to peonage and virtual slavery; all over the south it tends to crush labor and small business enterprises: and everywhere American prejudice, helped often by iniquitous laws, is making it more difficult for Negro-Americans to earn a decent living.

The Cleveland Gazette, July 22, 1905.

Common school education should be free to all American children and compulsory. High school training should be adequately provided for all, and college training should be the monopoly of no class or race in any section of our common country. We believe that in defense of its own institutions, the United States should aid common school education, particularly in the south, and we especially recommend concerted agitation to this end. We urge an increase in public high school facilities in the south, where the Negro-Americans are almost wholly without such provisions. We favor well-equipped trade and technical schools for the training of artisans, and the need of adequate and liberal endowment for a few institutions of higher education must be patent to sincere well-wishers of the race.

We demand upright judges in courts, juries selected without discrimination on account of color and the same measure of punishment, and the same efforts at reformation for black as for white offenders. We need orphanages and farm schools for dependent children, juvenile reformatories for delinquents, and the abolition of the dehumanizing convict-lease system. . . .

We hold up for public execration the conduct of two opposite classes of men; the practice among employers of importing ignorant Negro-American laborers in emergencies, and then affording them neither protection nor permanent employment; and the practice of labor unions of proscribing and boycotting and oppressing thousands of their fellow-toilers, simply because they are black. These methods have accentuated and will accentuate the war of labor and capital, and they are disgraceful to both sides. . . .

We regret that this nation has never seen fit adequately to reward the black soldiers who in its five wars, have defended their country with their blood, and yet have been systematically denied the promotions which their abilities deserve. And we regard as unjust, the exclusion of black boys from the military and navy training schools. . . .

The Negro race in America, stolen, ravished and degraded, struggling up through difficulties and oppression, needs sympathy and receives criticism, needs help and is given hindrance, needs protection and is given mob-violence, needs justice and is given charity, needs leadership and is given cowardice and apology, needs bread and is given a stone. This nation will never stand justified before God until these things are changed.

Especially are we surprised and astonished at the recent attitude of the church of Christ—on the increase of a desire to bow to racial prejudice, to narrow the bounds of human brotherhood, and to segregate black men in some outer sanctuary. This is wrong, unchristian and disgraceful to twentieth century civilization. . . .

And while we are demanding, and ought to demand, and will continue to demand the rights enumerated above, God forbid that we should ever forget to urge corresponding duties upon our people.

The duty to vote.
The duty to respect the rights of others.
The duty to work.
The duty to obey the laws.
The duty to be clean and orderly.

The duty to send our children to school.

The duty to respect ourselves, even as we respect others.

Black Pride

MARCUS GARVEY

I saw the injustice done my race because it was black, and I became dissatisfied on that account. I went traveling to South and Central America and parts of the West Indies to find out if it was so elsewhere, and I found the same situation. I set sail for Europe to find out if it was different there, and again I found the same stumbling block—"You are black." I read of the conditions in America. I read "Up From Slavery," by Booker T. Washington, and then my doom—if I may call it—of being a race leader dawned upon me in London after I had traveled through almost half of Europe.

I asked, "Where is the black man's Government?" "Where is his King and his kingdom?" "Where is his President, his country, and his ambassador, his army, his navy, his men of big affairs?" I could not find them, and then I declared, "I will help to make them."

Becoming naturally restless for the opportunity of doing something for the advancement of my race, I was determined that the black man would not continue to be kicked about by all the other races and nations of the world, as I saw in the West Indies, South and Central America and Europe and as I read of it in America. My young and ambitious mind led me into flights of great imagination. I saw before me, even as I do now, a new world of black men, not peons, serfs, dogs and slaves, but a nation of sturdy men making their impress upon civilization and causing a new light to dawn upon the human race. My brain was afire. There was a world of thought to conquer. I had to start ere it became too late and the work be not done. Immediately I boarded a ship at Southampton [England] for Jamaica, where I arrived on July 15, 1914. The Universal Negro Improvement Association and African Communities (Imperial) League was founded and organized five days after my arrival with the program of uniting all the negro peoples of the world into one great body to establish a country and Government absolutely their own. . . .

Being black, I have committed an unpardonable offense against the very light colored negroes in America and the West Indies by making myself famous as a negro leader of millions. In their view no black man must rise above them, but I still forge ahead determined to give to the world the truth about the new negro who is determined to make and hold for himself a place in the affairs of men. The Universal Negro Improvement Association has been misrepresented by my enemies. They have tried to make it appear that we are hostile to other races. This is absolutely false. We love all humanity. We are working for the peace of the world which we believe can only come about when all races are given their due.

Marcus Garvey, "The Negro's Greatest Enemy." Reprinted with permission from *Current History* magazine (18, September 1923), pp. 951–957. © 1923, Current History, Inc.

We feel that there is absolutely no reason why there should be any differences between the black and white races, if each stop to adjust and steady itself. We believe in the purity of both races. We do not believe the black man should be encouraged in the idea that his highest purpose in life is to marry a white woman, but we do believe that the white man should be taught to respect the black woman in the same way as he wants the black man to respect the white woman. It is a vicious and dangerous doctrine of social equality to urge, as certain colored leaders do, that black and white should get together, for that would destroy the racial purity of both.

We believe that the black people should have a country of their own where they should be given the fullest opportunity to develop politically, socially and industrially. The black people should not be encouraged to remain in white people's countries and expect to be Presidents, Governors, Mayors, Senators, Congressmen, Judges and social and industrial leaders. We believe that with the rising ambition of the negro, if a country is not provided for him in another 50 or 100 years, there will be a terrible clash that will end disastrously to him and disgrace our civilization. We desire to prevent such a clash by pointing the negro to a home of his own. We feel that all well disposed and broad minded white men will aid in this direction. It is because of this belief no doubt that my negro enemies, so as to prejudice me further in the opinion of the public, wickedly state that I am a member of the K Klux Klan, even though I am a black man.[1]

I have been deprived of the opportunity of properly explaining my work to the white people of America through the prejudice worked up against me by jealous and wicked members of my own race. My success as an organizer was much more than rival negro leaders could tolerate. They, regardless of consequences, either to me or to the race, had to destroy me by fair means or foul. The thousands of anonymous and other hostile letters written to the editors and publishers of the white press by negro rivals to prejudice me in the eyes of public opinion are sufficient evidence of the wicked and vicious opposition I have had to meet from among my own people, especially among the very lightly colored. But they went further than the press in their attempts to discredit me. They organized clubs all over the United States and the West Indies, and wrote both open and anonymous letters to city, State and Federal officials of this and other Governments to induce them to use their influence to hamper and destroy me. No wonder, therefore, that several Judges, District Attorneys and other high officials have been against me without knowing me. No wonder, therefore, that the great white population of this country and of the world has a wrong impression of the aims and objects of the Universal Negro Improvement Association and of the work of Marcus Garvey.

The Struggle of the Future

Having had the wrong education as a start in his racial career, the negro has become his own greatest enemy. Most of the trouble I have had in advancing the cause of

---

[1]Garvey was accused of cooperating with the Klan because he favored separation of the races, a position the Klan endorsed, though for different purposes from Garvey's—ED.

the race has come from negroes. Booker Washington aptly described the race in one of his lectures by stating that we were like crabs in a barrel, that none would allow the other to climb over, but on any such attempt all would continue to pull back into the barrel the one crab that would make the effort to climb out. Yet, those of us with vision cannot desert the race, leaving it to suffer and die.

Looking forward a century or two, we can see an economic and political death struggle for the survival of the different race groups. Many of our present-day national centres will have become over-crowded with vast surplus populations. The fight for bread and position will be keen and severe. The weaker and unprepared group is bound to go under. That is why, visionaries as we are in the Universal Negro Improvement Association, we are fighting for the founding of a negro nation in Africa, so that there will be no clash between black and white and that each race will have a separate existence and civilization all its own without courting suspicion and hatred or eyeing each other with jealousy and rivalry within the borders of the same country.

White men who have struggled for and built up their countries and their own civilizations are not disposed to hand them over to the negro or any other race without let or hindrance. It would be unreasonable to expect this. Hence any vain assumption on the part of the negro to imagine that he will one day become President of the Nation, Governor of the State, or Mayor of the city in the countries of white men, is like waiting on the devil and his angels to take up their residence in the Realm on High and direct there the affairs of Paradise.

6.3: The New Immigration and American Toleration (1912, 1916)

Although individual immigrants sometimes endured physical attack and intimidation, intolerance toward European immigrants in the early twentieth century primarily took verbal, economic, and legislative forms. Groups such as the Immigration Restriction League agitated for laws excluding immigrants unable to read and write (in any language) in the expectation that many from the newer regions of immigration would be disqualified. Other anti-immigrant organizations demanded laws capping the total admitted each year and setting quotas on specific nationality groups.

Americans had always worried that foreign newcomers would be difficult to assimilate culturally. But by the 1890s there were racial fears as well. The latest wave of foreigners, said many immigration restrictionists, derived from inferior human stock and so could never become a desirable element of American society, no matter how many classes they took in American civics or in the English language.

The selections below touch on several issues that concerned native-born Americans—and the immigrants as well—during the years 1890–1930.

Few American writers were more outspoken against immigration than Madison Grant. Educated at Yale and Columbia, he combined conventional scientific theories with social and legal concerns to formulate his belief that ethnic and social diversity would threaten American democracy. This selection, taken from his anti-immigration tract, The Passing of the Great Race, *is not only racist propaganda, but raises dangerous misconceptions about science and genetics that seem alarmingly relevant to our own time. What does Grant claim is the relationship between race and heredity? What does he mean by racial regression, and how is culture affected by it? What is obviously wrong with what he argues, and why would we consider such writing intolerable today?*

The final selection is from the autobiography of Mary Antin, a young Jewish woman born in Polotzk, Poland, who came to the United States with her family in 1894 at the age of thirteen and became a writer and social worker. In what way does she challenge the views of the Dillingham Commission? Do you think her experience was typical of that of the new immigrants in general? What role was the school system expected to play in the process of assimilating the immigrants? Is there any indication that her teacher encouraged Antin to retain any of her family heritage? Was her experience in school different from that of immigrants of our own day? Does the role of Antin's teacher tell us anything about the attitudes of some native-born Americans toward the newcomers?

The Passing of the Great Race

MADISON GRANT

Failure to recognize the clear distinction between race and nationality and the still greater distinction between race and language, the easy assumption that the one is indicative of the other, has been in the past a serious impediment to an understanding of racial values. Historians and philologists have approached the subject from the viewpoint of linguistics, and as a result we have been burdened with a group of mythical races, such as the Latin, the Aryan, the Caucasian, and, perhaps, most inconsistent of all, the "Celtic" race.

Madison Grant, *The Passing of the Great Race* (New York: C. Scribner's Sons, 1916), selected from the introduction pages 1–16.

Man is an animal differing from his fellow inhabitants of the globe, not in kind but only in degree of development, and an intelligent study of the human species must be preceded by an extended knowledge of other mammals, especially the primates. Instead of such essential training, anthropologists often seek to qualify by research in linguistics, religion, or marriage customs, or in designs of pottery or blanket weaving, all of which relate to ethnology alone.

The question of race has been further complicated by the effort of old-fashioned theologians to cramp all mankind into the scant six thousand years of Hebrew chronology, as expounded by Archbishop Ussher. Religious teachers have also maintained the proposition not only that man is something fundamentally distinct from other living creatures, but that there are no inherited differences in humanity that cannot be obliterated by education and environment.

It is, therefore, necessary at the outset for the reader to thoroughly appreciate that race, language, and nationality are three separate and distinct things, and that in Europe these three elements are only occasionally found persisting in combination, as in the Scandinavian nations.

To realize the transitory nature of political boundaries, one has only to consider the changes of the past century, to say nothing of those which may occur at the end of the present war. As to language, here in America we daily hear the English language spoken by many men who possess not one drop of English blood, and who, a few years since, knew not one word of Saxon speech.

As a result of certain religious and social doctrines, now happily becoming obsolete, race consciousness has been greatly impaired among civilized nations, but in the beginning all differences of class, of caste, and of color, marked actual lines of race cleavage.

In many countries the existing classes represent races that were once distinct. In the city of New York, and elsewhere in the United States, there is a native American aristocracy resting upon layer after layer of immigrants of lower races, and the native American, while, of course, disclaiming the distinction of a patrician class, nevertheless has, up to this time, supplied the leaders of thought and the control of capital, of education, and of the religious ideals and altruistic bias of the community.

In the democratic forms of government the operation of universal suffrage tends toward the selection of the average man for public office rather than the man qualified by birth, education, and integrity. How this scheme of administration will ultimately work out remains to be seen, but from a racial point of view, it will inevitably increase the preponderance of the lower types and cause a corresponding loss of efficiency in the community as a whole.

The tendency in a democracy is toward a standardization of type and a diminution of the influence of genius. A majority must of necessity be inferior to a picked minority, and it always resents specializations in which it cannot share. In the French Revolution the majority, calling itself "the people," deliberately endeavored to destroy the higher type, and something of the same sort was, in a measure, done after the American Revolution by the expulsion of the Loyalists and the confiscation of their lands.

In America we have nearly succeeded in destroying the privilege of birth; that is, the intellectual and moral advantage a man of good stock brings into the world with him. We are now engaged in destroying the privilege of wealth; that is, the reward of successful intelligence and industry, and in some quarters there is developing a tendency to attack the privilege of intellect and to deprive a man of the advantages of an early and thorough education. Simplified spelling is a step in this direction. Ignorance of English grammar or classic learning must not be held up as a reproach to the political and social aspirant.

Mankind emerged from savagery and barbarism under the leadership of selected individuals whose personal prowess, capacity, or wisdom gave them the right to lead and the power to compel obedience. Such leaders have always been a minute fraction of the whole, but as long as the tradition of their predominance persisted they were able to use the brute strength of the unthinking herd as part of their own force, and were able to direct at will the blind dynamic impulse of the slaves, peasants, or lower classes. Such a despot had an enormous power at this disposal which, if he were benevolent or even intelligent, could be used, and most frequently was used, for the general uplift of the race. Even those rulers who most abused this power put down with merciless rigor the antisocial elements, such as pirates, brigands, or anarchists, which impair the progress of a community, as disease or wounds cripple an individual.

True aristocracy is government by the wisest and best, always a small minority in any population. Human society is like a serpent dragging its long body on the ground, but with the head always thrust a little in advance and a little elevated above the earth. The serpent's tail, in human society represented by the antisocial forces, was in the past dragged by sheer force along the path of progress. Such has been the organization of mankind from the beginning, and such it still is in older communities than ours. What progress humanity can make under the control of universal suffrage, or the rule of the average, may find a further analogy in the habits of certain snakes which wiggle sideways and disregard the head with its brains and eyes. Such serpents, however, are not noted for their ability to make rapid progress.

To use another simile, in an aristocratic as distinguished from a plutocratic, or democratic organization, the intellectual and talented classes form the point of the lance, while the massive shaft represents the body of the population and adds by its bulk and weight to the penetrative impact of the tip. In a democratic system this concentrated force at the top is dispersed throughout the mass, supplying, to be sure, a certain amount of leaven, but in the long run the force and genius of the small minority is dissipated, if not wholly lost. *Vox populi,* so far from being *Vox Dei,* thus becomes an unending wail for rights, and never a chant of duty.

Where a conquering race is imposed on another race the institution of slavery often arises to compel the servient race to work, and to introduce it forcibly to a higher form of civilization. As soon as men can be induced to labor to supply their own needs slavery becomes wasteful and tends to vanish. Slaves are often more fortunate than freemen when treated with reasonable humanity, and when their elemental wants of food, clothing, and shelter are supplied. . . .

The continuity of physical traits and the limitation of the effects of environment to the individual only are now so throroughly recognized by scientists that it is at most a question of time when the social consequences which result from such crossings will be generally understood by the public at large. As soon as the true bearing and import of the facts are appreciated by lawmakers, a complete change in our political structure will inevitably occur, and our present reliance on the influences of education will be superseded by a readjustment based on racial values.

Bearing in mind the extreme antiquity of physical and spiritual characters and the persistency with which they outlive those elements of environment termed language, nationality, and forms of government, we must consider the relation of these facts to the development of the race in America. We may be certain that the progress of evolution is in full operation to-day under those laws of nature which control it, and that the only sure guide to the future lies in the study of the operation of these laws in the past.

We Americans must realize that the altruistic ideals which have controlled our social development during the past century, and the maudlin sentimentalism that has made America "an asylum for the oppressed," are sweeping the nation toward a racial abyss. If the Melting Pot is allowed to boil without control, and we continue to follow our national motto and deliberately blind ourselves to all "distinctions of race, creed, or color," the type of native American of Colonial descent will become as extinct as the Athenian of the age of Pericles, and the Viking of the days of Rollo.

The Promised Land

MARY ANTIN

The public school has done its best for us foreigners, and for the country, when it has made us into good Americans. I am glad it is mine to tell how the miracle was wrought in one case. You should be glad to hear of it, you born Americans; for it is the story of the growth of your country; of the flocking of your brothers and sisters from the far ends of the earth to the flag you love; of the recruiting of your armies of workers, thinkers, and leaders. And you will be glad to hear of it, my comrades in adoption; for it is a rehearsal of your own experience, the thrill and wonder of which your own hearts have felt.

How long would you say, wise reader, it takes to make an American? By the middle of my second year in school I had reached the sixth grade. When, after the Christmas holidays, we began to study the life of Washington, running through a summary of the Revolution, and the early days of the Republic, it seemed to me that all my reading and study had been idle until then. The reader, the arithmetic, the song book, that had so fascinated me until now, became suddenly sober exercise books, tools wherewith to hew a way to the source of inspiration. When the teacher

Mary Antin, *The Promised Land* (Boston: Houghton Mifflin Company, 1912), pp. 222–228.

read to us out of a big book with many bookmarks in it, I sat rigid with attention in my little chair, my hands tightly clasped on the edge of my desk; and I painfully held my breath, to prevent sighs of disappointment escaping, as I saw the teacher skip the parts between bookmarks. When the class read, and it came my turn, my voice shook and the book trembled in my hands. I could not pronounce the name of George Washington without a pause. Never had I prayed, never had I chanted the songs of David, never had I called upon the Most Holy, in such utter reverence and worship as I repeated the simple sentences of my child's story of the patriot. I gazed with adoration at the portraits of George and Martha Washington, till I could see them with my eyes shut. And whereas formerly my self-consciousness had bordered on conceit, and I thought myself an uncommon person, parading my schoolbooks through the streets, and swelling with pride when a teacher detained me in conversation, now I grew humble all at once, seeing how insignificant I was beside the Great.

As I read about the noble boy who would not tell a lie to save himself from punishment, I was for the first time truly repentant of my sins. Formerly I had fasted and prayed and made sacrifice on the Day of Atonement, but it was more than half play, in mimicry of my elders. I had no real horror of sin, and I knew so many ways of escaping punishment. I am sure my family, my neighbors, my teachers in Polotzk—all my world, in fact—strove together, by example and precept, to teach me goodness. Saintliness had a new incarnation in about every third person I knew. I did respect the saints, but I could not help seeing that most of them were a little bit stupid, and that mischief was much more fun than piety. Goodness, as I had known it, was respectable, but not necessarily admirable. The people I really admired, like my Uncle Solomon, and Cousin Rachel, were those who preached the least and laughed the most. My sister Frieda was perfectly good, but she did not think the less of me because I played tricks. What is loved in my friends was not inimitable. One could be downright good if one really wanted to. One could be learned if one had books and teachers. One could sing funny songs and tell anecdotes if one travelled about and picked up such things, like one's uncles and cousins. But a human being strictly good, perfectly wise, and unfailingly valiant, all at the same time, I had never heard or dreamed of. This wonderful George Washington was as inimitable as he was irreproachable. Even if I had never, never told a lie, I could not compare myself to George Washington; for I was not brave— I was afraid to go out when snowballs whizzed—and I could never be the First President of the United States.

So I was forced to revise my own estimate of myself. But the twin of my new-born humility, paradoxical as it may seem, was a sense of dignity I had never known before. For if I found that I was a person of small consequence, I discovered at the same time that I was more nobly related than I had ever supposed. I had relatives and friends who were notable people by the old standards,—I had never been ashamed of my family,—but this George Washington, who died long before I was born, was like a king in greatness, and he and I were Fellow Citizens. There was a great deal about Fellow Citizens in the patriotic literature we read at this time; and I knew from my father how he was a Citizen, through the process of naturalization, and how I also was a citizen, by virtue of my relation to him. Undoubtedly I was a Fellow Citizen, and George Washington was another. It thrilled me to realize what sudden greatness had fallen on me; and at the same time it sobered me, as with a sense of responsibility. I strove to conduct myself as befitted a Fellow Citizen.

Before books came into my life, I was given to stargazing and daydreaming. When books were given me, I fell upon them as a glutton pounces on his meat after a period of enforced starvation. I lived with my nose in a book, and took no notice of the alternations of the sun and stars. But now, after the advent of George Washington and the American Revolution, I began to dream again. I strayed on the common after school instead of hurrying home to read. I hung on fence rails, my pet book forgotten under my arm, and gazed off to the yellow-streaked February sunset, and beyond, and beyond. I was no longer the central figure of my dreams; the dry weeds in the lane crackled beneath the tread of Heroes.

What more could America give a child? Ah, much more! As I read how the patriots planned the Revolution, and the women gave their sons to die in battle, and the heroes led to victory, and the rejoicing people set up the Republic, it dawned on me gradually what was meant by *my country*. The people all desiring noble things, and striving for them together, defying their oppressors, giving their lives for each other—all this it was that made *my country*. It was not a thing that I *understood;* I could not go home and tell Frieda about it, as I told her other things I learned at school. But I knew one could say "my country" and *feel* it, as one felt "God" or "myself." My teacher, my schoolmates, Miss Dillingham, George Washington himself could not mean more than I when they said "my country," after I had once felt it. For the Country was for all the Citizens, and *I was a Citizen*. And when we stood up to sing "America," I shouted the words with all my might. I was in very earnest proclaiming to the world my love for my new-found country.

I love thy rocks and rills,
Thy woods and templed hills.

Boston Harbor, Crescent Beach, Chelsea Square—all was hallowed ground to me. As the day approached when the school was to hold exercises in honor of Washington's Birthday, the halls resounded at all hours with the strains of patriotic songs; and I, who was a model of the attentive pupil, more than once lost my place in the lesson as I strained to hear, through closed doors, some neighboring class rehearsing "The Star-Spangled Banner." If the doors happened to open, and the chorus broke out unveiled—

O! say, does that Star-Spangled Banner yet wave
O'er the land of the free, and the home of the brave?—

delicious tremors ran up and down my spine, and I was faint with suppressed enthusiasm.

Where had been my country until now? What flag had I loved? What heroes had I worshipped? The very names of these things had been unknown to me. Well

I knew that Polotzk was not my country. It was *goluth*—exile. On many occasions in the year we prayed to God to lead us out of exile. The beautiful Passover service closed with the words, "Next year, may we be in Jerusalem." On childish lips, indeed, those words were no conscious aspiration; we repeated the Hebrew syllables after our elders, but without their hope and longing. Still not a child among us was too young to feel in his own flesh the lash of the oppressor. We knew what it was to be Jews in exile, from the spiteful treatment we suffered at the hands of the smallest urchin who crossed himself; and thence we knew that Israel had good reason to pray for deliverance. But the story of the Exodus was not history to me in the sense that the story of the American Revolution was. It was more like a glorious myth, a belief in which had the effect of cutting me off from the actual world, by linking me with a world of phantoms. Those moments of exaltation which the contemplation of the Biblical past afforded us, allowing us to call ourselves the children of princes, served but to tinge with a more poignant sense of disinheritance the long humdrum stretches of our life. In very truth we were a people without a country. Surrounded by mocking foes and detractors, it was difficult for me to realize the persons of my people's heroes or the events in which they moved. Except in moments of abstraction from the world around me, I scarcely understood that Jerusalem was an actual spot on the earth, where once the Kings of the Bible, real people, like my neighbors in Polotzk, ruled in puissant majesty. For the conditions of our civil life did not permit us to cultivate a spirit of nationalism. The freedom of worship that was grudgingly granted within the narrow limits of the Pale by no means included the right to set up openly any ideal of a Hebrew State, any hero other than the Czar. What we children picked up of our ancient political history was confused with the miraculous story of the Creation, with the supernatural legends and hazy associations of Bible lore. As to our future, we Jews in Polotzk had no national expectations; only a lifeworn dreamer here and there hoped to die in Palestine. If Fetchke and I sang, with my father, first making sure of our audience, "Zion, Zion, Holy Zion, not forever is it lost," we did not really picture to ourselves Judæa restored.

So it came to pass that we did not know what *my country* could mean to a man. And as we had no country, so we had no flag to love. It was by no farfetched symbolism that the banner of the House of Romanoff became the emblem of our latter-day bondage in our eyes. Even a child would know how to hate the flag that we were forced, on pain of severe penalties, to hoist above our housetops, in celebration of the advent of one of our oppressors. And as it was with country and flag, so it was with heroes of war. We hated the uniform of the soldier, to the last brass button. On the person of a Gentile, it was the symbol of tyranny; on the person of a Jew, it was the emblem of shame.

So a little Jewish girl in Polotzk was apt to grow up hungry-minded and empty-hearted; and if, still in her outreaching youth, she was set down in a land of outspoken patriotism, she was likely to love her new country with a great love, and to embrace its heroes in a great worship. Naturalization, with us Russian Jews, may mean more than the adoption of the immigrant by America. It may mean the adoption of America by the immigrant.

6.4:   Asian-American Immigration
(1882, 1908)

Nativist prejudices against immigrants in the 1920s were expressed in the passing of restrictive legislation that established quota systems based upon national origin. Such quotas enabled American authorities to distinguish between "desirable" and "less desirable" or "undesirable" immigrants, based upon their birthplace. Long before Europeans were affected in this way, however, official U.S. policy aimed at controlling the influx of another group of immigrants—Asians. The Chinese Exclusion Act of 1882 and The Gentlemen's Agreement with Japan in 1908 both sought to curtail the flow of Asians into the United States. What native prejudices against Asians are displayed in these documents? To what extent do these seem related to race or class? Both documents were outgrowths of foreign policy negotiations. Why is this disturbing?

The Chinese Exclusion Act, May 6, 1882

An act to execute certain treaty stipulations relating to Chinese.

WHEREAS, in the opinion of the Government of the United States the coming of Chinese laborers to this country endangers the good order of certain localities within the territory thereof: Therefore,

Be it enacted, That from and after the expiration of ninety days next after the passage of this act, and until the expiration of ten years next after the passage of this act, the coming of Chinese laborers to the United States be. . . . suspended; and during such suspension it shall not be lawful for any Chinese laborer to come, or, having so come after the expiration of said ninety days, to remain within the United States.

SEC. 2. That the master of any vessel who shall knowingly bring within the United States on such vessel, and land or permit to be landed, any Chinese laborer, from any foreign port or place, shall be deemed guilty of a misdemeanor, and on conviction thereof shall be punished by a fine of not more than five hundred dollars for each and every such Chinese laborer so brought, and may be also imprisoned for a term not exceeding one year.

SEC. 3. That the two foregoing sections shall not apply to Chinese laborers who were in the United States on the seventeenth day of November, eighteen hundred and eighty, or who shall have come into the same before the expiration of ninety days next after the passage of this act, . . .

SEC. 6. That in order to the faithful execution of articles one and two of the treaty in this act before mentioned, every Chinese person other than a laborer who

The Chinese Exclusion Act, May 6, 1882 (*U.S. Statutes at Large,* vol. XXII, p. 58ff).

may be entitled by said treaty and this act to come within the United States, and who shall be about to come to the United States, shall be identified as so entitled by the Chinese Government in each case, such identity to be evidenced by a certificate issued under the authority of said government, which certificate shall be in the English language or (if not in the English language) accompanied by a translation into English, stating such right to come, and which certificate shall state the name, title, or official rank, if any, the age, height, and all physical peculiarities, former and present occupation or profession, and place of residence in China of the person to whom the certificate is issued and that such person is entitled conformably to the treaty in this act mentioned to come within the United States. . . .

SEC. 12. That no Chinese person shall be permitted to enter the United States by land without producing to the proper officer of customs the certificate in this act required of Chinese persons seeking to land from a vessel. And any Chinese person found unlawfully within the United States shall be caused to be removed therefrom to the country from whence he came, by direction of the President of the United States, and at the cost of the United States, after being brought before some justice, judge, or commissioner of a court of the United States and found to be one not lawfully entitled to be or remain in the United States.

SEC. 13. That this act shall not apply to diplomatic and other officers of the Chinese Government traveling upon the business of that government, whose credentials shall be taken as equivalent to the certificate in this act mentioned, and shall exempt them and their body and household servants from the provisions of this act as to other Chinese persons.

SEC. 14. That hereafter no State court or court of the United States shall admit Chinese to citizenship; and all laws in conflict with this act are hereby repealed.

SEC. 15. That the words "Chinese laborers," whenever used in this act, shall be construed to mean both skilled and unskilled laborers and Chinese employed in mining.

The Gentleman's Agreement, 1908

In order that the best results might follow from an enforcement of the regulations, an understanding was reached with Japan that the existing policy of discouraging emigration of its subjects of the laboring classes to continental United States should be continued, and should, by co-operation with the governments, be made as effective as possible. This understanding contemplates that the Japanese government shall issue passports to continental United States only to such of its subjects as are non-laborers or are laborers who, in coming to the continent, seek to resume a formerly acquired domicile, to join a parent, wife, or children residing there, or to assume active control of an already possessed interest in a farming enterprise in this country, so that the three classes of laborers entitled to receive passports have come

The Gentleman's Agreement with Japan of 1908. Quoted from *Report of the Commissioner General of Immigration,* 1908, p. 125.

to be designated "former residents," "parents, wives, or children of residents," and "settled agriculturists."

With respect to Hawaii, the Japanese government of its own volition stated that, experimentally at least, the issuance of passports to members of the laboring classes proceeding thence would be limited to "former residents" and "parents, wives, or children of residents." The said government has also been exercising a careful supervision over the subject of emigration of its laboring class to foreign contiguous territory.

☆ **7** ☆

World War I

In the summer of 1914 the great powers of Europe went to war. In a matter of weeks the armies and navies of two great coalitions, the Central Powers (Germany, Austria-Hungary, and later Turkey) and the Entente, or Allies (France, Great Britain, Russia, and later Italy), were locked in murderous combat in Europe and around the world.

For two and a half years the United States remained on the sidelines, the largest and most powerful neutral in a world at war. President Woodrow Wilson initially urged his compatriots to remain "impartial in thought as well as in action," but from the outset this proved impossible. Too many Americans were tied by sentiment or culture to one side or the other. Moreover, the United States, with its great industrial and financial resources, could not easily detach itself economically from Europe's confrontation.

Both sides sought to mold American policy for their own ends. The Allies saw the United States as a source of credit, supplies, and munitions and tried to insure free access to these resources. Beyond this, some Allied leaders hoped to draw the great American republic into the war as an actual military partner. The Central Powers also could not ignore the United States. Unable themselves to procure American goods through the Allied blockade and with no expectation of American alliance, they limited their goals to keeping the United States neutral and preventing the Allies from taking full advantage of America's financial, industrial, and military might.

Inevitably, America's relations with the belligerents were colored by disagreements over neutral rights in time of war. The Wilson administration defended the right of Americans under international law to trade a wide range of goods with whomever they wished, and to travel wherever and however they wished.

Neither the Allies nor Central Powers accepted America's broad definition of neutral rights, but the British and French benefited more from free trade with the United States than did the Germans and Austro-Hungarians, and so clashed with America less. Indeed, the Germans soon sought to block American trade with the Allies in the only way they could: by use of the U-boat, a torpedo-armed submarine that could sink without warning any merchant vessel suspected of carrying war material to the enemy. The tactic was often brutal. Crews and passengers could not be saved by the small, vulnerable U-boats and so often perished. To charges of inhumanity, the Germans responded that the Allied blockade of food to German civilians was as barbarous as submarine warfare.

Americans disagreed over which policies to pursue toward the warring powers during 1914–1917. Their views were affected by ethnicity, ideology, patriotism, politics, culture, material interest, and other considerations. These differing attitudes and the motives behind them are suggested in the documents that follow.

Eventually, intervention unleashed internationalist and idealistic feelings, much encouraged by Wilson's leadership. Wilson proposed that the nation assume a much larger role in world affairs, increasing its interest, commitments, and responsibilities. Patriotic sentiment supported the President while American soldiers fought in Europe during the last year of the war, but during the tense peace negotiations that followed, disillusionment and political impasse dashed the hopes of a new world order. Wilson's presidency ended in bitter stalemate over the Treaty of Versailles, which the United States never signed, and the nation once again returned to isolationism in the 1920s.

7.1: The Submarine Dimension (1915)

No belligerent action during World War I set off as explosive a response in the United States as did the German submarine campaign against Allied and neutral shipping. In February 1915 the German government announced that all merchant vessels, whether neutral or enemy, found in a broad zone surrounding the British Isles would be sunk on sight, even if this meant injury or death to crews and passengers. This "unrestricted" U-boat warfare violated the traditional usages of war, and the American government threatened to hold the Imperial German government "to a strict accountability" for any loss of American lives and property under the order. The first selection below is the note sent by Secretary of State William Jennings Bryan to the German government conveying the American position. In fact, Bryan correctly stated the normal practices of war, but the Germans felt they had no choice.

The second selection is the response of the German foreign minister, Gottlieb von Jagow, to the American protest against the sinking in May 1915 of the British passenger liner the Lusitania, *with the loss of 1,200 civilian lives, including 128 Americans. American opinion was outraged, and the attack had been almost universally condemned. But is it fair to see the Germans as barbarians, indifferent to human life? Does the German foreign minister make a convincing case for his country's use of the submarine weapon in the instances he describes? Why was the American government, do you suppose, so unsympathetic to German arguments? Was the American government ever willing, in later years, to limit the travel of its citizens in dangerous war zones?*

Protesting Unrestricted U-Boat Warfare

WILLIAM JENNINGS BRYAN

Washington, February 10, 1915

Please address a note immediately to the Imperial German Government to the following effect:

The Government of the United States, having had its attention directed to the proclamation of the German Admiralty issued on the 4th of February, . . . feels it to be its duty to call the attention of the Imperial German Government, with sincere respect and the most friendly sentiments but very candidly and earnestly, to the very serious possibilities of the course of action apparently contemplated under that proclamation.

The Government of the United States views those possibilities with such grave concern that it feels it to be its privilege, and indeed its duty in the circumstances, to request the Imperial German Government to consider before action is taken the critical situation in respect of the relations between this country and Germany which might arise were the German naval forces, in carrying out the policy foreshadowed in the Admiralty' proclamation, to destroy any merchant vessel of the United States or cause the death of American citizens.

It is of course not necessary to remind the German Government that the sole right of a belligerent in dealing with neutral vessels on the high seas is limited to visit and search, unless a blockade is proclaimed and effectively maintained, which this Government does not understand to be proposed in this case. To declare or exercise a right to attack and destroy any vessel entering a prescribed area of the high seas without first certainly determining its belligerent nationality and the contraband character of its cargo would be an act so unprecedented in naval warfare that this Gov-

[U.S. Department of State], *Papers Relating to the Foreign Relations of the United States, 1915. Supplement: The World War* (Washington: Government Printing Office, 1928), pp. 98–100.

ernment is reluctant to believe that the Imperial Government of Germany in this case contemplates it as possible. The suspicion that enemy ships are using neutral flags improperly can create no just presumption that all ships traversing a prescribed area are subject to the same suspicion. It is to determine exactly such questions that this Government understands the right of visit and search to have been recognized.

This Government has carefully noted the explanatory statement issued by the Imperial German Government at the same time with the proclamation of the German Admiralty, and takes this occasion to remind the Imperial German Government very respectfully that the Government of the United States is open to none of the criticisms for unneutral action to which the German Government believe the governments of certain other neutral nations have laid themselves open; that the Government of the United States has not consented to or acquiesced in any measures which may have been taken by the other belligerent nations in the present war which operate to restrain neutral trade, but has, on the contrary, taken in all such matters a position which warrants it in holding those governments responsible in the proper way for any untoward effects upon American shipping which the accepted principles of international law do not justify; and that it, therefore, regards itself as free in the present instance to take with a clear conscience and upon accepted principles the position indicated in this note.

If the commanders of German vessels of war should act upon the presumption that the flag of the United States was not being used in good faith and should destroy on the high seas an American vessel or the lives of American citizens, it would be difficult for the Government of the United States to view the act in any other light than as an indefensible violation of neutral rights which it would be very hard indeed to reconcile with the friendly relations now so happily subsisting between the two Governments.

If such a deplorable situation should arise, the Imperial German Government can readily appreciate that the Government of the United States would be constrained to hold the Imperial German Government to a strict accountability for such acts of their naval authorities and to take any steps it might be necessary to take to safeguard American lives and property and to secure to American citizens the full enjoyment of their acknowledged rights on the high seas.

The Government of the United States, in view of these considerations, which it urges with the greatest respect and with the sincere purpose of making sure that no misunderstanding may arise and no circumstance occur that might even cloud the intercourse of the two Governments, expresses the confident hope and expectation that the Imperial German Government can and will give assurance that American citizens and their vessels will not be molested by the naval forces of Germany otherwise than by visit and search, though their vessels may be traversing the sea area delimited in the proclamation of the German Admiralty.

It is added for the information of the Imperial Government that representations have been made to His Britannic Majesty's Government in respect to the unwarranted use of the American flag for the protection of British ships.

[Secretary of State William Jennings] Bryan

The Germans Defend Their Submarine Policy

GOTTLIEB VON JAGOW

Berlin, May 28, 1915

The Imperial Government has subjected the statements of the Government of the United States to a careful examination and has the lively wish on its part also to contribute in a convincing and friendly manner to clear up any misunderstandings which may have entered into the relations of the two Governments through the events mentioned by the American Government.

With regard firstly to the cases of the American steamers *Cushing* and *Gulflight,* the American Embassy has already been informed that it is far from the German Government to have any intention of ordering attacks by submarines or flyers on neutral vessels in the zone which have not been guilty of any hostile act; on the contrary, the most explicit instructions have been repeatedly given the German armed forces to avoid attacking such vessels. If neutral vessels have come to grief through the German submarine war during the past few months, by mistake, it is a question of isolated and exceptional cases which are traceable to the misuse of flags by the British Government in connection with carelessness or suspicious actions on the part of [the] captains of the vessels. In all cases where a neutral vessel through no fault of its own has come to grief through the German submarine or flyers according to the facts as ascertained by the German Government, this Government has expressed its regret at the unfortunate occurrence and promised indemnification where the facts justified it. The German Government will treat the cases of the American steamers *Cushing* and *Gulflight* according to the same principles. An investigation of these cases is in progress. Its results will be communicated to the Embassy shortly. The investigation might, if thought desirable, be supplemented by an international commission of inquiry, pursuant to Title III of the Hague Convention of October 18, 1907, for the pacific settlement of international disputes.

In the case of the sinking of the English steamer *Falaba,* the commander of the German submarine had the intention of allowing passengers and crew ample opportunity to save themselves. It was not until the captain disregarded the order to lay to and took to flight, sending up rocket signals for help, that the German commander ordered the crew and passengers by signals and megaphone to leave the ship within ten minutes. As a matter of fact he allowed them twenty-three minutes and did not fire the torpedo until suspicious steamers were hurrying to the aid of the *Falaba.*

With regard to the loss of life when the British passenger steamer *Lusitania* was sunk, the German Government has already expressed its deep regret to the neutral Governments concerned that nationals of those countries lost their lives on that occasion. The Imperial Government must state for the rest the impression that certain important facts most directly connected with the sinking of the *Lusitania* may have escaped the attention of the Government of the United States. It therefore considers

[U.S. Department of State]. *Papers Relating to the Foreign Relations of the United States, 1915. Supplement: The World War* (Washington: Government Printing Office, 1928), pp. 419–421.

it necessary in the interest of the clear and full understanding aimed at by either Government primarily to convince itself that the reports of the facts which are before the two Governments are complete and in agreement.

The Government of the United States proceeds on the assumption that the *Lusitania* is to be considered as an ordinary unarmed merchant vessel. The Imperial Government begs in this connection to point out that the *Lusitania* was one of the largest and fastest English commerce steamers, constructed with Government funds as auxiliary cruisers, and is expressly included in the navy list published by British Admiralty. It is moreover known to the Imperial Government from reliable information furnished by its officials and neutral passengers that for some time practically all the more valuable English merchant vessels have been provided with guns, ammunition, and other weapons, and reinforced with a crew specially practiced in manning guns. According to reports at hand here, the *Lusitania* when she left New York undoubtedly had guns on board which were mounted under decks and masked.

The Imperial Government furthermore has the honor to direct the particular attention of the American Government to the fact that the British Admiralty by a secret instruction of February of this year advised the British merchant marine not only to seek protection behind neutral flags and markings, but even when so disguised to attack German submarines by ramming them. High rewards have been offered by the British Government as a special incentive for the destruction of the submarines by merchant vessels, and such rewards have already been paid out. In view of these facts, which are satisfactorily known to it, the Imperial Government is unable to consider English merchant vessels any longer as "undefended territory" in the zone of maritime war designated by the Admiralty Staff of the Imperial German Navy, the German commanders are consequently no longer in a position to observe the rules of capture otherwise usual and with which they invariably complied before this. Lastly, the Imperial Government must specially point out that on her last trip the *Lusitania,* as on earlier occasions, had Canadian troops and munitions on board, including no less than 5,400 cases of ammunition destined for the destruction of brave German soldiers who are fulfilling with self-sacrifice and devotion their duty in the service of the Fatherland. The German Government believes that it acts in just self-defense when it seeks to protect the lives of its soldiers by destroying ammunition destined for the enemy with the means of war at its command. The English steamship company must have been aware of the dangers to which passengers on board the *Lusitania* were exposed under the circumstances. In taking them on board in spite of this the company quite deliberately tried to use the lives of American citizens as protection for the ammunition carried, and violated the clear provisions of American laws which expressly prohibit, and provide punishment for, the carrying of passengers on ships which have explosives on board. The company thereby wantonly caused the death of so many passengers. According to the express report of the submarine commander concerned, which is further confirmed by all other reports, there can be no doubt that the rapid sinking of the *Lusitania* was primarily due to the explosion of the cargo of ammunition caused by the torpedo. Otherwise, in all human probability, the passengers of the *Lusitania* would have been saved.

The Imperial Government holds the facts recited above to be of sufficient importance to recommend them to a careful examination by the American Government. The Imperial Government begs to reserve a final statement of its position with regard to the demand made in connection with the sinking of the *Lusitania* until a reply is received from the American Government.

[Foreign Minister Gottlieb] von Jagow

7.2:   Voices for Intervention (1915)

There was never any serious support in the United States for entering the war on the side of the Central Powers. But from the beginning some Americans sought to align the United States militarily with Britain and France. There have been many explanations for this tilt to the Allies. Below are three contemporary documents that suggest reasons for American sympathy for the Allied side and for the military support for Britain and France America finally provided.

The first is an excerpt from the Bryce Report of 1915, a British indictment of German behavior toward civilians in the German-occupied regions of France and Belgium. James Bryce, chief author of the report, was the former British ambassador to the United States, a respected figure who had written a famous book about America a generation before.

The Bryce Report was part of a concerted Allied propaganda campaign to influence American public opinion. Do the statements of the report ring true? Is it clear that the brutality against civilians described was deliberate German policy? How do Bryce and his colleagues link the Belgian and French atrocities to German, or "Prussian," militarism?

The second item is a memo from the private papers of Robert Lansing, the man who succeeded William Jennings Bryan as secretary of state in 1915. Although he represented an officially neutral nation, clearly Lansing himself was not neutral. What were the bases for his pro-Allies feelings? Were they shared by other influential Americans? Were his views of German policies and goals valid?

The third selection is a letter by Lansing to President Wilson on the issue of extending financial credits to the Allies to allow them to continue to buy American munitions and other war supplies. Earlier, in 1914, the American government had sought to discourage American loans to any of the belligerents as an unneutral act. Lansing's proposal represents a retreat from that policy. By April 1917 U.S. investors had bought $2.3 billion of Allied bonds.

Critics of American intervention in World War I have said that the liberal loan policy of the Wilson administration created an economic stake in Allied victory that powerfully influenced American policy. What were Lansing's reasons for wanting to liberalize American loan policies? Are his arguments convincing? Did America have an economic stake in the Allied cause and was this a significance factor in drawing the United States into the war in 1917?

British Report on German Atrocities in Belgium

AMBASSADOR JAMES BRYCE

In the minds of Prussian officers War seems to have become a sort of sacred mission, one of the highest functions of the omnipotent State, which is itself as much an Army as a State. Ordinary morality and the ordinary sentiment of pity vanish in its presence, superseded by a new standard which justifies to the soldier every means that can conduce to success, however shocking to a natural sense of justice and humanity, however revolting to his own feelings. The Spirit of War is deified. Obedience to the State and its War Lord leaves no room for any other duty or feeling. Cruelty becomes legitimate when it promises victory. Proclaimed by the heads of the army, this doctrine would seem to have permeated the officers and affected even the private soldiers, leading them to justify the killing of non-combatants as an act of war, and so accustoming them to slaughter that even women and children become at last the victims. It cannot be supposed to be a national doctrine, for it neither springs from nor reflects the mind and feelings of the German people as they have heretofore been known to other nations. It is a specifically military doctrine, the outcome of a theory held by a ruling caste who have brooded and thought, written and talked and dreamed about War until they have fallen under its obsession and been hypnotised by its spirit.

The doctrine is plainly set forth in the German Official Monograph on the usages of War on land, issued under the direction of the German staff. This book is pervaded throughout by the view that whatever military needs suggest becomes thereby lawful, and upon this principle, as the diaries show, the German officers acted. . . .

(a) Killing of Non-Combatants

The killing of civilians in Belgium has been already described sufficiently. Outrages on the civilian population of the invaded districts, the burning of villages, the shooting of innocent inhabitants and the taking of hostages, pillage and destruction continued as the German armies passed into France. . . .

Report of the Committee on Alleged German Outrages (London: His Majesty's Stationary Office, 1915), pp. 44–61.

(b) The Treatment of Women and Children

The evidence shows that the German authorities, when carrying out a policy of systematic arson and plunder in selected districts, usually drew some distinction between the adult male population on the one hand and the women and children on the other. It was a frequent practice to set apart the adult males of the condemned district with a view to the execution of a suitable number—preferably of the younger and more vigorous—and to reserve the women and children. . . .

We find many well-established cases of the slaughter (often accompanied by mutilation) of whole families, including not infrequently that of quite small children. In two cases it seems to be clear that preparations were made to burn a family alive. These crimes were committed over a period of many weeks and simultaneously in many places, and the authorities must have known or ought to have known that cruelties of this character were being perpetrated, nor can anyone doubt that they could have been stopped by swift and decisive action on the part of the heads of the German army. . . .

Whatever excuse may be offered by the Germans for the killing of grown-up women, there can be no possible defence for the murder of children, and if it can be shown that infants and small children were not infrequently bayoneted and shot it is a fair inference that many of the offences against women require no explanation more recondite than the unbridled violence of brutal or drunken criminals. . . .

Conclusions

From the foregoing pages it will be seen that the Committee have come to a definite conclusion upon each of the heads under which the evidence has been classified.

It is proved—

i. That there were in many parts of Belgium deliberate and systematically organised massacres of civil population, accompanied by many isolated murders and other outrages.
ii. That in the conduct of the war generally innocent civilians, both men and women, were murdered in large numbers, women violated, and children murdered.
iii. That looting, house burning, and the wanton destruction of property were ordered and countenanced by the officers of the German Army, that elaborate provision had been made for systematic incendiarism at the very outbreak of the war, and that the burnings and destruction were frequent where no military necessity could be alleged, being indeed part of a system of general terrorization.
iv. That the rules and usages of war were frequently broken, particularly by the using of civilians, including women and children, as a shield for advancing forces exposed to fire, to a less degree by killing the wounded and prisoners, and in the frequent abuse of the Red Cross and the White Flag.

Sensible as they are of the gravity of these conclusions, the Committee conceive that they would be doing less than their duty if they failed to record them as fully established by the evidence. Murder, lust, and pillage prevailed over many parts of Belgium on a scale unparalleled in any war between civilised nations during the last three centuries.

Our function is ended when we have stated what the evidence establishes, but we may be permitted to express our belief that these disclosures will not have been made in vain if they touch and rouse the conscience of mankind, and we venture to hope that as soon as the present war is over, the nations of the world in council will consider what means can be provided and sanctions devised to prevent the recurrence of such horrors as our generation is now witnessing.

Germany Must Not Be Allowed to Win the War

ROBERT LANSING

July 11, 1915

I have come to the conclusion that the German Government is utterly hostile to all nations with democratic institutions because those who compose it see in democracy a menace to absolutism and the defeat of the German ambition for world domination. Everywhere German agents are plotting and intriguing to accomplish the supreme purpose of their Government.

Only recently has the conviction come that democracy throughout the world is threatened. Suspicions of the vaguest sort only a few months [ago] have been more and more confirmed. From many sources evidence has been coming until it would be folly to close one's eyes to it.

German agents have undoubtedly been at work in Mexico arousing anti-American feeling and holding out false hopes of support. The proof is not conclusive but is sufficient to compel belief. Germans also appear to be operating in Haiti and San Domingo and are probably doing so in other Latin American republics.

I think that this is being done so that this nation will have troubles in America and be unable to take part in the European War if a repetition of such outrages as the LUSITANIA sinking should require us to act. It may even go further and have in mind the possibility of a future war with this Republic in case the Allies should be defeated.

In these circumstances the policies we adopt are vital to the future of the United States and, I firmly believe to the welfare of mankind, for I see in the perpetuation of democracy the one hope of universal peace and progress for the world. Today German absolutism is the great menace to democracy.

I think that we should, therefore, adopt the following for the present and pursue these policies until conditions materially change:

1. The settlement for the time being at least of present submarine controversy because the American people are still much divided on the merits of the war. As it progresses, I believe, that the real objects of the German Government will be disclosed and there will be united opposition. Meanwhile we should get ready to meet the worst.

Private Memoranda Books, The Papers of Robert Lansing, Manuscripts Division, Library of Congress, Washington, DC.

2. A rigorous and continuing prosecution of all plots in this country and a vigilant watch on Germans and their activities here.
3. Secret investigations of German activities in Latin America, particularly Mexico, and the adoption of means to frustrate them.
4. The cultivations of a Pan American doctrine with the object of alienating the American republics from European influence, especially the German influence. . . .
5. The actual participation of this country in the war in case it becomes evident that Germany will be the victor. A triumph for Germany imperialism *must not be*. We ought to look forward to this possibility and make ready to meet it.

There is a future possibility which does not change the foregoing policies but which emphasizes the last one. It is that the war may end in a draw or with the German Empire dominant over their enemies.

The argument could then be made by the German Government that, in spite of the fact that the world was arrayed against it, it succeeded in preventing the defeat of the Empire, and that having thus proved its superior efficiency it should be continued and supported as the agency best fitted to restore the German nation to a state of prosperity.

I believe that this argument would be potent with the German people, who are in the habit of unquestioning obedience to their rulers in thought as well as action. Of course the terrible cost of the war, when the time to consider that arrives, will weaken the argument for the people will ask what is the recompense for the great sacrifices they have made, the great sufferings which they have endured, and the Government will have nothing to show. The nation may then rise and demand a change to a political system in which their voice will be supreme. But, if the argument should prevail and the present military oligarchy should be perpetuated, then what?

My judgment is that the German Government, cherishing the same ambition of world empire which now possesses it, would with its usual vigor and thoroughness prepare to renew its attack on democracy. I think, however, that it would not pursue the course taken in this war which had failed because it would realize that the democratic nations would be more watchful and less trustful and better prepared to resist. It would probably endeavor to sow dissentions [*sic*] among the nations with liberal institutions and seek an alliance with other governments based to a more or less degree on the principle of absolutism.

The two powers, which would probably be approached by Germany, would be Russia and Japan, which are almost as hostile to democracy as Germany and which have similar ambitions of territorial expansion.

These three great empires would constitute an almost irresistible [*sic*] coalition against the nations with republican and liberal monarchical institutions. It would be the old struggle of absolutism against democracy, an even greater struggle than the one now in progress. The outcome would be doubtful, with, as it seems to me, the chances in favor of the autocratic allies.

The success of these three empires would mean a division for the time being at least of the world among them. I imagine that Germany would be master of Western Europe, of Africa and probably of the Americas; that Russia would dominate Scandinavia, and Western and Southern Asia; and Japan would control the Far East, the Pacific and possibly the West Coast of North America.

Their success would mean the overthrow of democracy in the world, the suppression of individual liberty, the setting up of evil ambitions, the subordination of the principles of right and justice to physical might directed by arbitrary will, and the turning back of the hands of human progress two centuries.

These, I believe, would be the consequences of the triumph of this triple alliance of autocratic empires, a triumph which even the most optimistic cannot deny to be a reasonable expectation.

The remedy seems to me to be plain. It is that Germany must not be permitted to win this war and to break even, though to prevent it this country is forced to take an active part. This ultimate necessity must be constantly in our minds in all our controversies with the belligerents. American public opinion must be prepared for the time, which may come, when we will have to cast aside our neutrality and become one of the champions of democracy.

We must in fact risk everything rather than leave the way open for a new combination of powers, stronger and more dangerous to liberty than the Central Allies are today.

Lending the Allies Money

ROBERT LANSING

Washington, September 6, 1915

My dear Mr. President:

Doubtless Secretary [William] McAdoo has discussed with you the necessity of floating government loans for the belligerent nations, which are purchasing such great quantities of goods in this country, in order to avoid a serious financial situation which will not only affect them but this country as well.

Briefly, the situation, as I understand it, is this: Since December 1st, 1914, to June 30, 1915, our exports have exceeded our imports by nearly a billion dollars, and it is estimated that the excess will be from July 1st to December 31, 1915, a billion and three quarters. Thus for the year 1915 the excess will be approximately two and [a] half billions of dollars.

It is estimated that the European banks have about three and [a] half billions of dollars in gold in their vaults. To withdraw any considerable amount would disastrously affect the credit of the European nations, and the consequence would be a general state of bankruptcy.

If the European countries cannot find means to pay for the excess of goods sold to them over those purchased from them, they will have to stop buying and our present export trade will shrink proportionately. The result would be restriction of outputs, industrial depression, idle capital and idle labor, numerous failures, financial demoralization, and general unrest and suffering among the laboring classes.

Probably a billion and three quarters of the excess of European purchases can be taken care of by the sale of American securities held in Europe and by the transfer of trade balances of oriental countries, but that will leave three quarters of a billion to be met in some other way. Furthermore, even if that is arranged, we will have to face a more serious situation in January, 1916, as the American securities held abroad will have been exhausted.

I believe that Secretary McAdoo is convinced and I agree with him that there is only one means of avoiding this situation which would so seriously affect economic conditions in the country, and that is the flotation of large bond issues by the belligerent governments. Our financial institutions have the money to loan and wish to do so. On account of the great balance of trade in our favor the proceeds of these loans would be expended here. The result would be a maintenance of the credit of the borrowing nations based on their gold reserve, a continuance of our commerce at its present volume and industrial activity with the consequent employment of capital and labor and national prosperity. . . .

Manifestly the Government has committed itself to the policy of discouraging general loans to belligerent governments. The practical reasons for the policy at the time we adopted it were sound, but basing it on the ground that loans are "inconsistent with the true spirit of neutrality" is now a source of embarrassment. This latter ground is as strong today as it was a year ago, while the practical reasons for discouraging loans have largely disappeared. We have more money than we can use. Popular sympathy has become crystallized in favor of one or another of the belligerents to such an extent that the purchase of bonds would in no way increase the bitterness of partisanship or cause a possibly serious situation.

Now, on the other hand, we are face to face with what appears to be a critical economic situation, which can only be relieved apparently by the investment of American capital in foreign loans to be used in liquidating the enormous balance of trade in favor of the United States.

Can we afford to let a declaration as to our conception of "the true spirit of neutrality" made in the first days of the war stand in the way of our national interests which seem to be seriously threatened?

If we cannot afford to do this, how are we to explain away the declaration and maintain a semblance of consistency?

My opinion is that we ought to allow the loans to be made for our own good, and I have been seeking some means of harmonizing our policy, so unconditionally announced, with the flotation of general loans. As yet I have found no solution to the problem.

Secretary McAdoo considers that the situation is becoming acute and that something should be done at once to avoid the disastrous results which will follow a continuance of the present policy.

Faithfully yours,

Robert Lansing

7.3: Opponents of Intervention (1917)

From the outset several groups opposed American intervention in the European war. First there were the pacifists, whether members of "peace churches," like the Quakers and Mennonites, or adherents of various secular pacifist groups. Many Socialists also opposed U.S. intervention, although on political, not moral, grounds. Ethnic considerations also played a role in opposing going to war. Many German Americans and Irish Americans either favored the Central Powers or disliked the Allies. Finally, some midwestern Progressives were "isolationists" who denied that America had any vital interest in European affairs and urged their fellow citizens to steer clear of overseas entanglements.

The antiwar forces were unable to keep America neutral, however. Soon after the German government announced resumption of unrestricted U-boat warfare in early 1917, the United States declared war on the Central Powers. The first selection below is a statement issued by the Socialist Party of America in early April, several days after the U.S. war declaration, expressing their opposition to the war. What were the bases of the Socialist position? Were they consistent with Socialist analyses of the nature of contemporary society? From this statement, can you deduce the Socialist attitude toward national loyalty and traditional patriotism?

The second selection is an excerpt from Wisconsin Senator Robert La Follette's remarks during the war-declaration debate in Congress. It is representative of the views of many midwestern Progressives. What is La Follette's analysis of the origins of the war? How does it differ from that of the Socialists? How does his analysis influence his view of the war's justice? Do his remarks betray national biases and prejudices? La Follette's own state, Wisconsin, was home to a very large German American population. Could the senator's views have been colored by that fact?

Socialist Party Convention: The Socialists Protest the War

The Socialist Party and the War[1]

The Socialist Party of the United States in the present grave crisis, solemnly reaffirms its allegiance to the principle of internationalism and working class solidarity the world over, and proclaims its unalterable opposition to the war just declared by the government of the United States.

The American Labor Yearbook, vol. 2 (1917–18), pp. 50–52.

[1]Majority report adopted at the St. Louis Convention of the Socialist Party, April 7–14, 1917, and ratified by referendum.

Modern wars as a rule have been caused by the commercial and financial rivalry and intrigues of the capitalist interests in the different countries. Whether they have been frankly waged as wars of aggression or have been hypocritically represented as wars of "defense," they have always been made by the classes and fought by the masses. Wars bring wealth and power to the ruling classes, and suffering, death and demoralization to the workers.

They breed a sinister spirit of passion, unreason, race hatred and false patriotism. They obscure the struggles of the workers for life, liberty and social justice. They tend to sever the vital bonds of solidarity between them and their brothers in other countries, to destroy their organizations and to curtail their civic and political rights and liberties.

The Socialist Party of the United States is unalterably opposed to the system of exploitation and class rule which is upheld and strengthened by military power and sham national patriotism. We, therefore, call upon the workers of all countries to refuse support to their governments in their wars. The wars of the contending national groups of capitalists are not the concern of the workers. The only struggle which would justify the workers in taking up arms is the great struggle of the working class of the world to free itself from economic exploitation and political oppression, and we particularly warn the workers against the snare and delusion of so-called defensive warfare. As against the false doctrine of national patriotism we uphold the ideal of international working-class solidarity. In support of capitalism, we will not willingly give a single life or a single dollar; in support of the struggle of the workers for freedom we pledge our all.

The mad orgy of death and destruction which is now convulsing unfortunate Europe was caused by the conflict of capitalist interests in the European countries.

In each of these countries, the workers were oppressed and exploited. They produced enormous wealth but the bulk of it was withheld from them by the owners of the industries. The workers were thus deprived of the means to repurchase the wealth which they themselves had created.

The capitalist class of each country was forced to look for foreign markets to dispose of the accumulated "surplus" wealth. The huge profits made by the capitalists could no longer be profitably reinvested in their own countries, hence, they were driven to look for foreign fields of investment. The geographical boundaries of each modern capitalist country thus became too narrow for the industrial and commercial operations of its capitalist class.

The efforts of the capitalists of all leading nations were therefore centered upon the domination of the world markets. Imperialism became the dominant note in the politics of Europe. The acquisition of colonial possessions and the extension of spheres of commercial and political influence became the object of diplomatic intrigues and the cause of constant clashes between nations.

The acute competition between the capitalist powers of the earth, their jealousies and distrusts of one another and the fear of the rising power of the working class forced each of them to arm to the teeth. This led to the mad rivalry of armament, which, years before the outbreak of the present war, had turned the leading countries of Europe into armed camps with standing armies of many millions, drilled and equipped for war in times of "peace."

Capitalism, imperialism and militarism had thus laid the foundation of an inevitable general conflict in Europe. The ghastly war in Europe was not caused by an accidental event, nor by the policy or institutions of any single nation. It was the logical outcome of the competitive capitalist system.

The six million men of all countries and races who have been ruthlessly slain in the first thirty months of this war, the millions of others who have been crippled and maimed, the vast treasures of wealth that have been destroyed, the untold misery and sufferings of Europe, have not been sacrifices exacted in a struggle for principles or ideals, but wanton offerings upon the altar of private profit.

The forces of capitalism which have led to the war in Europe are even more hideously transparent in the war recently provoked by the ruling class of this country.

When Belgium was invaded, the government enjoined upon the people of this country the duty of remaining neutral, thus clearly demonstrating that the "dictates of humanity," and the fate of small nations and of democratic institutions were matters that did not concern it. But when our enormous war traffic was seriously threatened, our government calls upon us to rally to the "defense of democracy and civilization."

Our entrance into the European war was instigated by the predatory capitalists in the United States who boast of the enormous profit of seven billion dollars from the manufacture and sale of munitions and war supplies and from the exportation of American food stuffs and other necessaries. They are also deeply interested in the continuance of war and the success of the allied arms through their huge loans to the governments of the allied powers and through other commercial ties. It is the same interests which strive for imperialistic domination of the Western Hemisphere.

The war of the United States against Germany cannot be justified even on the plea that it is a war in defense of American rights or American "honor." Ruthless as the unrestricted submarine war policy of the German government was and is, it is not an invasion of the rights of the American people, as such, but only an interference with the opportunity of certain groups of American capitalists to coin cold profits out of the blood and sufferings of our fellow men in the warring countries of Europe.

It is not a war against the militarist regime of the Central Powers. Militarism can never be abolished by militarism.

It is not a war to advance the cause of democracy in Europe. Democracy can never be imposed upon any country by a foreign power by force of arms.

It is cant and hypocrisy to say that the war is not directed against the German people, but against the Imperial Government of Germany. If we send an armed force to the battlefields of Europe, its cannont will mow down the masses of the German people and not the Imperial German Government.

Our entrance into the European conflict at this time will serve only to multiply the horrors of the war, to increase the toll of death and destruction and to prolong the fiendish slaughter. It will bring death, suffering and destitution to the people of the United States and particularly to the working class. It will give the powers of reaction in this country the pretext for an attempt to throttle our rights and to crush our democratic institutions, and to fasten upon this country a permanent militarism.

The working class of the United States has no quarrel with the working class of Germany or of any other country. The people of the United States have no quarrel with the people of Germany or any other country. The American people did not want and do not want this war. They have not been consulted about the war and have had no part in declaring war. They have been plunged into this war by the trickery and treachery of the ruling class of the country through its representatives in the National Administration and National Congress, its demagogic agitators, its subsidized press, and other servile instruments of public expression.

We brand the declaration of war by our government as a crime against the people of the United States and against the nations of the world.

In all modern history there has been no war more unjustifiable than the war in which we are about to engage.

No greater dishonor has ever been forced upon a people than that which the capitalist class is forcing upon this nation against its will.

A Progressive Opposes the Declaration of War

ROBERT LA FOLLETTE

Mr. LA FOLLETTE.   Mr. Chairman, when history records the truth about this awful act we are about to commit here, which means the maiming and dismembering of thousands of our noble boys and the deaths of thousands more, it will record that the Congress of the United States made this declaration of war under a misapprehension of the facts inexcusable in itself and that the people at large acquiesced in it on the theory that the Congress should have the facts, and would not make a declaration of war not justified by every rule of equity and fair dealing between nations, impartially applied by this country to all belligerents, and that after our following that course one of these contesting nations, despite our impartial action, had wantonly destroyed our legitimate commerce and destroyed the lives of some of our people.

I say the people acquiesce in our actions here to-day on exactly that false assumption of the facts. We have not treated, as a Government, these belligerents with any degree of impartiality; but, on the contrary, have demanded of one of them absolute obedience to our ideas and interpretations of international law, and have allowed at least one of the other belligerents to override at will the established rules and practice of all the civilized nations of the world for a hundred years with but feeble protest, and, in many cases, with no protest at all.

We surrendered to Great Britain practically all we contested for in the War of 1812. It is true, as far as we know, that she has not impressed our seamen, but she has seized and appropriated to her own use entire cargoes and the ships that carried them. Not carriers in European trade, but carriers to South America.

One of the underlying causes of the awful holocaust in Europe was because Germany had by her systematized reductions in cost of manufacturing, by subsidization of transportation lines and methods of credits made such serious inroads on Great

Congressional Record, 65th Cong., 1st sess. (1917), pp. 371–372.

Britain's trade in South America as to seriously disturb her equanimity and threaten her prestige as well as attendant profits.

Mr. Chairman, this war now devastating Europe so ruthlessly is not a war of humanity, but a war of commercialism, and there is not a student of economic conditions within the sound of my voice but knows that to be the fundamental cause of that war, although there are many primary and intermediate questions entering into it. . . .

The President of the United States in his message of the 2d of April [1917] said that the European war was brought on by Germany's rulers without the sanction or will of the people. For God's sake, what are we doing now? Does the President of the United States feel that the will of the American people is being consulted in regard to this declaration of war? The people of Germany surely had as much consideration as he has given the people of the United States. He has heard the cry of the Shylocks calling for their pound of flesh; later on he will hear the cry of Rachel weeping for her children and mourning because they are not, sacrificed to make good the pound of flesh in the name of liberty. The exclamation "O Liberty! Liberty! how many crimes are committed in thy name!" was well made.

Ours is the greatest Nation on the face of the globe. We have had a chance, if we had maintained a strict neutrality, to have bound up the wounds of the oppressed and to have upheld the tenets of the highest civilization throughout the world. But, no; we are asked to go into partnership with the country that has never allowed justice and right to have any weight with her when conquest and gold were placed in the balance. In India, which she held by right of conquest, as a punishment to those natives of that country who desired to be free of England's yoke and rebelled, even as did we in our Revolutionary period, she mercifully tied many of the rebels to the mouths of her cannon and humanely blew them to atoms as a sample of English Christianity. She destroyed the Boer Republic by intrigue and force of arms; she forced, for love of gold, the opium trade on China. Christian England, our would-be partner! In the Napoleonic wars she, by force of arms, confiscated the entire shipping of small but neutral nations to her own use, just as she has in a smaller degree appropriated ships of our citizens to her own use within the past two years. During the Civil War she fell over herself to recognize the Confederacy, and gave it every encouragement possible. Now we are asked to become her faithful ally against a country that, whatever her faults, surely has no blacker record than that of Christian England; to contribute our money and our people in the holy name of liberty to destroy one belligerent, which the President designates as Prussian militarism, a menace of the world; but English navalism, which is surely as great a menace, we enter into partnership with. George Washington said, "Avoid European entanglements," but we are recklessly entering a path to the end of which no man can foresee or comprehend, at the behest of, in many cases, a venal press and of a pacifist President.

God pity our country, gentlemen of the House of Representatives, if you desire that this cup be placed to our country's lips to quaff for crimes committed by a country for unneutral actions and that we enter into an alliance with another country which has been much less neutral. You may do so; I can not so vote at this time. . . .

Mr. Chairman, throughout the country patriotic meetings are being held to encourage enlistments of our young men and boys into the Army to engage in this war in advance of our declaration.

Mr. Chairman, I suggest a resolution, which should be passed and adhered to by the young men of our country and by our soldiers who are asked to enter the trenches of Europe:

"I hereby pledge myself to the service of my country and will guarantee to go and uphold its honor and its flag as soon as the sons of all the newspaper editors who have stood out for our entering the war, and who are of age for enlistment, have enlisted for the cause and the proprietors and editors themselves have patriotically enlisted, on the theory that they should feel it their duty to do so as instigators of the act."

Likewise, Mr. Chairman, the sons of manufacturers of ammunition and war supplies, and all stockholders making profits from such trade. They should freely offer their sons on the altar of their country and, in case of their being under military age, go themselves. Likewise, Mr. Chairman, the J. Pierpont Morgans and their associates, who have floated war loans running into millions which they now want the United States to guarantee by entering the European war; after they and all the holders of such securities have offered their sons and themselves, when of military age, on the altar of their country, and, Mr. Chairman, when the above-mentioned persons have no sons and are too old themselves to accept military service, then they shall, to make good their desire for the upholding of American honor and American rights, donate in lieu of such service of selves or sons one-half of all their worldly goods to make good their patriotic desire for our entering the European war in the name of liberty and patriotism.

Mr. Chairman, it will be fitting for those who have really nothing at stake in this war but death to enter into it and give their lives in the name of liberty and patriotism, after the persons covered by the above resolution have done their part as above suggested and many thousands of our citizens will see it that way ere long.

7.4:   Idealism and Disillusionment (1918, 1920)

Once the war ended, Woodrow Wilson quickly became preoccupied with the establishment of a new world order. America's military role at the end of the war had been small but significant, and it soon became apparent that America's economic role in the postwar world would be great. Wilson, like most Americans, held the institutions of Europe as largely responsible for the tragedy of World War I—monarchies that rarely extended political power to the masses and economic imperialism that ensured hostility and rivalry among nations. If corrupt diplomatic practices like secret treaties could be replaced by international law that would guarantee such rights as freedom of the seas, peace might have a chance. If the great autocratic and imperial political machines of the world loosened their grip, and individual peoples were each allowed national self-determination, then peace might have a chance. To replace Europe's sagging imperial structures and their inevitable rivalries, Wilson proposed a new scheme of international law to be called the League of Nations.

Wilson's philosophy was concisely defined in "The Fourteen Points" and permeated his thinking and diplomatic activity throughout the last three years of his presidency. The Fourteen Points have often been assailed as too idealistic to have been successful and full of basically unresolvable, inherent contradictions. Although the U.S. Senate never ratified the peace treaty that ended World War I, and the United States never joined the League of Nations that Wilson had worked so hard to establish, many of the main principles of "The Fourteen Points" found their way into the mainstream of American thinking on foreign policy years later.

Are "The Fourteen Points" an idealistic proclamation that should have been dismissed as mere rhetoric or propaganda? Did they have an economic component? Did Wilson have a legitimate point in saying that a war would remain inevitable if the institutions of Europe did not change? Most of all, how do "The Fourteen Points" reflect America's emerging role as a global economic and political force, and how, if implemented, would American interests have been served by them? Finally, although America retreated into isolationism in the 1920s and 1930s, how did the principles of Wilsonian idealism prove prophetic?

Finally, in evaluating the Senate's refusal to ratify the treaty unamended, yet another controversy was created. Did Wilson overstep the bounds of presidential authority by negotiating such a treaty without Congressional approval? Or did Wilson behave irrationally by refusing to sign an amended version that was acceptable to the Senate? Compare the Senate Resolution ratifying the treaty to "The Fourteen Points" and ask if the differences between the two are substantive or cosmetic.

The Fourteen Points
Wilson's Address to Congress, January 8, 1918

Gentlemen of the Congress:

. . . It will be our wish and purpose that the processes of peace, when they are begun, shall be absolutely open and that they shall involve and permit henceforth no secret understandings of any kind. The day of conquest and aggrandizement is gone

Wilson's Address to Congress, January 8, 1918. Quoted from *Supplement to the Messages and Papers of the Presidents Covering the Second Administration of Woodrow Wilson*, p. 8421 ff. Washington, D.C: United States Government Printing Office.

by; so is also the day of secret covenants entered into in the interest of particular governments and likely at some unlooked-for moment to upset the peace of the world. It is this happy fact, now clear to the view of every public man whose thoughts do not still linger in an age that is dead and gone, which makes it possible for every nation whose purposes are consistent with justice and the peace of the world to avow now or at any other time the objects it has in view.

We entered this war because violations of right had occurred which touched us to the quick and made the life of our own people impossible unless they were corrected and the world secured once for all against their recurrence. What we demand in this war, therefore, is nothing peculiar to ourselves. It is that the world be made fit and safe to live in; and particularly that it be made safe for every peace-loving nation which, like our own, wishes to live its own life, determine its own institutions, be assured of justice and fair dealing by the other peoples of the world as against force and selfish aggression. All the peoples of the world are in effect partners in this interest, and for our own part we see very clearly that unless justice be done to others it will not be done to us. The program of the world's peace, therefore, is our program; and that program, the only possible program, as we see it, is this:

I. Open covenants of peace, openly arrived at, after which there shall be no private international understandings of any kind but diplomacy shall proceed always frankly and in the public view.

II. Absolute freedom of navigation upon the seas, outside territorial waters, alike in peace and in war, except as the seas may be closed in whole or in part by international action of the enforcement of international covenants.

III. The removal, so far as possible, of all economic barriers and the establishment of an equality of trade conditions among all the nations consenting to the peace and associating themselves for its maintenance.

IV. Adequate guarantees given and taken that national armaments will be reduced to the lowest point consistent with domestic safety.

V. A free, open-minded, and absolutely impartial adjustment of all colonial claims, based upon a strict observance of the principle that in determining all such questions of sovereignty the interests of the populations concerned must have equal weight with the equitable claims of the government whose title is to be determined.

VI. The evacuation of all Russian territory and such a settlement of all questions affecting Russia as will secure the best and freest coöperation of the other nations of the world in obtaining for her an unhampered and unembarrassed opportunity for the independent determination of her own political development and national policy and assure her of a sincere welcome into the society of free nations under institutions of her own choosing; and, more than a welcome, assistance also of every kind that she may need and may herself desire. The treatment accorded Russia by her sister nations in the months to come will be the acid test of their good will, of their comprehension of her needs as distinguished from their own interests, and of their intelligent and unselfish sympathy.

VII. Belgium, the whole world will agree, must be evacuated and restored, without any attempt to limit the sovereignty which she enjoys in common with all other free nations. No other single act will serve as this will serve to restore confidence among the nations in the laws which they have themselves set and determined for the government of their relations with one another. Without this healing act the whole structure and validity of international law is forever impaired.

VIII. All French territory should be freed and the invaded portions restored, and the wrong done to France by Prussia in 1871 in the matter of Alsace-Lorraine, which has unsettled the peace of the world for nearly fifty years, should be righted, in order that peace may once more be made secure in the interest of all.

IX. A readjustment of the frontiers of Italy should be effected along clearly recognizable lines of nationality.

X. The peoples of Austria-Hungary, whose place among the nations we wish to see safe-guarded and assured, should be accorded the freest opportunity of autonomous development.

XI. Rumania, Serbia, and Montenegro should be evacuated; occupied territories restored; Serbia accorded free and secure access to the sea; and the relations of the several Balkan states to one another determined by friendly counsel along historically established lines of allegiance and nationality; and international guarantees of the political and economic independence and territorial integrity of the several Balkan states should be entered into.

XII. The Turkish portions of the present Ottoman Empire should be assured a secure sovereignty, but the other nationalities which are now under Turkish rule should be assured an undoubted security of life and an absolutely unmolested opportunity of autonomous development, and the Dardanelles should be permanently opened as a free passage to the ships and commerce of all nations under international guarantees.

XIII. An independent Polish state should be erected which should include the territories inhabited by indisputably Polish populations, which should be assured a free and secure access to the sea, and whose political and economic independence and territorial integrity should be guaranteed by international covenant.

XIV. A general association of nations must be formed under specific covenants for the purpose of affording mutual guarantees of political independence and territorial integrity to great and small states alike.

In regard to these essential rectifications of wrong and assertions of right we feel ourselves to be intimate partners of all the governments and peoples associated together against the Imperialists. We cannot be separated in interest or divided in purpose. We stand together until the end.

For such arrangements and covenants we are willing to fight and to continue to fight until they are achieved; but only because we wish the right to prevail and desire a just and stable peace such as can be secured only by removing the chief provocations to war, which this program does not remove. We have no jealousy of German greatness, and there is nothing in this program that impairs it. We grudge her no achievement or distinction of learning or of pacific enterprise such as have made her record very bright and very enviable. We do not wish to injure her or to block in any way her legitimate influence or power. We do not wish to fight her either with arms or with hostile arrangements of trade if she is willing to associate herself with us and the other peace-loving nations of the world in covenants of justice and law and fair dealing. We wish her only to accept a place of equality among the peoples of the world,—the new world in which we now live,—instead of a place of mastery.

Neither do we presume to suggest to her any alteration or modification of her institutions. But it is necessary, we must frankly say, and necessary as a preliminary to any intelligent dealings with her on our part, that we should know whom her spokesmen speak for when they speak to us, whether for the Reichstag majority or for the military party and the men whose creed is imperial domination.

We have spoken now, surely, in terms too concrete to admit of any further doubt or question. An evident principle runs through the whole program I have outlined. It is the principle of justice to all peoples and nationalities, and their right to live on equal terms of liberty and safety with one another, whether they be strong or weak. Unless this principle be made its foundation no part of the structure of international justice can stand. The people of the United States could act upon no other principle; and to the vindication of this principle they are ready to devote their lives, their honor, and everything that they possess. The moral climax of this the culminating and final war for human liberty has come, and they are ready to put their own strength, their own highest purpose, their own integrity and devotion to the test.

The Defeat of the League of Nations

RESOLUTION OF RATIFICATION OF TREATY OF PEACE WITH GERMANY AND THE LEAGUE OF NATIONS, MARCH 19, 1920

Resolution of ratification.

Resolved (two-thirds of the Senators present concurring therein), That the Senate advise and consent to the ratification of the treaty of peace with Germany concluded at Versailles on the 28th day of June, 1919, subject to the following reservations and understandings, which are hereby made a part and condition of this resolution of ratification, which ratification is not to take effect or bind the United States until the said reservations and understandings adopted by the Senate have been accepted as a part and a condition of this resolution of ratification by the allied and associated powers and a failure on the part of the allied and associated powers to make objection to said reservations and understandings prior to the deposit of ratification by the United States shall be taken as a full and final acceptance of such reservations and understandings by said powers:

1. The United States so understands and construes article 1 that in case of notice of withdrawal from the League of Nations, as provided in said article, the United States shall be the sole judge as to whether all its international obligations and all its obligations under the said covenant have been fulfilled, and notice of withdrawal by the United States may be given by a concurrent resolution of the Congress of the United States.

Resolution of Ratification of Treaty of Peace with Germany and the League of Nations, March 19, 1920. *Congressional Record,* vol. LIX, p. 4599.

2. The United States assumes no obligation to preserve the territorial integrity or political independence of any other country by the employment of its military or naval forces, its resources, or any form of economic discrimination, or to interfere in any way in controversies between nations, including all controversies relating to territorial integrity or political independence, whether members of the league or not, under the provisions of article 10, or to employ the military or naval forces of the United States, under any article of the treaty for any purpose, unless in any particular case the Congress, which, under the Constitution, has the sole power to declare war or authorize the employment of the military or naval forces of the United States, shall, in the exercise of full liberty of action, by act or joint resolution so provide.

3. No mandate shall be accepted by the United States under article 22, part 1, or any other provision of the treaty of peace with Germany, except by action of the Congress of the United States.

4. The United States reserves to itself exclusively the right to decide what questions are within its domestic jurisdiction and declares that all domestic and political questions relating wholly or in part to its internal affairs, including immigration, labor, coast-wise traffic, the tariff, commerce, the suppression of traffic in women and children and in opium and other dangerous drugs, and all other domestic questions, are solely within the jurisdiction of the United States and are not under this treaty to be submitted in any way either to arbitration or to the consideration of the council or of the assembly of the League of Nations, or any agency thereof, or to the decision or recommendation of any other power.

5. The United States will not submit to arbitration or to inquiry by the assembly or by the council of the League of Nations, provided for in said treaty of peace, any questions which in the judgment of the United States depend upon or relate to its long-established policy, commonly known as the Monroe doctrine; said doctrine is to be interpreted by the United States alone and is hereby declared to be wholly outside the jurisdiction of said League of Nations and entirely unaffected by any provision contained in the said treaty of peace with Germany.

6. The United States withholds its assent to articles 156, 157, and 158, and reserves full liberty of action with respect to any controversy which may arise under said articles.

7. No person is or shall be authorized to represent the United States, nor shall any citizen of the United States be eligible, as a member of any body or agency established or authorized by said treaty of peace with Germany, except pursuant to an act of the Congress of the United States providing for his appointment and defining his powers and duties.

8. The United States understands that the reparation commission will regulate or interfere with exports from the United States to Germany, or from Germany to the United States, only when the United States by act or joint resolution of Congress approves such regulation or interference.

9. The United States shall not be obligated to contribute to any expenses of the League of Nations, or of the secretariat, or of any commission, or committee, or conference, or other agency, organized under the League of Nations or under the treaty or for the purpose of carrying out the treaty provisions, unless and until an ap-

propriation of funds available for such expenses shall have been made by the Congress of the United States: *Provided.* That the foregoing limitation shall not apply to the United States' proportionate share of the expense of the office force and salary of the secretary general.

10. No plan for the limitation of armaments proposed by the council of the League of Nations under the provisions of article 8 shall be held as binding the United States until the same shall have been accepted by Congress, and the United States reserves the right to increase its armament without the consent of the council whenever the United States is threatened with invasion or engaged in war.

11. The United States reserves the right to permit, in its discretion, the nationals of a covenant-breaking State, as defined in article 16 of the covenant of the League of Nations, residing within the United States or in countries other than such covenant-breaking State, to continue their commercial, financial, and personal relations with the nationals of the United States.

12. Nothing in articles 296, 297, or in any of the annexes thereto or in any other article, section, or annex of the treaty of peace with Germany shall, as against citizens of the United States, be taken to mean any confirmation, ratification, or approval of any act otherwise illegal or in contravention of the rights of citizens of the United States.

13. The United States withholds its assent to Part XIII (articles 387 to 427, inclusive) unless Congress by act or joint resolution shall hereafter make provision for representation in the organization established by said Part XIII, and in such event the participation of the United States will be governed and conditioned by the provisions of such act or joint resolution.

14. Until Part I, being the covenant of the League of Nations, shall be so amended as to provide that the United States shall be entitled to cast a number of votes equal to that which any member of the league and its self-governing dominions, colonies, or parts of empire, in the aggregate shall be entitled to cast, the United States assumes no obligation to be bound, except in cases where Congress has previously given its consent, by any election, decision, report, or finding of the council or assembly in which any member of the league and its self-governing dominions, colonies, or parts of empire, in the aggregate have cast more than one vote.

The United States assumes no obligation to be bound by an decision, report, or finding of the council or assembly arising out of any dispute between the United States and any member of the league if such member, or any self-governing dominion, colony, empire, or part of empire united with it politically has voted.

15. In consenting to the ratification of the treaty with Germany the United States adheres to the principle of self-determination and to the resolution of sympathy with the aspirations of the Irish people for a government of their own choice adopted by the Senate June 6, 1919, and declares that when such government is attained by Ireland, a consummation it is hoped is at hand, it should promptly be admitted as a member of the League of Nations.

☆ **8** ☆

The Twenties Culture War

The 1920s have come down to us as the Jazz Age, a time when Americans, buoyed by prosperity, abandoned social concerns and gave themselves up to moneymaking and personal gratification. The conventional icons of the era include the Charleston, the flapper, the speakeasy, fast cars, the Greenwich Village bohemian, the real estate speculator, and the Wall Street bull market.

But this picture of a carefree, hedonistic society distorts reality. If economic and class conflict in the 1920s were muted by the bright glow of prosperity, cultural conflict was not. Indeed, few eras in our history witnessed such bitter clashes of contending values, credos, and loyalties. Although the battles were often confused, in general they pitted politically conservative, traditional, white Protestant rural and small-town Americans against various groups defined as outsiders by virtue of their liberal-to-radical politics, their religious or ethnic deviation, their urban cosmopolitanism, or sometimes all three.

The selections below illustrate three of the major cultural battlegrounds of the 1920s: political radicalism, religious and racial tolerance, and prohibition. There were other cultural struggles during the twenties as well as clashes over such issues as Darwinian evolution, sexual behavior, and the deportment of the young. All, however, were really aspects of the same cultural and ideological confrontation.

Keep in mind that the following documents refer to only a few facets of the twenties "cultural war" and do not present the full range of positions even on the controversies they discuss. As you read the selections, consider why the 1920s brought out cultural conflict in so lacerating a way.

8.1: Sacco-Vanzetti (1927)

*In May 1920 two Italian-born anarchists, Nicola Sacco and Bar-
tolomeo Vanzetti, were arrested for the murder of two shoe factory employees in the course of a payroll robbery in South Braintree, Massachusetts. The two men were tried and, in July 1921, convicted and
sentenced to death.*

*The case erupted into a cause célèbre and became the focus of sus-
picion, anger, and guilt. Many of the nation's liberal and radical intellectuals considered the trial a travesty of justice. The accused men,
they said, had been railroaded by a prosecutor and judge hostile to
their nationality and their political radicalism. Some of America's
brightest and most talented men and women, operating through Sacco-
Vanzetti defense committees, demanded a new trial to reverse the convictions. The far left staged protest rallies in major cities around the
world to demand the convicted men's exoneration.*

*In 1927 the friends of the two anarchists prevailed on Massachusetts
governor Alvan T. Fuller to review the trial. Fuller appointed a committee headed by A. Lawrence Lowell, president of Harvard University, to examine the trial record to see if an injustice had been done.
On the basis of this report the governor decided to let the sentences
stand. On August 23, 1927, the two men went to their deaths in the
electric chair still protesting their innocence. To this day questions of
their guilt and of the fairness of their trial arouse passionate feelings
among people who can still identify with the opposing sides as they
took shape more than seventy years ago.*

*The first selection is from Governor Fuller's message rejecting the
charge of unfairness and refusing to order a new trial. It is true that
this was an immensely complicated case, but is it possible to say anything valid about the probable fairness of the trial from Fuller's remarks as transcribed here?*

*The second selection is from a pamphlet by the poet Edna St. Vincent
Millay written a few months after the executions. It obviously reflects the
poet's own passionate commitment to the cause that had excited such
powerful emotions. Why do you suppose a person like Millay might have
been swept up in the Sacco-Vanzetti controversy? Are poets more sensitive to injustice than others? Were the creative people of this era more
alienated from mainstream American life than figures such as Governor
Fuller and A. Lawrence Lowell? Is there any sign of such alienation in
Millay's pamphlet? How do you explain her linkage of the execution of
Sacco and Vanzetti with the first World War?*

Trial of Sacco-Vanzetti Held to Be Fair

ALVAN T. FULLER

Boston, Massachusetts, August 3, 1927

On April 15th, 1920, a paymaster and his guard were held up, robbed and brutally murdered at South Braintree, Massachusetts. On May 5th, 1920, Nicola Sacco and Bartolomeo Vanzetti were arrested; they were later tried and found guilty of the murder. The verdict was followed by seven motions for a new trial and two appeals to the Supreme Court for the Commonwealth, all of which were heard and later denied. Prior to the trial of the two men in this case, Vanzetti had been arrested, tried and convicted of an attempted holdup on December 24, 1919, at Bridgewater, Massachusetts, and sentenced to fifteen years imprisonment.

The appeal to the Governor was presented by counsel for the accused on May 3rd of the present year. It was my first official connection with the case. . . .

The inquiry that I have conducted has had to do with the following questions:—

Was the jury trial fair?
Were the accused entitled to a new trial?
Are they guilty or not guilty?

As to the first question, complaint has been made that the defendants were prosecuted and convicted because they were anarchists. As a matter of fact, the issue of anarchy was brought in by them as an explanation of their suspicious conduct. Their counsel, against the advice of Judge Thayer, decided to attribute their actions and conduct to the fact that they were anarchists, suggesting that they were armed to protect themselves, that they were about to start out, at ten o'clock at night, to collect radical literature, and that the reason they lied was to save their friends.

I have consulted with every member of the jury now alive, eleven in number. They considered the judge fair; that he gave them no indication of his own opinion of the case. Affidavits have been presented claiming that the judge was prejudiced. I see no evidence of prejudice in his conduct of the trial. That he had an opinion as to the guilt or innocence of the accused after hearing the evidence is natural and inevitable.

The allegation has been made that conditions in the court room were prejudicial to the accused. After careful inquiry of the jury and others I find no evidence to support this allegation. I find the jurors were thoroughly honest men and that they were reluctant to find these men guilty but were forced to do so by the evidence. I can see no warrant for the assertion that the jury trial was unfair.

The charge of the judge was satisfactory to the counsel for the accused and no exceptions were taken to it. The Supreme Judicial Court for the Commonwealth has considered such of the more than 250 exceptions taken during the course of the trial

Alvan T. Fuller, *Decision of Gov. Alvan T. Fuller in the Matter of the Appeal of Bartolomeo Vanzetti and Nicola Sacco . . .* (Boston: 1928), pp. 3–8.

as counsel for the accused chose to argue and over-ruled them all, thus establishing that the proceedings were without legal flaw.

I have read the record and examined many witnesses and the jurymen to see from a layman's standpoint whether the trial was fairly conducted. I am convinced that it was.

The next question is whether newly discovered evidence was of sufficient merit to warrant a new trial.

After the verdict against these men, their counsel filed and argued before Judge Thayer seven distinct supplementary motions for a new trial six of them on the ground of newly discovered evidence, all of which were denied. I have examined all of these motions and read the affidavits in support of them to see whether they presented any valid reason for granting the accused men a new trial. I am convinced that they do not and I am further convinced that the presiding judge gave no evidence of bias in denying them all and refusing a new trial. The Supreme Judicial Court for the Commonwealth, which had before it appeals on four of the motions and had the opportunity to read the same affidavits which were submitted to Judge Thayer, declined to sustain the contentions of counsel for the accused. In my own investigations on the question of guilt, I have given these motions and their supporting affidavits and the witnesses every consideration. . . .

It has been a difficult task to look back six years through other people's eyes. Many of the witnesses told me their story in a way I felt was more a matter of repetition than the product of their memory. Some witnesses replied that during the six years they had forgotten; they could not remember; that it was a disagreeable experience and they had tried to forget it. I could not hope to put myself in the position of a juryman and have the advantage of seeing the witness on the stand and listening to the evidence and judging the spoken word. The motions for a new trial, however, were all made from affidavits and therefore they could be reviewed under the same circumstances as prevailed when the Judge heard them.

The next question, and the most vital question of all, is that of the guilt or innocence of the accused. In this connection I reviewed the Bridgewater attempted holdup for which Vanzetti had previously been tried before another jury and found guilty. At this trial Vanzetti did not take the witness stand in his own defense. He waived the privilege of telling his own story to the jury, and did not subject himself to cross examination. Investigating this case, I talked to the counsel for Vanzetti at the Plymouth trial, the jurymen, the trial witnesses, new witnesses, present counsel and Vanzetti. I have talked with the government witnesses who saw the Bridgewater holdup and who identified Vanzetti, and I believe their testimony to be substantially correct. I believe with the jury that Vanzetti was guilty and that his trial was fair. I found nothing unusual about this case except, as noted above, that Vanzetti did not testify.

In the Bridgewater case, practically everyone who witnessed the attempted holdup and who could have identified the bandits identified Vanzetti.

The South Braintree crime was particularly brutal. The murder of the paymaster (Parmenter) and the guard (Berardelli) was not necessary to the robbery. The murders were accomplished first, the robbery afterward. The first shot laid Berardelli low in the roadway, and after Parmenter was shot, he dropped the money box in the road and ran across the street. The money could then have been taken but the murderers pursued Parmenter across the road and shot him again, and then returned and fired three more shots into Berardelli, four in all, leaving his lifeless form in the roadway. The plan was evidently to kill the witnesses and terrorize the bystanders. The murderers escaped in an automobile driven by one of their confederates, the automobile being afterward located in the woods at Bridgewater, 18 miles distant.

Vanzetti when arrested on May 5th had in his hip pocket a fully loaded revolver. Sacco had a loaded pistol tucked into the front of his trousers and 20 loose carridges which fitted his pistol. Upon being questioned by the police, both men told what they afterward admitted was a tissue of lies. Sacco claimed to have been working at Kelly's shoe factory on April 15th, the date of the South Braintree crime. Upon investigation, it was proven that he was not at work on that day. He then claimed to have been at the Italian Consulate in Boston on that date but the only confirmation of this claim is the memory of a former employee of the Consulate who made a deposition in Italy that Sacco among forty others was in the office that day. This employee had no memorandum to assist his memory.

As the result of my study of the record and my personal investigation of the case, including my interviews with a large number of witnesses, I believe, with the jury, that Sacco and Vanzetti were guilty and that the trial was fair.

This crime was committed seven years ago. For six years, through dilatory methods, one appeal after another, every possibility for delay has been utilized, all of which lends itself to attempts to frighten and coerce witnesses, to influence changes in testimony, to multiply by the very years of time elapsed the possibilities of error and confusion.

It might be said that by undertaking this investigation I have contributed to the elaborate consideration accorded these men. My answer is that there was a feeling on the part of some people that the various delays that had dragged this case through the courts for six years were evidence that a doubt existed as to the guilt of these two men. The feeling was not justified. The persistent, determined efforts of an attorney of extraordinary versality and industry, the judge's illness, the election efforts of three District Attorneys, and dilatoriness on the part of most of those concerned are the principal causes of delay. The delays that have dragged this case out for six years are inexcusable.

This task of review has been a laborious one and I am proud to be associated in this public service with clear eyed witnesses, unafraid to tell the truth, and with jurors who discharged their obligations in accordance with their convictions and their oaths.

As a result of my investigation I find no sufficient justification for executive intervention.

I believe with the jury, that these men, Sacco and Vanzetti, were guilty, and that they had a fair trial. I furthermore believe that there was no justifiable reason for giving them a new trial.

(Signed) Alvan T. Fuller

Fear

EDNA ST. VINCENT MILLAY

There are two names you would not have me mention, for you are sick of the sound of them. All men must die, you say, and these men have died, and would that their names might die with them; would that their names were as names written in the sands, you say, to be dissipated by the next incoming tide! For you long to return to your gracious world of a year ago, where people had pretty manners and did not raise their voices; where people whom you knew, whom you had entertained in your houses, did not shout and weep and walk the streets vulgarly carrying banners, because two quite inconsequential people, two men who could not even speak good English, were about to be put forever out of mischief's way. *Do* let us forget, you say; after all, what *does* it matter?

You are right; it does not matter very much. In a world more beautiful than this it would have mattered more. On the surface of a Christianity already so spotted and defaced by the crimes of the Church this stain does not show very dark. In a freedom already so riddled and gashed by the crimes of the state this ugly rent is with difficulty to be distinguished at all.

And you are right; it is well to forget that men die. So far we have devised no way to defeat death, or to outwit him, or to buy him over. At any moment the cloud may split above us and the golden spear of death leap at the heart; at any moment the earth crack and the hand of death reach up from the abyss to grasp our ankles; at any moment the wind rise and sweep the roofs from our houses, making one dust of our ceilings and ourselves. And if not, we shall die soon, anyhow. It is well to forget that this is so.

But that man before his time, wantonly and without sorrow, is thrust from the light of the sun into the darkness of the grave by his brother's blindness or fear it is well to remember, at least until it has been shown to the satisfaction of all that this too is beyond our power to change.

Two months ago, in Massachusetts, these men whom I do not name were efficiently despatched out of the sunlight into the darkness of the grave. The executions of the death sentence upon them went forward without interference; there were no violent demonstrations. Whatever of agitation there was has steadily decreased since that night. Today things are very quiet. From time to time some small newspaper remarks editorially that the hysteria which swept the country has abated, and congratulates its readers upon having escaped disintegration. Aside from this there is little comment. The general opinion is that the affair has pretty well blown over. And the world sleeps easy on its pillow.

Yet if all is quiet today, it is more for this reason than for any other; that though you sit in the same room with a man you cannot hear his thoughts. And the tumult is in the mind; the shouting and rioting are in the thinking mind. Nothing has abated; nothing has changed; nothing is forgotten. It is as if the two months which have

Edna St. Vincent Millay, *Fear* (New York: The Sacco-Vanzetti National League, n.d. [1927]).

elapsed were but the drawing of a breath. In very truth, for those who sat in silence on that night of the 22nd of August, waiting for news from the prison, and in silence when the news came, it is still the night of the 22nd of August, for there has been no dawn.

I do not call these men by name, for I know how nervous and irritable you become at the sight of these names on the printed page; how your cheek flushes and you cluck with exasperation; how you turn to your family with words on your tongue which in former days you would not have used at all—"vipers, vermin, filth." This is because you were just dozing off nicely again after the shocking uproar of two months ago, and do not wish to be disturbed. You are as cross as an old dog asleep on the hearth if I shake you and try to get you out into the rainy wind. This is because what you most want out of life is not to be disturbed. You wish to lie peacefully asleep for a few years yet, and then to lie peacefully dead.

If you should rouse yourself for a moment and look about you at the world, you would be troubled, I think, and feel less peaceful and secure, seeing how it is possible for a man as innocent as yourself of any crime to be cast into prison and be killed. For whether or not these men whom I do not name were guilty of the crime of murder, it was not for murder that they died. The crime for which they died was the crime of breathing upon the frosty window and looking out.

"These Anarchists!" you say; "shall I never hear the last of them?"

Indeed, I fear it will be some time before you hear the last of them. I do not mean by this what you think I mean. I do not mean that plotting mischief is afoot, that thousands of people hitherto gentle and retired are now grimly engaged in fashioning engines of death to plant beneath the State House floor. This is not what I mean, although you will say it is what I meant.

It is of your children I was thinking, your young sons and daughters, your grandsons and granddaughters, these young people with whom you have already so much difficulty, because, as you say, they have so few illusions. How often already have they not stood looking at you coldly while with warm cheek and faltering accent you presented your pretty concepts: duty, honor, courage, purity, sacrifice—those fragile dolls of yours, that are always dressed for summer, no matter what the sky?

Your children heard you discussing the case in question. "Anarchists, murderers, Anarchists, Anarchists." This was your discussion of the case. They looked at you, yawned, and left the room.

Their minds are dark to you. But they are busy. Out of your sight they read, they ponder, they work things out. In your presence they often sit in a not too respectful silence, interrupting suddenly your placid remarks by their brisk utterance of some untidy truth never mentioned in your house before.

They are frankly occupied chiefly with the real business of life, which, as everybody knows, is having your own way, and getting as much as possible for as little as possible. It is you who have taught them this angular truth; you have failed only in that you have not been able to impart to them as well the ruffles and passementerie with which you are accustomed to adorn it. They were just beginning to look about them at life when war broke out and surrounded them with death. They know how important it is to have a good time while you can; in the next war it is they who will be taken.

As for their illusions, well, they have seen you at war, and they are beginning to understand why you went to war; they have seen you engaged in many another dubious and embarrassing activity; and now they have seen this. They who have been chidden time and again for having so little softness in them see now their parents, for all their gentle voices and courteous ways, more hard, more unscrupulous, more relentless, than themselves in their most iron moods. It is from these children, I fear, that you are likely to hear again on the subject, though not in so many words.

But, you say, what we did was done for the good of the country, to protect its honor, its institutions, the glory of its flag.

What is this honor, that a breath can tarnish? This glory, that a whisper can bring it low? What are these noble institutions, that a wind from any quarter can set to trembling like towers of jelly?

You do not know exactly what they are. For you do not live with them. They are not trees to shade you, water to quench your thirst. They are golden coins, hidden under the mattress in a very soiled wallet. The only pleasure they afford you is the rapturous dread lest some one may be taking them away. And some one is taking them away. But not the one you think.

Unkindness, hypocrisy, and greed—these are the forces that shall bring us low and enslave our children. Yet we quarter their troops in our houses without a murmur. We show them where the treasure is hid. But they know it already.

This is the way you look at it: These men were Anarchists, and they are well out of the way; you are fortunate to have escaped destruction at their hands; they were probably murderers; but, in any case, they are well out of the way. It was that word Anarchist which brought them to the chair; that word, and your ignorance of its meaning.

For you do not at all know what an Anarchist is. And all through this trial in which the word Anarchist has played such an important part you have not even looked up the word in the dictionary, your position being that, in the first place, you know quite well enough, and, in the second place, you would think shame to know.

An Anarchist, you insist, is a man who makes bombs and puts them under the State House, and that is that. On the contrary, that is by no means that. The person you have in mind is not an Anarchist, he is a bomber. You will find him everywhere—among Anarchists, among Fascists, among dry-law enforcers, among Modernists, among Fundamentalists, and freely distributed throughout the Ku Klux Klan. He is that person who, when he does not like a thing, lynches it, tars and feathers it, lays a curse upon it, or puts a bomb under it. His name is legion, and you will find him in every party.

An Anarchist, according to the dictionary, is a person who believes that human beings are naturally good, and that if left to themselves they would, by mutual agreement, govern themselves much better and much more peaceably than they are being governed now by a government based on violence. An interesting theory. Nonsense, of course, because man is not naturally good; man is naturally cruel, selfish and vain, and what he would be if left to his own devices it is horrible to contemplate. Still, it is an interesting concept, very idealistic, very pretty.

Of those who hold with the theory of Anarchism, the dictionary further tells us, there is one group whose members "occasionally resort to an act of violence against representatives of oppression to express a protest against, or to draw public attention to, existing social wrongs." (It is in this group that your bombers are happy and at home.) But "generally speaking," says the dictionary, "Anarchism repudiates violent methods, and hopes for a gradual evolution towards its goal."

Ah, you will say, but these men belonged to the violent group!

Their history would indicate otherwise. Up to the time of their detention for the crime for which they were later sentenced to die no slightest act of violence had ever been attributed to either of them. There are those who would have given much to be able to bring to light against them such an act of violence, and were unable to do so; it is to the counsel for the prosecution that I refer. "Throughout the entire trial" (I quote the uncontested statement of one who was in a position to know the facts)—"not one word of testimony was introduced against their character for honesty, peace, and good order."

I am going into this in some detail because I find it interesting. You, I fear, find it not only uninteresting, but vaguely and uncomfortably obscene. Yet, after all, you have very plentifully had your say on the subject—that action of yours, you know, that spoke so much louder than any words.

These men were castaways upon our shore, and we, an ignorant and savage tribe, have put them to death because their speech and their manners were different from our own, and because to the untutored mind that which is strange is in its infancy ludicrous, but in its prime evil, dangerous, and to be done away with.

These men were put to death because they made you nervous; and your children know it. The minds of your children are like clear pools, reflecting faithfully whatever passes on the bank; whereas in the pool of your own mind, whenever an alien image bends above, a fish of terror leaps to meet it, shattering its reflection.

I am free to say these things because I am not an Anarchist, although you will say that I am. It is unreasonable to you that a person should go to any trouble in behalf of another person unless the two are members of the same family, or of the same fraternity, or, at the remotest, of the same political party. As regards yourself and the man who lives next door to you, you wish him well, but not so very well. Even if he is a member of the same church as yourself, you do not wish him so inordinately well. Whereas if he does not belong to the same church as yourself, and if, in addition, he does things a little out of the ordinary, such as walk in the street without a hat, you do not wish him well at all. In any case, as regards your neighbor and yourself, although you have no desire to see his house burn down or his children killed in a motor accident, a most modest worldly success will do very well for him, as far as you are concerned. For these and other reasons sufficiently naive and self-revealing, you take it as a matter of course that, of the many persons involved in the recent agitation in Boston, those who were not in the ring for what they could get out of it were revolutionists of the most flagrant dye. It is impossible for you to conceive that men could weep in public and women permit themselves to be thrown in jail because (as it seemed to them) the blue hem of Justice was being dragged in the mire. In the world in which you live Justice is a woman of stone above a courthouse door.

As I said before, I am not sufficiently idealistic to share the political opinions of these men with whose fate I am concerned. It is impossible for me to be an Anarchist, for I do not believe in the essential goodness of man; man is quite patently, to my sight, the worm of the Moody and Sankey hymns.[1] Except for this fact, I should of course think twice before writing as I do. For, although I was born in this country, and am possessed of that simple right of the citizen to hold any opinions he may hold, yet to avail one's self of this right and express opinions contrary to the opinions of the majority may become, as we have lately seen, a folly punishable by the extreme correction. For surely you are not still insisting that these two poor wretches were put to death solely for the crime of murder? You and I both know that we must be careful, not only what we do, but also what we say, and even what we think, if we would not have one day our sleep brutally broken in upon and ourselves rudely forced to enter a place where we do not at all wish to go. And surely you will not deny that, if you would remain undisturbed, it is more important to be on the side of the established order of things than to be innocent of even the grossest crime?

As I said before, I dare say these things because I am not an Anarchist; but I dare say them for another reason, too: because my personal physical freedom, my power to go in and out when I choose, my personal life even, is no longer quite as important to me as it once was. Death even, that outrageous intrusion, appears to me at moments, and more especially when I think of what happened in Boston two months ago, death appears to me somewhat as a darkened room, in which one might rest one's battered temples out of the world's way, leaving the sweeping of the crossings to those who still think it important that the crossings be swept. As if indeed it mattered the least bit in the world whether the crossings be clean or foul, when of all the people passing to and from there in the course of an eight-hour day not one out of ten thousand has a spark of true courage in his heart, or any love at all, beyond the love of a cat for the fire, for any earthly creature other than himself. The world, the physical world, and that once was all in all to me, has at moments such as these no road through a wood, no stretch of shore, that can bring me comfort. The beauty of these things can no longer at such moments make up to me at all for the ugliness of man, his cruelty, his greed, his lying face.

8.2: The Ku Klux Klan (1924, 1921)

The most extreme expression of traditional America's hostility to "alien" trends and "alien" groups was the Ku Klux Klan. The Klan of the 1920s aped the Klan of the Reconstruction period, but it had both a broader agenda and a wider geographical range than its predecessor. With its program of racial and religious intolerance, cultural conformity, and superpatriotism, the Klan in the twenties spread beyond the

---

[1]Dwight Moody and Ira Sankey were two Protestant evangelists who wrote hymns—ED.

South and for a time threatened to become a decisive force in American politics on a national level.

The first selection below includes statements from two local Klan organizations, the first from New Jersey, the second from Louisiana. What are the essential ingredients of the Klan philosophy as expressed in these documents? Although they do not mention blacks and do not deal with political viewpoints, what do you suppose, judging from these documents, the Klan felt about black Americans and political dissenters?

The second selection is a brief letter written in 1921 by the famous editor of the Emporia Gazette, *the Progressive journalist, William Allen White. White despised the Klan in no uncertain terms. What tradition does he fall back on for his denunciation? Why would you expect a man like White to be proof against the appeal of the Klan? How could an editor like White have influenced the attitudes of the people of Emporia, Kansas, toward the Klan?*

Statements from the Ku Klux Klan

The New Jersey Klan Speaks Out

The Rising of the Ku Klux Klan—The New Reformation

"On account of the abuses of religion by the Roman Catholic hierarchy, civilization had reached a universal crisis in the sixteenth century; and Martin Luther, the chosen instrument of God, was placed in the breach to prevent the wheels of progress from being reversed and the world from being plunged into greater darkness than that of the Dark Ages.

"The thousand years preceding the Reformation, known by religions historians as Satan's Millennium, was brought on by the Romish Church with her paganistic worship and practices, during which time millions of men and women poured out their blood as martyrs of the Christian religion. . . .

The White-Robed Army

"Now come the Knights of the Ku Klux Klan in this crucial hour of our American history to contend for the faith of our fathers who suffered and died in behalf of freedom. At the psychological moment they have arrived to encourage the hearts of those who have been battling heroically for the rights and privileges granted them under the Constitution of the United States.

"How our hearts have been thrilled at the sight of this army! Words fail to express the emotions of the soul at the appearance of this mighty throng upon the battle-field, where a few faithful followers of the lowly Nazarene have been contending for the faith once delivered to the Saints, against Papal mobs who have torn down gospel tabernacles, wrecked buildings and imprisoned Protestant worshipers.

Our National Peril

"The World War was the signal for greater alarm than the average American has been willing to admit. Notwithstanding the sacrifices that had to be made at home and the thousands of our young men who crossed the sea and laid down their lives on the battlefields of the Old World, it has taken the Ku Klux Klan to awaken even a portion of the population of the United States to our national peril. Our religious and political foes are not only within our gates, but are coming by the hundreds of thousands, bringing the chaos and ruin of old European and Asiatic countries to un-Americanize and destroy our nation, and to make it subserve the purposes of the Pope in his aspirations for world supremacy.

Rome Would Overthrow Public Schools

"One of the great efforts of the Roman hierarchy toward this end is to get control of our public schools by placing Roman Catholics on school boards and in the schoolrooms and taking the Bible out of the schools. In the event of their success in their efforts to overthrow our present school system there would be a string of beads around every Protestant child's neck and a Roman Catholic catechism in his hand. 'Hail Mary, Mother of God,' would be on every child's lips, and the idolatrous worship of dead saints a part of the daily programme.

The Jewish and Catholic Alliance

"The money-grasping Jew, who has no use for the Christ of Calvary, does all in his power to bring discredit on Christianity, and would be pleased to see the whole structure broken down, and in this way get rid of his responsibility for crucifying the Christ on Calvary and bringing the curse on his race, which they have had to suffer since the beginning of the Christian era. The sons of Abraham have therefore become a strong ally to the Papacy, not because they have anything in common with it in religion, but in their political propaganda against American institutions and principles.

"While no true Christian has anything against the Jew, it must be admitted that this alliance with the Papacy is a dangerous menace to our flag and country. The Jew is insoluble and indigestible; and when he grows in numbers and power till he becomes a menace to Christianity and the whole moral fabric, drastic measures will have to be taken to counteract his destructive work, and more especially when he is in alliance with the old Papal religio-political machine."

The Louisiana Klan's Manifesto

Awake! Americans, Awake!

"Awake, Americans! You descendants of the patriots of the Revolution! You sons of the Pilgrim Fathers who fought back the hordes of the Tyrant! Gird on the armor of God who led you out of bondage and chased slavery from out of our land! There is an enemy without our gates ten thousand times more dangerous than the redcoats ever were!

"Catholic politicians are filling the air with propaganda which would lead you to believe that old Ship of State has broken loose from her moorings and is drifting far to sea. They cry out in tones of agony that people are growing intolerant and Protestants are seeking to abridge religious liberty. Catholics will prescribe our religion and forbid a Protestant funeral in a Catholic Church. Forbid Catholics attendance at Masonic funerals and then lay claim to a corner on tolerance. Now when Rome is caught red handed in her designs to make American Catholics and Protestants interfere, she cries intolerance and would have you believe that liberty is crushed and bleeding.

"When Protestants exercise a right guaranteed to all under the Constitution, when Americans meet in peaceable assembly, Catholics arm themselves with bludgeons and blunderbusses and try to beat down honest men and murder American citizens. Only fools resort to force to settle a dispute and bricks and rocks are only used by savages. Rome not having any grounds on which to fight in the realm of reason seeks to unite State and Church by the use of sandbags and billies. Reason and enlightenment with them are taboo. Blind passion is appealed to and ignorance is made a virtue. Intellectual darkness for the masses is sought by Rome as surely as a robber seeks the shadows. For when the bright light of reason shines upon her, priests lose their power, and her influence crumbles as hastily as would a snowbank in the nether regions.

"Catholic politicians, if intrusted with power, would pass laws to force American organizations out of existence and shackle liberty, as they have done in every clime wherein they have reigned supreme.

"There are men seeking high office in Louisiana to-day who if elected in numbers sufficient would jail Americans for assembling in peaceful meetings and give to Rome the revenue of our State. Take the Eagle from off the dollar and in its stead place a likeness of the unholy face of [Pope] Pius. Strip the stripes from the American Flag and rend the Stars asunder, and make for us a National banner with background dark and gloomy, and mount upon it a cluster of garlic to commemorate the odor that permeates the Vatican. Turn back the march of civilization and chain the Bible to a box. Tether the intellects of man and enslave reason. Place a statue of a priest where now stands the Goddess of Liberty and place in his hand the torch of intolerance. Demolish our free institutions of learning and imprison those bold enough to preach freedom of the masses. Have black-robed nuns who know only slavery teach our children and drown our art in miasmic ignorance.

"Not all Catholics are of this stripe, but those who seek high office are tainted woefully with Catholic teachings and some have been so bold as to proclaim no Protestant is fit for office and Catholics are the only hope of liberty."

Letter on the Ku Klux Klan

WILLIAM ALLEN WHITE

September 17, 1921

An organizer of the Ku-Klux Klan was in Emporia the other day, and the men whom he invited to join his band at ten dollars per join turned him down. Under the leadership of Dr. J. B. Brickell and following their own judgment after hearing his story, the Emporians told him that they had no time for him. The proposition seems to be:

Anti foreigners
Anti Catholics
Anti Negroes.

There are, of course, bad foreigners and good ones, good Catholics and bad ones, and all kinds of Negroes. To make a case against a birthplace, a religion, or a race is wickedly un-American and cowardly. The whole trouble with the Ku-Klux Klan is that it is based upon such deep foolishness that it is bound to be a menace to good government in any community. Any man fool enough to be Imperial Wizard would have power without responsibility and both without any sense. That is social dynamite.

American institutions, our courts, our legislators, our executive officers are strong enough to keep the peace and promote justice and good will in the community. If they are not, then the thing to do is to change these institutions and do it quickly, but always legally. For a self-constituted body of moral idiots, who would substitute the findings of the Ku-Klux Klan for the processes of law to try to better conditions, would be a most un-American outrage which every good citizen should resent.

It is to the everlasting credit of Emporia that the organizer found no suckers with $10 each to squander here. Whatever Emporia may be otherwise, it believes in law and order, and absolute freedom under the constitution for every man, no matter what birth or creed or race, to speak and meet and talk and act as a free law-abiding citizen. The picayunish cowardice of a man who would substitute Klan rule and mob law for what our American fathers have died to establish and maintain should prove what a cheap screw outfit the Klan is.

8.3:   Wets versus Drys (1915, 1924)

Another 1920s cultural fault line ran between supporters of nationwide prohibition ("drys") and defenders of the right to drink ("wets"). National prohibition had long been a goal of moral reformers and Protestant evangelicals, and, aided by wartime sentiment against German American brewers and by public concern for the moral safety of soldiers, these groups induced Congress to pass the Eighteenth

Amendment prohibiting the manufacture, sale, and transportation of alcoholic beverages anywhere in the United States. On January 16, 1920, the United States became officially "dry."

Many Americans disliked prohibition and refused to comply with the law. Opponents emphasized its denial of personal liberty. They claimed it encouraged bootlegging, rumrunning, and other criminal activities. Some insisted that it deprived working people of an innocent pleasure just to suit the prejudices of prudes and puritans. The drys fought back, defending the Eighteenth Amendment as "a noble experiment," an expression of decency, prudence, and wise concern for the health and well-being of the American people.

The first selection below, written while the debate over a prohibition amendment was reaching a crescendo, is a defense of moderate drinking that highlights many of the cultural and moral differences between wets and drys. As Percy Andreae sees it, what motivates the prohibitionists? What is the author referring to when he mentions "great wealth-producing industries"? What was the intellectual and cultural connection between the prohibitionists and the more conservative Protestant denominations?

The second selection is a resolution adopted by a pro-Eighteenth Amendment group in 1924, four years after national prohibition, as expressed through the Volstead Act[1] had been put into effect. Clearly the prohibitionists were now on the defensive. From their statement, what seems to be the vulnerable points of the dry position? How did the drys hope to make the law more effective? Do you know what finally happened to the "noble experiment"?

A Glimpse Behind the Mask of Prohibition

PERCY ANDREAE

I have met many active prohibitionists, . . . all of them thoroughly in earnest. In some instances I have found that their allegiance to the cause of prohibition took its origin in the fact that some near relative or friend had succumbed to overindulgence in liquor. In one or two cases the man himself had been the victim of this weakness, and had come to the conclusion, firstly, that every one else was constituted as he was; and secondly, that unless one were prevented from drinking, he would not be secure from the temptation to do so himself.

---

[1]Passed in October 1919, the Volstead Act spelled out the specifics of the anti-alcohol legislation permitted by the Eighteenth Amendment.

Percy Andreae, *The Prohibition Movement in Its Broader Bearings upon Social, Commercial, and Religious Liberties* (Chicago: Felix Mendelsohn, 1915), pp. 9–19.

This is one class of prohibitionists. The other, and by far the larger class, is made up of religious zealots, to whom prohibition is a word having at bottom a far wider application than that which is generally attributed to it. The liquor question . . . is merely put forth by them as a means to an end, an incidental factor in a fight which has for its object the supremacy of a certain form of religious faith. The belief of many of these people is that the Creator frowns upon enjoyment of any and every kind, and that he has merely endowed us with certain desires and capacities for pleasure in order to give us an opportunity to please Him by resisting them. They are, of course, perfectly entitled to this belief. . . . But are they privileged to force that belief on their fellow beings? That, in substance, is the question that is involved in the present-day prohibition movement. . . .

Prohibition is merely the title of the movement. Its real purpose is of a religious, sectarian character. . . . If any one doubts the truth of the statement, let me put this to him: How many Roman Catholics are prohibitionists? How many Jews, the most temperate race on earth, are to be found in the ranks of prohibition? Or Lutherans? Or German Protestants generally? What is the proportion of Episcopalians to that of Methodists, Baptists, and Presbyterians . . . in the active prohibition army? The answer to these questions will, I venture to say, prove conclusively the assertion that the fight for prohibition is synonymous with the fight of a certain religious sect, or group of sects, for the supremacy of its ideas. . . .

[T]he suppression of liquor . . . is [not] the ultimate end they have in view. . . . It is . . . part and parcel of their lugubrious notion of Godworship [sic] which they eventually hope to impose upon the rest of humanity; a Sunday without a smile, no games, no recreation, no pleasures, no music, card-playing tabooed, dancing anathematized, the beauties of art decried as impure—in short, this world reduced to a barren, forbidding wilderness in which we, its inhabitants, are to pass our time contemplating the joys of the next. . . .

Now if the habit of drinking to excess were a growing one, as our prohibitionist friends claim that it is, we should to-day . . . not be here at all to argue it; for the evil . . . has existed for so many ages that, if it were as general and contagious as is claimed, and its results as far-reaching as they are painted, the human race would have been destroyed by it long ago. Of course, the contrary is the case. The world has progressed in this as in all other respects. Compare, for instance, the drinking to-day with the drinking of a thousand years ago, nay, of only a hundred odd years ago, when a man, if he wanted to ape his so-called betters, did so by contriving to be carried to bed every night "drunk as a lord." Has that condition of affairs been altered by legislative measures restricting the right of the individual to control himself? No. It has been altered by that far greater power, the moral force of education and the good example which teaches mankind the very thing that prohibition would take from it: the virtue of self-control and moderation in all things. . . . Prohibition . . . is the direct negation of the term self-control. In order to save the small percentage of men who are too weak to resist their animal desires, it aims to put chains on every man, the weak and the strong alike. And if this is proper in one respect, why not in all respects? Yet what would one think of a proposition to keep all men locked up because a certain number have a propensity to steal . . .?

I consider the danger which threatens civilized society from the growing power of a sect whose views on prohibition are merely an exemplification of their generally low estimate of man's ability to rise to higher things by his own volition to be of infinitely greater consequence than the danger that, in putting their narrow theories to the test, a few billions of invested property will be destroyed, a number of great wealth-producing industries wiped out, the rate of individual taxation largely increased, and a million or so of struggling wage earners doomed to face starvation. These latter considerations, of course, must appeal to every thinking man, but what are they compared with the greater questions involved? Already the government of our State [Illinois], and indeed of a good many other States, has passed practically into the hands of a few preacher politicians of a certain creed. With the machine they have built up, by appealing to the emotional weaknesses of the more or less unintelligent masses, they have lifted themselves on to a pedestal of power that has enabled them to dictate legislation or defeat it at their will. . . .

And what does it all mean? It means that government by emotion is to be substituted for government by reason, and government by emotion . . . is . . . the most dangerous and pernicious of all forms of government. It has already crept into the legislative assemblies of most of the States of the Union, and is being craftily fostered by those who know how easily it can be made available for their purposes. . . . Prohibition is but one of its fruits, and the hand that is plucking this fruit is the same hand of intolerance that drove forth certain of our forefathers from the land of their birth to seek the sheltering freedom of these shores.

What a strange reversal of conditions! The intolerants of a few hundred years ago are the upholders of liberty to-day, while those they once persecuted, having multiplied by grace of the very liberty that has so long sheltered them here, are now planning to impose the tyranny of their narrow creed upon the descendants of their persecutors of yore.

Let the greater public, which is, after all, the arbiter of the country's destinies, pause and ponder these things before they are allowed to progress too far. Prohibition, though it must cause, and is already causing, incalculable damage, may never succeed in this country; but that which is behind it, as the catapults and the cannon were behind the battering rams in the battles of olden days, is certain to succeed unless timely measures of prevention are resorted to; and if it does succeed, we shall witness the enthronement of a monarch in this land of liberty compared with whose autocracy the autocracy of the Russian Czar is a mere trifle.

The name of this monarch is Religious Intolerance.

Citizenship Conference to the American People: Have Faith in Prohibition

1. We challenge those who are opposed to the Eighteenth Amendment to come out into the open, and have the courage to repeal the Amendment if they can and the manhood to observe it until they can. Hip-pocket guardians of liberty and defenders

"Message of the Citizenship Conference to the American People," in Ethan R. Shaw, *Prohibition: Going or Coming?* (Berwyn, IL: Shaw Publishing Company, 1924), pp. 423–28.

of the Constitution are teaching the doctrine of qualified allegiance. The man who upholds the Constitution must uphold the whole of it.

2. The Volstead Act must never be amended by its enemies. That way lies nullification. If it is ever to be amended, the amending must be done by its friends, not its foes. It must be amended not to prevent enforcement, but to perfect enforcement after a reasonable trial has demonstrated the way.

3. The time has arrived when the American people should see to it that only those are elected to public office who, in the words of Lincoln, will neither violate in the slightest particular the laws of the land, nor tolerate their violation by others. The state or federal official who does not respect the sanctity of his oath to support the federal Constitution should resign his office and give place to one who will neither violate his oath nor betray the confidence of the people. Too often members of Congress and of State Legislatures are violating the laws that they themselves have made. They should be retired to private life. Law-makers should not be law-breakers.

4. We emphasize the grave responsibility which rests upon the courts to compel obedience on the part of those who by open violation are bringing the administration of justice into disrepute. There is increasing evidence that after three years the judges are beginning to realize that the imposition of fines, which amount to nothing more than a small license tax on the vast profits of the illegal liquor traffic, is ineffectual to stop the criminal. We commend those judges who are promoting efficient enforcement of the Eighteenth Amendment by imposing jail sentences, and who, in injunction proceedings, are depriving offenders of the use of their property for saloons and other unlawful purposes.

Official tests show that over ninety per cent of the liquor seized in all sections of the country contains poison in greater or less degree and this iminent menace to life and health must be given increasing consideration by the Courts and juries in cases against illicit makers and sellers.

We urge upon the federal and state judges the need of more stringent action on the part of the courts to prevent the law's delays, and of extreme penalties for persistent offenders to compel the law-breaker to cease his lawlessness and arouse in the cynical and indifferent a new respect for law.

5. When the press of the country carried a report, although incorrect, that an incoming ocean liner had been blocked by the rum fleet in entering New York Harbor, it shocked the moral sense and wounded the pride of the American people. They are impatient at the disgrace which attends the successful operations of the rum runners. They will not believe that the most powerful nation in the world is impotent to prevent the landing of illicit liquor on American soil.

In this juncture we look with confidence to the President of the United States. We ask him to place every available craft and every available agency which may lawfully be used for the purpose, to police our shores. We assure him of our support in using every power at his command to compel respect for constituted authority. An expectant nation looks to him to assert and maintain the majesty of the law.

6. The Eighteenth Amendment places equal responsibility for law enforcement on state and nation. We demand that every Governor of every state shall fully cooperate with the President in securing the enforcement of the Eighteenth Amend-

ment and the Volstead Act. The states with many times the number of officers that the federal government has at its command, should face the responsibility of doing their share in this vital law enforcement work. With only 1,522 federal agents, and over 250,000 state and local agents, it must manifest that the citizens of the states must hold to greater responsibility their own officers.

7. Realizing the powerful influence of the press, and its vast opportunity through its editors, artists and reporters to mould public opinion, we earnestly ask that it will not permit its news columns, its editorial pages, or its cartoons and illustrations to be used to promote disrespect for law or to hold up to ridicule and contempt our Constitution and our laws.

8. A democracy has been truly defined as "government by public opinion." On the people of this country rests the ultimate responsibility for law enforcement. Public officials can go only so far as we will go with them.

Our final appeal is to the people. Our homes, our schools, and our universities must instill a respect for law into the hearts and minds of the youth of today who are to be the citizens of tomorrow. Our churches must preach the gospel of loyalty. Every liberty-loving, law-abiding citizen must stand up and be counted. When the supremacy of law is challenged, silence is acquiescence. Propaganda must be answered by truth. Complacency must give place to a militant spirit which shall awaken the conscience of the country.

"This is my covenant, saith the Lord, that I will put my laws in the hearts of the people and write them in their minds."

Inspired by this promise, we press on to achieve the realization of the aspiration of Lincoln that "reverence for law may become the political religion of the nation."

☆ **9** ☆

The New Deal

In October 1929 the stock market boom collapsed, triggering the longest and steepest economic slide in American history. At the Depression's worst, in the winter of 1932–1933, the nation's total output was 31 percent below its 1929 peak; unemployment reached 25 percent of the labor force. During that appalling period millions of citizens wondered whether the existing social order could long survive the economic collapse.

In their desperation Americans might have turned for salvation to extremist leaders outside the liberal tradition, as many did in Europe under similar pressures. Instead they chose as their president Franklin Roosevelt, the standard-bearer of the party out of power at the time of the crash. What followed was the New Deal, a legislative program more sweeping and comprehensive than any in our history.

The New Deal was many things simultaneously. It was a relief program to provide jobs and income to millions of unemployed men and women. It was a drive to stimulate the stalled economy and get private production moving again. It was a bid to reform the nation's financial institutions, provide insurance against social hazards, encourage trade union organization, and revitalize natural resource management. It was inconsistent and changeable. Roosevelt and his advisers had no clear idea of exactly what was wrong with the economy and no certain formula for fixing it. Their policies and programs were often improvised, although their reform agenda drew heavily on early twentieth-century Progressivism for inspiration.

Frightened by the devastating economic and financial breakdown, at first most Americans were willing to give Roosevelt and the Democrats a blank check for change. By 1934, however, many old conservatives had regained their confidence and were beginning to take aim at the president and his policies. The left too rallied, and Marxists and various neo-

Populists were soon attacking FDR as a friend of big business and even a covert fascist.

In the selections below you will encounter both defenders and opponents of the New Deal. But the voices are not simply pro and con. In their support or opposition the authors have individual perspectives that reward analysis.

9.1:   Roosevelt Explains His Policies (1934)

Franklin Delano Roosevelt was one of the most effective political leaders in American history. Himself a patrician from old, pre-Revolutionary stock, he communicated effectively with working-class and middle-class Americans of all origins through the new electronic medium, the radio, and won their support for his policies. In the selection below—one of his famous "fireside chats"—FDR explains his recovery program to a wide audience.

FDR was not a systematic thinker. He was a pragmatist and an improviser. Yet in this radio talk he makes it seem as if the New Deal program for industrial and financial recovery was part of a long-term plan. What is Roosevelt attempting to accomplish in this talk? Whom is he trying to appease? What position on the political spectrum is he seeking to establish for his policies? Why do you suppose he quotes the Republican politician Elihu Root at length?

The Second Fireside Chat of 1934

FRANKLIN DELANO ROOSEVELT

Three months have passed since I talked with you shortly after the adjournment of the Congress. Tonight I continue that report, though, because of the shortness of time, I must defer a number of subjects to a later date.

Recently the most notable public questions that have concerned us all have had to do with industry and labor and with respect to these, certain developments have taken place which I consider of importance. I am happy to report that after years of uncertainty, culminating in the collapse of the spring of 1933, we are bringing order out of the old chaos with a greater certainty of the employment of labor at a reasonable wage and of more business at a fair profit. These governmental and industrial developments hold promise of new achievements for the Nation.

Men may differ as to the particular form of governmental activity with respect to industry and business, but nearly all are agreed that private enterprise in times such

Franklin D. Roosevelt, *The Public Papers and Addresses of Franklin D. Roosevelt,* ed. Samuel Rosenman (New York: Random House, 1938), vol. 3, pp. 413–417, 420–422.

as these cannot be left without assistance and without reasonable safeguards lest it destroy not only itself but also our processes of civilization. The underlying necessity for such activity is indeed as strong now as it was years ago when Elihu Root said the following very significant words:

> Instead of the give and take of free individual contract, the tremendous power of organization has combined great aggregations of capital in enormous industrial establishments working through vast agencies of commerce and employing great masses of men in movements of production and transportation and trade, so great in the mass that each individual concerned in them is quite helpless by himself. The relations between the employer and the employed, between the owners of aggregated capital and the units of organized labor, between the small producer, the small trader, the consumer, and the great transporting and manufacturing and distributing agencies, all present new questions for the solution of which the old reliance upon the free action of individual wills appears quite inadequate. And in many directions, the intervention of that organized control which we call government seems necessary to produce the same result of justice and right conduct which obtained through the attrition of individuals before the new conditions arose.

It was in this spirit thus described by Secretary Root that we approached our task of reviving private enterprise in March, 1933. Our first problem was, of course, the banking situation because, as you know, the banks had collapsed. Some banks could not be saved but the great majority of them, either through their own resources or with Government aid, have been restored to complete public confidence. This has given safety to millions of depositors in these banks. Closely following this great constructive effort we have, through various Federal agencies, saved debtors and creditors alike in many other fields of enterprise, such as loans on farm mortgages and home mortgages; loans to the railroads and insurance companies and, finally, help for home owners and industry itself.

In all of these efforts the Government has come to the assistance of business and with the full expectation that the money used to assist these enterprises will eventually be repaid. I believe it will be.

The second step we have taken in the restoration of normal business enterprise has been to clean up thoroughly unwholesome conditions in the field of investment. In this we have had assistance from many bankers and business men, most of whom recognize the past evils in the banking system, in the sale of securities, in the deliberate encouragement of stock gambling, in the sale of unsound mortgages and in many other ways in which the public lost billions of dollars. They saw that without changes in the policies and methods of investment there could be no recovery of public confidence in the security of savings. The country now enjoys the safety of bank savings under the new banking laws, the careful checking of new securities under the Securities Act and the curtailment of rank stock speculation through the Securities Exchange Act. I sincerely hope that as a result people will be discouraged in unhappy efforts to get rich quick by speculating in securities. The average person almost always loses. Only a very small minority of the people of this country believe in gambling as a substitute for the old philosophy of Benjamin Franklin that the way to wealth is through work.

In meeting the problems of industrial recovery the chief agency of the Government has been the National Recovery Administration [N.R.A.]. Under its guidance, trades and industries covering over 90 percent of all industrial employees have adopted codes of fair competition, which have been approved by the President. Under these codes, in the industries covered, child labor has been eliminated. The work day and the work week have been shortened. Minimum wages have been established and other wages adjusted toward a rising standard of living. The emergency purpose of the N.R.A. was to put men to work and since its creation more than four million persons have been reemployed, in great part through the cooperation of American business brought about under the codes.

Benefits of the Industrial Recovery Program have come, not only to labor in the form of new jobs, in relief from overwork and in relief from underpay, but also to the owners and managers of industry because, together with a great increase in the payrolls, there has come a substantial rise in the total of industrial profits—a rise from a deficit figure in the first quarter of 1933 to a level of sustained profits within one year from the inauguration of N.R.A.

Now it should not be expected that even employed labor and capital would be completely satisfied with present conditions. Employed workers have not by any means all enjoyed a return to the earnings of prosperous times, although millions of hitherto underprivileged workers are today far better paid than ever before. Also, billions of dollars of invested capital have today a greater security of present and future earning power than before. This is because of the establishment of fair, competitive standards and because of relief from unfair competition in wage cutting which depresses markets and destroys purchasing power. But it is an undeniable fact that the restoration of other billions of sound investments to a reasonable earning power could not be brought about in one year. There is no magic formula, no economic panacea, which could simply revive overnight the heavy industries and the trades dependent upon them.

Nevertheless the gains of trade and industry, as a whole, have been substantial. In these gains and in the policies of the Administration there are assurances that hearten all forward-looking men and women with the confidence that we are definitely rebuilding our political and economic system on the lines laid down by the New Deal—lines which as I have so often made clear, are in complete accord with the underlying principles of orderly popular government which Americans have demanded since the white man first came to these shores. We count, in the future as in the past, on the driving power of individual initiative and the incentive of fair profit, strengthened with the acceptance of those obligations to the public interest which rest upon us all. We have the right to expect that this driving power will be given patriotically and whole-heartedly to our Nation. . . .

Closely allied to the N.R.A. is the program of public works provided for in the same Act and designed to put more men back to work, both directly on the public works themselves, and indirectly in the industries supplying the materials for these public works. To those who say that our expenditures for public works and other means for recovery are a waste that we cannot afford, I answer that no country, however rich, can afford the waste of its human resources. Demoralization caused by vast unemployment is our greatest extravagance. Morally, it is the greatest menace to our social order. Some people try to tell me that we must make up our minds that for the future we shall permanently have millions of unemployed just as other countries have had them for over a decade. What may be necessary for those countries is not my responsibility to determine. But as for this country, I stand or fall by my refusal to accept as a necessary condition of our future a permanent army of unemployed. On the contrary, we must make it a national principle that we will not tolerate a large army of unemployed and that we will arrange our national economy to end our present unemployment as soon as we can and then to take wise measures against its return. I do not want to think that it is the destiny of any American to remain permanently on relief rolls. . . .

In our efforts for recovery we have avoided, on the one hand, the theory that business should and must be taken over into an all-embracing Government. We have avoided, on the other hand, the equally untenable theory that it is an interference with liberty to offer reasonable help when private enterprise is in need of help. The course we have followed fits the American practice of Government, a practice of taking action step by step, or regulating only to meet concrete needs, a practice of courageous recognition of change. I believe with Abraham Lincoln, that "The legitimate object of Government is to do for a community of people whatever they need to have done but cannot do at all or cannot do so well for themselves in their separate and individual capacities."

I am not for a return to that definition of liberty under which for many years a free people were being gradually regimented into the service of the privileged few. I prefer and I am sure you prefer that broader definition of liberty under which we are moving forward to greater freedom, to greater security for the average man than he has ever known before in the history of America.

9.2:   The New Deal and the "Common Man" (1934, 1936)

Roosevelt and the New Deal proved immensely popular with middle- and lower-income Americans. In 1936 FDR won in an extraordinary popular landslide when he ran for reelection.

In the selections below—letters written by working class Americans to New Deal politicians, to FDR's wife, Eleanor, and to the president himself—we learn why the "common man" supported the administration's programs. How would you characterize the sources of this support? What New Deal programs particularly seemed to awaken the gratitude of ordinary Americans?

"Saint Roosevelt"

Cedarburg, Wis.
10:45 A.M. Mar. 5, 1934

Mrs. F. D. Roosevelt
Washington, D.C.

My dear Friend:

Just listened to the address given by your dear husband, our wonderful President. During the presidential campaign of 1932 we had in our home a darling little girl, three years old. My husband & I were great admirers of the Dem. candidate and so Dolores had to listen to much talk about the great man who we hoped and prayed would be our next Pres. We are Lutherans and she is Catholic so you'll get quite a thrill out of what I'm to tell you now. That fall Judge Karel of Mil. sent me a fine picture of our beloved President, which I placed in our Public Library. When I received this fine picture my dear mother (who has since been called Home) said to Dolores "Who is this man?" and Dolores answered without any hesitation "Why who else, but Saint Roosevelt!" The old saying goes fools and children often tell the truth and indeed we all feel if there ever was a Saint. He is one. As long as Pres. Roosevelt will be our leader under Jesus Christ we feel no fear. His speech this morning showed he feels for the "least of these" I am enclosing a snap shot of the dear little girl who acclaimed our President a Saint and rightly so.

I'm sure Pres. Roosevelt had a great day on Feb. 16, the world day of prayer, when many hearts were lifted in prayer for him all over this great land of ours.

We shall continue to ask our heavenly Father to guide and guard him in his great task as leader of the great American people.

With all good wishes for you and your fine family I am your most sincerely

Mrs. L.K.S.

Nov 25, 1934
Arkansas City, Kansas

Mrs. Eleanor Roosevelt
White House
Washington, D.C.

Dear Madam:

I beg to inform you that I have been reading your writings in the Wichita Beacon and I must say that the whole nation should be enthused over them. I especially was carried away with the one on Old Age Pensions. It brought my mind back to the day of the Chicago Convention, when Mr. Roosevelt was nominated for the presidency.

In our little home in Arkansas City, my family and I were sitting around the radio, to hear and we heard you when you flew over from N.Y. and entered the great hall and when he spoke it seems as though some Moses had come to alleviated us of our sufferings. Strange to say when he was speaking to see the moisten eyes and the deep feeling of emotions that gave vent to his every word and when you spoke then we knew that the white house would be filled with a real mother to the nation.

I am . . . glad to say . . . you have not failed us, you have visited the slums, the farms and homes of your people, and formed first handed ideas for their benefits. Oh what a blessing while you have always had a silver spoon in your own mouth you have not failed to try and place one in every mouth in the land and when I read in the Beacon your brilliant ideas of the Old Age Pensions. You said the only thing laking [sic] was the way to do it. So I said the first lady is seeking a way to help us and so let us help her to find it. . . .

Dear Madam, I am afraid to write more to you at this time as this is my first letter to the lady of the land as the others did not seem to be interested in the welfare of the people. Wife and I pray continually to God for your success. Every time the news boy hollers Extra our hearts are filled with fear that something has happened to the president, but as we go marching on to higher hills of prosperity through the new deal we are hoping and working to that point that all will be well. But one thing I was just about to forget I think that the home building program should be furnished means for back taxes included for repairs and etc. As many places are handicapped to get loans from government on account of being back taxes. Our heart in hand is ever with you and the Pres. to carry on.

Respectfuly Yours,
P.F.A. [male]

[Columbus, Ga.
October 24, 1934]

[Dear President Roosevelt:]

I hope you can spare the time for a few words from a cotton mill family, *out of work* and almost out of heart and in just a short while out of a house in which to live. you know of course that the realators are putting the people out when they cannot pay the rent promptly. and how are we to pay the rent so long as the mills refuse us work, merely because we had the nerve to ask or "demand," better working conditions.[1]

I realize *and* appreciate the aid and food which the government is giving to the poor people out of work *Thanks to you.*

but is it even partly right for us to be thrown out of our homes, when we have no chance whatever of paying, so long as the big corporations refuse of work. I for one am very disheartened *and* disappointed   guess my notice to move will come next.

---

[1]This is a reference to the unsuccessful 1934 textile workers' strike—ED.

what are we to do. wont you try to help us wont you appeal, "for *us* all," to the real estate people and the factories

hoping you'll excuse this, but I've always thought of F.D.R. as my personal friend.

C.L.F. [male]

[Akron, Ohio
February 1936]

My Dear Mrs Roosevelt.[2]

I thought I would write a letter hoping you would find time to read it, and if you thought it was worth while answering it, I would be glad of any advise you would care to give me. A few weeks ago, I heard your talk over the air, on the subject of the Old age pension, and I got to thinking what a blessing it would be to my mother, if it was possible for her to receive that pension, if the bill should pass. My mother has been in this country since April 1914 but she has never made herself a American Citizen, as she was sixty years old when she came here, and now she is eighty.

Mother come out to this country nineteen years ago [from Scotland][3]. . . .

I thought as long as I lived there was no need to worry about her being taken care of, but I never dreamed of a depression like we have had well it has changed the whole course of our lives we have suffered, and no one knowes but our own family, I have two children one nineteen, graduated from high school last June, and the girl graduates this coming June, and we have had the awfullest time trying to get the bare necessary things in life.

I am in no position to do the right thing for mother, I cant give her anything but her living but I thought if it was possible for her to get that pension it would be like a gift from heaven, as in all the years she has been in this country she has never had a dollar of her own.

I wish she could get it her days may not be long on this earth, and if she just had a little money coming once in a while, to make her feel independent of her family, I at least would know that if anything happened to me she could get a living, and not have to go back to the rest of her family, because she says she would rather go to a poor house, than live with any of the others.

Mrs Roosevelt you might think I have lots of nerve writing to you when you have so much to attend to but I could not help admiring you for the splended way you talked about the old people of this nation I feel sorry for all of them, they seem to be forgotten, and most young people think they have had there day and should be glad to die. but this is not my idea, I think that their last few years should be made as plesent for them as it is possible, I know that if it was in my power to make my mother happy by giving her what she justly deservs, I would gladly do so. Well whither my mother ever gets anything or not, I hope all the other old people that is intilted to it gets it soon, because there is noth-

[2]Misspellings are part of the original letter—ED.
[3]Eighteen years ago—ED.

ing sadder than old people who have struggled hard all there lives to give there family a start in life, then to be forgotten, when they them self need it most.

I will finish now but befor I do I want to thank you Mrs Roosevelt and also Mr Roosevelt for the good both of you are doing for this country you have gave people new hope and every real American has faith in you and may you both be spared to carry on the good work and lead this nation on to victory.

> Yours Respectfully,
> Mrs J. S.
> Akron, Ohio.

9.3:   Attack from the Right (1932, 1936)

Wherever it properly belongs on the political spectrum, the New Deal kindled opposition both to its right and to its left. Among conservatives no person was so determined an adversary as Herbert Hoover, the ex-president whom millions of Americans blamed for the Depression. In the first selection Hoover condemns big government. In the second selection, an excerpt from a speech he made during the 1936 election campaign in support of the Republican presidential candidate, Hoover tears into the New Deal. What are the grounds for his attack? What personal factors may have encouraged him in his opposition? What is his evaluation of the New Deal as an agency of recovery? Are Hoover's criticisms of the New Deal defensible?

America Has Not Yet Reached Its Zenith

HERBERT HOOVER

. . . I challenge the whole idea that we have ended the advance of America, that this country has reached the zenith of its power, the height of its development. That is the counsel of despair for the future of America. That is not the spirit by which we shall emerge from this depression. That is not the spirit that made this country. If it is true, every American must abandon the road of countless progress and unlimited opportunities. I deny that the promise of American life has been fulfilled, for that means we have begun the decline and fall. No nation can cease to move forward without degeneration of spirit.

I could quote from gentlemen who have emitted this same note of pessimism in economic depressions going back for 100 years. What Governor Roosevelt has overlooked is the fact that we are yet but on the frontiers of development of science, and of invention. I have only to remind you that discoveries in electricity, the internal-combustion engine, the radio—all of which have sprung into being since

Herbert Hoover, Speech in Madison Square Garden, New York City, October 31, 1932. Quoted from William Starr Myers, ed., *The State Papers and Other Public Writings of Herbert Hoover* (New York: Doubleday, Doran & Company, Inc., 1934), pp. 423–428.

our land was settled—have in themselves represented the greatest advances in America. This philosophy upon which the Governor of New York proposes to conduct the Presidency of the United States is the philosophy of stagnation, of despair. It is the end of hope. The destinies of this country should not be dominated by that spirit in action. It would be the end of the American system.

I have recited to you the progress of this last generation. Progress in that generation was not due to the opening up of new agricultural land; it was due to the scientific research, the opening of new invention, new flashes of light from the intelligence of our people. These brought the improvements in agriculture and in industry. There are a thousand inventions for comfort in the lockers of science and invention which have not yet come to light; all are but on their frontiers. As for myself I am confident that if we do not destroy this American system, if we continue to stimulate scientific research, if we continue to give it the impulse of initiative and enterprise, if we continue to build voluntary coöperative action instead of financial concentration, if we continue to build it into a system of free men, my children will enjoy the same opportunity that have come to me and to the whole 120,000,000 of my countrymen. I wish to see American Government conducted in this faith and in this hope.

If these measures, these promises, which I have discussed; or these failures to disavow these projects; this attitude of mind, mean anything, they mean the enormous expansion of the Federal Government; they mean the growth of bureaucracy such as we have never seen in our history. No man who has not occupied my position in Washington can fully realize the constant battle which must be carried on against incompetence, corruption, tyranny of government expanded into business activities. If we first examine the effect on our form of government of such a program, we come at once to the effect of the most gigantic increase in expenditure ever known in history. That alone would break down the savings, the wages, the equality of opportunity among our people. These measures would transfer vast responsibilities to the Federal Government from the states, the local governments, and the individuals. But that is not all; they would break down our form of government. Our legislative bodies can not delegate their authority to any dictator, but without such delegation every member of these bodies is impelled in representation of the interest of his constituents constantly to seek privilege and demand service in the use of such agencies. Every time the Federal Government extends its arm, 531 Senators and Congressmen become actual boards of directors of that business.

The New Deal Is a Danger to Freedom

HERBERT HOOVER

Through four years of experience this New Deal attack upon free institutions has emerged as the transcendent issue in America.

All the men who are seeking for mastery in the world today are using the same weapons. They sing the same songs. They all promise the joys of Elysium without effort.

New York Times, October 31, 1936.

But their philosophy is founded on the coercion and compulsory organization of men. True liberal government is founded on the emancipation of men. This is the issue upon which men are imprisoned and dying in Europe right now. . . .

Freedom does not die from frontal attack. It dies because men in power no longer believe in a system based upon liberty. . . .

I gave the warning against this philosophy of government four years ago from a heart heavy with anxiety for the future of our country. It was born from many years' experience of the forces moving in the world which would weaken the vitality of American freedom. It grew in four years of battle as President to uphold the banner of free men.

And that warning was based on sure ground from my knowledge of the ideas that Mr. Roosevelt and his bosom colleagues had covertly embraced despite the Democratic platform.

Those ideas were not new. Most of them had been urged upon me.

During my four years powerful groups thundered at the White House with these same ideas. Some were honest, some promising votes, most of them threatening reprisals, and all of them yelling "reactionary" at us.

I rejected the notion of great trade monopolies and price-fixing through codes. That could only stifle the little business man by regimenting him under the big brother. That idea was born of certain American Big Business and grew up to be the NRA.

I rejected the schemes of "economic planning" to regiment and coerce the farmer. That was born of a Roman despot 1,400 years ago and grew up into the AAA.

I refused national plans to put the government into business in competition with its citizens. That was born of Karl Marx.

I vetoed the idea of recovery through stupendous spending to prime the pump. That was born of a British professor.

I threw out attempts to centralize relief in Washington for politics and social experimentation. I defeated other plans to invade States' rights, to centralize power in Washington. Those ideas were born of American radicals.

I stopped attempts at currency inflation and repudiation of government obligation. That was robbery of insurance policy holders, savings bank depositors and wage-earners. That was born of the early Brain Trusters.

I rejected all these things because they would not only delay recovery but because I knew that in the end they would shackle free men.

Rejecting these ideas we Republicans had erected agencies of government which did start our country to prosperity without the loss of a single atom of American freedom. . . .

Our people did not recognize the gravity of the issue when I stated it four years ago. That is no wonder, for the day Mr. Roosevelt was elected recovery was in progress, the Constitution was untrampled, the integrity of the government and the institutions of freedom were intact.

It was not until after the election that the people began to awake. Then the realization of intended tinkering with the currency drove bank depositors into the panic that greeted Mr. Roosevelt's inauguration.

Recovery was set back for two years, and hysteria was used as the bridge to reach the goal of personal government.

I am proud to have carried the banner of free men to the last hour of the term my countrymen entrusted it to me. It matters nothing in the history of a race what happens to those who in their time have carried the banner of free men. What matters is that the battle shall go on.

The people know now the aims of this New Deal philosophy of government.

We propose instead leadership and authority in government within the moral and economic framework of the American System.

We propose to hold to the Constitutional safeguards of free men.

We propose to relieve men from fear, coercion and spite that are inevitable in personal government.

We propose to demobilize and decentralize all this spending upon which vast personal power is being built. We propose to amend the tax laws so as not to defeat free men and free enterprise.

We propose to turn the whole direction of this country toward liberty, not away from it.

The New Dealers say that all this that we propose is a worn-out system; that this machine age requires new measures for which we must sacrifice some part of the freedom of men. Men have lost their way with a confused idea that governments should run machines.

Man-made machines cannot be of more worth than men themselves. Free men made these machines. Only free spirits can master them to their proper use.

The relation of our government with all these questions is complicated and difficult. They rise into the very highest ranges of economics, statesmanship and morals.

And do not mistake. Free government is the most difficult of all government. But it is everlastingly true that the plain people will make fewer mistakes than any group of men no matter how powerful. But free government implies vigilant thinking and courageous living and self-reliance in a people.

Let me say to you that any measure which breaks our dikes of freedom will flood the land with misery.

9.4:   Thunder from the Left (1934)

The New Deal not only offended political conservatives; it also angered many radicals. During the opening years of the Roosevelt administration, no organized group was as hostile to it as the Communist Party of the United States. The following selection is from a 1934 Communist Party pamphlet presenting "a program for American labor" that interprets the New Deal as the enemy of the American working class.

Why did the American Communists compare the New Deal with contemporary fascism? What aspects of the New Deal did they have in mind? What did they mean by fascism? *Within a year or two the Communist Party of the United States would do a complete reversal on the Roosevelt administration. Can you guess why? What was the ultimate source of Communist attitudes toward American politics and politicians in these years?*

The Communist Party: The New Deal Means Fascism and War

Mass Starvation and Misery

... Sixteen million workers stand idle outside closed factories, mines, suffering from the lack of the very things they could produce in these industries. The total income of the working class is less than 40 per cent of what it was four years ago. The oppressed Negro masses are suffering new economic attacks, and a rising wave of lynch terror. Large sections of poor and middle farmers are being crushed and driven off their land or reduced to the position of tenants and peons for the bankers and monopolists. Great numbers of the middle class intellectuals, professionals, teachers, white collar workers, have likewise been cast into poverty. Especially hard hit as a result of the crisis is the youth of the working class, farmer and middle class. Millions of working class children are suffering from undernourishment and actual starvation, unable to go to school because of lack of food, clothing and even school facilities, which are everywhere reduced.

New Deal—Program of Fascism and War

... The "New Deal" of Roosevelt is the aggressive effort of the bankers and trusts to find a way out of the crisis at the expense of the millions of toilers. Under cover of the most shameless demagogy, Roosevelt and the capitalists carry through drastic attacks upon the living standards of the masses, increased terrorism against the Negro masses, increased political oppression and systematic denial of existing civil rights, and are strengthening the control of the big monopolists over the economic and political life of the country. The "New Deal" is a program of fascization and the most intense preparations for imperialist war. Its class character is especially seen in the policy of the subsidies to the railroads, banks, and insurance companies, accompanied by increased parasitism, corruption, and bureaucratism. The devaluation of the dollar has resulted in a rapid rise of prices of commodities, and the lowering of ... real wages. The N.R.A. machinery, with its labor boards on the one hand, and the most brutal police and military force on the other, has been used for the purpose of breaking up the workers' struggles and their organizations. Strike struggles, not only those of the independent class unions, against whom the attack has been most vicious, but also the struggles of the workers in the A. F. of L.,[1] have been violently

---

The Way Out: A Program for American Labor (New York: Workers' Library Publishers, 1934), pp. 33–35.
[1]The American Federation of Labor, a conservative labor group—ED.

suppressed. Its farm policy has helped to enrich the big farmers and capitalists at the expense of the agricultural workers, the poor and middle farmers.

. . . The right of organization which was so loudly hailed by the social-fascists, which was to be guaranteed by section 7a of the N.R.A., has been used as a new instrument in the hands of the employers for the development of company unions, to block the desire of the workers to organize into real trade unions, independent of the bosses and government. It is an instrument to prop up the boss-controlled A. F. of L. bureaucracy, where the workers cannot be forced into company unions, and a means to divert the fight and organization of the working class away from militant trade unions. The system of codes has been a step in the direction of government control and fascization of the trade unions. The codes fixed minimum wages in the face of inflation and rising prices. The so-called Public Works Program has been used for the building up of the army and navy—an additional important weapon for the whole program of Roosevelt, which is one of preparation for war. All of this proves that the Roosevelt regime is not, as the liberals and Socialist Party leaders claim, a progressive regime, but is a government serving the interests of finance capital and moving toward the fascist suppression of the workers' movement.

Threatening War Danger

. . . The capitalist class is feverishly preparing for war as a way out of the crisis. It has embarked on a naval race with its main imperialist rivals, Great Britain and Japan. The army has been further mechanized, and the world's largest air fleet has been provided for, coast defense has been strengthened, army cantonments throughout the country have been provided; and the C.C.C.[2] has served as a trial mobilization and training ground for a great army, both for imperialist war and for civil war against the workers at home, as openly admitted by Roosevelt's assistant secretary of war, Woodring.

In all the markets of the world, the struggle between Great Britain and the United States grows more acute. The Roosevelt regime, through its inflation, is engaged in a war on British goods and on British currency, in an effort to win world hegemony. The struggle for hegemony in the Pacific between the United States and Japan daily becomes more marked, with both nations building up their naval armaments in anticipation of war. All the chief imperialist powers are clashing for the lion's share in the dismemberment of China. The imperialist aggressiveness of Roosevelt's policies is shown most clearly in Cuba, in Latin America (Bolivia-Paraguay war), and in the Philippines. Roosevelt's policies are interlocked with the policies of world capitalism, characterized everywhere by the desperate attempt to get out of the crisis at the expense of the masses by means of fascism, war and intervention.

. . . The preparations for war are being carried through especially by Roosevelt under the cover of pacifist and "democratic" demagogy. In this trickery of the

---

[2]The Civilian Conservation Corps, a New Deal program to employ city youths in National Parks and forests under semi-military control—ED.

masses, Roosevelt has the utmost support of the A. F. of L. bureaucrats, Socialists and liberals. The A. F. of L. bureaucrats carry on the most violent attacks against the Socialist fatherland. They support the preparations for an army and navy on the plea that it gives employment. The Socialists have invested the "New Deal" war and fascist program with the halo of Socialism. Now openly and now covertly, they continue their attacks against the Soviet Union. . . .

The Fascization of the American Government

. . . American capitalism is more and more fascizing its rule. This is particularly being performed by the Roosevelt administration under the cover of the "New Deal." Under the mask of saving the "democratic institutions of the United States, the Roosevelt government and the bourgeoisie are: (a) increasing the violence against the workers, particularly revolutionary workers and Negro masses, against whom they have unleashed a wave of lynch terror; (b) increasing tendencies to suppress and deny the right to strike; (c) establishing labor Arbitration Boards with direct participation of the employers and the bureaucrats, with the object of preventing, suppressing, and disorganizing the struggles of the workers; (d) directly concentrating into the hands of the President almost dictatorial powers, and vesting power, formerly executed by Congress, in direct appointees of the President over matters of most vital concern to millions of toilers; (e) developing a wave of chauvinism and carrying through the whole N.R.A. campaign with the greatest emphasis upon nationalism.

☆ **10** ☆

World War II

By 1938 the attention of the Roosevelt administration was shifting rapidly from domestic to foreign concerns. Some scholars claim that this change of focus derived from the impasse over the nation's economic problems. Unemployment would simply not go away, and FDR and his colleagues, they say, found foreign affairs more congenial and politically rewarding than the intractable Depression. Other scholars feel there is no need to look beyond the growing menace abroad: the rise of the "dictators," especially the leader of Nazi Germany, Adolf Hitler, which truly threatened the world balance of power and the survival of the liberal democracies, including the United States.

In 1938, as tensions grew in Europe, the administration steeled itself for an eventual confrontation with the "aggressors." But the public's attitudes failed to keep in step. Through the 1920s and well into the 1930s most Americans felt that their country's World War I intervention had been a mistake and rejected any commitment to collective international action to preserve peace. Europe's—and Asia's—concerns were not ours.

The American isolationism of the period between the wars was compounded of many elements: traditional American xenophobia, pacifism, midwestern Progessivism, and an emotional backlash among ethnic groups humiliated during World War I by repressive superpatriotism. It was reinforced by a seductive intellectual construct. During the 1930s a rash of scholarly books and a burst of congressional hearings held by the Nye Committee in 1934–1936 blamed American involvement in World War I on the connivance of bankers and munitions manufacturers. The United States, it was argued, had been duped into the war to benefit the "merchants of death." Profits, rather than patriotism, had driven American foreign policy from 1914 to 1917.

Whatever the source of this distancing from foreign concerns, beginning in 1935 Congress enacted a number of Neutrality Acts designed to prevent U.S. entanglement in another great European conflict. These measures prohibited American loans to belligerents, restricted Americans' travel on belligerent ships, and forbade the export of American arms and munitions to belligerents. In effect, Congress sought to keep the United States from becoming enmeshed in Europe's problems, even if it meant surrendering some of its traditional rights.

But Congress had failed to take account of the deteriorating international environment. In 1932 Japan had seized Manchuria from China and five years later began a war to reduce all of the Chinese Republic to colonial status. In Africa the Italian fascist dictator, Benito Mussolini, attacked Ethiopia, virtually the last of Africa's free nations, and in 1936 annexed it as a colony. Most ominous of all was the aggressive posture of Germany under its brutal dictator, Adolf Hitler.

Hitler had risen to power pledged to undo the Versailles Treaty, rearm Germany, and restore it to its former level of influence. In 1936 he remilitarized the Rhineland border with France; in 1938 he annexed Austria to Germany. He was soon demanding Czech surrender of the Sudeten area, a part of the Czechoslovak Republic inhabited mainly by Germans. Meanwhile, in Germany itself he had destroyed the liberal Weimar Republic and imposed a viciously racist totalitarian regime that reversed a century of democratic progress in Europe.

It was against this background of Japanese, Italian, and German militarism and tyranny that Americans debated their country's role in international affairs. Isolationists remained unconvinced of the need for the United States to intrude into these conflicts. Interventionists believed that America's own vital interests, and indeed its very safety, were involved. In the selections below you will encounter samples of both the isolationist and interventionist arguments that shaped the intense debate over peace or war during the 1930s and in the months preceding the Japanese attack on Pearl Harbor in December 1941.

American foreign policy and public opinion were transformed by World War II. Intervention led to a bold new internationalism that would reveal itself in global war aims and major global commitments once the Allies began discussing the terms of the peace settlement and postwar order that would follow. The end of the war left the United States the world's undisputed economic, military, and diplomatic leader. In the thought of Franklin Roosevelt during the war years, it is easy to trace America's rise to globalism.

10.1:   Isolationism (1935, 1939)

One of the most prominent of the isolationist spokespersons during the1930s was the Democratic senator from Missouri, Bennett Champ Clark. A member of the Nye Committee, Clark was an ardent isolationist and opponent of the New Deal. In the following selection, taken from an address he delivered in May 1935, Clark defends the views and policies incorporated into the mid-thirties neutrality legislation.

Clark's attitudes are based on an analysis of how America became involved in World War I. Is the analysis valid? Could the United States have avoided war in 1917 if it had not insisted on its rights as a neutral nation? Had the Neutrality Acts passed in the 1930s been retained, would they have kept the United States out of the great new war emerging on the horizon?

Another prominent isolationist leader was the Republican senator from Ohio, Robert Taft, son of the twenty-seventh president of the United States. By early 1939, when Taft delivered the talk excerpted below, the world was already on the verge of war, and Roosevelt had begun to question the wisdom of the neutrality legislation, which, he believed, helped aggressors and penalized their victims. Roosevelt was particularly concerned that applying the American arms embargo would benefit the rebellion of the far right against the Spanish Loyalists then underway, led by General Francisco Franco and supported by fascist Italy and Nazi Germany.

Taft professes not to oppose collective action to stop aggressors, but he rejects unilateral American action. Is his position sincere, or was it a dodge? Did many isolationists favor American cooperation with other nations to prevent international aggression?

The Experience of the Last War Should Guide Us Today

BENNETT CHAMP CLARK

In the light of experience it is high time that we gave some thought to the hard, practical question of just how we propose to avoid war if it comes again. No one who has made an honest attempt to face the issue will assert that there is any easy answer. No one who has studied the history of our participation in the World War will tell you that there is a simple way out. There is none—no simple panacea, no magic formula. But if we have learned anything at all we know the inevitable and tragic end to a policy of drifting and trusting to luck. We know that however strong

28 May 1935, *Congressional Record*, 74th Cong., 1st sess., 8335-8338.

is the will of the American people to refrain from mixing in other peoples' quarrels, that will can only be made effective if we have a sound, definite policy from the beginning. No lesson of the last war is more clear than that such a policy cannot be improvised after war breaks out. It must be worked out in advance, before it is too late to apply reason. I say with all possible earnestness that if we want to avoid another war we must begin at once to formulate a policy based upon an understanding of the problem confronting us. . . .

The best way . . . is to examine the forces which are likely to involve us in war. In 1914 we knew very little about those forces. President Wilson issued his proclamation of neutrality and we went on with business as usual, in the happy belief that 3,000 miles of ocean would keep us out of the mess. Our professional diplomats were not much more astute. They assumed that all we had to do to keep out was to observe the rules of international law and insist upon our neutral rights. About 2 weeks after the outbreak of hostilities our State Department issued a public circular on the rights and duties of a neutral in war time. They took the position that "the existence of war between foreign governments does not suspend trade or commerce between this country and those at war." They told American merchants that there was nothing in international law to prevent them from trading with the warring nations. They told munitions makers that they were free to sell their war materials to either or both sides. They took no steps to warn American citizens of the dangers of travel on vessels of the warring nations, even after passenger ships had been sunk without warning. This attitude, strange as it may seem today, was in full accord with the rules of international law as generally understood at that time.

We are wiser today. We know more about war and much more about neutrality. And yet it is remarkable how much we seem to have forgotten. In the course of the Senate investigation of the munitions industry this winter Senator Nye and I have had occasion to go rather deeply into the activities of our arms merchants and other traders in war material during the early years of the conflict. We have examined again the tortuous record of our diplomatic correspondence. From this survey four broad conclusions stand out:

1. That a policy based on defense of our so-called "neutral rights" led us into serious diplomatic controversy with both the Allies and the Central Powers, and in the end brought us to a point where we were compelled to choose between surrendering those rights or fighting to defend them. In 1917 we chose to fight.

2. The "national honor" and "prestige" of the nation are inevitably involved when American ships are sunk on the high seas—even though the owners of these ships and their cargoes are private citizens seeking to profit from other nations' wars. Passions are quickly aroused when American lives are lost—even though the citizens who took passage on belligerent ships knew in advance the risks they ran.

3. That the economic forces, set in motion by our huge war trade with the Allies, made it impossible to maintain that "true spirit of neutrality" which President Wilson urged upon his fellow citizens at the outbreak of the conflict.

4. That among these economic forces, those which involved us most deeply were the huge trade in arms and ammunition and other war materials with the Allies.

Let Us Retain the Neutrality Acts

ROBERT TAFT

On January fourth [1939] the President of the United States devoted his annual message to Congress to an appeal for increased armament. He pictured a world about to be enveloped in the flames of war, and he pictured the United States as surrounded by deadly armaments and threats of new aggression. He appealed for increased appropriations for adequate defense. His message was followed several days later by a program calling for approximately $525,000,000, of which only $200,000,000 is to be spent in the fiscal year which ends July 1, 1940.

There can be no difference of opinion among Americans on the principle of providing for this country a completely adequate defense against attack by foreign nations. . . .

But the message of the President suggests that he favors a foreign policy very different from mere defense of the United States, and one which in the end would require much greater armament. A year ago, in Chicago, he declared his belief that we should "quarantine the aggressor nations." Now he says that "The defense of religion, of democracy and of good faith among nations is all the same fight. To save one, we must make up our minds to save all." It is somewhat difficult to see how we can save democracy and good faith among nations by any policy of mere defense of the United States. The President says that we cannot safely be indifferent to international lawlessness anywhere in the world, and cannot let pass, without effective protest, acts of aggression against sister nations. It is true that he assumes that the American people are not willing to go to war in other parts of the world, but he says, "There are many methods short of war, but stronger and more effective than mere words, of bringing home to aggressor government the aggregate sentiments of our own people." He declares against neutrality legislation and implies that he favors the repeal of the neutrality law. All this cannot mean anything except that the President wishes power granted to him by Congress to favor one nation or another in any dispute that arises, and to employ economic sanction or embargoes against a nation that he does not like at the same time that he assists those he does like. . . .

In my opinion, such a policy leads inevitably to foreign war. It is contrary to the traditional policy of the United States from the days of George Washington. The position of this country has always been that it would remain neutral in any foreign war, no matter how much its sympathies might be on one side, as long as its own rights or those of its citizens were not infringed upon. This is a policy which was emphatically reaffirmed by the American people in 1920 when it was proposed that we join the League of Nations.

There is something to be said in favor of a general agreement for collective security by which a number of nations, sufficiently strong to dominate the world, undertake to prevent aggression even though it leads to war. There is a reasonable chance

Robert Taft, *Vital Speeches,* vol. 5 (February 1, 1939), pp. 254–256. Mt. Pleasant, SC: South Carolina City News Publishing.

that such a policy must succeed. Our people, however, refused in 1920 to adopt it, and the efforts made under the League of Nations, without our cooperation, have now completely broken down. But the policy of the President . . . is not the policy of a League of Nations; it is completely original. No one has ever suggested before that a single nation should range over the world like a knight-errant, protecting democracy and ideals of good faith, and tilting, like Don Quixote, against the windmills of Fascism. . . .

Of course, such a policy is not only vain, but almost inevitably leads to war. If we enforce an effective embargo against Japan, driving its people to starvation . . . it would be only natural for Japan to attack the Philippines, and our whole standing and prestige would become involved in an Asiatic war. If the Spanish embargo is lifted and an American ship carrying munitions is sunk by an Italian cruiser as it approaches Barcelona, it is hard to see how we could avoid controversy with Italy, which might flame into a general war. We apparently are asked to line up with England and France, and probably Communist Russia, without even knowing what their policies may be or whether they will back up the stand that we may take. . . .

Congress was wise in adopting the neutrality bill, which prohibits the shipment of arms, ammunition, and implements of war to belligerent states, and to states where civil strife exists. I believe the President should long ago have found a state of war to exist between China and Japan, which he had full power to do, so that munitions might not be shipped to Japan. The neutrality bill intends that we shall not manufacture munitions for foreign wars. It provides further that in case of war, nations must come to this country and pay for all articles, other than munitions, to be shipped abroad before they are shipped. Its purpose is to reduce the chances of our becoming involved, and I believe it will assist very much the accomplishment of that purpose. It is in accord in spirit with the whole policy of American neutrality for 150 years.

But now it is suggested that the whole world is different. It is said that distances are so short we cannot possibly avoid being involved in a general war. I don't believe it. I think if we are sufficiently determined not to become involved, we can stay out. We learned our lesson in 1917. We learned that modern war defeats its own purposes. A war to preserve democracy resulted in the destruction of more democracies than it preserved. We may go in on the side of France and England because they are democracies, and find before we are through that they are Communist or Fascist.

Not only that, a war whether to preserve democracy or otherwise would almost certainly destroy democracy in the United States. We have moved far towards totalitarian government already. The additional powers sought by the President in case of war, the nationalization of all industry and all capital and all labor, already proposed in a bill before Congress, would create a socialist dictatorship which it would be impossible to dissolve when the war ended. . . .

There is a general illusion that we see in Germany and Italy forces which threaten to overwhelm England and France, and march on to attack the United States. But this is surely an imaginary fear at the present time. There is no reason to believe that Germany and Italy could defeat England and France in any protracted war. It is hard to see what they would gain even after a successful war by an attack on the United States. Certainly the strength of our position would make any nation hesitate, no matter how strong it might be.

It is natural that the sympathy of the people should be strongly aroused on one side when they see what is going on under the totalitarian governments. Perhaps the President should tell them what we think of them, especially as the day seems to have passed when nations go to war because others call them unpleasant names. But the great majority of the people are determined that those sympathies do not lead us into overt acts of embargo, blockade, or economic sanctions.

Considering the attitude which the President has taken, it seems essential that Congress shall strengthen the neutrality bill rather than repeal it. It seems essential that the President shall not have discretion to take sides in foreign wars, or impose sanctions against those nations which he might find to be aggressor nations. It seems wise not to repeal the Johnson Act, as it is now being suggested, and to maintain a policy of lending as little money as possible abroad. Congress is the body upon whom is conferred by the Constitution power to declare war. It should not permit the executive to go too far towards war, without consulting Congress, that Congress no longer has the power to prevent war.

I do not say that some special situation may not arise in the future, under which it may seem desirable to go to war as the first step in an effective defense. But if such a situation ever arises, it should be undertaken deliberately, after a public discussion by Congress as the representatives chosen by the people.

Many justifiable criticisms can be made of the neutrality act, and of any special type of neutrality. But the horrors of modern war are so great, its futility is so evident, its effect on democracy itself so destructive, that almost any alternative is more to be desired.

10.2: Interventionists (1935)

Not every American endorsed the prevailing isolationist mood of the 1930s. One dissenter was Henry L. Stimson, secretary of state under Herbert Hoover and later, following a long absence from public life, secretary of war under Roosevelt.

Stimson was the quintessential "eastern establishment" figure, a man from an affluent old family with an elite education. As secretary of state he had condemned Japanese aggression against China and, as the 1930s advanced, foresaw increasing danger for America in a chaotic world. Stimson delivered the following radio talk in October 1935, after the Italian attack on Ethiopia.

What is the basis for Stimson's desire that the United States cooperate with the League of Nations to stop Mussolini? Did the United States accept League of Nations sanctions against Italy? Did the sanctions work?

Repeal the Arms Embargo

HENRY L. STIMSON

In discussing the dangers and problems which confront us arising out of the war in Ethiopia, we start from the common ground that we all wish to keep our country out of war. The only differences of opinion between us are as to the methods which will serve to accomplish this common end and will avoid the danger to America of being ultimately embroiled in what is taking place on the other side of the world. The basic difficulty lies in the fact that the modern world has become interconnected and economically interdependent.

A great war anywhere in the world today will seriously affect all the nations, whether they go into that war or not. We have already been given a terrific lesson on this in the great war, but unfortunately in this country we have not all of us learned that lesson. Many of us are accustomed to say that in this great depression we are now suffering from the results of having gone into that war. This is not entirely true. We are really suffering principally from things which happened in that war long before we joined it. For three years we kept out. It was during those three years that the principal economic dislocations took place which have resulted in America's sufferings now.

When in 1914 the European farmers stopped farming and the European manufacturers, traders and laborers left manufacturing and commerce, and all of them concentrated on fighting, the dislocation was begun which has since resulted in the great depression. Our farmers began to plow up new marginal lands in Kansas and other places to take advantage of the high wheat prices which were thus offered; and our manufacturers and traders similarly enlarged their factories and facilities to seek the rich rewards in commerce which were thus thrown at their feet. Out of these dislocations came the foundation for our present trouble. We would have been suffering from them even if we had never entered the war.

From these patent facts we should have learned thoroughly that a war anywhere is dangerous and that a great war will ultimately make us suffer whether we go in or not. We should have learned that the chief problem of the world today is war prevention, not isolation; and that isolation in the modern world is a fantastic impossibility, so far as keeping out of economic trouble is concerned. Most of the other nations of the world have learned this lesson. They have learned that the only method of saving us from war's consequences is for all the nations of the world to cooperate to prevent war from starting. If it starts it must be at once stamped out before it spreads.

The League of Nations is the machinery which these other nations have adopted to secure such cooperation. No one questions the great difficulty of successfully securing cooperative action among the nations of the world, and the work of the League during the last fifteen years has met with much discouragement and opposition. Nevertheless, during those years they have been making progress and have achieved successes which we in this country have never fully appreciated. This au-

Congressional Digest, vol. 15 (January 1936), pp. 25–27.

tumn the League in its treatment of the war crisis between Italy and Ethiopia has taken more vigorous action and accomplished more signal results than ever before in its history. . . .

These nations of the League are now working upon the steps which shall be taken to stamp out this dangerous conflagration. They have pointed out to Premier [Benito] Mussolini the covenants of the League which he is breaking and have called upon him to stop, and he has thus far defied them and is pushing ahead. Without resorting to arms, they are seeking to hold him back by cutting off their trade with him and thus gradually depriving him of the necessary supplies for his expensive adventure. This is a most delicate undertaking, for it involves the stoppage of normal channels of trade between Italy and many other countries. The process may last a long time and lead to complications which no one can now foresee. Over fifty nations, however, have determined that it must be done. They feel that it is the last recourse left them for preventing a war which may spread to all the rest of the world.

In the face of this situation the conduct of our own government is prescribed by the terms of the joint resolution adopted by our Congress on the 31st of August last [1930], which directs the imposition of an embargo upon the export of "arms, ammunition or implements of war" from this country to either Italy or Ethiopia. Under this law the President on October 5 issued a proclamation containing a list of the commodities which are thus prohibited from export. This list covers only the actually completed articles which constitute arms, ammunition and other engines of warfare. It does not cover the raw materials out of which such arms are manufactured, nor does it cover food and other supplies which are just as necessary as arms to an army in the field. It does not cover copper which goes into shells, or cotton or nitrates which go into powder, or oil which goes into transport.

The evident purpose of our Congress in enacting this resolution was similar to that of the fifty nations who are now taking action against Italy at Geneva—namely, to check the progress of the war by cutting off supplies. But the joint resolution as interpreted in the President's proclamation is likely to do more harm than good. It will have very little deterrent effect upon Italy, who is the aggressor and who is able to manufacture her own arms and ammunition, and it is already threatening to be a serious obstacle to the peace efforts of the other nations. If they take no further action than we have taken, the prospect of stamping out the war by holding back the aggressor, Italy, is much diminished. On the other hand, if they put embargoes on these other supplies which are not on our list, the only effect may be to leave the field entirely open for American traders to rush in and take advantage of the enticing market which is thus presented for selling supplies to Italy. That would produce a very serious danger of ultimate trouble between us and the nations which are doing their best to stamp out this war. . . .

On the same day when [President Roosevelt] proclaimed his embargo on arms, ammunition and implements of war, he took a further step. He uttered a further warning in these words:

"In these specific circumstances I desire to be understood that any of our people who voluntarily engage in transactions *of any character* with either of the belligerents do so at their own risk."

By these words he virtually urged our people to cut off all relations with Italy and Ethiopia and to impose a voluntary boycott upon all transactions with them. If this was rendered necessary on account of the limitations of his Congressional authority, I think it was an act of wise leadership on the part of Mr. Roosevelt, taken to avoid future serious complications, and should be commended.

But in order to make this step effective I think eventually he will have to say more. The American President is the natural leader of the public opinion of his people in all matters of foreign relations, particularly in time of war. They look to him for their information and for their guidance. In this pending crisis not a word has yet been said by our government to indicate to our people the impelling moral reason why they should voluntarily make the sacrifices involved in this warning of the President. Not a word has been said to indicate that there is any moral difference between Italy, which has begun this war, and the other nations which are trying to stop it. Not a word has been uttered to point out that Italy has violated solemn covenants and treaties and that those other nations are endeavoring to uphold these treaties; not a word to recall to our people the promises which Italy made to us in the Pact of Paris in respect to renouncing war, promises which, according to the President's own proclamation of October 5, must have been violated.

In short, nothing has yet been said to rouse in our people any feeling that a moral issue is involved in the present crisis which should impel all patriotic men and women to follow the President's advice and to refrain from embarking on the tempting trade with Italy which the Congressional embargo has left open to them. They have not even been advised of the tremendous moral implications represented by the fact that over fifty nations of the world, with all their national differences and interests have been able to unite in a verdict against the nation which is now seeking our assistance to get supplies for an aggressive war. . . .

The public opinion of America is not indifferent to moral issues. The great masses of our countrymen do not wish to drift into a position of blocking the efforts of other nations to stamp out war. The only person who can effectively rouse and marshal moral opinion is the President of the United States, and when he tries to do so I have no doubt of his eventual success.

10.3: America First versus Aid to Britain (1940, 1941)

America's sense of security plumetted dramatically in September 1939, when Hitler invaded Germany's neighbor, Poland. Within hours Britain and France, pledged to defend Poland, declared war on Germany. Poland quickly collapsed under the awesome blows of the Nazi Wehrmacht, and then, in the spring and summer of 1940, the powerful German army attacked Denmark, Norway, Belgium, Holland, and

France. In a few weeks of blitzkrieg, the Nazi war machine had smashed all the Western armies arrayed against it.

By the end of 1940 Britain alone of Hitler's enemies held out, protected for the moment by its island position. But few believed Britain could stop the Nazi juggernaut. Meanwhile, in Nazi-occupied Europe a regime of unexampled savagery was being imposed on the helpless conquered people. At the same time, in the Far East militaristic Japan was taking advantage of the European colonial powers' preoccupation with Hitler to expand its empire in China and Southeast Asia.

The startling success of the aggressors, loosely organized as the Rome-Berlin-Tokyo Axis, dismayed most Americans. But public opinion split over how best to confront the international danger. Isolationists believed that the United States should continue to stay aloof from the Old World's wars while arming itself against any possible attack. In September 1940 they organized America First, headed by a prominent group of businesspeople, politicians, and civic leaders. The interventionists had their own organization, the Committee to Defend America by Aiding the Allies. Led by William Allen White, the Progressive Republican editor from Kansas, the committee sought to rally Americans to support the cause of faltering Britain and the surviving enemies of the Axis powers.

Many of the interventionists were, at heart, convinced that nothing short of full military involvement on Britain's side could protect America's vital interests. But the committee's public focus was on the repeal of the neutrality measures so that the United States could freely supply the anti-Axis forces with the guns, ships, tanks, and planes they needed to survive. The interventionists also sought, even more aggressively than their opponents, to build up America's own military power.

In the first selection below interventionist James B. Conant, president of Harvard University, expresses his views in a radio address in late May 1940. Conant's words were delivered just as Belgium surrendered to the Germans and as the defeated British forces in France gathered at the French port of Dunkirk for escape across the English Channel from the advancing Nazi army.

How does Conant seek to arouse American support for Britain? Is he trying to disguise the risk that the United States might be compelled to go to war? Are his arguments about the Nazis' designs on the United States correct? Was Hitler interested in conquering the United States? Could he have done so given the breadth of the Atlantic Ocean? Would a Nazi-dominated Europe have threatened the United States in any way?

The second selection is from a speech made by isolationist Senator Burton K. Wheeler of Montana in 1941. Like a number of other isolationists, Wheeler was a liberal from the American heartland who disliked Europe and its age-old quarrels. Here he is speaking in opposition to Roosevelt's recent proposal that Congress enact a measure allowing the president to lease vital arms and supplies to Britain for future repayment.

"Lend-lease," as this policy was known, was a late step in the dismantling of the neutrality legislation of the 1930s. At the end of 1939 Congress had repealed the arms embargo provision of the Neutrality Acts and replaced it with "cash and carry." But that was before the fall of France and the Dunkirk evacuation. Now Britain was running out of cash to pay for vital American supplies, and loans seemed the only way to guarantee it could fight on. In mid-December 1940 the president proposed that the United States "lend" or "lease" military equipment to Hitler's only remaining enemy with payment for the portion not returned after use to be postponed until after the war.[1]

Wheeler attacks the president's proposal on several grounds. What are these? To what American emotions and views is Wheeler playing?

We Must Aid the Allies

JAMES B. CONANT

There is no need for me to dwell on the agonizing news of the last few days. Tonight the Germans stand on the shores of the English Channel and along the Somme. Tomorrow looms before us like a menacing question-mark. A total victory for German arms is now well within the range of possibility. . . .

Let me ask you to visualize our future as a democratic free people in a world dominated by ruthless totalitarian states. There are those who argue that Hitler's war machine, when its task is done in Europe, will be converted to an instrument of peaceful industrial activity. I do not think so. There are those who imagine that a government which has broken promise after promise, which has scorned the democratic countries and all they stand for, which mocks and laughs at free institutions as a basis for civilization,—that such a government can live in a peaceful relationship with the United States. I do not think so.

To my mind a complete Nazi victory over France and England would be, by necessity, but a prelude to Hitler's attempt to dominate the world. If Germany were triumphant, at best there would result an armed truce. This country would be fever-

---

[1]The proposal was specious: The United States could not conceivably be interested in any used guns, tanks, and airplanes that might be returned after the war. Roosevelt was actually proposing nothing less than that the United States supply Britain with arms for free.

Congressional Record, 76th Cong., 3rd sess., Appendix, 3669–3670.

ishly endeavoring to put itself into an impregnable position based on a highly militarized society. Our way of life would be endangered for years to come. If this be so, what should we do in these desperate, tragic hours?

We must rearm at once, that much is clear. The vision rises before us of the United States suddenly left alone and unprotected in a totalitarian and destructive world. It is obvious we are unprepared to meet an emergency of this nature. It is also obvious that our first aim must be to prepare with all rapidity. England's failure to listen to Winston Churchill, warning of approaching danger, is responsible for her plight. We must not make the same mistake. We are all agreed on that. . . .

My purpose tonight is to urge another course of action equally important. I am advocating immediate aid to the Allies. I shall mince no words. *I believe the United States should take every action possible to insure the defeat of Hitler.* And let us face honestly the possible implications of such a policy. The actions we propose might eventuate in war. But fear of war is no basis for a national policy. In a free state public opinion must guide the Government, and a wise public opinion on matters of foreign policy can result only if there is a continuous, clear-headed, realistic discussion of all eventualities, including war.

At this moment, the entry of the United States into the war certainly does not seem necessary or wise. . . .

What are then the actions that can be taken at once?

Let us state a few of them: first, the release to France and England of army and navy airplanes and other implements of war, without impairing our own security; second, repeal of the laws which prevent United States citizens from volunteering to serve in foreign armies; third, control of exports with the purpose of aiding the Allies by avoiding leaks to Germany and giving priority to France and England; four, the cooperation of our Maritime Commission with the Allies in every way possible under our present laws to expedite the sending of supplies and munitions. These steps, if promptly taken by our Government, would render effective aid which some experts believe might tip the scales in favor of an Allied victory. Furthermore, they would be of infinite value in strengthening the morale of the Allied nations and would serve notice to the world that our resources were now enlisted in the democratic cause.

I have purposely avoided the use of the words "moral issues." The younger generation in particular is highly suspicious of this phrase. Their feeling is chiefly due to a widespread misinterpretation of the reasons for America's participation in the war in 1914–1918. I have avoided this issue, not because I sympathize with those who proclaim that there is no fundamental difference between the actions and aims of the democracies on the one hand and the totalitarian powers on the other. Far from it. There is to my mind all the difference between piracy and peaceful trade, all the difference between ruthless tyranny and enlightened intercourse among free men.

But I am endeavoring to confine my argument this evening to a realistic appraisal of our foreign policy. Let me make this clear. I advocate no moral crusade to distant lands. If crusading were a proper policy, we should have had more than one provocation for war in the last dozen years. I am arguing that the changed military situation in Europe actually threatens our way of life.

At this moment, today, the war is in effect veering towards our shores. The issue before the United States is, I repeat, can we live as a free, peaceful, relatively unarmed people in a world dominated by the totalitarian states? Specifically, can we look with indifference as a nation (as a nation, mind you, not as individuals) on the possible subjugation of England by a Nazi State? If your answer is yes, then my words are in vain. If your answer is no, I urge you as a citizen to act.

Write or telegraph to the President of the United States, to your Congressman and your Senators, stating your belief that this nation must give immediate, effective aid to the Allies. Let your elected agents of Government have your thoughts. Urge that Congress stay in session to consider emergency legislation as may be necessary, and speed the process of rearmament.

Above all else, let us consider the situation boldly. This is no time for defeatism or despair. The Allies may be expected to hold out if they have help from us and the promise of further help to come. The wrath of moral indignation is impotent in days like these. A struggle to the death is once again in progress on the fields of western Europe. The British Isles are making ready to stand a siege. . . . It is not too late but it is long past time to act. I urge you, let your voice be heard!

Lend-Lease Will Lead to War

BURTON K. WHEELER

The lend-lease policy, translated into legislative form, stunned a Congress and a nation wholly sympathetic to the cause of Great Britain. The Kaiser's blank check to Austria-Hungary in the first World War[1] was a piker compared to the Roosevelt blank check of World War II. It warranted my worst fears for the future of America, and it definitely stamps the President as war-minded.

The lend-lease-give program is the New Deal's triple A foreign policy; it will plow under every fourth American boy.[2]

Never before have the American people been asked or compelled to give so bounteously and so completely of their tax dollars to any foreign nation. Never before has the Congress of the United States been asked by any President to violate international law. Never before has this Nation resorted to duplicity in the conduct of its foreign affairs. Never before has the United States given to one man the power to strip this Nation of its defenses. Never before has a Congress coldly and flatly been asked to abdicate.

If the American people want a dictatorship—if they want a totalitarian form of government and if they want war—this bill should be steam-rollered through Congress, as is the wont of President Roosevelt.

Congressional Record, 77th Cong., 1st sess., Appendix, 178–179.
[1]Supposedly the German kaiser had promised to aid Austria-Hungary if war ensued from its 1914 ultimatum to Serbia—ED.
[2]A reference to the policy set by the Agricultural Adjustment Administration (AAA) in 1933 of destroying crops to raise farm prices—ED.

Approval of this legislation means war, open and complete warfare. I, therefore, ask the American people before they supinely accept it, Was the last World War worth while?

If it were, then we should lend and lease war materials. If it were, then we should lend and lease American boys. President Roosevelt has said we would be repaid by England. We will be. We will be repaid, just as England repaid her war debts of the first World War—repaid those dollars wrung from the sweat of labor and the toil of farmers with cries of "Uncle Shylock." Our boys will be returned—returned in caskets, maybe; returned with bodies maimed; returned with minds warped and twisted by sights of horrors and the scream and shriek of high-powered shells.

Considered on its merits and stripped of its emotional appeal to our sympathies, the lend-lease-give bill is both ruinous and ridiculous. Why should we Americans pay for war materials for Great Britain who still has $7,000,000,000 in credit or collateral in the United States? Thus far England has fully maintained rather than depleted her credits in the United States. The cost of the lend-lease-give program is high in terms of American tax dollars, but it is even higher in terms of our national defense. Now it gives to the President the unlimited power to completely strip our air forces of its every bomber, of its every fighting plane.

It gives to one man—responsible to no one—the power to denude our shores of every warship. It gives to one individual the dictatorial power to strip the American Army of our every tank, cannon, rifle, or antiaircraft gun. No one would deny that the lend-lease-give bill contains provisions that would enable one man to render the United States defenseless, but they will tell you, "The President would never do it." To this I say, "Why does he ask the power if he does not intend to use it?" Why not, I say, place some check on American donations to a foreign nation?

Is it possible that the farmers of America are willing to sell their birthright for a mess of pottage?

Is it possible that American labor is to be sold down the river in return for a place upon the Defense Commission, or because your labor leaders are entertained at pink teas?

Is it possible that the American people are so gullible that they will permit their representatives in Congress to sit supinely by while an American President demands totalitarian powers—in the name of saving democracy?

I say in the kind of language used by the President—shame on those who ask the powers—and shame on those who would grant them.

You people who oppose war and dictatorship, do not be dismayed because the war-mongers and interventionists control most of the avenues of propaganda, including the motion-picture industry.

Do not be dismayed because Mr. Willkie,[3] of the Commonwealth & Southern, agrees with Mr. Roosevelt. This merely puts all the economic and foreign "royalists" on the side of war.

Remember, the interventionists control the money bags, but you control the votes.

---

[3]Wendell Willkie, the Republican presidential nominee in 1940. He had been president of the Commonwealth and Southern Utility Company—ED.

10.4: Undeclared War (1941)

By mid-1941 Roosevelt was convinced that the United States could not avoid intervening militarily to stop the Axis powers. By defeating the German attempt to destroy the Royal Air Force, Britain had thwarted a cross-Channel Nazi invasion from occupied France, but it was losing the battle of supply against Axis U-boats on the Atlantic and was incapable of striking back effectively against the Germans on the continent. Meanwhile, by this time Japan was reeling in much of Southeast Asia like a large fish. Then, in June, Hitler attacked the Soviet Union, and in a few weeks Nazi columns had plunged deep into the Russian heartland, in the process destroying much of the Soviet army and air force.

In the fall of 1941, with the submarine menace growing more serious by the day, Roosevelt ordered the American navy to help escort lend-lease supplies to Britain and the Soviet Union. American navy ships and Nazi submarines were soon exchanging fire on the North Atlantic.

In the selection below from a speech of late October 1941, FDR reveals a new tone. Some historians believe that he was preparing the American public for an actual shooting war on the Atlantic as a back door to full American military participation in the anti-Axis struggle. Does Roosevelt seem to be setting things up for war? (It has been said that he also goaded the Japanese into attacking Pearl Harbor by freezing their financial assets in the United States and embargoing scrap iron and petroleum, both vital to Japan.) How convincing are Roosevelt's remarks about a secret map showing Nazi plans for conquest in the Western Hemisphere and his statement about Hitler's scheme to abolish all religion? Are they demagogic claims, playing on the ill-informed fears of the American people? Given the gravity of the Nazi menace, can the President be forgiven some exaggeration? Did the ends justify the means in this instance?

The German Menace

FRANKLIN DELANO ROOSEVELT

Five months ago tonight I proclaimed to the American people the existence of a state of unlimited emergency. Since then much has happened. Our Army and Navy are temporarily in Iceland in the defense of the Western Hemisphere.

New York Times, October 28, 1941.

Hitler has attacked shipping in areas close to the Americas in the North and South Atlantic.

Many American-owned ships have been sunk on the high seas. One American destroyer was attacked on September 4. Another destroyer was attacked and hit on October 17. Eleven brave and loyal men of our Navy were killed by the Nazis.

We have wished to avoid shooting. But the shooting has started. And history has recorded who fired the first shot. In the long run, however, all that will matter is who fired the last shot.

America has been attacked. . . .

The purpose of Hitler's attacks was to frighten, frighten the American people off the high seas—to force us to make a trembling retreat. This is not the first time that he has misjudged the American spirit. And today that spirit is . . . aroused.

If our national policy were to be dominated by the fear of shooting, then all of our ships and those of our sister republics would have to be tied up in home harbors. Our Navy would have to remain respectfully, abjectedly, behind any line which Hitler might decree on any ocean as his own dictated version of his own war zone.

Naturally we reject that absurd and insulting suggestion. We reject it because of our own self-interest, because of our own self-respect and because, most of all, of our own good faith. Freedom of the seas is now, as it always has been, the fundamental policy of your government and mine.

Hitler has often protested that his plans for conquest do not extend across the Atlantic Ocean. But his submarines and raiders prove otherwise. And so does the entire design of his new world order.

For example, I have in my possession a secret map made in Germany by Hitler's government, by the planners of the new world order. It is a map of South America and a part of Central America, as Hitler proposes to reorganize it. Today in this area there are fourteen separate countries. But the geographical experts of Berlin have ruthlessly obliterated all existing boundary lines. They have divided South America into five vassal States, bringing the whole continent under their domination. And they have also so arranged it that the territory of one of these new puppet States includes the Republic of Panama and our great life line, the Panama Canal.

That is his plan. It will never go into effect.

And that map, my friends, makes clear the Nazi design, not only against South America but against the United States as well.

And your government has in its possession another document, a document made in Germany by Hitler's government. It is a detailed plan, which, for obvious reasons, the Nazis do not wish to publicize just yet, but which they are ready to impose a little later on a dominated world, if Hitler wins.

It is a plan to abolish all existing religions, Catholic, Protestant, Mohammedan, Hindu, Buddhist and Jewish alike. The property of all churches will be seized by the Reich and its puppets. The cross and all other symbols of religion are to be forbidden. The clergy are to be ever liquidated, silenced under penalty of the concentration camps, where even now so many fearless men are being tortured because they have placed God above Hitler.

In the place of the churches of our civilization there is to be set up an international Nazi church, a church which will be served by orators sent out by the Nazi government. And in the place of the Bible, the words of "Mein Kampf"[1] will be imposed and enforced as Holy Writ. And in the place of the cross of Christ will be put two symbols, the swastika and the naked sword.

A god, the god of blood and iron, will take the place of the God of love and mercy. Let us well ponder that statement which I have made tonight.

These grim truths which I have told you of the present and future plans of Hitlerism will of course be hotly denied tonight and tomorrow in the controlled press and radio of the Axis powers. And some Americans, not many, will continue to insist that Hitler's plans need not worry us—that we should not concern ourselves with anything that goes on beyond rifle shot of our own shores.

The protestations of these few American citizens will, as usual, be paraded with applause through the Axis press and radio during the next few days in an effort to convince the world that the majority of Americans are opposed to their duly chosen government, and in reality are only waiting to jump on Hitler's band wagon when it comes this way.

The motive of such Americans is not the point at issue. The fact is that Nazi propaganda continues in desperation to seize upon such isolated statements as proof of American disunity.

The Nazis have made up their own list of modern American heroes. It is, fortunately, a short list and I am glad that it does not contain my name.

And so all of us Americans, of all opinions, in the last analysis are faced with the choice between the kind of world we want to live in and the kind of world which Hitler and his hordes would impose upon us.

None of us wants to burrow under the ground and live in total darkness like a comfortable mole.

The forward march of Hitler and of Hitlerism can be stopped, and it will be stopped.

Very simply and very bluntly—we are pledged to pull our own oar in the destruction of Hitlerism.

And when we have helped to end the curse of Hitlerism, we shall help to establish a new peace which will give to decent people everywhere a better chance to live and prosper in security and in freedom and in faith.

Every day that passes we are producing and providing more and more arms for the men who are fighting on actual battlefronts. That is our primary task.

And it is the nation's will that these vital arms and supplies of all kinds shall neither be locked up in American harbors nor sent to the bottom of the sea. It is the nation's will that America shall deliver the goods. In open defiance of that will, our ships have been sunk and our sailors have been killed.

---

[1]*Mein Kampf* was the title of Hitler's memoirs, an account of his life and ideology and a blueprint for his future career as Germany's ruler—ED.

And I say that we do not propose to take this lying down.

That determination of ours not to take it lying down has been expressed in the orders to the American Navy to shoot on sight. And those orders stand.

Furthermore, the House of Representatives has already voted to amend a part of the Neutrality Act of 1937, today outmoded by force of violent circumstances. And the Senate Committee on Foreign Relations has also recommended the elimination of other hamstringing provisions in that act. That is the course of honesty and of realism.

Our American merchant ships must be armed to defend themselves against the rattlesnakes of the sea.

Our American merchant ships must be free to carry our American goods into the harbors of our friends.

And our American merchant ships must be protected by our American Navy.

In the light of a good many years of personal experience I think that it can be said that it can never be doubted that the goods will be delivered by this nation, whose Navy believes in the tradition of "damn the torpedoes; full steam ahead!"

Yes, our nation will and must speak from every assembly line—yes, from every coal mine, the all-inclusive whole of our vast industrial machine. Our factories and our shipyards are constantly expanding. Our output must be multiplied. . . .

The lines of our essential defense now cover all the seas; and to meet the extraordinary demands of today and tomorrow our Navy grows to unprecedented size. Our Navy is ready for action. . . . Its officers and men need no praise from me.

Our new Army is steadily developing the strength needed to withstand the aggressors. Our soldiers of today are worthy of the proudest traditions of the United States Army. But tradition cannot shoot down dive-bombers or destroy tanks. That is why we must and shall provide for every one of our soldiers equipment and weapons, not merely as good but better than that of any other army on earth. And we are doing that right now.

For this, and all of this, is what we mean by total national defense.

The first objective of that defense is to stop Hitler. He can be stopped and can be compelled to dig in. And that will be the beginning of the end of his downfall, because dictatorship of the Hitler type can live only through continuing victories and increasing conquests.

The facts of 1918 are proof that a mighty German Army and a tired German people can crumble rapidly and go to pieces when they are faced with successful resistance.

Nobody who admires qualities of courage and endurance can fail to be stirred by the full-fledged resistance of the Russian people. The Russians are fighting for their own soil and their own homes. Russia needs all kinds of help—planes and tanks, guns and medical supplies and other aids—toward the successful defense against the invaders. From the United States and from Britain she is getting great quantities of these essential supplies. But the needs of her huge army will continue, and our help and British help will also continue.

The other day the Secretary of State of the United States was asked by a Senator to justify our giving aid to Russia. His reply was:

"The answer to that, Senator, depends on how anxious a person is to stop, to destroy the march of Hitler in his conquest of the world. If he were anxious enough to defeat Hitler, he would not worry about who was helping to defeat him."

Upon our American production falls the colossal task of equipping our own armed forces, and helping to supply the British and the Russians and the Chinese. In the performance of that task we dare not fail. And we will not fail.

10.5: A New American Internationalism (1941)

Franklin Roosevelt did not simply believe that the United States could or should play a greater role in world affairs; he believed that the world was changing rapidly, and that if Americans wished to preserve their way of life, they had no choice but to do so. Roosevelt was appalled by the forces of dictatorship and totalitarianism that swept the world into war, and he believed that the United States had a moral responsibility to do what it could to oppose these forces. But he also saw the economic and political consequences of these forces and realized their potential threat to American interests. Roosevelt's outlook became increasingly global as time went on. In his famous "Four Freedoms" speech, what is more apparent, idealism or realpolitik? *Can you discern an element of each? Why was the Atlantic Charter so well received?*

Roosevelt's "Four Freedoms" Speech
January 6, 1941

. . . Every realist knows that the democratic way of life is at this moment being directly assailed in every part of the world—assailed either by arms, or by secret spreading of poisonous propaganda by those who seek to destroy unity and promote discord in nations still at peace. During sixteen months this assault has blotted out the whole pattern of democratic life in an appalling number of independent nations, great and small. The assailants are still on the march, threatening other nations, great and small. . . .

As men do not live by bread alone, they do not fight by armaments alone. Those who man our defenses, and those behind them who build our defenses, must have

Franklin D. Roosevelt, Annual Message to Congress, January 6, 1941. Quoted from *The Public Papers of F. D. Roosevelt,* vol. 9, p. 663. Washington, D.C.: United States Government Printing Office.

the stamina and courage which come from an unshakable belief in the manner of life which they are defending. The mighty action which they are calling for cannot be based on a disregard of all things worth fighting for.

The Nation takes great satisfaction and much strength from the things which have been done to make its people conscious of their individual stake in the preservation of democratic life in America. Those things have toughened the fibre of our people, have renewed their faith and strengthened their devotion to the institutions we make ready to protect. Certainly this is no time to stop thinking about the social and economic problems which are the root cause of the social revolution which is today a supreme fact in the world.

There is nothing mysterious about the foundations of a healthy and strong democracy. The basic things expected by our people of their political and economic system are simple. They are: equality of opportunity for youth and for others: jobs for those who can work; security for those who need it; the ending of special privilege for the few, the preservation of civil liberties for all; the enjoyment of the fruits of scientific progress in a wider and constantly rising standard of living.

These are the simple and basic things that must never be lost sight of in the turmoil and unbelievable complexity of our modern world. The inner and abiding strength of our economic and political systems is dependent upon the degree to which they fulfill these expectations.

Many subjects connected with our social economy call for immediate improvement. As examples: We should bring more citizens under the coverage of old age pensions and unemployment insurance. We should widen the opportunities for adequate medical care. We should plan a better system by which persons deserving or needing gainful employment may obtain it.

I have called for personal sacrifice. I am assured of the willingness of almost all Americans to respond to that call. . . .

In the future days, which we seek to make secure, we look forward to a world founded upon four essential human freedoms.

The first is freedom of speech and expression—everywhere in the world.

The second is freedom of every person to worship God in his own way—everywhere in the world.

The third is freedom from want—which, translated into world terms, means economic understandings which will secure to every nation a healthy peace time life for its inhabitants—everywhere in the world.

The fourth is freedom from fear—which, translated into world terms, means a worldwide reduction of armaments to such a point and in such a thorough fashion that no nation will be in a position to commit an act of physical aggression against any neighbor—anywhere in the world.

That is no vision of a distant millenium. It is a definite basis for a kind of world attainable in our own time and generation. That kind of world is the very antithesis of the so-called new order of tyranny which the dictators seek to create with the crash of a bomb.

To that new order we oppose the greater conception—the moral order. A good society is able to face schemes of world domination and foreign revolutions alike without fear.

Since the beginning of our American history we have been engaged in change—in a perpetual peaceful revolution—a revolution which goes on steadily, quietly adjusting itself to changing conditions—without the concentration camp or the quicklime in the ditch. The world order which we seek is the cooperation of free countries, working together in a friendly, civilized society.

This nation has placed its destiny in the hands and heads and hearts of its millions of free men and women; and its faith in freedom under the guidance of God. Freedom means the supremacy of human rights everywhere. Our support goes to those who struggle to gain those rights or keep them. Our strength is in our unity of purpose.

To that high concept there can be no end save victory.

The Atlantic Charter, August 14, 1941

The President of the United States of America and the Prime Minister, Mr. Churchill, representing His Majesty's Government in the United Kingdom, being met together, deem it right to make known certain common principles in the national policies of their respective countries on which they base their hopes for a better future for the world.

First, their countries seek no agrandizement, territorial or other;

Second, they desire to see no territorial changes that do not accord with the freely expressed wishes of the peoples concerned;

Third, they respect the right of all peoples to choose the form of government under which they will live; and they wish to see sovereign rights and self government restored to those who have been forcibly deprived of them;

Fourth, they will endeavor, with due respect for their existing obligations, to further the enjoyment by all States, great or small, victor or vanquished, of access, on equal terms, to the trade and to the raw materials of the world which are needed for their economic prosperity;

Fifth, they desire to bring about the fullest collaboration between all nations in the economic field with the object of securing, for all, improved labor standards, economic advancement and social security;

Sixth, after the final destruction of the Nazi tyranny, they hope to see established a peace which will afford to all nations the means of dwelling in safety within their own boundaries, and which will afford assurance that all the men in all the lands may live out their lives in freedom from fear and want;

Seventh, such a peace should enable all men to traverse the high seas and oceans without hindrance:

The Public Papers of F. D. Roosevelt, vol. 10, p. 314. Washington, D.C.: United States Government Printing Office.

Eighth, they believe that all of the nations of the world, for realistic as well as spiritual reasons must come to the abandonment of the use of force. Since no future peace can be maintained if land, sea or air armaments continue to be employed by nations which threaten, or may threaten, aggression outside of their frontiers, they believe, pending the establishment of a wider and permanent system of general security, that the disarmament of such nations is essential. They will likewise aid and encourage all other practicable measures which will lighten for peace-loving peoples the crushing burden of armaments.

Franklin D. Roosevelt
Winston S. Churchill

☆ **11** ☆

The Fifties

The decade and a half following World War II was a period of mending and a time for Americans to get back to normal life. It was also an era of prosperity. Spurred by pent-up consumer demand and government programs to ease veterans' return to civilian life, the economy boomed. The new affluence produced a wave of optimism and self-congratulation that was startling for anyone who remembered the anxious, insecure, and painful days of the Depression and World War II.

The chief beneficiaries of the boom were the American middle-class and skilled workers. With steadily rising incomes they achieved the security that had escaped them since the 1920s. As if to make up for lost time they went on a buying spree, snapping up new cars, appliances, and, after 1950, television sets, by the millions.

No aspect of the postwar material culture was as consequential as the housing boom, however. After a period of difficult reconversion the construction industry churned out thousands of new homes, primarily for young families and predominantly in the suburbs. Suburban living ushered in a new way of life for millions of Americans marked by large families, house pride, and enhanced domesticity.

In reality the fifties were far from perfect. Minorities felt excluded from the postwar economic surge. Blacks continued to face legal inequality, job discrimination, and limited educational opportunity. To intellectuals the era seemed unpleasantly self-congratulatory, materialistic, conformist, and timid. And then there was the fear and intellectual intolerance triggered by the Cold War confrontation of the United States and the Soviet Union. Indeed, during the fifties all Americans felt oppressed in some degree by that superpower rivalry, since it threatened nuclear confrontation and possible world obliteration.

In the selections below you will encounter diverse views of three issues that stirred controversy during the fifties: the extent and significance of the new prosperity, the virtues of the new suburban lifestyle, and the validity of the anti-Communist panic.

11.1: Suburbia (1954, 1957)

Suburbia became a center of controversy during the fifties. Millions of Americans chose it as a place, and a way, to live. The detached private house, the automobile, domestic concerns, family and child rearing— all represented altered personal emphases for millions of young married couples.

Clearly a large number of Americans voted for suburbia "with their feet." Much of the suburban population were transplanted urbanites. And some of the nation's social observers approved heartily of their choice. In the first selection below, the editors of McCall's *magazine, a publication targeted at middle-class women, describe with undisguised delight one key aspect of the suburban surge—"togetherness." The second selection is by John Keats, a journalist and sociology popularizer, who expresses intense hostility toward suburbia.*

What special aspect of the suburban phenomenon was McCall's *referring to? What were the implications for women of the changes the magazine was highlighting and commending? Why might a magazine with a predominantly women's readership feature an article such as "A Man's Place Is in the Home"? Can you see any drawbacks to "togetherness"?*

What are Keat's objections to the suburban experience? How valid are his criticisms? What might have been the social or cultural sources of his opinions?

Live the Life of McCall's

Togetherness

If we'd made this suggestion in 1870, when *McCall's* was first published as the *Queen of Fashion* magazine, we would have been referring to a life of ease and elegance. For in the years before the turn of the century every woman aspired to be a lady and every lady envied Mrs. Astor. The world of women as reflected in their magazines was a rosy realm of fashion and folderol.

By 1902, when the *Queen of Fashion* broadened into *McCall's*, the ladies' magazines were mirroring the nature of life with Father. Those were the days

"Live the Life of *McCall's*," and "A Man's Place Is in the Home," *McCall's,* May 1954, pp. 27, 28–35.

when Papa ruled the roost, children were seen and not heard and women were delineated as mysterious and unpredictable creatures given to vagaries and vaporings.

Then came the battle of the sexes, followed by the First World War. You fought and won the fight for political equality. And *McCall's,* together with the other women's magazines, helped you to carve out large areas of living formerly forbidden to your sex.

Throughout the bright days of the Twenties and the twilight of the Thirties—the long years of the War, the bitter peace and the Korean conflict—in fact, right up to this moment, *McCall's* has been sensitive to [your] needs *as women first.*

In common with all other women's service magazines *McCall's* has been striving to widen your horizons, inspire you to lead lives of greater satisfaction, help you in your daily tasks. There's evidence that we're winning that victory.

Today women are not a sheltered sex. Men and women in ever increasing numbers are marrying at an earlier age, having children at an earlier age and rearing larger families. For the first time in our history the majority of men and women own their own homes and millions of these people gain their deepest satisfaction from making them their very own.

We travel more. We earn more, spend more, save more. We listen to finer music, read more and better books. We worship more. And in ever greater numbers we enjoy the advantages of higher education.

Thanks to our heritage of freedom, our national culture and our creative ingenuity, this wider range of living is an expression of the private conscience and the common hopes of the greatest number of people in this land of ours.

But the most impressive and the most heartening feature of this change is that men, women and children are achieving it *together.* They are creating this new and warmer way of life not as women *alone* or men *alone,* isolated from one another, but as a *family* sharing a common experience.

From this day forward *McCall's* will be edited to meet the needs and excite the interests of all who are or wish to be partners in this way of life—the life of *Mc-Call's.* And through exploring, interpreting and reporting that life we shall do our very best to help you—*as a family*—to live it well.

Otis Wiese
Editor and Publisher

A Man's Place Is in the Home

Meet a Modern American Husband and Father . . .

Here's Ed Richtscheidt of Pine Lake, New Jersey, his wife Carol and their three children. They live in a gray shingle split-level house with three bedrooms, one bath and an unfinished basement room that will one day be a game room. On the north side of their lot, where they plan to build a barbecue. Ed has made a play yard for the children.

We're introducing Ed and his family because, like millions of other married couples today, they're living the life of *McCall's,* a more casual but a richer life than that of even the fairly recent past.

Ed's place in this new way of living is something he takes for granted. He doesn't stop to think about the changes that have taken place since he was a boy. Had Ed been a father twenty-five years ago he would have had little time to think to play and work along with his children. The running of the household would have been left entirely in the hands of his wife. Husbands and fathers were loved and respected then, but they weren't friends and companions to their families. Household chores were beneath them.

Today the chores as well as the companionship make Ed part of his family. He and Carol have centered their lives almost completely around their children and their home. Every inch of their house and yard is lived in and enjoyed. And it's a very happy place. . . .

Ed and His Family Live Together and Love It

Caring for three lively children—Ricky, 6, Chris, 4, and Susie, 2—makes tremendous demands on Carol Richtscheidt. But Ed is a cheerful working partner to her, helps with the children and housework whenever he can, gives everything he has to make his family happy. In return they give him all the love and affection a husband and father could hope for.

Ed likes to	*Ed doesn't like to*
putter around the house, make things, paint	dust or vacuum, or to finish jobs he's started
select furniture, rugs and draperies	repair furniture, fix electrical connections and plumbing, hang draperies
dry dishes	wash pots and pans and dishes
read to the children and put them to bed	pick up after the children
work in the garden	shovel snow or mow the lawn
feed and dress the children and bathe them	change diapers
pick up the baby-sitter	take the baby-sitter home
attend P.T.A. meetings	visit school
cook	do the laundry, iron
buy clothes for his wife	buy clothes for the children
buy groceries	go back for groceries Carol forgot to list

Down with Suburbia

JOHN KEATS

Welcome to the Inquest

For literally nothing down—other than a simple two per cent and a promise to pay, and pay, and pay until the end of your life—you too, like a man I'm going to call

John Drone, can find a box of your own in one of the fresh-air slums we're building around the edges of America's cities. There's room for all in any price range, for even while you read this, whole square miles of identical boxes are spreading like gangrene throughout New England, across the Denver prairie, around Los Angeles, Chicago, Washington, New York, Miami—everywhere. In any one of these new neighborhoods, be it in Hartford or Philadelphia, you can be certain all other houses will be precisely like yours, inhabited by people whose age, income, number of children, problems, habits, conversation, dress, possessions and perhaps even blood type are also precisely like yours. In any one of these neighborhoods it is possible to make enemies of the folks next door with unbelievable speed. If you buy a small house, you are assured your children will leave you perhaps even sooner than they should, for at once they will learn never to associate home with pleasure. In short, ladies and gentlemen, we offer here for your inspection facts relative to today's housing developments—developments conceived in error, nurtured by greed, corroding everything they touch. They destroy established cities and trade patterns, pose dangerous problems for the areas they invade, and actually drive mad myriads of housewives shut up in them.

These facts are well known to responsible economists, sociologists, psychiatrists, city managers and bankers, and certainly must be suspected by the people who live in the suburban developments, yet there's no end in sight to the construction. Indeed, Washington's planners exult whenever a contractor vomits up five thousand new houses on a rural tract that might better have remained in hay, for they see in this little besides thousands of new sales of labor, goods and services. Jobs open for an army of bulldozer operators, carpenters, plasterers, plumbers, electricians, well-diggers, bricklayers, truck drivers, foremen and day laborers. Then come the new householders, followed by their needs. A shopping center and supermarket are hurriedly built, and into this pours another army of clerical and sales personnel, butchers, bakers, janitors, auto dealers, restaurateurs, waitresses, door-to-door salesmen, mail carriers, rookie cops, firemen, schoolteachers, medicine men of various degrees—the whole ruck and stew of civilization's auxiliaries. Thus, with every new development, jobs are born, money is earned, money is spent, and pretty soon everyone can afford a new television set, and Washington calls this prosperity.

That such prosperity is entirely material, possibly temporary and perhaps even illusory, causes little concern at present. It's money, isn't it? Well, maybe it is and maybe it isn't. A later chapter [in the book to which this is an introduction] will show whether any development householder really owns the house he thinks he's bought—whether he owns the things he uses. It's sufficient at this point to suggest the rooftrees of the nation's Levittowns[1] are held up by levitation.

Meanwhile, let's step back in time to consider the history of today's housing developments.

---

[1]Levittown became the generic name of large, mass-produced suburban developments after a Long Island builder William J. Levitt constructed his immensely successful community of small houses in the 1950s—ED.

The first good intentions which pave our modern Via Dolorosa were laid at war's end. Conscious of the fact that some 13,000,000 young men risked disfigurement, dismemberment and death in circumstances not of their choosing, a grateful nation decided to show its appreciation to the survivors. The GI Bill of Rights was enacted, and one of the articles provided an incentive for bankers to assume low-interest mortgages on houses purchased by veterans. The deal was, the bankers could recover a certain guaranteed sum from the government in event of the veteran's default. The real-estate boys read the Bill, looked at one another in happy amazement, and the dry, rasping noise they made rubbing their hands together could have been heard as far away as Tawi Tawi. Immediately, thanks to modern advertising, movable type, radio, television and other marvels, the absurdity was spread—and is still spread—that the veteran should own his home.

There was never the slightest justification for this nonsense. Never in the last 180 years of United States history was there an indication that a young man entering civil life from childhood or war should thereupon buy a house.

It is and has always been the nature of young people to be mobile. Rare indeed is the man whose life is a straight arrow's-flight from the classroom to the job he'll hold until he dies. Many a retiring corporate officer put in his early years driving a bread truck, then had a fling at a little unsuccessful business of his own, then wandered into the door-to-door sale of cemetery lots before catching on at the button-works he was one day to direct. Owning property implies a certain permanence—precisely that quality a bright young man should, and does, lack. A young man should be mobile until he finds his proper path. A man with a house is nailed to its floor.

The housing article in the GI Bill, however, opened vast vistas. Not only was there a government guarantee to be had, but there was also land to be sold, and since the veteran had been led both by private and government propaganda to believe he should own his home, the remaining consideration in the hard, practical minds of the real-estate men was how much house could be offered for how little money. Or, to put it in the more usual way, how little house could be offered for how much money. Cost became the sole criterion of the first postwar house, and the first economy was in space.

The typical postwar development operator was a man who figured how many houses he could possibly cram onto a piece of land and have the local zoning board hold still for it. Then he whistled up the bulldozers to knock down all the trees, bat the lumps off the terrain, and level the ensuing desolation. Then up went the houses, one after another, all alike, and none of those built immediately after the war had any more floor space than a moderately-priced, two-bedroom apartment. The dining room, the porch, the basement, and in many cases the attic, were dispensed with and disappeared from the American scene. The result was a little box on a cold concrete slab containing two bedrooms, bath, and an eating space the size of a broom closet tucked between the living room and the tiny kitchen. A nine-by-twelve rug spread across the largest room wall to wall, and there was a sheet of plate glass in the living-room wall. That, the builder said, was the picture window. The picture it framed was of the box across the treeless street. The young Americans who moved into these cubicles were not, and are not, to know the gracious dignity of living that their parents knew in the big two- and three-story family houses set well back on the grassy lawns off the shady streets of, say, Watertown, New York. For them and their children, there would be only the box on its slab. The Cape Cod Rambler had arrived.

It was inevitable that the development house was looked upon as an expedient by the young purchasers. It was most certainly not the house of their dreams, nor was the ready-made neighborhood a thing to make the soul sing. It was, simply, the only thing available. They had no choice—they couldn't afford to build their house, nor were they given a choice of architecture. Instead, they were offered a choice between a house they didn't much want and the fantastic rents that bobbed to the surface as soon as the real-estate lobby torpedoed rent control. The development house was the only living space on the market priced just within the means of the young veterans.

It is still a maxim with responsible land agents that you should never purchase a home in which you do not intend to dwell for at least ten years. Moreover, they'll say, a house in which you have no equity cannot be considered an investment. Despite these truths, houses were bought on the assumption they would serve only as brief campsites on life's wilderness trail, and incredibly enough, the government in the past two years has given encouragement to this singular point of view. With government blessing, purchasers are now being advised that buying a new house is like buying a new car. Old one too small for the growing family? Trade your old home in and buy a new one, the government suggests, meanwhile helping the developers to continue their dirty work in order that prosperity's bubble doesn't burst.

The first veterans' developments set a pattern for the builders. They sold the first houses like hotcakes, so they've been making hotcakes ever since. Today's new houses differ from those of 1947 only insofar as the materials are better and the workmen have now mastered their jobs. The basic living problems are unchanged—they're built right in. These problems will remain unchanged unless the whole construction pattern changes; until a housing development becomes something more than just a lot of houses.

First of all, a housing development cannot be called a community, for that word implies a balanced society of men, women and children wherein work and pleasure are found and the needs of all the society's members are served. Housing developments offer no employment and as a general rule lack recreational areas, churches, schools, or other cohesive influences.

A second present and future national danger lies in the fact that developments are creating stratified societies of singular monotony in a nation whose triumph to date has depended on its lack of a stratified society, on the diversity of its individuals. Yet today it is possible to drive through the various developments that surround one of our cities and tell at a glance the differing social strata.

Here is the $10,000 development—two bedrooms, low-priced cars, average income $75 a week after taxes, three children, average food budget $25 weekly; jobs vary from bus driver to house painter. Here is the $13,950 house—three bedrooms, available to foremen and successful newspapermen, medium-priced cars, two and a half children per average home; men's shoes cost $12 to $20 at this level. Next is the $17,450 split level, especially designed for split personalities, upper-medium cars; liquor bill is $25 weekly; inmates take fly-now-pay-later air rides to Europe.

The appearance of several square miles of new housing units in a once rural area adjacent to a city normally brings about a violent clash of interests. The young new householders, conscious only of their unmet needs, are intolerant of the political milieu they've invaded. Indeed, if there was any cohesive force acting on typical development householders, it would be that of hatred. Well might they form a sort of mutual loathing society where the first target of their wrath is the builder, the second, the community around them.

For its part, the invaded community eyes the newcomers with something less than wild enthusiasm. The administrative problems handed a county government by the sudden appearance of several thousand new families are enough to make a strong man blanch. And, when the guts of a city are deserted by a middle class that flocks to the suburbs, the tax problems created for the city fathers are even more frightening.

In any discussion of housing developments, however, we must first and last consider that poor devil, the householder. John Drone did not know it when he signed the deed, but appalling human tensions were a condition of the sale. Now these tensions are a tightening, knotted cord about his temples as he stands there on tiptoes, his hands tied, struggling for balance on the sharp roof of the house he may not own, nostril-deep in swirling debt.

11.2: The Red Scare (1950)

One serious blot on the comfort and complacency of the fifties was the era's anxiety over "disloyalty" and the "Communist menace." Whether the danger of subversion was real or a case of hysteria, the issue of domestic Communism roiled the placid surface of the decade as did few other issues.

At the center of the storm, although not its instigator, was the junior senator from Wisconsin, Joseph R. McCarthy. McCarthy came to the Senate in 1946, a banner year for conservative Republicans, and served much of his first term as an undistinguished backbench partisan. By 1950, without the record of achievement that an incumbent could normally show the voters, he faced the prospect of a hazardous reelection campaign two years down the road.

But there was an issue at hand that might bail him out—anti-Communism. This was a time of the emerging Cold War, when Americans perceived a remorseless spread of Communist influence over ever larger portions of the globe. This advance, many felt, did not derive solely from Communist aggression abroad; it must also stem from subversion within.

Out of this suspicion McCarthy would forge a potent political weapon. Day after day his charges of hidden Communists in the government, the media, the clergy, and other influential portions of American society made headlines and cast the Wisconsin senator in the role of champion of true Americanism. McCarthy won reelection in 1952 and, in tandem with other obsessive anti-Communists, helped make the remainder of the fifties a decade of fear and repression.

The following selections represent opening shots in the battles that would swirl around McCarthyism. The first is a speech by McCarthy himself before a women's Republican group in Wheeling, West Virginia, on Lincoln's Birthday in 1950.[1] Is McCarthy's indictment of Communism valid? Was his claim that Communism had made great gains since the end of World War II correct? What is McCarthy's explanation for these gains? Does his explanation hold up to examination? Are there qualities of his attack that might be disturbing to a prudent thinker and policy-maker?

The second selection is from a report by a Senate subcommittee, headed by Senator Millard Tydings of Maryland, that was empowered to investigate McCarthy's charges against the State Department. The subcommittee, clearly critical of the Wisconsin senator, held hearings and examined official files. It called the Wisconsin senator to testify in defense of his charges. McCarthy and his supporters fought back with angry attacks on Tydings and the investigating committee.

It is difficult for students to tell, without more information than it is possible to provide here, whether the charges of Communists in the State Department were correct. But you can evaluate Tydings' claims regarding the effects of charges like McCarthy's on public attitudes, the morale of government employees, and the climate of tolerance in the country.

In evaluating the McCarthy controversy, you should consider matters like the differences between subversion and espionage, the valid limits of political and ideological dissent in a democracy, and the connection between the Cold War and demands for internal intellectual and ideological conformity. You also should consider whether there was a political motive at work in the anti-Communist campaign. McCarthy was a Republican; Tydings a Democrat. Was the party difference significant?

---

[1]Actually, this text is a later reconstruction of the speech. The original seems lost forever.

Why Communism Is Gaining

JOSEPH R. MCCARTHY

Ladies and gentlemen, tonight as we celebrate the one hundred and forty-first birthday of one of the greatest men in American history, I would like to be able to talk about what a glorious day today is in the history of the world. As we celebrate the birth of this man who with his whole heart and soul hated war, I would like to be able to speak of peace in our time, of war being outlawed, and of worldwide disarmament. These would be truly appropriate things to be able to mention as we celebrate the birthday of Abraham Lincoln.

Five years after a world war has been won, men's hearts should anticipate a long peace, and men's minds should be free from the heavy weight that comes with war. But this is not such a period—for this is not a period of peace. This is a time of the "cold war." This is a time when all the world is split into two vast, increasingly hostile armed camps—a time of a great armaments race.

Today we can almost physically hear the mutterings and rumblings of an invigorated god of war. You can see it, feel it, and hear it all the way from the hills of Indochina, from the shores of Formosa, right over into the very heart of Europe itself.

The one encouraging thing is that the "mad moment" has not yet arrived for the firing of the gun or the exploding of the bomb which will set civilization about the final task of destroying itself. There is still a hope for peace if we finally decide that no longer can we safely blind our eyes and close our ears to those facts which are shaping up more and more clearly. And that is that we are now engaged in a showdown fight—not the usual war between nations for land areas or other material gains, but a war between two diametrically opposed ideologies.

The great difference between our western Christian world and the atheistic Communist world is not political, ladies and gentlemen, it is moral. There are other differences, of course, but those could be reconciled. For instance, the Marxian idea of confiscating the land and factories and running the entire economy as a single enterprise is momentous. Likewise, Lenin's invention of the one-party police state as a way to make Marx's idea work is hardly less momentous.

Stalin's resolute putting across of these two ideas, of course, did much to divide the world. With only those differences, however, the East and the West could most certainly still live in peace.

The real, basic difference, however, lies in the religion of immoralism—invented by Marx, preached feverishly by Lenin, and carried to unimaginable extremes by Stalin. This religion of immoralism, if the Red half of the world wins—and well it may—this religion of immoralism will more deeply wound and damage mankind than any conceivable economic or political system.

Karl Marx dismissed God as a hoax, and Lenin and Stalin have added in clear-cut, unmistakable language their resolve that no nation, no people who believe in a God, can exist side by side with their communistic state.

Congressional Record, 81st Cong., 2d sess., 96, 1950, 1954, 1956, 1957.

Karl Marx, for example, expelled people from his Communist Party for mentioning such things as justice, humanity, or morality. He called this soulful ravings and sloppy sentimentality.

While Lincoln was a relatively young man in his late thirties, Karl Marx boasted that the Communist specter was haunting Europe. Since that time, hundreds of millions of people and vast areas of the world have fallen under Communist domination. Today, less than 100 years after Lincoln's death, Stalin brags that this Communist specter is not only haunting the world, but is about to completely subjugate it.

Today we are engaged in a final, all-out battle between communistic atheism and Christianity. The modern champions of communism have selected this as the time. And, ladies and gentlemen, the chips are down—they are truly down.

Lest there be any doubt that the time has been chosen, let us go directly to the leader of communism today—Joseph Stalin. Here is what he said—not back in 1928, not before the war, not during the war—but 2 years after the last war was ended: "To think that the Communist revolution can be carried out peacefully, within the framework of a Christian democracy, means one has either gone out of one's mind and lost all normal understanding, or has grossly and openly repudiated the Communist revolution."

And this is what was said by Lenin in 1919, which was also quoted with approval by Stalin in 1947:

"We are living," said Lenin, "not merely in a state, but in a system of states, and the existence of the Soviet Republic side by side with Christian states for a long time is unthinkable. One or the other must triumph in the end. And before that end supervenes, a series of frightful collisions between the Soviet Republic and the Bourgeois states will be inevitable."

Ladies and gentlemen, can there be anyone here tonight who is so blind as to say that the war is not on? Can there be anyone who fails to realize that the Communist world has said, "The time is now"—that this is the time for the show-down between the democratic Christian world and the Communist atheistic world?

Unless we face this fact, we shall pay the price that must be paid by those who wait too long.

Six years ago, at the time of the first conference to map out the peace—Dumbarton Oaks[1]—there was within the Soviet orbit 180,000,000 people. Lined up on the antitotalitarian side there were in the world at that time roughly 1,625,000,000 people. Today, only 6 years later, there are 800,000,000 people under the absolute domination of Soviet Russia—an increase of over 400 percent. On our side, the figure has shrunk to around 500,000,000. In other words, in less than 6 years the odds have changed from 9 to 1 in our favor to 8 to 5 against us. This indicates the swiftness of the tempo of Communist victories and American defeats in the cold war. As one of our outstanding historical figures once said, "When a great democracy is destroyed, it will not be because of enemies from without, but rather because of enemies from within."

---

[1]Dumbarton Oaks near Washington, DC, was the site of a conference of the anti-Axis powers in 1944 where plans were made for a United Nations organization after victory—ED.

The truth of this statement is becoming terrifyingly clear as we see this country each day losing on every front.

At war's end we were physically the strongest nation on earth and, at least potentially, the most powerful intellectually and morally. Ours could have been the honor of being a beacon in the desert of destruction, a shining living proof that civilization was not yet ready to destroy itself. Unfortunately, we have failed miserably and tragically to arise to the opportunity.

The reason why we find ourselves in a position of impotency is not because our only powerful potential enemy has sent men to invade our shores, but rather because of the traitorous actions of those who have been treated so well by this Nation. It has not been the less fortunate or members of minority groups who have been selling this Nation out, but rather those who have had all the benefits that the wealthiest nation on earth has had to offer—the finest homes, the finest college education, and the finest jobs in Government we can give.

This is glaringly true in the Statement Department. There the bright young men who are born with silver spoons in their mouths are the ones who have been worst.

Now I know it is very easy for anyone to condemn a particular bureau or department in general terms. Therefore, I would like to cite one rather unusual case—the case of a man who has done much to shape our foreign policy.

When Chiang Kai-shek was fighting our war, the State Department had in China a young man named John S. Service. His task, obviously, was not to work for the communization of China. Strangely, however, he sent official reports back to the Statement Department urging that we torpedo our ally Chiang Kai-shek and stating, in effect, that communism was the best hope of China.

Later, this man—John Service—was picked up by the Federal Bureau of Investigation for turning over to the Communists secret State Department information. Strangely, however, he was never prosecuted. However, Joseph Grew, the Under Secretary of State, who insisted on his prosecution, was forced to resign. Two days after Grew's successor, Dean Acheson, took over as Under Secretary of State, this man—John Service—who had been picked up by the FBI and who had previously urged that communism was the best hope of China, was not only reinstated in the State Department but promoted. And finally, under Acheson, placed in charge of all placements and promotions.

Today, ladies and gentlemen, this man Service is on his way to represent the State Department and Acheson in Calcutta—by far and away the most important listening post in the Far East.

Now, let's see what happens when individuals with Communist connections are forced out of the State Department. Gustave Duran, who was labeled as (I quote) "a notorious international Communist," was made assistant to the Assistant Secretary of State in charge of Latin American affairs. He was taken into the State Department from his job as a lieutenant colonel in the Communist International Brigade. Finally, after intense congressional pressure and criticism, he resigned in 1946 from the State Department—and, ladies and gentlemen, where do you think he is now? He took over a high-salaried job as Chief of Cultural Activities Section in the office of the Assistant Secretary General of the United Nations.

Then there was a Mrs. Mary Jane Kenny, from the Board of Economic Warfare in the State Department, who was named in an FBI report and in a House committee report as a courier for the Communist Party while working for the Government. And where do you think Mrs. Kenny is—she is now an editor in the United Nations Document Bureau.

Another interesting case was that of Julian H. Wadleigh, economist in the Trade Agreements Section of the State Department for 11 years and [*sic*] was sent to Turkey and Italy and other countries as United States representative. After the statute of limitations had run [out] so he could not be prosecuted for treason, he openly and brazenly not only admitted but proclaimed that he had been a member of the Communist Party . . . that while working for the State Department he stole a vast number of secret documents . . . and furnished these documents to the Russian spy ring of which he was a part.

You will recall last spring there was held in New York what was known as the World Peace Conference—a conference which was labeled by the State Department and Mr. Truman as the sounding board for Communist propaganda and a front for Russia. Dr. Harlow Shapley was the chairman of that conference. Interestingly enough, according to the news release put out by the Department in July, the Secretary of State appointed Shapley on a commission which acts as liaison between UNESCO [United Nations Economic and Social Council] and the State Department.

This, ladies and gentlemen, gives you somewhat of a picture of the type of individuals who have been helping to shape our foreign policy. In my opinion the State Department, which is one of the most important government departments, is thoroughly infested with Communists.

I have in my hand 57 cases of individuals who would appear to be either card carrying members or certainly loyal to the Communist Party, but who nevertheless are still helping to shape our foreign policy.

One thing to remember in discussing the Communists in our Government is that we are not dealing with spies who get 30 pieces of silver to steal the blueprints of a new weapon. We are dealing with a far more sinister type of activity because it permits the enemy to guide and shape our policy. . . .

This brings us down to the case of one Alger Hiss[2] who is important not as an individual any more, but rather because he is so representative of a group in the State Department. It is unnecessary to go over the sordid events showing how he sold out the Nation which had given him so much. Those are rather fresh in all of our minds.

However, it should be remembered that the facts in regard to his connection with this international Communist spy ring were made known to the then Under Secretary of State [Adolf] Berle 3 days after Hitler and Stalin signed the Russo-German alliance pact. At that time one Whittaker Chambers—who was also part of the spy ring—apparently decided that with Russia on Hitler's side, he could no longer betray our Nation to Russia. He gave Under Secretary of State Berle—and this is all a

---

[2]Alger Hiss was a former New Deal official accused by Whittaker Chambers, a former editor of *Time,* of being a Soviet spy. Hiss' guilt or innocence became a major political issue between liberals and the left on the one hand, and conservatives on the other—ED.

matter of record—practically all, if not more, of the facts upon which Hiss' conviction was based.

Under Secretary Berle promptly contacted Dean Acheson and received word in return that Acheson (and I quote) "could vouch for Hiss absolutely"—at which time the matter was dropped. And this, you understand, was at a time when Russia was an ally of Germany. This condition existed while Russia and Germany were invading and dismembering Poland, and while the Communist groups here were screaming "warmonger" at the United States for their support of the allied nations.

Again in 1943, the FBI had occasion to investigate the facts surrounding Hiss' contacts with the Russian spy ring. But even after that FBI report was submitted, nothing was done.

Then late in 1948—on August 5—when the Un-American Activities Committee called Alger Hiss to give an accounting, President Truman at once issued a Presidential directive ordering all Government agencies to refuse to turn over any information whatsoever in regard to the Communist activities of any Government employee to a congressional committee.

Incidentally, even after Hiss was convicted—it is interesting to note that the President still labeled the exposé of Hiss as a "red herring."

If time permitted, it might be well to go into detail about the fact that Hiss was Roosevelt's chief adviser at Yalta when Roosevelt was admittedly in ill health and tired physically and mentally . . . and when, according to the Secretary of State, Hiss and Gromyko drafted the report on the conference.

According to the then Secretary of State Edward Stettinius, here are some of the things that Hiss helped to decide at Yalta. (1) The establishment of a European High Commission; (2) the treatment of Germany—this you will recall was the conference at which it was decided that we would occupy Berlin with Russia occupying an area completely circling the city, which, as you know, resulted in the Berlin airlift which cost 31 American lives; (3) the Polish question; (4) the relationship between UNRRA [United Nations Relief and Rehabilitation Administration] and the Soviet Union; (5) the rights of Americans on control commissions of Rumania, Bulgaria, and Hungary; (6) Iran; (7) China—here's where we gave away Manchuria; (8) Turkish Straits question; (9) international trusteeships; (10) Korea.

Of the results of this conference, Arthur Bliss Lane of the State Department had this to say: "As I glanced over the document, I could not believe my eyes. To me, almost every line spoke of a surrender to Stalin."

As you hear this story of high treason, I know that you are saying to yourself, "Well, why doesn't the Congress do something about it?" Actually, ladies and gentlemen, one of the important reasons for the graft, the corruption, the dishonesty, the disloyalty, the treason in high Government positions—one of the most important reasons why this continues is a lack of moral uprising on the part of the 140,000,000 American people. In the light of history, however, this is not hard to explain.

It is the result of an emotional hang-over and a temporary moral lapse which follows every war. It is the apathy to evil which people who have been subjected to the tremendous evils of war feel. As the people of the world see mass murder, the destruction of defenseless and innocent people, and all of the crime and lack of morals which go with war, they become numb and apathetic. It has always been thus after war.

However, the morals of our people have not been destroyed. They still exist. This cloak of numbness and apathy has only needed a spark to rekindle them. Happily, this spark has finally been supplied.

As you know, very recently the Secretary of State[3] proclaimed his loyalty to a man guilty of what has always been considered as the most abominable of all crimes—of being a traitor to the people who gave him a position of great trust.[4] The Secretary of State in attempting to justify his continued devotion to the man who sold out the Christian world to the atheistic world, referred to Christ's Sermon on the Mount as a justification and reason therefor, and the reaction of the American people to this would have made the heart of Abraham Lincoln happy.

When this pompous diplomat in striped pants, with a phony British accent, proclaimed to the American people that Christ on the Mount endorsed communism, high treason, and betrayal of a sacred trust, the blasphemy was so great that it awakened the dormant indignation of the American people.

He has lighted the spark which is resulting in a moral uprising and will end only when the whole sorry mess of twisted, warped thinkers are swept from the national scene so that we may have a new birth of national honesty and decency in Government.

McCarthy's Charges Are False

MILLARD TYDINGS COMMITTEE

Of the 81 alleged State Department employees,[1] only 40 were found to be employed by the State Department at the time of the review. Seven of the so-called 81 were never employed by the State Department and the remaining 33 are no longer in the Department, having been separated either through resignation, termination, or reduction in force. Specifically, of the 33 former employees, 3 were separated in 1949; 16, in 1948; 12, in 1947; and 2, in 1946. . . .

. . . We have carefully and conscientiously reviewed each and every one of the loyalty files relative to the individuals charged by Senator McCarthy. In no instance was any one of them now employed in the State Department found to be a "card-carrying Communist," a member of the Communist Party, or "loyal to the Communist Party." Furthermore, in no instance have we found in our considered judgment that the decision to grant loyalty and security clearance has been erroneously or improperly made in the light of existing loyalty standards. Otherwise stated, we do not

---

[3]Dean Acheson—ED.

[4]Acheson, without condoning any crime that Hiss might have committed, had stated publicly that he would not "turn his back" on his former colleague.

Senate Committee on Foreign Relations, *State Department Loyalty Investigation,* 81st Cong., 2d sess., 20 July 1950, S. Rept. 2108, pt. 1, 9–11, 149–152, 167.

[1]McCarthy had charged that 81 State Department employees were "loyalty risks"—ED.

find basis in any instance for reversing the judgment of the State Department officials charged with responsibility for employee loyalty; or concluding that they have not conscientiously discharged their duties. . . .

What the State Department knows concerning an employee's loyalty is to be found in its loyalty and security files. These files contain all information bearing on loyalty, obtained from any and all sources, including, of course, the reports of full field investigations by the FBI. Interestingly, in this regard, no sooner had the President indicated that the files would be available for review by the subcommittee than Senator McCarthy charged they were being "raped," altered, or otherwise subjected to a "housecleaning." This charge was found to be utterly without foundation in fact. The files were reviewed by representatives of the Department of Justice, and the Department has certified that all information bearing on the employee's loyalty as developed by the FBI appears in the files which were reviewed by the subcommittee. . . .

The Facts behind the Charge of "Whitewash"

Seldom, if ever, in the history of congressional investigations has a committee been subjected to an organized campaign of vilification and abuse comparable to that with which we have been confronted throughout this inquiry. This campaign has been so acute and so obviously designed to confuse and confound the American people that an analysis of the factors responsible therefor is indicated.

The first of these factors was the necessity of creating the impression that our inquiry was not thorough and sincere in order to camouflage the fact that the charges made by Senator McCarthy were groundless and that the Senate and the American people had been deceived. No sooner were hearings started than the cry of "whitewash" was raised along with the chant "investigate the charges and not McCarthy." This chant we have heard morning, noon, and night for almost 4 months from certain quarters for readily perceptible motives. Interestingly, had we elected to investigate Senator McCarthy, there would have been ample basis therefor, since we have been reliably informed that at the time he made the charges initially he had no information whatever to support them, and, furthermore, it early appeared that in securing Senate Resolution 231[2] a fraud had been perpetrated upon the Senate of the United States.

From the very outset of our inquiry, Senator McCarthy has sought to leave the impression that the subcommittee has been investigating him and not "disloyalty in the State Department." The reason for the Senator's concern is now apparent. He had no facts to support his wild and baseless charges, and lived in mortal fear that this situation would be exposed.

Few people, cognizant of the truth in even an elementary way, have, in the absence of political partisanship, placed any credence in the hit-and-run tactics of Senator McCarthy. He has stooped to a new low in his cavalier disregard of the facts.

---

[2]A resolution authorizing an investigation of disloyalty in the State Department—ED.

The simple truth is that in making his speech at Wheeling, Senator McCarthy was talking of a subject and circumstances about which he knew nothing. His extreme and irresponsible statements called for emergency measures. As Senator Wherry[3] told Emmanuel S. Larsen, "Oh, Mac has gone out on a limb and kind of made a fool of himself and we have to back him up now." Starting with nothing, Senator McCarthy plunged headlong forward, desperately seeking to develop some information, which colored with distortion and fanned by a blaze of bias, would forestall a day of reckoning.

Certain elements rallied to his support, particularly those who ostensibly fight communism by adopting the vile methods of the Communists themselves and in so doing actually hinder the fight of all right-minded people who detest and abhor communism in all its manifestations. We cannot, however, destroy one evil by the adoption of another. Senator McCarthy and McCarthyism have been exposed for what they are—and the sight is not a pretty one. . . .

General Observations

In concluding our report, we are constrained to make observations which we regard as fundamental.

It is, of course, clearly apparent that the charges of Communist infiltration of and influence upon the State Department are false. This knowledge is reassuring to all Americans whose faith has been temporarily shaken in the security of their Government by perhaps the most nefarious campaign of untruth in the history of our Republic.

We believe, however, that this knowledge and assurance, while important, will prove ultimately of secondary significance in contemplating the salutory aspects of our investigation. For, we believe that, inherent in the charges that have been made and the sinister campaign to give them ostensible verity, are lessons from which the American people will find inspiration for a rededication to the principles and ideals that have made this Nation great.

We have seen the technique of the "Big Lie," elsewhere employed by the totalitarian dictator with devastating success, utilized here for the first time on a sustained basis in our history. We have seen how, through repetition and shifting untruths, it is possible to delude great numbers of people.

We have seen the character of private citizens and of Government employees virtually destroyed by public condemnation on the basis of gossip, distortion, hearsay, and deliberate untruths. By the mere fact of their associations with a few persons of alleged questionable proclivities an effort has been made to place the stigma of disloyalty upon individuals, some of whom are little people whose only asset is their character and devotion to duty and country. This has been done without the slightest vestige of respect for even the most elementary rules of evidence or fair play or, indeed, common decency. Indeed, we have seen an effort not merely to establish guilt by association but guilt by accusation alone. The spectacle is one we would expect

---

[3]Conservative Republican Senator Kenneth Wherry of Nebraska—ED.

in a totalitarian nation where the rights of the individual are crushed beneath the juggernaut of statism and oppression; it has no place in America where government exists to serve our people, not to destroy them.

We have seen an effort to inflame the American people with a wave of hysteria and fear on an unbelievable scale in this free Nation. Were this campaign founded in truth it would be questionable enough; where it is fraught with falsehood from beginning to end, its reprehensible and contemptible character defies adequate condemnation.

We sincerely believe that charges of the character which have been made in this case seriously impair the efforts of our agencies of Government to combat the problem of subversion. Furthermore, extravagant allegations, which cannot be proved and are not subject to proof, have the inevitable effect of dulling the awareness of all Americans to the true menace of communism. . . .

At a time when American blood is again being shed to preserve our dream of freedom, we are constrained fearlessly and frankly to call the charges, and the methods employed to give them ostensible validity, what they truly are: A fraud and a hoax perpetrated on the Senate of the United States and the American people. They represent perhaps the most nefarious campaign of half-truths and untruth in the history of this Republic. For the first time in our history, we have seen the totalitarian technique of the "big lie" employed on a sustained basis. The result has been to confuse and divide the American people, at a time when they should be strong in their unity, to a degree far beyond the hopes of the Communists themselves whose stock in trade is confusion and division. In such a disillusioning setting, we appreciate as never before our Bill of Rights, a free press, and the heritage of freedom that has made this Nation great.

☆ **12** ☆

The Cold War

The international rivalry of the United States and the Soviet Union was, of course, the ultimate source of McCarthyism. Wartime allies against the Axis powers, America and the USSR became global antagonists after 1945 and remained so for almost half a century. During this period of Cold War, they battled ferociously for ideological, diplomatic, technological, and economic supremacy. Meanwhile, both the superpowers and their allies and satellites engaged in an immense, draining arms race that piled up mountains of weapons of mass destruction. At several points of crisis the world would cower under the threat of nuclear holocaust and the possible extinction of the human race. This disaster never happened, of course, but a number of times, through allies and stand-ins, superpower differences boiled over into costly conventional military confrontations.

Americans have disagreed over the origins of the Cold War. A majority have undoubtedly blamed it on Soviet aggression and the need to check it. A smaller group has seen the United States as primarily at fault: to protect capitalism, they say, America pursued unnecessarily provocative policies. And some have assigned responsibility more evenly than either of these two positions.

Below are documents that focus on early American moves to contain what most Washington policy makers perceived as dangerous and illegitimate Soviet expansionism. These actions set the stage, on the American side, for the long and menacing struggle that has finally subsided only since the end of the 1980s.

12.1: "Mr. X" and the Soviet Menace (1947, 1952)

Wartime British and American suspicions of the Soviet Union did not surface officially until the postwar peace-making process began. Then, after Germany's defeat, the Soviet Union imposed its will and system on the nations along its western borders and began to fish for political advantage in the waters of a troubled and impoverished Western Europe. Whether propelled by legitimate concern for its national security, Stalinist paranoia, or inherent Marxist imperatives, the USSR's actions set off alarm bells in Western capitals.

One man who detected aggressive Soviet designs early on was George Kennan, a scholarly American career diplomat familiar with the USSR from his service at the American embassy in Moscow and from his long study of Russian history. In late 1945 Kennan sent a riveting telegraphic dispatch to the U.S. State Department from Moscow predicting serious difficulties with the Soviet Union in the emerging postwar period.

In July 1947, back in Washington, Kennan published an article in the prestigious journal Foreign Affairs, *which he signed "X" to disguise his official position on the State Department's Policy Planning Staff. In it he clearly outlined the sources of Soviet foreign policy and recommended an approach—known as containment—for checking Soviet expansion. Containment soon became the guiding principle of American foreign policy and continued to govern America's relations with the Soviet Union until the 1990s.*

Not every American was impressed by the analysis of Mr. "X" and the policies that flowed from it. In 1948 a million voters would support former Vice President Henry Wallace in his demands for a more generous interpretation of Soviet motives and new American policies to restore the Soviet-American amity and cooperation of the World War II era. One such dissenter was William Appleman Williams, a foreign policy scholar who became an influential figure in the revisionist school of Cold War historiography.

The selections below mirror this division of opinion. The first is Kennan's Mr. "X" article. According to Kennan, what impelled Soviet leaders in their relations to the outside world? Does he say anything about the sources of American *policy? What would be required, in his view, to contain Soviet expansionism? How would containment achieve its goals? How long would it be necessary for the United States to continue its policies? In light of events since 1989, was Kennan a good prophet? Did containment work?*

The second selection is a 1952 article by Williams in the left-wing periodical Monthly Review *that is critical of containment. What are his objections to Kennan's analyses of the behavior of the Soviet leadership? How does he differ from Kennan on the role of the United States in instigating the Cold War? What does he say about the probable response of the Soviet Union to containment? Does he believe containment is likely to encourage or to undermine peace? Williams's observation that Kennan later retreated from his original views is correct. In fact, Kennan became still more of a "dove" in the 1980s. Does this defection by containment's author call into question his initial analysis?*

The Sources of Soviet Conduct

"X" [GEORGE KENNAN]

The political personality of Soviet power as we know it today is the product of ideology and circumstances: Ideology inherited by the present Soviet leaders from the movement in which they had their political origin, and circumstances of the power which they have now exercised for nearly three decades in Russia. . . .

It is difficult to summarize the set of ideological concepts with which the Soviet leaders came into power. Marxian ideology . . . has always been in process of subtle evolution. . . . But the outstanding features of Communist thought as it existed in 1916 may perhaps be summarized as follows: (a) that the central factor in the life of man, the fact which determines the character of public life and the "physiognomy of society," is the system by which material goods are produced and exchanged; (b) that the capitalist system of production is a nefarious one which inevitably leads to the exploitation of the working class by the capital-owning class and is incapable of developing adequately the economic resources of society or of distributing fairly the material goods produced by human labor; (c) that capitalism contains the seeds of its own destruction and must, in view of the inability of the capital-owning class to adjust itself to economic change, result eventually and inescapably in a revolutionary transfer of power to the working class; and (d) that imperialism, the final phase of capitalism, leads directly to war and revolution. . . .

The circumstances of the immediate post-Revolution period [after the Bolshevik takeover in November 1917]—the existence in Russia of civil war and foreign intervention,[1] together with the obvious fact that the Communists represented only a tiny minority of the Russian people—made the establishment of dictatorial power a ne-

---

"X" [George Kennan], "The Sources of Soviet Conduct," *Foreign Affairs,* July 1947, pp. 566–582.

[1] A combination of anger at the new Soviet regime for making peace with the Germans in 1918 while the Western Allies were still fighting the Central Powers and disdain for the radical Marxist government led to intervention by British, French, American, and Japanese forces in Russian affairs for a time.—ED.

cessity. . . . [Joseph] Stalin, and those whom he led in the struggle for succession to Lenin's position of leadership, were not the men to tolerate rival political forces in the sphere of power which they coveted. Their sense of insecurity was too great. Their particular brand of fanaticism, unmodified by any of the Anglo-Saxon traditions of compromise, was too fierce and too jealous to envisage any permanent sharing of power. From the Russian-Asiatic world out of which they had emerged they carried with them a skepticism as to the possibilities of permanent and peaceful coexistence of rival forces. Easily persuaded of their own doctrinaire "rightness," they insisted on the submission or destruction of all competing power. Outside of the Communist Party, Russian society was to have no rigidity. There were to be no forms of collective human activity or association which would not be dominated by the Party. No other force in Russian society was to be permitted to achieve vitality or integrity. Only the Party was to have structure. All else was to be an amorphous mass.

And within the Party the same principle was to apply. The mass of Party members might go through the motions of election, deliberation, decision and action, but in these motions they were to be animated not by their own individual wills but by the awesome breath of the Party leadership. . . .

Now the outstanding circumstance concerning the Soviet regime is that down to the present day this process of political consolidation has never been completed and the men in the Kremlin have continued to be predominantly absorbed with the struggle to secure and make absolute the power which they seized in November 1917. They have endeavored to secure it primarily against forces at home, within Soviet society itself. But they have also endeavored to secure it against the outside world. For ideology . . . taught them that the outside world was hostile and that it was their duty eventually to overthrow the political forces beyond their borders. . . .

Now it lies in the nature of the mental world of the Soviet leaders, as well as in the character of their ideology, that no opposition to them can be officially recognized as having any merit or justification whatsoever. Such opposition can flow . . . only from the hostile and incorrigible forces of dying capitalism. . . . [S]ince capitalism no longer existed in Russia and since it could not be admitted that there could be serious or widespread opposition to the Kremlin springing spontaneously from the . . . masses under its authority, it became necessary to justify the retention of the dictatorship by stressing the menace of capitalism abroad. . . .

By the same token, tremendous emphasis has been placed on the original Communist thesis of a basic antagonism between the capitalist and Socialist worlds. It is clear . . . that this emphasis is not founded in reality. . . . But there is ample evidence that the stress laid in Moscow on the menace confronting Soviet society from the world outside its borders is founded not on the realities of foreign antagonism but the necessity of explaining away the maintenance of dictatorial authority at home. . . .

So much for the historical background. What does it spell in terms of the political personality of Soviet power as we know it today?

Of the original ideology, nothing has been officially junked. Belief is maintained in the basic badness of capitalism, in the inevitability of its destruction, in the obligation of the proletariat to assist in that destruction and to take power into its own hands. But stress has come to be laid primarily on those concepts which relate most specifically to the Soviet regime itself: to its position as the sole truly Socialist regime in a dark and misguided world, and the relationships of power within it.

The first of these concepts is that of the innate antagonism between capitalism and Socialism. . . . It has profound implications for Russia's conduct as a member of international society. It means that there can never be on Moscow's side any sincere assumption of a community of aims between the Soviet Union and powers which are regarded as capitalist. It must invariably be assumed in Moscow that the aims of the capitalist world are antagonistic to the Soviet regime and, therefore, to the interests of the peoples it controls. If the Soviet government occasionally sets its signature to documents which would indicate the contrary, this is to be regarded as a tactical maneuver permissible in dealing with the enemy . . . and should be taken in the spirit of *caveat emptor*.[2] Basically, the antagonism remains. . . . And from it flow many of the phenomena which we find disturbing in the Kremlin conduct of foreign policy: the secretiveness, the lack of frankness, the duplicity, the . . . suspiciousness, and the basic unfriendliness of purpose. . . . [W]e should not be misled by tactical maneuvers. These characteristics of Soviet policy . . . are basic to the internal nature of Soviet power, and will be with us . . . until the internal nature of Soviet policy is changed.

This means that we are going to continue for a long time to find the Russians difficult to deal with. It does not mean that they should be considered as embarked upon a do-or-die program to overthrow our society by a given date. . . . The forces of progress can take their time in preparing the final *coup de grâce*. Meanwhile, what is vital is that the "Socialist fatherland"—that oasis of power which has already been won for Socialism in the person of the Soviet Union—should be cherished and defended by all good Communists at home and abroad, its fortunes promoted, its enemies badgered and confronted. The promotion of premature, "adventuristic" revolutionary projects abroad which might embarrass Soviet power in any way would be inexcusable. . . . The cause of Socialism is the support and promotion of Soviet power as defined in Moscow. . . .

But we have seen the Kremlin is under no ideological compulsion to accomplish its purposes in a hurry. Like the Church, it is dealing in ideological concepts which are of long-term validity, and it can afford to be patient. . . . The main thing is that there should always be pressure, increasing constant pressure, toward the desired goal. . . .

These considerations make Soviet diplomacy at once easier and more difficult to deal with than the diplomacy of individual aggressive leaders like Napoleon and Hitler. On the one hand it is more sensitive to contrary force. . . . On the other hand it cannot be easily defeated or discouraged by a single victory on the part of its opponents. And the patient persistence by which it is animated means that it can be effectively countered not by sporadic acts which represent the momentary whims of demo-

---

[2]Literally, "let the buyer beware," or, more or less, "you do so at your own risk"—ED.

cratic opinion but only by intelligent long-range policies on the part of Russia's adversaries—policies no less steady in their purpose, and no less variegated and resourceful in their application, than those of the soviet Union itself.

In these circumstances it is clear that the main element of any United States policy toward the Soviet Union must be that of a long-term, patient but firm and vigilant containment of Russian expansive tendencies. It is important to note, however, that such a policy has nothing to do with outward histrionics: with threats or blustering or superfluous gestures of outward "toughness." While the Kremlin is basically flexible in its reaction to political realities, it is by no means unamenable to considerations of prestige. Like almost any other government, it can be placed by tactless and threatening gestures in a position where it cannot afford to yield even though this might be dictated by its sense of realism. The Russian leaders are keen judges of human psychology, and as such they are highly conscious that loss of temper and of self-control is never a source of strength in political affairs. They are quick to exploit such evidences of weakness. . . .

In the light of the above, it will be clearly seen that the Soviet pressure against the free institutions of the Western world is something that can be contained by the adroit and vigilant application of counter-force at a series of constantly shifting geographical and political points, corresponding to the shifts and maneuvers of Soviet policy, but which cannot be charmed or talked out of existence. The Russians look forward to a duel of infinite duration, and they see that already they have scored great successes. . . .

It is clear that the United States cannot expect in the foreseeable future to enjoy political intimacy with the Soviet regime. It must continue to regard the Soviet Union as a rival, not a partner, in the political arena. It must continue to expect that Soviet policies will reflect no abstract love of peace and stability, no real faith in the possibility of a permanent happy coexistence of the Socialist and capitalist worlds, but rather a cautious, persistent pressure toward the disruption and weakening of all rival influence and rival power.

Balanced against this are the facts that Russia, as opposed to the Western world in general, is still by far the weaker party, that Soviet policy is highly flexible, and that Soviet society may well contain deficiencies which will eventually weaken its own total potential. This would of itself warrant the United States entering with reasonable confidence upon a policy of firm containment, designed to confront the Russians with unalterable counterforce at every point where they show signs of encroaching on the interests of a peaceful and stable world. . . .

It would be an exaggeration to say that American behavior unassisted and alone could exercise a power of life and death over the Communist movement and bring about the early fall of Soviet power in Russia. But the United States has it in its power to increase enormously the strains under which Soviet policy must operate, to force upon the Kremlin a far greater degree of moderation and circumspection than it has had to observe in recent years, and in this way promote tendencies which must eventually find their outlet in either the breakup or the gradual mellowing of Soviet power. . . .

Thus the decision will really fall in large measure on this country itself. The issue of Soviet-American relations is in essence a test of the over-all worth of the United States as a nation among nations. To avoid destruction the United States need only measure up to its own best traditions and prove itself worthy of preservation as a great nation.

A Second Look at Mr. X

WILLIAM APPLEMAN WILLIAMS

George Frost Kennan's appointment as United States Ambassador to the Soviet Union was a move of vital significance in the Cold War. For the choice of Kennan, self-acknowledged author of the policy of containment and publicly proclaimed "inside strategist" of the Cold War, reemphasized Washington's determination to press the original policy of containment—even though Kennan himself has hinted at the grave fallacy of his master plan. And while the Truman administration has yet to take note of its own expert's apparently changed views, the Republicans, under the guidance of John Foster Dulles,[1] bid fair to push containment to its logical conclusion—preventive or provoked war. Clearly, these aspects of current American policy toward Russia point up the need to take a second look at Kennan.

The errors of fact, violations of logic, and cases of judgment by double standard that may be found in Kennan's published writings comprise a total far beyond the scope of a single paper. But the fundamental character of his work is apparent in the famous "X" article, first printed in *Foreign Affairs* in July, 1947, and later republished in Kennan's volume on *American Diplomacy, 1900–1950*. Ostensibly an article on the Soviet political structure, Kennan's "X" article was originally written as a policy document for Secretary of Defense James Forrestal—and actually was but a condensation of the views Kennan had expressed as early as the first part of 1946. This background is important, for it reveals that Kennan's policy of containment was the product of long-term reflection on American-Russian relations; and Kennan was the leader of that small coterie of State Department personnel specifically trained in that field.

Despite the care that went into its preparation, the "X" article contains two signal weaknesses: Kennan's failure to probe the relationship between economic forces and foreign policy; and his attempt to analyze the history of the world since 1917 (and make recommendations for the present) without acknowledging, or addressing himself to, the fundamental challenge that the Bolshevik Revolution presented to the western world in general, and to the United States in particular. For the challenge of contemporary Russia is far more than that of a giant military machine: the Soviet Union is equally potent as the symbol of a fundamental critique of capitalist society that is currently the basis of action in many non-Russian areas of the world.

William Appleman Williams, "A Second Look at Mr. X," *Monthly Review,* vol. 4, no. 4, (August 1952), pp. 123–128, and back cover. Copyright © 1952 by Monthly Review Inc. Reprinted by permission of Monthly Review Foundation.
[1]Secretary of state under Dwight Eisenhower, 1953–59—ED.

To evade or ignore this aspect of American-Russian relations is to explain the past inadequately and to formulate current policy without comprehending the basic forces that condition day-to-day actions and decisions. It would require one to account for the non-Russian centers of Communism, for example, *solely* on the basis of pre-1917 concepts of political treason or a quite inexplicable index of psychiatric maladjustment. And the pattern of causation (while apparently accepted by many in the western world) has little relevance to the rise of Russian influence in China.

Even within his own frame of reference, however, Kennan's review of American-Soviet relations is open to serious question. There was "little" that the United States "could have done," he observes in *American Diplomacy,* "to moderate" the Soviet's "burning hostility" toward the West. Begging the question of what foundation in fact that antagonism might have had (both during and after the Bolshevik Revolution), Kennan concludes that "it was hardly to be altered by anything" the United States could have done directly, and observes that the "best reaction to it on our part would have been at all times an attitude of great reserve, consistency, and dignity" (p. 81).

That is certainly not a unique view of American-Soviet relations, but since Kennan is an expert on the question, his omission of several key aspects of history is difficult to understand. Surely Kennan is aware that Secretary of State Robert Lansing was avowedly and militantly opposed to the Bolshevik Revolution because of its economic and social goals; that the Wilson administration ignored several specific overtures from Lenin for collaboration against Germany and Japan; and that President Wilson openly "cast in his lot with the rest" and actively supported counter-revolutionary forces in an attempt to overthrow the Soviets.

Hard to comprehend, in the short, is Kennan's decision to ignore the fact that from the early days of the November Revolution to the failure of the 1937 Brussels Conference on Japanese aggression in China, the Soviet Union persistently wooed the United States in search of an understanding that would serve to decrease the probability of a conflict that Kennan describes as "at best a war of defense" for the West. Since Kennan is apparently unaware that Tsarist Russia made three overtures of a similar nature to the United States between 1905 and 1912, his failure to place these Soviet advances in a broad framework is perhaps understandable; but even considered as purely post-1917 moves, they can hardly be explained as examples of "burning hostility." Indeed, they document a remarkable Marxist heresy by the very torchbearers of the faith. For economic and political collaboration with the United States designed to preserve Moscow would also preserve Washington—a fact that could not have been missed by the men in the Kremlin. Far from being forced to alter unmitigated antagonism, as Kennan implies, the United States had a standing opportunity to respond to positive advances.

Nor does Kennan deal candidly with American foreign policy as a whole during the interwar years. Far from isolationism, Washington's policy is perhaps best described as an attempt to exercise dominant power within a framework of "freedom without responsibility." Political and economic (and in some cases military) intervention in Latin America, Europe, and China is not isolationism. And the Roosevelt administration's disinterest in the terms of appeasement offered to Mussolini and Hitler as long as they did not touch American interests is striking evidence of the refusal to accept responsibility. These are but the most glaring examples of Kennan's failure to grapple with basic problems in their entirety. The result is clear: Kennan's recommendations lack validity. That these conclusions can be accepted as a basis for action is a matter of record, but to expect them to promote the "national interest" (a well-worn generality that Kennan declines to define) is neither logical, necessary, nor possible.

Kennan's statement of the policy of containment is major evidence in support of this judgment. For when he came to apply his "theoretical foundation" to the specific problem of policy-making, the result was a recommendation for action designed to effect either a definitive change in, or the actual destruction of, the Soviet Union. To be sure, his point of departure is an admission that the sincerity of Soviet leaders cannot be questioned—that they do desire the betterment of life in Russia—but he immediately concludes that they have explained what Kennan takes to be lack of progress in that direction by the prior necessity to establish the security of the government.

Kennan's first problem, therefore, is to establish the validity of this thesis. For a review of the facts, however, he substitutes a statement that enables him to label the security argument as no more than a rationale by which the Soviet leaders maintain themselves in power—no more, in short, than a technique of control. "Tremendous emphasis," Kennan writes, "has been placed on the original Communist thesis of a basic antagonism between the capitalist and Socialist worlds." But, he continues, "it is clear, from many indications that this emphasis is not founded in reality. The real facts concerning it have been confused by the existence abroad of a genuine resentment provoked by Soviet philosophy and tactics and occasionally by the existence of great centers of military power, notably the Nazi regime in Germany and the Japanese Government of the late 1930's, which did indeed have aggressive designs against the Soviet Union." There is, Kennan then concludes, "ample evidence that the stress laid in Moscow on the menace confronting Soviet society . . . is founded not in the realities of foreign antagonism but in the necessity of explaining away the maintenance of dictatorial authority at home" (p. 113).

These comments and interpretations require further examination. Two notable omissions are Kennan's failure to point out that capitalist leaders militantly opposed socialism (both verbally and more actively) long years before the existence of the Soviet state, and his like failure to note Soviet overtures to the United States from 1917 to 1937. He also neglects to mention the fact and character of allied intervention in Russia. Nor does the reader find any reference to the avowed policy aims of Herbert Hoover (the "abandonment of their present economic system" on the part of the Bolsheviks) and Charles Evan Hughes[2] (who conditioned recognition on "fundamental changes" in the Soviet economic system). Likewise peculiar is the use of the word "occasionally" and the chronology "in the late 1930's" to characterize the threat to Russia from Germany and Japan.

"Occasionally" can hardly be applied to an armed challenge that concerned the world for the majority of the interwar years. And the phrase "in the late 1930's"

---

[2]Hughes, later Chief Justice of the Supreme Court, was Secretary of State in the early 1920s—ED.

does not take account of Japan's activities in the intervals from 1917 to 1922 and from 1931 to 1941—or Hitler's from 1934 forward. Kennan's argument that neither Japan's occupation of eastern Siberia and subsequent attacks along the border between Manchuria and Russia nor Hitler's expansion in Central Europe was a threat to Soviet security contrasts strangely with his claim that Moscow was a dire threat to America at a time when the United States had the only stockpile of atom bombs. Yet upon this questionable foundation Kennan proceeds to build his entire argument.

Kennan goes on to deal with two other factors that are central to an analysis of his policy recommendation. "The theory of the inevitability of the eventual fall of capitalism," he writes, "has the fortunate connotation that there is no hurry about it" (p. 116). And again, "the Kremlin is under no ideological compulsion to accomplish its purposes in a hurry" (p. 118). He points out, however, that the Soviet Government, "like almost any other government . . . can be placed in a position where it cannot afford to yield even though this might be dictated by its sense of realism" (p. 119).

For this reason, Kennan emphasizes, "it is a *sine qua non* of successful dealing with Russia that the foreign government in question should remain at all times cool and collected and that demands on Russian policy should be put forward in such a manner as to leave the way open for a compliance not too detrimental to Russian prestige" (p. 119). This statement would appear to indicate that Kennan (despite his inaccurate and misleading presentation of past policies toward Soviet Russia) envisaged some careful effort to establish a basic security accommodation with Moscow. His actual conclusion, however, can hardly be described in that manner.

Rather does Kennan prescribe the use of "unanswerable force," a coupling of words that has no meaning save in a military sense. Nor is his formulation vague. The United States, he concludes, "has it in its power to increase enormously the strains under which Soviet policy must operate, to force upon the Kremlin a far greater degree of moderation and circumspection than it has had to observe in recent years, and in this way promote tendencies which must eventually find their outlet in either the break-up or the gradual mellowing of Soviet power." . . . And Kennan's choice of words further emphasizes his resort to force: had he meant "a result to be expected," he would have used the phrase *will eventually.* Instead he wrote *must eventually,* an expression of obligation under "physical or logical necessity." But men do not surrender nations or social systems to the dictates of logic, as Kennan himself admits.

Thus Kennan disregards both his own warning about "tactless and threatening gestures" and his concern "to leave the way open for a compliance not too detrimental to Russian prestige." For his policy calls for the application of a steadily rising military pressure to challenge existing Soviet leadership (pp. 119, 120). To this the Soviet leaders can hardly be expected to reply other than by preparations for a short-range showdown. This will hardly bring a "mellowing" of internal controls in Russia. By the same token, Kennan's proposals destroy the "fortunate connotation" in Soviet theory that there is "no hurry." A more classic non-sequitur could hardly be conceived—even as an exercise in mental gymnastics. But the responsibility for the future of American-Russian relations cannot be classed as intellectual amusement, for upon their character depends the immediate future of the world. And freedom is not nurtured by nations preparing for war.

There is considerable evidence that Kennan later came to realize the fallacy of his 1946 policy recommendations. In 1951, while on leave of absence from the Department of State, he was a bit less disingenuous—and considerably more moderate—in his statements. First, he cautioned that no war (a more candid substitute for his earlier phrase "unanswerable force") with Russia "could be more than relatively successful" (pp. 129–30); took care to point out that even a defeated Russia would not emerge in the image of America (p. 131); sharply redefined the character of the role that the United States could play—from "has it in its power to increase enormously the strains" to "our role can be at best a marginal one"; and finally warned that any attempt "at direct talking by one nation to another about the latter's political affairs is a questionable procedure" (pp. 150, 53, 152).

Later still, on the eve of his departure for Moscow, Kennan more openly indicated doubts about his earlier analysis. "I want to assume that everything I've thought up to now is wrong," he is reported to have observed, "and see whether I come out at the same place this time." He remarked, however, that any change in his earlier conclusions was "improbable"—an admission that raised serious questions as to Kennan's ability to free himself from the thought patterns of the "X" article. Kennan left no doubt, though, that he was worried by the consequences of containment, for he expressed a fear that it was "a lesson that Americans have learned rather too well" (*The New Yorker,* May 17, 1952, pp. 111, 112). His concern is well founded, but nothing can alter the fact that it was Kennan himself who served as their tutor.

Central to Kennan's shift was his belated realization that the United States will never have enough power to force Russia to "unquestionably yield to it." Once he awoke to this basic error of his "X" article, Kennan quickly saw that his policy in action could well "increase [the Russians'] fear of being warred upon" (*The New Yorker,* pp. 112, 116). Small wonder that he seemed to be giving expression to a fear that his policy of containment is one for which he does not relish ultimate responsibility.

But Kennan cannot escape that responsibility. If he has in fact abandoned containment, he owes the world a formal statement of his decision—for his was the conception and the early implementation of the policy. To date, it has not been abandoned by the United States. If its author now finds it lacking in validity and dangerous in its consequences, then his is the responsibility to throw his weight on the side of revision.

Yet Kennan's greatest failure lies in his inability to define that "something which goes deeper and looks further ahead"—without which containment, by his own admission, "can only remain sterile and negative" (*American Diplomacy,* p. 153). That "something" is no less than the courage to acknowledge the broad challenge of the Bolshevik Revolution. One must conclude that so far, at any rate, Kennan is unaware of the challenge, and until he faces that issue candidly he cannot be expected to formulate an effective response to the challenge of Soviet power.

12.2:   The Truman Doctrine and the Marshall Plan (1947, 1949)

Intellectual formulations such as George Kennan's were important in shaping American Cold War policy, but actual events were even more compelling. In 1946–1947 the Soviet Union provoked a Western response by a series of moves in the Middle East and the Mediterranean designed to extend Soviet power. It refused at first to remove occupation troops that had been stationed in Iran during World War II. It next put pressure on Turkey to surrender control of the strategic Dardenelles Straits and to allow the USSR to base troops and ships on Turkish soil. It fed arms and money to a Communist-led guerrilla war in Greece against the existing pro-Western government.

Concerned with preserving its communications with India, Britain had been the traditional guarantor of autonomy for Greece and Turkey, but in January 1947 the war-exhausted British told the Americans that they could no longer afford to help them. The signal to the United States was clear: either the Americans stepped in or the eastern Mediterranean would fall under Soviet domination.

Meanwhile, a more diffuse crisis was developing in Western Europe. There, following Axis defeat, chaos threatened. On the continent war devastation, social disruption, and moral exhaustion, aggravated by the severe winter of 1946–1947, played into the hands of radical political forces that looked to the Soviet Union for leadership. During this grim period millions of Western Europeans lost their faith in capitalism and liberal democratic institutions and joined pro-Soviet Communist parties. If something were not done soon, said democratic leaders in Europe and America, the Communists might achieve power through legal parliamentary processes. They would then destroy democracy and impose pro-Soviet authoritarian regimes.

The American response to these crises took the form of the Truman Doctrine and the Marshall Plan. The first was announced on March 12, 1947, when President Harry Truman appeared before a joint session of Congress to request American aid to Greece and Turkey. The heart of his speech is excerpted in the first document below.

What were the bases for Truman's request for U.S. money for the Greek and Turkish governments? His reasons are couched in idealistic terms. Was it idealism alone that moved Truman? Many scholars consider the speech one of the most important ever made by a president. Why was it so important? What long-established precedents in American foreign policy might Truman be brushing aside?

The Marshall Plan, first announced by Secretary of State George Marshall at the Harvard University commencement in June 1947, sought to check Communist advance by restoring the prosperity of the whole European continent, East as well as West.[1] Eventually Congress appropriated billions of dollars to implement the plan, and, before long, food, equipment, coal, and steel were flowing to Europe in enormous volume.

What are Marshall's avowed motives for American aid? Why does he say that "our policy is directed not against any country or doctrine"? Was the Soviet Union excluded from Marshall Plan aid? Do you know what the results of the Marshall Plan were?

The final item is a critique of the Marshall Plan by a Marxist economist, Paul M. Sweezy, published in 1949, when the program was still new. Was Sweezy right about the failure of the Marshall Plan to restore European prosperity? Why might someone with Sweezy's political orientation have been skeptical of the plan? Is his claim that the authors of the Marshall Plan wished to save capitalism correct? What does he see as the only alternative to Marshall Plan aid as a way to prevent war?

Aid to Greece and Turkey

HARRY S TRUMAN

Mr. President, Mr. Speaker, Members of the Congress of the United States:

The gravity of the situation which confronts the world today necessitates my appearance before a joint session of the Congress.

The foreign policy and the national security of this country are involved.

One aspect of the present situation, which I wish to present to you at this time for your consideration and decision, concerns Greece and Turkey.

The United States has received from the Greek Government an urgent appeal for financial and economic assistance. Preliminary reports from the American Economic Mission now in Greece and reports from the American Ambassador in Greece corroborate the statement of the Greek Government that assistance is imperative if Greece is to survive as a free nation.

I do not believe that the American people and the Congress wish to turn a deaf ear to the appeal of the Greek Government.

Greece is not a rich country. Lack of sufficient natural resources has always forced the Greek people to work hard to make both ends meet. Since 1940 this in-

---

[1]In the end the Soviet Union and its satellites refused to accept Marshall Plan aid, considering it an American plot—ED.

The Public Papers of the Presidents . . . Harry S Truman . . . 1947 (Washington, DC: Government Printing Office, 1963), pp. 176–180.

dustrious and peace-loving country has suffered invasion, four years of cruel enemy occupation, and bitter internal strife. . . .

The very existence of the Greek state is today threatened by the terrorist activities of several thousand armed men, led by Communists, who defy the Government's authority at a number of points, particularly along the northern boundaries. A commission appointed by the United Nations Security Council is at present investigating disturbed conditions in northern Greece and alleged border violations along the frontier between Greece on the one hand and Albania, Bulgaria, and Yugoslavia on the other.

Meanwhile, the Greek Government is unable to cope with the situation. The Greek Army is small and poorly equipped. It needs supplies and equipment if it is to restore authority to the Government throughout Greek territory.

Greece must have assistance if it is to become a self-supporting and self-respecting democracy.

The United States must supply that assistance. We have already extended to Greece certain types of relief and economic aid, but these are inadequate.

There is no other country to which democratic Greece can turn.

No other nation is willing and able to provide the necessary support for a democratic Greek Government.

The British Government, which has been helping Greece, can give no further financial or economic aid after March 31. Great Britain finds itself under the necessity of reducing or liquidating its commitments in several parts of the world, including Greece.

We have considered how the United Nations might assist in this crisis. But the situation is an urgent one requiring immediate action, and the United Nations and its related organizations are not in a position to extend help of the kind that is required.

It is important to note that the Greek Government has asked for our aid in utilizing effectively the financial and other assistance we may give to Greece, and in improving its public administration. It is of the utmost importance that we supervise the use of any funds made available to Greece, in such a manner that each dollar spent will count toward making Greece self-supporting, and will help to build an economy in which a healthy democracy can flourish.

No government is perfect. One of the chief virtues of a democracy, however, is that its defects are always visible and under democratic processes can be pointed out and corrected. The Government of Greece is not perfect. Nevertheless it represents 85 percent of the members of the Greek Parliament who were chosen in an election last year. Foreign observers, including 692 Americans, considered this election to be a fair expression of the views of the Greek people.

The Greek Government has been operating in an atmosphere of chaos and extremism. It has made mistakes. The extension of aid by this country does not mean that the United States condones everything that the Greek Government has done or will do. We have condemned in the past, and we condemn now, extremist measures of the right or the left. We have in the past advised tolerance, and we advise tolerance now.

Greece's neighbor, Turkey, also deserves our attention.

The future of Turkey as an independent and economically sound state is clearly no less important to the freedom-loving peoples of the world than the future of Greece. The circumstances in which Turkey finds itself today are considerably different from those of Greece. Turkey has been spared the disasters that have beset Greece. And during the war the United States and Great Britain furnished Turkey with material aid.

Nevertheless, Turkey now needs our support.

Since the war Turkey has sought additional financial assistance from Great Britain and the United States for the purpose of effecting that modernization necessary for the maintenance of its national integrity.

That integrity is essential to the preservation of order in the Middle East.

The British Government has informed us that, owing to its own difficulties, it can no longer extend financial or economic aid to Turkey.

As in the case of Greece, if Turkey is to have the assistance it needs, the United States must supply it. We are the only country able to provide that help.

I am fully aware of the broad implications involved if the United States is the creation of conditions in which we and other nations will be able to work out a way of life free from coercion. This was a fundamental issue in the war with Germany and Japan. Our victory was won over countries which sought to impose their will, and their way of life upon other nations.

To insure the peaceful development of nations, free from coercion, the United States has taken a leading part in establishing the United Nations. The United Nations is designed to make possible lasting freedom and independence for all its members. We shall not realize our objectives, however, unless we are willing to help free peoples to maintain their free institutions and their national integrity against aggressive movements that seek to impose upon them totalitarian regimes. This is no more than a frank recognition that totalitarian regimes imposed upon free peoples, by direct or indirect aggression, undermine the foundations of international peace and hence the security of the United States.

The peoples of a number of countries of the world have recently had totalitarian regimes forced upon them against their will. The Government of the United States has made frequent protests against coercion and intimidation, in violation of the Yalta agreement, in Poland, Rumania, and Bulgaria. I must also state that in a number of other countries there have been similar developments.

At the present moment in world history nearly every nation must choose between alternative ways of life. The choice is too often not a free one.

One way of life is based upon the will of the majority, and is distinguished by free institutions, representative government, free elections, guaranties of individual liberty, freedom of speech and religion, and freedom from political oppression.

The second way of life is based upon the will of a minority forcibly imposed upon the majority. It relies upon terror and oppression, a controlled press and radio, fixed elections, and the suppression of personal freedoms.

I believe that it must be the policy of the United States to support free peoples who are resisting attempted subjugation by armed minorities or by outside pressures.

I believe that we must assist free peoples to work out their own destinies in their own way.

I believe that our help should be primarily through economic and financial aid which is essential to economic stability and orderly political processes.

The world is not static, and the *status quo* is not sacred. But we cannot allow changes in the *status quo* in violation of the Charter of the United Nations by such methods as coercion, or by such subterfuges as political infiltration. In helping free and independent nations to maintain their freedom, the United States will be giving effect to the principles of the Charter of the United Nations.

It is necessary only to glance at a map to realize that the survival and integrity of the Greek nation are of grave importance in a much wider situation. If Greece should fall under the control of an armed minority, the effect upon its neighbor, Turkey, would be immediate and serious. Confusion and disorder might well spread throughout the entire Middle East.

Moreover, the disappearance of Greece as an independent state would have a profound effect upon those countries in Europe whose peoples are struggling against great difficulties to maintain their freedoms and their independence while they repair the damages of war.

It would be an unspeakable tragedy if these countries, which have struggled so long against overwhelming odds, should lose that victory for which they sacrificed so much. Collapse of free institutions and loss of independence would be disastrous not only for them but for the world. Discouragement and possibly failure would quickly be the lot of neighboring peoples striving to maintain their freedom and independence.

Should we fail to aid Greece and Turkey in this fateful hour, the effect will be far-reaching to the West as well as to the East.

We must take immediate and resolute action.

I therefore ask the Congress to provide authority for assistance to Greece and Turkey in the amount of $400,000,000 for the period ending June 30, 1948. In requesting these funds, I have taken into consideration the maximum amount of relief assistance which would be furnished to Greece out of the $350,000,000 which I recently requested that the Congress authorize for the prevention of starvation and suffering in countries devastated by the war.

In addition to funds, I ask the Congress to authorize the detail of American civilian and military personnel to Greece and Turkey, at the request of those countries, to assist in the tasks of reconstruction, and for the purpose of supervising the use of such financial and material assistance as may be furnished. I recommend that authority also be provided for the instruction and training of selected Greek and Turkish personnel.

Finally, I ask that the Congress provide authority which will permit the speediest and most effective use, in terms of needed commodities, supplies, and equipment, of such funds as may be authorized.

If further funds, or further authority, should be needed for purposes indicated in this message, I shall not hesitate to bring the situation before the Congress. On this subject the Executive and Legislative branches of the Government must work together.

This is a serious course upon which we embark.

I would not recommend it except that the alternative is much more serious.

The United States contributed $341,000,000,000 toward winning World War II. This is an investment in world freedom and world peace.

The assistance that I am recommending for Greece and Turkey amounts to little more than one-tenth of one percent of this investment. It is only common sense that we should safeguard this investment and make sure that it was not in vain.

The seeds of totalitarian regimes are nurtured by misery and want. They spread and grow in the evil soil of poverty and strife. They reach their full growth when the hope of a people for a better life has died.

We must keep that hope alive.

The free peoples of the world look to us for support in maintaining their freedoms.

If we falter in our leadership, we may endanger the peace of the world—and we shall surely endanger the welfare of our own Nation.

Great responsibilities have been placed upon us by the swift movement of events.

I am confident that the Congress will face these responsibilities squarely.

We Must Help Europe Recover

GEORGE MARSHALL

I need not tell you gentlemen that the world situation is very serious. That must be apparent to all intelligent people. I think one difficulty is that the problem is one of such enormous complexity that the very mass of facts presented to the public by press and radio make it exceedingly difficult for the man in the street to reach a clear appraisement of the situation. Furthermore, the people of this country are distant from the troubled areas of the earth and it is hard for them to comprehend the plight and consequent reactions of the longsuffering peoples, and the effect of those reactions on their governments in connection with our efforts to promote peace in the world.

In considering the requirements for the rehabilitation of Europe, the physical loss of life, the visible destruction of cities, factories, mines, and railroads was correctly estimated, but it has become obvious during recent months that this visible destruction was probably less serious than the dislocation of the entire fabric of European economy. For the past ten years conditions have been highly abnormal. The feverish preparation for war and the more feverish maintenance of the war effort engulfed all aspects of national economies. Machinery has fallen into disrepair or is entirely obsolete. Under the arbitrary and destructive Nazi rule, virtually every possible enterprise was geared into the German war machine. Long-standing commercial ties, private institutions, banks, insurance companies, and shipping companies disappeared, through loss of capital, absorption through nationalization, or by simple destruction. In many countries, confidence in the local currency has been severely shaken. The breakdown of the business structure of Europe during the war was complete. Recovery has been seriously retarded by the fact that two years after the close of hostilities a peace settlement with Germany and Austria has not been agreed upon. But even given a more prompt solution of these difficult problems, the rehabilitation of the economic structure of Europe quite evidently will require a much longer time and greater effort than had been foreseen.

There is a phase of this matter which is both interesting and serious. The farmer has always produced the foodstuffs to exchange with the city dweller for the other necessities of life. This division of labor is the basis of modern civilization. At the present time it is threatened with breakdown. The town and city industries are not producing adequate goods to exchange with the food-producing farmer. Raw materials and fuel are in short supply. Machinery is lacking or worn out. The farmer or the peasant cannot find the goods for sale which he desires to purchase. So the sale of his farm produce for money which he cannot use seems to him an unprofitable transaction. He, therefore, has withdrawn many fields from crop cultivation and is using them for grazing. He feeds more grain to stock and finds for himself and his family an ample supply of food, however short he may be on clothing and the other ordinary gadgets of civilization. Meanwhile people in the cities are short of food and fuel. So the governments are forced to use their foreign money and credits to procure these necessities abroad. This process exhausts funds which are urgently needed for reconstruction. Thus a very serious situation is rapidly developing which bodes no good for the world. The modern system of the division of labor upon which the exchange of products is based is in danger of breaking down.

The truth of the matter is that Europe's requirements for the next three or four years of foreign food and other essential products—principally from America—are so much greater than her present ability to pay that she must have substantial additional help or face economic, social, and political deterioration of a very grave character.

The remedy lies in breaking the vicious circle and restoring the confidence of the European people in the economic future of their own countries and of Europe as a whole. The manufacturer and the farmer throughout wide areas must be able and willing to exchange their products for currencies the continuing value of which is not open to question.

Aside from the demoralizing effect on the world at large and the possibilities of disturbances arising as a result of the desperation of the people concerned, the consequences to the economy of the United States should be apparent to all. It is logical that the United States should do whatever it is able to do to assist in the return of normal economic health in the world, without which there can be no political stability and no assured peace. Our policy is directed not against any country or doctrine but against hunger, poverty, desperation, and chaos. Its purpose should be the revival of a working economy in the world so as to permit the emergence of political and social conditions in which the free institutions can exist. Such assistance, I am convinced, must not be on a piecemeal basis as various crises develop. Any assistance that this Government may render in the future should provide a cure rather than a mere palliative. Any government that is willing to assist in the task of recovery will find full cooperation, I am sure, on the part of the United States Government. Any government which maneuvers to block the recovery of other countries cannot expect help from us. Furthermore, governments, political parties, or groups which seek to perpetuate human misery in order to profit therefrom politically or otherwise will encounter the opposition of the United States.

It is already evident that, before the United States Government can proceed much further in its efforts to alleviate the situation and help start the European world on its way to recovery, there must be some agreement among the countries of Europe as to the requirements of the situation and the part of those countries themselves will take in order to giver proper effect to whatever action might be undertaken by this Government. It would be neither fitting nor efficacious for this Government to undertake to draw up unilaterally a program designed to place Europe on its feet economically. This is the business of the Europeans. The initiative, I think, must come from Europe. The role of this country should consist of friendly aid in the drafting of a European program and of later support of such a program so far as it may be practical for us to do so. The program should be a joint one, agreed to by a number, if not all, European nations.

An essential part of any successful action on the part of the United States is an understanding on the part of the people of America of the character of the problem and the remedies to be applied. Political passion and prejudice should have no part. With foresight, and a willingness on the part of our people to face up to the vast responsibility which history has clearly placed upon our country, the difficulties I have outlined can and will be overcome.

. . . This program will cost our country billions of dollars. It will impose a burden on the American taxpayer. It will require sacrifices today in order that we may enjoy security and peace tomorrow. Should the Congress approve the program for European recovery, as I urgently recommend, we Americans will have made an historic decision of our peacetime history.

A nation in which the voice of its people directs the conduct of its affairs cannot embark on an undertaking of such magnitude and significance for light or purely sentimental reasons. Decisions of this importance are dictated by the highest considerations of national interest. There are none higher, I am sure, than the establishment of enduring peace and the maintenance of true freedom for the individual. In the deliberations of the coming weeks I ask that the European Recovery Program be judged in these terms and on this basis. . . .

The program is *not* one of a series of piecemeal relief measures. I ask that you note this difference, and keep it in mind throughout our explanations. The difference is absolutely vital.

The Marshall Plan, An Instrument of Peace

PAUL M. SWEEZY

The annual question of how much money should be appropriated to carry out the purposes of the Marshall Plan is again before the Congress. It is a good time to recall what those purposes were supposed to be and to examine the extent to which they are being realized in practice.

The Marshall Plan was sold to the American people as a program of aid to the countries of western Europe which would enable them to achieve, within the space of about five years, full economic independence. That is certainly a praiseworthy aim. Economically independent countries can also afford to be politically independent. A politically independent western Europe, tied to no blocs and defending its own interests in the arena of international politics, would be a powerful force for peace. If the Marshall Plan were really calculated to create an independent Western Europe, it should receive support.

It is for precisely this reason that by far the most important fact about the Marshall Plan is that it is not creating an economically independent western Europe. There is not the slightest prospect that it will create an economically independent western Europe.

Official analyses of the Marshall Plan reveal this fact even though they dare not admit it. Honest evaluations of the Marshall Plan say it frankly and unequivocally.

Here, for example, is what Walter Lippman[1] had to say in his column in the *Herald-Tribune* of June 13:

> There is current a good deal of pretense and propaganda about how well in hand everything is. Yet ever since the report of the Marshall Plan countries which was made available at the end of 1948 it has been known to the relatively few who studied it that the goal of European recovery, in the official and popular sense of the words, was unattainable by 1952—during the period set by Congress and agreed to by the Marshall Plan countries. It was certain that even with almost unlimited wishful thinking the leading industrial countries of Europe could not become self-supporting and still achieve and maintain a tolerable standard of life by 1952, or in fact at any foreseeable date.

I believe this is a sober statement of the truth—the bedrock from which any rational evaluation of the Marshall Plan must start.

Why is the Marshall Plan failing to achieve its announced goals? Many theories are currently being put forward to explain this. Some say that it is because the United States is perverting the Marshall Plan into an instrument of American imperialism. Some say that it is because the British are selfishly looking out for their

Paul M. Sweezy, "The Marshall Plan, An Instrument of Peace?" *Monthly Review,* vol. 1, no. 3 (July 1949), pp. 80–84. Copyright © 1949 by Monthly Review Inc. Reprinted by permission of Monthly Review Foundation.

[1]Lippman was a famous columnist and political pundit—ED.

own recovery and neglecting the interests of western Europe as a whole. Some say that it is because of the maze of regulations and restrictions which are choking trade among the Marshall Plan countries themselves.

There is, of course, something to each one of these theories. But they are all essentially superficial, and even if the conditions to which they call attention were remedied the situation as a whole would not be decisively altered. The Marshall Plan might be administered without a thought for the interests of American business. The British might be as altruistic as they are alleged to be selfish. Trade restrictions among the Marshall Plan countries might be completely eliminated. There would still be no economically independent western Europe by the end of 1952.

The truth is that the Marshall Plan does not touch the real problem of western Europe. The Marshall Plan is based on the tacit assumption that western Europe was temporarily knocked out by the war and that what it needs is help in getting back on its feet again. This is a totally inadequate diagnosis. In fact the war was merely the climax of a long-term trend. The *status quo ante* in western Europe is dead; no amount of outside assistance can bring it to life again. To quote Thomas Balogh, an eminent Oxford economist: "Western Europe's crisis is not a temporary or short lived departure from an 'equilibrium position' to which it is easy to return. It is a historically unique, harsh break with all that has gone before, a fundamental crisis."

In broad outline the nature of this crisis is clear and simple. Western Europe was the original home of capitalism. During the 18th and 19th centuries it was economically by far the most advanced region in the world. It used its wealth and power to establish relations with the rest of the world which were enormously advantageous to western Europe. On the strength of these advantageous relations with the rest of the world, western Europe developed a very numerous population and provided it with a relatively high standard of living.

It is easy to see now, looking back, that the foundation of western Europe's extraordinary prosperity was temporary. The rest of the world was bound to catch up and to demand a redefinition of its relations with western Europe. When that happened western Europe could no longer go on living in the old way. It would have to face up to the problem of reconstructing and reorienting its economy to meet the requirements of a changed world.

The two world wars greatly accelerated this inevitable historical development. Already in the inter-war period, the day of reckoning was clearly approaching. By the end of World War II it was obvious that it had at last arrived.

What were the practical alternatives?

First, outside aid which would permit western Europe to evade the real problem but would in no sense contribute to its solution.

Or, second, a thorough-going economic revolution which would cut through centuries-old vested interests, drastically redirect and reorganize the utilization of human and material resources, and open the way for a planned coordination of the western European economy with the economies of other regions which would be both willing and able to enter into firm long-term commitments of a mutually beneficial nature. The watchword of such a revolution would have to be planning and still more planning—vigorous, disciplined, comprehensive.

Only a political imbecile could believe that the traditional ruling classes of western Europe would or could carry through such a revolution. It would have to be done by the working class which has few privileges to lose and is capable of toil and sacrifice for a communal goal. And in the very process of carrying out this great revolution, the workers of western Europe would inevitably be forced to scrap the old capitalist system of production for profit and to substitute a new socialist system of production for use.

In the actual circumstances which prevailed after World War II such a revolution was a very real possibility. On the continent the Resistance movements, under the leadership of Socialists and Communists, were everywhere spearheading the drive for radical economic reform. In England the Labor Party was swept into power on a wave of popular enthusiasm for its stated socialist aims. A firm Socialist-Communist front could have led the way forward despite all obstacles.

But the leaders of the United States, and especially those who have their offices in the skyscrapers of New York rather than in the government buildings of Washington, feared nothing so much as a real revolution in western Europe. They had one, and only one, weapon with which to fight it—economic subsidies which would give the old order a new lease on life and permit western Europe, for the time being at any rate, to evade rather than tackle the basic problem which confronted It. They used their weapon skillfully and ruthlessly; and they found valuable allies among the social democratic leaders of western Europe.

At first the subsidies took the form of a variety of loans and grants. Later they were systematized in the more effective form of the Marshall Plan with its centralized administrative apparatus, its network of bilateral treaties, and its agents in each of the countries affected.

Thus we see that while the Marshall Plan was sold to the American people as a *solution* to the crisis of western Europe, in reality it is just the opposite. It is the means by which American capitalism seeks to prevent western Europe from solving its own crisis in the only possible way it can solve the crisis, by the adoption of socialism.

It is only against this background that we can properly evaluate the relation of the Marshall Plan to peace and war. The relation is not a simple one and nothing is gained by pretending that it is.

If the ruling elements in the United States were prepared to continue the Marshall Plan indefinitely, if the support of the American people for such a policy could be secured, and if the economy of the United States could be stabilized by a continuing export surplus of this magnitude, then the Marshall Plan would have a tendency to reduce international tensions, at least for a considerable period. Western Europe would become the passive dumping ground for an economic system which is always in danger of choking on its own surplus product.

But none of these conditions is likely to be fulfilled. Subsidizing western Europe is not a directly profitable form of investment for American capitalists; the people of the United States are not sufficiently initiated into the mysteries of capitalist economics to understand the need for giving away 5 or 6 billion dollars a year forever; and in any case 5 or 6 billion dollars is not enough to keep American capitalism from choking.

Hence the Marshall Plan must be looked upon as a stopgap expedient which solves neither the problems of western Europe nor the problems of the United States. Being essentially temporary and inadequate by any standards, it cannot but play a disturbing role in international relations.

And yet it is hardly accurate to say that the Marshall Plan as such is a threat to peace.

The real threat to peace comes from the utter and complete inability of the rulers of the United States to devise a non-warlike program for dealing with the overwhelming problems which are pressing in on them from all sides.

When the Marshall Plan runs out, the crisis of western Europe will be no nearer solution than it was two years ago—and it may be added that the obvious and continued success of socialist planning in eastern Europe will by that time have shown the western Europeans how they can solve their crisis if they but have the will and the resolve. American capitalism is already giving signs of sliding into the inevitable depression which all the world expects and which our rulers know will deal a bodyblow to their prestige and authority. Worst of all from their point of view, if something isn't done, even the American people may wake up from their propaganda-created nightmare of Soviet aggression and Communist plots to discover that the real world is one in which those nations and peoples who manage their affairs in their own interests go forward in spite of all obstacles, while those who put their trust in the gods of free enterprise find themselves hopelessly stuck in the mire of economic insecurity and political reaction.

These are the problems which stare the rulers of America in the face. They do not know how to overcome them. In truth there is no way to overcome them within the framework of the self-contradictory system to which they are wedded. In the long run the replacement of capitalism by a rational socialist order is as certain in the United States as elsewhere. But in the meantime, the greatest danger to world peace, and indeed to much that is best in human civilization itself, is that the rulers of America will seek to put off the day of reckoning by embarking on a career of unlimited militarism and imperialism.

They are already moving in this direction—whether consciously or not is beside the point. If they continue, war may not come soon; but it is hard to see how it can be avoided indefinitely. Militarism and imperialism have their own logic, and its final term is war.

Is it too late to call a halt? That will depend on how quickly the people everywhere, but especially the people of western Europe and America, can be brought to understand that the only possibly guarantee of lasting peace is a new social order which puts the interests of producers and consumers above the interests of private capital.

☆ **13** ☆

The Civil Rights Revolution

Black Americans have struggled for respect and equal rights for generations, but except for the brief Reconstruction period, made little headway until after World War II. Well into the 1950s, black citizens virtually everywhere were victims of racial discrimination that denied them equal access to jobs, housing, training, education, and private amenities. In the South, state and local laws imposed a system of segregation (Jim Crow) that confined them to separate, and almost invariably inferior, public services and facilities, while legal sleight of hand, intimidation, and subterfuge also denied them the right to vote.

A victory over a malevolent racist ideology, World War II changed the racial climate. Many white Americans came to recognize the pernicious effects of racism; black soldiers returned from the fighting fronts with new determination to resist bigotry at home. Partially suspended during the war, the movement for racial justice vigorously revived after 1945.

During the late forties and early fifties the civil rights drive was led by the National Association for the Advancement of Colored People (NAACP), a coalition of white liberals and black activists that had as its ultimate goal an integrated society where race and color would cease to matter. The NAACP's chief weapon was suits in the federal courts to compel enforcement of the equal treatment principles enjoined by the Constitution but long ignored. Its strategy culminated in the 1954 Supreme Court decision *Brown* v. *Board of Education of Topeka,* declaring segregated schools in violation of the equal protection clause of the Fourteenth Amendment.

By the end of the 1950s nonviolent civil disobedience, as employed by the Southern Christian Leadership Conference (SCLC) headed by the Baptist minister Martin Luther King, Jr., had began to eclipse the NAACP's legal action approach. Yet even in this new period the civil rights movement remained committed to a color-blind, integrated society of "black and white together." King inspired millions of both races through his writings and through his highly visible protest tactics of boycotts and marches. The eloquence and bravery of King and his followers deeply moved the liberal public and helped undermine a tottering system of legal discrimination and disfranchisement.

By the mid-sixties, however, the civil rights movement had become more separatist and militant. Although Jim Crow was now virtually dead, blacks still remained poor and relatively powerless. These realities, amplified by the confrontational mood of the decade in general, encouraged black separatism and the willingness to consider aggressive means to force the larger society to confer greater political and economic equality.

In the selections below you will find a small sampling of the extensive literature of the civil rights movement. The writings include several competing varieties of civil rights thought as well as prosegregation, anti–civil rights documents. Carefully consider them for insight into the minds of participants in the momentous civil rights revolution.

13.1:   School Desegregation (1954, 1965)

After years of slow progress, the breakthrough in the legal attack on Jim Crow came in 1954 with the Supreme Court decision Brown v. Board of Education of Topeka. *The conclusion of a suit brought by the NAACP Legal Defense Fund headed by Thurgood Marshall, the* Brown *decision overthrew the precedent established by* Plessy v. Ferguson *(1896) allowing segregated public facilities for blacks, notwithstanding the Fourteenth Amendment, so long as they were* equal *to those provided for whites.* Separate, *by its very nature, said Chief Justice Earl Warren in the* Brown *decision, must be considered* unequal.

The Court would soon enjoin "all deliberate speed" for the implementation of its school desegregation order. In a few places in the Upper South school districts quickly complied. But in many southern communities the Brown *decision was met by massive resistance. The Ku Klux Klan revived and soon marshaled its weapons of violence and intimidation against school desegregation. More effective were the White Citizens' Councils, composed of "respectable" middle-class conservatives who deplored the crude methods of the Klan but used moral and economic pressure and legal maneuvering to preserve the Jim Crow system. In several southern states conservative administrations countered NAACP legal action with court suits of their own to delay application of the* Brown *decision.*

The two documents below represent the poles of opinion on the school desegregation issue. The first is an excerpt from the Brown *decision itself, written by Chief Justice Warren. Consider the basis for Warren's rejection of "separate but equal." Is his reasoning convincing? Why did the justices who originally announced the* Plessy v. Ferguson *doctrine in the 1890s see matters differently from Warren in 1954?*

The second selection is part of an article from The Citizen, *the official publication of the White Citizens' Councils. It was written for members of the Councils on the occasion of a leadership conference held in Chattanooga, Tennessee, in late 1965. Is the piece militantly racist? How convincing are the author's arguments for segregated schools? Consider the principle of segregation by ability, which is rejected. Is the argument against it convincing? Does the author find any gaps in the integrationists' armor? There is much in this article on the need to preserve religion in the schools. Was there a cultural link between segregationism and some kinds of traditional Christian faith? What seems to be the Citizens' Councils practical solution to the desegregation dilemma?*

Brown v. Board of Education of Topeka

WARREN, C. J. (Chief Justice). These cases come to us from the States of Kansas, South Carolina, Virginia, and Delaware. They are premised on different facts and different local conditions, but a common legal question justifies their consideration together in this consolidated opinion.

In each of these cases, minors of the Negro race, through their legal representatives, seek the aid of the courts in obtaining admission to the public schools of their community on a nonsegregated basis. In each instance, they have been denied admission to schools attended by white children under laws requiring or permitting segregation according to race. This segregation was alleged to deprive the plaintiffs of the equal protection of the laws under the Fourteenth Amendment. In each of the cases, other than the Delaware case, a three-judge federal district court denied relief to the plaintiffs on the so-called "separate but equal" doctrine announced by this Court in *Plessy* v. *Ferguson*. . . . Under that doctrine, equality of treatment is accorded when the races are provided substantially equal facilities, even though these facilities be separate. . . .

The plaintiffs contend that segregated public schools are not "equal": and cannot be made "equal," and hence they are deprived of the equal protection of the laws.

[*Brown* v. *Board of Education of Topeka*), 347 U.S. 483

Because of the obvious importance of the question presented, the Court took jurisdiction. Argument was heard in the 1952 Term, and reargument was heard this Term on certain questions propounded by the Court.

Reargument was largely devoted to the circumstances surrounding the adoption of the Fourteenth Amendment in 1868. It covered exhaustively consideration of the Amendment in Congress, ratification by the states, then existing practices in racial segregation, and the views of proponents and opponents of the Amendment. This discussion and our own investigation convince us that, although these sources cast some light, it is not enough to resolve the problem with which we are faced. At best they are inconclusive. . . .

In the first cases in the Court construing the Fourteenth Amendment, decided shortly after its adoption, the Court interpreted it as proscribing all state-imposed discrimination against the Negro race. The doctrine of "separate but equal" did not make its appearance in this Court until 1896 in the case of *Plessy* v. *Ferguson* . . . , involving not education but transportation. American courts have since labored with the doctrine for over half a century. In this Court, there have been six cases involving the "separate but equal" doctrine in the field of public education. . . . In none of these cases was it necessary to grant relief to the Negro plaintiff. And in *Sweatt* v. *Painter* . . . , the Court expressly reserved decision on the question whether *Plessy* v. *Ferguson* should be held inapplicable to public education.

In the instant case, that question is directly presented. Here . . . there are findings below that the Negro and white schools involved have been equalized, or are being equalized, with respect to buildings, curricula, qualifications and salaries of teachers, and other "tangible" factors. Our decision, therefore, cannot turn on merely a comparison of these tangible factors in the Negro and white schools involved in each of the cases. We must look instead to the effect of segregation itself on public education.

In approaching this problem, we cannot turn the clock back to 1868 when the Amendment was adopted, or even to 1896 when *Plessy* v. *Ferguson* was written. We must consider public education in the light of its full development and its present place in American life throughout the Nation. Only in this way can it be determined if segregation in public schools deprives these plaintiffs of the equal protection of the laws.

Today, education is perhaps the most important function of state and local governments. Compulsory school attendance and the great expenditures for education both demonstrate our recognition of the importance of education to our democratic society. It is required in the performance of our most basic responsibilities, even service in the armed forces. It is the very foundation of good citizenship. Today it is a principal instrument in awakening the child to cultural values, in preparing him for later professional training, and in helping him to adjust normally to his environment. In these days, it is doubtful that any child may reasonably be expected to succeed in life if he is denied the opportunity of an education. Such an opportunity, where the state has undertaken to provide it, is a right which must be made available to all on equal terms.

We come then to the question presented: Does segregation of children in public schools solely on the basis of race, even though the physical facilities and other "tangible" factors may be equal, deprive the children of the minority group of equal educational opportunities? We believe that it does.

In *Sweatt* v. *Painter,* . . . in finding that a segregated law school for Negroes could not provide them equal educational opportunities, this Court relied in large part on "those qualities which are incapable of objective measurement but which make for greatness in a law school." In *McLaurin* v. *Oklahoma State Regents,* . . . the Court, in requiring that a Negro admitted to a white graduate school be treated like all other students, again resorted to intangible considerations: " . . . his ability to study, to engage in discussion and exchange views with other students and, in general, to learn his profession." Such considerations apply with added force to children in grade and high schools. To separate them from others of similar age and qualifications solely because of their race generates a feeling of inferiority as to their status in the community that may affect their hearts and minds in a way unlikely ever to be undone. . . .

Whatever may have been the extent of psychological knowledge at the time of *Plessy* v. *Ferguson,* this finding is amply supported by modern authority. Any language contrary to this finding is rejected.

We conclude that in the field of public education the doctrine of "separate but equal" has no place. Separate educational facilities are inherently unequal. Therefore, we hold that the plaintiffs and other similarly situated for whom the actions have been brought are, by reason of the segregation complained of, deprived of the equal protection of the laws guaranteed by the Fourteenth Amendment. This disposition makes unnecessary any discussion whether such segregation also violates the Due Process Clause of the Fourteenth Amendment.

How Can We Educate Our Children?

WHITE CITIZENS' COUNCILS

Schools are not merely the mark of a civilization. They are the means of maintaining civilization.

Our American school system is at once an inheritance from Europe and an original contribution to the modern world. Ultimately, our system derives from the medieval universities such as Oxford and Cambridge, and from the "grammar" and other schools established to prepare for those universities. . . .

All the universities of the Middle Ages and the earliest universities or colleges in America were established by groups of Christians, whose basic concern was perpetuation of the gospel.

American state universities were frankly imitative of these educational institutions of the Christian church. Early American schools, like their European predecessors, aimed at beginning for children a course of study leading toward college. In this country, however, a new element came to be emphasized—the training of every child, whether he would or would not go to college. This vital feature of our society has now reached the point of undertaking to see that every child goes to college.

It is this widening of the doors of opportunity which has been the special contribution of America to the world, for to some degree the rest of the world is following us in it.

What needs to be remembered is that there is no point in widening the doors if the treasure within be lost in the process. Our schools and colleges became valuable because they led their student to skill in the arts and knowledge in the sciences, very specifically including the Holy Scripture and the Christian life.

Too often in our time the curriculum has been broadened at the expense of becoming shallower and recently all religious content has been dictatorially excluded from state operated schools. Of course some positive attitude toward religion is inseparable from an educational enterprise. . . .

In the world revolution now being everywhere attempted, the conscious overthrow of the traditional American school system, with its roots in the Christian culture of Western Europe, is a priority item. Many revolutionary techniques have been employed, many massive assaults have been made on the ramparts of the "three R's" and especially of the fourth "R," religion. . . .

No other blow against our educational structure has been quite so violent or damaging as the hysterical attack of the racial integrationists. The results in the District of Columbia are notorious. The school system of the nation's capital was once among the finest in the country. Today it is an educational desert—with one oasis in the far Northwest thanks to a process of *de facto* resegregation.

Central High School in Little Rock was found by a survey in the mid-1950's to be one of the 25 best secondary schools in the United States. Today, even though integration there is hardly more than a token, it is scarcely thought of in terms of overall excellence.

Dr. Henry Garrett and other experts have shown that a sound program of schooling is intrinsically impossible where significant numbers of white and black children are herded together in one classroom. The essential disparity, mentally and temperamentally, is just too great. The mania for homogenization has not yet reached the point where high school boys and girls are integrated in the same gym classes. Yet it would be hardly more absurd than the forced congregation of Negro with white children above the preschool level.

(In the Old South, white children played with Negro children regularly before reaching school age, and even later—outside the school. This fact sometimes caused painful personal readjustments later, which integrationists attribute to the eventual segregation, but which could just as well be attributed to the early integration. More reasonably, one could simply recognize that a full life involves many readjustments.)

Some object to segregationist arguments based on IQ differences by saying: "Well then, group them in class by IQ, or other ability test, without reference to race!" The rejoinder to this is twofold: (1) it is not at all what the militant integrationists want, since it would leave a racially unbalanced situation; and (2) it would create new psychological problems, possibly much more serious than any we now have, and would result in an ever widening gap between the predominantly white group, with its adopted superior Negroes, and the predominantly Negro group with its adopted subnormal whites.

Intelligence is not everything—not enough to justify breaking up groups with other sources of internal cohesion. But a group's average intelligence is important enough to justify separate education for groups with significantly different averages, even if there is some "overlap." By way of analogy, the existence of Amazonian women and effeminate men does not justify drafting women for combat military service (though the Russians have used women for such service).

Not to pursue further the speculative reasons for segregation, a recent analysis of practical school problems which gives the strongest kind of objective support to the segregationist position appeared in, of all places, the *New York Times Magazine* (May 2, 1965) by one Martin Mayer—subjectively, it would appear, an integrationist, but an intelligent observer and skillful writer. Following are excerpts from this revealing article:

> Public confidence in the [New York City] school system is fearfully low and dropping: White children are leaving the city public schools at a rate of 40,000 a year. . . . Of the leaders of the school system itself—the nine-member Board of Education and the 20-odd deputy and associate superintendents—only a handful have children who attend or ever did attend a New York Public school. . . . Of the Negro leaders of the integration drive, . . . not one has or has had a child in a New York public school. . . .

Integration is the main, but not the only threat to the American school system. Indeed, integration itself would not be promoted so fanatically if too many educators had not adopted a philosophy which says that the spirit of man is the result of material processes, and that there is no spirit beyond.

Materialism begins by exalting the schools, for it holds that through them society and the nature of man himself may undergo a revolutionary transformation. Yet materialism ends by destroying the schools, for it reduces them to budgets, buildings and bureaucracy, where blossom at best the beatniks of Berkeley,[1] and from which finer spirits escape altogether. . . .

Because of the integration-at-any-cost policy of both the Federal government and the majority of the nation's educational bureaucrats, the public is daily losing faith in the "serviceability of public education." This is not a condition which the Citizens' Councils have created, but it is one which we recognize. The purpose of the Chattanooga Leadership Conference is to promote the rapidly expanding private school movement as a means of protecting both racial integrity and American education.

---

[1] Nineteen-fifties social-cultural nonconformists whose dress, attitudes, and lifestyles offended many conventional middle class people—ED.

13.2:   Christian Love versus Racial Anger (1964, 1967)

The Brown *decision of 1954 unleashed forces that soon dismantled the entire system of legal discrimination. Each step of the way was marked by further court decisions and new federal legislation to enforce job equality and voting rights. But government agencies, whether the courts, Congress, or the Justice Department, would not have moved so fast without the bold challenges to southern practices by brave civil rights workers willing to face intimidation and physical attack. Inevitably, these challenges created martyrs, but they dramatized the plight of southern black people and revealed the continuing defiance of the law of the land by conservative whites. The process stirred waves of sympathy among white Americans that impressed Congress and the White House, accelerating the process of federal intervention.*

By the mid-sixties even these more militant tactics seemed too feeble to some civil rights activists. Driven by an emerging black nationalism and by frustration at the slow pace of economic progress for blacks, the militants lashed out angrily and defiantly at white America, including white liberal sympathizers. In place of the color-blind society, the ideal until this point, they proposed one where distinctive black institutions would function separately from those of the larger society. Infused with such "black power" views, the Student Non-Violent Coordinating Committee[1] (SNCC), along with the Congress of Racial Equality (CORE), expelled their white members and declared themselves separatist organizations. Meanwhile, organizations like the Black Panthers, a menacing paramilitary group from California, adopted Marxist or anticolonialist Third World revolutionary theories to guide their struggles against white America.

By this time outright violence had begun to sweep the inner-city black ghettos. Beginning in Watts in Los Angeles in 1965 and continuing for three years, riots erupted in the ghettos each summer. Often triggered by anger at police brutality, the uprisings expressed the frustrated expectations of the black urban poor. They culminated in April 1968, following the assassination of Martin Luther King, Jr., by a white supremacist, in a spasm of ghetto rage that raised visions of racial apocalypse.

---

[1]This group was originally a biracial offshoot of the 1960 student lunch counter sit-in movement of 1960 that helped desegregate restaurants and cafeterias in the South. Composed primarily of students and young men and women, it was affiliated with SCLC, although from the first it often refused to accept SCLC's direction.

White liberals urged compassion and understanding, but many white Americans resented and feared the new militancy. It soon triggered a surge of antiblack resentment labeled "white backlash." Backlash, King's tragic death, and the discouraging pace of African American economic progress stopped the civil rights movement in its tracks. Advance would eventually resume, but it would be once more primarily through the slow and quiet processes of legislation, legal challenge, bureaucratic ruling, and court review.

The first selection below is an SCLC statement of its approach and goals probably composed in 1964. It summarizes the philosophy that guided King and his supporters. What are the intellectual sources of SCLC's philosophy? Do SCLC's tactics place great psychological burdens on its practitioners? What were the SCLC's goals for the American society of the future? Were these goals realistic?

The second document is a statement made by SNCC after it had been taken over by the black power militants and repudiated SCLC and its tactics. How would you characterize the tone of this document? Was this late-period SNCC approach practical? Could its plan have been implemented? What do you think of the specific tactics to undermine the system suggested here? One element of this new mood was pan-Africanism. What forces or events help explain this identification of black Americans with Africa in the late 1960s? Have you encountered this view before in this volume? How would you expect most whites to respond to a manifesto such as this one?

This is SCLC

SOUTHERN CHRISTIAN LEADERSHIP CONFERENCE

Aims and Purposes of SCLC

The Southern Christian Leadership Conference has the basic aim of achieving full citizenship rights, equality, and the integration of the Negro in all aspects of American life. SCLC is a service agency to facilitate coordinated action of local community groups within the frame of their indigenous organizations and natural leadership. SCLC activity revolves around two main focal points: the use of nonviolent philosophy as a means of creative protest; and securing the right of the ballot for every citizen.

Philosophy of SCLC

The basic tenets of Hebraic-Christian tradition coupled with the Gandhian concept of *satyagraha*—truth force—is at the heart of SCLC's philosophy. Christian nonvi-

Southern Christian Leadership Conference, *This Is SCLC*, rev. ed., 1964.

olence actively resists evil in any form. It never seeks to humiliate the opponent, only to win him. Suffering is accepted without retaliation. Internal violence of the spirit is as much to be rejected as external physical violence. At the center of nonviolence is redemptive love. Creatively used, the philosophy of nonviolence can restore the broken community in America. SCLC is convinced that nonviolence is the most potent force available to an oppressed people in their struggle for freedom and dignity.

SCLC and Nonviolent Mass Direct Action

SCLC believes that the American dilemma in race relations can best and most quickly be resolved through the action of thousands of people, committed to the philosophy of nonviolence, who will physically identify themselves in a just and moral struggle. It is not enough to be intellectually dissatisfied with an evil system. The true nonviolent resister presents his physical body as an instrument to defeat the system. Through nonviolent mass direct action, the evil system is creatively dramatized in order that the conscience of the community may grapple with the rightness or wrongness of the issue at hand. . . .

SCLC and Voter-Registration

The right of the ballot is basic to the exercise of full citizenship rights. All across the South, subtle and flagrant obstacles confront the Negro when he seeks to register and vote. Poll taxes, long form questionnaires, harassment, economic reprisal, and sometimes death, meet those who dare to seek this exercise of the ballot. In areas where there is little or no attempt to block the voting attempts of the Negro, apathy generally is deeply etched upon the habits of the community. SCLC, with its specialized staff, works on both fronts: aiding local communities through every means available to secure the right to vote (e.g., filing complaints with the Civil Rights Commission) and arousing interest through voter-registration workshops to point up the importance of the ballot. Periodically, SCLC, upon invitation, conducts a voter-registration drive to enhance a community's opportunity to free itself from economic and political servitude. SCLC believes that the most important step the Negro can take is that short walk to the voting booth.

SCLC and Civil Disobedience

SCLC sees civil disobedience as a natural consequence of nonviolence when the resister is confronted by unjust and immoral laws. This does not imply that SCLC advocates either anarchy or lawlessness. The Conference firmly believes that all people have a moral responsibility to obey laws that are just. It recognizes, however, that there also are unjust laws. From a purely moral point of view, an unjust law is one that is out of harmony with the moral law of the universe, or, as the religionist would say, out of harmony with the Law of God. More concretely, an unjust law is one in which the minority is compelled to observe a code which is not binding on the majority. An unjust law is one in which people are required to obey a code that they had no part in making because they were denied the right to vote. In the face of such obvious inequality, where difference is made legal, the nonviolent resister has no alternative but to disobey the unjust law. In disobeying such a law, he does so peacefully, openly and nonviolently. Most important, he *willingly* accepts the penalty for breaking the law. This distinguishes SCLC's position on civil disobedience from the "uncivil disobedience" of the racist opposition in the South. In the face of laws they consider unjust, they seek to defy, evade, and circumvent the law, BUT they are *unwilling* to accept the penalty for breaking the law. The end result of their defiance is anarchy and disrespect for the law. SCLC, on the other hand, believes that civil disobedience involves the highest respect for the law. He who openly disobeys a law that conscience tells him is unjust and willingly accepts the penalty is giving evidence that he so respects the law that he belongs in jail until it is changed. . . .

SCLC and Segregation

SCLC is firmly opposed to segregation in any form that it takes and pledges itself to work unrelentingly to rid every vestige of its scars from our nation through nonviolent means. Segregation is an evil and its presence in our nation has blighted our larger destiny as a leader in world affairs. Segregation does as much harm to the *segregator* as it does to the *segregated*. The *segregated* develops a false sense of inferiority and the *segregator* develops a false sense of superiority, both contrary to the American ideal of democracy. America must rid herself of segregation not alone because it is politically expedient, but because it is morally right!

SCLC and Constructive Program

SCLC's basic program fosters nonviolent resistance to all forms of racial injustice, including state and local laws and practices, even when this mean going to jail; and imaginative, bold constructive action to end the demoralization caused by the legacy of slavery and segregation—inferior schools, slums, and second-class citizenship. Thus, the Conference works on two fronts. On the one hand, it resists continuously the system of segregation which is the basic cause of lagging standards; on the other hand, it works constructively to improve the standards themselves. There MUST be a balance between attacking the causes and healing the effects of segregation.

SCLC and the Beloved Community

The ultimate aim of SCLC is to foster and create the "beloved community" in America where brotherhood is a reality. It rejects any doctrine of black supremacy for this merely substitutes one kind of tyranny for another. The Conference does not foster moving the Negro from a position of disadvantage to one of advantage for this would thereby subvert justice. SCLC works for integration. Our ultimate goal is genuine intergroup and interpersonal living—*integration*. Only through nonviolence can reconciliation and the creation of the beloved community be effected. The international focus on America and her internal problems against the dread prospect of a hot war, demand our seeking this end.

We Want Black Power

STUDENT NON-VIOLENT COORDINATING COMMITTEE

Black Men of America Are a Captive People

The black man in America is in a perpetual state of slavery no matter what the white man's propaganda tells us.

The black man in America is exploited and oppressed the same as his black brothers are all over the face of the earth by the same white man. We will never be free until we are all free and that means all black oppressed people all over the earth.

We are not alone in this fight, we are a part of the struggle for self-determination of all black men everywhere. We here in America must unite ourselves to be ready to help our brothers elsewhere.

We must first gain BLACK POWER here in America. Living inside the camp of the leaders of the enemy forces, it is our duty to our Brothers to revolt against the system and create our own system so that we can live as MEN.

We must take over the political and economic systems where we are in the majority in the heart of every major city in this country as well as in the rural areas. We must create our own black culture to erase the lies the white man has fed our minds from the day we were born.

The Black Man in the Ghetto Will Lead the Black Power Movement

The black Brother in the ghetto will lead the Black Power Movement and make the changes that are necessary for its success.

The black man in the ghetto has one big advantage that the bourgeois Negro does not have despite his 'superior' education. He is already living outside the value system white society imposes on all black Americans.

He has to look at things from another direction in order to survive. He is ready. He received his training in the streets, in the jails, from the ADC[1] check his mother did not receive in time and the head-beatings he got from the cop on the corner.

Once he makes that first important discovery about the great pride you feel inside as a BLACK MAN and the great heritage of the mother country, Africa, there is no stopping him from dedicating himself to fight the white man's system.

This is why the Black Power Movement is a true revolutionary movement with the power to change men's minds and unmask the tricks the white man has used to keep black men enslaved in modern society.

The Bourgeois Negro Cannot Be a Part of the Black Power Movement

The bourgeois Negro has been force-fed the white man's propaganda and has lived too long in the half-world between white and phony black bourgeois society. He

Student Non-Violent Coordinating Committee, Chicago Office, *We Want Black Power,* 1967.
[1]Aid to Dependent Children, a major feature of the federal welfare system—ED.

cannot think for himself because he is a shell of a man full of contradictions he cannot resolve. He is not to be trusted under any circumstances until he has proved himself to be "cured." There are a minute handful of these "cured" bourgeois Negroes in the Black Power Movement and they are most valuable but they must not be allowed to take control. They are aware intellectually but under stress will react emotionally to the pressures of white society in the same way a white 'liberal' will expose an unconscious prejudice that he did not even realize he possessed.

What Brother Malcolm X Taught Us about Ourselves

Malcolm X[2] was the first black man from the ghetto in America to make a real attempt to get the white man's fist off the black man. He recognized the true dignity of man—without the white society prejudices about status, education and background that we all must purge from our minds.

Even today, in the Black Power Movement itself we find Brothers who look down on another Brother because of the conditions that life has imposed upon him. The most beautiful thing that Malcolm X taught us is that once a black man discovers for himself a pride of his blackness, he can throw off the shackles of mental slavery and become a MAN in the truest sense of the word. We must move on from the point our Great Black Prince had reached.

We Must Become Leaders for Ourselves

We must not get hung-up in the bag of having one great leader who we depend upon to make decisions. This makes the Movement too vulnerable to those forces the white man uses to keep us enslaved, such as the draft, murder, prison or character assassination.

We have to all learn to become leaders for ourselves and remove all white values from our minds. When we see a Brother using a white value through error it is our duty to the Movement to point it out to him. We must thank our Brothers who show us our own errors. We must discipline ourselves so that if necessary we can leave family and friends at a moment's notice, maybe forever, and know our Brothers have pledged themselves to protect the family we have left behind.

As a part of our education, we must travel to other cities and make contracts with the Brothers in all the ghettos in America so that when the time is right we can unite as one under the banner of BLACK POWER.

**Learning to Think Black and Remove White Things
from Our Minds**

We have got to begin to say and understand with complete assuredness what black is. Black is an inner pride that the white man's language hampers us from expressing. Black is being a complete fanatic, who white society considers insane.

We have to learn that black is so much better than belonging to the white race with the blood of millions dripping from their hands that it goes far beyond any prejudice or resentment. We must fill ourselves with hate for all white things. This

---

[2]The former Malcolm Little, a convert to the Nation of Islam, a black separatist group. He was eventually assassinated, apparently by a rival black group—ED.

is not vengeance or trying to take the white oppressors' place to become new black oppressors but is a oneness with a worldwide black brotherhood.

We must regain respect for the lost religion of our fathers, the spirits of the black earth of Africa. The white man has so poisoned our minds that if a Brother told you he practiced Voodoo you would roll around on the floor laughing at how stupid and superstitious he was.

We have to learn to roll around on the floor laughing at the black man who says he worships the white Jesus. He is truly sick.

We must create our own language for these things that the white man will not understand because a Black Culture exists and it is not the wood-carvings or native dancing it is the black strength inside of true men.

Ideas on Planning for the Future of Black Power

We must infiltrate all government agencies. This will not be hard because black clerks work in all agencies in poor paying jobs and have a natural resentment of the white men who run these jobs.

People must be assigned to seek out these dissatisfied black men and women and put pressure on them to give us the information we need. Any man in overalls, carrying a tool box, can enter a building if he looks like he knows what he is doing.

Modern America depends on many complex systems such as electricity, water, gas, sewerage and transportation and all are vulnerable. Much of the government is run by computers that must operate in air conditioning. Cut off the air conditioning and they cannot function.

We must begin to investigate and learn all of these things so that we can use them if it becomes necessary. We cannot train an army in the local park but we can be ready for the final confrontation with the white man's system.

Remember your Brothers in South Africa and do not delude yourselves that it could not happen here. We must copy the white man's biggest trick, diversion, (Hitler taught them that) and infiltrate all civil rights groups, keep them in confusion so they will be neutralized and cannot be used as a tool of the white power structure.

The civil rights, integrationist movement says to the white man, "If you please, Sir, let us, the 10 percent minority of American have our rights. See how nice and nonviolent we are?"

This is why SNCC calls itself a Human Rights Organization. We believe that we belong to the 90 percent majority of the people on earth that the white man oppresses and that we should not beg the white man for anything. We want what belongs to us as human beings and we intend to get it through BLACK POWER.

How to Deal with Black Traitors

Uncle Tom is too kind of a word. What we have are black traitors, quisslings [sic], collaborators, sell-outs, white Negroes.

We have to expose these people for once and for all for what they are and place them on the side of the oppressor where they belong. Their black skin is a lie and their guilt the shame of all black men. We must ostracize them and if necessary exterminate them.

We must stop fighting a "fair game." We must do whatever is necessary to win BLACK POWER. We have to hate and disrupt and destroy and blackmail and lie and steal and become blood-brothers like the Mau-Mau.

We must eliminate or render ineffective all traitors. We must make them fear to stand up like puppets for the white men, and we must make the world understand that these so-called men do not represent us or even belong to the same black race because they sold out their birthright for a mess of white society pottage. Let them choke on it.

Pitfalls to Avoid on the Path to Black Power

We must learn how close America and Russia are politically. The biggest lie in the world is the cold-war. Money runs the world and it is controlled completely by the white man.

Russia and America run the two biggest money systems in the world and they intend to keep it under their control under any circumstances. Thus, we cannot accept any help from Communism or any other "ism."

We must seek out poor peoples movements in South America, Africa and Asia and make our alliances with them. We must not be fooled into thinking that there is a ready-made doctrine that will solve all our problems.

There are only white man's doctrines and they will never work for us. We have to work out our own systems and doctrines and culture.

Why Propaganda Is Our Most Important Tool

The one thing that the white man's system cannot stand is the TRUTH because his system is all based on lies.

There is no such thing as "justice" for a black man in America. The white man controls everything that is said in every book, newspaper, magazine, TV and radio broadcast.

Even the textbooks used in the schools and the bible that is read in the churches are designed to maintain the system for the white man. Each and every one of us is forced to listen to the white man's propaganda every day of our lives.

The political system, economic system, military system, educational system, religious system and anything else you name is used to preserve the status quo of white America getting fatter and fatter while the black man gets more and more hungry.

We must spend our time telling our Brothers the truth.

We must tell them that any black woman who wears a diamond on her finger is wearing the blood of her Brothers and Sisters in slavery in South Africa where one out of every three black babies die before the age of one, from starvation, to make the white man rich.

We must stop wearing the symbols of slavery on our fingers.

We must stop going to other countries to exterminate our Brothers and Sisters for the white man's greed.

We must ask our Brothers which side they are on.

Once you know the truth for yourself it is your duty to dedicate your life to recruiting your Brothers and to counteract the white man's propaganda.

We must disrupt the white man's system to create our own. We must publish newspapers and get radio stations. Black Unity is strength—let's use it now to get BLACK POWER.

☆ **14** ☆

The Great Society

The nation's political climate was transformed by the election of John F. Kennedy as president in 1960. JFK was not a flaming liberal, but he was young and bold, and his victory, after eight years of the grandfatherly old soldier, Dwight Eisenhower, in the White House, created a sense of new political possibilities.

In fact, the Kennedy administration's domestic achievements were rather modest. The president aroused the idealism of youth with his Peace Corps program and fed American pride by his program to land a human being on the moon during the decade. But virtually all of his liberal New Frontier legislation stalled in Congress. By the time of his tragic assassination in November 1963 little of it had been enacted into law.

Most of the bold legislative advances of the decade started with Kennedy's successor. Lyndon B. Johnson was a very different person from the young man he succeeded. A physically massive Texan, LBJ lacked the polish, glamour, and personal magnetism of his predecessor, but he made up for them by his extraordinary political skills honed by twenty years in Congress and a decade of Democratic party leadership in the Senate. Johnson was able to break the legislative logjam through persuasion, cajolery, deal-making, and arm-twisting. Between early 1964 and 1968 Congress enacted most of his Great Society program, the most sweeping reform agenda since the New Deal a generation before.

These programs established new systems of health-care benefits for retirees (Medicare) and for the needy (Medicaid). They provided massive aid to public education and scholarships for college students. Clean air, clean water, and highway beautification measures supplemented the environmental legislation of the New Deal era. There were also new federal subsidies for the arts and for academic scholarship. Most innovative and dramatic of all was the War on Poverty, a federal campaign to eliminate want in America through Headstart, the Job Corps, subsidized legal services, a Community Action Program, and many more initiatives, all under an Office of Economic Opportunity.

The Great Society clearly benefited from initial public support. Running in 1964 for president in his own right against conservative Barry Goldwater, Johnson achieved one of the most sweeping electoral victories in this century, carrying every state but Arizona and a few in the South, and leading his party to unprecedented majorities in both houses of Congress.

LBJ interpreted this success as a liberal mandate, and it was. With prices stable and economic growth high, the nation felt flush—and generous, and Congress was quick to approve the costly new social programs.

In the selections below you will find responses to the Great Society by three groups: defenders, detractors on the right, and detractors on the left. Try to analyze the reasons and reasoning behind each position. Also consider the validity of each viewpoint.

14.1:　Defenders (1964)

No one was as eloquent on the goals of the Great Society as Lyndon Johnson himself. The following extract is from the president's speech at the University of Michigan graduation ceremonies in May 1964, where he laid out his ambitious Great Society plan.

Was Johnson's vision utopian, or was it realistic? Can you detect in it antecedents in the form of similar views held by previous reformers? Although a one-time protégé of Franklin Roosevelt, in his previous career as a representative and senator, Johnson was not considered a liberal. At most he seemed a centrist who reflected the racial views and economic interests of his native Texas. How do you explain the apparent shift, as exemplified by the Great Society, when he became president? Can you think of other political leaders whose perspectives changed when they changed office?

The Great Society[1]

LYNDON B. JOHNSON

I have come today from the turmoil of your capital to the tranquility of your campus to speak about the future of your country.

Public Papers of the Presidents of the United States: Lyndon B. Johnson, 1963–64, vol. 1, (Washington, DC: U.S. Government Printing Office, 1965), pp. 704–707.
[1]Footnotes deleted.

The purpose of protecting the life of our nation and preserving the liberty of our citizens is to pursue the happiness of our people. Our success in that pursuit is the test of our success as a nation.

For a century we labored to settle and to subdue a continent. For half a century we called upon unbounded invention and untiring industry to create an order of plenty for all of our people.

The challenge of the next half century is whether we have the wisdom to use that wealth to enrich and elevate our national life, and to advance the quality of our American civilization.

Your imagination, your initiative, and your indignation will determine whether we build a society where progress is the servant of our needs, or a society where old values and new visions are buried under unbridled growth. For in your time we have the opportunity to move not only toward the rich society and the powerful society, but upward to the Great Society.

The Great Society rests on abundance and liberty for all. It demands an end to poverty and racial injustice, to which we are totally committed in our time. But that is just the beginning.

The Great Society is a place where every child can find knowledge to enrich his mind and to enlarge his talents. It is a place where leisure is a welcome chance to build and reflect, not a feared cause of boredom and restlessness. It is a place where the city of man serves not only the needs of the body and the demands of commerce but the desire for beauty and the hunger for community.

It is a place where man can renew contact with nature. It is a place which honors creation for its own sake and for what it adds to the understanding of the race. It is a place where men are more concerned with the quality of their goals than the quantity of their goods.

But most of all, the Great Society is not a safe harbor, a resting place, a final objective, a finished work. It is a challenge constantly renewed, beckoning us toward a destiny where the meaning of our lives matches the marvelous products of our labor.

So I want to talk to you today about three places where we begin to build the Great Society—in our cities, in our countryside, and in our classrooms.

Many of you will live to see the day, perhaps fifty years from now, when there will be 400 million Americans—four-fifths of them in urban areas. In the remainder of this century urban population will double, city land will double, and we will have to build homes, highways, and facilities equal to all those built since this country was first settled. So in the next forty years we must rebuild the entire urban United States.

Aristotle said: "Men come together in cities in order to live, but they remain together in order to live the good life." It is harder and harder to live the good life in American cities today.

The catalogue of ills is long: there is the decay of the centers and the despoiling of the suburbs. There is not enough housing for our people or transportation for our traffic. Open land is vanishing and old landmarks are violated.

Worst of all expansion is eroding the precious and time-honored values of community with neighbors and communion with nature. The loss of these values breeds loneliness and boredom and indifference.

Our society will never be great until our cities are great. Today the frontier of imagination and innovation is inside those cities and not beyond their borders. . . .

A second place where we begin to build the Great Society is in our countryside. We have always prided ourselves on being not only America the strong and America the free, but America the beautiful. Today that beauty is in danger. The water we drink, the food we eat, the very air that we breathe, are threatened with pollution. Our parks are overcrowded, our seashores overburdened. Green fields and dense forests are disappearing.

A few years ago we were greatly concerned about the "Ugly American." Today we must act to prevent an ugly America.

For once the battle is lost, once our natural splendor is destroyed, it can never be recaptured. And once man can no longer walk with beauty or wonder at nature his spirit will wither and his sustenance be wasted.

A third place to build the Great Society is in the classrooms of America. There your children's lives will be shaped. Our society will not be great until every young mind is set free to scan the farthest reaches of thought and imagination. We are still far from that goal. . . .

Each year more than 100,000 high school graduates, with proved ability, do not enter college because they cannot afford it. And if we cannot educate today's youth, what will we do in 1970 when elementary school enrollment will be 5 million greater than 1960? And high school enrollment will rise by 5 million. College enrollment will increase by more than 3 million.

In many places, classrooms are overcrowded and curricula are outdated. Most of our qualified teachers are underpaid, and many of our paid teachers are unqualified. So we must give every child a place to sit and a teacher to learn from. Poverty must not be a bar to learning, and learning must offer an escape from poverty.

But more classrooms and more teachers are not enough. We must seek an educational system which grows in excellence as it grows in size. This means better training for our teachers. It means preparing youth to enjoy their hours of leisure as well as their hours of labor. It means exploring new techniques of teaching, to find new ways to stimulate the love of learning and the capacity for creation.

These are three of the central issues of the Great Society. While our government has many programs directed at those issues, I do not pretend that we have the full answer to those problems. . . .

But I do promise this: We are going to assemble the best thought and the broadest knowledge from all over the world to find those answers for America. I intend to establish working groups to prepare a series of White House conferences and meetings—on the cities, on natural beauty, on the quality of education, and on other emerging challenges. And from these meetings and from this inspiration and from these studies we will begin to set our course toward the Great Society.

The solution to these problems does not rest on a massive program in Washington, nor can it rely solely on the strained resources of local authority. They require us to create new concepts of cooperation, a creative federalism, between the national capital and the leaders of local communities.

Within your lifetime powerful forces, already loosed, will take us toward a way of life beyond the realm of our experience, almost beyond the bounds of our imagination.

For better or for worse, your generation has been appointed by history to deal with those problems and to lead America toward a new age. You have the chance never before afforded to any people in any age. You can help build a society where the demands of morality, and the needs of the spirit, can be realized in the life of the nation.

So, will you join in the battle to give every citizen the full equality which God enjoins and the law requires, whatever his belief, or race, or the color of his skin?

Will you join in the battle to give every citizen an escape from the crushing weight of poverty?

Will you join in the battle to make it possible for all nations to live in enduring peace—as neighbors and not as mortal enemies?

Will you join in the battle to build the Great Society, to prove that our material progress is only the foundation on which we will build a richer life of mind and spirit?

There are those timid souls who say this battle cannot be won; that we are condemned to a soulless wealth. I do not agree. We have the power to shape the civilization that we want. But we need your will, your labor, your hearts, if we are to build that kind of society.

Those who came to this land sought to build more than just a new country. They sought a new world. So I have come here today to your campus to say that you can make their vision our reality. So let us from this moment begin our work so that in the future men will look back and say: It was then, after a long and weary way, that man turned the exploits of his genius to the full enrichment of his life.

14.2: The Attack from the Right (1964)

Conservative opponents of the Great Society responded promptly by raising familiar charges of socialist encroachment by government. Not only was the program hopelessly collectivist in nature, they said, it also fostered the inefficient growth of big government, diminished traditional American values such as self-reliance and pride in one's work, and in the long run probably wouldn't accomplish what it hoped to achieve. Barry Goldwater, Johnson's opponent in the 1964 presidential race, raised these objections repeatedly. In the following selection, do you see a connection between Goldwater's way of thinking and the ideas presented by conservatives earlier in the twentieth century? In what ways were Goldwater's ideas similar to those of today's conservatives?

The Conscience of a Conservative

BARRY GOLDWATER

For many years it appeared that the principal domestic threat to our freedom was contained in the doctrines of Karl Marx. The collectivists—non-Communists as well as Communists—had adopted the Marxist objective of "socializing the means of production." And so it seemed that if collectivization were imposed, it would take the form of a State owned and operated economy. I doubt whether this is the main threat any longer.

The collectivists have found, both in this country and in other industrialized nations of the West, that free enterprise has removed the economic and social conditions that might have made a class struggle possible. Mammoth productivity, wide distribution of wealth, high standards of living, the trade union movement—these and other factors have eliminated whatever incentive there might have been for the "proletariat" to rise up, peaceably or otherwise, and assume direct ownership of productive property. Significantly, the bankruptcy of doctrinaire Marxism has been expressly acknowledged by the Socialist Party of West Germany, and by the dominant faction of the Socialist Party of Great Britain. In this country the abandonment of the Marxist approach (outside the Communist Party, of course) is attested to by the negligible strength of the Socialist Party, and more tellingly perhaps, by the content of left wing literature and by the programs of left wing political organizations such as the Americans For Democratic Action.

The currently favored instrument of collectivization is the Welfare State. The collectivists have not abandoned their ultimate goal—to subordinate the individual to the State—but their strategy has changed. They have learned that Socialism can be achieved through Welfarism quite as well as through Nationalization. They understand that private property can be confiscated as effectively by taxation as by expropriating it. They understand that the individual can be put at the mercy of the State—not only by making the State his employer—but by divesting him of the means to provide for his personal needs and by giving the State the responsibility of caring for those needs from cradle to grave. Moreover, they have discovered—and here is the critical point—that *Welfarism is much more compatible with the political processes of a democratic society.* Nationalization ran into popular opposition, but the collectivists feel sure the Welfare State can be erected by the simple expedient of buying votes with promises of "free" hospitalization, "free" retirement pay and so on . . . The correctness of this estimate can be seen from the portion of the federal budget that is now allocated to welfare, an amount second only to the cost of national defense.[1]

Barry Goldwater, *The Conscience of a Conservative* (New York: Hillman Books, 1960), pp. 70–77. (Copyright owned by Victor Publishing Company.)

[1]The total figure is substantially higher than the $15,000,000,000 noted above if we take into account welfare expenditures outside the Department of Health, Education and Welfare—for federal housing projects, for example.

I do not welcome this shift of strategy. Socialism-through-Welfarism poses a far greater danger to freedom than Socialism-through-Nationalization precisely because it *is* more difficult to combat. The evils of Nationalization are self-evident and immediate. Those of Welfarism are veiled and tend to be postponed. People can understand the consequences of turning over ownership of the steel industry, say, to the State; and they can be counted on to oppose such a proposal. But let the government increase its contribution to the "Public Assistance" program and we will, at most, grumble about excessive government spending. The effect of Welfarism on freedom will be felt later on—after its beneficiaries have become its victims, after dependence on government has turned into bondage and it is too late to unlock the jail.

But a far more important factor is Welfarism's strong emotional appeal to many voters, and the consequent temptations it presents the average politician. It is hard, as we have seen, to make out a case for State ownership. It is very different with the rhetoric of humanitarianism. How easy it is to reach the voters with earnest importunities for helping the needy. And how difficult for Conservatives to resist these demands without appearing to be callous and contemptuous of the plight of less fortunate citizens. Here, perhaps, is the best illustration of the failure of the Conservative demonstration.

I know, for I have heard the questions often. Have you no sense of social obligation? the Liberals ask. Have you no concern for people who are out of work? for sick people who lack medical care? for children in overcrowded schools? Are you unmoved by the problems of the aged and disabled? Are you *against* human welfare?

The answer to all of these questions is, of course, no. But a simple "no" is not enough. I feel certain that Conservatism is through unless Conservatives can demonstrate and communicate the difference between being concerned with these problems and believing that the federal government is the proper agent for their solution.

The long range political consequences of Welfarism are plain enough: as we have seen, the State that is able to deal with its citizens as wards and dependents has gathered unto itself unlimited political and economic power and is thus able to rule as absolutely as any oriental despot.

Let us, however, weigh the consequences of Welfarism on the citizen.

Consider, first, the effect of Welfarism on the donors of government welfare—not only those who pay for it but also the voters and their elected representatives who decide that the benefits shall be conferred. Does some credit redound on them for trying to care for the needs of their fellow citizens? Are they to be commended and rewarded, at some moment in eternity, for their "charity"? I think not. Suppose I should vote for a measure providing for free medical care: I am unaware of any moral virtue that is attached to my decision to confiscate the earnings of X and give them to Y.

Suppose, however, that X approves of the program—that he has voted for welfarist politicians with the idea of helping his fellow man. Surely the wholesomeness of his act is diluted by the fact that he is voting not only to have his own money taken but also that of his fellow citizens who may have different ideas about their social obligations. Why does not such a man, instead, contribute what he regards as his just share of human welfare to a private charity?

Consider the consequences to the recipient of welfarism. For one thing, he mortgages himself to the federal government. In return for benefits—which, in the majority of cases, he pays for—he concedes to the government the ultimate in political power—the power to grant or withhold from him the necessities of life as the government sees fit. Even more important, however, is the effect on him—the elimination of any feeling of responsibility for his own welfare and that of his family and neighbors. A man may not immediately, or ever, comprehend the harm thus done to his character. Indeed, this is one of the great evils of Welfarism—that it transforms the individual from a dignified, industrious, self-reliant *spiritual* being into a dependent animal creature without his knowing it. There is no avoiding this damage to character under the Welfare State. Welfare programs cannot help but promote the idea that the government *owes* the benefits it confers on the individual, and that the individual is entitled, by right, to receive them. Such programs are sold to the country precisely on the argument that government has an *obligation* to care for the needs of its citizens. Is it possible that the message will reach those who vote for the benefits, but not those who receive them? How different it is with private charity where both the giver and the receiver understand that charity is the product of the humanitarian impulses of the giver, not the due of the receiver.

Let us, then, not blunt the noble impulses of mankind by reducing charity to a mechanical operation of the federal government. Let us, by all means, encourage, those who are fortunate and able to care for the needs of those who are unfortunate and disabled. But let us do this in a way that is conducive to the spiritual as well as the material well-being of our citizens—and in a way that will preserve their freedom. Let welfare be a private concern. Let it be promoted by individuals and families, by churches, private hospitals, religious service organizations, community charities and other institutions that have been established for this purpose. If the objection is raised that private institutions lack sufficient funds, let us remember that every penny the federal government does *not* appropriate for welfare is potentially available for private use—and without the overhead charge for processing the money through the federal bureaucracy. Indeed, high taxes, for which government Welfarism is so largely responsible, is the biggest obstacle to fund raising by private charities.

Finally, if we deem public intervention necessary, let the job be done by local and state authorities that are incapable of accumulating the vast political power that is so inimical to our liberties.

The Welfare State is *not* inevitable, as its proponents are so fond of telling us. There is nothing inherent in an industrialized economy, or in democratic processes of government that *must* produce de Tocqueville's "guardian society." Our future, like our past, will be what we make it. And we can shatter the collectivists' designs on individual freedom if we will impress upon the men who conduct our affairs this one truth: that the material and spiritual sides of man are intertwined; that it is impossible for the State to assume responsibility for one without intruding on the essential nature of the other; that if we take from a man the personal responsibility for caring for his material needs, we take from him also the will and the opportunity to be free.

14.3: The Attack from the Left (1962)

The years of the Great Society also witnessed a powerful revival of left-wing political activism in the United States. During this period university students, civil rights militants, and cultural dissenters all came to view white, middle-class, liberal America as repressive, exploitative, and stultifying. To most of the new radicals the Great Society was at best a feeble response to the country's real problems, and at worst an effort to evade those problems and deflect any fundamental attempt to solve them.

No organization better articulated the political aspirations of the emerging New Left more comprehensively and persistently than the Students for a Democratic Society, which by the late 1960s had an active chapter on most college campuses. The following excerpt is taken from the famed "Port Huron Statement," drafted by the group's leaders after lengthy and intense debate in June 1962. Intended to be both a manifesto and a strategic plan, the Statement is probably the most thorough explanation of the philosophy of "the movement" that would soon devote its energy to political protest and civil disobedience. These radicals found the liberalism of Johnson's Great Society to be even more distasteful than conservatism. Running through each sentence lingers a fundamental anger toward the American way of life. Why were they so bitter? How would you compare the New Left to previous radicals? Would you say that they had socialist leanings, or would you consider them anarchistic? Finally, what specifically made them hate liberal programs like the Great Society so much?

The Port Huron Statement

STUDENTS FOR A DEMOCRATIC SOCIETY

We are the people of this generation, bred in at least modest comfort, housed now in universities, looking uncomfortably to the world we inherit.

When we were kids, the United States was the wealthiest and strongest country in the world: the only one with the atom bomb, the least scarred by war, an initiator of

Students for a Democratic Society, *Statement of the National Convention, June 11–15, 1962,* Port Huron, Michigan.

the United Nations that we thought would distribute Western influence throughout the world. Freedom and equality for each individual, government of, by, and for the people—these American values we found good, principles by which we could live as men. Many of us began maturing in complacency.

As we grew, however, our comfort was penetrated by events too troubling to dismiss. First, the permeating and victimizing fact of human degradation, symbolized by the Southern struggle against racial bigotry, compelled most of us from silence to activism. Second, the enclosing fact of the Cold War, symbolized by the presence of the Bomb, brought awareness that we ourselves, and our friends, and millions of abstract "others" . . . might die at any time. We might deliberately ignore, or avoid, or fail to feel all other human problems, but not these two, for these were too immediate and crushing in their impact, too challenging in the demand that we as individuals take responsibility for encounter and resolution. . . .

We witnessed, and continue to witness, other paradoxes. With nuclear energy whole cities can easily be powered, yet the dominant nation-states seem more likely to unleash destruction greater than that incurred in all wars of human history. Although our own technology is destroying old and creating new forms of social organization, men still tolerate meaningless work and idleness. While two-thirds of mankind suffers undernourishment, our own upper classes revel amidst superfluous abundance. Although world population is expected to double in forty years, the nations still tolerate anarchy as a major principle of international conduct and uncontrolled exploitation governs the sapping of the earth's physical resources. Although mankind desperately needs revolutionary leadership, America rests in national stalemate, its goals ambiguous and tradition-bound instead of informed and clear, its democratic system apathetic and manipulated rather than "of, by, and for the people. . . ."

Our work is guided by the sense that we may be the last generation in the experiment of living. But we are a minority—the vast majority of our people regard the temporary equilibriums of our society and the world as eternally functional parts. In this is perhaps the outstanding paradox: We ourselves are imbued with urgency, yet the message of our society is that there is no viable alternative to the present. Beneath the reassuring tones of the politicians, beneath the common opinion that America will "muddle through," beneath the stagnation of those who have closed their minds to the future, is the pervading feeling that there simply are no alternatives, that our times have witnessed the exhaustion not only of Utopias, but of any new departures as well. Feeling the press of complexity upon the emptiness of life, people are fearful of the thought that at any moment things might thrust out of control. They fear change itself, since change might smash whatever invisible framework seems to hold back chaos for them now. For most Americans all crusades are suspect, threatening. . . . Then, too, we are a materially improved society, and by our own improvements we seem to have weakened the case for further change.

Some would have us believe that Americans feel contentment amidst prosperity—but might it not better be called a glaze above deeply felt anxieties about their role in the new world? And if these anxieties produce a developed indifference to human affairs, do they not as well produce a yearning to believe there *is* an alternative to the present, that something *can* be done to change circumstances in the school, the workplace, the bureaucracies, the government? It is to this latter yearning, at once the spark and engine of change, that we direct our present appeal. The search for truly democratic alternatives to the present, and a commitment to social experimentation with them, is a worthy and fulfilling enterprise, one which moves us and, we hope, others today. On such a basis do we offer this document of our convictions and analysis: as an effort in understanding and changing the conditions of humanity in the late twentieth century, an effort rooted in the ancient, still unfinished conception of man attaining and determining influence over his circumstances of life.

Values

Making values explicit . . . is an activity that has been devalued and corrupted. . . . But neither has our experience in the universities brought us moral enlightenment. Our professors and administrators sacrifice controversy to public relations; their curriculums change more slowly than the living events of the world; their skills and silence are purchased by investors in the arms race; passion is called unscholastic. The questions we might want raised—what is really important? can we live in a different and better way? if we wanted to change society, how would we do it?—are not thought to be questions of a "fruitful, empirical nature," and thus are brushed aside.

Unlike youth in other countries, we are used to moral leadership being exercised and moral dimensions being clarified by our elders. But today, for us, not even the liberal and socialist preachments of the past seem adequate to the forms of the present. . . . [A]nd there are few new prophets. It has been said that our liberal and socialist predecessors were plagued by vision without program, while our own generation is plagued by program without vision. All around us there is astute grasp of method, technique, . . . but if pressed critically, such expertise is incompetent to explain its implicit ideals. . . .

Theoretic chaos has replaced the idealistic thinking of old. . . . Doubt has replaced hopefulness—and men act out of a defeatism that is labelled realistic. The decline of utopia and hope is in fact one of the defining features of social life today. . . .

We regard *men* as infinitely precious and possessed of unfulfilled capacities for reason, freedom, and love. In affirming these principles we are aware of countering perhaps the dominant conceptions of man in the twentieth century: that he is a thing to be manipulated, and that he is inherently incapable of directing his own affairs. We oppose the depersonalization that reduces human beings to the status of things. . . . We oppose, too, the doctrine of human incompetence because it rests essentially on the modern fact that men have been "competently" manipulated into incompetence—we see little reason why men cannot meet with increasing skill the complexities and responsibilities of their situation, if society is organized not for minority, but for majority, participation in decision-making.

Men have unrealized potential for self-cultivation, self-direction, self-understanding, and creativity. It is this potential that we regard as crucial and to which we appeal, not to the human potentiality for violence, unreason, and submission to authority. The goal of man and society should be human independence: a concern not with image [or] popularity but with finding a meaning in life that is personally authentic; a quality of mind not compulsively driven by a sense of powerlessness, nor one which unthinkingly adopts status values, nor one which represses all threats to its habits, but one which has full, spontaneous access to present and past experiences, one which easily unites the fragmented parts of personal history, one which openly faces problems which are troublesome and unresolved; one with an intuitive awareness of possibilities, an active sense of curiosity, an ability and willingness to learn. . . .

Loneliness, estrangement, isolation describe the vast distance between man and man today. These dominant tendencies cannot be overcome by better personnel management, nor by improved gadgets, but only when a love of man overcomes the idolatrous worship of things by man. . . .

As a *social system* we seek the establishment of a democracy of individual participation, governed by two central aims: that the individual share in those social decisions determining the quality and direction of his life; that society be organized to encourage independence in men and provide the media for their common participation.

In a participatory democracy, the political life would be based in several root principles:

—that decision-making of basic social consequence be carried out by public groupings;
—that politics be seen positively, as the art of collectively creating an acceptable pattern of social relations;
—that politics has the function of bringing people out of isolation and into community, thus being a necessary, though not sufficient, means of finding meaning in personal life;
—that the political order should serve to clarify problems in a way instrumental to their solution; it should provide outlets for the expression of personal grievance and aspiration; opposing views should be organized so as to illuminate choices and facilitate the attainment of goals. . . .

The economic sphere would have as its basis the principles:

—that work should involve incentives worthier than money or survival. It should be educative, not stultifying; creative, not mechanical; self-direct[ed], not manipulated; encouraging independence, a respect for others, a sense of dignity, and a willingness to accept social responsibility. . . .
—that the economic experience is so personally decisive that the individual must share in its full determination;
—that the economy itself is of such social importance that its major resources should be open to democratic participation and subject to democratic social regulation.

Like the political and economic ones, major social institutions . . . should be generally organized with the well-being and dignity of man as the essential measure of success.

The Students

In the last few years, thousands of American students demonstrated that they at least felt the urgency of the times. They moved actively and directly against racial injustices, the threat of war, violations of individuals rights of conscience and, less frequently, against economic manipulation. They succeeded in restoring a small measure of controversy to the campuses after the stillness of the McCarthy period. They succeeded, too, in gaining some concessions from the people and institutions they opposed, especially in the fight against racial bigotry.

The significance of these scattered movements lies . . . in the fact the students are breaking the crust of apathy and overcoming the inner alienation that remain the defining characteristics of American college life.

If student movements for change are rarities still on the campus scene, what is commonplace there? The real campus . . . is a place of private people engaged in their notorious "inner emigration." It is a place of commitment to business-as-usual, getting ahead, playing it cool. It is a place of mass affirmation of the Twist, but mass reluctance toward the controversial public stance. Rules are accepted as "inevitable," bureaucracy as "just circumstances," irrelevance as "scholarship," selflessness as "martyrdom," . . .

Almost no students value activity as a citizen. . . . Attention is being paid to social status . . . ; much too is paid to academic status. . . . But neglected generally is real intellectual status, the personal cultivation of the mind. . . .

Under these conditions university life loses all relevance to some. Four hundred thousand of our classmates leave college every year.

But apathy is not simply an attitude; it is a product of social institutions, and of the structure and organization of higher education itself. The extracurricular life is ordered according to *in loco parentis* theory, which ratifies the Administration as the moral guardian of the young. The accompanying "let's pretend" theory of student extracurricular affairs validates student government as a training center for those who want to spend their lives in political pretense and discourages initiative from more articulate, honest, and sensitive students. . . .

The Society Beyond

Look beyond the campus to America itself. . . . Americans are in withdrawal from public life, from any collective effort at directing their own affairs.

Some regard this national doldrum as a sign of healthy approval of the establishment order—but is it approval by consent or manipulated acquiescence? Others declare that the people are withdrawn because compelling issues are fast disappearing—perhaps there are fewer breadlines in America, but is Jim Crow gone, is there enough work and work more fulfilling, is world war a diminishing threat, and what of the revolutionary new peoples? . . .

There are no convincing apologies for the contemporary malaise. While the world tumbles toward the final war, while men in other nations are trying desperately to alter events, while the very future qua future is uncertain—America is without community, impulse, without the inner momentum necessary for an age when societies cannot successfully perpetuate themselves by their military weapons, when democracy must be viable because of the quality of its life, not the quantity of its rockets.

The apathy here is first *subjective*—the felt powerlessness of ordinary people, the resignation before the enormity of events. But subjective apathy is encouraged by the *objective* American situation—the actual structural separation of people from power, from relevant knowledge, from pinnacles of decision-making. . . .

Politics without Publics

A crucial feature of the political apparatus in America is that greater differences are harbored within each major party than the differences between them. Instead of two parties representing distinctive and significant differences of approach, what dominates the system is a natural interlocking of Democrats from Southern states and the more conservative elements of the Republican party. The arrangement of forces is blessed by the seniority system of Congress which guarantees congressional committee domination by conservatives. . . .

A most alarming fact is that few, if any, politicians are calling for changes in these conditions. . . . In such a setting of status quo politics, where most if not all government activity is rationalized in Cold War anti-communist terms, it is somewhat natural that discontented, super-patriotic groups would emerge . . . and explain their ultra-conservatism as the best means of victory over Communism. They have become a politically influential force within the Republican party, at a national level, through Senator Goldwater. . . .

The Economy

American capitalism today advertises itself as the Welfare State. Many of us comfortably expect pensions, medical care, unemployment compensation, and other social services in our lifetimes. Even with one-fourth of our productive capacity unused, the majority of Americans are living in relative comfort. . . . In many places, unrestrained bosses, uncontrolled machines, and sweatshop conditions have been reformed or abolished and suffering tremendously relieved. But in spite of the benign yet obscuring effects of the New Deal reforms . . . the paradoxes and myths of the economy are sufficient to irritate our complacency and reveal to us some essential causes of the American malaise.

We live amidst a national celebration of economic prosperity while poverty and deprivation remain an unbreakable way of life for millions in the "affluent society," including many of our own generation. . . . Work, too, is often unfilling and victimizing, accepted as a channel to status . . . rarely as a means of understanding and controlling self and events. . . .

The Military-Industrial Complex

The most spectacular and important creation of the authoritarian and oligopolistic structure of economic decision-making in America is the institution called "the military-industrial complex" by former President Eisenhower, the powerful congruence of interest and structure among military and business elites which affects so much of our development and destiny. Not only is ours the first generation to live with the possibility of worldwide cataclysm—it is the first to experience the actual social preparation for cataclysm, the general militarization of American society. . . .

Automation, Abundance, and Challenge

Automation, the process of machines replacing men in performing sensory, motoric, and complex logical tasks, is transforming society in ways that are scarcely comprehensible. . . . Automation is destroying whole categories of work, . . . in blue-collar, service, and even middle management occupations. In addition, it is eliminating employment opportunities for a youth force that numbers one million more than it did in 1950. . . . The consequences of this economic drama . . . are momentous: Five million becomes an acceptable unemployment tabulation, and misery, uprootedness and anxiety become the lot of increasing numbers of Americans. . . . Hard-core poverty exists just beyond the neon lights of affluence, and the "have-nots" may be driven still further from opportunity as the high-technology society demands better education to get into the production mainstream and more capital to get into "business." . . .

The Stance of Labor

Amidst all this, what of organized labor, the historic institutional representative of the exploited, the presumed "countervailing power" against the excesses of Big Business? Today labor remains the most liberal "mainstream" institution, but often its liberalism represents vestigial commitments. . . . In some measure labor has succumbed to institutionalization, its social idealism waning under the tendencies of bureaucracy, materialism, business ethics. . . .

The Individual in the Warfare State

Business and politics, when significantly militarized, affect the whole living condition of each American citizen. Worker and family depend on the Cold War for life. Half of all research and development is concentrated on military ends. . . . To a decisive extent, the means of defense, the military technology itself, determines the political and social character of the state being defended. . . . So it has been with America, as her democratic institutions and habits have shriveled in almost direct proportion to the growth of her armaments. Decision about military strategy, including the monstrous decision to go to war, are more and more the property of the military and the industrial arms race machine, with the politicians assuming a ratifying role instead of a determining one. . . .

Deterrence Policy

Deterrence advocates, all of them prepared at least to threaten mass extermination, advance arguments of several kinds. At one pole are the minority of open advocates of preventive war. . . . Perhaps more disturbing for their numbers within the Kennedy administration, are the many advocates of the "counterforce" theory of aiming strategic nuclear weapons at military installations. . . . Others would support fighting "limited wars" which use conventional . . . weapons backed by deterrents so mighty that both sides would fear to use them . . . [with] the potential tendency for a "losing side" to push limited protracted fighting on the soil of underdeveloped countries. Still other deterrence artists proposed limited, clearly defensive and retaliatory nuclear capacity, always potent enough to deter an opponent's aggressive designs. . . .

All the deterrence theories . . . allow insufficient attention to preserving, extending, and enriching democratic values. . . . [T]hey inadequately realize the inherent instabilities of the continuing arms race and balance of fear. They . . . tend to eclipse . . . disarmament by solidifying economic, political, and even moral investments in the continuation of tensions. [T]hey offer a disinterested and even patriotic rationale for the boondoggling, belligerence, and privilege of military and economic elites. . . .

Anti-Communism

An unreasoning anti-communism has become a major social problem for those who want to construct a more democratic America. McCarthyism and other forms of exaggerated and conservative anti-communism seriously weaken democratic institutions and spawn movements contrary to the interests of basic freedoms and peace. In such an atmosphere even the most intelligent of Americans fear to join political organizations, sign petitions, speak out on serious issues. . . . Thus much of American anti-communism takes on the characteristics of paranoia. . . .

Communism and Foreign Policy

As democrats we are in basic opposition to the communist system. The Soviet Union . . . rests on the total suppression of organized opposition, as well as on a vision of the future in the name of which human life has been sacrificed and numerous small and large denials of human dignity rationalized. . . . The communist movement has failed, in every sense, to achieve its stated intentions of leading a worldwide movement for human emancipation.

But present trends in American anti-communism are not sufficient for the creation of appropriate policies with which to relate and counter communist movements in the world. In no instance is this better illustrated than in our basic national policy-making assumption that the Soviet Union is inherently expansionist and aggressive, prepared to dominate the rest of the world by military means. On this assumption rests the monstrous American structure of military "preparedness"; because of it we sacrifice values and social programs to the alleged needs of military power. . . .

Discrimination

Our America is still white. Consider the plight, statistically, of its greatest nonconformists, the "nonwhites." . . .

[Here follows a page reviewing the inferior circumstances of black Americans in regard to literacy, salaries, skill and professional levels, employment, housing, education, and voting rights.]

Even against this background, some will say progress is being made. The facts belie it, however, unless it is assumed that America has another century to deal with its racial inequalities. . . .

It has been said that the Kennedy administration did more in two years than the Eisenhower administration did in eight. Of this there can be no doubt. But it is analogous to comparing whispers to silence when positively stentorian tones are demanded. . . . To avoid conflict with the Dixiecrat-Republican alliance, President Kennedy has developed a civil rights philosophy of "enforcement, not enactment," implying that existing statutory tools are sufficient to change the lot of the Negro. . . .

The Industrialization of the World

The United States' principal goal should be creating a world where hunger, poverty, disease, ignorance, violence, and exploitation are replaced as central features by abundance, reason, love, and international cooperation. To many this will seem the product of juvenile hallucination: but we insist it is a more realistic goal than is a world of nuclear stalemate. . . .

We should undertake here and now a fifty-year effort to prepare for all nations the conditions of industrialization. . . . We should not depend significantly on private enterprise to do the job. . . . We should not lock the development process into the Cold War: We should use it as a way to end that conflict. . . . America should show its commitment to democratic institutions not by withdrawing support from undemocratic regimes, but by making domestic democracy exemplary. . . . Democratic theory must confront the problems inherent in social revolutions. . . .

Towards American Democracy

America must abolish its political party stalemate. Two genuine parties, centered around issue and essential values, demanding allegiance to party principles shall supplant the current system of organized stalemate. . . .

Institutions and practices which stifle dissent should be abolished, and the promotion of peaceful dissent should be actively promoted. . . .

Corporations must be made publicly responsible. It is not possible to believe that true democracy can exist where a minority utterly controls enormous wealth and power. . . .

The allocation of resources must be based on social needs. A truly "public sector" must be established, and its nature debated and planned. . . .

America should concentrate on its genuine social priorities: abolish squalor, terminate neglect, and establish an environment for people to live with dignity and creativeness. . . . A program against poverty . . . must . . . be directed to the abolition of the structural circumstances of poverty. . . . *Medical care* must become recognized as a lifetime human right just as vital as food, shelter, clothing. . . . Existing institutions should be extended so the Welfare State cares for *everyone's* welfare according to need. . . . A full-scale public initiative for civil rights should be undertaken despite the clamor among conservatives (and liberals) about gradualism, property rights, and law and order. . . . We must meet the growing complex of "city" problems. . . . Juvenile delinquency, untended mental illness, crime increase, slums, urban tenancy and uncontrolled housing, the isolation of the individual in the city—are all problems of the city. . . . The *model* city must be projected—more community decision making and participation, true integration of classes, races, vocations—provision for beauty, access to nature and the benefits of the central city as well. . . .

The University and Social Change.   [T]he civil rights and peace and student movements are too poor and socially slighted, and the labor movement too quiescent, to be counted with enthusiasm [as agents of change]. From where else can power and vision be summoned? We believe that the universities are an overlooked seat of influence. . . .

1. Any new left in America must be . . . a left with real intellectual skills, committed to the deliberativeness, honesty, [and] reflection as working tools. The university permits the political life to be an adjunct to the academic one, and action to be informed by reason.
2. A new left must be distributed in significant social roles throughout the country. The universities are distributed in such a manner.
3. A new left must consist of younger people who matured in the post-war world, and partially be directed to the recruitment of younger people. The university is the obvious beginning point.
4. A new left must include liberals and socialists. . . . The university is a more sensible place than a political party for these two traditions to begin to discuss their differences and look for political synthesis.
5. A new left must start controversy across the land, if national policies and national apathy are to be reversed. The ideal university is a community of controversy, within itself and in its effects on communities beyond.
6. A new left must transform modern complexity into issues that can be understood and felt close-up by every human being. It must give form to the feelings of helplessness and indifference, so that people may see the political, social, and economic sources of their private troubles and organize to change society. In a time of supposed prosperity, moral complacency and political manipulation, a new left cannot rely on only aching stomachs to be the engine force of social reform. The case for change, for alternatives that will involve uncomfortable personal efforts, must be argued as never before. The university is a relevant place for all these activities.

But we need not indulge in illusions: the university system cannot complete a movement of ordinary people making demands for a better life. From its schools and colleges across the nation, a militant left might awaken its allies, and by beginning the process towards peace, civil rights, and labor struggles, reinsert theory and idealism where too often reign confusion and political barter. The power of students and faculty united is not only potential; it has shown its actuality in the South, and in the reform movements of the North.

The bridge to political power, though, will be built through genuine cooperation, locally, nationally, and internationally, between a new left of young people, and an awakening community of allies. In each community we must look within the university and act with confidence that we can be powerful, but we must look outwards to the less exotic but more lasting struggles for justice.

To turn these possibilities into realities will involve national efforts at university reform by an alliance of students and faculty. They must wrest control of the educational process from the administrative bureaucracy. They must make fraternal and functional contact with allies in labor, civil rights, and other liberal forces outside the campus. They must import major public issues into the curriculum—research and teaching on problems of war and peace is an outstanding example. They must make debate and controversy, not dull pedantic cant, the common style for educational life. They must consciously build a base for their assault upon the loci of power.

As students for a democratic society we are committed to stimulating this kind of social movement, this kind of vision and program in campus and community across the country. If we appear to seek the unattainable, as it has been said, then let it be known that we do so to void the unimaginable.

☆ **15** ☆

The New Feminism

The social insurgency of the 1960s extended beyond the civil rights movement. Other Americans besides blacks, feeling denied respect, excluded from power, or kept from economic advancement, also mobilized for collective action against the social and economic status quo. During the sixties and seventies Hispanic Americans, gay Americans, Native Americans, and others formed defense or liberation organizations, often closely modeled on the black civil rights groups.

None of these liberation movements had such pervasive consequences as the New Feminism. Like the others, it owed much to the civil rights crusade, but it had distinctive roots of its own. The new movement was in part a rebound from the 1950s, when most women had acquiesced in the domestic suburban lifestyle and feminism as an ideology virtually disappeared. It also drew sustenance from the frustration of well-educated postwar American women with bright, well-furnished minds and no interesting and rewarding place to go. It differed from the feminism of the past, which emphasized political and civil rights, by its focus on social and economic equality and its sharper challenge to traditional gender roles.

The New Feminism can probably be dated from 1961 with the creation by John F. Kennedy of the President's Commission on the Status of Women. Although it accomplished little directly, the commission helped create a network of activists dedicated to expanding women's rights and improving women's lot. Two years later a Long Island housewife and magazine writer, Betty Friedan, jolted the New Feminism into full life with a three hundred-page manifesto, *The Feminine Mystique,* that denounced the gilded cage of postwar suburbia and called for a revitalized woman's movement.

In 1966 the activists organized NOW, the National Organization for Women, with Friedan as president. Dedicated to bringing "women into full participation in the mainstream of American society . . . [and] exercising all the privileges and responsibilities thereof in truly equal partnership with men," NOW was middle class in membership and hierarchical in structure. It accepted male members. It lobbied for its goals in Congress and the state legislatures and supported politicians who favored its programs. By the 1970s one of NOW's chief goals was to secure adoption of the Equal Rights Amendment to the Constitution forbidding both the states and the federal government to deny "equality of rights under the law . . . on account of sex."

Toward the end of the sixties still newer groups of feminists who favored more militant tactics and supported more radical goals challenged NOW's positions and leadership. Many of these activists were recruits from the student New Left that had appeared in the early sixties and caught the public's attention for its attacks on university administrations, racism, and the Vietnam War.

The militants favored more than reforming of "sexist" society by laws expanding and protecting women's rights. Rather, they sought to overthrow the "patriarchal" system they considered fundamental to all oppressive societies and to replace it with one where gender was socially and politically irrelevant. Many demanded the radical transformation of existing male-female relationships and the total reordering of the family. Such militants generally had little faith in electoral politics or legislative lobbying. Some favored inciting socialist revolution to destroy patriarchy. Others believed change would come through the transformation of social sensibility by propaganda, civil disobedience, militant demonstrations, and "consciousness-raising." Most radical feminist groups sought to avoid top-down, hierarchical control of their organizations and often grouped themselves into egalitarian "collectives."

The selections below provide an opportunity to discuss and evaluate the New Feminism, both the middle-of-the-road sort and the more radical kind. You will also find antifeminist viewpoints. Feminism is still a controversial issue today, and it may not be easy to be objective about some of the opinions expressed below. But once again try to use your critical judgment in considering the competing positions.

15.1: The National Organization for Women's Bill of Rights (1967)

At its first annual conference in 1967 NOW adopted the following Bill of Rights. The document of course was intended to parallel the first ten amendments to the federal Constitution, which are the original Bill of Rights. Does the NOW manifesto put forth a program that was bold for its time? Does it still seem bold today? Are any parts of the NOW Bill of Rights still controversial? Which one(s)? Why?

Bill of Rights

NOW (NATIONAL ORGANIZATION FOR WOMEN)

Adopted at NOW's first national conference, Washington, D.C., 1967

I. Equal Rights Constitutional Amendment
II. Enforce Law Banning Sex Discrimination in Employment
III. Maternity Leave Rights in Employment and in Social Security Benefits
IV. Tax Deduction for Home and Child Care Expenses for Working Parents
V. Child Day Care Centers
VI. Equal and Unsegregated Education
VII. Equal Job Training Opportunities and Allowances for Women in Poverty
VIII. The Right of Women to Control Their Reproductive Lives

WE DEMAND:

I. That the U.S. Congress immediately pass the Equal Rights Amendment to the Constitution to provide that "Equality of rights under the law shall not be denied or abridged by the United States or by any State on account of sex," and that such then be immediately ratified by the several States.

II. That equal employment opportunity be guaranteed to all women, as well as men, by insisting that the Equal Employment Opportunity Commission enforces the prohibitions against racial discrimination.

III. That women be protected by law to ensure their rights to return to their jobs within a reasonable time after childbirth without loss of seniority or other accrued benefits, and be paid maternity leave as a form of social security and/or employee benefit.

IV. Immediate revision of tax laws to permit the deduction of home and child-care expenses for working parents.

V. That child-care facilities be established by law on the same basis as parks, libraries, and public schools, adequate to the needs of children from the preschool years through adolescence, as a community resource to be used by all citizens from all income levels.

VI. That the right of women to be educated to their full potential equally with men be secured by Federal and State legislation, eliminating all discrimination and segregation by sex, written and unwritten, at all levels of education, including colleges, graduate and professional schools, loans and fellowships, and Federal and State training programs such as the Job Corps.

VII. The right of women in poverty to secure job training, housing, and family allowances on equal terms with men, but without prejudice to a parent's right to remain at home to care for his or her children; revision of welfare legislation and poverty programs which deny women dignity, privacy, and self-respect.

VIII. The right of women to control their own reproductive lives by removing from the penal code laws limiting access to contraceptive information and devices, and by repealing penal laws governing abortion.

15.2:   Radical Feminism (1969, 1968)

Radical feminism came in several varieties. Some radical feminists emphasized the economic roots of women's oppression. Others saw sexism as independent of economic systems. In some ways the second version was more radical than the first, since its partisans often attacked the nuclear family itself as inherently oppressive to women—and children.

Below are two examples of radical feminist views dating from the late 1960s. The first item is a statement adopted by the New York Radical Feminists to express their overall philosophy at their founding meeting in 1969. The second is a manifesto issued by the Radical Feminists' precursors, Radical Women, shortly before the group held a widely publicized protest demonstration at the 1968 Miss America Beauty Pageant in Atlantic City.

Is the Radical Feminists' statement antimale, as critics have charged? What forces does it emphasize as crucial for molding women's attitudes and characteristics? Is its grim picture of women as totally oppressed valid?

The Miss America Pageant protest created a sensation and undoubtedly made a broad public aware of radical feminist views. But it probably did not endear the group or their positions to a majority of Americans. Although none of the protesters at Atlantic City actually burned their brassieres, the media dismissively labeled them "bra-burners," and the tag stuck.

Why would the demonstration at the Miss America Pageant have offended conventional Americans? How might you defend the radical feminist positions and tactics? Was the pageant a valid target for feminists? What feminist attitudes lay behind their attack on such a public ritual?

Politics of the Ego: A Manifesto for New York Radical Feminists[1]

ANNE KOEDT

Radical feminism recognizes the oppression of women as a fundamental political oppression wherein women are categorized as an inferior class based upon their sex. It is the aim of radical feminism to organize politically to destroy this sex class system.

As radical feminists we recognize that we are engaged in a power struggle with men, and that the agent of our oppression is man insofar as he identifies with and carries out the supremacy privileges of the male role. For while we realize that the

[Anne Koedt], "Politics of the Ego: A Manifesto for New York Radical Feminists," in *Notes from the Second Year* (n.p., n.d.).
[1]Footnotes deleted.

liberation of women will ultimately mean the liberation of men from their destructive role as oppressor, we have no illusion that men will welcome this liberation without a struggle.

Radical feminism is political because it recognizes that a group of individuals (men) have organized together for power over women, and that they have set up institutions throughout society to maintain this power.

A political power institution is set up for a purpose. We believe that the purpose of male chauvinism is primarily to obtain psychological ego satisfaction, and that only secondarily does this manifest itself in economic relationships. For this reason we do not believe that capitalism, or any other economic system, is the cause of female oppression, nor do we believe that female oppression will disappear as a result of a purely economic revolution. The political oppression of women has its own class dynamic; and that dynamic must be understood in terms previously called "non-political"—namely the politics of the ego.[2]

Thus the purpose of the male power group is to fulfill a need. That need is psychological, and derives from the supremacist assumptions of the male identity—namely that the male identity be sustained through is ability to have power over the female ego. Man establishes his "manhood" in direct proportion to his ability to have his ego override woman's, and derives his strength and self-esteem through this process. This male need, though destructive, is in that sense impersonal. It is not out of a desire to hurt the woman that man dominates and destroys her; it is out of a need for a sense of power that he necessarily must destroy her ego and make it subservient to his. Hostility to women is a secondary effect, to the degree that a man is not fulfilling his own assumptions of male power he hates women. Similarly, a man's failure to establish himself supreme among other males (as for example a poor white male) may make him channel his hostility into his relationship with women, since they are one of the few political groups over which he can still exercise power.

As women we are living in a male power structure, and our roles become necessarily a function of men. The services we supply are services to the male ego. We are rewarded according to how well we perform these services. Our skill—our profession—is our ability to be feminine—that is, dainty, sweet, passive, helpless, ever-giving and sexy. In other words, everything to help reassure man that he is primary. If we perform successfully, our skills are rewarded. We "marry well"; we are treated with benevolent paternalism; we are deemed successful women, and may even make the "women's pages."

If we do not choose to perform these ego services, but instead assert ourselves as primary to ourselves, we are denied the necessary access to alternatives to express our self-assertion. Decision-making positions in the various job fields are closed to us; politics (left, right or liberal) are barred in other than auxiliary roles; our creative efforts are *a priori* judged not serious because we are females; our day-to-day lives are judged failures because we have not become "real women."

---

[2]Ego: We are using the classical definition rather than the Freudian: that is, the sense of individual self as distinct from others.

Rejection is economic in that women's work is underpaid. It is emotional in that we are cut off from human relationships because we choose to reject the submissive female role. We are trapped in an alien system, just as the worker under capitalism is forced to sell his economic services in a system which is set up against his self-interest.

Sexual Institutions

The oppression of women is manifested in particular institutions, constructed and maintained to keep women in their place. Among these are the institutions of marriage, motherhood, love, and sexual intercourse (the family unit is incorporated by the above). Through these institutions the woman is taught to confuse her biological sexual differences with her total human potential. Biology is destiny, she is told. Because she has childbearing capacity, she is told that motherhood and child rearing is her function, not her option. Because she has childbearing capacity she is told that it is her function to marry and have the man economically maintain her and "make the decisions." Because she has the physical capacity for sexual intercourse, she is told that sexual intercourse too is her function, rather than just a voluntary act which she may engage in as an expression of her general humanity.

In each case *her* sexual difference is rationalized to trap her within it, while the male sexual difference is rationalized to imply an access to all areas of human activity.

Love, in the context of an oppressive male-female relationship, becomes an emotional cement to justify the dominant-submissive relationship. The man "loves" the woman who fulfills her submissive ego-boosting role. The woman "loves" the man she is submitting to—that is, after all, why she "lives for him." LOVE, magical and systematically unanalyzed, becomes the emotional rationale for the submission of one ego to the other. And it is deemed every woman's natural function to love.

Radical feminism believes that the popularized version of love has thus been politically to cloud and justify an oppressive relationship between men and women, and that in reality there can be no genuine love until the need to *control* the growth of another is replaced by love *for* the growth of another.

Learning to Become Feminine

The process of training women for their female role begins as far back as birth, when a boy child is preferred over a girl child. In her early years, when the basic patterns of her identity are being established, it is reinforced in her that her female role is not a choice but a fact. Her future will be spent performing the same basic functions as her mother and women before her. Her life is already determined. She is not given the choice of exploring activity toys. Her brothers play astronaut, doctor, scientist, race-car driver. She plays little homemaker, future mother (dolls), and nurse (doctor's helper). Her brothers are given activity toys; the world is their future. She is given service toys. She is already learning that her future will be in the maintenance of others. Her ego is repressed at all times to prepare her for this future submissiveness. She must dress prettily and be clean; speak politely; seek approval; please. Her brothers are allowed to fight, get dirty, be aggressive and be self-assertive.

As she goes through school she learns that subjects which teach mastery and control over the world, such as science and math, are male subjects; while subjects which teach appearance, maintenance, or sentiment, such as home economics or literature, are female subjects. School counselors will recommend nursing for girls, while they will encourage boys to be doctors. Most of the best colleges will accept only a token sprinkling of women (quota system), regardless of academic abilities.

By the time she is of marrying age she has been prepared on two levels. One, she will realize that alternatives to the traditional female role are both prohibitive and prohibited; two, she will herself have accepted on some levels the assumptions about her female role.

Internalization

It is not only through denying women human alternatives that men are able to maintain their positions of power. It is politically necessary for any oppressive group to convince the oppressed that they are in fact inferior, and therefore deserve their situation. For it is precisely through the destruction of women's egos that they are robbed of their ability to resist.

For the sake of our own liberation, we must learn to overcome this damage to ourselves through internalization. We must begin to destroy the notion that we are indeed only servants to the male ego, and must begin to reverse the systematic crushing of women's egos by constructing alternate selves that are healthy, independent and self-assertive. We must, in short, help each other to transfer the ultimate power of judgment about the value of our lives from men to ourselves.

It remains for us as women to fully develop a new dialectic of sex class—an analysis of the way in which sexual identity and institutions reinforce one another.

No More Miss America![1]

RADICAL WOMEN (ORGANIZATION)

August 1968

On September 7th in Atlantic City, the Annual Miss America Pageant will again crown "your ideal." But this year, reality will liberate the contest auction-block in the guise of "genyooine" de-plasticized, breathing women. Women's Liberation Groups, black women, high-school and college women, women's peace groups, women's welfare and social-work groups, women's job-equality groups, pro-birth control and pro-abortion groups—women of every political persuasion—all are invited to join us in a day-long boardwalk-theater event, starting at 1:00 p.m. on the Boardwalk in front of Atlantic City's Convention Hall. We will protest the image of Miss America, an image that oppresses women in every area in which it purports to

[1]Footnotes deleted.

represent us. There will be: Picket Lines; Guerrilla Theater; Leafleting; Lobbying Visits to the contestants urging our sisters to reject the Pageant Farce and join us; a huge Freedom Trash Can (into which we will throw bras, girdles, curlers, false eyelashes, wigs, and representative issues of *Cosmopolitan, Ladies' Home Journal, Family Circle,* etc.—bring any such woman-garbage you have around the house); we will also announce a Boycott of all those commercial products related to the Pageant, and the day will end with a Women's Liberation rally at midnight when Miss America is crowned on live television. Lots of other surprises are being planned (come and add your own!) but we do not plan heavy disruptive tactics and so do not expect a bad police scene. It should be a groovy day on the Boardwalk in the sun with our sisters. In case of arrests, however, we plan to reject all male authority and demand to be busted by policewomen only. (In Atlantic City, women cops are not permitted to make arrests—dig that!)

Male chauvinist-reactionaries on this issue had best stay away, nor are male liberals welcome in the demonstrations. But sympathetic men can donate money as well as cars and drivers.

Male reporters will be refused interviews. We reject patronizing reportage. *Only newswomen will be recognized.*

The Ten Points

We Protest:

1. *The Degrading Mindless-Boob-Girlie Symbol.* The Pageant contestants epitomize the roles we are all forced to play as women. The parade down the runway blares the metaphor of the 4-H Club county fair, where the nervous animals are judged for teeth, fleece, etc., and where the best "specimen" gets the blue ribbon. So are women in our society forced daily to compete for male approval, enslaved by ludicrous "beauty" standards we ourselves are conditioned to take seriously.
2. *Racism with Roses.* Since its inception in 1921, the Pageant has not had one Black finalist, and this has not been for a lack of test-case contestants. There has never been a Puerto Rican, Alaskan, Hawaiian, or Mexican-American winner. Nor has there ever been a *true* Miss America—an American Indian.
3. *Miss America as Military Death Mascot.* The highlight of her reign each year is a cheerleader-tour of American troops abroad—last year she went to Vietnam to pep-talk our husbands, fathers, sons and boyfriends into dying and killing with a better spirit. She personifies the "unstained patriotic American womanhood our boys are fighting for." The Living Bra and the Dead Soldier. We refuse to be used as Mascots for Murder.
4. *The Consumer Con-Game.* Miss America is a walking commercial for the Pageant's sponsors. Wind her up and she plugs your product on promotion tours and TV—all in an "honest, objective" endorsement. What a shill.
5. *Competition Rigged and Unrigged.* We deplore the encouragement of an American myth that oppresses men as well as women: the win-or-you're-worthless competitive disease. The "beauty contest" creates only one winner to be "used" and forty-nine losers who are "useless."
6. *The Woman as Pop Culture Obsolescent Theme.* Spindle, mutilate, and then discard tomorrow. What is so ignored as least year's Miss America? This only reflects the gospel of our society, according to Saint Male: women must be young, juicy, mal-

leable—hence age discrimination and the cult of youth. And we women are brain-washed into believing this ourselves!

7. *The Unbeatable Madonna-Whore Combination.* Miss America and Playboy's centerfold are sisters over the skin. To win approval, we must be both sexy and wholesome, delicate but able to cope, demure yet titillatingly bitchy. Deviation of any sort brings, we are told, disaster: "You won't get a man!!"

8. *The Irrelevant Crown on the Throne of Mediocrity.* Miss America represents what women are supposed to be: unoffensive, bland, apolitical. If you are tall, short, over or under what weight The Man prescribes you should be, forget it. Personality, articulateness, intelligence, commitment—unwise. Conformity is the key to the crown—and, by extension, to success in our society.

9. *Miss America as Dream Equivalent To—?* In this reputedly democratic society, where every little boy supposedly can grow up to be President, what can every little girl hope to grow to be? Miss America. That's where it's at. Real power to control our own lives is restricted to men, while women get patronizing pseudopower, an ermine cloak and a bunch of flowers; men are judged by their actions, women by their appearance.

10. *Miss America as Big Sister Watching You.* The Pageant exercises Thought Control, attempts to sear the Image onto our minds, to further make women oppressed and men oppressors; to enslave us all the more in high-heeled, low-status roles; to inculcate false values in young girls; to use women as beasts of buying; to seduce us to prostitute ourselves before our own oppression.

NO MORE MISS AMERICA

15.3: The Counterattack (1977)

The opposition of many men to the feminist campaign, especially to its more militant versions, was predictable. But the feminist movement also made enemies among women. One of the most ardent of these was Phyllis Schlafly, a successful Illinois lawyer and mother of six. In the 1970s Schlafly would become a leading opponent of the Equal Rights Amendment to the Constitution, and her conservative Eagle Forum would take credit for preventing its final adoption.

The document below is Schlafly's indictment of the New Feminism in all its versions, moderate and radical alike, and her defense of traditional views of women and femininity. Do you find her position convincing in whole or in part? Schlafly emphasizes the biological bases for male–female differences. Does biology profoundly influence the roles and achievements of the two sexes? What group of women, defined socially or culturally, might consider her views congenial? Why? Schlafly was herself a well-educated professional woman. Was her appeal largely to women like herself?

Understanding the Difference

PHYLLIS SCHLAFLY

The first requirement for the acquisition of power by the Positive Woman[1] is to understand the differences between men and women. Your outlook on life, your faith, your behavior, your potential for fulfillment, all are determined by the parameters of your original premise. The Positive Woman starts with the assumption that the world is her oyster. She rejoices in the creative capability within her body and the power potential of her mind and spirit. She understands that men and women are different, and that those very differences provide the key to her success as a person and fulfillment as a woman.

The women's liberationist, on the other hand, is imprisoned by her own negative view of herself and of her place in the world around her. This view of women was most succinctly expressed in an advertisement designed by the principal women's liberationist organization, the National Organization for Women (NOW), and run in many magazines and newspapers and as spot announcements on many television stations. The advertisement showed a darling curlyheaded girl with the caption: "This healthy, normal baby has a handicap. She was born female."

This is the self-articulated dog-in-the-manger, chip-on-the-shoulder, fundamental dogma of the women's liberation movement. Someone—it is not clear who, perhaps God, perhaps the "Establishment," perhaps a conspiracy of male chauvinist pigs—dealt women a foul blow by making them female. It becomes necessary, therefore, for women to agitate and demonstrate and hurl demands on society in order to wrest from an oppressive male-dominated social structure the status that has been wrongfully denied to women through the centuries.

By its very nature, therefore, the women's liberation movement precipitates a series of conflict situations—in the legislatures, in the courts, in the schools, in industry—with man targeted as the enemy. Confrontation replaces cooperation as the watchword of all relationships. Women and men become adversaries instead of partners.

The second dogma of the women's liberationists is that, of all the injustices perpetrated upon women through the centuries, the most oppressive is the cruel fact that women have babies and men do not. Within the confines of the women's liberationist ideology, therefore, the abolition of this overriding inequality of women becomes the primary goal. This goal must be achieved at any and all costs—to the woman herself, to the baby, to the family, and to society. Women must be made equal to men in their ability *not* to become pregnant and *not* to be expected to care for babies they may bring into the world.

This is why women's liberationists are compulsively involved in the drive to make abortion and child-care centers for all women, regardless of religion or income, both socially acceptable and government-financed. Former Congresswoman

[1]This is Schlafly's version of the fulfilled modern woman, someone, one assumes, like herself—ED.

Bella Abzug has defined the goal: "to enforce the constitutional right of females to terminate pregnancies that they do not wish to continue."

If man is targeted as the enemy, and the ultimate goal of women's liberation is independence from men and the avoidance of pregnancy and its consequences, then lesbianism is logically the highest form in the ritual of women's liberation. Many, such as Kate Millett, come to this conclusion, although many others do not.

The Positive Woman will never travel that dead-end road. It is self-evident to the Positive Woman that the female body with its baby-producing organs was not designed by a conspiracy of men but by the Divine Architect of the human race. Those who think it is unfair that women have babies, whereas men cannot, will have to take up their complaint with God because no other power is capable of changing that fundamental fact. On some college campuses, I have been assured that other methods of reproduction will be developed. But most of us must deal with the real world rather than with the imagination of dreamers.

Another feature of the woman's natural role is the obvious fact that women can breast-feed babies and men cannot. This functional role was not imposed by conspiratorial males seeking to burden women with confining chores, but must be recognized as part of the plan of the Divine Architect for the survival of the human race through the centuries and in the countries that know no pasteurization of milk or sterilization of bottles.

The Positive Woman looks upon her femaleness and her fertility as part of her purpose, her potential, and her power. She rejoices that she has a capability for creativity that men can never have.

The third basic dogma of the women's liberation movement is that there is no difference between male and female except the sex organs, and that all those physical, cognitive, and emotional differences you *think* are there, are merely the result of centuries of restraints imposed by a male-dominated society and sex-stereotyped schooling. The role imposed on women is, by definition, inferior, according to the women's liberationists.

The Positive Woman knows that, while there are some physical competitions in which women are better (and can command more money) than men, including those that put a premium on grace and beauty, such as figure skating, the superior physical strength of males over females in competitions of strength, speed, and short-term endurance is beyond rational dispute. . . .

The Positive Woman remembers the essential validity of the old prayer: "Lord, give me the strength to change what I can change, the serenity to accept what I cannot change, and the wisdom to discern the difference." The women's liberationists are expending their time and energies erecting a make-believe world in which they hypothesize that *if* schooling were gender-free, and *if* the same money were spent on male and female sports programs, and *if* women were permitted to compete on equal terms, *then* they would prove themselves to be physically equal. Meanwhile, the Positive Woman has put the ineradicable physical differences into her mental computer, programmed her plan of action, and is already on the way to personal achievement. . . .

Despite the claims of the women's liberation movement, there are countless physical differences between men and women. The female body is 50 to 60 percent water, the male 60 to 70 percent water, which explains why males can dilute alcohol better than women and delay its effect. The average woman is about 25 percent fatty tissue, while the male is 15 percent, making women more buoyant in water and able to swim with less effort. Males have a tendency to color blindness. Only 5 percent of persons who get gout are female. Boys are born bigger. Women live longer in most countries of the world, not only in the United States where we have a hard-driving competitive pace. Women excel in manual dexterity, verbal skills, and memory recall. . . .

Does the physical advantage of men doom women to a life of servility and sub-servience? The Positive Woman knows that she has a complementary advantage which is at least as great—and, in the hands of a skillful woman, far greater. The Divine Architect who gave men a superior strength to lift weights also gave women a different kind of superior strength.

The women's liberationists and their dupes who try to tell each other that the sex-ual drive of men and women is really the same, and that it is only societal restraints that inhibit women from an equal desire, an equal enjoyment, and an equal freedom from the consequences, are doomed to frustration forever. It just isn't so, and pre-tending cannot make it so. The differences are not a woman's weakness but her strength. . . .

The new generation can brag all it wants about the new liberation of the new morality, but it is still the woman who is hurt the most. The new morality isn't just a "fad"—it is a cheat and a thief. It robs the woman of her virtue, her youth, her beauty, and her love—for nothing, just nothing. It has produced a generation of young women searching for their identity, bored with sexual freedom, and despon-dent from the loneliness of living a life without commitment. They have abandoned the old commandments, but they can't find any new rules that work.

The Positive Woman recognizes the fact that, when it comes to sex, women are simply not the equal of men. The sexual drive of men is much stronger than that of women. That is how the human race was designed in order that it might perpetuate itself. The other side of the coin is that it is easier for women to control their sexual appetites. A Positive Woman cannot defeat a man in a wrestling or boxing match, but she can motivate him, inspire him, encourage him, teach him, restrain him, re-ward him, and have power over him that he can never achieve over her with all his muscle. How or whether a Positive Woman uses her power is determined solely by the way she alone defines her goals and develops her skills.

The differences between men and women are also emotional and psychological. Without woman's innate maternal instinct, the human race would have died out cen-turies ago. There is nothing so helpless in all earthly life as the newborn infant. It will die within hours if not cared for. Even in the most primitive, uneducated societies, women have always cared for their newborn babies. They didn't need any schooling to teach them how. They didn't need any welfare workers to tell them it is their social obligation. Even in societies to whom such concepts as "ought," "social responsibility," and "com-passion for the helpless," were unknown, mothers cared for their new babies.

Why? Because caring for a baby serves the natural maternal need of a woman. Although not nearly so total as the baby's need, the woman's need is nonetheless real. . . .

This is not to say that every woman must have a baby in order to be fulfilled. But it is to say that fulfillment for most women involves expressing their natural maternal urge by loving and caring for someone.

The women's liberation movement complains that traditional stereotyped roles assume that women are "passive" and that men are "aggressive." The anomaly is that a woman's most fundamental emotional need is not passive at all, but active. A woman naturally seeks to love affirmatively and to show that love in an active way by caring for the object of her affections.

The Positive Woman finds somebody on whom she can lavish her maternal love so that it doesn't well up inside her and cause psychological frustrations. Surely no woman is so isolated by geography or insulated by spirit that she cannot find someone worthy of her maternal love. All persons, men and women, gain by sharing something of themselves with their fellow humans, but women profit most of all because it is part of their very nature.

15.4:   *Roe* v. *Wade* (1973)

In January 1973, the famous court decision Roe *v.* Wade *struck down a Texas law prohibiting abortion, thus paving the way to legalized abortion in the United States. Few issues have remained as passionate to the feminist movement as maintaining a "pro-choice" stance on abortion. Few issues have been as incendiary to the pro-life movement as ending legalized abortion.*

Roe *v.* Wade *is a complex and multifaceted ruling. What are its major legal and philosophical assumptions? Does the decision seem consistent with feminist principles expressed earlier in this chapter? Did the ruling cite practical or moral issues as well as legal ones? What ideas behind* Roe *v.* Wade *are contrary to the beliefs of the Right to Life Party?*

Roe v. *Wade*

A pregnant single woman (Roe) brought a class action suit challenging the constitutionality of the Texas criminal abortion laws, which proscribe procuring or attempting an abortion except on medical advice for the purpose of saving the mother's life. A licensed physician (Hallford), who had two state abortion prosecutions pending against him, was permitted to intervene. A childless married couple (the Does), the wife not being pregnant separately, attacked the laws, basing alleged injury on the future possibilities of contraceptive failure, pregnancy, unpreparedness for par-

Appeal from the United States District Court for the Northern District of Texas. Argued December 13, 1971; reargued October 11, 1972; decided January 22, 1973.)

enthood, and impairment of the wife's health. A three-judge District Court, which consolidated the actions, held that Roe and Hallford, and members of their classes, had standing to sue and present justiciable controversies. . . .[1] Ruling . . . the abortion statutes void as vague and overbroadly infringing those plaintiffs' Ninth and Fourteenth Amendment rights,[2] the court ruled the Does' complaint not justiciable. Appellants directly appealed to this Court . . . and appellee [the state of Texas] cross-appealed from the District Court's grant of . . . relief to Roe and Hallford. *Held:*

[Here follow several paragraphs in which the Court explains why it allowed the Roe case to be heard but not those of Hallford and the Does.]

3. State criminal abortion laws, like those involved here, that except from criminality only a life-saving procedure on the mother's behalf without regard to the stage of her pregnancy and other interests involved violate the Due Process Clause of the Fourteenth Amendment, which protects against state action the right to privacy, including a woman's qualified right to terminate her pregnancy. Though the State cannot override that right, it has legitimate interests in protecting both the pregnant woman's health and the potentiality of human life, each of which interests grows and reaches a "compelling" point at various stages of the woman's approach to term.

(a) For the stage prior to approximately the end of the first trimester, the abortion decision and its effectuation must be left to the medical judgment of the pregnant woman's attending physician.

(b) For the stage subsequent to approximately the end of the first trimester, the state, in promoting its interest in the health of the mother, may, if it chooses, regulate the abortion procedure in ways that are reasonably related to maternal health.

(c) For the stage subsequent to viability [of the fetus] the State, in promoting its interest in the potentiality of human life, may, if it chooses, regulate, and even proscribe abortion except where necessary, in appropriate medical judgment, for the preservation of the life or health of the mother.

4. The state may define the term "physician" to mean only a physician currently licensed by the State, and may proscribe any abortion by a person who is not a physician as so defined. . . .

Opinion of the Court

Mr. Justice Blackmun delivered the opinion of the Court.

This Texas federal appeal . . . present (s) constitutional challenges to state criminal abortion legislation. The Texas statutes under attack here are typical of those that have been in effect in many states for approximately a century.

We forthwith acknowledge our awareness of the sensitive and emotional nature of the abortion controversy, of the vigorous opposing views even among physi-

---

[1]"Justiciable" means that the issue is a legal matter valid for the courts to decide.
[2]That is, essentially, the right of privacy extracted from the Fourteenth Amendment by the Warren Court.

cians, and of the deep and seemingly absolute convictions that the subject inspires. One's philosophy, one's religious training, one's attitudes toward life and family and their values, and the moral standards one establishes and seeks to observe are all likely to influence and to color one's thinking and conclusions about abortion.

In addition, population growth, pollution, poverty, and racial overtones tend to complicate and not to simplify the problem.

Our task, of course, is to resolve the issue by constitutional measurement, free of emotion and of predilection. We seek earnestly to do this, and because we do, we have inquired into, and in this opinion place some emphasis upon, medical and medical-legal history and what this history reveals about man's attitudes toward the abortion procedure over the centuries. . . .

I

The Texas statutes that concern us here are [articles] 1191–1194 and 1196 of the state's Penal Code. These make it a crime to "procure an abortion," as therein defined, or attempt one, except with respect to "an abortion procured or attempted by medical advice for the purpose of saving the life of the mother." Similar statutes are in existence in a majority of the states. . . .

[Here follows a section on the legislative history of the Texas anti-abortion laws.]

II

Jane Roe [a pseudonym for Norma McCorvey], a single woman who was residing in Dallas County, Texas, instituted this federal action in March 1970 against the District Attorney of the county. She sought a declaratory judgment that the Texas criminal abortion statutes were unconstitutional on their face, and an injunction restraining the defendant from enforcing the statutes.

Roe alleged that she was unmarried and pregnant; that she wished to terminate her pregnancy by an abortion "performed by a competent, licensed physician under safe, clinical conditions"; that she was unable to get a "legal" abortion in Texas because her life did not appear to be threatened by the continuation of her pregnancy; and that she could not afford to travel to another jurisdiction in order to secure a legal abortion under safe conditions. She claimed that the Texas statutes were unconstitutionally vague and that they abridged her right of personal privacy protected by the First, Fourth, Ninth, and Fourteenth Amendments. By an amendment to her complaint Roe purported to sue "on behalf of herself and all other women" similarly situated. . . .

[Here follow the circumstances of the parallel suits of Dr. Hallford and the Doe couple.]

The . . . actions were consolidated and heard together by a duly convened three-judge district court. . . . Upon the filing of affidavits, motions were made for dismissal and for summary judgment. . . . On the merits, the District Court held that the "fundamental right of a single woman and married persons to decide whether to have children is protected by the Ninth Amendment, through the Fourteenth Amendment," and that the Texas criminal abortion statutes were void on their face because they were both unconstitutionally vague and constituted an overbroad infringement of the plaintiffs' Ninth Amendment rights. The court then held that abstention was warranted with respect to the requests for an injunction. . . .

The plaintiffs . . . have appealed to this Court from that part of the District Court's judgment denying the injunction. . . .

[Here follow several sections regarding the Court's willingness to take jurisdiction in the case and why it did not consider in this decision the cases of Dr. Hallford and the Does. Blackmun also includes a lengthy history of anti-abortion laws, the thrust of which is that: "Those laws, generally proscribing abortion, or its attempt at any time during pregnancy except when necessary to preserve the pregnant woman's life, are not of ancient or even of common-law origin. Instead, they derive from statutory changes effected for the most part in the latter half of the 19th century." He also describes the historical and recent views of the American Medical Association and of the American Public Health Association and the American Bar Association.]

VII

Three reasons have been advanced to explain historically the enactment of criminal abortion laws in the 19th century and to justify their continued existence.

It has been argued occasionally that these laws were the product of a Victorian social concern to discourage illicit sexual conduct. Texas, however, does not advance this justification in the present case, and it appears that no court or commentator has taken the argument seriously. . . .

A second reason is concerned with abortion as a medical procedure. When most criminal abortion laws were first enacted, the procedure was a hazardous one for the woman. This was particularly true prior to the development of antisepsis. . . .

Modern medical techniques have altered this situation. . . . Consequently, any interest of the state in protecting the woman from an inherently hazardous procedure . . . has largely disappeared. . . . The state has a legitimate interest in seeing to it that abortion, like any other medical procedure, is performed under circumstances that insure maximum safety for the patient. . . . [T]he state retains a definite interest in protecting a woman's own health and safety when an abortion is proposed at a late stage of pregnancy.

The third reason is the state's interest—some phrase it in terms of duty—in protecting prenatal life. Some of the arguments for this justification rest on the theory that a new human life is present from the moment of conception. The state's interest and general obligation to protect life then extends, it is argued, to prenatal life. Only when the life of the pregnant mother herself is at stake, balanced against the life she carries within her, should the interest of the embryo or fetus not prevail. . . .

Parties challenging state abortion laws have sharply disputed in some courts the contention that a purpose of these laws, when enacted, was to protect prenatal life. Pointing to the absence of legislative history to support the contention, they claim that most state laws were designed solely to protect the woman. Because medical advances have lessened this concern . . . they argue that with respect to such abortions the laws can no longer be justified by any state interest. There is some scholarly support for this view of original purpose. The few state courts called upon to interpret their laws in the 19th and early 20th centuries did focus on the state's interest in protecting the woman's health rather than in preserving the embryo and fetus. . . .

It is with these interests and the weight to be attached to them, that this case is concerned.

VIII

The Constitution does not explicitly mention any right of privacy. In a line of decisions, however, . . . the Court has recognized that a right of personal privacy, or a guarantee of certain areas or zones of privacy, does exist under the Constitution. . . . These decisions make it clear that only personal rights that can be deemed "fundamental" or "implicit in the concept or ordered liberty," . . . are included in this guarantee of personal privacy. They also make it clear that the right has some extension to activities relating to marriage, . . . procreation, . . . contraception, . . . family relationships, . . . and child rearing and education. . . .

This right of privacy . . . is broad enough to encompass a woman's decision whether or not to terminate her pregnancy. The detriment that the state would impose upon the pregnant woman by denying this choice altogether is apparent. Specific and direct harm medically diagnosable even in early pregnancy may be involved. Maternity, or additional offspring, may force upon the woman a distressful life and future. Psychological harm may be imminent. Mental and physical health may be taxed by child care. There is also the distress, for all concerned, associated with the unwanted child, and there is the problem of bringing a child into a family already unable, psychologically or otherwise, to care for it. In other cases, as in this one, the additional difficulties and continuing stigma of unwed motherhood may be involved. All these are factors the woman and her responsible physician necessarily will consider in consultation.

On the basis of elements such as these, appellant [that is, Roe] and some *amici* [that is, her legal supporters] argue that the woman's right is absolute and that she is entitled to terminate her pregnancy at whatever time, in whatever way, and for whatever reason she alone chooses. With this we do not agree. Appellant's arguments that Texas either has no valid interest at all in regulating the abortion decision, or no interest strong enough to support any limitation upon the woman's sole determination, are unpersuasive. The Court's decision recognizing a right of privacy also acknowledges that some state regulation in areas protected by that right is appropriate. As noted above, a State may properly assert important interests in safeguarding health, in maintaining medical standards, and in protecting potential life. . . . The privacy right involved, therefore, cannot be said to be absolute. In fact, it is not clear to us that the claim asserted by some *amici* that one has an unlimited right to do with one's body as one pleases bears a close relationship to the right of privacy previously articulated in the Court's decisions. The Court has refused to recognize an unlimited right of this kind in the past.

We, therefore, conclude that the right of personal privacy includes the abortion decision, but that this right is not unqualified and must be considered against important state interests in regulation. . . .

[Here follow sections reviewing state court decisions agreeing with the idea of limitation on the right of privacy.]

IX

A. Texas argues that, apart from the Fourteenth Amendment, life begins at conception and is present throughout pregnancy, and that, therefore, the state has a compelling interest in protecting that life from and after conception. We need not resolve the difficult question of when life begins. When those trained in the respective disciplines of medicine, philosophy, and theology are unable to arrive at any consensus, the judiciary, at this point in the development of man's knowledge, is not in a position to speculate as to the answer.

It should be sufficient to note briefly the wide divergence of thinking on this most sensitive and difficult question. There has always been strong support for the view that life does not begin until live birth. . . .

[Here follows a review of past opinion as to when life begins and of what the current law is on the subject. In regard to the latter, Blackmun concludes: "In short, the unborn have never been recognized in the law as persons in the whole sense."]

X

In view of this, we do not agree that, by adopting one theory of life, Texas may override the rights of the pregnant woman that are at stake. We repeat, however, that the state does have an important and legitimate interest in preserving and protecting the health of the pregnant woman. . . .

With respect to the state's important and legitimate interest in the health of the mother, the "compelling" point, in the light of present medical knowledge, is at approximately the end of the first trimester. This is so because of the now-established medical fact . . . that until the end of the first trimester mortality in abortion may be less than mortality in normal childbirth. . . .

This means . . . that for the period of pregnancy prior to this "compelling" point, the attending physician, in consultation with his patient, is free to determine, without regulation by the state, that, in his medical judgment, the patient's pregnancy should be terminated. If that decision is reached, the judgment may be effectuated by an abortion free of interference by the state. . . .

☆ **16** ☆

The Vietnam War

The Vietnam War has been described as America's longest war. It was also America's most demoralizing, divisive, and ultimately most despised war.

The Vietnam conflict was an extension into Southeast Asia of the Cold War between the superpowers and their clients. As viewed by American policy makers in the 1960s, the United States, as prime defender of the free world, had to prevent the conquest of pro-Western South Vietnam by a pro-Soviet regime in North Vietnam led by the Communist leader Ho Chi Minh. If we failed in our mission, it would consign much of the region to ultimate Communist domination.

Whatever the rationale, the United States drifted, almost absentmindedly, into a military and political commitment in the region. Vietnam had been part of French Indochina, a dependency of France since the nineteenth century. The Japanese occupied the country during World War II, and when they left in 1945 the French sought to reestablish political control. They were opposed by Indochinese groups determined to oust France and establish independent nations in the former colony.

The most effective of these insurgent forces was the Viet Minh, concentrated around Hanoi in northern Vietnam and led by the Moscow-trained Ho Chi Minh. Ho and his supporters were determined to unite all of Vietnam as a Marxist state under their leadership.

Despite a flood of American money and military supplies, the French failed to subdue the Viet Minh, and after their defeat in battle at Dien Bien Phu in 1954, they agreed to leave their former colony. Their departure left Indochina divided into four small countries: Communist-dominated North Vietnam with its capital at Hanoi; a pro-Western South Vietnam governed from Saigon; and two small states, Laos and Cambodia, which tried to maintain a neutral position.

The Geneva Accords of 1954, confirming French defeat, mandated national elections in two years to decide on the unification of the two

Vietnams. But the vote was never held. In the south the pro-Western regime led by Ngo Dinh Diem, fearing defeat, ignored the election provision of the Geneva agreement. Frustrated by this check to reunification of both Vietnams under its control, Ho's regime in the north supported a guerrilla war by the Communist Vietcong (the National Liberation Front) against the Saigon government.

The American government tried to prop up the Diem regime in South Vietnam with arms, food, and money. In 1961 President Kennedy dispatched the first American military personnel to South Vietnam, although they were advisers to the South Vietnamese armed forces, not combat troops. This aid was not enough. The Diem regime was corrupt, arbitrary, and bigoted, and, while failing to win over South Vietnam's peasants, offended the influential Buddhists.

In late 1963 the United States encouraged the overthrow of the Diem regime by pro-American generals. For the next few years confusion reigned in Saigon as various factions and individuals fought for power. By now Lyndon Johnson was president, and the American commitment to preserving the status quo in Vietnam was about to get a major boost.

Soon after LBJ's election in 1964 he escalated the American military investment in Vietnam. In March 1965 he ordered a major bombing campaign ("Rolling Thunder") against North Vietnam to discourage further aid to the Vietcong. Soon after, the first American combat troops arrived in South Vietnam. By the end of the year there would be almost 200,000 U.S. fighting men in the country. Each month thereafter the number grew. At the peak of the Vietnam War in late 1968, some 536,000 American troops would be engaged in a struggle to stop Hanoi from reuniting the two Vietnams under its sole authority.

At home the war proved to be the most divisive in American history. Constrained by fears of Chinese or Soviet intervention, the administration refused to employ nuclear weapons. It also failed to make an effective case to the American people for an all-out war and in fact sought to hide the costs of the American commitment lest they arouse too much domestic opposition. To make matters worse, the American client regime in Saigon never seemed to care as much about saving itself as the United States did; its generals and troops seldom engaged the enemy aggressively.

Significant domestic opposition to the war erupted in early 1965, and thereafter the antiwar movement grew with each new increment of U.S. military investment. Antiwar feelings were amplified by the nightly TV news, which showed the bombings, the firefights, and the daily "body counts" in Vietnam to an appalled American viewership. The president and his advisers kept reassuring the public that there was "light at the end of the tunnel," and that with a few thousand more men and a little more effort, the enemy would collapse. Americans soon greeted each new claim with derision. In late January 1968, after months of optimistic predictions, the prowar "hawks" suffered a devastating setback when a coordinated, multicity Vietcong attack on South Vietnamese and American posts and installations during the Vietnamese Tet new year festival caught the Americans by surprise. The Vietcong captured the provincial capital of Hue and penetrated the American embassy compound in Saigon.

In the end Vietcong losses were appalling, but the Tet Offensive demolished the administration's claim of imminent victory. To the very end a bloc of "hawk" loyalists continued to support the war. But by this time many Americans had lost faith in their government, a mood that fed the political and cultural left and propelled a stream of recruits into such organizations as Students for a Democratic Society, the Resistance, and the Yippies.

In 1968 antiwar Democrats, led by Senators Eugene McCarthy of Minnesota and Robert Kennedy of New York, forced Johnson to drop his reelection bid. The Democratic presidential candidate that year, Hubert Humphrey, was hobbled by his loyalty to Johnson and lost narrowly to Richard Nixon in November. Once in office Nixon began to reduce American combat troops and turn the fighting over to the South Vietnamese, a process he called "Vietnamization." Meanwhile American and North Vietnamese officials conducted frustrating peace negotiations in Paris, out of the public's sight. Yet the fighting continued, and the antiwar activists accused Nixon of hypocrisy.

In January 1973 the United States, North Vietnam, South Vietnam, and the Vietcong finally concluded an agreement to stop the fighting, exchange prisoners, and form a National Council of Reconciliation to determine future relations between Hanoi and Saigon. In March 1973 the last American troops left South Vietnam.

The Nixon administration claimed that the South Vietnamese could protect themselves if the United States continued to provide money and equipment. It was untrue, however, and in any event Congress was unwilling to provide the resources. In April 1975, under powerful attack by North Vietnamese forces, the South Vietnamese government collapsed. As the Communist tanks rumbled into Saigon, the United States hurriedly evacuated the remaining Americans and hundreds of South Vietnamese supporters from the U.S. embassy grounds by helicopter. Over the next few years, as the North Vietnamese imposed a totalitarian regime in the South, hundreds of thousands of South Vietnamese "boat people" fled the Communists, many eventually finding haven in the United States.

America's longest war had ended on a bitter note, leaving behind a legacy of neo-isolationism, internal domestic division, dismay at excessive presidential power, and skepticism of American goals and purposes. It would take years before the wounds healed.

The selections below represent the positions of various groups on the American role in Vietnam. Included are defenders of the administration policies, American peace advocates, and even the Communist North Vietnamese. Needless to say, the disagreements among the parties are striking.

16.1: The Hawk Position (1954, 1965)

As far back as the 1950s American leaders saw a victory for the Viet-namese Communists as a grave danger to the other non-Communist regimes in East Asia. Influenced by the containment policy in Europe and the experience of the Korean War, they warned that if the North Vietnamese were not stopped, the Communist virus would soon spread to neutral or pro-Western East Asian nations. This in turn would ex-pand the power of the Soviet Union and the Communist People's Re-public of China at the free world's expense.

The most famous expression of this pessimistic view came at a 1954 press conference, reported below, at which President Dwight Eisen-hower likened the non-Communist nations of the region to a row of dominoes that would tip over one by one if the Hanoi regime were suc-cessful in reuniting Vietnam under its aegis. Yet despite his convic-tions, Eisenhower proved unwilling to commit American combat forces to Vietnam. Students will want to ask if there were plausible reasons to believe in the "domino effect"? Did events prove Eisen-hower to be correct?

It took more than a decade before the sort of thinking behind Eisen-hower's statement produced a full-scale American military commit-ment to the defense of South Vietnam. The second item below is a Feb-ruary 1965 memo from National Security Adviser McGeorge Bundy to President Lyndon Johnson expressing what came to be called the hawk position. Bundy was writing from Vietnam, where he had gone on a scouting trip for the president. At the time of his visit Vietcong guerrillas were engaged in a major offensive against the forces of the South Vietnamese government and had recently inflicted severe casu-alties on them. American military "advisers," moreover, were already stationed in Vietnam, and just the day before the Bundy memo the Vi-etcong had attacked U.S. military installations at Pleiku, killing nine Americans.

What is Bundy's estimate of the situation in South Vietnam? What are his recommendations to meet that situation? What seems to be his estimate of the will and capacity of the South Vietnamese to defend themselves? Did events ultimately confirm or refute Bundy's estimate? What sort of reprisals actually followed soon after his recommendations?

The Domino Theory

DWIGHT D. EISENHOWER

Q: Robert Richards, Copley Press: Mr. President, would you mind commenting on the strategic importance of Indochina to the free world? I think there has been, across the country, some lack of understanding on just what it means to us.

The President: You have, of course, both the specific and the general when you talk about such things.

First of all, you have the specific value of a locality in its production of materials that the world needs.

Then you have the possibility that many human beings pass under a dictatorship that is inimical to the free world.

Finally, you have broader considerations that might follow what you would call the "falling domino" principle. You have a row of dominoes set up, you knock over the first one, and what will happen to the last one is the certainly that it will go over very quickly. So you could have a beginning of a disintegration that would have the most profound influences.

Now, with respect to the first one, two of the items from this particular area that the world uses are tin and tungsten. They are very important. There are others, of course, the rubber plantations and so on.

Then with respect to more people passing under this domination, Asia, after all, has already lost some 450 million of its people to the Communist dictatorship, and we simply can't afford greater losses.

But when we come to the possible sequence of events, the loss of Indochina, of Burma, of Thailand, of the Peninsula, and Indonesia following, now you begin to talk about areas that not only multiply the disadvantages that you would suffer through loss of materials, sources of materials, but now you are talking really about millions and millions and millions of people.

Finally, the geographical position achieved thereby does many things. It turns the so-called island defensive chain of Japan, Formosa, of the Philippines and to the southward; it moves in to threaten Australia and New Zealand.

It takes away, in its economic aspects, that region that Japan must have as a trading area or Japan, in turn, will have only one place in the world to go—that is, toward the Communist areas in order to live.

So, the possible consequences of the loss are just incalculable to the free world.

Public Papers of the Presidents of the United States: Dwight D. Eisenhower, 1954 (Washington, DC: Government Printing Office, 1958), pp. 381–390.

The Situation in Vietnam

McGEORGE BUNDY

Re: The Situation in Vietnam

This memorandum attempts to describe the situation, the stakes and the measures which I think should now . . . [be] taken.

I. Summary Conclusions

The situation in Vietnam is deteriorating, and without new U.S. action defeat appears inevitable—probably not in a matter of weeks or perhaps even months, but within the next year or so. There is still time to turn it around, but not much.

The stakes in Vietnam are extremely high. The American investment is very large, and American responsibility is a fact of life which is palpable in the atmosphere of Asia, and even elsewhere. The international prestige of the United States, and a substantial part of our influence, are directly at risk in Vietnam. There is no way of unloading the burden on the Vietnamese themselves, and there is no way of negotiating ourselves out of Vietnam which offers any serious promise at present. It is possible that at some future time a neutral non-Communist force may emerge, perhaps under Buddhist leadership, but no such force currently exists, and any negotiated U.S. withdrawal today would mean surrender on the installment plan.

The policy of graduated and continuing reprisal . . . is the most promising course available, in my judgment. The judgment is shared by all who accompanied me from Washington, and I think by all members of the country team.

The events of the last twenty-four hours have produced a practicable point of departure for this policy of reprisal, and for the removal of U.S. dependents. They may also have catalyzed the formation of a new Vietnamese government. If so, the situation may be at a turning point. There is much that can and should be done to support and to supplement our present effort, while adding sustained reprisals. . . .

II. The General Situation

For the last year—and perhaps for longer—the overall situation in Vietnam has been deteriorating. The Communists have been gaining and the anti-Communist forces have been losing. As a result there is now great uncertainty among Vietnamese as well as Americans as to whether Communist victory can be prevented. There is nervousness about the determination of the U.S. Government. There is recrimination and fear among Vietnamese political leaders. There is an appearance of wariness among some military leaders. There is a worrisome lassitude among the Vietnamese generally. There is a distressing absence of positive commitment to any serious social or political purpose. Outside observers are ready to write the patient off. All of this tends to bring latent anti-Americanism dangerously near to the surface.

Moreover, the Vietnamese people, although war weary, are also remarkably tough and resilient, and they do not find the prospect of Communist domination at-

Gareth Porter, ed., *Vietnam: The Definitive Documentation of Human Decisions* (Stanfordville, NY: Earl M. Coleman Enterprises, Inc., Publishers, 1979), vol. 2, pp. 349–354.

tractive. Their readiness to quit is much lower than the discouraging events of recent months might lead one to expect. It is probable that most Vietnamese think American withdrawal is more likely than an early switch to neutralism or surrender by major elements within Vietnam.

Nevertheless the social and political fabric is stretched thin, and extremely unpleasant surprises are increasingly possible—both political and military.

And it remains a stubborn fact that the percentage of the countryside which is dominated or threatened by the Viet Cong continues to grow. Even in areas which are "cleared," the follow-on pacification is stalled because of widespread belief that the Viet Cong are going to win in the long run. The areas which can be regarded as truly cleared and pacified and safe are few and shrinking. . . .

III. The Political Situation

Next only to the overall state of the struggle against the Viet Cong, the shape and structure of the government is [sic] the most important element of the Saigon situation. We made it our particular business to examine the question whether and to what degree a stable government is a necessity for the successful prosecution of our policy in Vietnam. We reached a mixed conclusion.

For immediate purposes—and especially for the initiation of reprisal policy, we believe that the government need be no stronger than it is today with General Khanh[1] as the focus of raw power while a weak caretaker government goes through the motions. Such a government can execute military decisions and it can give formal political support to joint US/GVN[2] policy. That is about all it can do.

In the longer run, it is necessary that a government be established which will in one way or another be able to maintain its political authority against all challenges over a longer time than the governments of the last year and a half.

The composition and direction of such a government is [sic] a most difficult problem, and we do not wholly agree with the mission in our estimate of its nature.

The mood of the mission with respect to the prospect of obtaining such a government is one of pessimism and frustration.

Specifically, we believe that General Khanh, with all his faults, is by long odds the outstanding military man currently in sight—and the most impressive personality generally. We do not share the conclusion of Ambassador [Maxwell] Taylor that he must somehow be removed from the military and political scene.

There are strong reasons for the Ambassador's total lack of confidence in Khanh. At least twice Khanh has acted in ways that directly spelled Ambassador Taylor's high hopes for December. When he abolished the High National Council he undercut the prospect of the stable government needed for Phase II action against the North. In January he overthrew Huong just when the latter, in the Embassy's view, was about to succeed in putting the bonzes[3] in their place.

---

[1]Nguyen Khanh, leader of a group of South Vietnamese junior officers who overthrew the junta that had, in November 1963, overthrown Ngo Dinh Diem, the former tyrannical client of the United States—ED.
[2]The GVN means government of Vietnam, the regime in Saigon—ED.
[3]Buddhist monks—ED.

Khanh is not an easy man to deal with. It is clear that he takes a highly tactical view of truth, although General Westmoreland asserts that Khanh has never deceived him. He is intensely ambitious and intent above all else on maintaining and advancing his own power. He gravely lacks the confidence of many of his colleagues—military and civilian—and he seems not to be personally popular with the public. He is correctly assessed as tricky. He remains able, energetic, perceptive and resilient, and in our judgment he will pursue the fight against the Communists as long as he can count on U.S. help. (If he should conclude that the U.S. was violently against him personally, he might well seek a way to power by some anti-American path, a path which would lead to disaster for both Vietnam and the United States.)

But our principal reason for opposing any sharp break with Khanh is that we see no one else in sight with anything like his ability to combine military authority with some sense of politics.

We also differ from the Embassy in our estimate of the Buddhist leaders. The dominant Embassy view is that "the Buddhists" are really just a handful of irresponsible and designing clerics and that they must be curbed by firmness. We agree that they may well have to be limited at some point, especially in their use of mobs, but we also think they must be offered some accommodation.

We feel that the operative concept should be *incorporation* into the affairs of government rather than confrontation. This is easier said than done, because the Buddhists have many of the bad habits of men who have prospered by irresponsible opposition. Still there are signs that both Buddhist laymen and bonzes are now taking a more positive stance. We feel that the mission might do more in attempting to direct or channel the Buddhists into a more useful and positive role—an active rather than a passive approach. The Buddhists now play a key role in the balance of political forces, so that something more than "confrontation" must be achieved if there is to be any active government at all.

IV. Strengthening the Pacification Program

If we suppose that new hopes are raised—at least temporarily—by a reprisal program, and if we suppose further that a government somewhat better than the bare minimum is established, the most urgent order of business will then be the improvement and broadening of the pacification program, especially in its non-military elements.

The mission fully concurs in the importance of this effort. We believe, however, that consideration should be given to important modifications in its organization for this purpose. In particular we believe that there should be intensive effort to strengthen our program at the margin between military advice and economic development—in the area which implies civil government for the soldiers and police action for the aid mission. These efforts, important as they are understood to be, are somehow at the edge of vision for both parties. General Westmoreland and his people inevitably think first of military programs, though they have been imaginative and understanding about the importance of other aspects. Mr. Killen and the USOM people are centrally concerned with problems of aid and of economic improvement, although they talk with conviction and energy about their increasing police effort. It remains a fact that its own organization for helping to provide real security for an area which has been "cleared" in crude military terms is unfinished business for the U.S. mission. What is true of our side is doubly true of the Vietnamese.

We do not offer a definite solution to this problem. We are inclined to suggest, however, that one important and unemployed asset is the Special Forces of the Defense Department. Because of the predominant role of the U.S. military, and because of the generous spirit and broad mind of General Westmoreland himself, we are inclined to believe that the easiest growing edge for this work may be through the use of some of these versatile and flexible units.

We would think it important, however, that an effort of this kind be coordinated at a high level between the Defense Department and AID, and we believe that a joint mission which would include either Director Bell or Mr. Gaud from AID is urgently needed for the purpose of building this missing link into our program.

V. A Sense of Positive Hope

Vietnamese talk is full of the need for "revolution." Vietnamese practice is empty of action to match the talk—so much so that the word "revolution" sometimes seems to have no real meaning. Yet in fact there is plainly a deep and strong yearning among the young and the unprivileged for a new and better social order. This is what the Buddhist leaders are groping toward; this is what the students and young Turk generals are seeking. This yearning does not find an adequate response in American policy as Vietnamese see it. This is one cause of latent anti-American feeling. We only perceived this problem toward the end of our visit. We think it needs urgent further attention. We make no present recommendations. We do believe that over the long pull our military and political firmness must be matched by our political and economic support for the hopes that are embodied to Vietnamese in the word "revolution."

VI. The Basic U.S. Commitment

The prospect in Vietnam is grim. The energy and persistence of the Viet Cong are astonishing. They can appear anywhere—and at almost any time. They have accepted extraordinary losses and they come back for more. They show skill in their sneak attacks and ferocity when cornered. Yet the weary country does not want them to win.

There are a host of things the Vietnamese need to do better and areas in which we need to help them. The place where we can help most is in the clarity and firmness of our own commitment to what is in fact as well as in rhetoric a common cause. There is one grave weakness in our posture in Vietnam which is within our own power to fix—and that is a widespread belief that we do not have the will and force and patience and determination to take the necessary action and stay the course.

This is the overriding reason for our present recommendation of a policy of sustained reprisal. Once such a policy is put in force, we shall be able to speak in Vietnam on many topics and in many ways, with growing force and effectiveness.

One final word. At its very best the struggle in Vietnam will be long. It seems to us important that this fundamental fact be made clear and our understanding of it be made clear to our people and to the people of Vietnam. Too often in the past we have conveyed the impression that we expect an early solution when those who live with this war know that no early solution is possible. It is our own belief that the people of the United States have the necessary will to accept and to execute a policy that rests upon the reality that there is no shortcut to success in South Vietnam.

16.2: The North Vietnamese Analyze American Intervention (1965)

During their decade of conflict with the United States, the North Vietnamese often displayed a more realistic capacity for analysis than the Americans. The selection below is from a July 1965 talk by Le Duan, a high-ranking official in the North Vietnamese Communist Party. His remarks, which were a "pep talk" to a group of Communist leaders, also represent a careful dissection of American options. What factors, according to Le Duan, would influence American choices in Vietnam? Does he emphasize American military weakness or political vulnerability? Was his assessment shrewd or wide of the mark?

The North Vietnamese Analyze American Intervention

LE DUAN

We know that the U.S. sabotaged the Geneva Agreement and encroached on South Vietnam in order to achieve three objectives:

1. To turn the South into a colony of a new type.
2. To turn the South into a military base, in order to prepare to attack the North and the Socialist bloc.
3. To establish a South Vietnam-Cambodia-Laos defensive line in order to prevent the socialist revolution from spreading through Southeast Asia.

At present, we fight the U.S.in order to defeat their first two objectives to prevent them from turning the South into a new-type colony and military base.

We do not yet aim at their third objective, essentially to divide the ranks of the imperialist and to make other imperialists disagree with the U.S. in broadening the war in Vietnam and also to attract the support of other democratic and independent countries for our struggle in the South. Our revolutionary struggle in the South has the character of a conflict between the two camps in fact, but we advocate not making that conflict grow but limiting it in order to concentrate our forces to resolve the

Gareth Porter, ed., *Vietnam: The Definitive Documentation of Human Decisions* (Stanfordville, NY: Earl M. Coleman Enterprises, Inc., Publishers, 1979), vol. 2, pp. 383–385.

contradiction between the people and U.S. imperialism and its lackeys, to complete the national democratic revolution in the whole country. It is for this reason that we put forward the slogan "peace and neutrality" for the South, a flexible slogan to win victory step by step. We are not only determined to defeat the U.S. but must know how to defeat the U.S. in the manner most appropriate to the relation of forces between the enemy and us during each historical phase. Putting forward the slogan peace and neutrality for the South as well as the five points of the National Liberation Front of South Vietnam and the four points in our government's declaration read before the National Assembly as bases for the revolution of the Vietnamese problem, means that we know how to fight and defeat the Americans most advantageously.

. . . [T]he U.S. is still strong enough to enter into a limited war in Vietnam, by sending not only 200,00–250,000 but 300,000–400,000 troops to South Vietnam. But if it switches to limited war, the U.S. still will have weaknesses which it cannot overcome. The U.S. rear area is very far away, and American soldiers are "soldiers in chains," who cannot fight like the French, cannot stand the weather conditions, and don't know the battlefield but on the contrary have many weaknesses in their opposition to people's war. If the U.S. puts 300–400,000 [sic] troops into the South, it will have stripped away the face of its neocolonial policy and revealed the face of an old style colonial invader, contrary to the whole new-style annexation policy of the U.S. in the world at present. Thus, the U.S. will not be able to maintain its power with regard to influential sectors of the United States. If the U.S. itself directly enters the war in the South it will have to fight for a prolonged period with the people's army of the South,[1] with the full assistance of the North and the Socialist bloc.[2] To fight for a prolonged period is a weakness of U.S. imperialism. The Southern revolution can fight a protracted war, while the U.S. can't, because American military, economic and political resources must be distributed throughout the world. If it is bogged down in one place and can't withdraw, the whole effort will be violently shaken. The U.S. would lose its preeminence in influential sectors at home and create openings for other competing imperialists, and lose the American market. Therefore at present, although the U.S. can immediately send 300,000 to 400,000 troops at once, why must the U.S. do it step by step? Because even if it does send many troops like that, the U.S. would still be hesitant; because that would be a passive policy full of contradictions; because of fear of protracted war, and the even stronger opposition of the American people and the world's people, and even of their allies who would also not support widening the war.

With regard to the North, the U.S. still carries out its war of destruction, primarily by its air force: Besides bombing military targets, bridges and roads to obstruct transport and communications, the U.S. could also indiscriminately bomb economic targets, markets, villages, schools, hospitals, dikes, etc., in order to create confusion and agitation among the people. But the North is determined to fight back at the U.S. invaders in a suitable manner, determined to punish the criminals, day or night,

---

[1]The Vietcong—ED.
[2]That is, the other Communist nations of the world, especially China and the Soviet Union—ED.

and determined to make them pay the blood debts which they have incurred to our people in both zones. The North will not flinch for a moment before the destructive acts of the U.S., which could grow increasingly mad with every passing day. The North will not count the cost but will use all of its strength to produce and fight, and endeavor to help the South. For a long time, the Americans have boasted of the strength of their air force and navy but during five to six months of directly engaging in combat with the U.S. in the North, we see clearly that the U.S. cannot develop that strength in relation to the South as well as in relation to the North, but revealed more clearly every day its weak-points. We have shot down more than 400 of their airplanes, primarily with rifles, anti-aircraft guns; [but] the high level of their hatred of the aggressors, and the spirit of determination to defeat the U.S. invaders [are strong]. Therefore, if the U.S. sends 300,000–400,000 troops into the South, and turns special war into direct war in the South, escalating the war of destruction in the North, they still can't hope to avert defeat, and the people of both North and South will still be determined to fight and determined to win.

If the U.S. is still more adventurous and brings U.S. and puppet troops of all their vassal states to attack the North, broadening it into a direct war in the entire country, the situation will then be different. Then it will not be we alone who still fight the U.S. but our entire camp. First the U.S. will not only be doing battle with 17 million people in the North but will also have to battle with hundreds of millions of Chinese people. Attacking the North would mean that the U.S. intends to attack China, because the North and China are two socialist countries linked extremely closely with each other, and the imperialists cannot attack this socialist country without also intending to attack the other. Therefore the two countries would resist together. Could the American imperialists suppress hundreds of millions of people? Certainly they could not. If they reach a stage of desperation, would the U.S. use the atomic bomb? Our camp also has the atomic bomb. The Soviet Union has sufficient atomic strength to oppose any imperialists who wish to use the atomic bomb in order to attack a socialist country, and threaten mankind. If U.S. imperialism uses the atomic bomb in those circumstances they would be committing suicide. The American people themselves would be the ones to stand up and smash the U.S. government when that government used atomic bombs. Would the U.S. dare to provoke war between the two blocks, because of the Vietnam problem; would it provoke a third world war in order to put an early end to the history of U.S. imperialism and of the entire imperialist system in general? Would other imperialist countries, factions in the U.S., and particularly the American people, agree to the U.S. warmongers throwing them into suicide? Certainly, the U.S. could not carry out their intention, because U.S. imperialism is in a weak position and not in a position of strength.

But the possibility of the broadening [of] the direct war to the North is a possibility which we must pay utmost attention, because U.S. imperialism could be adventurous. We must be vigilant and prepared to cope with each worst possibility. The best way to cope, and not to let the U.S. broaden the direct warfare in the South or in the North is to fight even more strongly and more accurately in the South, and make the puppet military units—the primary mainstay of the U.S.—rapidly fall apart, push military and political struggle forward, and quickly create the opportune moment to advance to complete defeat of U.S. imperialism and its lackeys in the South.

16.3:   The Antiwar Movement Strikes Back (1965, 1966)

As the dreary and painful months and years passed with no resolution of the Vietnam conflict, more and more Americans began to question the wisdom of their country's commitment and demand that it extricate itself from the East Asian morass.

The opposition to the war took many forms. Some Americans opposed it primarily on pragmatic grounds: The United States had no vital interest in Vietnam and no reason to pay a high price for a dispute not ours. Others considered the war wicked: America was acting as a brutal imperialist nation determined to impose its will on a weaker people.

A majority of the war's opponents confined themselves to petitions, marches, rallies, and protests. For young men of draft age, these measures often did not suffice. Many sought to avoid military service through fraudulent medical exemptions, conscientious objector status, or flight from the country. Organized opposition to Vietnam began with campus "teach-ins" in response to Lyndon Johnson's bombing campaign in the spring of 1965. Thereafter, numerous peace groups— moderates demanding early negotiations, radicals demanding immediate withdrawal—held rallies and demonstrations in major American cities around the country. Professional bodies, religious associations, and circles of intellectuals and artists denounced the war in resolutions and paid advertisements that often depicted Johnson as a coarse and brutal murderer of innocents. Militant black civil rights groups demanded that America get out of Vietnam.

The first reading below is from a pamphlet distributed by the Vietnam Day Committee (VDC) to army inductees and enlisted men at military bases in northern California. The VDC had been the organizing agency for the Berkeley teach-in in May 1965 following Johnson's "Rolling Thunder" attack. Afterward it became a semipermanent antiwar organization that drew support largely from the student radicals who, some months before, had led the Berkeley Free Speech Movement, the first of the major campus uprisings of the 1960s.

What seems to be the basis for the VDC case against American involvement in Vietnam? Is it ideological? Is it pragmatic? Does it seem to be anti-American? Why do the authors draw an analogy between the American cause in Vietnam and the Nazi rampage in Europe during World War II? Is the analogy valid? Why might the authorities have been particularly dismayed by the circulation of this pamphlet?

The second selection is a statement by the Student Nonviolent Coordinating Committee, the militant civil rights group that emerged from the 1960 student lunch-counter sit-ins in the South. By 1966, when SNCC launched this attack, its members were thoroughly disenchanted with American policy in Vietnam. Other groups were also hostile, but SNCC felt that blacks had special reasons to deplore the nation's involvement in Southeast Asia.

What were these reasons? Consider the costs of the war. Were blacks paying a disproportionate price? In what ways? What other attitudes common in the civil rights movement after 1965 might have influenced SNCC's views? Do you know if Martin Luther King, Jr., a centrist civil rights leader, ever broke with the Johnson administration over Vietnam?

Attention All Military Personnel

VIETNAM DAY COMMITTEE

You may soon be sent to Vietnam. You have heard about the war in the news; your officers will give you pep talks about it. But you probably feel as confused and uncertain as most Americans do. Many people will tell you to just follow orders and leave the thinking to others. But you have the right to know as much about this war as anyone. After all, it's you—not your Congressman—who might get killed.

Why Are We Fighting in Vietnam?

We are supposed to be fighting to protect democracy in Vietnam, and yet your own government admits that South Vietnam is run by a dictatorship. Generally Ky,[1] the latest military dictator, is as bad as they come. In a recent interview he said: "People ask me who my heroes are. I have only one—Hitler. I admire Hitler because he pulled his country together when it was in a terrible state" (*London Sunday Mirror*, July 4, 1965).

General Ky doesn't mean much to us; we're not even sure how to pronounce his name, but the South Vietnamese have lived under men like him for years. As far as the Vietnamese are concerned, we are fighting on the side of Hitlerism: and they hope we lose.

Vietnam Day Committee, "Attention All Military Personnel" (pamphlet, May 1965).

[1]Nguyen Cao Ky, a South Vietnamese air force general who, along with Nguyen Van Thieu, emerged as successor to Ngo Dinh Diem as ruler in Saigon—ED.

Who Is the Enemy?

U.S. military spokesmen have often said that their greatest problem is finding the enemy. The enemy, they say, is everywhere. The old woman feeding her chickens may have a stock of hand grenades in her hut. The little boy who trails after the American soldiers during the day slips out to give information to the guerrillas at night. The washerwoman at the American air base brings a bomb to work one day. It is impossible, say the military, to tell which are the Viet Cong and which are the civilians.

And so, because the whole Vietnamese people seem to be the enemy, the military is taking no chances. They use tear gas—a weapon designed for use against civilians. They order American troops to fire at women and children—because women and children, after all, are firing at American troops. American fighter planes destroy civilian villages with napalm; American B-52s are flattening whole regions. That is why the war in Vietnam is so often called a "dirty war."

When the South Vietnamese people see you in your foreign uniform, they will think of you as *their* enemy. You are the ones bombing their towns. They don't know whether you're a draftee or a volunteer, whether you're for the war or against it; but they're not taking any chances either.

Free Elections

The Vietnamese would like to *vote* the foreigners out of their country, but they have been denied the chance. According to the Geneva Agreement of 1954, there were supposed to be elections throughout Vietnam in 1956. But the U.S. government was certain that our man in Vietnam, Premier Diem, would lose. So we decided not to allow any election until we were sure we could win. Diem set up a political police force and put all political opposition—Communist and anti-Communist—in jail. By 1959, it was clear there weren't going to be any elections, and the guerrillas known as the Viet Cong began to fight back. By 1963 our government was fed up with Diem, but still wasn't willing to risk elections. Our CIA helped a group of Vietnamese generals to overthrow Diem and kill him. Since then there have been a series of "better" military dictators. General Ky—the man who admires Hitler—is the latest one.

Fighting for Democracy

Your job as a soldier is supposed to be "to win the people of South Vietnam." Win them to what—democracy? No, we keep military dictators in power. What then? The American way of life? But why should they care any more about our way of life than we care about theirs? We can't speak their language or even pronounce their names. We don't know anything about their religion or even what it is. We never even heard of Vietnam until Washington decided to run it.

You are supposed to be fighting "to save the Vietnamese people from Communism." Certainly Communist influence is very strong in the National Liberation Front [NLF], the rebel government. Yet most of the people support the NLF. Why? Many of the same people who now lead the NLF led the Vietnamese independence movement against the Japanese during World War II, and then went on to fight against French colonial rule. Most Vietnamese think of the NLF leaders as their country's outstanding patriots. In fact, many anti-Communists have joined the guerrilla forces in the belief that the most important thing is to get rid of foreign domination and military dictators. On the other hand, very few Vietnamese support the official government of General Ky. His army has low morale and a high desertion rate.

The Guerrillas

The newspapers and television have told us again and again what a tough fighter the Vietnamese guerrilla is. Short of ammunition and without any air cover, he can beat forces that outnumber him five or ten to one. Why do they have such high morale? They are not draftees; no draftees over fight like that. They are not high-paid, professional soldiers. Most of them are peasants who work their fields; they can't even spare the ammunition for target practice.

Their secret is that they know why they are fighting. They didn't hear about Vietnam in the newspapers; they've lived there all their lives. While we were in high school, they were living under the Diem regime and hating it. Now American planes are bombing their towns and strafing their fields; American troops have occupied their country; and if they complain out loud, an American-supported dictator sentences them to jail or the firing squad. Is it any wonder that they fight so fiercely?

Crushing the Resistance

The war in Vietnam is not being fought according to the rules. Prisoners are tortured. Our planes drop incendiary bombs on civilian villages. Our soldiers shoot at women and children. Your officers will tell you that it is all necessary, that we couldn't win the war any other way. *And they are right.* Americans are no more cruel than any other people; American soldiers don't enjoy this kind of war. But if you are going to wage war against an entire people, you have to become cruel.

The ordinary German soldier in occupied Europe wasn't especially cruel, either. But as the resistance movements grew, he *became* cruel. He shot at women and children because they were shooting at him; he never asked himself *why* they were shooting at him. When a certain town became a center of resistance activity, he followed his orders and destroyed the whole town. He knew that SS men were torturing captured resistance fighters, but it wasn't his business to interfere.

Following Orders

As a soldier you have been trained to obey orders, but as a human being you must take responsibility for your own acts. International and American law recognize that an individual soldier, even if acting under orders, must bear final legal and moral responsibility for what he does. This principle became a part of law after World War II, when the Allied nations, meeting in London, decided that German war criminals must be punished even if they committed war crimes under orders. This principle was the basis of the Nuremberg trials. We believe that the entire war in Vietnam is criminal and immoral. We believe that the atrocities which are necessary to wage this war against the people of Vietnam are inexcusable.

Oppose the War

We hope that you too find yourself, as a human being, unable to tolerate this nightmare war, and we hope that you will oppose it. We don't know what kind of risks we are taking in giving you this leaflet; you won't know what risk you will be taking in opposing the war. A growing number of GIs have already refused to fight in Vietnam and have been court-martialed. They have shown great courage. We believe that they, together with other courageous men who will join them, will have influence far out of proportion to their numbers.

There may be many other things you can do; since you are in the service, you know better than civilians what sorts of opposition are possible. But whatever you do, keep your eyes open. Draw your own conclusions from the things you see, read, and hear. At orientation sessions, don't be afraid to ask questions, and if you're not satisfied with the answers, keep asking. Take every chance you get to talk to your fellow soldiers about the war.

You may feel the war is wrong, and still decide not to face a court-martial. You may then find yourself in Vietnam under orders. You might be forced to do some fighting—but don't do any more than you have to. Good luck.

The U.S. Government Has Deceived Us

STUDENT NON-VIOLENT COORDINATING COMMITTEE

The Student Nonviolent [sic] Coordinating Committee has a right and a responsibility to dissent with United States foreign policy on any issue when it sees fit. The Student Nonviolent Coordinating Committee now states its opposition to United States' involvement in Vietnam on these grounds:

We believe the United States government has been deceptive in its claims of concern for the freedom of the Vietnamese people, just as the government has been deceptive in claiming concern for the freedom of colored people in such other countries as the Dominican Republic, the Congo, South Africa, Rhodesia, and in the United States itself.

We, the Student Nonviolent Coordinating Committee, have been involved in the black people's struggle for liberation and self-determination in this country for the past five years. Our work, particularly in the South, has taught us that the United States government has never guaranteed the freedom of oppressed citizens, and is not yet truly determined to end the rule of terror and oppression within its own borders.

We ourselves have often been victims of violence and confinement executed by United States governmental officials. We recall the numerous persons who have

Student Non-Violent Coordinating Committee, "The U.S. Government Has Deceived Us" (broadside, 1966).

been murdered in the South because of their efforts to secure their civil and human rights, and whose murderers have been allowed to escape penalty for their crimes.

The murder of Samuel Young [a young black man] in Tuskegee, Alabama, is no different than the murder of peasants in Vietnam, for both Young and the Vietnamese sought, and are seeking, to secure the rights guaranteed them by law. In each case, the United States government bears a great part of the responsibility for these deaths.

Samuel Young was murdered because United States law is not being enforced. Vietnamese are murdered because the United States is pursuing an aggressive policy in violation of international law. The United States is no respecter of persons or law when such persons or laws run counter to its needs or desires.

We recall the indifference, suspicion, and outright hostility with which our reports of violence have been met in the past by government officials.

We know that for the most part, elections in this country, in the North as well as the South, are not free. We have seen that the 1965 Voting Rights Act and the 1964 Civil Rights Act have not yet been implemented with full federal power and sincerity.

We question, then, the ability and even the desire of the United States government to guarantee free elections abroad. We maintain that our country's cry of "preserve freedom in the world" is a hypocritical mask behind which it squashes liberation movements which are not bound, and refuse to be bound, by the expediencies of United States Cold War policies.

We are in sympathy with, and support, the men in this country who are unwilling to respond to a military draft which would compel them to contribute their lives to United States aggression in Vietnam in the name of "freedom" we find so false in this country.

We recoil with horror at the inconsistency of a supposedly "free" society where responsibility to freedom is equated with the responsibility to lend oneself to military aggression. We take note of the fact that 16 percent of the draftees from this country are Negroes called on to stifle the liberation of Vietnam, to preserve a "democracy" which does not exist for them at home.

We ask, where is the draft for the freedom fight in the United States?

We therefore encourage those Americans who prefer to use their energy in building democratic forms within this country. We believe that work in the civil rights movement and with other human relations organizations is a valid alternative to the draft. We urge all Americans to seek this alternative, knowing full well that it may cost them their lives—as painfully as in Vietnam.

☆ **17** ☆

Watergate

Watergate is the name of a luxury apartment complex on the Potomac River in Washington, DC. It is also the name given to a political scandal that reached the highest levels of the American government and ultimately forced a president to resign. The president was Richard Nixon.

Nixon fought ferociously for every political success he achieved. As Dwight Eisenhower's vice-presidential running mate in 1952, he was almost pushed off the ticket by a scandal over political contributions. In 1960 he lost the presidential race by the narrowest of margins to John Kennedy and, when he ran for governor of California in 1962, he lost again. Six years later he defeated Hubert Humphrey for the presidency but the result was a squeaker. Running for reelection in 1972, he would leave nothing to chance. This time he intended to win big to make up for all the disappointments and close races of the past.

The collection of crimes and deceptions called Watergate grew out of this win-at-all-costs attitude. Running Nixon's 1972 reelection campaign was former attorney general John Mitchell, head of the Committee for the Re-Election of the President (CRP). Under him was a collection of political operators and tricksters. The CRP (called "CREEP" by the Democrats) had large amounts of money, much of it extracted from corporations by promises of government favors or threats of disfavor, and laundered to disguise its origins.

If the CRP had stopped at drowning the Democrats in cash, disaster could have been avoided. But Mitchell and other Nixon cronies insisted on using every trick in the book to confuse, distract, unbalance, and obstruct their opponents. One of these "dirty trick" operations was a break-in on June 18, 1972, at the Democratic National Committee headquarters in the Watergate complex by a group nicknamed the "plumbers," apparently to rifle files for incriminating information on the Democrats and to bug their telephones. The break-in was discovered by the police while underway, and the Watergate burglars were arrested and indicted.

Nixon apparently did not order the break-in, nor, it seems, did he know about it until his aides told him a week later that the men caught at the Watergate worked for either the White House or the CRP. His accusers would claim, however, that he approved the efforts of aides H. R. Haldeman, John Dean, and John D. Ehrlichman to hide the connection between the Watergate "plumbers" and the administration and, still more serious, to offer the arrested men executive clemency and money in exchange for their silence. In the end, it was this cover-up attempt that brought the president down.

During the summer and fall of 1972, George McGovern, the Democratic presidential candidate, sought to make the mysterious Watergate break-in a campaign issue, but the administration was able to hide it until after the Republican election sweep in November. Then the cover-up began to come apart. In January 1973 the "plumbers" were tried before Judge John Sirica, and one of them confessed that he and his fellow defendants had committed perjury in denying their connection to the White House. In February the Senate established a select committee to investigate Watergate, headed by Sam Ervin of North Carolina, and in May the committee began televised hearings that revealed that the break-in had originated with the CRP and that the president may have condoned an attempt to obstruct justice. On July 16, 1973, one of the witnesses before the Ervin committee revealed that since 1971 all confidential discussions in the Oval Office and the Executive Office Building had been taped, which meant that everything that Nixon and his colleagues had said and done about Watergate could be checked. Meanwhile, two *Washington Post* reporters, Carl Bernstein and Robert Woodward, intrigued by the mysterious events at the Watergate, began to follow a trail of proliferating leads. Their sensational revelations soon ignited a race among the media to ferret out details of the complex operations of the CRP and other administration agents. The public watched transfixed as almost daily new details emerged of misdeeds by the White House.

Nixon resisted every effort to make him surrender the tapes to a special prosecutor he had agreed, under pressure, to appoint. When the prosecutor, Archibald Cox, became too aggressive, Nixon fired him in what came to be called the "Saturday Night Massacre." The storm of public outrage that followed forced Nixon to appoint another prosecutor, Leon Jaworski, a conservative Texas lawyer who refused to be intimidated. In late April 1974, under the prodding of Jaworski and Congress, Nixon released 1200 pages of edited tape transcript that revealed the president as a mean-spirited, bigoted, win-at-any-price man, but contained no "smoking gun" directly linking him to an illegal attempt to obstruct justice.

On May 1 the House Judiciary Committee denied that the transcripts submitted represented full compliance with their demands; Nixon had held back crucial sections. In July, with support for the president fast dropping away, the Judiciary Committee began public debate on impeachment, and on the twenty-seventh voted three articles of impeachment against Nixon for attempting to "delay, impede, and obstruct the investigation" of the Watergate incident and to "cover-up, conceal, and protect those responsible" for the break-in.

The next step in the constitutional procedure would have been trial by the Senate under the House articles for "high crimes and misdemeanors," with conviction bringing removal from office. This would have been the first impeachment trial of a president since Andrew Johnson's in 1868. It was not to be. On August 5, under order by the Supreme Court, Nixon surrendered the last of the tapes, which included the long-sought "smoking gun": on June 23, 1972, the president had discussed the break-in with Haldeman, and had told him that the FBI and CIA must be ordered to desist from any further investigation of the incident on national security grounds.

This second batch of tapes ended the charade. On August 7, 1974, Senators Barry Goldwater of Arizona and Hugh Scott of Pennsylvania, representing both wings of the Republican Party, advised Nixon to resign to spare the country the long agony of an impeachment trial. Goldwater told reporters that he had counted only fifteen senators who would vote against conviction. The next evening Nixon appeared on national television to tell the American people that he had decided to resign the presidency. Shortly after noon the following day, as Nixon and his family flew to California, Gerald Ford took the oath of office as thirty-eighth president of the United States.

Watergate was a devastating blow to American pride and self-confidence. Coming so soon after defeat in Vietnam, it further eroded the legitimacy of the American political process. But did it deserve the response it evoked? In June 1972 White House press secretary Ronald Ziegler had called the break-in a "third-rate burglary," and to this day some people accept this conclusion. To many Nixon loyalists, not to speak of Nixon himself, the president had done nothing seriously wrong, and they see the destruction of his administration as a politically partisan act by liberal enemies. As you read the selections that follow, see if you can objectively evaluate the significance of the acts and the decisions that destroyed the Nixon presidency and shook Americans' faith in "the system."

17.1: The Tapes (1972)

The Watergate transcipts doomed the Nixon presidency. The House Judiciary Committee, the media, and the American people all concluded from their contents that the president was guilty of obstructing

*justice and deserved to be impeached. Most Americans were also ap-
palled by the glimpse they afforded of the president's personality and
of the slipshod way a great nation was being governed.*

*The excerpt from the Watergate tapes below is the "smoking-gun"
segment of June 23, 1972. Does it prove that Nixon sought to obstruct
justice? What does it tell us about his view of the American political
process and his opponents? Does it provide any insight into Nixon's
personality? What, if anything, does it tell us about the American presidency in those years?*

*Everyone was appalled by the vulgarity of the president's remarks
("expletive deleted") and his weak syntax and unfocused quality. But
remember, this conversation was an unguarded private one between
close associates. How many private conversations of people under
stress would sound better if reported verbatim? Would your own?*

The Smoking Gun

RICHARD NIXON

June 23, 1972

[H. R.] Haldeman: Now, on the investigation, you know the Democratic break-in
thing, we're back in the problem area because the FBI is not under control, because
[Director Patrick] Gray doesn't exactly know how to control it and they have—their
investigation is now leading into some productive area. . . . They've been able to
trace the money—not through the money itself—but through the bank sources—the
banker. And it goes in some directions we don't want it to go. Ah, also there have
been some [other] things—like an informant came in off the street to the FBI in
Miami who was a photographer or has a friend who is a photographer who developed some films through this guy [Bernard] Barker and the films had pictures of
Democratic National Committee letterhead documents and things. So it's things
like that that are filtering in. . . . [John] Mitchell came up with yesterday, and John
Dean analyzed very carefully last night and concludes, concurs now with Mitchell's
recommendation that the only way to solve this . . . is for us to have [CIA Assistant
Director Vernon] Walters call Pat Gray and just say, "Stay to hell out of this—this
is ah, [our] business here. We don't want you to go any further on it." That's not an
unusual development, and ah, that would take care of it.

President: What about Pat Gray—you mean Pat Gray doesn't want to?

Haldeman: Pat does want to. He doesn't know how to, and he doesn't have any
basis for doing it. Given this, he will then have the basis. He'll call [FBI Assistant

Hearings before the Committee on the Judiciary, House of Representatives, 93rd Congress, 2d Session
(Washington, DC: Government Printing Office, 1974), pp. 512–514.

Director] Mark Felt in, and the two of them—and Mark Felt wants to cooperate because he's ambitious—

President: Yeah.

Haldeman: He'll call him in and say, "We've got the signal from across the river[1] to put the hold on this." And that will fit rather well because the FBI agents who are working the case, at this point, feel that's what it is.

President: This is CIA? They've traced the money? Who'd they trace it to?

Haldeman: Well, they've traced it to a name, but they haven't gotten to the guy yet.

President: Would it be somebody here?

Haldeman: Ken Dahlberg.

President: Who the hell is Ken Dahlberg?

Haldeman: He gave $25,000 in Minnesota and, ah, the check went directly to this guy Barker.

President: It isn't from the Committee though, from [Maurice] Stans?

Haldeman: Yeah. It is. It's directly traceable and there's some more through some Texas people that went to the Mexican bank which can also be traced to the Mexican bank—they'll get their names today.

President: Well, I mean, there's no way—I'm just thinking if they don't cooperate, what do they say? That they were approached by the Cubans? That's what Dahlberg has to say, the Texans too.

Haldeman: Well, if they will. But then we're relying on more and more people all the time. That's the problem and they'll [the FBI] . . . stop if we could take this other route.

President: All right.

Haldeman: [Mitchell and Dean] say the only way to do that is from White House instructions. And it's got to be to [CIA Director Richard] Helms and to—ah, what's his name? . . . Walters.

President: Walters.

Haldeman: And the proposal would be that . . . [John] Ehrlichman and I call them in, and say, ah—

President: All right, fine. How do you call him in—I mean you just—well, we protected Helms from one hell of a lot of things.

Haldeman: That's what [John] Erhlichman says.

President: Of course; this [Howard] Hunt [business.] That will uncover a lot of things. You open that scab there's a hell of a lot of things and we just feel that it

[1]The CIA headquarters were located in Virginia, across the Potomac from the White House—ED.

would be very detrimental to have this thing go any further. This involves these Cubans, Hunt, and a lot of hanky-panky that we have nothing to do with ourselves. Well, what the hell, did Mitchell know about this?

Haldeman: I think so. I don't think he knew the details, but I think he knew.

President: He didn't know how it was going to be handled though—with Dahlberg and the Texans and so forth? Well who was the asshole that did? Is it [G. Gordon] Liddy? Is that the fellow? He must be a little nuts!

Haldeman: He is.

President: I mean he just isn't well screwed on, is he? Is that the problem?

Haldeman: No, but he was under pressure, apparently, to get more information, and as he got more pressure, he pushed the people harder.

President: Pressure from Mitchell?

Haldeman: Apparently. . . .

President: All right, fine, I understand it all. We won't second-guess Mitchell and the rest. Thank God it wasn't [Special White House Counsel Charles] Colson.

Haldeman: The FBI interviewed Colson yesterday. They determined that would be a good thing to do. To have him take an interrogation, which he did, and the FBI guys working the case concluded that there were one or two possibilities—one, that this was a White House (they don't think that there is anything at the Election Committee) they think it was either a White House operation and they have some obscure reasons for it—non-political, or it was a—Cuban [operation] and [involved] the CIA. And after their interrogation of Colson yesterday, they concluded it was not the White House, but are now convinced it is a CIA thing, so the CIA turnoff would—

President: Well, not sure of their analysis, I'm not going to get that involved. I'm (unintelligible).

Haldeman: No, sir, we don't want you to.

President: You call them in.

Haldeman: Good deal.

President: Play it tough. That's the way they play it and that's the way we are going to play it. . . .

President: O.K. . . . Just say (unintelligible) very bad to have this fellow Hunt, ah, he knows too damned much. . . . If it gets out that this is all involved, the Cuba thing, it would be a fiasco. It would make the CIA look bad, it's going to make Hunt look bad, and it is likely to blow the whole Bay of Pigs thing which we think would be very unfortunte—both for CIA, and for the country, at this time, and for American foreign policy. Just tell him to lay off. Don't you [think] so?

Haldeman: Yep. That's the basis to do it on. Just leave it at that. . . .

17.2:   Nixon Defends Himself (1973)

As the details of Watergate unfolded, the president sought to staunch the political hemorrhage by appealing to the voters. On April 30, 1973, he went on television to defend himself and to announce the "resignations" of three of his top aides who, he said, had failed to inform him of the "plumbers" operation. The selection that follows is an excerpt from that speech.

What is Nixon's strategy in delivering this speech? Is he throwing Erhlichman, Haldeman, and Dean to the wolves to save his neck, as critics charged? Does he deal with the question of obstruction of justice? Or does he focus purely on the illegality of the break-in and the failure of his aides to admit its authorization by the CRP? Compare Nixon's words here with his private remarks made in the Oval Office on June 23 of the previous year.

I Did Not Know about Watergate

RICHARD M. NIXON

Good evening:

I want to talk to you tonight from my heart on a subject of deep concern to every American.

In recent months, members of my Administration and officials of the Committee for the Re-election of the President—including some of my closest friends and most trusted aides—have been charged with involvement in what has come to be known as the Watergate affair. These include charges of illegal activity during and preceding the 1972 Presidential election and charges that responsible officials participated in efforts to cover up that illegal activity.

The inevitable result of these charges has been to raise serious questions about the integrity of the White House itself. Tonight I wish to address those questions.

Last June 17, while I was in Florida trying to get a few days rest after my visit to Moscow, I first learned from news reports of the Watergate break-in. I was appalled at this senseless, illegal action, and I was shocked to learn that employees of the Re-election Committee were apparently among those guilty. I immediately ordered an investigation by appropriate Government authorities. On September 15, as you will recall, indictments were brought against seven defendants in the case.

As the investigations went forward, I repeatedly asked those conducting the investigation whether there was any reason to believe that members of my Administration were in any way involved. I received repeated assurances that there were not. Because of these continuing reassurances, because I believed the reports I was

Congressional Quarterly, *Historic Documents, 1973* (Washington, DC: Congressional Quarterly, Inc., 1974), pp. 502–506.

getting, because I had faith in the persons from whom I was getting them, I discounted the stories in the press that appeared to implicate members of my Administration or other officials of the campaign committee.

Until March of this year, I remained convinced that the denials were true and that the charges of involvement by members of the White House Staff were false. The comments I made during this period, and the comments made by my Press Secretary in my behalf, were based on the information provided to us at the time we made those comments. However, new information then came to me which persuaded me that there was a real possibility that some of these charges were true, and suggesting further that there had been an effort to conceal the facts both from the public, from you, and from me.

As a result, on March 21, I personally assumed the responsibility for coordinating intensive new inquiries into the matter, and I personally ordered those conducting the investigations to get all the facts and to report them directly to me, right here in this office.

I again ordered that all persons in the Government or at the Re-election Committee should cooperate fully with the FBI, the prosecutors, and the grand jury. I also ordered that anyone who refused to cooperate in telling the truth would be asked to resign from government service. And, with ground rules adopted that would preserve the basic constitutional separation of powers between the Congress and the Presidency, I directed that members of the White House Staff should appear and testify voluntarily under oath before the Senate committee which was investigating Watergate.

I was determined that we should get to the bottom of the matter, and that the truth should be fully brought out—no matter who was involved.

At the same time, I was determined not to take precipitate action, and to avoid, if at all possible, any action that would appear to reflect on innocent people. I wanted to be fair. But I knew that in the final analysis, the integrity of this office—public faith in the integrity of this office—would have to take priority over all personal considerations.

Announcement of Resignations

Today, in one of the most difficult decisions of my Presidency, I accepted the resignations of two of my closest associates in the White House—Bob Haldeman, John Ehrlichman—two of the finest public servants it has been my privilege to know.

I want to stress that in accepting these resignations, I mean to leave no implication whatever of personal wrongdoing on their part, and I leave no implication tonight of implication on the part of others who have been charged in this matter. But in matters as sensitive as guarding the integrity of our democratic process, it is essential not only that rigorous legal and ethical standards be observed, but also that the public, you, have total confidence that they are both being observed and enforced by those in authority and particularly by the President of the United States. They agreed with me that this move was necessary in order to restore that confidence.

Because Attorney General [Richard] Kleindienst—though a distinguished public servant, my personal friend for 20 years, with no personal involvement whatever in this matter—has been a close personal and professional associate of some of those who are involved in this case, he and I both felt that it was also necessary to name a new Attorney General.

The Counsel to the President, John Dean, has also resigned.

As the new Attorney General, I have today named Elliot Richardson, a man of unimpeachable integrity and rigorously high principle. I have directed him to do everything necessary to ensure that the Department of Justice has the confidence and the trust of every law abiding person in this country.

I have given him absolute authority to make all decisions bearing upon the prosecution of the Watergate case and related matters. I have instructed him that if he should consider it appropriate, he has the authority to name a special supervising prosecutor for matters arising out of the case.

Whatever may appear to have been the case before, whatever improper activities may yet be discovered in connection with this whole sordid affair, I want the American people, I want you to know beyond the shadow of a doubt that during my term as President, justice will be pursued fairly, fully, and impartially, no matter who is involved. This office is a sacred trust and I am determined to be worthy of that trust.

Looking back at the history of this case, two questions arise:

How could it have happened?
Who is to blame?

Political commentators have correctly observed that during my 27 years in politics I have always previously insisted on running my own campaigns for office.

But 1972 presented a very different situation. In both domestic and foreign policy, 1972 was a year of crucially important decisions, of intense negotiations, of vital new directions, particularly in working toward the goal which has been my overriding concern throughout my political career—the goal of bringing peace to America, peace to the world.

That is why I decided, as the 1972 campaign approached, that the Presidency should come first and politics second. To the maximum extent possible, therefore, I sought to delegate campaign operations, to remove the day-to-day campaign decisions from the President's office and from the White House. I also, as you recall, severely limited the number of my own campaign appearances.

Who Is to Blame?

Who, then, is to blame for what happened in this case?

For specific criminal actions by specific individuals, those who committed those actions must, of course, bear the liability and pay the penalty.

For the fact that alleged improper actions took place within the White House or within my campaign organization, the easiest course would be for me to blame those to whom I delegated the responsibility to run the campaign. But that would be a cowardly thing to do.

I will not place the blame on subordinates—on people whose zeal exceeded their judgment, and who may have done wrong in a cause they deeply believed to be right.

In any organization, the man at the top must bear the responsibility. That responsibility, therefore, belongs here, in this office. I accept it. And I pledge to you tonight, from this office, that I will do everything in my power to ensure that the guilty are brought to justice, and that such abuses are purged from our political processes in the years to come, long after I have left this office.

Some people, quite properly appalled at the abuses that occurred, will say that Watergate demonstrates the bankruptcy of the American political system. I believe precisely the opposite is true. Watergate represented a series of illegal acts and bad judgments by a number of individuals. It was the system that has brought the facts to light and that will bring those guilty to justice—a system that in this case has included a determined grand jury, honest prosecutors, a courageous judge, John Sirica, and a vigorous free press.

It is essential now that we place our faith in that system—and especially in the judicial system. It is essential that we let the judicial process go forward, respecting those safeguards that are established to protect the innocent as well as to convict the guilty. It is essential that in reacting to the excesses of others, we not fall into excesses ourselves.

It is also essential that we not be so distracted by events such as this that we neglect the vital work before us, before this Nation, before America, at a time of critical importance to America and the world.

Since March, when I first learned that the Watergate affair might, in fact, be far more serious than I had been led to believe, it has claimed far too much of my time and my attention.

Whatever may now transpire in the case, whatever the actions of the grand jury, whatever the outcome of any eventual trials, I must now turn my full attention—and I shall do so—once again to the larger duties of this office. I owe it to this great office that I hold, and I owe it to you—to my country.

I know that as Attorney General, Elliot Richardson will be both fair and he will be fearless in pursuing this case wherever it leads. I am confident that with him in charge, justice will be done.

There is vital work to be done toward our goal of a lasting structure of peace in the world—work that cannot wait, work that I must do.

Tomorrow, for example, Chancellor Brandt of West Germany will visit the White House for talks that are a vital element of "The Year of Europe," as 1973 has been called. We are already preparing for the next Soviet-American summit meeting later this year.

This is also a year in which we are seeking to negotiate a mutual and balanced reduction of armed forces in Europe, which will reduce our defense budget and allow us to have funds for other purposes at home so desperately needed. It is the year when the United States and Soviet negotiators will seek to work out the second and even more important round of our talks on limiting nuclear arms, and of reducing the danger of a nuclear war that would destroy civilization as we know it. It is a year in which we confront the difficult tasks of maintaining peace in Southeast Asia and in the potentially explosive Middle East.

There is also vital work to be done right here in America: to ensure prosperity, and that means a good job for everyone who wants to work; to control inflation, that I know worries every housewife, everyone who tries to balance a family budget in America; to set in motion new and better ways of ensuring progress toward a better life for all Americans.

When I think of this office—of what it means—I think of all the things that I want to accomplish for this Nation, of all the things I want to accomplish for you.

17.3:   The Vote for Impeachment (1974)

In July 1974, for the first time in over a century, the Judiciary Committee of the House of Representatives voted articles of impeachment against a president. The selection below is a transcription of these articles. They would have become the basis for Nixon's trial by the Senate had he not resigned first.

Based on the evidence you have seen, were the articles valid? Note that none of the articles were adopted unanimously. Most of the negative votes came from Republicans. Does this support a political interpretation of Watergate? Keep in mind that Nixon himself was a highly partisan politician. He seldom sought or expected consensus, and his partisanship aroused similar responses in his Democratic and liberal opponents. Would a less partisan president have avoided the searching investigation of Watergate that destroyed him? Do you know if other presidents have employed political espionage or "dirty tricks" against their enemies?

Impeachment Articles

HOUSE JUDICIARY COMMITTEE

Article I

In his conduct of the office of President of the United States, Richard M. Nixon, in violation of his constitutional oath faithfully to execute the office of President of the United States and, to the best of his ability, preserve, protect, and defend the Constitution of the United States, and in violation of his constitutional duty to take care that the laws be faithfully executed, had prevented, obstructed, and impeded the administration of justice, in that:

Congressional Quarterly, *Historic Documents, 1974* (Washington, DC: Congressional Quarterly Inc., 1975), pp. 656–660.

On June 17, 1972, and prior thereto, agents of the Committee for the Re-election of the President committed unlawful entry of the headquarters of the Democratic National Committee in Washington, District of Columbia, for the purpose of securing political intelligence. Subsequent thereto, Richard M. Nixon, using the powers of his high office, engaged personally and through his close subordinates and agents, in a course of conduct or plan designed to delay, impede, and obstruct the investigation of such unlawful entry; to cover up, conceal and protect those responsible; and to conceal the existence and scope of other unlawful covert activities.

The means used to implement this course of conduct or plan included one or more of the following:

1. making false or misleading statements to lawfully authorized investigative officers and employees of the United States;
2. withholding relevant and material evidence or information from lawfully authorized investigative officers and employees of the United States;
3. approving, condoning, acquiescing in, and counseling witnesses with respect to the giving of false or misleading statements to lawfully authorized investigative officers and employees of the United States and false or misleading testimony in duly instituted judicial and congressional proceedings;
4. interfering or endeavoring to interfere with the conduct of investigations by the Department of Justice of the United States, the Federal Bureau of Investigation, the Office of Watergate Special Prosecution Force, and Congressional Committees;
5. approving, condoning, and acquiescing in, the surreptitious payment of substantial sums of money for the purpose of obtaining the silence or influencing the testimony of witnesses, potential witnesses or individuals who participated in such unlawful entry and other illegal activities;
6. endeavoring to misuse the Central Intelligence Agency, an agency of the United States;
7. disseminating information received from officers of the Department of Justice of the United States to subjects of investigations conducted by lawfully authorized investigative officers and employees of the United States, for the purpose of aiding and assisting such subjects in their attempts to avoid criminal liability.
8. making or causing to be made false or misleading public statements for the purpose of deceiving the people of the United States into believing that a thorough and complete investigation had been conducted with respect to allegations of misconduct on the part of personnel of the executive branch of the United States and personnel of the Committee for the Re-election of the President, and that there was no involvement of such personnel in such misconduct; or
9. endeavoring to cause prospective defendants, and individuals duly tried and convicted, to expect favored treatment and consideration in return for their silence or false testimony, or rewarding individuals for their silence or false testimony.

In all of this, Richard M. Nixon has acted in a manner contrary to his trust as President and subversive of constitutional government, to the great prejudice of the cause of law and justice and to the manifest injury of the people of the United States.

Wherefore Richard M. Nixon, by such conduct, warrants impeachment and trial, and removal from office.

—Adopted July 27 by a 27–11 vote

Article II

Using the powers of the office of President of the United States, Richard M. Nixon, in violation of his constitutional oath faithfully to execute the office of President of the United States and, to the best of his ability, preserve, protect, and defend the Constitution of the United States, and in disregard of his constitutional duty to take care that the laws be faithfully executed, has repeatedly engaged in conduct violating the constitutional rights of citizens, impairing the due and proper administration of justice and the conduct of lawful inquiries, or contravening the laws governing agencies of the executive branch and the purposes of these agencies.

This conduct has included one or more of the following:

1. He has, acting personally and through his subordinates and agents, endeavored to obtain from the Internal Revenue Service, in violation of the constitutional rights of citizens, confidential information contained in income tax returns for purposes not authorized by law, and to cause, in violation of the constitutional rights of citizens, income tax audits or other income tax investigations to be initiated or conducted in a discriminatory manner.
2. He misused the Federal Bureau of Investigation, the Secret Service, and other executive personnel, in violation or disregard of the constitutional rights of citizens, by directing or authorizing such agencies or personnel to conduct or continue electronic surveillance or other investigations or purposes unrelated to national security, the enforcement of laws, or any other lawful function of his office; he did direct, authorize, or permit the use of information obtained thereby for purposes unrelated to national security, the enforcement of laws, or any other lawful function of his office; and he did direct the concealment of certain records made by the Federal Bureau of Investigation of electronic surveillance.
3. He has, acting personally and through his subordinates and agents, in violation or disregard of the constitutional rights of citizens, authorized and permitted to be maintained a secret investigative unit within the office of the President, financed in part with money derived from campaign contributions, which unlawfully utilized the resources of the Central Intelligence Agency, engaged in covert and unlawful activities, and attempted to prejudice the constitutional right of an accused to a fair trial.
4. He has failed to take care that the laws were faithfully executed by failing to act when he knew or had reason to know that his close subordinates endeavored to impede and frustrate lawful inquiries by duly constituted executive, judicial, and legislative entities concerning the unlawful entry into the headquarters of the Democratic National Committee, and the cover up thereof, and concerning other unlawful activities including those relating to the confirmation of Richard Kleindienst as Attorney General of the United States, the electronic surveillance of private citizens, the break-in into the offices of Dr. Lewis Fielding and the campaign financing practices of the Committee to Re-elect the President [sic].
5. In disregard of the rule of law, he knowingly misused the executive branch, including the Federal Bureau of Investigation, the Criminal Division, and the Office of Watergate Special Prosecution Force, of the Department of Justice, and the Central Intelligence Agency, in violation of his duty to take care that the laws be faithfully executed.

In all of this, Richard M. Nixon has acted in a manner contrary to his trust as President and subversive of constitutional government, to the great prejudice of the cause of law and justice and to the manifest injury of the people of the United States.

Wherefore Richard M. Nixon, by such conduct, warrants impeachment and trial, and removal from office.

—Adopted July 29, by a 28–10 vote

Article III

In his conduct of the office of President of the United States, Richard M. Nixon, contrary to his oath faithfully to execute the office of President of the United States and, to the best of his ability, preserve, protect, and defend the Constitution of the United States, and in violation of his constitutional duty to take care that the laws be faithfully executed, has failed without lawful cause of excuse to produce papers and things as directed by duly authorized subpoenas issued by the Committee on the Judiciary of the House of Representatives on April 11, 1974, May 15, 1974, May 30, 1974, and June 24, 1974, and willfully disobeyed such subpoenas. The subpoenaed papers and things were deemed necessary by the Committee in order to resolve by direct evidence fundamental, factual questions relating to Presidential direction, knowledge, or approval of actions demonstrated by other evidence to be substantial grounds for impeachment of the President. In refusing to produce these papers and things Richard M. Nixon, substituting his judgment as to what materials were necessary for the inquiry, interposed the powers of the Presidency against the lawful subpoenas of the House of Representatives, thereby assuming to himself functions and judgments necessary to the exercise of the sole power of impeachment vested by the Constitution in the House of Representatives.

In all of this, Richard M. Nixon has acted in a manner contrary to his trust as President and subversive of constitutional government, to the great prejudice of the cause of law and justice, and to the manifest injury of the people of the United States.

Wherefore, Richard M. Nixon by such conduct, warrants impeachment and trial, and removal from office.

—Adopted July 30 by a 21–17 vote

☆ **18** ☆

The Reagan Revolution

By the late 1970s the public mood in America had turned sour. Abroad the United States seemed on the defensive. During these years the Soviet Union expanded its military strength and extended its influence into Central America, West Africa, and Afghanistan. Meanwhile, in the wake of the 1973 Arab-Israeli War, the Organization of Petroleum Exporting Countries (OPEC) raised oil prices to levels that threatened to strangle the American economy. At home, the worst of the sixties turmoil was past, but crime, drugs, illegitimacy, divorce, sexual permissiveness, pornography, and other social problems lingered and indeed seemed to become worse.

The American economy also seemed sick. A chronic condition called "stagflation"—simultaneous price inflation and stagnant economic growth—had gripped the nation and would not yield. At the same time the United States seemed to be losing its competitive edge in the international economy. Japan, Germany, and other Asian and European nations had captured many of America's foreign customers as well as the American domestic market for cars, steel, clothing, cameras, and electronics goods.

Perceptions of decline and retreat reawakened a dormant conservative movement, which in 1980 triumphed with the presidential election of Ronald Reagan, the former Hollywood actor and recent governor of California.

The Reagan administration that came to power in January 1981 promised to reduce inflation, restore America's international prestige, unleash economic energies, and improve the nation's moral climate. The documents that follow touch on several aspects of this conservative movement that culminated in what has been called the "Reagan Revolution." You will encounter defenders as well as detractors of conservative policies and programs, and as usual you should thoughtfully consider their contending views. The final evaluation, however, as always, is yours to make.

18.1: The New Right (1981, 1980, 1978)

The political right of the late 1970s and eighties was a composite movement. One strand derived from the individualistic conservatism that had coalesced around Barry Goldwater in 1964. Inspired by the frontier tradition, this brand was sustained and financed by self-made entrepreneurs from California, Texas, the mountain states, and the newly prosperous South.

The first document, "Why the New Right is Winning" by Richard Viguerie, focuses on what the author sees as wrong with liberalism. Can you sense a backlash against that which had been conventional in this article? Which specific complaints about liberalism reflect traditional American conservative values? Which complaints are tied specifically to political issues of the Carter years? Did the right win, or the liberals lose, the election of 1980?

The second document represents another thread in 1980s conservatism: the new religious right. It is written by the Reverend Jerry Falwell, the pastor of the Thomas Road Baptist Church in Lynchburg, Virginia. A fundamentalist who believed in the "inerrancy" of the Bible and deplored the moral damage of weakening Christian faith, Falwell had attacked the social activism of Martin Luther King, Jr., and other clerical defenders of civil rights during the 1960s. By the end of the next decade, however, he had concluded that without the active intervention of traditional religion the country would go to the dogs—or to the sinners.

In 1979, in collaboration with a new breed of secular conservative activists, Falwell and other religious conservatives organized the Moral Majority to imprint their moral vision on American public life. The Moral Majority urged pious Americans to express their beliefs at the ballot box in order to bring the reprobate nation back to virtue. The 1980 defeat of liberal candidates for Congress opposed by the Moral Majority convinced many Americans that the religious right had become a formidable political force.

The selection included here is from Falwell's Listen America!, *a 1980 book that conveys the spirit of his concerns. Falwell refers to "situation ethics" and "secular humanism." What are these, and why does he abhor them? Why does he urge the defeat of the Equal Rights*

Amendment? There is a strong patriotic theme in the excerpt from Listen America! *Is there a logical connection between Falwell's religious faith and a passionately pro-America position? Can liberals be patriots too?*

The third selection incorporates still another theme of the new right revival of the 1980s: "supply-side" economics. A creation of Arthur Laffer, Robert Mundell, and other conservative economists, the new theory sought to explain, and proposed a remedy for, stagflation. The economy's poor performance, supply-siders claimed, was the result of high taxes, government deficit spending, and the excessive emphasis on consumption (demand), all of which discouraged enterprise and investment. Rather than worrying about insufficient demand, *they argued, the government should encourage a greater* supply *of goods and services by stimulating economic effort and increased investment through tax cuts. Higher investment and production would put money in the pockets of the public in the form of wages and dividends and indirectly increase demand as well. Not only would the economy rebound in the short run, but American would be better prepared for sustained long-term growth as well.*

One of the most eloquent supply-side publicists was Jude Wanniski, a conservative journalist who wrote for the Wall Street Journal. *The article excerpted here represents Arthur Laffer's ideas as interpreted by Wanniski. In what way is supply-side economic theory consistent with other conservative views? How were the supply-siders able to test their theories in practice during the Reagan administration? Did events confirm the value of the theories? Who gained and who lost by the application of supply-side economics to federal policies?*

The New Right: We're Ready to Lead

RICHARD VIGUERIE

The election of 1980 came as a great shock to Americans who depended on the establishment media for their forecasts.

Not only did Ronald Reagan win the Presidency in an electoral landslide of historic proportions, for the first time in nearly a generation, Republicans took over the Senate.

Nationally known liberal Democrats—George McGovern, Frank Church, John Culver, Warren Magnuson, Gaylord Nelson, Birch Bayh—went down to defeat.

Richard Viguerie, *The New Right: We're Ready to Lead* (Falls Church, Virginia: Viguerie Company, 1980), pp. 1–7.

The nation's leading liberal Republican senator (one of the few remaining after the 1978 elections) went down too: Jacob Javits lost to Alfonse D'Amato.

Americans learned early on the evening of November 4 that the election the media had called a "cliffhanger" was going to be, instead, a rout.

It was not until the next morning, when they woke to find the Senate in Republican hands, that they began to sense the full dimensions of the conservative revolution.

Suddenly it was the most cautious forecasters who looked most foolish. It was the people who had played it "safe" who had proved wildly wrong.

A few of us were not surprised. We in the New Right had been working for this moment for many years. We saw that our labors were bearing fruit, and we said so.

In the first edition of this book, written in the summer of 1980 and published six weeks *before* the election, I wrote:

"I firmly believe that we are on the brink of capturing one of those Houses, the U.S. Senate, perhaps this year and almost surely by 1982."

At the same time it must have sounded as if I hadn't been reading the papers!

On the night of November 4, history walked in on the liberals uninvited.

- Ronald Reagan, the country's foremost conservative politician since 1966, won the Presidency of the United States.
- His popular vote total topped that of the incumbent President, the highly-publicized third-party candidate John Anderson, and all the splinter-party standard-bearers *combined*.
- His electoral college margin—489 to 49—was among the greatest in history. And among challengers facing incumbents, only Franklin Roosevelt in 1932—with a three-year Depression on his side—did better.

Meanwhile, in the Senate races, the results were just as astonishing.

Backed by the support and organization of the New Right, conservatives like Steve Symms of Idaho, Don Nickles of Oklahoma, Bob Kasten of Wisconsin, Jeremiah Denton of Alabama, John East of North Carolina, Charles Grassley of Iowa, James Abdnor of South Dakota, Dan Quayle of Indiana, and the only woman to win, Paula Hawkins of Florida, stepped forth to offer the nation a new generation of conservative congressional leadership.

It has been obvious for a long time that conservatism is rising and liberalism is declining. Despite all the talk in the media about "trends," "cliffhangers," and "last-minute shifts," the plain truth is that more and more Americans are sick of liberalism—and aren't afraid to say so.

The election of 1980 was the first modern conservative landslide. But it wasn't the first anit-liberal landslide.

In 1968 two anti-liberal candidates, Richard Nixon and George Wallace, won a combined 57 percent of the popular vote against the well-liked—but liberal—incumbent Vice President, Hubert Humphrey.

In 1972 Nixon, never very popular, won more than 60% of the total vote against the flamingly liberal George McGovern, who carried only one state (not even his home state of South Dakota).

Jimmy Carter didn't win election as a liberal. In the 1976 primaries he presented himself as the most conservative candidate in the field, and it was not until after he was safely in office that it became clear he intended to be a liberal President.

Even in 1980, when Democrats were sick of Carter, he won primaries—when his opponent was the even further left Edward Kennedy. Meanwhile, Ronald Reagan piled up victories against conservative, moderate and liberal candidates in his own party.

After the televised debate a week before the election, an ABC phone-in poll gave Reagan a 2 to 1 edge over Carter. Many others in media denounced the poll as "unscientific."

Maybe it was. But the election on November 4 wasn't conducted in a laboratory either. The ABC poll was just one more sign of the times—for anyone who was interested.

All the signs pointed one way. They've been pointing that way for years, and years, and years. They still do.

America is basically a conservative country. The potential for conservative revolt has always been there, under the most favorable conditions. But those conditions have to be made.

That's where the New Right comes in.

For many years, conservatives were frustrated. We had no way to translate our vision into reality.

Most importantly, we lacked a vehicle to carry our message to the voters without going through the filter of the liberal-leaning news media.

During the 1950s, 1960s, and most of the 1970s liberal politicians were able to make speeches that sounded as if they were written by Barry Goldwater. The liberals could come home on weekends and make speeches calling for a strong America, attacking waste in Washington, and complaining about big government. Then, on Monday, they could go back to Washington and vote to block new weapons systems, to give away the Panama Canal, to increase taxes, to create new government agencies, and to weaken the CIA and FBI.

Occasionally, liberal politicians would visit Communist leaders like Fidel Castro and return to the U.S. with wonderful words of praise for the Cuban dictator, praise that most voters in South Dakota or Idaho never heard.

Why did the voters in South Dakota, Idaho, Iowa, Indiana, and Wisconsin not know about their congressmen's and senators' double lives—conservative-sounding at home, actively liberal in Washington or abroad?

Because most of the national (and some of the local) media didn't report the double life the politicians were leading.

Thanks to the New Right, the "people's right to know"—which the establishment media pay loud lip-service to, when it serves their own purposes—finally became a reality.

"You can't turn back the clock."

How often we hear this line from liberals. What they really mean is that we shouldn't try to correct their mistakes.

Well, the New Right has news for them. We aren't in the business of turning back clocks.

It's the Left that has tried to stop the clock and even bring back evils civilization has left behind.

- It's the Left that has re-introduced guild privileges based on compulsory unionism, government-imposed racial and sexual discrimination, and oppressive taxes.
- It's the Left that favors a society based on state regulation, supervision, and coercion.
- It's the Left that has defended and even promoted pornography and abortion. (The clock has stopped forever for eight million unborn American children.)
- It's the Left that focuses its compassion on the criminal rather than his victims.
- It's the Left that attacks our allies rather than our enemies.
- It's the Left that favors the non-producers over the people who work.
- It's the Left that encourages American women to feel that they are failures if they want to be wives and mothers.
- It's the Left that tears apart families and neighbors by the forced busing of children.
- It's the Left that has failed to protest Communist slavery and religious persecution— evils afflicting 1.8 *billion* human beings.
- It's the Left that's fought to keep prayer out of the schools.
- It's the Left that allowed ruthless Communist take-overs in Vietnam, Laos, Cambodia and Afghanistan.
- It's the Left that allowed the takeover of Iran, one of America's strongest allies, by a group of terrorists and extremists.
- It's the Left who crippled the CIA and FBI.
- It's the Left who sold the Russians computers and other sophisticated equipment used to oppress their people.

Liberalism has pitted itself against the best instincts of the American people. Journalist Tom Bethell says the abortion issue alone has destroyed the liberals' "moral monopoly."

Put simply, most Americans no longer look up to liberals. They look down on them.

Liberals have long sensed this. They have tried to make their mistakes irreversible and election-proof. As far as possible, they have sought to turn the powers of government over to the courts and administrative agencies—that is, to unelected and unaccountable public officials.

They have found other ways to impose their will. One of the most sophisticated has been deficit spending—producing an inflation that reduces blue-collar workers' real pay by pushing them into what used to be executive tax brackets. By such means liberals have increased government's grip on our wealth without openly raising tax rates.

Somebody had to call a halt to this devious elitism. What used to be liberalism has turned into socialism on the installment plan.

With the New Right, America has found a new voice. In 1980, that voice rang out—loud and clear.

The voters of Idaho and South Dakota finally got to know the *real* Frank Church and the *real* George McGovern—the ones Fidel Castro knows.

Because conservatives have mastered the new technology, we've been able to by-pass the Left's near-monopoly of the national news media.

The New Right has also had its own ready-made network: the thousands of conservative Christian ministers whose daily broadcasts on local and national radio and TV reach an audience of 27 million. Every week, approximately 20 million people view just three such ministers—Jerry Falwell, Pat Robertson, and James Robison.

Until now this whole culture has been a dark continent to the Northeast, coastal-based national media. But these ministers are attacking issues the national media hardly mention: issues like worldwide Communist aggression, school prayer, sex on TV, the failures of the public schools. The conservative ministers are in touch with the people, and now they are in touch with each other.

The conservatism was always there. It took the New Right to give it leadership, organization, and direction.

The key word is *leadership.* Conservatives have had no lack of brilliant thinkers, brilliant writers, brilliant debaters, brilliant spokesmen. But none of these is the same thing as a leader.

George Gallup has found that 49% of registered voters in the U.S. now place themselves "right of center"—as against only 29% who say they are "left of center" and only 10% who call themselves "middle of the road."

And yet, with this tremendous potential support, the Republican Party has proved itself incapable of even mounting a consistent and effective opposition, much less rallying that 49% behind an agenda of its own. If it can't find its base with both hands, how is it going to lead the whole nation?

The New Right has proved it can lead. We're doing it. Leadership doesn't just show up on the first Tuesday in November. It has to be out there ahead of time—organizing, mailing, phoning, advertising, informing, getting names on the ballot.

The simple truth is that there is a new majority in America—and it's being led by the New Right.

We Must Return to Traditional Religious Values

JERRY FALWELL

We must reverse the trend America finds herself in today. Young people between the ages of twenty-five and forty have been born and reared in a different world than Americans of years past. The television set has been their primary baby-sitter. From the television set they have learned situation ethics and immorality—they have learned a loss of respect for human life. They have learned to disrespect the family as God has established it. They have been educated in a public-school system that is permeated with secular humanism. They have been taught that the Bible is just another book of literature. They have been taught that there are no absolutes in our world today. They have been introduced to the drug culture. They have been reared by the family and by the public school in a society that is greatly void of discipline and character-building. These same young people have been reared under the influence of a government that has taught them socialism and welfarism. They have been taught to believe that the world owes them a living whether they work or not.

I believe that America was built on integrity, on faith in God, and on hard work. I do not believe that anyone has ever been successful in life without being willing to add that last ingredient—diligence or hard work. We now have second- and third-generation welfare recipients. Welfare is not always wrong. There are those who do need welfare, but we have reared a generation that understands neither the dignity nor the importance of work.

Every American who looks at the facts must share a deep concern and burden for our country. We are not unduly concerned when we say that there are some very dark clouds on America's horizon. I am not a pessimist, but it is indeed a time for truth. If Americans will face the truth, our nation can be turned around and can be saved from the evils and the destruction that have fallen upon every other nation that has turned its back on God.

There is no excuse for what is happening in our country. We must, from the highest office in the land right down to the shoe shine boy in the airport, have a return to biblical basics. If the Congress of our United States will take its stand on that which is right and wrong, and if our President, our judiciary system, and our state and local leaders will take their stand on holy living, we can turn this country around.

I personally feel that the home and the family are still held in reverence by the vast majority of the American public. I believe there is still a vast number of Americans who love their country, are patriotic, and are willing to sacrifice for her. I remember that time when it was positive to be patriotic, and as far as I am concerned, it still is. I remember as a boy, when the flag was raised, everyone stood proudly and put his hand upon his heart and pledged allegiance with gratitude. I remember when the band struck up "The Stars and Stripes Forever," we stood and goose pimples would run all over me. I remember when I was in elementary school during World War II, when every report from the other shores meant something to us. We were not out demonstrating against our boys who were dying in Europe and Asia. We were praying for them and thanking God for them and buying war bonds to help pay for the materials and artillery they needed to fight and win and come back.

I believe that Americans went to see this country came back to basics, back to values, back to biblical morality, back to sensibility, and back to patriotism. Americans are looking for leadership and guidance. It is fair to ask the question, "If 84 per cent of the American people still believe in morality, why is America having such internal problems?" We must look for the answer to the highest places in every level of government. We have a lack of leadership in America. But Americans have been lax in voting in and out of office the right and the wrong people.

My responsibility as a preacher of the Gospel is one of influence, not of control, and that is the responsibility of each individual citizen. Through the ballot box Americans must provide for strong moral leadership at every level. If our country will get back on the track in sensibility and moral sanity, the crises that I have herein mentioned will work out in the course of time and with God's blessings.

It is now time to take a stand on certain moral issues, and we can only stand if we have leaders. We must stand against the Equal Rights Amendment, the feminist revolution, and the homosexual revolution. We must have a revival in this country. . . .

As a preacher of the Gospel, I not only believe in prayer and preaching, I also believe in good citizenship. If a labor union in America has the right to organize and improve its working conditions, then I believe that the churches and the pastors, the priests, and the rabbis of America have a responsibility, not just the right, to see to it that the moral climate and conscience of Americans is such that this nation can be healed inwardly. If it is healed inwardly, then it will heal itself outwardly. . . .

Americans have been silent much too long. We have stood by and watched as American power and influence have been systematically weakened in every sphere of the world.

We are not a perfect nation, but we are still a free nation because we have the blessing of God upon us. We must continue to follow in a path that will ensure that blessing. . . .

Let us never forget that as our Constitution declares, we are endowed by our Creator with certain inalienable rights. It is only as we abide by those laws established by our Creator that He will continue to bless us with these rights. We are endowed our rights to freedom and liberty and the pursuit of happiness by the God who created man to be free and equal.

The hope of reversing the trends of decay in our republic now lies with the Christian public in America. We cannot expect help from the liberals. They certainly are not going to call our nation back to righteousness and neither are the pornographers, the smut peddlers, and those who are corrupting our youth. Moral Americans must be willing to put their reputations, their fortunes, and their very lives on the line for this great nation of ours. Would that we had the courage of our forefathers who knew the great responsibility that freedom carries with it. . . .

Our Founding Fathers separated church and state in function, but never intended to establish a government void of God. As is evidenced by our Constitution, good people in America must exert an influence and provide a conscience and climate of morality in which it is difficult to go wrong, not difficult for people to go right in America.

I am positive in my belief regarding the Constitution that God led in the development of that document, and as a result, we here in America have enjoyed 204 years of unparalleled freedom. The most positive people in the world are people who believe the Bible to be the Word of God. The Bible contains a positive message. It is a message written by 40 men over a period of approximately 1,500 years under divine inspiration. It is God's message of love, redemption, and deliverance for a fallen race. What could be more positive than the message of redemption in the Bible? But God will force Himself upon no man. Each individual American must make His choice. . . .

Americans must no longer linger in ignorance and apathy. We cannot be silent about the sins that are destroying this nation. The choice is ours. We must turn America around or prepare for inevitable destruction. I am listening to the sounds that threaten to take away our liberties in America. And I have listened to God's admonitions and His direction—the only hopes of saving America. Are you listening too?

Taxes, Revenues, and the "Laffer Curve"

JUDE WANNISKI

As Arthur Laffer has noted, "There are always two tax rates that yield the same revenues." When an aide to President Gerald Ford asked him once to elaborate, Laffer (who is Professor of Business Economics at the university of Southern California) drew a simple curve to illustrate his point. The point, too, is simple enough—though, like so many simple points, it is also powerful in its implications.

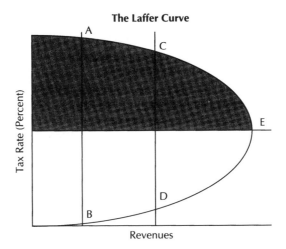

The Laffer Curve

When the tax rate is 100 percent, all production ceases in the money economy (as distinct from the barter economy, which exists largely to escape taxation). People will not work in the money economy if all the fruits of their labors are confiscated by the government. And because production ceases, there is nothing for the 100-percent rate to confiscate, so government revenues are zero.

On the other hand, if the tax rate is zero, people can keep 100 percent of what they produce in the money economy. There is no governmental "wedge" between earnings and after-tax income, and thus no governmental barrier to production. Production is therefore maximized, and the output of the money economy is limited only by the desire of workers for leisure. But because the tax rate is zero, government revenues are again zero, and there can be no government. So at a 0-percent tax

Jude Wanniski, "Taxes, Revenues, and the 'Laffer Curve.'" Reprinted from *The Public Interest,* No. 50 (Winter 1978), pp. 3–16. © 1978 by National Affairs, Inc.

rate the economy is in a state of anarchy, and at a 100-percent tax rate the economy is functioning entirely through barter.

In between lies the curve. If the government reduces its rate to something less than 100 percent, say to point A, some segment of the barter economy will be able to gain so many efficiencies by being in the money economy that, even with near-confiscatory tax rates, after-tax production would still exceed that of the barter economy. Production will start up, and revenues will flow into the government treasury. By lowering the tax rate, we find an increase in revenues.

On the bottom end of the curve, the same thing is happening. If people feel that they need a minimal government and thus institute a low tax rate, some segment of the economy, finding that the marginal loss of income exceeds the efficiencies gained in the money economy, is shifted into either barter or leisure. But with that tax rate, revenues do flow into the government treasury. This is the situation at point B. Point A represents a very high tax rate and very low production. Point B represents a very low tax rate and very high production. Yet they both yield the same revenue to the government.

The same is true of points C and D. The government finds that by a further lowering of the tax rate, say from point A to point C, revenues increase with the further expansion of output. And by raising the tax rate, say from point B to point D, revenues also increase, by the same amount.

Revenues and production are maximized at point E. If, at point E, the government lowers the tax rate again, output will increase, but revenues will fall. And if, at point E, the tax rate is raised, both output and revenue will decline. The shaded area is *the prohibitive range for government,* where rates are unnecessarily high and can be reduced with gains in *both* output and revenue.

Tax Rates and Tax Revenues

The next important thing to observe is that, except for the 0-percent and 100-percent rates, there are no numbers along the "Laffer curve." Point E is not 50 percent, although it may be, but rather a variable number: *It is the point at which the electorate desires to be taxed.* At points B and D, the electorate desires more government goods and services and is willing—without reducing its productivity—to pay the higher rates consistent with the revenues at point E. And at points A and C, the electorate desires more private goods and services in the money economy, and wishes to pay the lower rates consistent with the revenues at point E. It is the task of the statesman to determine the location of point E, and follow its variations as closely as possible. . . .

Work vs. Productivity

The idea behind the "Laffer curve" is no doubt as old as civilization, but unfortunately politicians have always had trouble grasping it. In his essay, *Of Taxes,* written in 1756, David Hume pondered the problem:

> Exorbitant taxes, like extreme necessity, destroy industry by producing despair; and even before they reach this pitch, they raise the wages of the labourer and manufacturer, and heighten the price of all commodities. An attentive disinter-

ested legislature will observe the point when the emolument ceases, and the prejudice begins. But as the contrary character is much more common, 'tis to be feared that taxes all over Europe are multiplying to such a degree as will entirely crush all art and industry; tho' perhaps, their first increase, together with other circumstances, might have contributed to the growth of these advantages.

The chief reason politicians and economists throughout history have failed to grasp the idea behind the "Laffer curve" is their confusion of work and productivity. Through both introspection and observation, the politician understands that when tax rates are raised, there is a tendency to work harder and longer to maintain after-tax income. What is no so apparent, because it requires analysis *at the margin,* is this: As taxes are raised, individuals in the system may indeed work harder, but their productivity declines. . . .

Imagine that there are three men who are skilled at building houses. If they work together, one works on the foundation, one on the frame, and the third on the roof. Together they can build three houses in three months. If they work separately, each building his own home, they need six months to build the three houses. If the tax rate on homebuilding is 49 percent, they will work together, since the government leaves them a small gain from their division of labor. But if the tax rate goes to 51 percent, they suffer a net loss because of their teamwork, and so they will work separately. When they were pooling their efforts, since they could produce six houses in the same time it would take them to build three houses working alone, the government was collecting revenues almost equivalent to the value of three completed homes. At the 51-percent tax rate, however, the government loses all the revenue, and the economy loses the production of the three extra homes that could have been built by their joint effort. . . .

The Politics of the "Laffer Curve"

The "Laffer curve" is a simple but exceedingly powerful analytical tool. In one way or another, all transactions, even the simplest, take place along it. The homely adage, "You can catch more flies with molasses than with vinegar," expresses the essence of the curve. But empires are built on the bottom of this simple curve and crushed against the top of it. The Caesars understood this, and so did Napoleon (up to a point) and the greatest of the Chinese emperors. The Founding Fathers of the United States knew it well; the arguments for union (in *The Federalist Papers*) made by [Alexander] Hamilton, [James] Madison, and [John] Jay reveal an understanding of the notion. Until War I—when progressive taxation was sharply increased to help finance it—the United States successfully remained out of the "prohibitive range."

In the 20th century, especially since World War I, there has been a constant struggle by all the nations of the world to get down the curve. The United States managed to do so in the 1920's, because Andrew Mellon understood the lessons of the "Laffer curve" for the domestic economy. . . .

The stock market crash of 1929 and the subsequent global depression occurred because Herbert Hoover unwittingly contracted the world economy with his high-tariff policies, which pushed the West, as an economic unit, up the "Laffer curve."

Hoover compounded the problem in 1934 by raising personal tax rates almost up to the levels of 1920. . . .

The British empire was built on the lower end of the "Laffer curve" and dismantled on the upper end. The high wartime rates imposed to finance the Napoleonic wars were cut back sharply in 1816, despite warnings from "fiscal experts" that the high rates were needed to reduce the enormous public debt of £900 million. For the following 60 years, the British economy grew at an unprecedented pace, as a series of finance ministers used ever-expanding revenues to lower steadily the tax rates and tariffs.

In Britain, though, unlike the United States, there was no Mellon to risk lowering the extremely high tax rates imposed to finance World War I. As a result, the British economy struggled through the 1920's and 1930's. After World War II, the British government again made the mistake of not sufficiently lowering tax rates to spur individual initiative. Instead, the postwar Labour government concentrated on using tax policy for Keynesian objectives—i.e., increasing consumer demand to expand output. On October 23, 1945, tax rates were cut on lower-income brackets and surtaxes were added to the already high rates on the upper-income brackets. Taxes on higher incomes were increased, according to Chancellor of the Exchequer Hugh Dalton, in order to "continue that steady advance toward economic and social equality which we have made during the war and which the Government firmly intends to continue in peace."

From that day in 1945, there has been no concerted political voice in Britain arguing for are reduction of the high tax rates. Conservatives have supported and won tax reductions for business, especially investment-tax income credits. But while arguing for a reduction of the 83-percent rate on incomes above £20,000 (roughly $35,000 at current exchange rates) of earned income and the 98-percent rate on "unearned income" from investments, they have insisted that government *first* lower its spending, in order to permit the rate reductions. Somehow, the spending levels never can be cut. Only in the last several months of 1977 has Margaret Thatcher, the leader of the opposition Conservative Party, spoken of reducing the high tax rates as a way of expanding revenues.

In the United States, in September 1977, the Republic National Committee unanimously endorsed the plan of Representative Jack Kemp of New York for cutting tax rates as a way of expanding revenues through increased business activity. This was the first time since 1953 that the GOP had embraced the concept of tax cuts! In contrast, the Democrats under President Kennedy sharply cut tax rates in 1962–64 (though making their case in Keynesian terms). The reductions successfully moved the United States economy down the "Laffer curve," expanding the economy and revenues.

It is crucial to Western economic expansion, peace, and prosperity that "conservative" parties move in this direction. They are, after all, traditionally in favor of income growth, with "liberals" providing the necessary political push for income redistribution. A welfare state is perfectly consistent with the "Laffer curve," and can function successfully along its lower range. But there must be income before there can be income redistribution. Most of the economic failures of this century can rightly be charged to the failure of conservatives to press for tax rates along the lower range of the "Laffer curve." Presidents Eisenhower, Nixon and Ford were timid in this crucial area of public policy. The Goldwater Republicans of 1963–64, in fact, emphatically opposed the Kennedy tax-rate cuts!

If, during the remainder of this decade, the United States and Great Britain demonstrate the power of the "Laffer curve" as an analytical tool, its use will spread, in the developing countries as well as the developed world. Politicians who understand the curve will find that they can defeat politicians who do not, other things being equal. Electorates all over the world always know when they are unnecessarily perched along the upper edge of the "Laffer curve," and will support political leaders who can bring them back down.

18.2: The Liberals Hit Back (1982, 1981)

Needless to say, many Americans never accepted the views of the revived political right. Liberal and left-of-center publications and critics disliked virtually everything about the New Right and denounced the Reagan administration and its policies. The first selection is an attack from the political left by economist Robert L. Heilbroner on Reaganite economic policy that goes beyond objections to supply-side tax policies. What is Heilbroner really indicting? Are his characterizations of the prevailing socioeconomic system well taken? Is it fair to hold the Reagan administration, or conservatives generally, responsible for the failings that Heilbroner sees in American society in the 1980s?

The religious right also encountered opposition. Religious liberals objected to the theology as well as the social philosophy of the Moral Majority and of the Protestant fundamentalists who formed its core. In the second selection Robert McAfee Brown, a prominent Presbyterian minister and professor of religion at New York's liberal Union Theological Seminary, takes issue with Falwell and his colleagues. What is the stated religious basis for Brown's disagreements with the Moral Majority? Do you think Brown is solely concerned with what the Bible teaches? In what way do his politics disagree with Falwell's? Why do the two clergymen reach such different social and political conclusions?

The third selection is an attack on Reagan's policies by liberal public interest attorney Mark Green. Written in early 1981, just as the first Reagan budget proposals were wending their way through Congress, the piece takes issue with the underlying premises of supply-side economic theories. What are Green's major objections to "Reaganomics"? Why does he call the Reagan program "Cowboy Economics"? What does he anticipate will happen if the Reagan proposals pass? Has time confirmed or refuted Green's predictions?

The Demand for the Supply-Side

ROBERT L. HEILBRONER

Supply-side economics has taken Washington by storm. Both a diagnosis and a prescription, supply-side economics comprises ideas about what is wrong with the economy and remedies to put it right. As its name would indicate, both diagnosis and prescription emphasize the actual production of goods and services rather than the buying of them. From this vantage point, supply-siders see our fundamental difficulties as constraints, mainly caused by taxes that deter productive effort, rather than as problems deriving from a lack of purchasing power. We catch a vision of the economy as a coiled spring held down by the weight of government. Remove the weight, and the spring will reveal its inherent force.

Most of the heated discussions about supply-side economics are concerned with how much tension the spring really has and how vigorously it will respond to the removal of various tax disincentives. I shall come back to these matters later. But it seems foolish to begin an appraisal of supply-side economics with debates about how far we must cut income taxes to achieve renewed growth, or how quickly inflation will be overcome by increased output. At the root of all supply-side remedies lie profoundly held if sometimes implicit convictions about the nature of the capitalist system itself. Since I am convinced that these views are wrong, I cannot get much exercised about the particular prescription on supply-side medicines. . . .

To turn to . . . strictly economic matters: supply-side economics puts forward two policy prescriptions. First, it advocates a substantial reduction in marginal tax rates, in order to create a burst of response. A response of what? The supply-siders are convinced that more hours will be worked, that less effort will be diverted into the underground economy, that more risks will be taken. In a word, we will produce more, giving rise to more employment, and ultimately to a diminution of inflationary pressure.

Here everything hinges on the crucial matter of how individuals or firms respond to tax cuts. The fact of the matter is that we do not know very much about this problem. Worse, it is possible to construct two quite opposing, but equally convincing predictions. The supply-siders[1] see individuals using their tax bonanzas, such as the Kemp-Roth proposed reduction of taxes by 10 percent a year for three years, to add to their savings, or as a spur to more effort because more income will be kept. Skeptics see an entirely different picture. They see families reacting to a tax bonanza the way they react to all income increases: they will spend about 95 percent of it. They also see an increase in their after-tax incomes permitting a lot of people to give up moonlighting, overtime, or other distasteful tasks to which high taxes have driven them. Thus the skeptics see the impact of supply-side policies as boosting inflation far more than production. I number myself among the skeptics.

Robert L. Heilbroner, "The Demand for the Supply-Side," in Robert Fink, ed., *Supply-Side Economics: A Critical Appraisal* (Frederick, MD: University Publications of America, 1982), pp. 80–91. An imprint of Greenwood Publishing Group, Inc., Westport, CT. Reprinted with permission.
[1]A supply-side measure introduced in Congress by Representative Jack Kemp of New York and Senator William Roth of Delaware to federal income taxes—ED.

And what about the stimulus to production that firms will experience, as taxes are rolled back and onerous regulations repealed? In all likelihood there will be some response: the crucial question is how much. Again two views are plausible. One of them, exemplified by George Gilder's[2] stress on the creative efforts of individual entrepreneurs, sees a great burst of small business formation, not only creating jobs but providing the innovative zest needed to restore economic vitality. The other, more skeptical view looks to the great corporations that dominate so much of economic life and asks whether tax reductions or milder regulation will suffice to turn the automobile industry around, to reinvigorate the steel industry, to strengthen the transportation system, to solve the energy problem, and the like. Once again, I number myself among the skeptics.

Second, supply-siders want to roll back government, not merely to get it off our backs, but also because government is perceived as essentially a wasteful, not a productive, use of resources. This last is a very interesting contention. I would be the last to deny the presence of government waste: the MX missile system, the space shuttle, the tax subsidies to various upper-income groups, not to mention the petty cadging and occasional grand larceny among welfare clients. However, I want to call attention to a curious aspect of the question of waste. It is that there is no waste in the private sector. This is the case because all "wasteful" activities are eliminated by the market, like the famous Edsel. On the other hand, whatever survives the test of the market is not waste. The five giant buildings that will be erected between 53rd and 57th Streets along Madison Avenue are not waste, whatever chaos they create, unless they cannot be rented. The $100,000 Rolls Royce is not waste, assuming that it sells. There is not waste in the production of *anything* that sells, because the very act of purchase provides the justification for whatever resources have been used.

Clearly there are entirely different criteria for waste in the public and private domains. Suppose that the scrutiny usually directed at government were brought to bear on private output, and that each act of private production had to justify itself by the *noneconomic* criteria we apply to public output. Would we not find a great deal of waste in the private sphere? And suppose that the government limited its production to those things it could sell—pocket-sized missiles and salable services of all kinds. Would not all waste disappear from the public sphere? This leads one to think about the meaning of the "waste" perceived from the supply side.

It leads one also to reflect on the ideological element within supply-side thinking. To be sure, all social orders have ideologies, and none could exist without them. Therefore societies never think of their prevailing views as being "ideological," but rather as expressing self-evident or natural truths. As [historian] Immanuel Wallerstein has acutely remarked, during most periods of history there is effectively only one class that is conscious of itself, and this dominant class sincerely expresses its own views as representing those of the entire society. Thus the senators of Rome, the lords of the manor, the monarchs of France and England, and the members of the Soviet elite all speak with unself-conscious assurance in the name of their soci-

---

[2]A conservative writer on social and economic themes—ED.

eties. None feels itself to be a "privileged" class or thinks its views to be other than universal. . . .

The question to be pondered is why supply-side economics has attracted the worst ideology, and why it has dulled the sensibilities of the best ideologists. I am ashamed to say the one convincing reason that occurs to me: supply-side economics has as its immediate objective the improvement of the conditions of the rich. What bonanzas will result from the lowering of the high marginal rate on property income and on the reduction of the capital gains tax! I too rub my hands at the prospect. To be sure, like all policies, the *ultimate* objective of supply-side economics is the improvement of the condition of everyone. Just the same, I do not think supply-side economics would adduce quite the same fervor, or quite the same dulling of critical sensibilities, if its *immediate* aim were the improvement of the poor and its ultimate aim the bettering of the rich. Self-interest has extraordinary powers of persuasion. . . .

What is likely to happen over the next decade? Nothing. I say so from a profound skepticism about the efficacy of supply-side stimuli. But from a more history-laden point of view, I mean something different by "nothing." I mean that the slow, almost invisible trends of the past will continue to have their way, not because these trends have a life of their own but because they express the inner motions, the self-created dynamic of the system. I will mention only two of these trends:

1. *State-owned or state-dependent organizations will emerge as the leading agents of accumulation.* We are all familiar with the slow drift in the texture of the representative firm, from a single-product, single-plant, single-family enterprise to a multi-product, multi-plant, multi-national managerial bureaucracy. This has been the consequence of the continuing division of labor and of technologies of control which have brought concentration and centralization in virtually every field of human endeavor.

   This trend now seems likely to move to a new level of organizational size and strength by combining the capital-mobilizing and competition-buffering abilities of the state with the independence and drive of private management. Most capitalist nations today have public-private firms in airlines or airframes, in steel, automobiles, chemicals, and the like.

   Many of these public-private firms have been formed to prevent private bankruptcies. That in no way weakens my argument. But the Japanese present a more interesting case. Japan is evidently now preparing to enter the semiconductor industry on a public-private basis with one or two huge firms. That industry today is still dominated by the United States, where numerous businesses compete vigorously for market shares. The result, as Lester Thurow[3] has written, is that in the U.S. the market is likely to eliminate the losers, and the Japanese will thereafter eliminate the winners.

   Whether or not the Japanese "model" of public-private coordination can be exported, I would think that statist enterprise of some sort is very likely to be the form in which the accumulation of capital is carried on in the coming years.

2. As part of this statist movement, I would also expect to see the emergence of an ever more explicit reliance on national planning. This will assume two forms. One

[3]Thurow is a liberal economist—ED.

will be macroplanning for adequate employment, probably through government work programs, for acceptable price behavior through a network of controls and mandatory incomes policies, and for international buffers through protectionism. The other form of planning will be microplanning aimed at channeling labor and capital into socially advantageous uses and at coping with disruptive problems such as energy, urban decay, etc.

It may be objected that planning does not "work," that we are now in retreat from it—a retreat led by supply-side economics. That depends on what one means by "work." As I see it, *no organizational system can smoothly combine the explosive technology, restless polity, and deadening work experience of contemporary industrial society.* This is as true for self-styled socialist societies as for capitalist ones. Hence I do not expect state capitalism to "work" particularly well, but I expect it to survive and to continue the function that is the driving force of capitalism—the accumulation of capital by means of wage labor.

It is possible, of course, that ideological opposition may reverse this two-century-long trend toward centralization. Social orders sometimes refuse to adopt changes which, to outsiders, would preserve their regimes: one thinks of the refusal of the Roman senators to undertake land reform, or of the opposition of the French aristocracy to tax reform. To identify historical trends is not to deny social orders the right to commit suicide.

These considerations lead inescapably to the question of how long capitalism is likely to survive. I would think for quite a long while. No one can project an "indefinite" life span for capitalism. It is by its nature dynamic, and is constantly changing. Today it is pressing against the absorptive limits of the environment and thereby threatening the pace and scope of accumulation. Its moral cement, as I have remarked, is dissolving in its commercial ethic. It faces the contradictions of its antagonistic policy and economy, and the Laocoön-like struggles of its accumulation mechanics. Its broad movement today seems toward a bureaucratic statist regime. After that, who can tell?

Nonetheless, I do not see any immediate "end" of capitalism. Much of the world remains to be penetrated by its formidable mode of labor organization, its seductive technology, its intellectual brilliance. However decadent at its center, capitalism is today without a serious rival as an economic system, dangerous though the Soviet Union may be as a military rival.

This expectation of continued life seems all the more likely because, as I have just said, there is really nothing yet visible beyond capitalism. As an imaginable institutional arrangement, socialism has become a word almost without content. If it means the nationalization of industry or private-public planning, it can be seen—at least, so I suggest—as the extension of capitalism. As a deindustrialization of society it holds forth the specter of a catastrophic decline in living standards. As a vast extension of worker participation, it suffers from a complete lack of any economic and political institutions—or conception of such institutions—within which workers' autonomy could be expressed. In the underdeveloped world it is all too likely that socialist revolutions will usher in narrow, inefficient, and xenophobic regimes.

Hence there is little enthusiasm for socialism today, always excepting the burning desire of oppressed peoples or abused workers to throw off cruel or simply sclerotic regimes. After that, the realities of the industrial process, the impatient expectations of the masses, the contagion of Western ideas and goods must somehow be accommodated. The next stage of economic history, whatever its label, will not be a pleasant one. That supply-side economics, the darling and fad of conservative thought, imagines itself to be the vehicle of this next stage strikes me as an extraordinary fantasy. It is to confuse a small eddy, located in a few board rooms and academic centers, with the Gulf Stream of history.

The Need for a Moral Minority

ROBERT McAFEE BROWN

Some of you may have misread the title "The Need for a Moral Minority," and assumed that I was going to address the Moral Majority. I am going to make some references to the Moral Majority in the course of these remarks, but I do not want to concentrate exclusively on that movement. I particularly do not want to have the Moral Majority setting my agenda, or our agendas, for the eighties. I think that agenda is somewhat politically naive and theologically un-Biblical; I will try to footnote that in a little while.

My overall concern is much more how we can relate religion and politics positively. If along the way we can learn some things from the Moral Majority, about how not to do it, I am willing to call that a gain.

This whole problem of a religious presence on the political scene which has been highlighted for us in this rather recent emergence of the theological right wing, the problem of religion of the political scene is illustrated for me by a comment from an anonymous 17th century writer, one of my favorite anonymous comments. This writer wrote: "I had rather see coming toward me a whole regiment with drawn swords, than one lone Calvinist convinced that he is doing the will of God." Now that statement illustrates both the glory and demonry of Calvinism, and by a not very difficult extension, the potential glory and potential demonry of all political involvement on the part of religiously minded persons. On the one hand, there is something immensely freeing and energizing about the feeling that one is doing God's will, and that the outcome of one's activity is therefore safe in God's hands. Such an attitude can liberate one to new kinds of courage, to immense risk taking, even to the point of death. . . .

But there can be a demonry as well in the invoking of God's support which we find exhibited when individuals or groups decide what they want to impose on others, and then claim divine sanction for it. This gives them carte blanche to do whatever they feel is necessary to stop their opponents since their opponents, being opposed to them, are clearly opposed to God as well, and do not finally deserve the right to speak or act or persuade, and Christians have often been guilty of this. The Crusades were an example, Christian anti-Semitism is another, and sometimes the Christian willingness to

Robert McAfee Brown, "The Need for a Moral Minority," in Herbert Vetter, ed., *Speak Out Against the New Right* (Boston: Beacon Press, 1982), pp. 118–126.

kill, whether in support of a Nazi ideology, or extreme nationalism, whether of the Russian or American variety, these are other instances that come to mind. And as I look at the current American religious scene, it is this tendency that seems to me in danger of characterizing this recently emerged religious right of which [the] Moral Majority is at least one very clear-cut example.

Mr. Falwell, Jerry Falwell, the leader of that movement, states that he knows just what is wrong with our country, and tells us: "God has called me to action. I have a divine mandate to go into the halls of Congress and fight for laws that will save America." As this position develops, it turns out that those who disagree with him are really by definition disagreeing with God, since he, and not they, have access to God's will. Liberals, for example, who Mr. Falwell abominates, are not just political liberals or theological liberals, they are godless liberals. They are the ones who must be removed from public office, since they are not only wrong, but evil. What we must have in office are God-fearing, Bible-believing Christians, which is bad news to Jews and secularists.

I do not for a moment challenge Mr. Falwell's right or anybody's right to get into the American political process, to work for change, to support candidates, urge people to vote and all the rest. That is the way the American system works, and the more people that are doing that, the better for the health of the system. And it would be a very perverse logic to claim that only people with whom I agree ought to be engaging in political activity and I want no part of such an argument. I have taken my own political stands in the past; I intend to keep doing so in the present and in the future, so can and should everyone, whether named Billy Graham or Bill Coffin, whether named Jerry Falwell or Robert Drinan.[1]

Furthermore, this emergence of the Radical Right on the political scene, means that there is one ancient battle we are not going to have to fight for a while. For the most of my adult life, at any rate, people on the theological right have been saying religion and politics do not mix. The rest of us have been saying, "They do too mix." And now, for better or for worse, that message has been heard.

The question is no longer, "Do religion and politics mix?" The question is simply, "What is the nature of the mix?" And it is the nature of the mix, as far as groups like [the] Moral Majority are concerned, that is increasingly concerning me, and even on some levels beginning to frighten me. Now let me say just enough about that kind of mix so that I can then set the stage in the latter part of these comments, for what seems to me a more appropriate alternative.

In Christian terms, and I think in terms with which all Jews could also agree, my real complaint about the Moral Majority's intrusion of the Bible into American politics, is that they are not biblical enough. I do not for a moment concede that they have the Bible on their side and that the rest of us are nothing but godless liberals or secular humanists which, in Mr. Falwell's lexicon, is very close to being either a Socialist or a Communist.

---

[1]Billy Graham, a conservative Protestant revivalist; William Sloane Coffin, a liberal Protestant minister; Robert Drinan, a liberal Catholic priest—ED.

So let me illustrate that in two ways. First of all, it seems to me that the Moral Majority's biblically inspired political agenda involves a very selective, very partial, and therefore very distorted use of the Bible. They have isolated a set of concerns that they say get to the heart of what is wrong with America—homosexuality, abortion, and pornography. These are the things that are wrong and that are destroying our nation. What we need to do, what we need to be for, basically for prayer in public schools, and for more bombs. Jesus wants our kids to pray and he wants the Pentagon to be able to kill more people if necessary. I know that sounds a little crude, but I believe it is. I am not denying that there are moral dimensions involved in all those issues and that people can take different moral positions in response to them, but the notion that they represent what the Hebrew and Christian scriptures offer us as the key for understanding what is wrong with the world today, is one that strikes me as grotesque.

Take the issue of homosexuality. If one turns to the scriptures as a whole, to try to come up with their central concerns, homosexuality is going to be very low on such a list even if indeed it makes the list at all. There are perhaps seven very ambiguous verses in the whole biblical canon that even allude to it and I will any day subordinate the minuscule import of those seven verses, isolated verses, to hundreds and hundreds of places where the scriptures are dealing over and over again with questions of social justice, the tendency of the rich to exploit the poor, the need for all of us to have a commitment to the hungry, the need for nations not to put their major trust in armaments, the concern for the sick, the recognition that all people are children of God, even if they are Russians or Cubans or Salvadoreans. The Moral Majority creates an agenda and then proceeds to impose that agenda on scripture by developing little strings of unrelated verses to give divine sanction to the position. As those who work with the Bible know, one can prove absolutely anything that way. You can make a biblical case for militarism or pacifism, nationalism or internationalism, for male dominance or for women's rights, though it is a bit more difficult with women's rights. One can make a case for capital punishment or for letting the prisoners go free. One can make a case for socialism or for capitalism, simply by selecting a few verses very carefully and ignoring all the others.

It seems clear to me that there are great and central overriding themes and concerns in the scriptures. You and I might have slightly different lists of what these themes would be, but there would be certain ones that simply could not be ignored if we were going to respond honestly to the text. There are huge sections, for example, on the dangers of national idolatry, that is to say, making the nation into God, accepting uncritically whatever we have to do as a nation against other nations.

Those major emphases stand in very sharp contrast to Mr. Falwell's assessment that we should have done whatever we needed to win in Vietnam because our national honor was at stake. That was the criterion and I submit that national honor is a criterion that the Bible unremittingly attacks. There are long sections in scripture dealing with the need to be concerned about the poor and the destitute. There are treatments of the "virus" of racism. There are many recognitions that those with wealth will always be tempted to act repressively against the poor and so on and so on. It is breathtaking that when one looks over the agendas of the Moral Majority there is absolutely no mention of such things, there is a total silence. We seem to be living in two different worlds, reading two different books. . . .

So let me now to conclude, suggest very briefly five characteristics that I think would be appropriate to the moral minority. . . .

First . . . the Bible does not talk about minorities as much as about remnants. Since the demise of . . . Constantinian Christianity[2] where Christians were running the show . . . this remnant posture has become both appropriate and descriptive for Christians. We are a small percentage, a remnant, of the whole human family, particularly when we look at ourselves globally. . . .

[One remnant within the remnant might be to dissent from the prevailing views of local church establishments. Our model for this might be the circumstances of Latin America.] For centuries . . . the Catholic Church in Latin America was at the beck and call of the little group of the wealthy who had all the power, who had all the money, all the prestige. . . . But in recent years the churches have been getting away from that uncritical alliance with those in power [and speaking up and working for social justice]. . . .

Secondly . . . if we could break out of the kind of "culturally conditioned" ways we have read the Bible, we could find it an explosive arsenal of material for creative change. . . . When the Bible talks about good news for the poor we immediately interpret that to mean the spiritually poor. . . . Now, I am sure that is part of what was meant, but it seems to me very clear what is also meant [is] that when Jesus is talking about the poor, he also meant the materially poor, the really impoverished, who do not have enough to eat, . . . who do not have enough power. . . .

The third thing the moral minority could stress, perhaps the most important thing in the time in which we live, would be the necessity of a global perspective. This world is now just too small to allow for anything else. And to look at the world simply in terms of what is good for the United States, is ultimately going to be self-defeating. To put the main stress and priority on more weapons, as the national debate is now suggesting, is truly likely to increase the likelihood that we will use them. . . .

That suggests a fourth thing the moral minority might become; it could become that group in our society which is genuinely committed to the powerless and voiceless. . . . [T]he church . . . must be that place where the voiceless are empowered to speak on their own behalf, and are guaranteed a hearing. . . .

Fifth, and finally, a moral minority must . . . set its own agendas. . . . Our agendas must not be set by the Moral Majority movement. We must not fall into the trap of single-issue politics. . . . I find it kind of morally oppressive to be told, again and again, some kind of obsession about other people's sex life [sic] is the burning issue of the day, when the majority of the human family went to bed hungry every night or to be told to rally around getting prayers back into schools when millions of people are unable to find jobs, or get minimal help if they are unemployed and disadvantaged. . . . [T]he whole human family is hurting from the mad escalation of the

---

[2]The emperor Constantine the Great in the fourth century A.D. made Christianity the supreme religion of the Roman world—ED.

arms race, the need for more equitable distribution of food, coming to terms with denials, both abroad and home, of basic human rights, such as education and medical care and jobs and all the rest.

I think we need to rally around these problems in a context which provides a forum for seeking the good of all, not just small segments of the population. We must try to present issues without demagoguery cheating. We must acknowledge that problems are complex and that simplistic solutions will be misleading and wrong, and acknowledge also that ambiguities abound not only within the positions of those with whom we disagree, but within our own positions as well. With some such way of engaging in political life, we might be able to create a moral minority that could propose convictions without arrogance but insight without absolutism, with commitment but without coercion and with democracy but without demagoguery.

☆ **19** ☆

The New Environmentalism

As we move through the last decade of the twentieth century, we can see that the Cold War's end will not free America of global concerns. If nothing else, the 1991 Gulf War has made that clear. But it is also apparent that more of our attention and resources will have to be devoted to domestic matters and to the sort of peaceful international issues that the United States seldom had to consider in the past. None of these concerns and issues will be as vital as preserving the physical environment, for the air, the land, and the waters are the very foundations of human existence.

Our environmental worries are not new. The conservation-preservation movement of almost a century ago foreshadowed our present concerns. But the modern surge of environmentalism dates from the writings of Rachel Carson, whose 1962 book, *The Silent Spring,* describing the blighting effects of DDT and other pesticides, alerted millions to new environmental dangers.

Since then environmental awareness has blossomed into a worldwide consciousness of the delicate ecological balances of nature and humankind's dependence on those balances. During the 1960s the new concerns generated a flood of federal legislation designed to eliminate pollutants, protect the nation's air and waters, and preserve its natural heritage. Robust public interest in the environment coincided with the winding down of the Vietnam War and the demise of the New Left, and served as an alternative to campus protest for many idealistic young men and women. In their staging, their spirit, and their personnel, the rallies for the first Earth Day in 1970 resembled the antiwar demonstrations of the same era. Later in the decade, particularly in Europe, various "Green" parties would make environmental reform into a political force that challenged centrist as well as traditional left-wing parties.

In the following selections you will encounter a variety of environmentalist positions as well as critiques of the environmental movement. See if you can detect, behind the contending pronouncements and formulas, the fundamentally different views of humanity's proper relations with nature.

19.1:   The Ecology Ethic (1949, 1975, 1973)

Rachel Carson may be the source of the modern public's environmental fears, but the founder of the larger post–World War II ecological consciousness was Aldo Leopold, a naturalist who worked successively for the U.S. Forestry Service, the Arms and Ammunition Manufacturers' Institute,[1] and the University of Wisconsin. As a disciple of Gifford Pinchot, Leopold was initially a utilitarian conservationist who sought to advance the rational use of natural resources. He later moved beyond that position to defend the preservation of unspoiled nature and to insist that humans no more "owned" the land than they "owned" other human beings. The first selection in this chapter is from his book A Sand County Almanac, *published in 1949, just after his death, in which Leopold announced a new "land ethic" of respect, even reverence, for nature coupled with a belief that humankind was merely a part of nature, not its lord and master.*

Does Leopold dismiss economic factors in considering how people should manage natural resources? In his view, what other factors must they take into account? Would Leopold's opinions be considered bold or radical today?

The second item is by Harvard professor George Wald, a Nobel Prize winner in biology and charter member of Friends of the Earth, an influential voice for environmental-ecological concerns. It is part of an address Wald delivered in 1975 to a conference in Switzerland on "The Limits to Medicine."

Wald speaks with a different voice from Leopold. Leopold is thoughtful and philosophical about the environment; Wald sounds a note of alarm at the environmental havoc that people have caused. And yet it is possible to see a connection between the ideas of the two men. What is that connection? On the other hand, there are differ-

---

[1]Given the general linkage of modern environmentalism with liberal political causes, this connection is surprising. Yet those interested in game hunting have long sought to preserve the natural environment, for only if it survives will the animals they stalk survive. Theodore Roosevelt epitomizes this marriage between big game hunting and the wilderness preservation side of the environmental movement.

ences. How can we explain them? What events that occurred in the intellectual, economic, and political worlds between 1949 and 1975 might account for the differences in the tones of their statements? The Wald selection raises another question: Does an ecological consciousness imply a political viewpoint? Can you detect an implicit political position in Wald's remarks? If so, what is it? Is his political perspective common among those who view the environment as he does?

The third selection, on the critical environmental issue of nuclear energy, is by Ernst Schumacher. Author of Small Is Beautiful, *an influential book advocating limits on economic and population growth, the German-born Schumacher is one of many environmentalists who have warned of the grave dangers to human life posed by nuclear energy.*

His is a contribution to an important force behind the recent environmental movement: the health and safety fears of millions confronted with the power and mystery of modern technology. Are these fears exaggerated? Can we meet our energy needs if we abandon the nuclear option? What are some alternate energy choices? Would adopting alternative energy sources impose crippling costs on society? Have the antinuclear forces been effective in slowing the use of nuclear energy?

The Land Ethic

ALDO LEOPOLD

When god-like Odysseus returned from the wars in Troy, he hanged all on one rope a dozen slave-girls of his household whom he suspected of misbehavior during his absence.

This hanging involved no question of propriety. The girls were property. The disposal of property was then, as now, a matter of expediency, not of right and wrong.

Concepts of right and wrong were not lacking from Odysseus' Greece: witness the fidelity of his wife through the long years before at last his black-prowed galleys clove the wine-dark seas for home. The ethical structure of that day covered wives, but had not yet been extended to human chattels. During the three thousand years which have since elapsed, ethical criteria have been extended to many fields of conduct, with corresponding shrinkages in those judged by expediency only.

The Ethical Sequence

This extension of ethics, so far studied only by philosophers, is actually a process in ecological evolution. Its sequences may be described in ecological as well as in philo-

Aldo Leopold, "The Land Ethic," *A Sand County Almanac: With Other Essays from Round River* (New York: Oxford University Press, 1949), pp. 201–4, 223–6.

sophical terms. An ethic, ecologically, is a limitation on freedom of action in the struggle for existence. An ethic, philosophically, is a differentiation of social from anti-social conduct. These are two definitions of one thing. The thing has its origin in the tendency of interdependent individuals or groups to evolve modes of co-operation. The ecologist calls these symbioses. Politics and economics are advanced symbioses in which the original free-for-all competition has been replaced, in part, by co-operative mechanisms with an ethical content.

The complexity of co-operative mechanisms has increased with population density, and with the efficiency of tools. It was simpler, for example, to define the anti-social uses of sticks and stones in the days of the mastodons than of bullets and billboards in the age of motors.

The first ethics dealt with the relation between individuals; the Mosaic Decalogue is an example. Later accretions dealt with the relation between the individual and society. The Golden Rule tries to integrate the individual to society; democracy to integrate social organization to the individual.

There is as yet no ethic dealing with man's relation to land and to the animals and plants which grow upon it. Land, like Odysseus' slave-girls, is still property. The land-relation is still strictly economic, entailing privileges but not obligations.

The extension of ethics to this third element in human environment is, if I read the evidence correctly, an evolutionary possibility and an ecological necessity. It is the third step in a sequence. The first two have already been taken. Individual thinkers since the days of Ezekiel and Isaiah have asserted that the despoliation of land is not only inexpedient but wrong. Society, however, has not yet affirmed their belief. I regard the present conservation movement as the embryo of such an affirmation.

An ethic may be regarded as a mode of guidance for meeting ecological situations so new or intricate, or involving such deferred reactions, that the path of social expediency is not discernible to the average individual. Animal instincts are modes of guidance for the individual in meeting such situations. Ethics are possibly a kind of community instinct in-the-making.

The Community Concept

All ethics so far evolved rest upon a single premise: that the individual is a member of a community of interdependent parts. His instincts prompt him to compete for his place in that community, but his ethics prompt him also to co-operate (perhaps in order that there may be a place to compete for).

The land ethic simply enlarges the boundaries of the community to include soils, waters, plants, and animals, or collectively, the land.

This sounds simple: Do we not already sing our love for and obligation to the land of the free and the home of the brave? Yes, but just what and whom do we love? Certainly not the soil, which we are sending helter-skelter downriver. Certainly not the waters, which we assume have no function except to turn turbines, float barges, and carry off sewage. Certainly not the plants, of which we exterminate whole communities without batting an eye. Certainly not the animals, of which we have already extirpated many of the largest and most beautiful species. A land ethic of course cannot prevent the alteration, management, and use of these "resources," but it does affirm their right to continued existence, and, at least in spots, their continued existence in a natural state.

In short, a land ethic changes the role of *Homo sapiens* from conqueror of the land-community to plain member and citizen of it. It implies respect for his fellow-members, and also respect for the community as such.

The Outlook

It is inconceivable to me that an ethical relation to land can exist without love, respect, and admiration for land, and a high regard for its value. By value, I of course mean something far broader than mere economic value; I mean value in the philosophical sense.

Perhaps the most serious obstacle impeding the evolution of a land ethic is the fact that our educational and economic system is headed away from, rather than toward, an intense consciousness of land. Your true modern is separated from the land by many middlemen, and by innumerable physical gadgets. He has no vital relation to it; to him it is the space between cities on which crops grow. Turn him loose for a day on the land, and if the spot does not happen to be a golf links or "scenic" area, he is bored stiff. If crops could be raised by hydroponics instead of farming, it would suit him very well. Synthetic substitutes for wood, leather, wool, and other natural land products suit him better than the originals. In short, land is something he has "outgrown."

Almost equally serious as an obstacle to a land ethic is the attitude of the farmer for whom the land is still an adversary, or a taskmaster that keeps him in slavery. Theoretically, the mechanization of farming ought to cut the farmer's chains, but whether it really does is debatable.

One of the requisites for an ecological comprehension of land is an understanding of ecology, and this is by no means co-extensive with "education," in fact, much higher education seems deliberately to avoid ecological concepts. An understanding of ecology does not necessarily originate in courses bearing ecological labels; it is quite as likely to be labeled geography, botany, agronomy, history, or economics. This is as it should be, but whatever the label, ecological training is scarce.

The case for a land ethic would appear hopeless but for the minority which in obvious revolt against these "modern" trends.

The "key-log" which must be moved to release the evolutionary process for an ethic is simply this: quit thinking about decent land-use as solely an economic problem. Examine each question in terms of what is ethically and esthetically right, as well as what is economically expedient. A thing is right when it tends to preserve the integrity, stability, and beauty of the biotic community. It is wrong when it tends otherwise.

It of course goes without saying that economic feasibility limits the tether of what can or cannot be done for land. It always has and it always will. The fallacy the economic determinists have tied around our collective neck, and which we now need to cast off, is the belief that economics determines *all* land-use. This is simply not true. An innumerable host of actions and attitudes, comprising perhaps the bulk of all land relations, is determined by the land-users' tastes and predilections, rather than by his purse. The bulk of all land relations hinges on investments of time, forethought, skill, and faith rather than on investments of cash. As a land-user thinketh, so is he.

I have purposely presented the land ethic as a product of social evolution because nothing so important as an ethic is ever "written." Only the most superficial student of history supposes that Moses "wrote" the Decalogue; it evolved in the minds of a thinking community, and Moses wrote a tentative summary of it for a "seminar." I say tentative because evolution never stops.

The evolution of a land ethic is an intellectual as well as emotional process. Conservation is paved with good intentions which prove to be futile, or even dangerous, because they are devoid of critical understanding either of the land, or of economic land-use. I think it is a truism that as the ethical frontier advances from the individual to the community, its intellectual content increases.

The mechanism of operation is the same for any ethic: social approbation for right actions; social disapproval for wrong actions.

By and large, our present problem is one of attitudes and implements. We are remodeling the Alhambra with a steam-shovel, and we are proud of our yardage. We shall hardly relinquish the shovel, which after all has many good points, but we are in need of gentler and more objective criteria for its successful use.

The Lethal Society[1]

GEORGE WALD

I've had the strange feeling in this meeting, listening to the papers on the limits of medicine, that they seem to disregard what I think is our major trouble. That is that we are talking about the limits of medicine in a highly lethal society, and indeed one that is threatening to die, perhaps soon. And that makes a special set of problems.

Why do I say a highly lethal society? Well, because no society in human history has cultivated the killing and destruction as has Western society under Christianity. It's a commentary on this that our Western world has been so shocked that India produced an atom bomb, a very small one by present standards. The shock was not in the atom bomb (we have lots of those, and big ones). The shock consisted in an atom bomb being produced in the wrong place, by the wrong kind of nation. A Third World country has no business producing an atom bomb. . . .

My own nation, the United States, is now making three hydrogen warheads per day. The Soviet Union keeps pace with us. You must think of the limits of medicine, and how to humanize medicine, against the background of the production in my country of three hydrogen warheads per day.

It is not only atomic bombs we need to fear. Nuclear power, that enticing thing, in all its present forms threatens our future as a civilization and as people. . . .

George Wald, "The Lethal Society," in Mary Lou Deventer, ed., *Earthworks: Ten Years on the Environmental Front* (San Francisco: Friends of the Earth, 1980), pp. 230–35.
[1]Illustrations deleted.

Every nuclear reactor of any type now at work produces as a by-product pluto-nium 239, probably the most toxic substance known. One milligram inhaled is enough to kill a person within hours by massive fibrosis of the lungs. One micro-gram is likely eventually to cause lung or bone cancer. Also, this is the most conve-nient material out of which to make fission bombs. The "trigger" quantity, the quan-tity of plutonium 239 with which one can make an atom bomb, is *two kilograms.* You could carry that amount perfectly safely in a brown paper grocery bag. A plu-tonium 239 bomb of the explosive force of the bomb that leveled Hiroshima and killed 100,000 persons would take six to seven kilograms. You'd have to put that in a shopping bag. . . .

The Workplace Environment

I have not yet heard spoken of in this meeting a terrible problem. It is the danger of the workplace, the problem for workers to stay alive while making a living. I have heard several times here the auto referred to as a big killer of healthy persons. In the United States, the workplaces are at least as big a killer. We register about 22,000 deaths by industrial accident every year and 2.2 million disabling accidents. But those statistics don't touch the slow killing: the black lung of the coal mines; the brown lung that is produced by exposure to the dust of cotton and hemp and flax in the textile mills; the silicosis, asbestosis, and uranium poisoning, and the large num-ber and variety of cancers associated with these conditions. None of these chronic conditions is in the statistics. And indeed, this kind of statistics is hard to come by, because the industry fights tooth and nail to keep them concealed. The reason is ob-vious. Every attempt to make the workplaces safer increases the cost of production; every alleged work injury represents an insurance or compensation cost. So it is in the interest of industry to conceal these disabilities. In the US, the only physicians who concern themselves with these disabilities, or who are available at the work-place, are almost without exception employed by the industry and make their re-ports to the industry, not to the workers. . . .

The whole of humanity now suffers from a series of exceedingly threatening new developments, all coming to a head at about the same time, close to the year 2000. I am one of those scientists—and believe me, it is no pleasure—who, trying as we will, hoping as we do that something in our view of things is wrong, still find it very difficult to see how the human race is to get itself much past the year 2000. So there isn't much time.

The Jolly Green Giant

Every few years one is told that [Thomas] Malthus was wrong: that he was "naive" in thinking that we might eventually overpopulate the globe relative to our food re-sources. The last event said to demonstrate that Malthus was wrong was the Green Revolution.[2]

---

[2]The Green Revolution is a name given to a surge in agricultural productivity of the 1960s based on modern genetic science—ED.

In fact, the Green Revolution has a terrible contradiction at its core. The biggest single event in the history of life on this planet was the development of photosynthesis. That made us independent of the accumulation of organic molecules upon which life depended from its origin until—through photosynthesis, using the energy of sunlight—life could make its own organic molecules. Well, the Green Revolution has reversed this development by making us dependent again upon fossil organic molecules. It is a poor bargain. The total energy consumed by U.S. agriculture per year is equivalent to more than 30 billion gallons of gasoline. This represents more than *five times the energy content of the food produced.* The Green Revolution means that we use fossil fuels produced by early ages of photosynthesis to promote present-day photosynthesis.

The Green Revolution rests upon huge amounts of synthetic fertilizers and synthetic pesticides and herbicides, all produced with fossil fuels—with coal and oil. That worked as long as coal and oil were cheap. But they no longer are cheap; and with that, much of the Green Revolution, particularly for the Third World, has gone bankrupt. . . .

The Cultivation of "Marginal Men"

Until recently, the intensifying food shortages in the world could be ascribed mainly to increase in population. To this a new element has been added, mainly within the last decade: a sudden large increase in the demand for meat—for beef and pork—in the developed nations. I was in Japan twice, six years apart, and was amazed by the change in Japanese dietary habits during that short period. This places an enormous burden upon the poorer and hungrier parts of the world, because making that meat strikes a very bad nutritional bargain. It takes about eight pounds of grain to make one pound of meat. The grain that might otherwise go to feeding a starving peasantry is instead fed to hogs and cattle to supply this enormously increased demand for meat in the affluent world. Dr. Georg Borgstrom has calculated that U.S. livestock consume enough food materials to feed 1.3 billion persons and world livestock consume enough to feed 15 billion persons.

Another development greatly aggravates these troubles. Most of human work used to be done with human muscles; but now, increasingly, it is done by machines—even in agriculture. Agriculture is rapidly going over from farming to agribusiness. In my own country, 51 percent of the vegetables, 85 percent of the citrus fruits, 97 percent of the chickens, and 100 percent of the sugar cane are being produced by the same companies that make our aircraft, control our soil and coal, and run our transportation system. That kind of thing is happening all over the world. It is another aspect of the Green Revolution; and everywhere it is throwing people out of work. Unemployment is rising all over the world—and something much worse. It is not just that many persons are unemployed, which one thinks of as a temporary condition, but that there is no further use for them in the free-market economy. They are wanted neither as workers nor as consumers. They are not wanted at all. Their existence is looked on as an embarrassment—even as a potential threat, for they continue to demand food, clothing, and shelter. Even education. Robert MacNamara, in his report to the World Bank of September 21, 1970, referred to such superfluous persons as "marginal men." He estimated that there were then 500 million of them, that by 1980 there would be one billion, and by 1990, two billion. That would be close to half the world population. . . .

The Limits of Research

What are we to do? It is easy to say what is wrong, but how to make it right?

Our kind of person has one answer all prepared. Research. If people are hungry, set up a well-funded project on hunger. If our world is coming to an end, set up a well-funded Project Apocalypse.

As a research person, I should like to say something about this. Research is a fine thing. We never know enough about anything. But research must not be allowed to become a trap, a means of endlessly putting off action. And that's the way it is frequently being exploited. That's the way it is with the big industrial diseases, with pollution, with tobacco smoking and cancer. We are told that "all the facts are not yet in." How inane! All the facts are never in. Each of these situations changes as one studies it. So let's by all means have more research. But let us also act; let us do what is needed.

We already know enough to *begin* to cope with all the major problems that are now threatening human life and much of the rest of life on Earth. Our crisis is not a crisis of information; it is a crisis of decision, of policy.

Though we already know enough to begin to cope with all the major problems, I don't know one of those major problems that we could begin to cope with *while maximizing profits*. And I think that a society such as our own that puts the maximization of profits above all other considerations is thereby headed for destruction and is doomed. . . .

What we need is a reorganization of our society, a fundamental change in its direction, so as better to meet human needs, to fulfill human values, to humanize what is now increasingly alienating, to serve life rather than death. To fulfill short-term goals for an increasingly narrow power structure, we are devastating the Earth; and the business of killing—armaments—is now by far the world's biggest business. . . .

Toward a Non-Lethal Society

As I try to think in terms of a reorganization of society, it seems to me increasingly clear that the really significant journey to make is not to the moon, but to China. One sees things going on in China that are altogether surprising to middle-class persons who have grown up in our society. . . . With famine in much of the Third World, no Chinese is expected to starve this year. You don't have to take that from the Chinese or from me. Twenty American agricultural experts went over as a delegation a couple of months ago, and they came out saying that China seems well supplied with food—that the hunger prevalent in other parts of the Third World is not afflicting the Chinese. Then they said something more that has a wonderfully ironic twist: that the Chinese are not producing agricultural experts, and that unless they begin quickly to produce agricultural experts, they'll soon be in trouble! . . .

The only solutions for the problems I have spoken of are *political.* They must come out in the form of political power exercised by an aroused people who insist on taking their lives back into their own hands.

What we fondly call the free world is composed almost entirely (in its Third World components) of military dictatorships. That phrase, the free world, used to trouble me until I finally realized what it meant. The free world consists of those nations that get their armaments free from the U.S.

In our free world—perhaps you feel differently in Switzerland—the governments are not masters. . . . Then who are the masters? I think that our so-called free world is now wholly controlled by such multinational super-enterprises as General Motors, Exxon, the Chase Manhattan Bank, ITT, Royal Dutch Shell, and British Petroleum. . . .

I don't know myself where to turn politically. We don't have a politics in the United States at present that promises to go in the direction I think our society needs to go. That's no accident. We now sell and buy political candidates in exactly the same way we sell and buy toothpaste and soap. The same advertising methods are used, and the same people are paying for it. . . .

Our present society seems to me to have the following structure. In control is a very small power elite, in which is concentrated more power and wealth than ever before in human history. At the other end of the social scale is a great, faceless mass of workers—increasingly urban, and hence increasingly dependent on their employment. In between is the middle class to which we ourselves belong. It includes all government officials, high and low; all military and police officials; professors, journalists and clergymen; physicians and lawyers. The role laid out for it is to mediate between the power elite and the working masses; to keep the system running, if possible smoothly, but to keep it running at all costs; to rationalize the system's contradictions; to foster its acceptance through education, indoctrination, and religious exhortation; to fragment and dilute any opposition, and in the event of serious challenge, to control or crush it.

Conceivably, such a system could work to social advantage. At times and places in the past, it may have done so. But in recent history, it has turned destructive. It is leading our society rapidly toward disaster. In an obsessive pursuit of short-term profit and power, it threatens to bring an end to the human enterprise. And our role as the middle class, the role for which we are designed, trained, employed, and paid, is to help that to happen—to do what we can to smooth the way to that disaster.

But we do not have to accept that role. We have a choice. We can opt for life rather than death. Rather than serve the power elite in its present plunge toward destruction, we can turn the other way; we can *serve the people.*

The Energy Assumption

Urbanization and the availability of energy arc closely related. The emergence of the first cities was closely associated with agricultural breakthroughs such as the harnessing of draft animals, the domestication of new agricultural plants, and the development of irrigation systems. In effect, these enabled humans to harness more energy for their own purposes—to capture more solar energy in plants or, in the case of draft animals, to convert otherwise unusable roughage into a form that could be used to increase the food supply. Important though these new energy sources were, the agricultural surpluses they made possible were never enough to support more than a small proportion of the population living away from the land. Indeed, as recently as 1800, only 2.2 percent of the population of Europe lived in cities of 100,000 or more.

The energy breakthrough that permitted much larger populations—even majorities—to live in cities was the discovery of fossil fuels, initially coal and later oil. The harnessing of fossil fuels to generate steam for industrial power gave birth to the industrial revolution, permitted the concentration of economic activity, and ushered in a new era of urbanization.

The large-scale migration of people from countryside to city required an abundance of energy. Cities require more energy to satisfy food, fuel, housing, and transport needs. Assuming no change in consumption levels, each person who moves from the countryside to the city raises world energy requirements.

With food, urbanization raises energy requirements on two fronts. As the urban population increases relative to the rural food-producing population, more energy is required in agriculture to generate this requisite food surplus. At the same time, more energy is needed to process the food and transport it to urban areas.

As more and more people move into the cities, each person remaining in agriculture must produce an ever-larger surplus. This, in turn, requires the broad substitution of mechanical energy for labor in food production. In a world where energy is becoming scarce and unemployment is rising, it makes little sense to continue this substitution in countries with large, unemployed rural populations.

It is customary to point with pride to the small percentage of the population living on the land in industrial nations such as the U.S. where 5 percent of the people provide food for the rest. This level of labor productivity in agriculture requires vast amounts of energy. Professor David Pimentel, writing in *Science* (November 2, 1973), illustrates how much. If the current four billion world population were to be fed at U.S. consumption levels, using U.S. energy-intensive agricultural production techniques, and "if *petroleum* were the only source of energy, and if we used "all *petroleum* reserves solely to feed the world population, the 415-billion barrel reserve would last a mere 29 years."

Although the amounts required for food production are large, they are dwarfed by comparison with the amount of energy used to transport, process, and distribute food. Within the U.S., one-fourth of the energy used in the food system is used to produce food. Three-fourths of the total is used to transport, process, and distribute that same food.

Urbanization also increases energy requirements for waste disposal. At the village level, waste disposal is not a major problem. Organic wastes are returned to the soil to enrich it, an important and integral part of nature's nutrient cycles of phosphorus, sulfur, and nitrogen. In this way they contribute to the food supply. But once large numbers of people congregate in cities, waste may no longer be an asset. Indeed, efforts to safely dispose of it are often an additional drain on scarce energy resources.

The rapid urbanization of this century, so far, occurred during an era of cheap energy, an era which may be historically unique. Oil production has already peaked in some major producing countries, including the U.S. Production declines in other countries will follow. With the end of the petroleum age now clearly in sight, the world must turn to other forms of energy, forms which may, by their very natures, affect the pattern of human settlement.

Until recently, it was assumed that the world would move from the fossil fuel era into the nuclear age. After a quarter-century of experience with nuclear power, the world is beginning to have second thoughts about continuing down the nuclear path. Failure to devise any satisfactory techniques of waste disposal, the inevitable spread of nuclear weapons along with nuclear power, and the prospect of terrorist groups acquiring nuclear materials and weapons are all beginning to raise doubts in even the most sanguine of minds.

Beyond the seemingly insoluble waste disposal and security problems, the economics associated with nuclear power are becoming questionable. In 1975 there were 25 times as many nuclear reactors cancelled or deferred in the U.S. as there were new orders placed. The industry is undoubtedly sick; the real question is whether or not it may be terminally ill.

The world may well move not from fossil fuel to nuclear, but toward growing reliance on solar energy. If the world moves toward a solar age, the population will need to be broadly distributed, for the simple reason that solar energy itself is broadly dispersed.

The Dangers of Nuclear Energy

ERNST SCHUMACHER

Of all the changes introduced by man into the household of nature, large-scale nuclear fission is undoubtedly the most dangerous and profound. As a result, ionising radiation has become the most serious agent of pollution of the environment and the greatest threat to man's survival on earth. The attention of the layman, not surprisingly, has been captured by the atom bomb, although there is at least a chance that it may never be used again. The danger to humanity created by the so-called peaceful users of atomic energy may be much greater.

A new dimension is given also by the fact that while man now can—and does—create radioactive elements, there is nothing he can do to reduce their radioactivity once he has created them. No chemical reaction, no physical interference, only the passage of time reduces the intensity of radiation once it has been set going. Carbon-14 has a half-life of 5900 years, which means that it takes nearly 6000 years for its radioactivity to decline to one-half of what it was before. The half-life of strontium-90 is twenty-eight years. But whatever the length of the half-life, some radiation continues almost indefinitely, and there is nothing that can be done about it, except to try and put the radioactive substance into a safe place.

Ernst Schumacher, "Production in Service to Life," in Hugh Nash, ed., *Progress As if Survival Mattered: A Handbook for a Conserver Society* (San Francisco: Friends of the Earth, 1981), pp. 236-37.

But what is a safe place, let us say, for the enormous amounts of radioactive waste products created by nuclear reactors? No place on earth can be shown to be safe.

The most massive wastes are, of course, the nuclear reactors themselves after they have become unserviceable. There is a lot of discussion on the trivial economic question of whether they will last for twenty, twenty-five, or thirty years. No one discusses the humanly vital point that they cannot be dismantled and cannot be shifted but have to be left standing where they are, probably for centuries, perhaps for thousands of years, an active menace to all life, silently leaking radioactivity into air, water and soil. No one has considered the number and location of these satanic mills which will relentlessly accumulate. Earthquakes, of course, are not supposed to happen, nor wars, nor civil disturbances, nor riots like those that infested American cities. Disused nuclear power stations will stand as unsightly monuments to unquiet man's assumption that nothing but tranquility, from now on, stretches before him, or else—that the future counts as nothing compared with the slightest economic gain now.

No degree of prosperity could justify the accumulation of large amounts of highly toxic substances which nobody knows how to make "safe" and which remain an incalculable danger to the whole of creation for historical or even geological ages. To do such a thing is a transgression against life itself, a transgression infinitely more serious than any crime ever perpetrated by man. The idea that a civilisation could sustain itself on the basis of such a transgression is an ethical, spiritual, and metaphysical monstrosity. It means conducting the economic affairs of man as if people really did not matter at all.

19.2: The Critics (1971, 1970)

The contemporary environmental movement has had its detractors as well as its defenders. Its opponents have accused it of encouraging "ecoterrorists" who release mice and dogs from scientific laboratories to stop animal testing, drive spikes into trees to discourage lumbering, and cut power lines to sabotage nuclear energy reactors. They say it has fostered alarmists who exaggerate the dangers of technology and seek an impossible risk-free society. The new ecologists, they believe, often put abstract nature before human needs.

The first of the selections is by Richard Neuhaus, a Lutheran pastor[1] who has written extensively on conservative social and political themes. Neuhaus is responding to a group of "Neo-Malthusian" environmentalists who, inspired by the eighteenth-century English economist Thomas Malthus, warned that human population growth, if unchecked, will soon exhaust the earth's resources and lead to mass

---

[1]Neuhaus later converted to Catholicism.

poverty and even starvation. The Neo-Malthusians believe that the potential threat of demographic disaster justifies limiting economic growth and reducing resource exploitation.

In what way does Neuhaus challenge the Neo-Malthusians? What principle does Neuhaus elevate above that of nature's sovereignty? Why might a Christian clergyman object to some of the views of environmentalists in general and of Neo-Malthusians in particular?

The second selection is a critique of environmentalism from the political left. Reflecting the views of Ramparts *magazine, a radical publication founded in the 1960s, it was written on the occasion of the first Earth Day in the spring of 1970, at a time when the New Left was still a flourishing ideology. What are the editor's reservations about the environmental movement of the day? From a radical political perspective, is the assessment valid? Since 1970, have fears such as those expressed by the* Ramparts *editors been validated or refuted?*

People vs. Trees

RICHARD NEUHAUS

Because they agree that "not much time is available" many policy planners and promoters of survival are not inclined to wait for "the intricate processes and symbol-systems of whole societies" to take their course. At a highly secretive symposium in New York City, Professor Garrett Hardin[1] broke the question down into some simple propositions: Population + Prosperity = Pollution. "To reduce pollution, one must reduce either population or prosperity, and it is better to reduce population rather than prosperity." The American people—not to mention the people of the Third World—are not yet ready for the implications of this simple proposition. In the symposium, sponsored by the Population Council in May 1970, Hardin suggested that the implications must be slipped to the general public in small doses accompanied by a new understanding of what is moral and what is immoral. According to the report of the meeting, Hardin urged that "we should go lightly in encouraging rising expectations [among the poor] . . . for if everyone in the world had the same standard of living as do we, we would increase pollution by a factor of 20. . . . Therefore, it is a questionable morality to seek to increase the food supply. We should hesitate to make sacrifices locally for the betterment of the rest of the world."

Proponents of "nature's rights" might ponder Hardin's resolution of the problem posed by someone suggesting that the redwood trees should be cut down in order to grow potatoes on that land and ship the potatoes to the victims of famine. "If the

[1]A professor of ecology at the University of California at Santa Barbara who warned of the dire consequences of excessive population growth—ED.

space required to grow four redwood trees could be devoted to growing food for one person, we should say directly and bluntly that four redwood trees are more important than a person." If this sounds callous, we are piously reminded that "We are guardians of the future, not owners of the trees, but trustees of the trees, trustees for the future. We are trustees of the grandchildren of the world, ours included." Oh yes, *ours* especially. Hardin acknowledges that the predictions of disaster that make such ethical transformations necessary may turn out to be wrong. In that case, we are assured, there is no great loss. "You can always produce more babies." The redwoods are irreplaceable.

Hardin, like Ehrlich,[2] is no ecological eccentric but is one of the movement's formative voices and has authored some of the more influential statements on population policy. Their views are echoed in an editorial in the February 1969 issue of *Bioscience:* "Because it creates a vicious cycle that compounds human suffering at a high rate, the provision of food to the malnourished populations of the world that cannot or will not take very substantial measures to control their own reproductive rates is inhuman, immoral, and irresponsible." Writing in the *New Republic,* Wayne Davis of the University of Kentucky, asserts, "It is time we faced our responsibilities. Those who call for increased food production in the world are asking that we make a grave problem still more grave. Responsible people must oppose any food distribution plan that is not tied to a program of birth control and a genuine effort to help the recipients break the poverty cycle." In its myriad forms, the logic of the "triage" solution is on the ascendancy. The long drum roll has begun for two-thirds of humanity. We are called to the banners of the rich, led by America, in righteous crusade against the wretched of the earth who will either surrender to our terms or die in their wretchedness. But please do not be misled. This is not the old warfare of nationalist pride, racial prejudice and the arrogance of power; this warfare, made possible by a revolution in values, is the battle of a new morality. It is human, it is responsible, and the poor who survive it will some day understand that we did only what was best for them.

The dispassionate observer of the present ecology movement cannot help but be struck by the ironies and contradictions coexisting under that one banner. Compassion and callousness, altruism and greed, world vision and nationalistic *hubris,* all join in what some presume to term the ultimate revolution, the revolution to end revolutions, the reordering of man's place in nature. It is as though, in the same movement and often within the same persons, the left hand refuses to know what the right hand is doing. The literature of the movement is marked by a moving reverence for "the seamless web of life," accompanied by a shocking indifference to the weaker and less convenient forms of human life and by an almost cavalier readiness to disrupt the carefully woven web of civility and humane values. Threatened forms of fauna and animal life are passionately protected while the threatened and oppressed forms of human existence are too often ignored. The insight of Abraham

[2]Paul Ehrlich, a Stanford University biology professor and author of *The Population Bomb,* which warns about world population exceeding world resources—ED.

Heschel's[3] axiom, "The health of a society is measured by the protection it affords its weakest members," is applied to extra-human nature which must be preserved even at the expense of violating the axiom with regard to human society.

The language and its implicit value assumptions have infiltrated far beyond the ecology movement itself. Economist Robert Heilbroner speaks of "the most fearsome reality of all—a population that is still increasing like an uncontrollable cancer on the surface of the globe." An official and conservative Lutheran church periodical pronounces "every effort for social change is futile unless we first take realistic measures to reduce the earth's population." The printed programs for symphony orchestra concerts at Carnegie Hall have interspersed in their pages the little boxed cartoon of a round bomb (plant earth) with a lighted fuse and the legend, "The Population Bomb Keeps Ticking." It is no doubt a comforting thought for the affluent patrons of Carnegie Hall to believe that the world's inequities, so glaringly apparent when contrasted with Americans at the symphony, can be attributed not to economic and political injustice but to the evasively anonymous "population explosion." The cartoon reappears on matchbook covers at Marchi's, one of New York's more expensive restaurants. Remember the old-fashioned Thanksgiving dinner when in the saying of grace we were reminded of the hungry of the world? It made us uncomfortable about the lavishness of the meal, but it seemed only right to acknowledge the outrageous inequities in the distribution of the world's wealth, and no doubt some of us did then and there resolve to do something about righting the wrong. No longer need the edge of guilt impinge upon the enjoyment of our good fortune. We need not, indeed we should not, do anything about feeding the hungry. Such misguided compassion "can only make an already grave problem more grave." The fault lies not with the structure of American power that works so well to our advantage but with the heathen hordes who resist conversion to our enlightened policies whereby some of them may survive and, as Ehrlich says, "none represents a threat to the developed sections of the world." The fault lies not with our rapacity but with their fertility. On with the symphony; on with the feast; up America!

Ironies and contradictions abound among the gentle people of ecology's public springtime. Charles Lindbergh devotes his latter years to protecting the environment. In his *Wartime Journals* he describes flying over Nuremberg after it had been devastated by allied bombing: "Pushing my head further out, I can see one spire of the cathedral, gutted but still beautiful, dimly silhouetted in the light. Above there are broken clouds, and the stars are coming. I feel surrounded by death. Only in the sky is there hope, only in that which man has never touched and which God forbid we ever will." He seems unaware that the death all around him came from the air, from the pristine sky of his poetic ardor. The sky is absolved of responsibility, as others absolve American power of any responsibility for the sufferings of the Third World. The sky, nature, is the illusion of innocence, so unlike the earth that has been tainted, corrupted, maggot-infested, by the archenemy People. The popular press views Lindbergh's devotion to conservationism as a balance to the oppro-

---

[3] A professor of religion at Jewish Theological Seminary—ED.

brium of his past sympathies for Nazi Germany. It is probably more accurate to see his inclinations and passions in dramatic continuity. It is apparent from his *Journals* that Lindbergh, guided by the lights of "nature's order," shared many of Hitler's views on inherently superior and inferior races. How natural that he should toward the end of his life turn away from the artificial contrivances of man and his politics and seek solace in the eternal verities of nature.

"Man is the measure of all things" was never entirely satisfying. But it is a thousand times preferable to "Nature is the measure of all things"—especially if by "Nature" one means everything apart from man. For the believer, man himself was measured in light of the transcendent and this enhanced his glory as cantor, caretaker and celebrant of the universe. From the Renaissance and Enlightenment, discovery and delight in mankind have emerged the values that have made Western civilization, with all its grievous faults, a reasonably tolerable form of the human condition. One does not wish to praise civilization too highly, lest he give false comfort to those responsible for its widespread injustices. At the same time, we dare not despise and reject the assumptions that have made possible whatever good there is in it. Undergirding these assumptions is the reverence and delight in humanity itself.

Are we now to reject Shakespeare's declaration of human dignity? "What a piece of work is a man! How noble in reason! how infinite in faculty! in form, in moving, how express and admirable! in action how like an angel! in apprehension how like a god! the beauty of the world! the paragon of animals!" We have been wearied by our failures and are now advised to conclude with Hamlet, "And, yet, to me, what is this quintessence of dust? man delights not me; no, nor woman neither. . . ." Shall we now accept Loren Eiseley's[4] view, so pervasive among those who write on ecology? "It is with the coming of man that a vast hole seems to open in nature, a vast black whirlpool spinning faster and faster, consuming flesh, stones, soil, minerals, sucking down the lightning, wrenching power from the atom, until the ancient sounds of nature are drowned in the cacophony of something which is no longer nature, something instead which is loose and knocking at the world's heart, something demonic and no longer planned—escaped, it may be—spewed out of nature, contending in a final giant's game against its master."

> *O Lord, our Lord,*
> *how majestic is thy name in all the earth!*
>
> *When I look at thy heavens, the work of thy fingers,*
> *the moon and the stars which thou hast established;*
> *what is man that thou art mindful of him,*
> *and the son of man that thou dost care for him?*
>
> *Yet thou hast made him little less than God,*
> *and dost crown him with glory and honor.*
> *Thou hast given him dominion over*
> *the works of thy hands;*

---

[4]A prominent American anthropologist and writer on environmental issues—ED.

thou hast put all things under his feet,
all sheep and oxen, and also the beasts of the field,
the birds of the air, and the fish of the sea,
whatever passes along the paths of the sea.

O Lord, our Lord,
   how majestic is thy name in all the earth!

Psalm 8, RSV

Is it all a lie? Are we rather something unnatural, a hateful mutant, spewed out and rejected by the natural order, a cancer besmirching Spaceship Earth's green and pleasant land? Our vanity cries out to deny it. But it is not vanity alone that protests. There is the sure intuition that, for all our abuse of our dominion, God has no other instrument to divine and fulfill his work. There is the sure intuition that our failures do not excuse us from further duty. And there is the sure intuition that, if we learn to despise ourselves, we will shortly despise also our sisters and brothers; losing our nerve, we will become the victims of the few who seize the authority of nature's law to crush our proud illusions of human dignity.

Editorial on Environmentalism

EDITORS OF *RAMPARTS*

The environment may well be the gut issue that can unify a polarized nation in the 1970's, writes *Time* magazine. The Hearst Press sees it as a movement "that could unite the generations." And *The New York Times* solemnly predicts that ecology "will replace Vietnam as the major issue with students."

The wishful thinking of a frightened Establishment? Perhaps. But the organizers of the officially sanctioned April 22 Teach-In movement are doing their best to give life to the media's daydream about the co-optive potential of ecology. If they succeed, thousands of young people across the country will engage in a series of environmental extravaganzas, embellished to capture the excitement of the original Vietnam teach-ins, but structured to encourage the young to forsake the "less important issues" and enlist in a crusade to save the earth.

We think that any analogy between what is supposed to happen around April 22 and the organization of the Vietnam teach-ins is obscene. We think that the Environmental Teach-In apparatus is the first step in a con game that will do little more than abuse the environment even further. We do not think it will succeed.

The originators of the Vietnam teach-ins worked at great odds and against the lies and opposition of government, university administrations and the media. They raised their own money and had offices in student apartments or small storefronts. "Earth Day" came to life in the offices of Senator Gaylord Nelson, received blessings from Nixon's Department of Health, Education and Welfare, was funded by foundations, and has worked out of facilities lent by the Urban Coalition.

Editors of *Ramparts, Eco-Catastrophe* (New York: Harper and Row, 1970), pp. vii–xii.

Vietnam protestors had to create their own reading lists, fact sheets and white papers; they had to work against the "expertise" of Southeast Asia scholars. The Environmental Teach-In comes prepackaged; a well-paid and well-staffed national office sends local organizers an official brochure which avoids mentioning the social and economic environment with which Mother Nature has to cope. Friends of the Earth (FOE) provides, through Ballantine Books, a semi-official "Environmental Handbook," which insists that saving the environment "transcends the other issues" and that we should in nonpartisan fashion "support a man from any political party if he is a true Friend of the Earth."

Never mind if he's a racist. Don't worry about whether or not he supports American imperialism. This spring the Nixon Administration is busy undoing 15 years of struggle for school integration: the police continue to murder black people in the streets; the American judicial system is disintegrating and, in the eyes of the State, every radical has become a conspirator; the war machine in Washington has made clear its intention to stay in Vietnam indefinitely and to spread its war to Laos. All this—and the Teach-In organizers want to banish everything but environment to the back pages of our minds. They must be blind, or perverse, or both.

How can anyone in this dark springtime believe kind words—about environment or anything else—from the men in power? Once we might have been able to believe that because a President had embraced the civil rights issue, apartheid in the Deep South was dead. But such illusions can hardly be sustained any longer. The Open Housing Act, the chief legislative victory of those years, finds use this season only for its "H. Rap Brown Amendment"—the interstate travel ban on which the Justice Department hung the Chicago 7.

Lyndon Johnson promised that We Shall Overcome. Now Richard Nixon promises to clean up America. Even TV's "Laugh-In"[1] knows the punch-line: "If Nixon's War on Pollution is as successful as Johnson's War on Poverty, we're going to have an awful lot of dirty poor people around."

Haven't we learned after a decade of social struggle that major problems like Vietnam, Race, Poverty—now Environment—can't be packaged separately, each protected from contamination by "other issues"? Even the Kerner Commission[2] realized that white racism was systematic, structural and linked to economic and social institutions. Even the most determined skeptic has now been shown by the Nixon Administration that the Vietnam war was no honest mistake, but the result of a long history of American expansion into Asia and a long-term policy of subjecting poor nations to the imperatives of American investors. To understand why Washington has persisted in its genocidal war in Indo-China, don't look at the politicians who come and go; look at the structures of power and interest that remain.

Threats to the environment are no different. At their source is the same division of society—those with power against those without: the corporations, which organize for their own benefit, against the people whom they organize destructively.

[1] A popular TV comedy program of the 1960s—ED.
[2] A Presidential Commission of the late 1960s that investigated the causes of ghetto rioting—ED.

Look at the values which galvanize energies and allocate resources in the business system: pursuit of money, enrichment of self, the exploitation of man—and of nature—to generate still more money. Is it surprising that a system seeking to turn everything into gold ends up turning everything into garbage? The market is master. Business makes money meeting consumer demands; it makes even more money creating new demands. More money is spent on advertising and sales promotion in America, on planned obsolescence and consumer manipulation, than on all education—public and private, elementary school through the university. This is pollution of the mind, and it has its own costs. Some students estimate that socially useless, ecologically disastrous waste products make up nearly half of the Gross National Product. Nixon has already predicted a 50 per cent increase in the GNP by 1980, ostensibly to finance new priorities like environmental reform. It would be better if he had questioned how much waste the dynamic American economy will have to produce in the next decade simply to clean up the waste of past decades.

Others, like the organizers of the National Teach-In, tell us that it is in the interest even of the corporate rich to clean up the environment. If all their customers are asphyxiated by air pollution, explain these optimists, business (and businessmen) would expire as well. By this same logic, the military-industrial complex should bar the ABM[3] from its cities, and the corporations, always eager to bring new consumers into the market, should make the war on poverty work. But no businessman, alone or with other businessmen, can change the tendencies of this ultimately ecocidal process unless he puts the system out of business. As long as society organizes production around the incentive to convert man's energies and nature's resources into profit, no planned, equable, ecologically balanced system of production can ever exist. Teach-ins which fail to confront this fact of life do worse than teach nothing. They obstruct knowledge and stand in the way of a solution. They join the struggle on the side which permits them truly to say—not of mankind, but of themselves—"We have found the enemy and he is us."

Perhaps the Teach-Ins could teach better if, instead of their present brochure, they distributed a full-page ad from Fortune's special environment issue. Sponsored by the New York State Department of Commerce, the ad pictures Governor Nelson Rockefeller inviting businessmen to come grow with New York. The pitch is simple: "Personal property of manufacturers is completely exempt from taxation in New York . . . During the past eleven years, there has not been one single new business tax in New York." Nowhere does the ad mention New York's long series of new *nonbusiness* taxes. In 11 years in office, Rocky has first imposed, then hiked a new state sales tax; quadrupled the cigarette tax; tripled the gasoline tax; and lowered the minimum income below which poor people are free of the state income tax. Businesses apparently aren't expected to care who subsidizes their growth. But the ad does want them to know that Governor Rockefeller, author of the "soak-the-poor

---

[3]Anti-Ballistic Missile, a missile designed to shoot down attacking missiles. It was said to be an invitation to nuclear attacks—ED.

program," considers "economic growth—a continuing expansion of the private economy—to be the indispensable ingredient of all progress."

Rockefeller doesn't say this only because he's a Rockefeller; he says it because he's Governor and every governor wants business to invest in his state. Private business accounts for 85 per cent of the GNP; it must be kept happy and expanding, or, short of revolution, there will be nothing for anyone at all. Regulation of business consequently can never be more than self-regulation, federal intervention into the business sector never more than federal intervention on behalf of the business sector.

But regulation is not the question. We simply don't need any more gross national product, any more unnecessary goods and factories. What we do need is a *redistribution* of existing real wealth, and a *reallocation* of society's resources. Everyone knows what this redistribution and reallocation should do; the crises of the last ten years have made it all so obvious: The poor must have adequate income, the cities must be rebuilt to fit human requirements, the environment must be de-polluted, the educational system must be vastly expanded, and social energies now poured into meaningless pursuits (like advertising and sales promotion) must be rechanneled into humanly edifying and creative activities.

We must, in short, junk the business system and its way of life, and create revolutionary new institutions to embody new goals—human and environmental.

All this sounds utopian. Well, utopias are relative. More utopian by far than revolution is the idea that the present society, dominated by business, can create lasting, meaningful reforms sufficient, for example, to permit mankind to survive the century.

At a recent "Survival Faire" in San Jose, California, ecology organizers bought a new car and buried it as a symbol of the task which they saw confronting ecology action groups. This was an indication of dangerous political naivete that must be overcome. To buy the car in the first place was to pay the criminal and strengthen him. But this act also pointed the finger of guilt at the consumer, who has only the choice of traveling to work by auto or walking 30 miles to work on the freeway. In opposition to this misdirected gesture of revolt, San Jose's black students angrily demanded that the car be raffled to provide defense funds for their brothers on trial. The blacks made their point very clearly. "Don't bury the car," their placard said, "bury the system."

In contrast to this Survival Faire, the week after the Conspiracy defendants were sentenced in Chicago, angry students razed the local branch of the Bank of America in Santa Barbara, California. The only bank in the Isla Vista youth ghetto, B of A had long treated young people as a class apart. It had opposed the grape strikers centered in Delano. It had supported, with branches in Saigon and Bangkok and with its leadership of the investment build-up in the Pacific, the American occupation of Southeast Asia. Two of its directors sit on the board of Union Oil, which had for so many months desecrated the once-beautiful beaches of Santa Barbara and destroyed their wildlife. Most important, as the branch manager explained to the press, it had been the major local symbol of capitalism and the business system.

Burning a bank is not the same as putting the banks and their system out of business. To do that, millions of people in this country will first have to wake up to the real source of their misery. The action in Santa Barbara, a community which has seen its environment destroyed by corporate greed, might spark that awakening. If it does, the students who burned the Bank of America in Santa Barbara will have done more to save the environment than all the Survival Faires and "Earth Day Teach-Ins" put together.

☆ 20 ☆

Defining America at the Century's End

During the late 1980s, public education in America was shaken by a series of disputes that became known as the "Culture Wars." Throughout the nation, school districts grappled with controversial questions about curriculum, which often exploded into public spectacles and political imbroglios. Before fanaticism and sensationalism gave way to reasoned debate, several painful trends began to emerge. First, defining what an American is or should be continued to be no simple task, and second, matters of race and class were hazardously close to America's political fault lines.

On the surface, domestic politics during the 1990s seemed to drift in a moderate or centrist direction. The Republican ascendancy that had repudiated liberalism in the 1980s seemed to reach its zenith in the Congressional election of 1994 and receive the message that "enough was enough" in the reelection of Bill Clinton in 1996. Had American politics finally come to rest in middle ground as the century neared its conclusion? Or had just the opposite happened, with the noisy extremes canceling each other out and leaving behind a stalemate? Bill Clinton's failed effort to launch a national health-care crusade seemed to reveal the difficulties to be faced by any political leader hoping to accomplish something on a grand scale. Clinton quickly redirected his energies toward achieving more limited "incremental" goals for much of his presidency.

Scandal and crime fascinated the nation more than ever, and a series of trials commanded unprecedented media attention: O.J. Simpson; the Oklahoma City bombing; and, finally, the transformation of the Whitewater investigation into the "White House Sex Scandal." Angry voices filled the air waves as radio and television talk shows seemed to attest daily that a revolution of rising expectations had in fact created a permanent culture of complaint.

What became of public life and the public purpose in America as the century neared its end? Had it become a victim of its own success? Had American politics solved all substantive problems, leaving behind only relatively minor matters and thus more competitive scrambles for media attention? Were the 1990s just atypically tranquil? Or was it the reverse—had particularism, litigation, and self-interest simply eroded common ground, leaving a disjointed and atomistic body politic behind? Few political climates could contain more apparent contradictions: The Clinton economy boomed, but pockets of severe misery persisted. The Cold War was over and won, but fanaticism, terrorism, and the deployment of nuclear and biochemical weapons left peace and national security as fragile and vulnerable as ever.

The last selection of readings reflects the ways Americans tried to define themselves as the century neared its conclusion. Conflicting visions of conservatives and liberals, left and right, and Democrats and Republicans often revealed questions of identity and definition.

In the first reading, Dinesh D'Souza, a conservative, argues that identity politics and multiculturalism promote racism and discrimination rather than effectively combatting them. In the second reading, Henry Louis Gates, Jr. disagrees, giving his reasons why minority identities must be preserved in a pluralistic society such as our own. Next, Todd Gitlin bemoans the loss of common ground and raises traditional radical views as to how to recover it. Finally, a beleaguered Bill Clinton attempts to persuade an unsympathetic Congress which items should be on the American political agenda for the twenty-first century.

To what extent are these new issues? How have Americans answered them in the past, and how do you think they will be likely to answer them in the future?

The End of Racism

DINESH D'SOUZA

An Alternative Vision

[I] examine[s] the credibility of the claim that racism is to blame for black failure and test[s] the viability of the multicultural vision being promoted to fight Eurocentrism and institutional racism. My conclusion is that antiracism, in its current form, is intellectually bankrupt and may have run its course. Thus the contemporary phenomena of black rage, white backlash, and liberal despair are part of the debris of a liberal intellectual edifice that is now imploding. Virtually all the contemporary liberal assumptions about the origin of racism, its historical significance, its contemporary effects, and what to do about it are wrong. In a sense, pessimists like Andrew Hacker and Derrick Bell are right: Liberal hope is dead. The only questions are how

Dinesh D'Souza, *The End of Racism. Principles for a Multiracial Society* (New York: The Free Press, 1995), pp. 22–24.

a seemingly noble vision went awry, and whether there are grounds for a restoration of a realistic liberal belief in a solution to the race problem. Here are some of the issues I examine and—admittedly in condensed and simplified form—some of my main findings.

Is racism a Western idea? Yes. Contrary to popular impression, racism is not universal. Indeed, there are no clear examples of racism anywhere in the world before the year 1500 A.D. Racism arose in the West during the modern era as a rational and eventually scientific ideology to explain large differences in civilizational development that could not be explained by environment. Thus racism originated not in ignorance and fear but as part of an enlightened enterprise of intellectual discovery. The good news is that since racism had a beginning, it is conceivable that it may have an end.

Was slavery a racist institution? No. Slavery was practiced for thousands of years in virtually all societies: in China, India, Europe, the Arab world, sub-Saharan Africa, and the Americas. In the United States, slave-owning was not confined to whites: American Indians and free blacks owned thousands of slaves. Thus slavery is neither distinctively Western nor racist. What is uniquely Western is the abolition of slavery. The American founders articulated principles of equality and consent which formed the basis for emancipation and the civil rights movement.

Why did white liberals and black activists abandon color blindness as a basis for law and policy? The civil rights movement in which both groups participated embodied from the outset the assumptions of cultural relativism: the presumed equality of all cultures or groups. Martin Luther King, Jr., emphasized one serious problem faced by blacks (racial discrimination) while ignoring another equally serious one (cultural deficiencies) which inhibited black competitiveness. Thus equal rights for blacks could not and did not produce equality of results. Consequently, many liberals and civil rights activists invoked equality of results to prove that white racism continues unabated. They supported affirmative action and racial preferences in order to fight the effects of past and present racism.

Why have charges of racism multiplied while clear evidence of racism has declined? There is now in place a civil rights establishment which has a vested interest in making exaggerated accusations of racism. Promiscuous charges of bigotry are used to cajole and intimidate whites into acquiescing in programs which financially and politically benefit the civil rights establishment. If racism were to disappear, many of these activists and bureaucrats would be out of a job.

Why is the black underclass worse off while the black middle class is better off? As the main beneficiary of affirmative action, blacks with better skills and motivation have moved out of their old neighborhoods, taking with them middle-class norms and social and financial resources. Consequently, in the inner city, civilizing institutions such as the church and small business have greatly eroded. Moreover, the civil rights establishment has a vested interest in the persistence of the underclass, because the scandalous pathologies of poor blacks create the public sympathy that legitimizes continuing subsidies to the black middle class.

Can blacks be racist? Yes. Many liberals find it difficult to recognize black racism because they are ideologically committed to view it as a mere reaction to white racism. In fact, African American racism is a coherent ideology of black supremacy, promoted in Afrocentric courses and institutionally embodied in the Nation of Islam. In an increasingly meritocratic society, black racism becomes a rationalization for black failure. Thus African American antagonism is most vehemently directed against groups such as Jews and Asian Americans that have no history of persecuting blacks but that outcompete them.

Does contemporary liberalism have a future? No. Many white liberals are so embarrassed by low levels of academic performance and high levels of criminal and antisocial behavior by blacks, that they are destroying liberal institutions such as free speech, race neutrality, the legal presumption of innocence, and equal rights under the law in order to compel equal results for racial groups. Ultimately white liberals are trapped in a logic in which they must blame themselves for African American problems, and condone the demise of their cherished principles in order to camouflage black failure.

Is racism the main problem facing blacks today? No. The main contemporary obstacle facing African Americans is neither white racism, as many liberals claim, nor black genetic deficiency, as Charles Murray and others imply. Rather it involves destructive and pathological cultural patterns of behavior: excessive reliance on government, conspiratorial paranoia about racism, a resistance to academic achievement as "acting white," a celebration of the criminal and outlaw as authentically black, and the normalization of illegitimacy and dependency. These group patterns arose as a response to past oppression, but they are now dysfunctional and must be modified.

Are you saying that racial discrimination no longer exists? On the contrary. Evidence for the old discrimination has declined, but there are many indications that black cultural pathology has contributed to a new form of discrimination: rational discrimination. High crime rates of young black males, for example, make taxi drivers more reluctant to pick them up, storekeepers more likely to follow them in stores, and employers less willing to hire them. Rational discrimination is based on accurate group generalizations that may nevertheless be unfair to particular members of a group.

If racism is not the main problem for blacks, what is? Liberal antiracism. By asserting the equality of all cultures, cultural relativism prevents liberals from dealing with the nation's contemporary crisis—a civilizational breakdown that affects all groups, but is especially concentrated among black underclass. Many liberals continue to blame African American pathologies on white racism and oppose all measures that impose civilizational standards on the grounds that they are nothing more than "blaming the victim." Meanwhile, the pathologies persist unchecked.

Loose Canons

HENRY LOUIS GATES, JR.

To both its proponents and its antagonists, multiculturalism represents—either refreshingly or frighteningly—a radical departure. Like most claims of cultural novelty, this one is more than a little exaggerated. For both the challenge of cultural pluralism and the varied forms of political resistance to it go back to the founding of our republic.

Henry Louis Gates, Jr., *Loose Canons: Notes on the Culture Wars* (New York: Oxford University Press, 1992), pp. xiv–xvii.

In the university today, it must be admitted, the challenge has taken on a peculiar inflection. But the underlying questions are time-tested. What does it mean to be an American? Must academic inquiry be subordinated to the requirements of national identity? Should scholarship and education reflect our actual diversity, or should they, rather, forge a communal identity that may not yet have been achieved?

For answers, you can, of course, turn to the latest jeremiad on the subject from, say, George Will, Dinesh D'Souza, or Roger Kimball. But in fact, these questions have always occasioned lively disagreement among American educators. In 1917, William Henry Hulme decried "the insidious introduction into our scholarly relations of the political propaganda of a wholly narrow, selfish, and vicious nationalism and false patriotism." His opponents were equally emphatic in their beliefs. "More and more clearly," Fred Lewis Pattee ventured in 1919, "is it seen now that the American soul, the American conception of democracy, Americanism should be made prominent in our school curriculums, as a guard against the rising spirit of experimental lawlessness." Sound familiar?

Given the political nature of the debate over education and the national interest, the conservative penchant of charging the multiculturalists with "politics" is a little perplexing. For conservative critics, to their credit, have never hesitated to provide a political defense of what they consider the "traditional" curriculum: The future of the republic, they argue, depends on the inculcation of proper civic virtues. What these virtues are is a matter of vehement dispute. But to speak of a curriculum untouched by political concerns is to imagine—as no one does—that education could take place in a vacuum.

Stated simply, the thrust of the pieces gathered here is this: Ours is a late-twentieth-century world profoundly fissured by nationality, ethnicity, race, class, and gender. And the only way to transcend those divisions—to forge, for once, a civic culture that respects both differences and commonalities—is through education that seeks to comprehend the diversity of human culture. Beyond the hype and the high-flown rhetoric is a pretty homely truth: There is no tolerance without respect—and no respect without knowledge. Any human being sufficiently curious and motivated can fully possess another culture, no matter how "alien" it may appear to be.

Indeed, the historical architects of the university always understood this. As Cardinal Newman wrote over a century ago, the university should promote "the power of viewing many things at once as one whole, referring them severally to their true place in the universal system, of understanding their respective values, and determining their mutual dependence." In just this vein, the critic Edward Said has recently suggested that "Our model for academic freedom should therefore be the migrant or traveler: for if, in the real world outside the academy, we must needs be ourselves and only ourselves, inside the academy we should be able to discover and travel among other selves, other identities, other varieties of the human adventure. But most essentially, in this joint discovery of self and other, it is the role of the academy to transform what might be conflict, or context, or assertion into reconciliation, mutuality, recognition, creative interaction."

But if multiculturalism represents the culmination of an age-old ideal—the dream known, in the seventeenth century, as *mathesis universalis*—why has it been the target of such ferocious attacks?

The conservative desire has been to cast the debate in terms of the West versus the Rest. And yet that's the very opposition that the pluralist wants to challenge. Pluralism sees culture as porous, dynamic, and interactive, rather than as the fixed property of particular ethnic groups. Thus the idea of a monolithic, homogeneous "West" itself comes into question (nothing new here: literary historians have pointed out that the very concept of "Western culture" may date back only to the eighteenth century). But rather than mourning the loss of some putative ancestral purity, we can recognize what's valuable, resilient, even cohesive in the hybrid and variegated nature of our modernity.

Cultural pluralism is not, of course, everyone's cup of tea. Vulgar cultural nationalists—like Allan Bloom or Leonard Jeffries—correctly identify it as the enemy. These polemicists thrive on absolute partitions: between "civilization" and "barbarism," between "black" and "white," between a thousand versions of Us and Them. But they are whistling in the wind.

For whatever the outcome of the culture wars in the academy, the world we live in is multicultural already. Mixing and hybridity are the rule, not the exception. As a student of African American culture, of course, I've come to take this kind of cultural palimpsest for granted. Duke Ellinon, Miles Davis, and John Coltrane have influenced popular musicians the world over. Wynton Marsalis is as comfortable with Mozart as with jazz. Anthony Davis writes in a musical idiom that combines Bartok with the blues. In the dance, Judith Jameson, Alvin Alley, and Katherine Dunham all excelled at "Western" cultural forms, melding these with African American styles to produce performances that were neither, and both. In painting, Romare Bearden and Jacob Lawrenee, Martin Puryear and Augusta Savage, learned to paint and sculpt by studying Western artists, yet each has pioneered the construction of a distinctly African American visual art. And in literature, of course, the most formally complex and compelling black writers—such as Jean Toomer, Sterling Brown, Langston Hughes, Zora Hurston, Richard Wright, Ralph Ellison, James Baldwin, Toni Morrison, and Gwendolyn Brooks—have always blended forms of Western literature with African American vernacular and written traditions. Then again, even a vernacular form like the spirituals took as its texts the King James version of the Old and New Testaments. Morrison's master's thesis was on Virginia Woolf and Faulkner: Rita Dove is as conversant with German literature as she is with that of her own country. African American culture, then, has been a model of multiculturalism and plurality. And it is this cultural impulse, I believe, that represents the very best hope for us, collectively, to forge a new, and vital, common American culture in the twenty-first century.

The Twilight of Common Dreams

TODD GITLIN

It is [the] mobilization for equality and against arbitrary power that is the Left's main business—if there is to be a Left. Just how can a democratic society regulate

Todd Gitlin, *The Twilight of Common Dreams: Why America Is Wracked by Culture Wars* (New York: Metropolitan Books, Henry Holt and Company, 1995) pp. 236–237.

the demons of technology and the strains of competition? How can multinational corporations be brought under democratic control without resorting to the heavy hand of the state? In the United States, though, the mindset of identity politics—including the panic against political correctness—aborts the necessary discussion. Cultivating unity within minority groups, the obsession with difference stands in the way of asking the right questions.

To recognize diversity, more than diversity is needed. The commons is needed. To affirm the rights of minorities, majorities must be formed. Democracy is more than a license to celebrate (and exaggerate) differences. It cannot afford to live in the past—anyone's past. It is a political system of mutual reliance and common moral obligations. Mutuality needs tending. If multiculturalism is not tempered by a stake in the commons, then centrifugal energy overwhelms any commitment to a larger good. This is where multiculturalism as a faith has proved a trap even—or especially—for people in the name of whom the partisans of identity politics purport to speak. Affirming the virtues of the margins, identity politics has left the centers of power uncontested. No wonder the threatened partisans of "normality" have seized the offensive.

The dialogue today is inflamed and incoherent in part because the symbolic stakes are overloaded on every side. There is a lot of fantasy in circulation. The melting pot never melted as thoroughly as Henry Ford would have liked: The golden years were mighty white. And the monocultures of Afrocentrists and goddess-worshippers, however foolish, are far less prevalent than their advocates wish or their antagonists fear. But if the Right magnifies the multiculturalist menace, identity partisans inflate the claims they make for multiculturalism. All suffer from a severe lack of proportion. Most of all, while critics of identity politics are looting society, the politics of identity is silent on the deepest sources of social misery: the devastation of cities, the draining of resources away from the public and into the private hands of the few. It does not organize to reduce the sickening inequality between rich and poor. Instead, in effect, it struggles to change the color of inequality. In this setting, the obsession with cultural identity at the expense of political citizenship distracts what must be the natural constituencies of a Left if there is to be one: the poor, those fearful of being poor, intellectuals with sympathies for the excluded.

Make no mistake—the path of commonality offers no utopian destination. It offers, in fact, difficulties galore. Majorities come and go: they are not easy to stitch together under the best of circumstances. A diversity of customs and rages is here to stay—and nowhere more than in amazingly profuse, polychrome, polyglot America. Plainly people are motivated by loyalties to clan, religion, race. Meanwhile, capital moves across frontiers at the speed of light as labor lumbers along at a human pace. Capital can always threaten to take off for lower-wage pastures and bring national reformers to their knees. At the same time, the nation-states that people expect to protect them against the flux may be obsolescent in an age of global markets, but they haven't gotten the news. They exist. They have weight. They wave flags; they recruit armies; they build monuments; people are willing to kill and die for their symbols. By contrast, commonality offers—what? The discredited red flag? The blue banner of UN bureaucracy? The green flag is fine, as far as it goes, and so is the flag of human rights, but neither stirs enough human hearts.

Still, we will not see what lies on the other side of the politics of identity unless, unflinchingly, without illusions, we look, look again, and are willing to go on looking. For too long, too many Americans have busied themselves digging trenches to fortify their cultural borders, lining their trenches with insulation. Enough bunkers! Enough of the perfection of differences! We ought to be building bridges.

Let Us Strengthen Our Nation for the 21st Century

BILL CLINTON

January 27, 1998

. . . [C]ommunity means living by the defining American value—the ideal heard round the world that we are all created equal. Throughout our history, we haven't always honored that ideal and we've never fully lived up to it. Often it's easier to believe that our differences matter more than what we have in common. It may be easier, but it's wrong.

What we have to do in our day and generation to make sure that America becomes truly one nation—what do we have to do? We're becoming more and more and more diverse. Do you believe we can become one nation? The answer cannot be to dwell on our differences, but to build on our shared values. We all cherish family and faith, freedom and responsibility. We all want our children to grow up in a world where their talents are matched by their opportunities.

I've launched this national initiative on race to help us recognize our common interests and to bridge the opportunity gaps that are keeping us from becoming one America. Let us begin by recognizing what we still must overcome. Discrimination against any American is un-American.

We must vigorously enforce the laws that make it illegal. I ask your help to end the backlog at the Equal Employment Opportunity Commission. Sixty thousand of our fellow citizens are waiting in line for justice, and we should act now to end their wait.

We also should recognize that the greatest progress we can make toward building one America lies in the progress we make for all Americans, without regard to race. When we open the doors of college to all Americans, when we rid all our streets of crime, when there are jobs available to people from all our neighborhoods, when we make sure all parents have the child care they need, we're helping to build one nation.

We, in this chamber and in this government, must do all we can to address the continuing American challenge to build one America. But we'll only move forward if all our fellow citizens—including every one of you at home watching tonight—is also committed to this cause.

We must work together, learn together, live together, serve together. On the forge of common enterprise Americans of all backgrounds can hammer out a common identity. We see it today in the United States military, in the Peace Corps, in Ameri-

Bill Clinton, "Let us Strengthen Our Nation for the 21st Century," The 1998 State of the Union, January 27, 1998 *(Vital Speeches of the Day,* February 15, 1998 pp. 263–264).

Corps. Wherever people of all races and backgrounds come together in a shared endeavor and get a fair chance, we do just fine. With shared values and meaningful opportunities and honest communication and citizen service, we can unite a diverse people in freedom and mutual respect. We are many; we must be one.

In that spirit, let us lift our eyes to the new millennium. How will we mark that passage? It just happens once every thousand years. This year, Hillary and I launched the White House Millennium Program to promote America's creativity and innovation, and to preserve our heritage and culture into the 21st century. Our culture lives in every community, and every community has places of historic value that tell our stories as Americans. We should protect them. I am proposing a public-private partnership to advance our arts and humanities, and to celebrate the millennium by saving American's treasures, great and small.

And while we honor the past, let us imagine the future. Think about this—the entire store of human knowledge now doubles every five years. In the 1980s, scientists identified the gene causing cystic fibrosis—it took nine years. Last year, scientists located the gene that causes Parkinson's Disease—in only nine days. Within a decade, "gene chips" will offer a road map for prevention of illnesses throughout a lifetime. Soon we'll be able to carry all the phone calls on Mother's Day on a single strand of fiber the width of a human hair. A child born in 1998 may well live to see the 22nd century.

Tonight, as part of our gift to the millennium, I propose a 21st Century Research Fund for path-breaking scientific inquiry—the largest funding increase in history for the National Institutes of Health, the National Science Foundation, the National Cancer Institute.

We have already discovered genes for breast cancer and diabetes. I ask you to support this initiative so ours will be the generation that finally wins the war against cancer, and begins a revolution in our fight against all deadly diseases.

As important as all this scientific progress is, we must continue to see that science serves humanity, not the other way around. We must prevent the misuse of genetic tests to discriminate against any American.

And we must ratify the ethical consensus of the scientific and religious communities, and ban the cloning of human beings.

We should enable all the world's people to explore the far reaches of cyberspace. Think of this—the first time I made a State of the Union speech to you, only a handful of physicists used the World Wide Web. Literally, just a handful of people. Now, in schools, in libraries, homes and businesses, millions and millions of Americans surf the Net every day. We must give parents the tools they need to help protect their children from inappropriate material on the Internet. But we also must make sure that we protect the exploding global commercial potential of the Internet. We can do the kinds of things that we need to do and still protect our kids.

For one thing, I ask Congress to step up support for building the next generation Internet. It's getting kind of clogged, you know. And the next generation Internet will operate at speeds up to a thousand times faster than today.

Even as we explore this inner space in a new millennium we're going to open new frontiers in outer space. Throughout all history, humankind has had only one place to call home—our planet Earth. Beginning this year, 1998, men and women from 16 countries will build a foothold in the heavens—the international space station. With its vast expanses, scientists and engineers will actually set sail on an unchartered sea of limitless mystery and unlimited potential.

And this October, a true American hero, a veteran pilot of 149 combat missions and one, five-hour space flight that changed the world, will return to the heavens. Godspeed, John Glenn.

John, you will carry with you America's hopes. And on your uniform, once again, you will carry America's flag, marking the unbroken connection between the deeds of America's past and the daring of America's future.

Nearly 200 years ago, a tattered flag, its broad stripes and bright stars still gleaming through the smoke of a fierce battle, moved Francis Scott Key to scribble a few words on the back of an envelope—the words that became our national anthem. Today, that Star Spangled Banner, along with the Declaration of Independence, the Constitution and the Bill of Rights, are on display just a short walk from here. They are America's treasures and we must also save them for the ages.

I ask all Americans to support our project to restore all our treasures so that the generations of the 21st century can see for themselves the images and the words that are the old and continuing glory of America; an America that has continued to rise through every age, against every challenge, of people of great works and greater possibilities, who have always, always found the wisdom and strength to come together as one nation—to widen the circle of opportunity, to deepen the meaning our freedom, to form that "more perfect union." Let that be our gift to the 21st century.

God bless you, and God bless the United States.